Economic Freedom of the World

2011 Annual Report

James Gwartney
Florida State University

Robert Lawson
Southern Methodist University

Joshua Hall
Beloit College

with

Jean-Pierre Chauffour
World Bank

Michael D. Stroup
Stephen F. Austin State University

2011

Published in cooperation with the Economic Freedom Network
Editing, design, and typesetting by Lindsey Thomas Martin
Cover design by Bill Ray
Printed and bound in Canada

Data available to researchers

The full data set, including all of the data published in this report as well as data omitted due to limited space, can be downloaded for free at <http://www.freetheworld.com>. The data file available there contains the most up-to-date and accurate data for the Economic Freedom of the World index. Some variable names and data sources have evolved over the years since the first publication in 1996; users should consult earlier editions of the Economic Freedom of the World annual reports for details regarding sources and descriptions for those years. All editions of the report are available in PDF and can be downloaded for free from <http://www.freetheworld.com/datasets_efw.html>. However, users are always strongly encouraged to use the data from this most recent data file as updates and corrections, even to earlier years' data, do occur. Users doing long-term or longitudinal studies are encouraged to use the chain-linked index as it is the most consistent through time. If you have problems downloading the data, please contact Jean-François Minardi via e-mail to <freetheworld@fraserinstitute.org> or via telephone +1.514.281.9550 ext. 306. If you have technical questions about the data itself, please contact Robert Lawson via e-mail to <rlawson@smu.edu>. Please cite the data set as:

> Authors: James Gwartney, Robert Lawson, and Joshua Hall
> Title: 2011 Economic Freedom Dataset, published in *Economic Freedom of the World: 2011 Annual Report*
> Publisher: Fraser Institute
> Year: 2011
> URL: <http://www.freetheworld.com/datasets_efw.html>

Cite this publication

Authors: James Gwartney, Robert Lawson, and Joshua Hall
Title: *Economic Freedom of the World: 2011 Annual Report*
Publisher: Fraser Institute
Date of publication: 2011
Digital copy available from <www.fraserinstitute.org> and <www.freetheworld.com>

Cataloguing Information

Gwartney, James D.
     Economic freedom of the world ... annual report / James D. Gwartney.

Annual.
     Description based on: 1997
     2011 issue by James Gwartney, Robert Lawson, and Joshua Hall,
     with Jean-Pierre Chauffour and Michael D. Stroup.
     Issued also online.
     ISSN 1482-471X; ISBN 978-0-88975-252-8 (2011 edition).

1. Economic history--1990- --Periodicals.   2. Economic indicators--Periodicals.
I. Fraser Institute (Vancouver, B.C.)   II. Title

Table of Contents

Executive Summary

Economic Freedom of the World

The index published in *Economic Freedom of the World* measures the degree to which the policies and institutions of countries are supportive of economic freedom. The cornerstones of economic freedom are personal choice, voluntary exchange, freedom to compete, and security of privately owned property. Forty-two data points are used to construct a summary index and to measure the degree of economic freedom in five broad areas:

1 Size of Government: Expenditures, Taxes, and Enterprises;
2 Legal Structure and Security of Property Rights;
3 Access to Sound Money;
4 Freedom to Trade Internationally;
5 Regulation of Credit, Labor, and Business.

Economic freedom has suffered another setback

- The chain-linked summary index (exhibit 1.4) permits comparisons over time. The average economic freedom score rose from 5.53 (out of 10) in 1980 to 6.74 in 2007, but fell back to 6.67 in 2008, and to 6.64 in 2009, the most recent year for which data are available. (See chapter 1 for a discussion.)

- In this year's index, Hong Kong retains the highest rating for economic freedom, 9.01 out of 10. The other nations among the top 10 are: Singapore (8.68); New Zealand (8.20); Switzerland (8.03); Australia (7.98); Canada (7.81); Chile (7.77); United Kingdom (7.71); Mauritius (7.67); and the United States (7.60).

- The rankings (and scores) of other large economies are Germany, 21 (7.45); Japan, 22 (7.44); France, 42 (7.16); Italy, 70 (6.81); Mexico, 75 (6.74); Russia, 81 (6.55); China, 92 (6.43); India, 94 (6.40); and Brazil, 102 (6.19).

- The bottom 10 nations are: Zimbabwe (4.08); Myanmar (4.16); Venezuela (4.28); Angola (4.76); Democratic Republic of Congo (4.84); Central African Republic (4.88); Guinea-Bissau (5.03); Republic of Congo (5.04); Burundi (5.12); and Chad (5.32).

The world's largest economy, the United States, has suffered one of the largest declines in economic freedom over the last 10 years, pushing it into tenth place. Much of this decline is a result of higher government spending and borrowing and lower scores for the legal structure and property rights components. Over the longer term, the summary chain-linked ratings of Venezuela, Zimbabwe, United States, and Malaysia fell by eight-tenths of a point or more between 1990 and 2009, causing their rankings to slip.

The chain-linked summary ratings of Uganda, Zambia, Nicaragua, Albania, and Peru have increased by three or more points since 1990. The summary ratings of eight other countries—Bulgaria, Poland, El Salvador, Romania, Ghana, Nigeria, Hungary, and Guinea-Bissau—increased by between two and three points during this same period.

Nations that are economically free out-perform non-free nations in indicators of well-being

- Nations in the top quartile of economic freedom had an average per-capita GDP of $31,501 in 2009, compared to $4,545 for those nations in the bottom quartile, in constant 2005 international dollars (exhibit 1.9).

- Nations in the top quartile of economic freedom had an average growth in per-capita GDP between 1990 and 2009 of 3.07%, compared to 1.18% for those nations in the bottom quartile, in constant 2005 international dollars (exhibit 1.10).

- In the top quartile, the average income of the poorest 10% of the population was $8,735, compared to $1,061 for those in the bottom quartile, in constant 2005 international dollars (exhibit 1.12). Interestingly, the average income of the poorest 10% in the top quartile is almost double the overall income per capita in the bottom quartile ($4,545, exhibit 1.9): the poorest people in the most economically free countries are nearly twice as rich as the average people in the least free countries.

- Life expectancy is 79.4 years in the top quartile compared to 60.7 years in the bottom quartile (exhibit 1.13).

- The $1.25-per-day poverty rate is 2.7% in the top quartile compared to 41.5% in the bottom quartile (exhibit 1.17).

Chapter 1: Economic Freedom of the World

The principal authors of the report, James Gwartney (Florida State University), Robert Lawson (Southern Methodist University), and Joshua Hall (Beloit College), provide an overview of the report and discuss why economic freedom is important.

Chapter 2: Country Data Tables

Detailed historical data is provided for each of the 141 countries and territories in the index. For many countries, this covers years 1980, 1985, 1990, 1995, 2000, 2005, 2008, and 2009.

Chapter 3: What Matters for Development: Freedom or Entitlement?

Jean-Pierre Chauffour, Lead Economist, Middle East and North Africa Region, World Bank, examines policies that promote "freedom" compared to "entitlement" in relation to economic development. He notes that, depending on the balance between free choices and more coerced decisions, individual opportunities to learn, own, work, save, invest, trade, protect, and so forth could vary greatly across countries and over time. Chauffour's empirical findings suggest that fundamental freedoms are paramount in explaining long-term economic growth. For a given set of exogenous conditions, countries that favor free choice—economic freedom and civil and political liberties—over entitlement rights are likely to achieve higher sustainable economic growth and to achieve many of the distinctive proximate characteristics of success identified by the Commission on Growth and Development (World Bank, 2008). In contrast, pursuing entitlement rights through greater coercion by the state is likely to be self-defeating in the long run.

These findings provide potentially important policy lessons for all countries. For developed countries, they suggest that prioritizing economic freedom over social entitlements could be an effective way to reform the welfare state and make it more sustainable and equitable in the long run. For middle-income countries (such as countries in the midst of the Arab Spring and countries in Asia and Latin America), they indicate that the quest for civil and political rights and for economic freedom could create the conditions for new social contracts. For low-income countries, they provide an opportunity to reflect on the achievements under the Millennium Development Goals (MDG) and the potential role that economic freedom and other fundamental freedoms that could play in a post-2015 MDG development agenda.

Chapter 4: Does Economic Freedom Promote Women's Wellbeing?

Michael D. Stroup, Stephen F. Austin State University, examined the impact of economic freedom on women's wellbeing based on a recent United Nations Development Project (UNDP) report. He finds that a one-point increase in the average EFW index, controlling for other relevant factors, was found to be associated with:

- a decline in the UNDP Gender Inequality (GI) index of 0.03 with the sample average at 0.53;

- a decline in the maternal death rate by 131 women per 100,000 births with the sample average at 300;

- a reduction of over six births per 1,000 births to females age 15–19 when the sample average is 53;

- an increase of almost five percentage points in the percentage of women with a secondary education when the sample average is 52%;

- an increase of two percentage points in the number of women holding seats in parliament in the legislative branch of a national government when the sample average is 18%.

Data available to researchers

The full data set, including all of the data published in this report as well as data omitted due to limited space, can be downloaded for free at <http://www.freetheworld.com>. The data file available there contains the most up-to-date and accurate data for the Economic Freedom of the World index. Some variable names and data sources have evolved over the years since the first publication in 1996; users should consult earlier editions of the *Economic Freedom of the World* annual reports for details regarding sources and descriptions for those years. All editions of the report are available in PDF and can be downloaded for free from <http://www.freetheworld.com/datasets_efw.html>. However, users are always strongly encouraged to use the data from this most recent data file as updates and corrections, even to earlier years' data, do occur. Users doing long-term or longitudinal studies are encouraged to use the chain-linked index as it is the most consistent through time. If you have problems downloading the data, please contact Jean-François Minardi via e-mail to <freetheworld@fraserinstitute.org> or via telephone +1.514.281.9550 ext. 306. If you have technical questions about the data itself, please contact Robert Lawson via e-mail to <rlawson@smu.edu>. Please cite the data set as:

> Authors: James Gwartney, Robert Lawson, and Joshua Hall
> Title: 2011 Economic Freedom Dataset, published in *Economic Freedom of the World: 2011 Annual Report*
> Publisher: Fraser Institute
> Year: 2011
> URL: <http://www.freetheworld.com/datasets_efw.html>

Chapter 1
Economic Freedom of the World, 2009

This year's *Economic Freedom of the World* reflects a quarter of a century of research and development in the measurement of economic freedom. Numerous scholars, including Nobel Prize winners Milton Friedman, Douglass North, and Gary Becker, have contributed to this project. The EFW measure now covers 141 countries and provides reliable data for approximately 100 of them back to 1980.

The concept of economic freedom

The key ingredients of economic freedom are:

- personal choice,
- voluntary exchange coordinated by markets,
- freedom to enter and compete in markets, and
- protection of persons and their property from aggression by others.

These four cornerstones imply that economic freedom is present when individuals are permitted to choose for themselves and engage in voluntary transactions as long as they do not harm the person or property of others. Individuals have a right to decide how they will use their time, talents, and resources, but they do not have a right to the time, talents, and resources of others. Put another way, individuals do not have a right to take things from others or demand that others provide things for them. Use of violence, theft, fraud, and physical invasions are not permissible but, otherwise, individuals are free to choose, trade, and cooperate with others, and compete as they see fit.

In an economically free society, the primary role of government is to protect individuals and their property from aggression by others. The EFW index is designed to measure the extent to which the institutions and policies of a nation are consistent with this protective function. In order to achieve a high EFW rating, a country must provide secure protection of privately owned property, even-handed enforcement of contracts, and a stable monetary environment. It also must keep taxes low, refrain from creating barriers to both domestic and international trade, and rely more fully on markets rather than the political process to allocate goods and resources.

Why economic freedom is important

Numerous scholarly articles have used the EFW data to examine the relationship between economic freedom and various measures of economic and social performance. This research indicates why economic freedom is vitally important to a society. We will mention just four areas of research below. Exhibt 1.1 provides a list of selected scholarly articles in each of these areas.

1 Economic freedom and investment, income, and growth

Economic freedom leads to more investment, higher per-capita incomes, and growth rates. Dozens of studies have investigated the relationship between economic freedom on the one hand and investment, economic growth, and per person income on the other. These studies typically control for geographic, locational, political, educational, and numerous other factors. Most of them have found that higher levels of economic freedom, or certain components of economic freedom, exert an independent positive impact on investment, economic growth, and income per capita.

2 Economic freedom, reductions in poverty, and improvements in human welfare

Economic freedom leads to less poverty and improvements in the general living conditions of a society. Critics sometimes charge that economic freedom and market allocation often result in the poor being left behind but research in this area is inconsistent with this view. As seen in exhibit 1.17 at the end of this chapter, countries with persistently high levels of economic freedom have lower poverty rates. Moreover, those that move toward more economic freedom enjoy better living standards across multiple dimensions.

3 Economic freedom, cooperation, tolerance, and peaceful relations

Economic freedom encourages cooperation, tolerance, and peaceful relations. Voluntary exchange is the centerpiece of economically free economies. Both parties to an exchange gain and therefore buyers and sellers are encouraged to interact with those who give them the best deal, regardless of their racial, religious, ethnic, gender, or tribal characteristics. Markets reward those who serve others, including those they do not necessarily like. When markets thrive, people with vastly different characteristics often interact peacefully with each other. In turn, the peaceful interaction among diverse groups encourages tolerance and promotes understanding. In contrast, political allocation promotes divisiveness and polarization. When resources are allocated politically, individuals and groups get ahead by taking from others or imposing regulations that provide them with an advantage relative to others. This encourages various groups to bind together in order to gain advantages relative to other groups. Thus, political allocation leads to polarization and bitterness toward groups favored by the political process. In cases where a racial, religious, ethnic, or tribal group forms a majority, the political process is often used to oppress the minority. The empirical studies are consistent with this view. Countries with higher levels of economic freedom are less likely to experience both internal and external use of violence.

4 Economic freedom, entrepreneurship, and honesty in government
Economic freedom leads to entrepreneurial business activity; political allocation leads to crony capitalism and political corruption. When the function of government is limited to protection of people and their property and even-handed enforcement of contracts and settlement of disputes, entrepreneurs will get ahead by discovering highly valued products and lower-cost methods of production. Profits will direct resources toward productive projects—those that increase the value of resources. Similarly, losses will channel resources away from wasteful projects that reduce the value of resources. When resources are allocated by political decision-making, a system of crony capitalism will emerge. Predictably, politicians will allocate resources toward the politically powerful—those who can provide them with the most votes, campaign funds, high-paying jobs for political allies and, yes, even bribes. Unlike true entrepreneurs, crony capitalists do not create wealth; instead they form a coalition with political officials to plunder wealth from taxpayers and other citizens.

Will goods and resources be directed by markets or political officials? This is the great debate of our time. This debate highlights the importance of an accurate and objective measure of economic freedom. The index published in *Economic Freedom of the World* provides a measure that will help one track the direction of this debate, which is sure to affect the prosperity of the world in the years immediately ahead.

Exhibit 1.1: Selected scholarly articles on the importance of economic freedom

1 Economic freedom and investment, income, and growth

Aixala, J., and G. Fabro (2009). Economic Freedom, Civil Liberties, Political Rights and Growth: A Causality Analysis. *Spanish Economic Review* 11, 3: 165–178.

Azman-Saini, W.N.W., A.Z. Baharumshah, and S.H. Law (2010). Foreign Direct Investment, Economic Freedom and Economic Growth: International Evidence. *Economic Modelling* 27, 5: 1079–1089.

Berggren, Niclas (2003). The Benefits of Economic Freedom: A Survey. *Public Choice* 8, 2: 193–211.

Bergh, A., and M. Karlsson (2010). Government Size and Growth: Accounting for Economic Freedom and Globalization. *Public Choice* 142, 1-2: 195–213.

Carlsson, F., and S. Lundstrom (2002). Economic Freedom and Growth: Decomposing the Effects. *Public Choice* 112, 3-4: 335–344.

Cole, Julio H. (2003). The Contribution of Economic Freedom to World Economic Growth. *Cato Journal* 23, 2: 189–198.

Dawson, J.W. (1998). Institutions, Investment, and Growth: New Cross-Country and Panel Data Evidence. *Economic Inquiry* 36, 4: 603–619.

de Haan, J., S. Lundstrom, and J.-E. Sturm (2006). Market-Oriented Institutions and Policies and Economic Growth: A Critical Survey. *Journal of Economic Surveys* 20, 2: 157–191.

de Hann, J., and J.-E. Sturm (2000). On the Relationship between Economic Freedom and Growth. *European Journal of Political Economy* 16, 2: 215–241.

Djankov, S., T. Ganser, C. McLiesh, R. Ramalho, and A. Shleifer (2010). The Effect of Corporate Taxes on Investment and Entrepreneurship. *American Economic Journal-Macroeconomics* 2, 3: 31–64.

Fabro, G., and J. Aixala (2009). Economic Growth and Institutional Quality: Global and Income-Level Analyses. *Journal of Economic Issues* 43, 4: 997–1023.

Faria, H.J., and H.M. Montesinos (2009). Does Economic Freedom Cause Prosperity? An IV Approach. *Public Choice* 141, 1-2: 103–127.

Gwartney, J.D., R.G. Holcombe, and R.A. Lawson (2006). Institutions and the Impact of Investment on Growth. *Kyklos* 59, 2: 255–273.

Gwartney, J.D., R.A. Lawson, and R.G. Holcombe (1999). Economic Freedom and the Environment for Economic Growth. *Journal of Institutional and Theoretical Economics—Zeitschrift fur die Gesamte Staatswissenschaft* 155, 4: 643–663.

Hall, J.C., R.S. Sobel, and G.R. Crowley (2010). Institutions, Capital, and Growth. *Southern Economic Journal* 77, 2: 385–405.

Harms, P., and H.W. Ursprung (2002). Do Civil and Political Repression Really Boost Foreign Direct Investments? *Economic Inquiry* 40, 4: 651–663.

Heckelman, J.C., and S. Knack (2009). Aid, Economic Freedom, and Growth. *Contemporary Economic Policy* 27, 1: 46–53.

Heckelman, J.C., and M.D. Stroup (2000). Which Economic Freedoms Contribute to Growth? *Kyklos* 53, 4: 527–544.

Justesen, M.K. (2008). The Effect of Economic Freedom on Growth Revisited: New Evidence on Causality from a Panel of Countries 1970–1999. *European Journal of Political Economy* 24, 3: 642–660.

Lothian, J.R. (2006). Institutions, Capital Flows and Financial Integration. *Journal of International Money and Finance* 25, 3: 358–369.

N'Da, K., A. Robin, and T. Tribunella (2009). Economic Freedom and the Impact of Technology on Productivity. *Journal of Global Information Management* 17, 3: 42–58.

Scully, G.W. (2002). Economic Freedom, Government Policy and the Trade-Off between Equity and Economic Growth. *Public Choice* 113, 1-2: 77–96.

2 Economic freedom, reductions in poverty, and improvements in human welfare

Ashby, N.J. (2010). Freedom and International Migration. *Southern Economic Journal* 77, 1: 49–62.

Bjornskov, C., A. Dreher, and J.V.A. Fischer (2008). Cross-Country Determinants of Life Satisfaction: Exploring Different Determinants across Groups in Society. *Social Choice and Welfare* 30, 1: 119–173.

Bjornskov, C., A. Dreher, and J.V.A. Fischer (2010). Formal Institutions and Subjective Well-Being: Revisiting the Cross-Country Evidence. *European Journal of Political Economy* 26, 4: 419–430.

Connors, Joseph (2011). Global Poverty: The Role of Economic Freedom, Democracy, and Foreign Aid. Ph.D. dissertation, Department of Economics, Florida State University.

Connors, Joseph, and James D. Gwartney (2010). Economic Freedom and Global Poverty. In Mark D. White, ed., *Accepting the Invisible Hand* (Palgrave Macmillan): 43–68.

de Soysa, I., and E. Neumayer (2005). False Prophet, or Genuine Savior? Assessing the Effects of Economic Openness on Sustainable Development, 1980–99. *International Organization* 59, 3: 731–772.

Leeson, P. (2010). Two cheers for capitalism? *Society* 47, 3: 227–233.

Ott, J. (2010). Greater Happiness for a Greater Number: Some Non-Controversial Options for Governments. *Journal of Happiness Studies* 11, 5: 631–647.

Ott, J.C. (2010). Good Governance and Happiness in Nations: Technical Quality Precedes Democracy and Quality Beats Size. *Journal of Happiness Studies* 11, 3: 353–368.

Shleifer, A. (2009). The Age of Milton Friedman. *Journal of Economic Literature* 47, 1: 123–135.

Stroup, M.D. (2007). Economic Freedom, Democracy, and the Quality of Life. *World Development* 35, 1: 52–66.

Stroup, M.D. (2008). Separating the Influence of Capitalism and Democracy on Women's Well-Being. *Journal of Economic Behavior & Organization* 67, 3-4: 560–572.

3 Economic freedom, cooperation, tolerance, and peaceful relations

Burkhart, R.E. (2002). The Capitalist Political Economy and Human Rights: Cross-National Evidence. *Social Science Journal* 39, 2: 155–170.

de Soysa, I., and H. Fjelde (2010). Is the Hidden Hand an Iron Fist? Capitalism and Civil Peace, 1970–2005. *Journal of Peace Research* 47, 3: 287–298.

Eriksen, S., and I. de Soysa (2009). A Fate Worse than Debt? International Financial Institutions and Human Rights, 1981–2003. *Journal of Peace Research* 46, 4: 485–503.

Gartzke, E. (2007). The Capitalist Peace. *American Journal of Political Science* 51, 1: 166–191.

Strong, M. (2009). Peace through Access to Entrepreneurial Capitalism for All. *Journal of Business Ethics* 89: 529–538.

Kurrild-Klitgaard, P., M.K. Justesen, and R. Klemmensen (2006). The Political Economy of Freedom, Democracy and Transnational Terrorism. *Public Choice* 128, 1-2: 289–315.

Steinberg, D.A., and S.M. Saideman (2008). Laissez Fear: Assessing the Impact of Government Involvement in the Economy on Ethnic Violence. *International Studies Quarterly* 52, 2: 235–259.

4   Economic freedom, entrepreneurship, and honesty in government

Bjornskov, C., and N.J. Foss (2008). Economic Freedom and Entrepreneurial Activity: Some Cross-Country Evidence. *Public Choice* 134, 3-4: 307–328.

Carden, A., and L. Verdon (2010). When Is Corruption a Substitute for Economic Freedom? *Law and Development Review* 3, 1: 41–62.

Dreher, A., C. Kotsogiannis, and S. McCorriston (2007). Corruption around the World: Evidence from a Structural Model. *Journal of Comparative Economics* 35, 3: 443–466.

Freytag, A., and R. Thurik (2007). Entrepreneurship and Its Determinants in a Cross-Country Setting. *Journal of Evolutionary Economics* 17, 2: 117–131.

Heckleman, J., and B. Powell (2010). Corruption and the Environment for Growth. *Comparative Economic Studies* 52, 3: 351–378.

Swaleheen, M., and D. Stansel (2007). Economic Freedom, Corruption, and Growth. *Cato Journal* 27, 3: 343–358.

Nystrom, K. (2008). The Institutions of Economic Freedom and Ewntrepreneurship: Evidence from Panel Data. *Public Choice* 136, 3-4: 269–282.

Quinn, J.J. (2008). The Effects of Majority State Ownership of Significant Economic Sectors on Corruption: A Cross-Regional Comparison. *International Interactions* 34, 1: 84–128.

The *Economic Freedom of the World* index, 2009

The construction of the index published in *Economic Freedom of the World* is based on three important methodological principles. First, objective components are always preferred to those that involve surveys or value judgments. Given the multi-dimensional nature of economic freedom and the importance of legal and regulatory elements it is sometimes necessary to use data based on surveys, expert panels, and generic case studies. To the fullest extent possible, however, the index uses objective components. Second, the data used to construct the index ratings are from external sources such as the International Monetary Fund, World Bank, and World Economic Forum that provide data for a large number of countries. Data provided directly from a source within a country are rarely used, and only when the data are unavailable from international sources. Importantly, the value judgments of the authors or others in the Economic Freedom Network are never used to alter the raw data or the rating of any country. Third, transparency is present throughout. The report provides information about the data sources, the methodology used to transform raw data into component ratings, and how the component ratings are used to construct both the area and summary ratings. Complete methodological details can be found in the Appendix: Explanatory Notes and Data Sources (pp. 191). The entire data set used in the construction of the index is freely available to researchers at <www.freetheworld.com>.

Exhibit 1.2 indicates the structure of the EFW index. The index measures the degree of economic freedom present in five major areas: [1] Size of Government: Expenditures, and Taxes, Enterprises; [2] Legal Structure and Security of Property Rights; [3] Access to Sound Money; [4] Freedom to Trade Internationally; [5] Regulation of Credit, Labor, and Business.

Within the five major areas, there are 23 components in this year's index. Many of those components are themselves made up of several sub-components. In total, the index comprises 42 distinct variables. Each component and sub-component is placed on a scale from 0 to 10 that reflects the distribution of the underlying data. The sub-component ratings are averaged to determine each component. The component ratings within each area are then averaged to derive ratings for each of the five areas. In turn, the five area ratings are averaged to derive the summary rating for each country. The following section provides an overview of the five major areas.

Exhibit 1.2: The Areas, Components, and Sub-Components of the EFW Index

1 Size of Government: Expenditures, Taxes, and Enterprises

  A General government consumption spending as a percentage of total consumption

  B Transfers and subsidies as a percentage of GDP

  C Government enterprises and investment

  D Top marginal tax rate

    i Top marginal income tax rate

    ii Top marginal income and payroll tax rates

2 Legal Structure and Security of Property Rights

  A Judicial independence (GCR)

  B Impartial courts (GCR)

  C Protection of property rights (GCR)

  D Military interference in rule of law and the political process (ICRG)

  E Integrity of the legal system (ICRG)

  F Legal enforcement of contracts (DB)

  G Regulatory restrictions on the sale of real property (DB)

3 Access to Sound Money

  A Money growth

  B Standard deviation of inflation

  C Inflation: Most recent year

  D Freedom to own foreign currency bank accounts

4 Freedom to Trade Internationally

  A Taxes on international trade

    i Revenues from trade taxes (% of trade sector)

    ii Mean tariff rate

    iii Standard deviation of tariff rates

  B Regulatory trade barriers

    i Non-tariff trade barriers (GCR)

    ii Compliance cost of importing & exporting (DB)

  C Size of trade sector relative to expected

  D Black-market exchange rates

  E International capital market controls

    i Foreign ownership / investment restrictions (GCR)

    ii Capital controls

5 Regulation of Credit, Labor, and Business

  A Credit market regulations

    i Ownership of banks

    ii Foreign bank competition

    iii Private sector credit

    iv Interest rate controls / negative real interest rates

  B Labor market regulations

    i Hiring regulations and minimum wage (DB)

    ii Hiring and firing regulations (GCR)

    iii Centralized collective bargaining (GCR)

    iv Hours regulations (DB)

    v Mandated cost of worker dismissal (DB)

    vi Conscription

  C Business regulations

    i Price controls

    ii Administrative requirements (GCR)

    iii Bureaucracy costs (GCR)

    iv Starting a business (DB)

    v Extra payments / bribes / favoritism (GCR)

    vi Licensing restrictions (DB)

    vii Cost of tax compliance (DB)

GCR = *Global Competitiveness Report*; ICRG = *International Country Risk Guide*; DB = *Doing Business*.

See Appendix: Explanatory Notes and Data Sources (page 191) for bibliographical information.

Area 1: Size of Government: Expenditures, Taxes, and Enterprises

The four components of Area 1 indicate the extent to which countries rely on the political process to allocate resources and goods and services. When government spending increases relative to spending by individuals, households, and businesses, government decision-making is substituted for personal choice and economic freedom is reduced. The first two components address this issue. Government consumption as a share of total consumption (1A) and transfers and subsidies as a share of GDP (1B) are indicators of the size of government. When government consumption is a larger share of the total, political choice is substituted for personal choice. Similarly, when governments tax some people in order to provide transfers to others, they reduce the freedom of individuals to keep what they earn.

The third component (1C) in this area measures the extent to which countries use private rather than government enterprises to produce goods and services. Government firms play by rules that are different from those to which private enterprises are subject. They are not dependent on consumers for their revenue or on investors for capital. They often operate in protected markets. Thus, economic freedom is reduced as government enterprises produce a larger share of total output.

The fourth component (1D) is based on (1Di) the top marginal income tax rate and (1Dii) the top marginal income and payroll tax rate and the income threshold at which these rates begin to apply. These two sub-components are averaged to calculate the top marginal tax rate (1D). High marginal tax rates that apply at relatively low income levels are also indicative of reliance upon government. Such rates deny individuals the fruits of their labor. Thus, countries with high marginal tax rates and low income thresholds are rated lower.

Taken together, the four components of Area 1 measure the degree to which a country relies on personal choice and markets rather than government budgets and political decision-making. Therefore, countries with low levels of government spending as a share of the total, a smaller government enterprise sector, and lower marginal tax rates earn the highest ratings in this area.

Area 2: Legal Structure and Security of Property Rights

Protection of persons and their rightfully acquired property is a central element of economic freedom and a civil society. Indeed, it is the most important function of government. Area 2 focuses on this issue. The key ingredients of a legal system consistent with economic freedom are rule of law, security of property rights, an independent judiciary, and an impartial court system. Components indicating how well the protective function of government is performed were assembled from three primary sources: the *International Country Risk Guide*, the *Global Competitiveness Report*, and the World Bank's *Doing Business* project.

Security of property rights, protected by the rule of law, provides the foundation for both economic freedom and the efficient operation of markets. Freedom to exchange, for example, is meaningless if individuals do not have secure rights to property, including the fruits of their labor. When individuals and businesses lack confidence that contracts will be enforced and the fruits of their productive efforts protected, their incentive to engage in productive activity is eroded. Perhaps more than any other area, this area is essential for the efficient allocation of resources. Countries with major deficiencies in this area are unlikely to prosper regardless of their policies in the other four areas.

Area 3: Access to Sound Money

Money oils the wheels of exchange. An absence of sound money undermines gains from trade. As Milton Friedman informed us long ago, inflation is a monetary phenomenon, caused by too much money chasing too few goods. High rates of monetary growth invariably lead to inflation. Similarly, when the rate of inflation increases, it also tends to become more volatile. High and volatile rates of inflation distort relative prices, alter the fundamental terms of long-term contracts, and make it virtually impossible for individuals and businesses to plan sensibly for the future. Sound money is essential to protect property rights and, thus, economic freedom. Inflation erodes the value of property held in monetary instruments. When governments finance their expenditures by creating money, in effect, they are expropriating the property and violating the economic freedom of their citizens.

The important thing is that individuals have access to sound money: who provides it makes little difference. Thus, in addition to data on a country's inflation and its government's monetary policy, it is important to consider how difficult it is to use alternative, more credible, currencies. If bankers can offer saving and checking accounts in other currencies or if citizens can open foreign bank accounts, then access to sound money is increased and economic freedom expanded.

There are four components in Area 3 of the EFW index. All of them are objective and relatively easy to obtain and all have been included in the earlier editions of the index. The first three are designed to measure the consistency of monetary policy (or institutions) with long-term price stability. Component 3D is designed to measure the ease with which other currencies can be used via domestic and foreign bank accounts. In order to earn a high rating in this area, a country must follow policies and adopt institutions that lead to low (and stable) rates of inflation and avoid regulations that limit the ability to use alternative currencies.

Area 4: Freedom to Trade Internationally

In our modern world of high technology and low costs for communication and transportation, freedom of exchange across national boundaries is a key ingredient of economic freedom. Many goods and services are now either produced abroad or contain resources supplied from abroad. Voluntary exchange is a positive-sum activity: both trading partners gain and the pursuit of the gain provides the motivation for the exchange. Thus, freedom to trade internationally also contributes substantially to our modern living standards.

In response to protectionist critics and special-interest politics, virtually all countries adopt trade restrictions of various types. Tariffs and quotas are obvious examples of roadblocks that limit international trade. Because they reduce the convertibility of currencies, controls on the exchange rate also hinder international trade. The volume of trade is also reduced if the passage of goods through customs is onerous and time consuming. Sometimes these delays are the result of administrative inefficiency while in other instances they reflect the actions of corrupt officials seeking to extract bribes. In both cases, economic freedom is reduced.

The components in this area are designed to measure a wide variety of restraints that affect international exchange: tariffs, quotas, hidden administrative restraints, and exchange rate and capital controls. In order to get a high rating in this area, a country must have low tariffs, a trade sector larger than expected, easy clearance and efficient administration of customs, a freely convertible currency, and few controls on the movement of capital.

Area 5: Regulation of Credit, Labor, and Business

When regulations restrict entry into markets and interfere with the freedom to engage in voluntary exchange, they reduce economic freedom. The fifth area of the index focuses on regulatory restraints that limit the freedom of exchange in credit, labor, and product markets. The first component (5A) reflects conditions in the domestic credit market. The first two sub-components provide evidence on the extent to which the banking industry is dominated by private firms and whether foreign banks are permitted to compete in the market. The final two sub-components

indicate the extent to which credit is supplied to the private sector and whether controls on interest rates interfere with the market in credit. Countries that use a private banking system to allocate credit to private parties and refrain from controlling interest rates receive higher ratings for this regulatory component.

Many types of labor-market regulations infringe on the economic freedom of employees and employers. Among the more prominent are minimum wages, dismissal regulations, setting of wages by a centralized agency, extension of union contracts to non-participating parties, and military conscription. The labor-market component (5B) is designed to measure the extent to which these restraints upon economic freedom are present. In order to earn high marks in the component rating regulation of the labor market, a country must allow market forces to determine wages and establish the conditions of hiring and firing, and refrain from the use of conscription.

Like the regulation of credit and labor markets, the regulation of business activities (5C) inhibits economic freedom. The sub-components of 5C are designed to identify the extent to which regulations and bureaucratic procedures restrain entry and reduce competition. In order to earn a high score in this portion of the index, countries must allow markets to determine prices and refrain from regulatory activities that retard entry into business and increase the cost of producing products. They also must refrain from "playing favorites," that is, from using their power to extract financial payments and reward some businesses at the expense of others.

Construction of Summary and Area ratings

Theory provides us with direction regarding elements that should be included in the five areas and the summary index, but it does not indicate what weights should be attached to the components within the areas or among the areas in the construction of the summary index. It would be nice if these factors were independent of each other and a weight could be attached to each of them. During the past several years, we have investigated several methods of weighting the various components, including principle component analysis and a survey of economists. We have also invited others to use their own weighting structure if they believe that it is preferable. In the final analysis, the summary index is not very sensitive to substantial variations in the weights.

Furthermore, there is reason to question whether the areas (and components) are independent or work together as a team. Put another way, they may be linked more like the wheels, motor, transmission, drive shaft, and frame of a car. Just as it is the bundle of these factors that underlies the mobility of an auto, it may be a bundle of factors that underlies the composition of economic freedom. With regard to an automobile, which is more important for mobility: the motor, wheels, or transmission? The question cannot be easily answered because the parts work together. If any of these key parts break down, the car is immobile. Institutional quality may be much the same. If any of the key parts are absent, the overall effectiveness is undermined.

As the result of these two considerations, we organize the elements of the index in a manner that seems sensible to us but we make no attempt to weight the components in any special way when deriving either area or summary ratings. Of course, the data for the components and sub-components are available to researchers who would like to consider alternative weighting schemes and we encourage them to do so.

Summary Economic Freedom Ratings, 2009

Exhibit 1.3 presents summary economic freedom ratings, sorted from highest to lowest. These ratings are for the year 2009, the most recent year for which comprehensive data are available. Hong Kong and Singapore, once again, occupy the top two positions. The other nations in the top 10 are New Zealand, Switzerland, Australia, Canada, Chile, United Kingdom, Mauritius, and the United States. The rankings of other major countries include Germany (21st), Japan (22nd), Korea (30th), France (42nd), Spain (54th), Italy (70th), Mexico (75th), Russia (81st), China (92nd), India (94th), and Brazil (102nd). The ten lowest-rated countries are Chad, Burundi, Republic of Congo, Guinea-Bissau, Central African Republic, Democratic Republic of Congo, Angola, Venezuela, Myanmar, and, again in last place, Zimbabwe.

The EFW index is calculated back to 1970 as the availability of data allows; see the Country Data Tables in chapter 2 or our website, <http://www.freetheworld.com>, for information from past years. Because some data for earlier years may have been updated or corrected, researchers are always encouraged to use the data from the most recent annual report to assure the best-quality data.

Area Economic Freedom Ratings (and Rankings), 2009

Exhibit 1.4 presents the ratings (and, in parentheses, the rankings) for each of the five areas of the index and for components 5A, 5B, and 5C. A number of interesting patterns emerge from an analysis of these datas. High-income industrial economies generally rank quite high for Legal Structure and Security of Property Rights (Area 2), Access to Sound Money (Area 3), and Freedom to Trade Internationally (Area 4). Their ratings were lower, however, for Size of Government: Expenditures, Taxes, and Enterprises (Area 1) and Regulation of Credit, Labor, and Business (Area 5). This was particularly true for western European countries.

On the other hand, a number of developing nations have a small fiscal size of government, but rate poorly in other areas. Madagascar and Togo illustrate this point. Madagascar ranks fourth and Togo second for size of government (Area 1). However, Madagascar ranks 132nd in Area 2, 89th in Area 4, 126th in Area 5, and its summary rating places it 96th. In a similar fashion, Togo ranks 139th in Area 2, 109th in Area 4, 140th in Area 5, and its overall summary ranking is 123rd. Clearly, a small size of government is insufficient for the provision of economic freedom. The institutions of economic freedom, such as the rule of law and property rights, as well as sound money, trade openness, and sensible regulation are also required.

Weakness in the rule of law and property rights is particularly pronounced in sub-Saharan Africa, among Islamic nations, and for several nations that were part of the former Soviet bloc, though some of these nations have made strides toward improvement. Many Latin American and Southeast Asian nations also score poorly for rule of law and property rights. The nations that rank poorly in this category also tend to score poorly in the trade and regulation areas, even though several have reasonably sized governments and sound money.

The economies most open to foreign trade are Hong Kong and Singapore, while the most closed economies are Myanmar and Venezuela. The least regulated countries—those at the top in Regulation of Credit, Labor, and Business (Area 5)—are a diverse lot: Belize, Bahamas, Hong Kong, Fiji, New Zealand, and Singapore.

Exhibit 1.3: Summary Economic Freedom Ratings, 2009

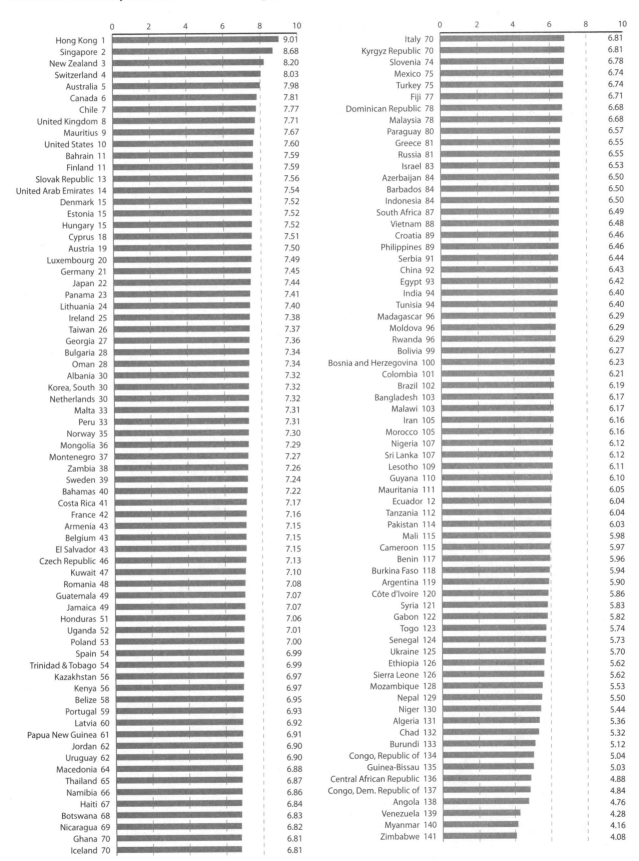

Hong Kong 1	9.01
Singapore 2	8.68
New Zealand 3	8.20
Switzerland 4	8.03
Australia 5	7.98
Canada 6	7.81
Chile 7	7.77
United Kingdom 8	7.71
Mauritius 9	7.67
United States 10	7.60
Bahrain 11	7.59
Finland 11	7.59
Slovak Republic 13	7.56
United Arab Emirates 14	7.54
Denmark 15	7.52
Estonia 15	7.52
Hungary 15	7.52
Cyprus 18	7.51
Austria 19	7.50
Luxembourg 20	7.49
Germany 21	7.45
Japan 22	7.44
Panama 23	7.41
Lithuania 24	7.40
Ireland 25	7.38
Taiwan 26	7.37
Georgia 27	7.36
Bulgaria 28	7.34
Oman 28	7.34
Albania 30	7.32
Korea, South 30	7.32
Netherlands 30	7.32
Malta 33	7.31
Peru 33	7.31
Norway 35	7.30
Mongolia 36	7.29
Montenegro 37	7.27
Zambia 38	7.26
Sweden 39	7.24
Bahamas 40	7.22
Costa Rica 41	7.17
France 42	7.16
Armenia 43	7.15
Belgium 43	7.15
El Salvador 43	7.15
Czech Republic 46	7.13
Kuwait 47	7.10
Romania 48	7.08
Guatemala 49	7.07
Jamaica 49	7.07
Honduras 51	7.06
Uganda 52	7.01
Poland 53	7.00
Spain 54	6.99
Trinidad & Tobago 54	6.99
Kazakhstan 56	6.97
Kenya 56	6.97
Belize 58	6.95
Portugal 59	6.93
Latvia 60	6.92
Papua New Guinea 61	6.91
Jordan 62	6.90
Uruguay 62	6.90
Macedonia 64	6.88
Thailand 65	6.87
Namibia 66	6.86
Haiti 67	6.84
Botswana 68	6.83
Nicaragua 69	6.82
Ghana 70	6.81
Iceland 70	6.81

Italy 70	6.81
Kyrgyz Republic 70	6.81
Slovenia 74	6.78
Mexico 75	6.74
Turkey 75	6.74
Fiji 77	6.71
Dominican Republic 78	6.68
Malaysia 78	6.68
Paraguay 80	6.57
Greece 81	6.55
Russia 81	6.55
Israel 83	6.53
Azerbaijan 84	6.50
Barbados 84	6.50
Indonesia 84	6.50
South Africa 87	6.49
Vietnam 88	6.48
Croatia 89	6.46
Philippines 89	6.46
Serbia 91	6.44
China 92	6.43
Egypt 93	6.42
India 94	6.40
Tunisia 94	6.40
Madagascar 96	6.29
Moldova 96	6.29
Rwanda 96	6.29
Bolivia 99	6.27
Bosnia and Herzegovina 100	6.23
Colombia 101	6.21
Brazil 102	6.19
Bangladesh 103	6.17
Malawi 103	6.17
Iran 105	6.16
Morocco 105	6.16
Nigeria 107	6.12
Sri Lanka 107	6.12
Lesotho 109	6.11
Guyana 110	6.10
Mauritania 111	6.05
Ecuador 12	6.04
Tanzania 112	6.04
Pakistan 114	6.03
Mali 115	5.98
Cameroon 115	5.97
Benin 117	5.96
Burkina Faso 118	5.94
Argentina 119	5.90
Côte d'Ivoire 120	5.86
Syria 121	5.83
Gabon 122	5.82
Togo 123	5.74
Senegal 124	5.73
Ukraine 125	5.70
Ethiopia 126	5.62
Sierra Leone 126	5.62
Mozambique 128	5.53
Nepal 129	5.50
Niger 130	5.44
Algeria 131	5.36
Chad 132	5.32
Burundi 133	5.12
Congo, Republic of 134	5.04
Guinea-Bissau 135	5.03
Central African Republic 136	4.88
Congo, Dem. Republic of 137	4.84
Angola 138	4.76
Venezuela 139	4.28
Myanmar 140	4.16
Zimbabwe 141	4.08

Exhibit 1.4: Area Economic Freedom Ratings (Ranks), 2009

	AREAS					COMPONENTS OF AREA 5		
	1 Size of Government	2 Legal System & Property Rights	3 Sound Money	4 Freedom to Trade Internationally	5 Regulation	5A Credit Market Regulation	5B Labor Market Regulations	5C Business Regulations
	Rating (Rank)	Rating (Rank)	Rating (Rank)	Rating (Rank)	Rating (Rank)	Rating (Rank)	Rating (Rank)	Rating (Rank)
Albania	8.2 (8)	5.4 (79)	9.6 (6)	6.6 (72)	6.7 (83)	8.1 (78)	5.9 (86)	6.1 (55)
Algeria	3.6 (138)	4.6 (100)	7.0 (105)	6.3 (94)	5.4 (131)	5.5 (136)	5.3 (111)	5.3 (105)
Angola	3.5 (139)	3.3 (130)	5.2 (139)	6.4 (85)	5.4 (133)	7.2 (114)	3.9 (136)	5.0 (118)
Argentina	6.2 (77)	4.5 (105)	7.0 (102)	5.8 (112)	6.0 (116)	8.2 (75)	5.3 (108)	4.4 (130)
Armenia	7.7 (21)	5.5 (78)	9.4 (30)	6.5 (79)	6.7 (86)	8.1 (83)	6.2 (77)	5.7 (88)
Australia	6.7 (58)	8.2 (11)	9.6 (9)	7.1 (38)	8.2 (9)	9.5 (14)	8.4 (16)	6.8 (25)
Austria	4.8 (119)	8.3 (9)	9.6 (14)	7.3 (26)	7.4 (34)	9.2 (33)	6.2 (79)	6.8 (20)
Azerbaijan	5.4 (106)	6.0 (54)	7.8 (87)	6.4 (80)	6.9 (66)	7.8 (96)	6.8 (60)	6.2 (51)
Bahamas	8.3 (7)	7.0 (28)	7.2 (98)	4.8 (135)	8.9 (2)	9.8 (8)	9.4 (3)	7.4 (8)
Bahrain	6.6 (62)	6.6 (37)	9.0 (50)	7.5 (21)	8.3 (7)	9.3 (28)	8.7 (8)	7.0 (16)
Bangladesh	8.1 (12)	3.6 (128)	6.7 (114)	5.7 (118)	6.8 (78)	8.1 (77)	6.5 (68)	5.7 (89)
Barbados	5.6 (96)	7.8 (18)	6.7 (117)	5.1 (128)	7.3 (44)	8.5 (62)	7.6 (35)	5.9 (77)
Belgium	4.1 (135)	6.8 (31)	9.6 (5)	7.7 (15)	7.5 (30)	8.9 (46)	7.4 (45)	6.3 (45)
Belize	6.6 (61)	5.5 (75)	8.3 (68)	5.4 (123)	8.9 (1)	9.4 (23)	9.3 (4)	8.1 (1)
Benin	7.0 (39)	4.4 (106)	6.7 (115)	5.0 (133)	6.6 (88)	9.2 (32)	5.8 (91)	4.8 (123)
Bolivia	6.3 (75)	3.8 (125)	8.7 (57)	6.8 (59)	5.7 (123)	8.0 (85)	4.6 (124)	4.5 (129)
Bosnia & Herzeg.	5.5 (103)	3.9 (121)	8.3 (69)	6.5 (77)	6.9 (65)	8.7 (58)	6.6 (66)	5.4 (99)
Botswana	4.4 (132)	6.9 (30)	8.4 (66)	6.7 (63)	7.8 (18)	9.5 (14)	7.2 (51)	6.6 (32)
Brazil	6.7 (59)	5.3 (82)	7.9 (84)	6.0 (105)	5.1 (136)	6.6 (124)	4.4 (130)	4.2 (132)
Bulgaria	7.3 (31)	5.1 (85)	9.4 (29)	7.2 (36)	7.7 (23)	9.7 (12)	7.8 (28)	5.5 (97)
Burkina Faso	6.4 (71)	4.1 (117)	6.7 (113)	5.2 (127)	7.3 (51)	8.5 (63)	7.2 (50)	6.0 (64)
Burundi	4.6 (124)	3.2 (133)	6.8 (110)	4.4 (138)	6.6 (90)	6.6 (125)	8.2 (20)	5.1 (115)
Cameroon	6.8 (51)	3.6 (126)	6.6 (120)	6.0 (103)	6.8 (79)	8.0 (85)	7.6 (38)	4.7 (126)
Canada	6.1 (80)	8.1 (15)	9.6 (19)	6.9 (51)	8.3 (8)	9.2 (31)	8.5 (12)	7.1 (12)
Central African Rep.	6.3 (73)	2.0 (141)	7.0 (100)	3.9 (139)	5.0 (137)	7.3 (110)	3.8 (138)	4.1 (133)
Chad	6.9 (43)	2.7 (136)	5.7 (134)	6.0 (104)	5.3 (135)	6.1 (128)	6.0 (83)	3.7 (139)
Chile	7.7 (23)	7.2 (25)	9.0 (51)	7.8 (9)	7.2 (55)	8.7 (56)	5.8 (93)	7.1 (13)
China	4.5 (128)	6.4 (45)	8.0 (79)	7.2 (30)	6.0 (115)	7.4 (106)	5.5 (103)	5.0 (119)
Colombia	6.0 (84)	4.4 (108)	8.1 (76)	5.7 (120)	6.9 (72)	8.5 (67)	5.9 (89)	6.2 (49)
Congo, Dem. Rep.	5.2 (110)	2.7 (137)	7.0 (107)	4.6 (136)	4.8 (139)	4.8 (139)	5.7 (98)	4.0 (134)
Congo, Rep. of	5.0 (115)	4.2 (115)	4.7 (140)	5.7 (119)	5.6 (127)	6.3 (127)	6.4 (73)	4.0 (135)
Costa Rica	7.4 (30)	6.5 (39)	7.9 (86)	7.3 (27)	6.9 (70)	7.6 (99)	6.7 (64)	6.4 (43)
Côte d'Ivoire	7.0 (40)	3.2 (135)	6.6 (119)	6.2 (97)	6.3 (106)	8.0 (85)	5.7 (97)	5.2 (107)
Croatia	5.1 (111)	5.6 (74)	8.5 (64)	6.3 (91)	6.8 (75)	8.9 (48)	6.4 (72)	5.1 (114)
Cyprus	7.3 (32)	6.8 (32)	9.4 (31)	6.7 (67)	7.3 (49)	9.5 (14)	6.3 (74)	6.1 (58)
Czech Republic	4.9 (118)	6.4 (44)	9.5 (27)	7.6 (18)	7.3 (46)	8.7 (54)	7.6 (36)	5.6 (92)

Exhibit 1.4 (continued): Area Economic Freedom Ratings (Ranks), 2009

| | AREAS | | | | | COMPONENTS OF AREA 5 | | |
| | 1
Size of
Government | 2
Legal System &
Property Rights | 3
Sound Money | 4
Freedom to Trade
Internationally | 5
Regulation | 5A
Credit Market
Regulation | 5B
Labor Market
Regulations | 5C
Business
Regulations |
	Rating (Rank)	Rating (Rank)	Rating (Rank)	Rating (Rank)	Rating (Rank)	Rating (Rank)	Rating (Rank)	Rating (Rank)
Denmark	4.1 (134)	8.5 (4)	9.5 (24)	7.4 (23)	8.1 (11)	9.3 (27)	7.5 (41)	7.4 (6)
Dominican Rep.	7.7 (20)	4.8 (93)	8.1 (77)	6.4 (87)	6.5 (98)	7.4 (104)	6.3 (75)	5.8 (85)
Ecuador	7.9 (14)	4.0 (119)	6.4 (125)	6.2 (98)	5.8 (120)	8.0 (90)	4.1 (135)	5.3 (102)
Egypt	6.0 (85)	5.5 (77)	8.7 (60)	6.4 (82)	5.6 (124)	6.0 (130)	5.0 (121)	5.8 (86)
El Salvador	8.9 (3)	4.4 (109)	9.3 (36)	6.5 (75)	6.7 (81)	8.7 (59)	5.0 (120)	6.5 (37)
Estonia	5.5 (102)	7.2 (26)	9.5 (22)	7.8 (10)	7.7 (22)	9.9 (5)	5.9 (87)	7.2 (11)
Ethiopia	6.0 (87)	5.2 (83)	5.7 (132)	5.0 (129)	6.2 (108)	4.4 (140)	7.6 (37)	6.5 (38)
Fiji	7.0 (42)	5.8 (62)	6.8 (112)	5.3 (126)	8.7 (4)	10.0 (1)	9.0 (6)	7.3 (10)
Finland	5.2 (109)	8.7 (3)	9.6 (18)	7.2 (35)	7.4 (40)	9.8 (9)	5.5 (100)	6.8 (21)
France	4.7 (123)	7.5 (22)	9.7 (4)	7.1 (41)	6.9 (71)	8.4 (71)	5.9 (88)	6.3 (46)
Gabon	6.0 (83)	4.4 (112)	5.7 (133)	5.8 (110)	7.2 (53)	7.5 (102)	8.7 (9)	5.4 (98)
Georgia	7.8 (15)	5.1 (86)	9.2 (40)	7.4 (24)	7.2 (56)	6.8 (119)	7.5 (40)	7.4 (7)
Germany	5.4 (105)	8.2 (14)	9.5 (21)	7.5 (20)	6.6 (92)	8.0 (89)	5.3 (112)	6.6 (33)
Ghana	6.7 (55)	5.5 (76)	8.2 (72)	6.9 (57)	6.7 (82)	7.8 (93)	6.2 (78)	6.1 (57)
Greece	6.0 (88)	5.6 (71)	9.6 (8)	6.1 (101)	5.4 (129)	6.0 (132)	4.5 (128)	5.8 (87)
Guatemala	7.8 (19)	4.6 (98)	9.4 (32)	7.2 (33)	6.4 (103)	8.6 (60)	4.5 (126)	6.0 (69)
Guinea-Bissau	4.3 (133)	3.3 (131)	6.3 (126)	5.0 (130)	6.3 (105)	9.3 (25)	3.8 (137)	5.8 (83)
Guyana	3.8 (137)	4.8 (92)	7.9 (83)	6.6 (73)	7.4 (42)	8.1 (81)	7.8 (27)	6.2 (48)
Haiti	8.5 (6)	2.5 (140)	8.6 (61)	6.9 (58)	7.6 (25)	8.6 (61)	9.7 (1)	4.7 (127)
Honduras	8.2 (9)	4.3 (113)	9.2 (41)	7.1 (42)	6.5 (99)	8.0 (84)	5.0 (119)	6.4 (40)
Hong Kong	9.4 (1)	8.2 (13)	9.3 (35)	9.3 (2)	8.8 (3)	9.3 (26)	9.5 (2)	7.8 (3)
Hungary	6.2 (79)	6.5 (40)	9.5 (20)	7.9 (8)	7.4 (35)	8.8 (51)	7.3 (46)	6.1 (56)
Iceland	5.0 (114)	8.3 (7)	7.8 (88)	5.4 (125)	7.6 (28)	7.3 (112)	7.8 (25)	7.6 (4)
India	6.7 (57)	5.7 (67)	6.6 (121)	6.5 (76)	6.5 (97)	6.7 (123)	7.9 (23)	4.9 (121)
Indonesia	7.6 (26)	4.4 (107)	7.7 (91)	6.7 (65)	6.1 (112)	8.1 (80)	4.8 (122)	5.3 (101)
Iran	6.5 (67)	5.8 (64)	8.2 (75)	5.0 (134)	5.4 (130)	6.7 (122)	4.4 (131)	5.2 (110)
Ireland	4.6 (125)	7.8 (17)	9.1 (46)	8.3 (4)	7.0 (60)	6.5 (126)	7.8 (30)	6.8 (24)
Israel	4.6 (127)	6.0 (53)	8.8 (55)	7.1 (45)	6.2 (107)	7.0 (117)	5.3 (109)	6.4 (41)
Italy	5.3 (108)	5.8 (63)	9.6 (12)	6.9 (55)	6.6 (94)	7.5 (103)	6.8 (62)	5.5 (96)
Jamaica	8.7 (5)	5.4 (80)	8.2 (73)	6.1 (102)	6.9 (69)	7.3 (113)	7.7 (32)	5.7 (91)
Japan	6.5 (68)	7.5 (21)	9.8 (1)	5.8 (114)	7.7 (19)	8.9 (47)	8.4 (18)	6.0 (70)
Jordan	4.4 (130)	6.3 (47)	9.3 (38)	7.2 (32)	7.4 (43)	7.3 (107)	8.4 (15)	6.3 (44)
Kazakhstan	6.8 (49)	5.9 (58)	8.3 (71)	6.2 (95)	7.5 (31)	9.3 (24)	7.2 (53)	6.1 (54)
Kenya	7.7 (22)	4.6 (101)	8.6 (62)	6.7 (66)	7.3 (50)	8.4 (73)	7.8 (26)	5.7 (90)
Korea, South	6.8 (50)	6.6 (36)	9.5 (26)	7.1 (40)	6.6 (93)	9.3 (28)	4.4 (129)	6.0 (63)
Kuwait	5.1 (112)	7.0 (27)	9.3 (39)	6.2 (100)	8.0 (13)	10.0 (1)	7.3 (48)	6.6 (34)

Exhibit 1.4 (continued): Area Economic Freedom Ratings (Ranks), 2009

	AREAS					COMPONENTS OF AREA 5		
	1 Size of Government	2 Legal System & Property Rights	3 Sound Money	4 Freedom to Trade Internationally	5 Regulation	5A Credit Market Regulation	5B Labor Market Regulations	5C Business Regulations
	Rating (Rank)	Rating (Rank)	Rating (Rank)	Rating (Rank)	Rating (Rank)	Rating (Rank)	Rating (Rank)	Rating (Rank)
Kyrgyz Republic	7.1 (37)	4.7 (95)	8.2 (74)	6.7 (68)	7.4 (41)	9.0 (37)	6.4 (71)	6.7 (28)
Latvia	4.8 (120)	6.4 (43)	8.9 (53)	7.1 (44)	7.4 (38)	8.9 (45)	7.2 (54)	6.1 (61)
Lesotho	4.4 (129)	4.6 (99)	7.7 (92)	6.4 (81)	7.4 (39)	9.8 (9)	7.1 (55)	5.3 (104)
Lithuania	6.7 (54)	6.5 (41)	9.2 (45)	6.9 (53)	7.7 (21)	9.5 (20)	7.1 (56)	6.5 (35)
Luxembourg	4.4 (131)	8.3 (10)	9.6 (17)	8.0 (7)	7.3 (48)	9.4 (21)	5.5 (102)	7.0 (15)
Macedonia	6.9 (46)	5.0 (90)	8.0 (82)	6.7 (70)	7.9 (17)	9.1 (35)	7.9 (24)	6.6 (31)
Madagascar	8.8 (4)	3.2 (132)	7.5 (93)	6.3 (89)	5.6 (126)	5.6 (134)	5.2 (113)	5.9 (79)
Malawi	5.7 (92)	5.6 (73)	7.0 (106)	5.7 (117)	6.9 (68)	7.8 (94)	7.0 (59)	5.8 (82)
Malaysia	5.5 (101)	6.5 (38)	6.5 (124)	7.2 (29)	7.6 (26)	9.0 (40)	7.8 (31)	6.1 (59)
Mali	6.4 (70)	4.4 (111)	6.8 (111)	5.9 (108)	6.5 (100)	8.0 (88)	5.5 (101)	5.9 (75)
Malta	5.8 (90)	7.5 (20)	9.5 (28)	7.0 (50)	6.9 (67)	8.5 (65)	7.7 (33)	4.5 (128)
Mauritania	6.5 (66)	4.5 (103)	5.6 (136)	6.4 (86)	7.2 (52)	9.2 (34)	7.1 (57)	5.4 (100)
Mauritius	7.8 (18)	6.3 (46)	9.2 (44)	7.2 (34)	7.9 (15)	9.5 (14)	7.5 (42)	6.7 (29)
Mexico	6.8 (48)	5.1 (89)	8.0 (81)	6.9 (54)	7.0 (62)	9.9 (6)	5.5 (104)	5.6 (93)
Moldova	5.6 (97)	5.6 (70)	7.7 (89)	6.3 (88)	6.1 (110)	7.7 (97)	5.4 (106)	5.3 (103)
Mongolia	7.6 (24)	5.7 (68)	8.0 (80)	7.5 (19)	7.6 (29)	9.0 (41)	7.2 (49)	6.5 (39)
Montenegro	6.0 (86)	6.1 (52)	9.5 (25)	6.8 (62)	8.0 (12)	9.8 (7)	8.3 (19)	5.9 (71)
Morocco	6.3 (72)	5.9 (56)	7.0 (104)	6.0 (106)	5.6 (125)	6.8 (119)	4.1 (134)	5.9 (80)
Mozambique	4.7 (121)	4.1 (116)	6.5 (122)	6.3 (92)	6.0 (114)	9.0 (42)	3.1 (140)	6.0 (68)
Myanmar	6.3 (73)	3.2 (134)	5.7 (135)	1.3 (141)	4.3 (141)	3.9 (141)		
Namibia	6.5 (63)	7.5 (19)	6.1 (129)	6.2 (96)	7.9 (14)	10.0 (1)	7.7 (34)	6.1 (53)
Nepal	6.1 (81)	3.9 (124)	6.1 (128)	5.4 (124)	6.0 (117)	6.9 (118)	5.9 (90)	5.2 (112)
Netherlands	3.4 (140)	8.1 (16)	9.5 (23)	8.1 (6)	7.4 (36)	9.0 (43)	6.7 (63)	6.5 (36)
New Zealand	6.1 (82)	8.8 (1)	9.7 (2)	7.7 (13)	8.7 (5)	10.0 (1)	8.5 (11)	7.6 (5)
Nicaragua	7.0 (41)	4.4 (110)	8.7 (58)	7.0 (47)	7.0 (61)	8.4 (68)	6.8 (61)	5.8 (84)
Niger	6.7 (56)	4.2 (114)	6.5 (123)	4.5 (137)	5.3 (134)	7.7 (98)	3.3 (139)	4.9 (122)
Nigeria	7.1 (38)	3.9 (122)	6.2 (127)	6.3 (93)	7.2 (54)	8.9 (44)	8.4 (17)	4.3 (131)
Norway	4.9 (116)	8.8 (2)	9.2 (42)	6.5 (78)	7.1 (59)	9.5 (14)	5.1 (117)	6.6 (30)
Oman	5.6 (99)	7.4 (23)	8.9 (54)	7.2 (37)	7.7 (20)	7.4 (105)	8.8 (7)	6.9 (18)
Pakistan	8.0 (13)	4.0 (118)	6.0 (130)	5.7 (116)	6.4 (102)	8.5 (66)	5.6 (99)	5.2 (106)
Panama	7.8 (16)	5.1 (87)	9.1 (48)	8.2 (5)	6.8 (76)	9.3 (28)	5.3 (110)	5.9 (76)
Papua New Guinea	7.2 (33)	4.7 (96)	7.0 (101)	7.7 (12)	7.9 (16)	8.2 (76)	8.6 (10)	6.8 (22)
Paraguay	7.4 (28)	3.6 (127)	8.7 (59)	7.2 (31)	5.9 (119)	7.3 (109)	4.3 (132)	6.0 (67)
Peru	7.6 (27)	5.4 (81)	9.2 (43)	7.5 (22)	6.9 (73)	7.3 (108)	7.3 (47)	5.9 (73)
Philippines	7.8 (17)	4.6 (102)	6.8 (109)	6.5 (74)	6.6 (87)	8.8 (52)	6.0 (84)	5.2 (113)
Poland	5.6 (95)	6.3 (48)	9.3 (33)	6.8 (60)	6.9 (64)	8.4 (69)	7.5 (43)	5.0 (120)

Exhibit 1.4 (continued): Area Economic Freedom Ratings (Ranks), 2009

	1 Size of Government	2 Legal System & Property Rights	3 Sound Money	4 Freedom to Trade Internationally	5 Regulation	5A Credit Market Regulation	5B Labor Market Regulations	5C Business Regulations
	Rating (Rank)	Rating (Rank)	Rating (Rank)	Rating (Rank)	Rating (Rank)	Rating (Rank)	Rating (Rank)	Rating (Rank)
Portugal	5.6 (100)	6.7 (35)	9.6 (10)	7.1 (46)	5.7 (122)	6.1 (129)	5.2 (116)	5.9 (72)
Romania	6.3 (76)	5.9 (61)	9.0 (49)	7.4 (25)	6.8 (74)	7.5 (101)	7.0 (58)	5.9 (74)
Russia	6.8 (52)	5.7 (66)	8.3 (70)	5.8 (111)	6.1 (111)	8.3 (74)	6.1 (81)	4.0 (136)
Rwanda	5.6 (98)	6.2 (50)	7.5 (94)	5.0 (131)	7.1 (58)	6.0 (131)	8.5 (13)	6.8 (23)
Senegal	5.4 (104)	3.9 (123)	7.0 (103)	6.2 (99)	6.2 (109)	8.8 (50)	4.6 (125)	5.1 (117)
Serbia	6.9 (47)	4.7 (97)	7.7 (90)	6.3 (90)	6.6 (89)	9.1 (36)	5.7 (94)	5.1 (116)
Sierra Leone	5.9 (89)	3.9 (120)	7.5 (95)	5.0 (132)	5.7 (121)	5.7 (133)	5.4 (105)	6.2 (50)
Singapore	8.1 (11)	8.3 (8)	9.1 (47)	9.4 (1)	8.5 (6)	9.8 (9)	7.8 (29)	8.0 (2)
Slovak Republic	6.4 (69)	6.0 (55)	9.7 (3)	8.3 (3)	7.3 (45)	9.4 (22)	7.4 (44)	5.2 (108)
Slovenia	4.6 (126)	6.2 (49)	9.6 (7)	6.7 (64)	6.7 (80)	8.4 (72)	6.0 (85)	5.9 (78)
South Africa	5.0 (113)	6.2 (51)	7.9 (85)	6.4 (84)	7.0 (63)	8.7 (57)	6.1 (80)	6.1 (60)
Spain	5.6 (94)	6.5 (42)	9.6 (15)	6.9 (56)	6.4 (101)	8.4 (70)	5.0 (118)	5.8 (81)
Sri Lanka	6.7 (60)	5.1 (88)	6.7 (116)	5.7 (121)	6.5 (96)	7.5 (100)	6.5 (69)	5.5 (95)
Sweden	3.2 (141)	8.4 (5)	9.6 (16)	7.6 (17)	7.3 (47)	9.5 (14)	5.4 (107)	7.1 (14)
Switzerland	7.6 (25)	8.4 (6)	9.3 (34)	6.6 (71)	8.1 (10)	9.0 (38)	8.5 (14)	7.0 (17)
Syria	6.2 (78)	4.5 (104)	7.3 (97)	5.8 (113)	5.4 (132)	4.8 (137)	6.1 (82)	5.2 (111)
Taiwan	6.9 (44)	6.7 (34)	9.3 (37)	7.2 (28)	6.7 (85)	8.5 (64)	5.2 (115)	6.4 (42)
Tanzania	4.7 (122)	5.9 (59)	7.5 (96)	5.7 (115)	6.3 (104)	7.9 (91)	5.8 (92)	5.2 (109)
Thailand	7.1 (36)	5.7 (65)	7.1 (99)	7.7 (16)	6.8 (77)	8.7 (55)	5.7 (96)	6.0 (66)
Togo	9.0 (2)	2.6 (139)	6.6 (118)	5.9 (109)	4.6 (140)	4.8 (138)	4.2 (133)	4.8 (124)
Trinidad & Tobago	7.4 (29)	5.2 (84)	8.1 (78)	6.8 (61)	7.5 (32)	8.8 (53)	7.5 (39)	6.2 (52)
Tunisia	5.3 (107)	6.8 (33)	6.8 (108)	5.9 (107)	7.2 (57)	8.1 (82)	6.6 (65)	6.8 (19)
Turkey	6.9 (45)	5.6 (72)	8.9 (52)	6.4 (83)	5.9 (118)	6.7 (121)	4.8 (123)	6.2 (47)
Uganda	7.1 (34)	4.9 (91)	8.4 (67)	7.0 (49)	7.7 (24)	8.9 (49)	8.1 (22)	6.0 (62)
Ukraine	5.7 (91)	4.7 (94)	5.3 (138)	6.7 (69)	6.0 (113)	8.1 (79)	6.2 (76)	3.8 (138)
United Arab Emir.	7.1 (35)	6.9 (29)	8.4 (65)	7.8 (11)	7.5 (33)	7.8 (95)	7.2 (52)	7.4 (9)
United Kingdom	5.7 (93)	8.2 (12)	9.6 (13)	7.7 (14)	7.4 (37)	7.3 (111)	8.2 (21)	6.7 (26)
United States	6.5 (65)	7.3 (24)	9.6 (11)	7.0 (48)	7.6 (27)	7.0 (116)	9.1 (5)	6.7 (27)
Uruguay	6.5 (64)	5.7 (69)	8.8 (56)	6.9 (52)	6.5 (95)	7.0 (115)	6.6 (67)	6.0 (65)
Venezuela	4.9 (117)	2.6 (138)	5.4 (137)	3.0 (140)	5.6 (128)	9.0 (38)	4.5 (127)	3.2 (140)
Vietnam	6.7 (53)	5.9 (57)	5.9 (131)	7.1 (43)	6.7 (84)	9.6 (13)	5.7 (95)	4.8 (125)
Zambia	8.1 (10)	5.9 (60)	8.5 (63)	7.1 (39)	6.6 (91)	7.9 (92)	6.5 (70)	5.5 (94)
Zimbabwe	4.1 (136)	3.5 (129)	2.5 (141)	5.5 (122)	4.9 (138)	5.6 (135)	5.2 (114)	3.8 (137)

The Chain-Linked Summary Index, 1970–2009

The EFW data are available for many countries back to 1970. Through time, the index has become more comprehensive and the available data more complete. As a result, the number and composition of the components for many countries will vary across time. This presents a problem similar to that confronted when calculating GDP or a price index over time when we know that the underlying goods and services are changing from one year to another. In order to correct for this problem and assure comparability across time, we have done the same thing that statisticians analyzing national income do: we have chain-linked the data.

The base year for the chain-linked index is 2000, and as a result the chain-linked index is not available for any countries added since that year. Changes in a country's chain-linked index through time are based only on changes in components that were present in adjoining years. For example, the 2005 chain-linked rating is based on the 2004 rating but is adjusted based on the changes in the underlying data between 2004 and 2005 for those components that were present in both years. If the common components for a country in 2005 were the same as in 2004, then no adjustment was made to the country's 2005 summary rating. However, if the 2005 components were lower than those for 2004 for the components present in both years, then the country's 2005 summary rating was adjusted downward proportionally to reflect this fact.

Correspondingly, in cases where the ratings for the common components were higher in 2005 than for 2004, the country's 2005 summary rating was adjusted upward proportionally. The chain-linked ratings were constructed by repeating this procedure backward in time to 1970 and forward in time to 2009. The chain-linked methodology means that a country's rating will change across time periods only when there is a change in ratings for components present during adjacent years. This is precisely what one would want when making comparisons across time periods.

Exhibit 1.5 shows the average chain-linked economic freedom index rating for the 102 countries with ratings since 1980. The average level of economic freedom, as measured by the chain-linked EFW index, has increased to 6.64 in 2009 from 5.53 in 1980. During the past two years, however, the average summary rating has declined, slipping from 6.74 in 2007 to 6.64 in 2009. Much of the long-term increase since 1980 was driven by reductions in marginal income-tax rates, improvements in monetary policy, and global trade liberalization.

The Chain-Linked Summary ratings for all years are found in exhibit 1.6. Researchers using the data for long-term studies should use these chain-linked data. These longitudinal data make it possible to follow the changes in economic freedom and analyze their impact over a lengthy period of time.

Exhibit 1.5: Average Chain-linked EFW Rating for the 102 countries with ratings since 1980

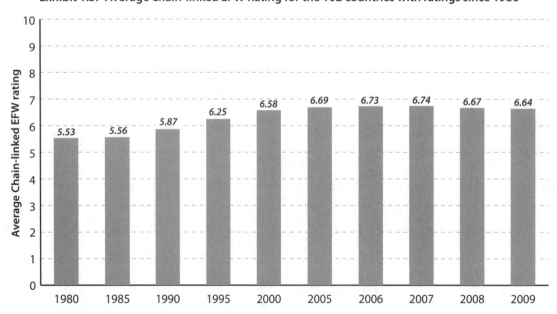

The chain-linked methodology was also used to derive area ratings. The ratings (and rankings) for the chain-linked summary and area ratings are presented in the country tables. The country tables also present the unadjusted summary and area ratings, but when tracking ratings across time, the chain-linked ratings will present a more accurate picture.

Big movers

The chain-linked summary ratings of Uganda, Zambia, Nicaragua, Albania, and Peru have improved by three or more points since 1990. The summary ratings of eight other countries—Bulgaria, Poland, El Salvador, Romania, Ghana, Nigeria, Hungary, and Guinea-Bissau—improved

by between two and three points during this same period. The rankings of these countries improved substantially. In contrast, the summary ratings of Venezuela, Zimbabwe, United States, and Malaysia fell by eight tenths of a point or more between 1990 and 2009, causing their rankings to slip.

Several economies that were centrally planned for many years have made remarkable progress during the past decade. Eight of them—the Slovak Republic, Estonia, Hungary, Lithuania, Bulgaria, Albania, Mongolia, and Georgia—now rank in the top 40. By way of comparison, only three Latin American countries—Chile, Panama, and Peru – place in the top 40. All of these countries now rank higher than Sweden and France, for example.

Exhibit 1.6: The Chain-Linked Summary Index of Ratings, 1970–2009

	1970	1975	1980	1985	1990	1995	2000	2001	2002	2003	2004	2005	2006	2007	2008	2009
Albania					4.24	4.87	6.04	6.10	6.40	6.87	6.60	7.06	7.23	7.38	7.38	7.54
Algeria			4.30	4.05	3.89	4.53	4.98	4.97	4.89	4.90	5.00	5.83	5.73	5.52	5.34	5.39
Angola																
Argentina	5.29	3.35	4.41	3.98	4.78	6.77	7.19	6.49	6.16	5.99	6.20	5.94	6.06	6.27	6.01	5.92
Armenia																
Australia	7.24	6.30	7.13	7.35	7.66	7.80	7.88	7.65	7.71	7.84	7.81	7.85	7.91	7.93	7.84	7.91
Austria	6.63	6.28	6.76	6.72	7.22	7.04	7.37	7.21	7.22	7.76	7.74	7.70	7.69	7.67	7.57	7.48
Azerbaijan																
Bahamas		6.67	6.57	6.51	6.54	6.40	6.63	6.69	6.67	6.78	6.88	7.10	6.95	7.07	7.11	7.10
Bahrain			7.46	6.85	6.85	6.93	7.28	7.18	7.16	7.19	7.07	6.92	7.22	7.35	7.27	7.24
Bangladesh		3.16	3.63	3.94	4.68	5.45	5.82	5.76	5.93	5.77	5.69	5.88	6.00	5.92	5.94	6.11
Barbados		5.69	5.86	6.23	6.14	6.08	6.09	6.08	6.00	6.07	6.16	6.26	6.01	6.21	5.95	6.06
Belgium	7.81	7.05	7.27	7.30	7.54	7.26	7.74	7.41	7.34	7.53	7.43	7.23	7.20	7.29	7.13	7.08
Belize			5.63	5.48	5.98	6.40	6.41	6.33	6.73	6.82	6.80	6.84	6.77	6.73	6.72	6.74
Benin			5.04	4.80	5.06	4.70	5.25	5.28	5.39	5.29	5.23	5.36	5.63	5.55	5.52	5.54
Bolivia			4.39	3.55	5.39	6.40	6.79	6.51	6.44	6.36	6.30	6.40	6.43	6.18	6.15	6.28
Bosnia & Herzeg.																
Botswana			5.55	5.80	6.04	6.29	7.10	7.05	7.06	6.85	6.86	6.74	6.71	7.14	6.89	6.64
Brazil	5.66	4.78	4.45	3.87	4.54	4.58	5.85	5.83	5.98	5.86	5.82	6.25	6.21	6.15	6.25	6.20
Bulgaria				5.51	4.23	4.58	5.27	5.79	6.38	6.60	6.54	6.94	7.08	7.17	7.18	7.21
Burkina Faso																
Burundi		4.31	4.44	4.74	4.88	4.39	4.78	4.96	4.89	4.38	4.28	4.59	4.95	5.11	4.62	4.87
Cameroon			5.74	5.77	5.70	5.58	5.84	6.03	6.04	6.06	6.10	5.94	6.00	5.90	5.86	6.00
Canada	8.05	7.13	7.67	7.75	8.07	7.90	8.15	8.03	8.04	8.13	8.11	8.06	8.03	7.98	7.92	7.78

Exhibit 1.6 (continued): The Chain-Linked Summary Index of Ratings, 1970–2009

	1970	1975	1980	1985	1990	1995	2000	2001	2002	2003	2004	2005	2006	2007	2008	2009
Central African Rep.				4.70	5.11	4.68	5.09	5.15	5.01	5.55	5.44	4.96	5.20	5.25	5.16	5.26
Chad				5.05	5.05	5.02	5.47	5.95	6.06	5.95	5.83	5.69	5.77	5.37	5.28	5.63
Chile	4.31	3.93	5.56	6.18	7.02	7.47	7.28	7.47	7.59	7.75	7.67	7.94	7.97	8.08	8.08	7.83
China			4.23	5.15	4.96	5.30	5.73	5.79	5.79	5.85	5.66	6.08	6.13	6.23	6.20	6.24
Colombia	5.32	5.01	4.83	5.19	5.12	5.45	5.31	5.42	5.44	5.63	5.63	5.87	6.05	6.19	6.14	6.27
Congo, Dem. Rep.	4.47	4.02	3.00	3.87	3.39	3.56	4.10	4.05	4.69	4.56	4.68	4.66	5.27	4.95	4.86	4.77
Congo, Rep. of			4.63	4.43	5.12	5.24	4.50	4.83	4.68	4.71	4.73	4.66	4.79	4.61	4.77	5.06
Costa Rica		6.33	5.61	5.36	6.76	6.85	7.31	7.17	7.04	7.30	7.14	7.28	7.45	7.24	7.10	7.08
Côte d'Ivoire			5.59	6.15	5.60	5.24	6.07	6.14	5.99	5.93	5.92	6.03	6.07	6.03	5.67	5.88
Croatia						4.91	6.10	6.07	6.21	6.31	6.42	6.40	6.47	6.58	6.54	6.49
Cyprus		5.77	5.57	5.51	5.98	6.16	6.17	6.26	6.66	6.61	7.25	7.34	7.29	7.42	7.50	7.48
Czech Republic						5.79	6.48	6.55	6.66	6.82	6.85	6.70	6.69	6.92	6.87	6.82
Denmark	7.05	6.33	6.53	6.68	7.41	7.46	7.65	7.44	7.57	7.78	7.76	7.72	7.72	7.74	7.70	7.54
Dominican Rep.			5.33	4.98	4.60	5.86	6.54	6.49	6.46	6.08	5.41	6.30	6.15	6.26	6.25	6.58
Ecuador	4.07	5.03	5.40	4.63	5.31	5.98	5.69	5.48	5.97	5.92	5.28	5.79	5.85	5.81	6.04	6.02
Egypt		3.97	4.83	5.36	5.01	5.84	6.60	6.43	6.16	6.07	6.16	6.63	6.77	6.92	6.79	6.55
El Salvador			4.84	4.49	4.77	7.00	7.30	7.28	7.22	7.25	7.32	7.60	7.56	7.60	7.58	7.29
Estonia						5.70	7.36	7.42	7.50	7.58	7.57	7.84	7.81	7.77	7.55	7.45
Ethiopia																
Fiji		5.34	5.70	6.03	5.90	6.09	6.23	6.09	6.02	5.99	6.06	6.48	6.62	6.56	6.57	6.56
Finland	7.13	6.39	6.95	7.15	7.40	7.32	7.51	7.39	7.43	7.70	7.62	7.72	7.66	7.67	7.56	7.58
France	6.86	6.01	6.22	6.13	7.07	6.80	7.06	6.73	6.87	7.11	7.16	6.97	7.01	7.18	7.20	7.05
Gabon			4.55	5.09	5.33	5.26	5.75	5.57	5.51	5.50	5.52	5.49	5.68	5.60	5.64	5.66
Georgia																
Germany	7.69	7.11	7.37	7.40	7.80	7.52	7.52	7.31	7.39	7.71	7.65	7.64	7.60	7.54	7.47	7.45
Ghana		4.10	3.27	3.41	5.04	5.43	5.86	5.98	6.21	6.68	6.43	6.73	7.33	7.25	7.26	7.15
Greece	6.35	5.99	5.97	5.38	6.04	6.18	6.66	6.57	6.66	7.00	6.87	7.00	6.91	6.96	6.82	6.53
Guatemala	6.17	6.63	6.03	4.90	5.56	6.67	6.38	6.43	6.49	6.61	6.68	7.09	7.16	7.28	7.14	7.10
Guinea-Bissau					3.15	3.71	4.51	4.96	5.05	4.89	4.84	4.78	5.22	4.91	4.89	5.16
Guyana						5.27	6.66	6.56	6.35	6.30	6.09	6.66	6.51	6.71	6.74	6.59
Haiti				6.29	5.66	5.36	5.29	6.54	6.36	6.33	6.49	6.51	6.61	6.62	6.50	6.66	6.84
Honduras				6.06	5.46	5.52	6.07	6.51	6.38	6.65	6.68	6.73	6.85	7.17	7.34	7.14	6.92
Hong Kong	8.99	8.85	9.21	8.81	8.76	9.11	8.82	8.76	8.76	8.81	8.75	8.94	8.95	9.00	9.04	8.98
Hungary			4.63	5.24	5.39	6.14	6.55	6.82	6.82	7.39	7.50	7.39	7.34	7.32	7.38	7.47
Iceland	6.45	4.78	5.43	5.75	7.03	7.40	7.76	7.67	7.60	7.72	7.73	7.71	7.61	7.46	6.89	6.72
India	5.43	4.56	5.41	5.08	5.13	5.76	6.27	6.11	6.32	6.42	6.43	6.55	6.49	6.45	6.45	6.38
Indonesia	4.74	5.39	5.24	6.16	6.53	6.57	6.04	5.72	5.98	6.26	6.19	6.41	6.38	6.55	6.56	6.53
Iran	5.64	5.48	3.75	4.07	4.77	4.50	5.76	6.17	6.10	6.04	6.18	6.30	6.28	6.15	6.15	6.22
Ireland	7.12	6.20	6.73	6.75	7.32	8.20	8.16	7.96	7.99	7.93	8.02	8.07	7.94	7.87	7.71	7.32

Exhibit 1.6 (continued): The Chain-Linked Summary Index of Ratings, 1970–2009

	1970	1975	1980	1985	1990	1995	2000	2001	2002	2003	2004	2005	2006	2007	2008	2009
Israel	5.11	4.44	3.79	4.34	4.79	5.87	6.55	6.49	6.95	6.90	6.92	7.03	6.88	6.61	6.55	6.43
Italy	6.08	5.33	5.53	5.68	6.59	6.50	7.11	6.96	7.03	6.81	6.91	7.01	6.92	6.84	6.75	6.67
Jamaica			4.22	5.03	5.59	6.43	7.23	7.06	7.09	7.08	7.23	7.26	7.23	7.08	6.89	6.86
Japan	7.04	6.57	7.08	7.12	7.47	7.11	7.45	7.08	7.16	7.53	7.43	7.47	7.48	7.58	7.46	7.37
Jordan		5.46	5.50	5.84	6.05	6.42	7.24	6.97	7.14	7.11	7.03	7.38	7.29	7.41	7.14	6.84
Kazakhstan																
Kenya	5.11	4.84	5.04	5.41	5.58	5.88	6.68	6.76	6.72	6.92	6.74	7.28	7.20	7.37	6.99	7.17
Korea	5.49	5.37	5.71	5.65	6.19	6.42	6.58	6.90	7.00	7.09	7.18	7.36	7.52	7.56	7.39	7.37
Kuwait			5.01	6.88	5.47	6.69	6.72	7.06	7.10	7.22	7.21	7.25	7.47	7.46	7.55	7.13
Kyrgyz Republic																
Latvia						5.19	6.62	6.66	6.97	6.83	6.89	7.18	7.21	7.03	6.88	6.73
Lesotho																
Lithuania						5.10	6.28	6.32	6.77	6.74	6.68	7.11	7.09	7.15	7.08	7.02
Luxembourg	7.59	7.64	7.58	7.94	7.88	7.70	7.87	7.85	7.71	7.73	7.76	7.47	7.49	7.51	7.52	7.42
Macedonia																
Madagascar			4.55	4.79	4.68	4.67	5.94	6.27	5.82	6.07	5.90	5.94	6.00	6.29	6.28	6.40
Malawi		5.38	4.94	5.16	5.48	4.69	5.01	5.52	5.58	6.00	5.68	5.46	5.33	5.79	5.95	6.00
Malaysia	6.63	6.42	7.07	7.12	7.49	7.55	6.72	6.35	6.55	6.64	6.80	6.89	6.92	6.96	6.71	6.68
Mali		5.68	5.78	4.93	5.16	5.26	6.23	6.07	5.73	6.12	5.93	6.03	6.28	6.35	5.98	6.03
Malta			5.57	5.23	5.42	6.56	6.45	6.42	6.49	6.18	6.94	7.10	7.09	7.25	7.02	6.98
Mauritania																
Mauritius		5.21	5.16	6.25	6.23	7.29	7.39	7.16	7.01	6.89	6.83	7.17	7.16	7.53	7.61	7.47
Mexico	6.53	5.80	5.69	4.91	6.28	6.46	6.39	6.24	6.52	6.48	6.61	7.00	6.97	6.92	6.87	6.75
Moldova																
Mongolia																
Montenegro																
Morocco	5.76	5.16	4.54	5.25	5.27	6.15	6.12	6.10	6.11	6.28	6.09	6.31	6.29	6.29	6.29	6.25
Mozambique																
Myanmar			4.84	4.42	3.46	4.02	4.00	3.77	3.41	3.21	3.54	3.67	3.87	3.36	3.49	3.59
Namibia					5.33	6.28	6.47	6.49	6.49	6.59	6.32	6.56	6.51	6.75	6.63	6.63
Nepal			5.75	5.31	5.42	5.37	5.75	5.78	5.70	5.21	5.27	5.38	5.42	5.58	5.44	5.40
Netherlands	7.64	6.96	7.51	7.65	7.82	7.80	8.05	7.76	7.78	7.70	7.69	7.59	7.50	7.52	7.45	7.25
New Zealand	6.72	6.02	6.73	6.57	7.95	8.64	8.35	8.22	8.37	8.38	8.38	8.37	8.16	8.30	8.22	8.15
Nicaragua			4.17	2.11	2.96	5.38	6.50	6.30	6.57	6.67	6.57	6.82	6.92	7.09	6.83	6.76
Niger			4.69	5.06	5.06	4.43	5.42	5.05	5.02	5.09	5.47	5.40	5.49	5.42	5.35	5.47
Nigeria	3.82	3.76	3.76	4.04	3.73	4.20	5.52	5.31	5.77	5.82	5.84	6.01	6.21	6.21	5.96	5.84
Norway	6.38	5.90	6.17	6.70	7.26	7.34	7.04	6.84	6.78	7.35	7.32	7.47	7.42	7.45	7.36	7.24
Oman				6.70	6.23	6.73	7.03	7.11	7.07	7.30	7.26	7.33	7.37	7.50	7.40	7.64
Pakistan	4.57	3.83	4.65	5.09	5.13	5.73	5.55	5.61	5.70	5.49	5.49	5.90	5.92	5.94	5.83	6.00

Exhibit 1.6 (continued): The Chain-Linked Summary Index of Ratings, 1970–2009

	1970	1975	1980	1985	1990	1995	2000	2001	2002	2003	2004	2005	2006	2007	2008	2009
Panama		6.68	5.66	6.22	6.53	7.36	7.41	7.38	7.36	7.40	7.38	7.47	7.53	7.52	7.32	7.30
Papua New Guinea				6.16	6.31	6.53	5.96	5.99	5.91	5.89	5.93	6.51	6.51	6.92	6.94	6.98
Paraguay			5.76	5.12	5.78	6.50	6.28	6.35	6.23	6.22	6.15	6.46	6.53	6.49	6.62	6.65
Peru	4.75	4.03	4.27	3.11	4.13	6.31	7.07	7.05	7.06	7.07	7.09	7.19	7.18	7.24	7.36	7.29
Philippines	5.73	5.42	5.42	5.11	5.85	7.24	6.98	6.81	6.91	6.95	6.72	7.09	7.00	6.91	6.77	6.45
Poland				4.07	4.00	5.30	6.19	5.97	6.30	6.26	6.71	6.78	6.80	6.85	6.88	6.90
Portugal	6.37	4.28	5.99	5.74	6.54	7.32	7.37	7.25	7.41	7.38	7.48	7.11	7.16	7.16	7.07	6.90
Romania				4.64	4.54	3.90	5.19	5.25	5.75	6.04	6.01	6.82	6.73	6.95	6.72	6.93
Russia						4.49	5.27	5.15	5.57	5.64	5.93	6.37	6.36	6.50	6.57	6.50
Rwanda					5.08	3.89	5.45	5.65	5.96	5.49	5.48	5.70	6.00	6.22	6.61	6.43
Senegal			4.65	5.31	5.41	4.83	5.90	5.72	5.81	5.70	5.73	5.70	5.61	5.67	5.56	5.67
Serbia																
Sierra Leone		5.43	5.51	3.89	4.04	4.47	5.31	5.12	5.42	5.68	5.49	5.35	5.43	5.79	5.42	5.44
Singapore	7.89	7.58	7.93	8.13	8.73	8.81	8.53	8.44	8.66	8.57	8.57	8.82	8.75	8.79	8.75	8.73
Slovak Rep						5.54	6.16	6.49	6.47	6.81	7.36	7.67	7.56	7.56	7.55	7.53
Slovenia						4.76	6.36	6.49	6.47	6.56	6.55	6.41	6.49	6.47	6.52	6.46
South Africa	6.69	5.97	6.12	5.78	5.62	6.44	6.96	6.92	6.98	7.10	6.93	6.77	6.75	6.79	6.53	6.39
Spain	6.71	6.02	6.19	6.18	6.51	7.04	7.31	7.06	7.10	7.50	7.50	7.35	7.28	7.27	7.19	6.92
Sri Lanka			5.10	5.17	5.02	6.02	6.10	6.02	5.95	6.11	5.93	5.97	6.04	6.02	5.90	5.98
Sweden	5.77	5.64	5.95	6.66	7.08	7.14	7.44	7.16	7.39	7.52	7.29	7.35	7.31	7.29	7.26	7.22
Switzerland	7.95	7.78	8.18	8.28	8.22	7.96	8.39	8.14	8.28	8.26	8.21	8.07	8.07	8.11	7.91	7.93
Syria	4.27	4.47	3.67	3.36	3.87	4.53	4.91	5.22	4.96	4.82	5.21	5.46	5.20	5.48	5.08	5.31
Taiwan	6.88	6.10	6.92	7.10	7.39	7.33	7.31	7.19	7.38	7.39	7.60	7.69	7.74	7.68	7.54	7.42
Tanzania	4.79	3.72	4.06	3.73	4.24	5.53	5.95	6.05	5.89	5.91	6.02	6.02	6.10	5.99	5.89	6.02
Thailand	6.06	6.05	6.19	6.21	6.97	7.19	6.52	6.20	6.67	6.66	6.68	6.92	7.02	7.04	7.04	6.96
Togo			4.22	5.16	5.65	5.38	5.84	6.07	6.22	5.84	5.67	5.87	6.00	5.70	5.65	5.63
Trinidad & Tobago		4.80	5.07	4.92	5.64	6.93	7.18	7.11	6.89	6.77	6.78	6.75	6.85	6.81	6.83	6.68
Tunisia	4.80	4.78	5.09	4.80	5.48	5.75	6.03	6.05	5.95	5.93	5.97	6.05	6.03	6.01	5.98	5.96
Turkey	4.06	4.19	3.95	5.08	5.14	5.72	5.75	5.25	5.51	6.00	6.12	6.36	6.47	6.53	6.91	6.84
Uganda			3.42	3.01	3.00	5.17	6.57	6.51	6.52	6.62	6.61	6.85	7.01	7.15	7.12	7.10
Ukraine						3.72	4.70	4.80	5.39	5.29	5.55	5.60	5.68	5.76	5.60	5.69
United Arab Emir.			5.92	6.79	7.18	6.77	7.02	6.99	7.07	7.11	6.96	7.22	7.35	7.27	7.38	7.26
United Kingdom	6.56	6.29	6.73	7.66	8.14	8.04	8.25	8.11	8.15	8.25	8.10	8.04	7.96	7.84	7.78	7.68
United States	7.74	7.83	8.03	8.18	8.43	8.32	8.45	8.23	8.22	8.17	8.15	8.07	8.01	8.08	7.89	7.58
Uruguay			5.95	5.86	6.17	6.11	6.68	6.50	6.75	6.63	6.74	6.74	6.67	6.69	6.67	6.64
Venezuela	6.81	5.80	6.29	5.95	5.45	4.34	5.61	5.50	4.51	4.07	4.53	4.74	4.82	4.37	4.30	4.23
Vietnam																
Zambia		4.60	5.08	3.97	3.52	4.87	6.63	6.58	6.56	6.72	6.76	6.99	7.31	7.36	7.30	7.35
Zimbabwe			4.93	4.85	5.05	5.81	4.59	3.62	3.59	3.77	3.32	3.37	3.39	2.96	4.03	4.06

Exhibit 1.7 shows the five countries whose ratings on the Chain-Linked Summary Index have improved the most since 2000. Cyprus and Ghana achieved the greatest improvement: Cyprus jumped from a rating of 6.17 in 2000 to 7.48 in 2009, pushing its ranking to 18th; Ghana's rating improved from 5.86 in 2000 to 7.15 in 2009, pushing its ranking up from 90th to 70th. The ratings of Colombia, Malawi, and Turkey improved by approximately one point between 2000 and 2009. Clearly, the countries with the greatest improvements were a diverse group.

Exhibit 1.8 shows the five countries, among the 123 for which the data were available, whose ratings on the Chain-Linked Summary Index declined the most since 2000: Argentina, Iceland, Ireland, United States, and Venezuela. Argentina's rating fell from 7.19 in 2000 to 5.92 in 2009, causing its ranking to plummet from 32nd to 102nd. Venezuela's rating declined from 5.61 in 2000 to 4.23 in 2009, pushing its ranking down from 101st to 121st. The ratings of Iceland and Ireland fell sharply beginning in 2005 as they both ran into financial difficulties.

The chain-linked rating of the United States fell from 8.45 in 2000 to 7.58 in 2009, causing the accompanying ranking to slip from 3rd to 10th. Lower ratings in the legal structure area and government borrowing that dominated the credit market (5Aiii) were primarily responsible for the decline in the overall rating of the United States.

Exhibit 1.7: Countries showing the greatest improvement on the chain-linked EFW index, 2000–2009

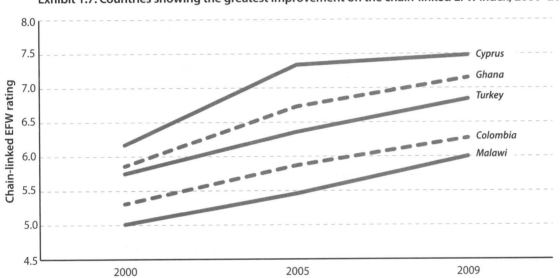

Exhibit 1.8: Countries showing the greatest decline on the chain-linked EFW index, 2000–2009

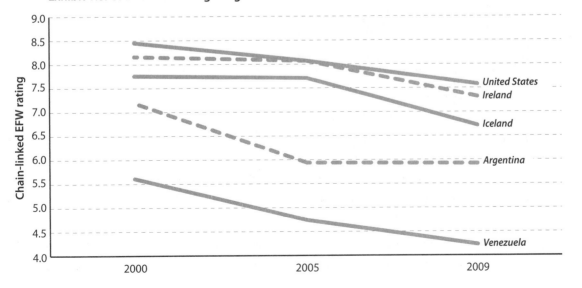

Economic Freedom and other indicators of human and political progress

This graphs shown in exhibits 1.9 to 1.17 illustrate simple relationships between economic freedom and some other indicators of human and political progress. They use the average of the chain-linked EFW index for the period from 1990 to 2009, breaking the data into four quartiles ordered from least free to most free. Because persistence is important and the impact of economic freedom will be felt over a lengthy time period, it is better to use the average rating over a fairly long time span rather than the current rating to observe the impact of economic freedom on performance.

The graphs begin with the data on the relationship between economic freedom and the level of per-capita GDP and economic growth.[1] In recent years, numerous scholarly studies have analyzed these relationships in detail. Almost without exception, these studies have found that countries with higher and improving economic freedom grow more rapidly and achieve higher levels of per-capita GDP.

Many of the relationships illustrated in the graphs below reflect the impact of economic freedom as it works through increasing economic growth. In other cases, the observed relationships may reflect the fact that some of the variables that influence economic freedom may also influence political factors like trust, honesty in government, and protection of civil liberties. Thus, we are not necessarily arguing that there is a direct causal relation between economic freedom and the variables considered below. In other words, these graphics are no substitute for real, scholarly investigation that controls for other factors. Nonetheless, we believe that the graphs provide some insights about the contrast between the nature and characteristics of market-oriented economies and those dominated by government regulation and planning. At the very least, these figures suggest potential fruitful areas for future research.

---

1 The bar chart in exhibit 1.10, Economic Freedom and Economic Growth, is based on a regression in which we controlled for the initial level of development. The regression was: (Growth, 1990–2009) = 3.06 (Most Free Quartile) + 2.43 (Second Quartile) + 2.27 (Third Quartile) + 1.18 (Least Free Quartile) − 0.046 (GDP per capita, 1990).

Exhibit 1.9: Economic Freedom and Income per Capita

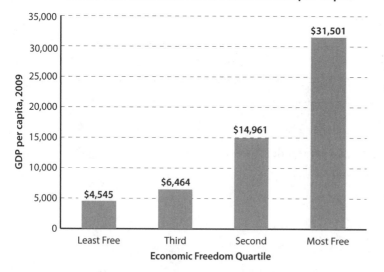

Countries with more economic freedom have substantially higher per-capita incomes.

Sources: Fraser Institute, *Economic Freedom of the World: 2011 Annual Report*; World Bank, *World Development Indicators*.

Exhibit 1.10: Economic Freedom and Economic Growth

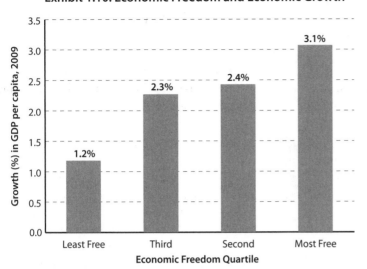

The economies of countries with more economic freedom tend to grow more rapidly.

Note: The data for growth were adjusted to control for the initial level of income.

Sources: Fraser Institute, *Economic Freedom of the World: 2011 Annual Report*; World Bank, *World Development Indicators*.

Exhibit 1.11: Economic Freedom and the Income Share of the Poorest 10%, 1990–2009

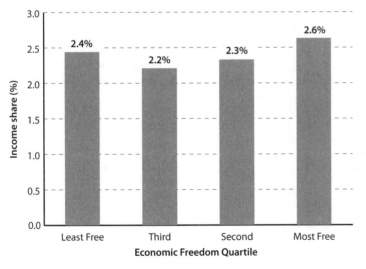

The share of income earned by the poorest 10% of the population is unrelated to economic freedom.

Sources: Fraser Institute, *Economic Freedom of the World: 2011 Annual Report*; World Bank, *World Development Indicators*.

Exhibit 1.12: Economic Freedom and Income per Capita among the Poorest 10%, 2009

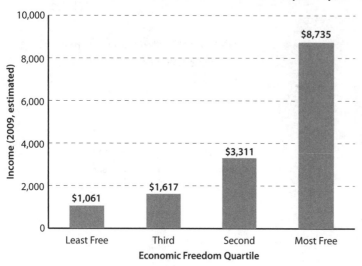

The amount, as opposed to the share, of income earned by the poorest 10% of the population is much higher in countries with greater economic freedom.

Sources: Fraser Institute, *Economic Freedom of the World: 2011 Annual Report*; World Bank, *World Development Indicators.*

Exhibit 1.13: Economic Freedom and Life Expectancy, 2009

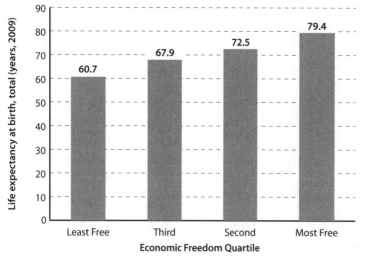

Life expectancy is about 20 years longer in countries with the greatest economic freedom than it is in countries with the least.

Sources: Fraser Institute, *Economic Freedom of the World: 2011 Annual Report*; World Bank, *World Development Indicators.*

Exhibit 1.14: Economic Freedom and Literacy, 2000–2009

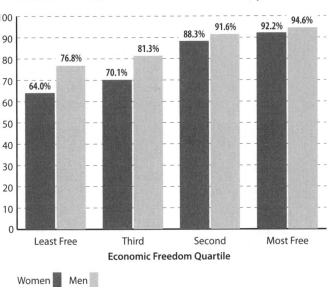

Sources: Fraser Institute, *Economic Freedom of the World: 2011 Annual Report*; World Bank, *World Development Indicators*.

Literacy increases as economic freedom increases, especially for women.

Exhibit 1.15: Economic Freedom and Educational Quality, 2009

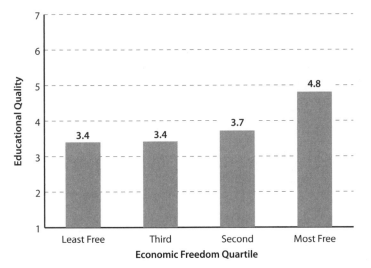

Sources: Fraser Institute, *Economic Freedom of the World: 2011 Annual Report*; World Economic Forum, *Executive Opinion Survey*.

Perceived educational quality increases with economic freedom.

Based on the question: "How well does the educational system in your country meet the needs of a competitive economy? 1 = Not well at all; 7 = Very well" (*Executive Opinion Survey*).

Exhibit 1.16: Economic Freedom and Quality of Healthcare, 2009

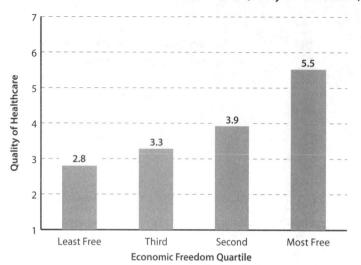

Perceived quality of healthcare increases with economic freedom.

Based on the question: "How would you assess the quality of healthcare provided for ordinary citizens in your country? 1 = Very poor, 7 = Excellent, among the best" (*Executive Opinion Survey*).

Sources: Fraser Institute, *Economic Freedom of the World: 2011 Annual Report*; World Economic Forum, *Executive Opinion Survey*.

Exhibit 1.17: Economic Freedom and Poverty, 2000–2005

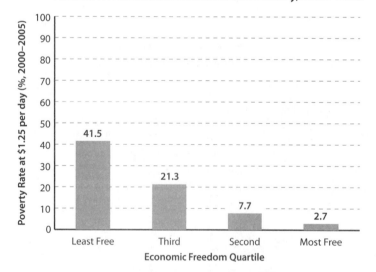

The rate of extreme poverty decreases as economic freedom increases.

Sources: Fraser Institute, *Economic Freedom of the World: 2011 Annual Report*; World Bank, *World Development Indicators* and calculations by Joe Connors (Duke University).

Chapter 2
Country Data Tables

This chapter presents detailed data on the components used in constructing the EFW index for the 141 countries included in this study. For each country for which data were available, we present the overall EFW index rating and the rank of that country for the years 1980, 1985, 1990, 1995, 2000, 2005, 2008, and 2009. (Ratings are also available for many countries for 1970, 1975, 2001, 2002, 2003, 2004, 2006, and 2007, but these data are not shown in the tables due to limited space.) Like all the ratings in the index, these are values out of 10; 10 is the highest possible rating and zero (0) is the lowest. A higher rating indicates a greater degree of economic freedom.

Chain-Linked   The country data tables show both unadjusted and chain-linked ratings and ranks. See chapter 1 for a full explanation of the chain-linked method. The top row under the "Chain-linked" section shows the country's chain-linked summary rating for each year and, in parentheses, its overall rank. In the rows below, titles on the left in bold face indicate the five areas of economic freedom that are combined to generate an overall rating. The cells to their right give the chain-linked rating and, in parentheses, the rank for that particular area for each year.

Unadjusted   The top row under the "Unadjusted" section shows the country's summary rating for each year and, in parentheses, its overall rank. In the rows below, titles on the left in bold face indicate the five areas of economic freedom that are combined to generate an overall score. The cells to their right give the rating for that area for each year. Underneath each area title are the titles of the components and sub-components that are combined to generate that area's score. In these rows are the scores for each year presented, where data are available. Shown in italic beside some scores are the actual data used to derive that particular component rating. For some countries, data for other components for certain years may be reported even though there were insufficient data to compute area or summary ratings. A more complete description of each component, including the methodology used to calculate the ratings, can be found in the Appendix: Explanatory Notes and Data Sources (p. 191).

Data available to researchers
The full data set, including all of the data published in this report as well as data omitted due to limited space, can be downloaded for free at <http://www.freetheworld.com>. The data file available there contains the most up-to-date and accurate data for the Economic Freedom of the World index. Some variable names and data sources have evolved over the years since the first publication in 1996; users should consult earlier editions of the *Economic Freedom of the World* annual reports for details regarding sources and descriptions for those years. All editions of the report are available in PDF and can be downloaded for free from <http://www.freetheworld.com/datasets_efw.html>. However, users are always strongly encouraged to use the data from this most recent data file as updates and corrections, even to earlier years' data, do occur. Users doing long-term or longitudinal studies are encouraged to use the chain-linked index as it is the most consistent through time. If you have problems downloading the data, please contact Jean-François Minardi via e-mail to <freetheworld@fraserinstitute.org> or via telephone +1.514.281.9550 ext. 306. If you have technical questions about the data itself, please contact Robert Lawson via e-mail to <rlawson@smu.edu>.

Published work using research ratings from *Economic Freedom of the World*
A selected list of published papers that have used the economic freedom ratings from *Economic Freedom of the World* is available on line at <http://www.freetheworld.com/>. In most cases, a brief abstract of the article is provided. If you know of any other papers current or forthcoming that should be included on this page, or have further information about any of these papers or authors, please write to <freetheworld@fraserinstitute.org>.

Albania

Chain-Linked

	1980 Rating (Rank)	1985 Rating (Rank)	1990 Rating (Rank)	1995 Rating (Rank)	2000 Rating (Rank)	2005 Rating (Rank)	2008 Rating (Rank)	2009 Rating (Rank)
Summary Rating (Rank) ➤			4.24 (99)	4.87 (99)	6.04 (83)	7.06 (47)	7.38 (27)	7.54 (12)
Area 1. Size of Government			3.51 (102)	6.54 (40)	7.63 (18)	8.89 (4)	9.10 (2)	9.06 (3)
Area 2. Legal Structure and Security of Property Rights		5.25 (54)	5.21 (57)	4.64 (97)	4.58 (85)	5.46 (70)	6.02 (56)	6.19 (50)
Area 3. Access to Sound Money		4.89 (94)	4.90 (91)	3.26 (105)	7.40 (71)	9.64 (9)	9.40 (25)	9.63 (6)
Area 4. Freedom to Trade Internationally				5.38 (97)	5.32 (112)	5.41 (106)	6.16 (85)	6.50 (70)
Area 5. Regulation of Credit, Labor, and Business			2.58 (117)	4.55 (99)	5.27 (98)	6.03 (87)	6.39 (70)	6.44 (69)

Unadjusted

	1980 Rating Data	1985 Rating Data	1990 Rating Data	1995 Rating Data	2000 Rating Data	2005 Rating Data	2008 Rating Data	2009 Rating Data
Summary Rating (Rank) ➤			4.60 (98)	4.83 (101)	6.04 (83)	6.86 (69)	7.18 (46)	7.32 (30)
1. Size of Government			4.19	6.54	7.63	8.00	8.24	8.20
A. Government consumption	7.70 (13.81)	7.83 (13.39)	4.87 (23.44)	7.78 (13.55)	9.10 (9.07)	9.00 (9.40)	8.86 (9.87)	8.70 (10.43)
B. Transfers and subsidies			3.51 (24.30)	7.85 (8.40)	7.80 (8.57)	9.70 (1.70)	9.59 (2.01)	9.59 (2.01)
C. Government enterprises and investment				4.00 (39.00)	6.00 (26.70)	8.00 (19.50)	6.00 (26.38)	6.00 (28.93)
D. Top marginal tax rate						5.50	8.50	8.50
(i) Top marginal income tax rate						9.00 (25)	10.00 (10)	10.00 (10)
(ii) Top marginal income and payroll tax rates						2.00 (51)	7.00 (35)	7.00 (35)
2. Legal Structure and Security of Property Rights		5.25	5.21	4.64	4.58	4.80	5.30	5.45
A. Judicial independence						2.40	3.23	3.77
B. Impartial courts				3.94	4.31	2.70	4.39	4.70
C. Protection of property rights						3.40	3.72	3.91
D. Military interference in rule of law and politics				3.65	6.67	8.30	8.33	8.33
E. Integrity of the legal system				6.96	3.33	3.70	4.17	4.17
F. Legal enforcement of contracts						5.20	5.17	5.17
G. Regulatory restrictions on sale of real property						8.10	8.09	8.09
3. Access to Sound Money		6.52	6.54	3.26	7.40	9.60	9.40	9.63
A. Money growth				0.00 (78.90)	9.57 (2.16)	9.50 (2.50)	8.88 (5.60)	9.24 (3.80)
B. Standard deviation of inflation		9.64 (0.91)	9.62 (0.95)	0.00 (86.94)	5.03 (12.43)	9.50 (1.16)	9.37 (1.57)	9.75 (0.63)
C. Inflation: most recent year		9.93 (0.35)	10.00 (0.00)	8.03 (9.83)	9.99 (0.05)	9.50 (2.37)	9.33 (3.36)	9.54 (2.28)
D. Freedom to own foreign currency bank accounts	0.00	0.00	0.00	5.00	5.00	10.00	10.00	10.00
4. Freedom to Trade Internationally				5.18	5.32	5.50	6.29	6.63
A. Taxes on international trade				5.70	6.11	8.20	8.44	8.45
(i) Revenues from trade taxes (% of trade sector)				5.70 (6.45)	5.14 (7.29)	8.10 (2.80)	8.57 (2.14)	8.57 (2.14)
(ii) Mean tariff rate					6.60 (17.00)	8.70 (6.30)	8.96 (5.20)	9.00 (5.00)
(iii) Standard deviation of tariff rates					6.60 (8.50)	7.80 (5.40)	7.78 (5.56)	7.78 (5.55)
B. Regulatory trade barriers						4.90	6.86	6.90
(i) Non-tariff trade barriers						4.40	6.27	6.35
(ii) Compliance cost of importing and exporting						5.40	7.45	7.45
C. Size of trade sector relative to expected	0.51	0.00	0.00	0.00	0.74	1.20	2.97	2.36
D. Black-market exchange rates	0.00	0.00	0.00	10.00	10.00	10.00	10.00	10.00
E. International capital market controls	0.00	0.00	0.00	2.00	1.54	3.30	3.16	5.44
(i) Foreign ownership/investment restrictions						5.00	5.50	6.26
(ii) Capital controls	0.00	0.00	0.00	2.00	1.54	1.50	0.83	4.62
5. Regulation of Credit, Labor, and Business			2.47	4.55	5.27	6.30	6.67	6.72
A. Credit market regulations			0.00	4.55	4.61	7.90	8.12	8.12
(i) Ownership of banks			0.00	2.00	2.00	5.00	5.00	5.00
(ii) Foreign bank competition						9.00	9.00	9.00
(iii) Private sector credit				5.64	2.83	8.50	8.46	8.46
(iv) Interest rate controls/negative real interest rates			0.00	6.00	9.00	9.00	10.00	10.00
B. Labor market regulations						6.00	5.79	5.94
(i) Hiring regulations and minimum wage						5.60	5.60	5.57
(ii) Hiring and firing regulations						6.70	6.15	6.05
(iii) Centralized collective bargaining						7.70	7.20	7.02
(iv) Hours regulations						8.00	8.00	8.00
(v) Mandated cost of worker dismissal						4.80	4.81	6.03
(vi) Conscription	0.00	0.00	0.00	3.00	10.00	3.00	3.00	3.00
C. Business regulations						5.00	6.10	6.10
(i) Price controls			0.00	4.00	4.00	6.00	6.00	6.00
(ii) Administrative requirements						2.70	3.97	5.01
(iii) Bureaucracy costs						1.00	6.66	6.30
(iv) Starting a business						8.40	9.66	9.66
(v) Extra payments/bribes/favoritism						4.90	4.29	4.91
(vi) Licensing restrictions						4.60	4.82	4.83
(vii) Cost of tax compliance						7.30	7.26	5.96

Algeria

	1980	1985	1990	1995	2000	2005	2008	2009
Chain-Linked	Rating (Rank)	Rating (Rank)	Rating (Rank)	Rating (Rank)	Rating (Rank)	Rating (Rank)	Rating (Rank)	Rating (Rank)
Summary Rating (Rank) ➤	**4.30** (87)	**4.05** (95)	**3.89** (105)	**4.53** (109)	**4.98** (115)	**5.83** (103)	**5.34** (113)	**5.39** (114)
Area 1. Size of Government	4.72 (64)	3.55 (95)	5.02 (73)	6.71 (36)	5.65 (80)	4.84 (106)	3.49 (122)	3.56 (119)
Area 2. Legal Structure and Security of Property Rights	3.77 (60)	3.52 (82)	3.50 (83)	3.68 (112)	2.87 (120)	5.45 (71)	4.67 (88)	4.80 (86)
Area 3. Access to Sound Money	5.23 (89)	6.30 (74)	4.50 (97)	5.37 (84)	7.00 (80)	7.51 (79)	7.61 (80)	7.01 (93)
Area 4. Freedom to Trade Internationally	4.29 (70)	3.58 (78)	3.38 (100)	3.95 (108)	5.72 (104)	6.32 (82)	5.94 (95)	6.40 (72)
Area 5. Regulation of Credit, Labor, and Business			2.96 (110)	2.92 (122)	3.66 (122)	5.12 (113)	5.03 (115)	5.21 (114)

Unadjusted								
Summary Rating (Rank) ➤	**4.49** (83)	**4.24** (92)	**3.87** (106)	**4.53** (109)	**4.98** (115)	**5.81** (116)	**5.32** (130)	**5.36** (131)
	Rating Data	Rating Data	Rating Data	Rating Data	Rating Data	Rating Data	Rating Data	Rating Data
1. Size of Government	**4.32**	**3.25**	**4.60**	**6.71**	**5.65**	**4.80**	**3.49**	**3.56**
A. Government consumption	4.65 (24.19)	4.50 (24.69)	5.19 (22.35)	5.29 (22.01)	4.53 (24.60)	3.90 (26.70)	2.44 (31.72)	2.48 (31.56)
B. Transfers and subsidies				7.84 (8.43)	8.41 (6.32)	8.60 (5.50)	8.04 (7.68)	8.18 (7.16)
C. Government enterprises and investment	4.00 (32.50)	2.00 (47.90)	4.00 (30.40)	7.00 (24.90)	4.00 (37.80)	2.00 (48.40)	0.00 (61.26)	0.00 (61.26)
D. Top marginal tax rate								
(i) Top marginal income tax rate								
(ii) Top marginal income and payroll tax rates								
2. Legal Structure and Security of Property Rights	**3.77**	**3.52**	**3.50**	**3.68**	**2.87**	**5.20**	**4.46**	**4.58**
A. Judicial independence						4.60	3.02	3.00
B. Impartial courts				3.61	3.84	5.10	3.52	3.62
C. Protection of property rights						5.80	3.54	4.29
D. Military interference in rule of law and politics				0.00	0.00	5.00	5.00	5.00
E. Integrity of the legal system				6.96	3.33	5.00	5.00	5.00
F. Legal enforcement of contracts						4.40	4.39	4.39
G. Regulatory restrictions on sale of real property						6.60	6.78	6.78
3. Access to Sound Money	**5.23**	**6.30**	**4.50**	**5.37**	**7.00**	**7.50**	**7.61**	**7.01**
A. Money growth	8.35 (8.24)	7.81 (10.96)	9.35 (3.25)	8.11 (9.44)	7.95 (10.26)	7.80 (10.80)	7.57 (12.17)	8.01 (9.95)
B. Standard deviation of inflation	7.70 (5.75)	8.33 (4.17)	5.53 (11.17)	4.07 (14.83)	5.14 (12.16)	7.50 (6.20)	8.78 (3.05)	6.19 (9.52)
C. Inflation: most recent year	4.87 (25.66)	9.07 (4.64)	3.12 (34.40)	4.31 (28.46)	9.93 (0.34)	9.70 (1.64)	9.11 (4.44)	8.85 (5.74)
D. Freedom to own foreign currency bank accounts	0.00	0.00	0.00	5.00	5.00	5.00	5.00	5.00
4. Freedom to Trade Internationally	**4.66**	**3.88**	**3.67**	**3.95**	**5.72**	**6.20**	**5.82**	**6.27**
A. Taxes on international trade	7.66	5.66	5.08	3.72	4.95	7.00	6.87	6.90
(i) Revenues from trade taxes (% of trade sector)				3.58 (9.63)	6.36 (5.46)	8.20 (2.70)	8.49 (2.26)	8.58 (2.13)
(ii) Mean tariff rate	7.66 (11.70)	5.66 (21.70)	5.08 (24.60)	5.42 (22.90)	5.08 (24.60)	6.80 (15.80)	6.28 (18.60)	6.28 (18.60)
(iii) Standard deviation of tariff rates				2.16 (19.60)	3.40 (16.50)	5.80 (10.50)	5.83 (10.42)	5.83 (10.42)
B. Regulatory trade barriers						6.30	6.63	6.76
(i) Non-tariff trade barriers						5.20	5.95	6.21
(ii) Compliance cost of importing and exporting						7.50	7.30	7.30
C. Size of trade sector relative to expected	7.39	5.50	5.02	5.77	5.99	6.20	5.96	6.42
D. Black-market exchange rates	0.00	0.00	0.00	0.00	7.78	7.90	8.16	9.18
E. International capital market controls	0.00	0.00	0.00	2.00	1.67	3.50	1.47	2.09
(i) Foreign ownership / investment restrictions						6.10	2.94	3.41
(ii) Capital controls	0.00	0.00	0.00	2.00	1.67	0.90	0.00	0.77
5. Regulation of Credit, Labor, and Business			**3.07**	**2.92**	**3.66**	**5.30**	**5.20**	**5.37**
A. Credit market regulations	0.00	0.00	0.87	0.48	2.26	5.30	5.32	5.54
(i) Ownership of banks	0.00	0.00	0.00	0.00	0.00	0.00	0.00	0.00
(ii) Foreign bank competition						8.00	8.00	8.00
(iii) Private sector credit			1.74	1.44	1.78	3.30	4.28	4.17
(iv) Interest rate controls / negative real interest rates				0.00	5.00	10.00	9.00	10.00
B. Labor market regulations						5.20	4.93	5.32
(i) Hiring regulations and minimum wage						5.60	5.60	5.57
(ii) Hiring and firing regulations						4.40	3.66	4.70
(iii) Centralized collective bargaining						5.60	4.91	5.85
(iv) Hours regulations						6.00	6.00	6.00
(v) Mandated cost of worker dismissal						8.40	8.42	8.79
(vi) Conscription	5.00	0.00	1.00	1.00	1.00	1.00	1.00	1.00
C. Business regulations						5.40	5.35	5.26
(i) Price controls			2.00	2.00	4.00	4.00	4.00	4.00
(ii) Administrative requirements						3.30	2.34	2.12
(iii) Bureaucracy costs						3.70	6.45	5.91
(iv) Starting a business						8.90	9.00	8.98
(v) Extra payments / bribes / favoritism						5.70	3.75	3.92
(vi) Licensing restrictions						6.90	6.93	6.93
(vii) Cost of tax compliance						4.90	4.94	4.94

Angola

	1980	1985	1990	1995	2000	2005	2008	2009
Chain-Linked						Rating (Rank)	Rating (Rank)	Rating (Rank)
Summary Rating (Rank) ➤								
Area 1. Size of Government								
Area 2. Legal Structure and Security of Property Rights								
Area 3. Access to Sound Money								
Area 4. Freedom to Trade Internationally								
Area 5. Regulation of Credit, Labor, and Business								

	1980	1985	1990	1995	2000	2005	2008	2009
Unadjusted								
Summary Rating (Rank) ➤						**3.47** (140)	**3.89** (140)	**4.76** (138)
						Rating *Data*	Rating *Data*	Rating *Data*
1. Size of Government						**1.30**	**0.00**	**3.48**
A. Government consumption						2.60 *(31.20)*	0.00 *(45.48)*	0.95 *(36.76)*
B. Transfers and subsidies								
C. Government enterprises and investment						0.00 *(62.50)*	0.00 *(85.23)*	0.00 *(83.75)*
D. Top marginal tax rate								9.50
(i) Top marginal income tax rate								10.00 *(17)*
(ii) Top marginal income and payroll tax rates								9.00 *(25)*
2. Legal Structure and Security of Property Rights						**3.20**	**3.34**	**3.30**
A. Judicial independence						3.10		3.26
B. Impartial courts						2.90	3.30	3.37
C. Protection of property rights						4.10		3.11
D. Military interference in rule of law and politics						3.30	3.33	3.33
E. Integrity of the legal system						5.00	5.00	5.00
F. Legal enforcement of contracts						2.30	2.30	2.30
G. Regulatory restrictions on sale of real property						1.40	2.78	2.74
3. Access to Sound Money						**1.30**	**5.03**	**5.24**
A. Money growth						0.00 *(53.90)*	3.35 *(33.23)*	4.81 *(25.94)*
B. Standard deviation of inflation						0.00 *(40.17)*	4.27 *(14.32)*	3.89 *(15.28)*
C. Inflation: most recent year						5.00 *(24.76)*	7.51 *(12.47)*	7.25 *(13.73)*
D. Freedom to own foreign currency bank accounts						0.00	5.00	5.00
4. Freedom to Trade Internationally						**7.10**	**6.00**	**6.40**
A. Taxes on international trade						7.90	7.93	7.91
(i) Revenues from trade taxes (% of trade sector)								
(ii) Mean tariff rate						8.50 *(7.60)*	8.54 *(7.30)*	8.54 *(7.30)*
(iii) Standard deviation of tariff rates						7.40 *(6.60)*	7.31 *(6.72)*	7.28 *(6.79)*
B. Regulatory trade barriers						4.00	1.32	3.62
(i) Non-tariff trade barriers						6.70		4.49
(ii) Compliance cost of importing and exporting						1.40	1.32	2.75
C. Size of trade sector relative to expected						10.00	10.00	8.24
D. Black-market exchange rates						10.00	10.00	10.00
E. International capital market controls						3.70	0.77	2.23
(i) Foreign ownership/investment restrictions						5.80		3.70
(ii) Capital controls						1.50	0.77	0.77
5. Regulation of Credit, Labor, and Business						**4.50**	**5.10**	**5.36**
A. Credit market regulations						6.20	6.45	7.16
(i) Ownership of banks						5.00	5.00	5.00
(ii) Foreign bank competition						9.00	9.00	9.00
(iii) Private sector credit						5.60	4.78	5.65
(iv) Interest rate controls/negative real interest rates						5.00	7.00	9.00
B. Labor market regulations						4.00	2.98	3.87
(i) Hiring regulations and minimum wage						3.30	3.30	3.33
(ii) Hiring and firing regulations						4.40		4.60
(iii) Centralized collective bargaining						7.60		6.34
(iv) Hours regulations						4.00	4.00	4.00
(v) Mandated cost of worker dismissal						4.60	4.62	4.98
(vi) Conscription						0.00	0.00	0.00
C. Business regulations						3.50	5.86	5.04
(i) Price controls								
(ii) Administrative requirements						2.20		1.67
(iii) Bureaucracy costs						0.50		7.93
(iv) Starting a business						3.10	6.14	6.02
(v) Extra payments/bribes/favoritism						4.90		3.47
(vi) Licensing restrictions						3.20	4.49	4.31
(vii) Cost of tax compliance						7.00	6.95	6.84

Argentina

Chain-Linked	1980		1985		1990		1995		2000		2005		2008		2009	
	Rating	(Rank)	Rating	(Rank)	Rating	(Rank)	Rating	(Rank)	Rating	(Rank)	Rating	(Rank)	Rating	(Rank)	Rating	(Rank)
Summary Rating (Rank) ➤	4.41	(85)	3.98	(97)	4.78	(91)	6.77	(35)	7.19	(32)	5.94	(96)	6.01	(93)	5.92	(102)
Area 1. Size of Government	6.10	(23)	5.22	(51)	6.18	(41)	8.22	(7)	7.78	(17)	7.56	(24)	6.37	(63)	6.24	(64)
Area 2. Legal Structure and Security of Property Rights	4.51	(53)	4.90	(61)	6.48	(37)	5.45	(61)	5.41	(68)	4.53	(92)	4.45	(96)	4.45	(94)
Area 3. Access to Sound Money	2.50	(104)	2.50	(106)	2.50	(109)	6.57	(63)	9.71	(4)	5.44	(114)	6.90	(89)	7.03	(90)
Area 4. Freedom to Trade Internationally	4.00	(73)	2.59	(91)	4.14	(89)	6.98	(43)	6.29	(82)	6.01	(91)	6.38	(81)	5.81	(93)
Area 5. Regulation of Credit, Labor, and Business	5.10	(58)	5.02	(59)	4.85	(81)	6.65	(22)	6.74	(33)	6.17	(76)	5.95	(94)	6.10	(91)

Unadjusted	1980		1985		1990		1995		2000		2005		2008		2009	
Summary Rating (Rank) ➤	4.35	(86)	3.92	(101)	4.65	(96)	6.76	(38)	7.19	(32)	5.92	(112)	5.99	(113)	5.90	(119)
	Rating	Data	Rating	Data	Rating	Data	Rating	Data	Rating	Data	Rating	Data	Rating	Data	Rating	Data
1. Size of Government	**6.10**		**5.22**		**6.18**		**8.22**		**7.78**		**7.60**		**6.37**		**6.24**	
A. Government consumption	6.91	(16.50)	7.94	(13.00)	8.53	(11.00)	8.06	(12.60)	6.88	(16.62)	7.00	(16.30)	6.20	(18.92)	5.68	(20.68)
B. Transfers and subsidies	7.49	(9.70)	6.95	(11.70)	8.17	(7.20)	7.33	(10.30)	7.22	(10.69)	8.30	(6.80)	8.28	(6.82)	8.28	(6.82)
C. Government enterprises and investment	4.00	(39.50)	4.00	(38.30)	4.00	(30.00)	10.00	(8.50)	10.00	(6.44)	10.00	(11.00)	6.00		6.00	
D. Top marginal tax rate	6.00		2.00		4.00		7.50		7.00		5.00		5.00		5.00	
(i) Top marginal income tax rate	6.00	(45)	2.00	(62)	7.00	(35)	9.00	(30)	8.00	(35)	7.00	(35)	7.00	(35)	7.00	(35)
(ii) Top marginal income and payroll tax rates					1.00	(57)	6.00	(40)	6.00	(36-43)	3.00	(46)	3.00	(46)	3.00	(49)
2. Legal Structure and Security of Property Rights	**4.20**		**4.56**		**6.03**		**5.45**		**5.41**		**4.50**		**4.45**		**4.45**	
A. Judicial independence							3.87		3.17		2.00		2.35		2.60	
B. Impartial courts							4.20		5.18		2.60		2.21		2.40	
C. Protection of property rights							4.57		3.72		3.20		3.19		2.75	
D. Military interference in rule of law and politics							7.66		6.67		7.20		7.50		7.50	
E. Integrity of the legal system							6.96		8.33		5.00		4.17		4.17	
F. Legal enforcement of contracts											5.00		5.02		5.02	
G. Regulatory restrictions on sale of real property											6.70		6.72		6.72	
3. Access to Sound Money	**2.50**		**2.50**		**2.50**		**6.57**		**9.71**		**5.40**		**6.90**		**7.03**	
A. Money growth	0.00	(90.34)	0.00	(252.73)	0.00	(441.58)	7.07	(14.66)	9.50	(−2.48)	3.30	(33.40)	7.39	(13.06)	7.80	(10.99)
B. Standard deviation of inflation	0.00	(119.77)	0.00	(208.29)	0.00	(1198.84)	0.00	(52.44)	9.52	(1.20)	5.40	(11.56)	8.33	(4.18)	8.50	(3.74)
C. Inflation: most recent year	0.00	(92.02)	0.00	(620.84)	0.00	(2064.19)	9.23	(3.87)	9.81	(−0.94)	8.10	(9.64)	6.87	(15.66)	6.80	(16.00)
D. Freedom to own foreign currency bank accounts	10.00		10.00		10.00		10.00		10.00		5.00		5.00		5.00	
4. Freedom to Trade Internationally	**4.42**		**2.87**		**4.29**		**6.93**		**6.29**		**6.00**		**6.38**		**5.81**	
A. Taxes on international trade	4.05		3.07		3.19		7.46		7.47		6.50		6.55		6.26	
(i) Revenues from trade taxes (% of trade sector)	3.67	(9.50)	1.53	(12.70)	3.40	(9.90)	7.53	(3.70)	7.92	(3.12)	5.60	(6.60)	5.58	(6.62)	5.58	(6.62)
(ii) Mean tariff rate	4.44	(27.80)	4.60	(27.00)	5.90	(20.50)	7.90	(10.50)	7.48	(12.60)	7.90	(10.60)	7.68	(11.60)	7.48	(12.60)
(iii) Standard deviation of tariff rates					0.28	(24.30)	6.96	(7.60)	7.00	(7.50)	6.00	(10.00)	6.38	(9.05)	5.72	(10.71)
B. Regulatory trade barriers							7.17		6.42		5.70		5.94		5.56	
(i) Non-tariff trade barriers							7.17		6.18		3.80		3.80		3.05	
(ii) Compliance cost of importing and exporting									6.66		7.60		8.08		8.08	
C. Size of trade sector relative to expected	0.00		0.99		0.00		0.49		0.98		4.90		4.90		3.82	
D. Black-market exchange rates	9.80		2.00		10.00		10.00		10.00		10.00		10.00		10.00	
E. International capital market controls	0.00		0.00		0.00		9.53		6.58		2.90		4.51		3.40	
(i) Foreign ownership / investment restrictions							9.06		9.31		5.90		5.17		5.26	
(ii) Capital controls	0.00		0.00		0.00		10.00		3.85		0.00		3.85		1.54	
5. Regulation of Credit, Labor, and Business	**4.53**		**4.46**		**4.27**		**6.63**		**6.74**		**6.10**		**5.86**		**5.99**	
A. Credit market regulations	4.45		4.20		3.70		7.92		7.68		8.20		7.94		8.19	
(i) Ownership of banks	5.00		5.00		5.00		5.00		5.00		5.00		5.00		5.00	
(ii) Foreign bank competition							8.63		7.33		8.00		8.00		8.00	
(iii) Private sector credit	8.34		7.61		6.09		7.61		6.95		9.80		9.78		9.78	
(iv) Interest rate controls / negative real interest rates	0.00		0.00		0.00		10.00		10.00		10.00		9.00		10.00	
B. Labor market regulations	3.73		3.70		3.46		5.94		6.11		5.10		5.18		5.32	
(i) Hiring regulations and minimum wage							5.95		4.42		5.60		5.60		3.90	
(ii) Hiring and firing regulations					3.00		3.00		5.28		2.50		2.87		2.76	
(iii) Centralized collective bargaining	5.18		5.18		5.18		5.18		4.83		4.60		3.44		3.32	
(iv) Hours regulations	5.01		4.93		4.66		5.55		6.01		8.00		8.00		10.00	
(v) Mandated cost of worker dismissal											0.00		1.19		1.97	
(vi) Conscription	1.00		1.00		1.00		10.00		10.00		10.00		10.00		10.00	
C. Business regulations							6.02		6.44		4.90		4.44		4.44	
(i) Price controls							8.00		8.00		1.00		0.00		0.00	
(ii) Administrative requirements									6.78		2.50		2.79		2.68	
(iii) Bureaucracy costs							6.70		7.50		7.10		5.52		5.74	
(iv) Starting a business							6.22		4.83		8.90		9.01		9.01	
(v) Extra payments / bribes / favoritism							3.16		5.07		5.00		3.72		3.57	
(vi) Licensing restrictions											4.90		5.14		5.16	
(vii) Cost of tax compliance											4.90		4.92		4.92	

Armenia

	1980	1985	1990	1995	2000	2005	2008	2009
Chain-Linked						Rating (Rank)	Rating (Rank)	Rating (Rank)
Summary Rating (Rank) ➤								
Area 1. Size of Government								
Area 2. Legal Structure and Security of Property Rights								
Area 3. Access to Sound Money								
Area 4. Freedom to Trade Internationally								
Area 5. Regulation of Credit, Labor, and Business								

Unadjusted	1980	1985	1990	1995	2000	2005	2008	2009
Summary Rating (Rank) ➤						**7.16** (44)	**7.11** (50)	**7.15** (43)
						Rating *Data*	Rating *Data*	Rating *Data*
1. Size of Government						**7.70**	**7.62**	**7.67**
A. Government consumption						8.20 *(12.30)*	7.64 *(14.04)*	7.82 *(13.42)*
B. Transfers and subsidies						8.30 *(6.60)*	7.84 *(8.44)*	7.87 *(8.32)*
C. Government enterprises and investment						6.00	6.00	6.00
D. Top marginal tax rate						8.50	9.00	9.00
(i) Top marginal income tax rate						9.00	10.00 *(20)*	10.00 *(20)*
(ii) Top marginal income and payroll tax rates						8.00	8.00 *(26)*	8.00 *(26)*
2. Legal Structure and Security of Property Rights						**5.50**	**5.49**	**5.47**
A. Judicial independence						2.10	2.10	2.71
B. Impartial courts						3.00	3.13	3.40
C. Protection of property rights						5.50	5.37	4.45
D. Military interference in rule of law and politics						5.80	5.83	5.83
E. Integrity of the legal system						5.00	5.00	5.00
F. Legal enforcement of contracts						7.20	7.16	7.16
G. Regulatory restrictions on sale of real property						9.80	9.83	9.77
3. Access to Sound Money						**9.20**	**8.88**	**9.44**
A. Money growth						7.60 *(12.20)*	8.14 *(9.30)*	9.46 *(2.71)*
B. Standard deviation of inflation						9.40 *(1.48)*	9.18 *(2.05)*	8.97 *(2.57)*
C. Inflation: most recent year						9.90 *(0.64)*	8.21 *(8.95)*	9.32 *(3.41)*
D. Freedom to own foreign currency bank accounts						10.00	10.00	10.00
4. Freedom to Trade Internationally						**6.60**	**6.61**	**6.49**
A. Taxes on international trade						7.70	8.77	8.82
(i) Revenues from trade taxes (% of trade sector)						9.40 *(1.00)*	8.75 *(1.88)*	8.91 *(1.64)*
(ii) Mean tariff rate						9.40 *(3.00)*	9.44 *(2.80)*	9.44 *(2.80)*
(iii) Standard deviation of tariff rates						4.40 *(14.10)*	8.11 *(4.73)*	8.11 *(4.73)*
B. Regulatory trade barriers						5.20	6.42	6.64
(i) Non-tariff trade barriers						5.30	5.35	5.33
(ii) Compliance cost of importing and exporting						5.00	7.49	7.95
C. Size of trade sector relative to expected						2.60	0.29	0.00
D. Black-market exchange rates						10.00	10.00	10.00
E. International capital market controls						7.60	7.56	6.98
(i) Foreign ownership / investment restrictions						6.80	5.95	5.63
(ii) Capital controls						8.50	9.17	8.33
5. Regulation of Credit, Labor, and Business						**6.70**	**6.94**	**6.67**
A. Credit market regulations						8.90	8.95	8.06
(i) Ownership of banks						10.00	10.00	10.00
(ii) Foreign bank competition						7.00	7.00	7.00
(iii) Private sector credit						9.70	9.82	6.22
(iv) Interest rate controls / negative real interest rates						9.00	9.00	9.00
B. Labor market regulations						6.00	6.12	6.23
(i) Hiring regulations and minimum wage						6.70	6.70	5.00
(ii) Hiring and firing regulations						5.10	6.03	5.79
(iii) Centralized collective bargaining						7.60	7.19	7.02
(iv) Hours regulations						8.00	8.00	10.00
(v) Mandated cost of worker dismissal						8.80	8.79	9.60
(vi) Conscription						0.00	0.00	0.00
C. Business regulations						5.20	5.75	5.72
(i) Price controls						5.00	5.00	5.00
(ii) Administrative requirements						3.00	3.73	3.42
(iii) Bureaucracy costs						2.90	6.31	6.52
(iv) Starting a business						9.40	9.49	9.49
(v) Extra payments / bribes / favoritism						5.20	3.74	3.64
(vi) Licensing restrictions						7.50	8.50	8.46
(vii) Cost of tax compliance						3.50	3.49	3.49

Australia

	1980	1985	1990	1995	2000	2005	2008	2009
Chain-Linked	Rating (Rank)	Rating (Rank)	Rating (Rank)	Rating (Rank)	Rating (Rank)	Rating (Rank)	Rating (Rank)	Rating (Rank)
Summary Rating (Rank) ➤	**7.13** (11)	**7.35** (10)	**7.66** (11)	**7.80** (9)	**7.88** (10)	**7.85** (10)	**7.84** (8)	**7.91** (5)
Area 1. Size of Government	5.08 (51)	4.42 (74)	5.35 (65)	5.68 (74)	5.47 (81)	6.38 (70)	6.80 (47)	6.67 (47)
Area 2. Legal Structure and Security of Property Rights	8.57 (14)	9.29 (9)	9.27 (15)	8.96 (10)	9.49 (3)	8.63 (9)	8.31 (11)	8.22 (11)
Area 3. Access to Sound Money	9.00 (9)	9.35 (10)	9.15 (18)	9.40 (28)	9.40 (27)	9.44 (30)	9.43 (21)	9.62 (9)
Area 4. Freedom to Trade Internationally	6.26 (38)	6.88 (26)	7.33 (24)	7.65 (26)	7.76 (32)	6.79 (58)	6.76 (65)	7.15 (38)
Area 5. Regulation of Credit, Labor, and Business	6.87 (11)	6.96 (11)	7.28 (10)	7.29 (9)	7.26 (12)	8.03 (15)	7.91 (14)	7.89 (14)

Unadjusted								
Summary Rating (Rank) ➤	**6.89** (13)	**7.10** (9)	**7.28** (14)	**7.78** (10)	**7.88** (10)	**7.92** (9)	**7.91** (7)	**7.98** (5)
	Rating Data	Rating Data	Rating Data	Rating Data	Rating Data	Rating Data	Rating Data	Rating Data
1. Size of Government	**5.08**	**4.42**	**5.35**	**5.68**	**5.47**	**6.40**	**6.80**	**6.67**
A. Government consumption	4.93 (23.23)	4.77 (23.79)	5.20 (22.33)	5.47 (21.40)	4.79 (23.70)	4.70 (24.00)	4.54 (24.55)	4.69 (24.05)
B. Transfers and subsidies	7.38 (10.10)	6.89 (11.90)	7.22 (10.70)	6.27 (14.20)	7.09 (11.17)	6.80 (12.30)	7.15 (10.96)	6.51 (13.32)
C. Government enterprises and investment	6.00 (28.40)	4.00 (30.20)	6.00 (25.20)	7.00 (21.50)	7.00 (21.50)	10.00 (10.60)	10.00 (11.20)	10.00 (11.20)
D. Top marginal tax rate	2.00	2.00	3.00	4.00	3.00	4.00	5.50	5.50
(i) Top marginal income tax rate	2.00 (62)	2.00 (60)	3.00 (49)	4.00 (47)	3.00 (47)	4.00 (47)	6.00 (45)	6.00 (45)
(ii) Top marginal income and payroll tax rates			3.00 (49)	4.00 (48)	3.00 (49)	4.00 (49)	5.00 (47)	5.00 (47)
2. Legal Structure and Security of Property Rights	**7.26**	**7.88**	**7.86**	**8.96**	**9.49**	**8.60**	**8.31**	**8.22**
A. Judicial independence				9.05	9.52	8.80	9.07	8.79
B. Impartial courts				9.00	9.69	8.30	6.77	6.99
C. Protection of property rights				7.32	8.27	9.00	8.62	8.11
D. Military interference in rule of law and politics				9.46	10.00	10.00	10.00	10.00
E. Integrity of the legal system				10.00	10.00	9.80	9.17	9.17
F. Legal enforcement of contracts						6.20	6.23	6.23
G. Regulatory restrictions on sale of real property						8.30	8.29	8.26
3. Access to Sound Money	**9.00**	**9.35**	**9.15**	**9.40**	**9.40**	**9.40**	**9.43**	**9.62**
A. Money growth	8.57 (7.17)	9.50 (2.50)	8.06 (9.70)	8.43 (7.83)	9.19 (4.04)	8.60 (6.90)	8.71 (6.45)	8.94 (5.30)
B. Standard deviation of inflation	9.40 (1.51)	9.13 (2.17)	9.19 (2.02)	9.74 (0.64)	9.31 (1.72)	9.70 (0.79)	9.86 (0.34)	9.92 (0.20)
C. Inflation: most recent year	8.03 (9.84)	8.79 (6.06)	9.35 (3.26)	9.42 (2.90)	9.10 (4.48)	9.50 (2.67)	9.13 (4.35)	9.64 (1.82)
D. Freedom to own foreign currency bank accounts	10.00	10.00	10.00	10.00	10.00	10.00	10.00	10.00
4. Freedom to Trade Internationally	**6.57**	**7.23**	**7.48**	**7.51**	**7.76**	**6.80**	**6.76**	**7.15**
A. Taxes on international trade	7.35	7.60	6.46	7.71	8.43	8.40	8.52	8.76
(i) Revenues from trade taxes (% of trade sector)	7.60 (3.60)	7.87 (3.20)	7.93 (3.10)	8.80 (1.80)	9.06 (1.41)	9.00 (1.60)	9.17 (1.24)	9.17 (1.24)
(ii) Mean tariff rate	7.10 (14.50)	7.34 (13.30)	7.16 (14.20)	8.36 (8.20)	8.84 (5.80)	9.10 (4.30)	9.30 (3.50)	9.30 (3.50)
(iii) Standard deviation of tariff rates			4.28 (14.30)	5.96 (10.10)	7.40 (6.50)	7.20 (7.10)	7.10 (7.25)	7.80 (5.50)
B. Regulatory trade barriers				6.42	8.78	8.20	8.13	8.04
(i) Non-tariff trade barriers				6.42	8.07	7.40	7.35	7.16
(ii) Compliance cost of importing and exporting					9.50	8.90	8.91	8.91
C. Size of trade sector relative to expected	5.52	5.36	4.77	5.17	5.47	2.40	2.40	4.14
D. Black-market exchange rates	9.80	10.00	10.00	10.00	10.00	10.00	10.00	10.00
E. International capital market controls	2.00	5.00	8.00	8.27	6.11	4.90	4.77	4.80
(i) Foreign ownership/investment restrictions				8.53	9.14	7.60	7.22	7.29
(ii) Capital controls	2.00	5.00	8.00	8.00	3.08	2.30	2.31	2.31
5. Regulation of Credit, Labor, and Business	**6.53**	**6.62**	**6.56**	**7.34**	**7.26**	**8.40**	**8.24**	**8.22**
A. Credit market regulations	8.38	8.67	9.68	9.04	8.95	9.50	9.50	9.50
(i) Ownership of banks	8.00	8.00	10.00	10.00	10.00	10.00	10.00	10.00
(ii) Foreign bank competition				7.92	6.53	8.00	8.00	8.00
(iii) Private sector credit	7.14	8.00	9.03	9.19	10.00	10.00	10.00	10.00
(iv) Interest rate controls/negative real interest rates	10.00	10.00	10.00	10.00	10.00	10.00	10.00	10.00
B. Labor market regulations				6.56	5.43	5.57	8.40	8.48	8.39
(i) Hiring regulations and minimum wage				3.58	4.55	10.00	10.00	10.00
(ii) Hiring and firing regulations			4.50	4.50	3.08	4.60	4.95	4.64
(iii) Centralized collective bargaining	5.18	5.18	5.18	5.18	5.52	5.90	6.28	5.69
(iv) Hours regulations				3.88	4.68	10.00	10.00	10.00
(v) Mandated cost of worker dismissal						9.60	9.63	10.00
(vi) Conscription	10.00	10.00	10.00	10.00	10.00	10.00	10.00	10.00
C. Business regulations				7.54	7.26	7.20	6.74	6.76
(i) Price controls			6.00	7.00	7.00	7.00	7.00	7.00
(ii) Administrative requirements					6.73	3.50	3.66	3.99
(iii) Bureaucracy costs				7.21	6.20	5.30	1.93	2.00
(iv) Starting a business				6.80	7.37	9.90	9.93	9.93
(v) Extra payments/bribes/favoritism				9.16	9.01	8.90	8.59	8.35
(vi) Licensing restrictions						7.30	7.29	7.29
(vii) Cost of tax compliance						8.80	8.80	8.78

Austria

Chain-Linked	1980		1985		1990		1995		2000		2005		2008		2009	
	Rating	(Rank)	Rating	(Rank)	Rating	(Rank)	Rating	(Rank)	Rating	(Rank)	Rating	(Rank)	Rating	(Rank)	Rating	(Rank)
Summary Rating (Rank) ➤	**6.76**	(16)	**6.72**	(20)	**7.22**	(20)	**7.04**	(28)	**7.37**	(21)	**7.70**	(15)	**7.57**	(14)	**7.48**	(15)
Area 1. Size of Government	3.14	(95)	3.05	(102)	3.11	(106)	2.82	(115)	2.77	(122)	5.23	(94)	5.07	(105)	4.85	(102)
Area 2. Legal Structure and Security of Property Rights	9.47	(5)	9.27	(11)	9.82	(11)	8.85	(12)	9.34	(5)	8.63	(9)	8.41	(9)	8.29	(10)
Area 3. Access to Sound Money	8.40	(13)	8.31	(23)	9.63	(10)	9.55	(18)	9.63	(9)	9.55	(17)	9.54	(7)	9.58	(12)
Area 4. Freedom to Trade Internationally	6.86	(26)	6.91	(24)	7.43	(21)	8.10	(16)	8.51	(10)	7.66	(23)	7.54	(33)	7.35	(27)
Area 5. Regulation of Credit, Labor, and Business	6.08	(30)	6.26	(27)	6.21	(34)	5.91	(52)	6.59	(37)	7.40	(27)	7.28	(26)	7.33	(25)

Unadjusted

	1980		1985		1990		1995		2000		2005		2008		2009	
Summary Rating (Rank) ➤	**6.38**	(18)	**6.35**	(22)	**6.78**	(20)	**7.03**	(29)	**7.37**	(21)	**7.72**	(14)	**7.59**	(16)	**7.50**	(19)
	Rating	Data	Rating	Data	Rating	Data	Rating	Data	Rating	Data	Rating	Data	Rating	Data	Rating	Data
1. Size of Government	**3.14**		**3.05**		**3.11**		**2.82**		**2.77**		**5.20**		**5.07**		**4.85**	
A. Government consumption	4.46	(24.82)	4.35	(25.22)	4.40	(25.03)	4.01	(26.37)	4.16	(25.86)	4.60	(24.40)	4.22	(25.66)	3.87	(26.86)
B. Transfers and subsidies	4.11	(22.10)	3.84	(23.10)	4.03	(22.40)	3.27	(25.20)	2.93	(26.44)	2.80	(26.80)	2.54	(27.86)	2.02	(29.80)
C. Government enterprises and investment	2.00	(44.50)	2.00	(42.00)	2.00	(42.00)	2.00	(42.00)	2.00	(42.00)	10.00	(5.20)	10.00	(5.18)	10.00	(5.65)
D. Top marginal tax rate	2.00		2.00		2.00		2.00		2.00		3.50		3.50		3.50	
(i) Top marginal income tax rate	2.00	(62)	2.00	(62)	4.00	(50)	4.00	(50)	4.00	(50)	4.00	(50)	4.00	(50)	4.00	(50)
(ii) Top marginal income and payroll tax rates					0.00	(62)	0.00	(66)	0.00	(66)	3.00	(54)	3.00	(54)	3.00	(54)
2. Legal Structure and Security of Property Rights	**8.04**		**7.88**		**8.35**		**8.85**		**9.34**		**8.60**		**8.41**		**8.29**	
A. Judicial independence							8.82		9.02		8.10		8.46		7.96	
B. Impartial courts							7.72		9.02		8.60		7.17		6.98	
C. Protection of property rights							7.73		8.65		9.10		8.95		8.59	
D. Military interference in rule of law and politics							9.97		10.00		10.00		10.00		10.00	
E. Integrity of the legal system							10.00		10.00		10.00		10.00		10.00	
F. Legal enforcement of contracts											6.70		6.38		6.38	
G. Regulatory restrictions on sale of real property											7.90		7.92		8.12	
3. Access to Sound Money	**8.40**		**8.31**		**9.63**		**9.55**		**9.63**		**9.60**		**9.54**		**9.58**	
A. Money growth	9.97	(−0.17)	9.36	(3.22)	9.46	(2.69)	8.92	(5.39)	9.18	(4.10)	8.80	(6.10)	8.96	(5.21)	8.67	(6.67)
B. Standard deviation of inflation	9.64	(0.90)	9.51	(1.23)	9.75	(0.63)	9.69	(0.78)	9.80	(0.50)	9.90	(0.23)	9.85	(0.37)	9.74	(0.64)
C. Inflation: most recent year	9.00	(5.00)	9.38	(3.08)	9.31	(3.45)	9.57	(2.13)	9.53	(2.35)	9.50	(2.30)	9.36	(3.18)	9.90	(0.49)
D. Freedom to own foreign currency bank accounts	5.00		5.00		10.00		10.00		10.00		10.00		10.00		10.00	
4. Freedom to Trade Internationally	**6.91**		**6.95**		**7.28**		**8.04**		**8.51**		**7.70**		**7.54**		**7.35**	
A. Taxes on international trade	8.61		8.80		7.92		8.72		9.18		8.40		8.03		8.22	
(i) Revenues from trade taxes (% of trade sector)	9.53	(0.70)	9.60	(0.60)	9.53	(0.70)	9.87	(0.20)	9.78	(0.33)	9.60	(0.60)	9.61	(0.59)	9.44	(0.84)
(ii) Mean tariff rate	7.68	(11.60)	8.00	(10.00)	8.26	(8.70)	8.66	(6.70)	9.52	(2.40)	9.50	(2.70)	8.88	(5.60)	8.94	(5.30)
(iii) Standard deviation of tariff rates					5.96	(10.10)	7.64	(5.90)	8.24	(4.40)	6.10	(9.70)	5.61	(10.98)	6.29	(9.28)
B. Regulatory trade barriers							8.13		9.15		8.40		8.36		8.31	
(i) Non-tariff trade barriers							8.13		8.80		7.80		7.64		7.53	
(ii) Compliance cost of importing and exporting									9.50		8.90		9.08		9.08	
C. Size of trade sector relative to expected	5.74		5.78		5.33		4.83		6.12		6.00		5.89		5.02	
D. Black-market exchange rates	10.00		10.00		10.00		10.00		10.00		10.00		10.00		10.00	
E. International capital market controls	2.00		2.00		5.00		8.50		8.11		5.50		5.40		5.18	
(i) Foreign ownership / investment restrictions							9.00		9.30		7.90		7.71		7.29	
(ii) Capital controls	2.00		2.00		5.00		8.00		6.92		3.10		3.08		3.08	
5. Regulation of Credit, Labor, and Business	**5.39**		**5.55**		**5.52**		**5.89**		**6.59**		**7.50**		**7.39**		**7.43**	
A. Credit market regulations	6.96		7.59		7.46		6.96		8.59		9.30		9.44		9.23	
(i) Ownership of banks	5.00		5.00		5.00		5.00		10.00		10.00		10.00		10.00	
(ii) Foreign bank competition							6.52		5.73		8.00		8.00		8.00	
(iii) Private sector credit	7.88		7.78		7.39		7.47		9.16		9.20		9.74		8.91	
(iv) Interest rate controls / negative real interest rates	8.00		10.00		10.00		8.00		10.00		10.00		10.00		10.00	
B. Labor market regulations	4.63		4.63		4.63		4.28		3.86		5.90		5.92		6.21	
(i) Hiring regulations and minimum wage							4.58		4.56		8.90		10.00		10.00	
(ii) Hiring and firing regulations					4.82		4.82		3.05		4.30		3.85		3.94	
(iii) Centralized collective bargaining	4.49		4.49		4.49		4.49		3.50		2.80		2.15		2.33	
(iv) Hours regulations	4.40		4.40		4.22		4.50		5.18		6.70		6.70		8.00	
(v) Mandated cost of worker dismissal											9.80		9.81		10.00	
(vi) Conscription	5.00		5.00		5.00		3.00		3.00		3.00		3.00		3.00	
C. Business regulations							6.43		7.33		7.30		6.81		6.84	
(i) Price controls					5.00		8.00		8.00		8.00		9.00		9.00	
(ii) Administrative requirements									7.53		4.30		4.22		4.39	
(iii) Bureaucracy costs							6.52		7.43		5.50		1.34		1.46	
(iv) Starting a business							3.72		5.42		8.80		8.88		8.87	
(v) Extra payments / bribes / favoritism							7.48		8.27		8.90		8.49		8.41	
(vi) Licensing restrictions											7.60		7.63		7.62	
(vii) Cost of tax compliance											8.10		8.08		8.09	

Azerbaijan

	1980	1985	1990	1995	2000	2005	2008	2009
Chain-Linked						Rating (Rank)	Rating (Rank)	Rating (Rank)
Summary Rating (Rank) ➤								
Area 1. Size of Government								
Area 2. Legal Structure and Security of Property Rights								
Area 3. Access to Sound Money								
Area 4. Freedom to Trade Internationally								
Area 5. Regulation of Credit, Labor, and Business								

Unadjusted								
Summary Rating (Rank) ➤						**6.11** (104)	**6.55** (86)	**6.50** (84)
				Rating *Data*	Rating *Data*	Rating *Data*	Rating *Data*	Rating *Data*
1. Size of Government						**5.00**	**5.27**	**5.37**
A. Government consumption						6.00 *(19.60)*	4.65 *(24.19)*	5.02 *(22.92)*
B. Transfers and subsidies					7.09 *(11.19)*	7.10 *(11.20)*	9.44 *(2.57)*	9.44 *(2.57)*
C. Government enterprises and investment						2.00	2.00	2.00
D. Top marginal tax rate						5.00	5.00	5.00
(i) Top marginal income tax rate						7.00 *(35)*	7.00 *(35)*	7.00 *(35)*
(ii) Top marginal income and payroll tax rates						3.00 *(49)*	3.00 *(49)*	3.00 *(49)*
2. Legal Structure and Security of Property Rights						**5.70**	**6.40**	**5.96**
A. Judicial independence						3.00	4.79	3.86
B. Impartial courts						3.40	4.88	4.19
C. Protection of property rights						4.40	5.36	4.76
D. Military interference in rule of law and politics						6.70	6.67	5.83
E. Integrity of the legal system						6.00	5.83	5.83
F. Legal enforcement of contracts						7.30	7.55	7.55
G. Regulatory restrictions on sale of real property						8.80	9.73	9.73
3. Access to Sound Money						**7.30**	**7.55**	**7.83**
A. Money growth						8.60 *(7.20)*	6.88 *(15.60)*	7.58 *(12.09)*
B. Standard deviation of inflation						7.80 *(5.58)*	7.49 *(6.27)*	4.00 *(14.99)*
C. Inflation: most recent year						7.70 *(11.59)*	5.84 *(20.79)*	9.72 *(1.40)*
D. Freedom to own foreign currency bank accounts						5.00	10.00	10.00
4. Freedom to Trade Internationally						**6.60**	**6.66**	**6.44**
A. Taxes on international trade						6.90	7.91	8.07
(i) Revenues from trade taxes (% of trade sector)							9.19 *(1.21)*	9.19 *(1.21)*
(ii) Mean tariff rate						7.90 *(10.40)*	8.18 *(9.10)*	8.22 *(8.90)*
(iii) Standard deviation of tariff rates						5.90 *(10.30)*	6.36 *(9.10)*	6.80 *(8.01)*
B. Regulatory trade barriers						3.50	4.00	3.95
(i) Non-tariff trade barriers						4.40	4.81	4.21
(ii) Compliance cost of importing and exporting						2.60	3.19	3.69
C. Size of trade sector relative to expected						7.70	5.67	4.59
D. Black-market exchange rates						10.00	10.00	10.00
E. International capital market controls						4.90	5.74	5.61
(i) Foreign ownership / investment restrictions						6.70	6.48	5.84
(ii) Capital controls						3.10	5.00	5.38
5. Regulation of Credit, Labor, and Business						**6.00**	**6.86**	**6.90**
A. Credit market regulations						6.60	7.50	7.75
(i) Ownership of banks						5.00	5.00	5.00
(ii) Foreign bank competition						6.00	6.00	6.00
(iii) Private sector credit				7.66	6.52	6.50	10.00	10.00
(iv) Interest rate controls / negative real interest rates						9.00	9.00	10.00
B. Labor market regulations						6.50	6.89	6.80
(i) Hiring regulations and minimum wage						6.70	10.00	8.33
(ii) Hiring and firing regulations						7.80	6.77	6.66
(iii) Centralized collective bargaining						7.60	7.59	8.02
(iv) Hours regulations						8.00	8.00	8.00
(v) Mandated cost of worker dismissal						8.00	7.96	8.79
(vi) Conscription						1.00	1.00	1.00
C. Business regulations						4.90	6.18	6.16
(i) Price controls						6.00	6.00	6.00
(ii) Administrative requirements						4.00	5.29	4.49
(iii) Bureaucracy costs						5.90	5.18	5.58
(iv) Starting a business						8.30	9.65	9.71
(v) Extra payments / bribes / favoritism						4.60	4.51	3.90
(vi) Licensing restrictions						5.70	6.87	6.84
(vii) Cost of tax compliance						0.00	5.79	6.57

Bahamas

Chain-Linked	1980 Rating (Rank)	1985 Rating (Rank)	1990 Rating (Rank)	1995 Rating (Rank)	2000 Rating (Rank)	2005 Rating (Rank)	2008 Rating (Rank)	2009 Rating (Rank)
Summary Rating (Rank) ➤	**6.57** (20)	**6.51** (26)	**6.54** (30)	**6.40** (50)	**6.63** (50)	**7.10** (43)	**7.11** (45)	**7.10** (39)
Area 1. Size of Government	8.45 (6)	8.47 (2)	8.51 (3)	8.19 (11)	7.79 (16)	8.06 (13)	8.29 (9)	8.29 (7)
Area 2. Legal Structure & Security of Property Rights		6.08 (39)	6.06 (43)	5.19 (74)	6.35 (46)	7.85 (18)	7.64 (20)	7.49 (21)
Area 3. Access to Sound Money	6.25 (54)	6.48 (66)	7.02 (44)	7.05 (55)	6.87 (87)	6.82 (92)	6.82 (92)	7.15 (86)
Area 4. Freedom to Trade Internationally	4.80 (58)	4.89 (63)	4.33 (85)	4.65 (105)	5.24 (113)	4.37 (118)	4.30 (118)	4.06 (119)
Area 5. Regulation of Credit, Labor, and Business	6.43 (18)	6.70 (14)	6.82 (12)	6.90 (14)	6.90 (23)	8.32 (7)	8.49 (5)	8.50 (4)

Unadjusted

	1980 Rating Data	1985 Rating Data	1990 Rating Data	1995 Rating Data	2000 Rating Data	2005 Rating Data	2008 Rating Data	2009 Rating Data
Summary Rating (Rank) ➤	**6.63** (15)	**6.57** (19)	**6.49** (31)	**6.41** (46)	**6.63** (50)	**7.22** (42)	**7.24** (40)	**7.22** (40)
1. Size of Government	**8.45**	**8.47**	**8.51**	**8.19**	**7.79**	**8.10**	**8.29**	**8.29**
A. Government consumption	6.81 (16.85)	6.90 (16.54)	7.18 (15.60)	6.21 (18.90)	5.18 (22.40)	6.50 (18.00)	7.16 (15.66)	7.27 (15.28)
B. Transfers and subsidies	10.00 (0.50)	10.00 (0.10)	9.86 (1.00)	9.56 (2.10)	8.97 (4.29)	8.80 (5.00)	8.99 (4.20)	8.88 (4.63)
C. Government enterprises and investment	7.00 (24.20)	7.00 (24.20)	7.00 (24.20)	7.00	7.00	7.00	7.00	7.00
D. Top marginal tax rate	10.00	10.00	10.00	10.00	10.00	10.00	10.00	10.00
(i) Top marginal income tax rate	10.00 (0)	10.00 (0)	10.00 (0)	10.00 (0)	10.00 (0)	10.00 (0)	10.00 (0)	10.00 (0)
(ii) Top marginal income and payroll tax rates					10.00 (5–9)	10.00 (5–9)	10.00 (5–9)	10.00 (9)
2. Legal Structure and Security of Property Rights		**5.72**	**5.70**	**5.19**	**6.35**	**8.50**	**7.13**	**6.99**
A. Judicial independence				5.00	5.00			
B. Impartial courts				6.56	7.07	7.90	7.70	7.00
C. Protection of property rights				3.00	3.00			
D. Military interference in rule of law and politics				7.30	10.00	10.00	10.00	10.00
E. Integrity of the legal system				4.11	6.67	7.50	7.50	7.50
F. Legal enforcement of contracts							5.49	5.49
G. Regulatory restrictions on sale of real property							4.98	4.98
3. Access to Sound Money	**6.25**	**6.48**	**7.02**	**7.05**	**6.87**	**6.80**	**6.82**	**7.15**
A. Money growth	8.43 (7.84)	9.72 (1.41)	9.38 (3.08)	9.40 (2.99)	8.05 (9.74)	8.60 (6.90)	8.99 (5.05)	9.47 (2.66)
B. Standard deviation of inflation	8.58 (3.54)	7.88 (5.29)	9.32 (1.70)	9.35 (1.63)	9.64 (0.90)	9.00 (2.57)	9.20 (2.01)	9.56 (1.11)
C. Inflation: most recent year	8.00 (10.01)	8.31 (8.46)	9.37 (3.16)	9.44 (2.81)	9.79 (1.04)	9.70 (1.59)	9.10 (4.49)	9.59 (2.06)
D. Freedom to own foreign currency bank accounts	0.00	0.00	0.00	0.00	0.00	0.00	0.00	0.00
4. Freedom to Trade Internationally	**4.83**	**4.92**	**4.38**	**4.71**	**5.24**	**4.40**	**5.10**	**4.81**
A. Taxes on international trade	4.32	3.67	3.60	3.13	3.33	4.30	4.59	3.66
(i) Revenues from trade taxes (% of trade sector)	4.60 (8.10)	3.80 (9.30)	3.60 (9.60)	3.13 (10.30)	3.67 (9.50)	4.10 (8.80)	5.15 (7.28)	5.15 (7.28)
(ii) Mean tariff rate	4.04 (29.80)	3.54 (32.30)			3.00 (35.00)	4.00 (30.20)	4.02 (29.90)	2.84 (35.80)
(iii) Standard deviation of tariff rates						4.70 (13.30)	4.62 (13.46)	2.98 (17.54)
B. Regulatory trade barriers							8.01	7.76
(i) Non-tariff trade barriers								
(ii) Compliance cost of importing and exporting							8.01	7.76
C. Size of trade sector relative to expected	5.63	4.93	2.69	2.57	3.10	1.90	2.11	1.89
D. Black-market exchange rates	6.00	7.80	7.40	9.60	10.00	10.00	10.00	10.00
E. International capital market controls	0.00	0.00	0.00	0.00	1.54	1.50	0.77	0.77
(i) Foreign ownership / investment restrictions								
(ii) Capital controls	0.00	0.00	0.00	0.00	1.54	1.50	0.77	0.77
5. Regulation of Credit, Labor, and Business	**6.98**	**7.27**	**6.82**	**6.90**	**6.90**	**8.30**	**8.85**	**8.86**
A. Credit market regulations	8.62	9.38	9.73	10.00	10.00	9.80	9.75	9.75
(i) Ownership of banks	10.00	10.00	10.00	10.00	10.00	10.00	10.00	10.00
(ii) Foreign bank competition								
(iii) Private sector credit	7.86	8.13	9.20	10.00	10.00	9.30	9.25	9.25
(iv) Interest rate controls / negative real interest rates	8.00	10.00	10.00	10.00	10.00	10.00	10.00	10.00
B. Labor market regulations							9.40	9.44
(i) Hiring regulations and minimum wage							10.00	10.00
(ii) Hiring and firing regulations								
(iii) Centralized collective bargaining								
(iv) Hours regulations							10.00	10.00
(v) Mandated cost of worker dismissal							7.59	7.78
(vi) Conscription	10.00	10.00	10.00	10.00	10.00	10.00	10.00	10.00
C. Business regulations							7.40	7.39
(i) Price controls			4.00	4.00	4.00	4.00	4.00	4.00
(ii) Administrative requirements								
(iii) Bureaucracy costs								
(iv) Starting a business							8.92	8.91
(v) Extra payments / bribes / favoritism								
(vi) Licensing restrictions							7.33	7.30
(vii) Cost of tax compliance							9.35	9.35

Bahrain

Chain-Linked	1980 Rating (Rank)	1985 Rating (Rank)	1990 Rating (Rank)	1995 Rating (Rank)	2000 Rating (Rank)	2005 Rating (Rank)	2008 Rating (Rank)	2009 Rating (Rank)
Summary Rating (Rank) ➤	**7.46** (8)	**6.85** (17)	**6.85** (27)	**6.93** (31)	**7.28** (28)	**6.92** (55)	**7.27** (34)	**7.24** (32)
Area 1. Size of Government	7.26 (11)	6.00 (28)	5.91 (47)	6.18 (59)	6.80 (43)	6.48 (67)	6.58 (55)	6.56 (51)
Area 2. Legal Structure and Security of Property Rights		5.72 (46)	5.70 (51)	5.90 (47)	5.86 (59)	5.39 (73)	6.09 (52)	6.07 (53)
Area 3. Access to Sound Money	8.10 (18)	8.61 (19)	8.79 (22)	9.43 (27)	9.12 (35)	8.82 (49)	9.09 (37)	9.00 (47)
Area 4. Freedom to Trade Internationally	7.70 (13)	7.31 (16)	7.30 (26)	6.81 (50)	7.71 (35)	7.44 (31)	7.82 (18)	7.74 (12)
Area 5. Regulation of Credit, Labor, and Business	6.70 (13)	6.59 (20)	6.54 (20)	6.33 (34)	6.90 (23)	6.50 (63)	6.77 (49)	6.80 (50)

Unadjusted

	1980 Rating Data	1985 Rating Data	1990 Rating Data	1995 Rating Data	2000 Rating Data	2005 Rating Data	2008 Rating Data	2009 Rating Data
Summary Rating (Rank) ➤	**7.54** (4)	**6.90** (14)	**6.85** (18)	**6.93** (35)	**7.28** (28)	**7.03** (54)	**7.62** (14)	**7.59** (11)
1. Size of Government	**7.26**	**6.00**	**5.91**	**6.18**	**6.80**	**6.50**	**6.58**	**6.56**
A. Government consumption	3.25 (28.95)	0.00 (43.46)	0.00 (43.78)	1.41 (35.20)	3.78 (27.15)	2.90 (30.00)	2.81 (30.44)	2.72 (30.75)
B. Transfers and subsidies	9.81 (1.20)	10.00 (0.00)	9.64 (1.80)	9.30 (3.06)	9.43 (2.59)	9.00 (4.20)	9.52 (2.25)	9.53 (2.24)
C. Government enterprises and investment	6.00 (29.80)	4.00 (31.70)	4.00 (31.70)	4.00 (31.70)	4.00 (31.70)	4.00	4.00	4.00
D. Top marginal tax rate	10.00	10.00	10.00	10.00	10.00	10.00	10.00	10.00
(i) Top marginal income tax rate	10.00 (0)	10.00 (0)	10.00 (0)	10.00 (0)	10.00 (0)	10.00 (0)	10.00 (0)	10.00 (0)
(ii) Top marginal income and payroll tax rates			10.00 (0)	10.00 (0)			10.00 (17)	10.00 (17)
2. Legal Structure and Security of Property Rights		**5.72**	**5.70**	**5.90**	**5.86**	**5.60**	**6.60**	**6.58**
A. Judicial independence						4.10	6.61	6.73
B. Impartial courts				6.74	6.30	4.10	4.87	4.95
C. Protection of property rights						6.60	7.49	7.71
D. Military interference in rule of law and politics				6.11	5.00	5.00	5.00	5.00
E. Integrity of the legal system				6.96	8.33	8.30	8.33	8.33
F. Legal enforcement of contracts							4.79	4.79
G. Regulatory restrictions on sale of real property							9.12	8.53
3. Access to Sound Money	**8.10**	**8.61**	**8.79**	**9.43**	**9.12**	**8.80**	**9.09**	**9.00**
A. Money growth	6.38 (18.10)	8.46 (7.70)	9.60 (1.99)	9.24 (−3.82)	9.71 (1.46)	8.40 (8.00)	7.71 (11.44)	8.05 (9.77)
B. Standard deviation of inflation	6.81 (7.98)	6.33 (9.17)	6.92 (7.71)	8.70 (3.26)	6.91 (7.73)	7.40 (6.54)	9.35 (1.62)	8.51 (3.72)
C. Inflation: most recent year	9.22 (3.90)	9.64 (−1.82)	8.63 (6.84)	9.80 (1.00)	9.86 (−0.70)	9.50 (2.59)	9.29 (3.53)	9.44 (2.80)
D. Freedom to own foreign currency bank accounts	10.00	10.00	10.00	10.00	10.00	10.00	10.00	10.00
4. Freedom to Trade Internationally	**7.70**	**7.24**	**7.30**	**6.81**	**7.71**	**7.20**	**7.56**	**7.48**
A. Taxes on international trade	9.39	9.17	9.27	9.07	9.19	8.40	8.19	8.25
(i) Revenues from trade taxes (% of trade sector)	9.39 (0.91)	9.53 (0.70)	9.27 (1.10)	9.07 (1.40)	9.19 (1.21)	8.80 (1.80)	9.53 (0.70)	9.53 (0.70)
(ii) Mean tariff rate		8.80 (6.00)				9.00 (5.10)	8.96 (5.20)	8.96 (5.20)
(iii) Standard deviation of tariff rates						7.30 (6.70)	6.07 (9.83)	6.26 (9.36)
B. Regulatory trade barriers						7.60	7.84	8.19
(i) Non-tariff trade barriers						7.60	7.62	8.07
(ii) Compliance cost of importing and exporting							8.05	8.31
C. Size of trade sector relative to expected	8.95	6.87	7.07	4.82	4.26	3.20	4.52	3.36
D. Black-market exchange rates	10.00	10.00	10.00	10.00	10.00	10.00	10.00	10.00
E. International capital market controls	2.00	2.00	2.00	2.00	6.92	6.60	7.24	7.62
(i) Foreign ownership / investment restrictions						7.10	7.80	7.75
(ii) Capital controls	2.00	2.00	2.00	2.00	6.92	6.20	6.67	7.50
5. Regulation of Credit, Labor, and Business	**7.07**	**6.95**	**6.54**	**6.33**	**6.90**	**7.10**	**8.28**	**8.32**
A. Credit market regulations	8.71	8.35	8.80	8.11	10.00	9.50	9.25	9.25
(i) Ownership of banks	8.00	8.00	8.00	8.00	10.00	10.00	10.00	10.00
(ii) Foreign bank competition						8.00	8.00	8.00
(iii) Private sector credit	9.42	8.71	8.41	8.32	10.00	10.00	10.00	10.00
(iv) Interest rate controls / negative real interest rates			10.00	8.00	10.00	10.00	9.00	9.00
B. Labor market regulations						7.00	8.64	8.74
(i) Hiring regulations and minimum wage							10.00	10.00
(ii) Hiring and firing regulations						3.20	4.26	4.15
(iii) Centralized collective bargaining						7.90	7.96	8.28
(iv) Hours regulations							10.00	10.00
(v) Mandated cost of worker dismissal							9.63	10.00
(vi) Conscription	10.00	10.00	10.00	10.00	10.00	10.00	10.00	10.00
C. Business regulations						4.60	6.96	6.98
(i) Price controls			4.00	4.00	4.00	4.00	4.00	4.00
(ii) Administrative requirements						4.00	4.53	5.01
(iii) Bureaucracy costs						2.90	4.01	3.82
(iv) Starting a business							9.07	8.81
(v) Extra payments / bribes / favoritism						7.50	7.62	7.76
(vi) Licensing restrictions							9.90	9.86
(vii) Cost of tax compliance							9.60	9.60

Bangladesh

	1980		1985		1990		1995		2000		2005		2008		2009	
Chain-Linked	Rating	(Rank)	Rating	(Rank)	Rating	(Rank)	Rating	(Rank)	Rating	(Rank)	Rating	(Rank)	Rating	(Rank)	Rating	(Rank)
Summary Rating (Rank) ➤	**3.63**	(99)	**3.94**	(99)	**4.68**	(94)	**5.45**	(80)	**5.82**	(94)	**5.88**	(100)	**5.94**	(99)	**6.11**	(92)
Area 1. Size of Government	4.52	(70)	4.56	(70)	7.37	(12)	8.07	(13)	8.07	(11)	8.12	(12)	8.08	(12)	8.07	(12)
Area 2. Legal Structure and Security of Property Rights	2.34	(81)	2.27	(104)	2.25	(107)	4.63	(98)	3.47	(112)	3.17	(113)	3.27	(115)	3.78	(109)
Area 3. Access to Sound Money	4.64	(97)	6.10	(83)	6.95	(49)	6.42	(67)	7.02	(79)	6.65	(97)	6.39	(103)	6.74	(101)
Area 4. Freedom to Trade Internationally	2.12	(91)	2.01	(97)	1.75	(102)	3.08	(111)	5.05	(115)	5.19	(111)	5.52	(104)	5.40	(106)
Area 5. Regulation of Credit, Labor, and Business	4.42	(77)	4.67	(75)	5.20	(63)	5.00	(84)	5.47	(89)	6.28	(67)	6.43	(67)	6.57	(63)

Unadjusted

	1980		1985		1990		1995		2000		2005		2008		2009	
Summary Rating (Rank) ➤	**3.75**	(100)	**4.06**	(96)	**4.68**	(94)	**5.46**	(80)	**5.82**	(94)	**5.94**	(109)	**6.00**	(112)	**6.17**	(103)
	Rating	Data	Rating	Data	Rating	Data	Rating	Data	Rating	Data	Rating	Data	Rating	Data	Rating	Data
1. Size of Government	**4.30**		**4.33**		**7.00**		**7.67**		**8.07**		**8.10**		**8.08**		**8.07**	
A. Government consumption	9.89	(6.38)	10.00	(5.39)	10.00	(4.82)	10.00	(5.33)	10.00	(5.60)	9.70	(7.00)	9.81	(6.63)	9.83	(6.59)
B. Transfers and subsidies									9.28	(3.15)	9.80	(1.30)	9.50	(2.32)	9.47	(2.45)
C. Government enterprises and investment	2.00	(44.40)	2.00	(46.60)	2.00	(47.10)	4.00	(34.00)	4.00	(30.03)	4.00	(30.00)	4.00		4.00	
D. Top marginal tax rate	1.00		1.00		9.00		9.00		9.00		9.00		9.00		9.00	
(i) Top marginal income tax rate	1.00	(60)	1.00	(60)	9.00	(25)	9.00	(25)	9.00	(25)	9.00	(25)	9.00	(25)	9.00	(25)
(ii) Top marginal income and payroll tax rates					9.00	(25)	9.00	(25)	9.00	(25)	9.00	(25)	9.00	(25)	9.00	(25)
2. Legal Structure and Security of Property Rights	**2.54**		**2.46**		**2.44**		**5.02**		**3.47**		**3.00**		**3.07**		**3.55**	
A. Judicial independence											2.50		4.13		3.98	
B. Impartial courts							3.91		4.22		3.00		3.41		3.30	
C. Protection of property rights									2.02		4.70		4.13		4.07	
D. Military interference in rule of law and politics							5.25		3.33		4.60		2.50		5.00	
E. Integrity of the legal system							6.96		3.33		3.30		4.17		4.17	
F. Legal enforcement of contracts											1.20		1.15		1.15	
G. Regulatory restrictions on sale of real property											1.60		2.02		3.20	
3. Access to Sound Money	**4.64**		**6.10**		**6.95**		**6.42**		**7.02**		**6.60**		**6.39**		**6.74**	
A. Money growth	7.03	(14.86)	7.84	(10.82)	9.62	(1.89)	7.99	(10.03)	9.07	(4.64)	8.60	(7.20)	8.05	(9.77)	8.63	(6.85)
B. Standard deviation of inflation	4.23	(14.43)	8.76	(3.10)	9.16	(2.10)	9.05	(2.38)	9.46	(1.36)	9.40	(1.38)	9.28	(1.81)	9.40	(1.51)
C. Inflation: most recent year	7.32	(13.39)	7.79	(11.07)	9.03	(4.87)	8.65	(6.73)	9.56	(2.21)	8.60	(7.04)	8.22	(8.90)	8.92	(5.42)
D. Freedom to own foreign currency bank accounts	0.00		0.00		0.00		0.00		0.00		0.00		0.00		0.00	
4. Freedom to Trade Internationally	**2.24**		**2.12**		**1.79**		**3.14**		**5.05**		**5.50**		**5.81**		**5.68**	
A. Taxes on international trade	0.53		0.00		0.64		1.42		5.19		5.80		6.48		6.53	
(i) Revenues from trade taxes (% of trade sector)	1.07	(13.40)	0.00	(17.90)	1.93	(12.10)	4.27	(8.60)	5.33	(7.00)	4.10	(8.80)	5.89	(6.17)	5.99	(6.01)
(ii) Mean tariff rate	0.00	(99.90)	0.00	(86.00)	0.00	(102.20)	0.00	(81.20)	5.68	(21.60)	6.60	(16.80)	7.04	(14.80)	7.06	(14.70)
(iii) Standard deviation of tariff rates					0.00	(50.40)	0.00	(26.10)	4.56	(13.60)	6.50	(8.70)	6.51	(8.73)	6.53	(8.67)
B. Regulatory trade barriers									4.73		4.50		5.86		5.66	
(i) Non-tariff trade barriers									4.73		5.40		5.46		5.18	
(ii) Compliance cost of importing and exporting											3.70		6.26		6.13	
C. Size of trade sector relative to expected	2.39		2.33		0.00		1.63		2.41		2.80		4.31		3.92	
D. Black-market exchange rates	0.00		0.00		0.00		4.40		10.00		10.00		10.00		10.00	
E. International capital market controls	0.00		0.00		0.00		0.00		2.93		4.10		2.39		2.31	
(i) Foreign ownership/investment restrictions									5.86		7.50		4.79		4.62	
(ii) Capital controls	0.00		0.00		0.00		0.00		0.00		0.80		0.00		0.00	
5. Regulation of Credit, Labor, and Business	**5.03**		**5.31**		**5.22**		**5.03**		**5.47**		**6.50**		**6.67**		**6.80**	
A. Credit market regulations	3.44		4.19		5.76		5.12		5.91		8.20		8.19		8.14	
(i) Ownership of banks	0.00		0.00		0.00		0.00		2.00		5.00		5.00		5.00	
(ii) Foreign bank competition									5.85		8.00		8.00		8.00	
(iii) Private sector credit	4.31		6.56		7.28		7.37		8.05		9.60		9.74		9.57	
(iv) Interest rate controls/negative real interest rates	6.00		6.00		10.00		8.00		10.00		10.00		10.00		10.00	
B. Labor market regulations									6.55		6.80		6.37		6.54	
(i) Hiring regulations and minimum wage									4.60		6.70		5.60		5.57	
(ii) Hiring and firing regulations									4.97		6.00		5.94		6.09	
(iii) Centralized collective bargaining									6.63		7.50		6.35		6.86	
(iv) Hours regulations											10.00		10.00		10.00	
(v) Mandated cost of worker dismissal											0.40		0.36		0.73	
(vi) Conscription	10.00		10.00		10.00		10.00		10.00		10.00		10.00		10.00	
C. Business regulations									3.96		4.50		5.45		5.71	
(i) Price controls					0.00		0.00		0.00		6.00		6.00		6.00	
(ii) Administrative requirements									7.55		2.40		2.44		3.15	
(iii) Bureaucracy costs									5.73		2.40		6.41		6.37	
(iv) Starting a business									4.58		7.90		8.21		9.04	
(v) Extra payments/bribes/favoritism									1.91		2.30		2.46		2.67	
(vi) Licensing restrictions											5.20		5.98		6.14	
(vii) Cost of tax compliance											5.50		6.61		6.61	

Barbados

	1980	1985	1990	1995	2000	2005	2008	2009
Chain-Linked	Rating (Rank)	Rating (Rank)	Rating (Rank)	Rating (Rank)	Rating (Rank)	Rating (Rank)	Rating (Rank)	Rating (Rank)
Summary Rating (Rank) ➤	**5.86** (36)	**6.23** (28)	**6.14** (41)	**6.08** (62)	**6.09** (81)	**6.26** (87)	**5.95** (97)	**6.06** (93)
Area 1. Size of Government	6.27 (22)	6.38 (17)	6.42 (32)	6.40 (46)	6.85 (39)	6.59 (63)	5.58 (90)	5.61 (80)
Area 2. Legal Structure and Security of Property Rights		6.11 (37)	6.09 (42)	4.76 (92)	5.20 (73)	5.63 (65)	5.34 (75)	5.32 (74)
Area 3. Access to Sound Money	5.06 (92)	6.67 (52)	6.67 (57)	7.19 (50)	6.70 (91)	6.29 (107)	6.10 (109)	6.68 (104)
Area 4. Freedom to Trade Internationally	5.57 (44)	5.42 (54)	5.02 (72)	5.49 (95)	5.07 (114)	4.54 (117)	4.47 (116)	4.47 (117)
Area 5. Regulation of Credit, Labor, and Business	6.19 (26)	6.61 (18)	6.57 (19)	6.56 (26)	6.61 (35)	8.25 (9)	8.35 (6)	8.35 (8)

Unadjusted								
Summary Rating (Rank) ➤	**5.88** (37)	**6.22** (27)	**6.04** (42)	**6.02** (66)	**6.09** (81)	**6.60** (79)	**6.33** (95)	**6.50** (84)
	Rating Data	Rating Data	Rating Data	Rating Data	Rating Data	Rating Data	Rating Data	Rating Data
1. Size of Government	**6.27**	**6.38**	**6.42**	**6.40**	**6.85**	**6.60**	**5.58**	**5.61**
A. Government consumption	6.09 (19.28)	4.52 (24.62)	4.69 (24.07)	5.09 (22.70)	3.91 (26.70)	4.40 (24.90)	3.32 (28.71)	3.44 (28.30)
B. Transfers and subsidies	10.00 (0.20)	10.00 (0.00)	10.00 (0.50)	10.00 (0.00)	10.00 (0.00)	8.40 (6.30)	5.50 (17.02)	5.50 (17.02)
C. Government enterprises and investment	8.00 (19.00)	10.00 (11.90)	8.00 (18.30)	7.00 (22.78)	10.00 (12.00)	10.00 (3.70)	10.00 (3.68)	10.00 (3.68)
D. Top marginal tax rate	1.00	1.00	3.00	3.50	3.50	3.50	3.50	3.50
(i) Top marginal income tax rate	1.00 (60)	1.00 (60)	4.00 (50)	5.00 (40)	5.00 (40)	5.00 (40)	5.00 (40)	5.00 (40)
(ii) Top marginal income and payroll tax rates			2.00 (54)	2.00 (53)	2.00 (53)	2.00 (53)	2.00 (53)	2.00 (53)
2. Legal Structure and Security of Property Rights		**5.72**	**5.70**	**4.60**	**5.20**	**8.00**	**7.83**	**7.80**
A. Judicial independence				5.00	5.00	8.10	7.84	7.89
B. Impartial courts				6.29	7.61	7.20	6.46	6.40
C. Protection of property rights				3.00	3.00	7.30	7.83	7.69
D. Military interference in rule of law and politics						9.40	9.20	9.20
E. Integrity of the legal system				4.11				
F. Legal enforcement of contracts								
G. Regulatory restrictions on sale of real property								
3. Access to Sound Money	**5.06**	**6.67**	**6.67**	**7.19**	**6.70**	**6.30**	**6.10**	**6.68**
A. Money growth	7.17 (14.16)	8.92 (5.41)	9.12 (4.38)	9.32 (−3.38)	7.89 (10.55)	7.70 (11.70)	7.11 (14.45)	8.22 (8.88)
B. Standard deviation of inflation	7.59 (6.03)	8.59 (3.52)	8.64 (3.39)	9.49 (1.28)	9.40 (1.50)	8.70 (3.23)	8.92 (2.71)	9.21 (1.96)
C. Inflation: most recent year	5.49 (22.56)	9.18 (4.12)	8.91 (5.45)	9.95 (0.25)	9.51 (2.44)	8.80 (6.08)	8.38 (8.11)	9.27 (3.64)
D. Freedom to own foreign currency bank accounts	0.00	0.00	0.00	0.00	0.00	0.00	0.00	0.00
4. Freedom to Trade Internationally	**5.73**	**5.46**	**4.85**	**5.37**	**5.07**	**5.20**	**5.10**	**5.10**
A. Taxes on international trade	7.53	7.17	6.06	6.58	6.20	5.60	5.81	5.81
(i) Revenues from trade taxes (% of trade sector)	7.53 (3.70)	7.73 (3.40)	7.60 (3.60)	7.80 (3.30)		7.90 (3.20)	8.39 (2.41)	8.39 (2.41)
(ii) Mean tariff rate		6.60 (17.00)		7.18 (14.10)	6.20 (19.00)	7.30 (13.50)	7.30 (13.50)	7.30 (13.50)
(iii) Standard deviation of tariff rates			4.52 (13.70)	4.76 (13.10)		1.70 (20.80)	1.74 (20.66)	1.74 (20.66)
B. Regulatory trade barriers						5.20	5.49	5.47
(i) Non-tariff trade barriers						5.20	5.49	5.47
(ii) Compliance cost of importing and exporting								
C. Size of trade sector relative to expected	5.09	4.12	1.99	2.66	1.12	1.30	1.36	1.49
D. Black-market exchange rates	7.80	7.80	8.00	9.40	9.80	10.00	10.00	10.00
E. International capital market controls	0.00	0.00	0.00	0.00	0.00	3.70	2.82	2.71
(i) Foreign ownership/investment restrictions						7.40	5.64	5.43
(ii) Capital controls	0.00	0.00	0.00	0.00	0.00	0.00	0.00	0.00
5. Regulation of Credit, Labor, and Business	**6.45**	**6.89**	**6.57**	**6.56**	**6.61**	**6.90**	**7.06**	**7.34**
A. Credit market regulations	7.19	8.36	8.25	8.21	8.37	8.30	8.52	8.53
(i) Ownership of banks	8.00	8.00	8.00	8.00	8.00	8.00	8.00	8.00
(ii) Foreign bank competition								
(iii) Private sector credit	7.58	7.08	6.74	6.62	7.11	7.00	7.55	7.60
(iv) Interest rate controls/negative real interest rates	6.00	10.00	10.00	10.00	10.00	10.00	10.00	10.00
B. Labor market regulations						7.20	6.97	7.62
(i) Hiring regulations and minimum wage								
(ii) Hiring and firing regulations						5.00	4.73	4.60
(iii) Centralized collective bargaining						6.60	6.17	5.88
(iv) Hours regulations								10.00
(v) Mandated cost of worker dismissal								
(vi) Conscription	10.00	10.00	10.00	10.00	10.00	10.00	10.00	10.00
C. Business regulations						5.30	5.69	5.87
(i) Price controls			6.00	6.00	6.00	6.00	6.00	6.00
(ii) Administrative requirements						4.00	5.04	5.47
(iii) Bureaucracy costs						3.40	4.45	4.51
(iv) Starting a business								
(v) Extra payments/bribes/favoritism						7.60	7.28	7.51
(vi) Licensing restrictions								
(vii) Cost of tax compliance								

Belgium

	1980		1985		1990		1995		2000		2005		2008		2009	
Chain-Linked	Rating	(Rank)	Rating	(Rank)	Rating	(Rank)	Rating	(Rank)	Rating	(Rank)	Rating	(Rank)	Rating	(Rank)	Rating	(Rank)
Summary Rating (Rank) ➤	7.27	(10)	7.30	(11)	7.54	(12)	7.26	(23)	7.74	(13)	7.23	(36)	7.13	(43)	7.08	(42)
Area 1. Size of Government	3.62	(90)	3.60	(93)	4.19	(91)	4.04	(102)	4.57	(102)	4.34	(115)	4.20	(113)	4.06	(114)
Area 2. Legal Structure and Security of Property Rights	8.97	(11)	9.03	(13)	9.57	(14)	7.52	(24)	8.29	(18)	6.97	(29)	6.92	(28)	6.83	(28)
Area 3. Access to Sound Money	9.58	(2)	9.58	(3)	9.74	(3)	9.73	(6)	9.62	(10)	9.53	(20)	9.48	(14)	9.64	(5)
Area 4. Freedom to Trade Internationally	8.66	(4)	8.87	(3)	8.74	(3)	8.66	(5)	8.96	(6)	8.06	(11)	7.95	(14)	7.68	(15)
Area 5. Regulation of Credit, Labor, and Business	5.69	(37)	5.56	(48)	5.66	(49)	6.34	(32)	7.28	(10)	7.24	(33)	7.12	(35)	7.15	(33)

Unadjusted

	1980		1985		1990		1995		2000		2005		2008		2009	
Summary Rating (Rank) ➤	7.06	(8)	7.09	(10)	7.30	(13)	7.23	(23)	7.74	(13)	7.32	(36)	7.22	(41)	7.15	(43)
	Rating	Data	Rating	Data	Rating	Data	Rating	Data	Rating	Data	Rating	Data	Rating	Data	Rating	Data
1. Size of Government	3.62		3.60		4.19		4.04		4.57		4.30		4.20		4.06	
A. Government consumption	5.43	(21.55)	5.79	(20.30)	6.44	(18.10)	6.20	(18.93)	3.45	(28.26)	3.00	(30.00)	2.88	(30.20)	2.35	(32.00)
B. Transfers and subsidies	3.05	(26.00)	2.62	(27.60)	3.32	(25.00)	2.97	(26.30)	3.81	(23.21)	3.40	(24.80)	2.91	(26.53)	2.91	(26.53)
C. Government enterprises and investment	6.00	(26.80)	6.00	(25.30)	6.00	(27.00)	6.00	(27.00)	10.00	(11.86)	10.00	(8.70)	10.00	(7.31)	10.00	(8.31)
D. Top marginal tax rate	0.00		0.00		1.00		1.00		1.00		1.00		1.00		1.00	
(i) Top marginal income tax rate	0.00	(76)	0.00	(76)	2.00	(55-61)	1.00	(58-64)	2.00	(58-62.7)	2.00	(50-55)	2.00	(50-55)	2.00	(50-55)
(ii) Top marginal income and payroll tax rates					0.00	(70)	1.00	(58-64)	0.00	(71)	0.00	(67-71)	0.00	(68-71)	0.00	(68-71)
2. Legal Structure and Security of Property Rights	7.83		7.88		8.35		7.52		8.29		7.00		6.92		6.83	
A. Judicial independence							5.78		7.35		7.00		7.27		7.01	
B. Impartial courts							6.42		8.18		6.30		4.91		5.10	
C. Protection of property rights							6.90		7.57		8.20		7.93		7.41	
D. Military interference in rule of law and politics							8.49		10.00		10.00		10.00		10.00	
E. Integrity of the legal system							10.00		8.33		8.30		8.33		8.33	
F. Legal enforcement of contracts											5.70		5.65		5.65	
G. Regulatory restrictions on sale of real property											3.30		4.33		4.33	
3. Access to Sound Money	9.58		9.58		9.74		9.73		9.62		9.50		9.48		9.64	
A. Money growth	9.78	(1.10)	9.78	(1.11)	9.97	(0.17)	9.63	(1.85)	9.10	(4.48)	8.80	(6.10)	8.94	(5.30)	8.73	(6.33)
B. Standard deviation of inflation	9.38	(1.56)	9.76	(0.59)	9.62	(0.95)	9.64	(0.90)	9.89	(0.28)	9.90	(0.28)	9.88	(0.30)	9.85	(0.38)
C. Inflation: most recent year	9.16	(4.18)	8.79	(6.05)	9.37	(3.14)	9.67	(1.67)	9.49	(2.54)	9.40	(2.78)	9.10	(4.50)	9.99	(−0.05)
D. Freedom to own foreign currency bank accounts	10.00		10.00		10.00		10.00		10.00		10.00		10.00		10.00	
4. Freedom to Trade Internationally	8.78		8.99		8.72		8.54		8.96		8.10		7.95		7.68	
A. Taxes on international trade	9.02		9.15		8.46		8.68		9.18		8.40		8.03		8.22	
(i) Revenues from trade taxes (% of trade sector)	9.80	(0.30)	9.80	(0.30)	9.73	(0.40)	9.73	(0.40)	9.78	(0.33)	9.60	(0.60)	9.61	(0.59)	9.44	(0.84)
(ii) Mean tariff rate	8.24	(8.80)	8.50	(7.50)	8.52	(7.40)	8.66	(6.70)	9.52	(2.40)	9.50	(2.70)	8.88	(5.60)	8.94	(5.30)
(iii) Standard deviation of tariff rates					7.12	(7.20)	7.64	(5.90)	8.24	(4.40)	6.10	(9.70)	5.61	(10.98)	6.29	(9.28)
B. Regulatory trade barriers							8.28		8.86		8.10		8.43		8.53	
(i) Non-tariff trade barriers							8.28		8.22		7.20		7.92		8.12	
(ii) Compliance cost of importing and exporting									9.50		8.90		8.93		8.93	
C. Size of trade sector relative to expected	6.74		7.67		7.02		6.42		7.59		7.10		7.23		5.61	
D. Black-market exchange rates	10.00		10.00		10.00		10.00		10.00		10.00		10.00		10.00	
E. International capital market controls	10.00		10.00		10.00		9.31		9.17		6.70		6.08		6.01	
(i) Foreign ownership/investment restrictions							8.61		9.87		8.10		7.54		7.41	
(ii) Capital controls	10.00		10.00		10.00		10.00		8.46		5.40		4.62		4.62	
5. Regulation of Credit, Labor, and Business	5.52		5.39		5.50		6.30		7.28		7.70		7.54		7.55	
A. Credit market regulations	8.60		8.11		8.40		8.66		9.26		9.20		9.38		8.92	
(i) Ownership of banks	10.00		10.00		10.00		10.00		10.00		10.00		10.00		10.00	
(ii) Foreign bank competition							7.90		7.98		8.00		8.00		8.00	
(iii) Private sector credit	5.80		4.33		5.21		8.41		10.00		8.80		9.51		7.68	
(iv) Interest rate controls/negative real interest rates	10.00		10.00		10.00		10.00		10.00		10.00		10.00		10.00	
B. Labor market regulations	3.49		3.49		3.63		4.93		5.01		6.60		6.90		7.39	
(i) Hiring regulations and minimum wage							3.87		5.12		8.90		8.90		8.90	
(ii) Hiring and firing regulations					3.77		3.77		3.10		2.60		3.29		3.15	
(iii) Centralized collective bargaining	4.49		4.49		4.49		4.49		4.17		3.80		4.71		4.27	
(iv) Hours regulations	2.99		2.99		3.25		2.55		2.67		6.00		6.00		8.00	
(v) Mandated cost of worker dismissal											8.50		8.52		10.00	
(vi) Conscription	3.00		3.00		3.00		10.00		10.00		10.00		10.00		10.00	
C. Business regulations							5.30		7.56		7.20		6.35		6.34	
(i) Price controls					2.00		5.00		6.00		5.00		6.00		6.00	
(ii) Administrative requirements									8.20		3.00		2.78		2.70	
(iii) Bureaucracy costs							6.49		8.88		7.90		2.12		1.90	
(iv) Starting a business							4.60		6.42		9.00		9.75		9.75	
(v) Extra payments/bribes/favoritism							5.11		8.28		8.10		7.50		7.72	
(vi) Licensing restrictions											8.00		8.05		8.05	
(vii) Cost of tax compliance											9.30		8.25		8.25	

Belize

	1980	1985	1990	1995	2000	2005	2008	2009
Chain-Linked	Rating (Rank)	Rating (Rank)	Rating (Rank)	Rating (Rank)	Rating (Rank)	Rating (Rank)	Rating (Rank)	Rating (Rank)
Summary Rating (Rank) ➤	**5.63** (45)	**5.48** (51)	**5.98** (45)	**6.40** (50)	**6.41** (66)	**6.84** (60)	**6.72** (68)	**6.74** (61)
Area 1. Size of Government	5.19 (47)	5.38 (45)	5.20 (69)	6.79 (34)	6.68 (47)	6.84 (51)	6.56 (58)	6.57 (50)
Area 2. Legal Structure and Security of Property Rights				5.35 (68)	6.19 (48)	5.34 (74)	5.23 (78)	5.04 (81)
Area 3. Access to Sound Money	6.18 (56)	6.56 (60)	7.01 (45)	7.16 (52)	6.65 (93)	8.27 (62)	8.18 (61)	8.32 (65)
Area 4. Freedom to Trade Internationally	5.19 (52)	4.07 (73)	5.16 (66)	5.72 (91)	5.68 (105)	5.01 (114)	4.98 (113)	4.98 (112)
Area 5. Regulation of Credit, Labor, and Business	5.96 (33)	5.88 (39)	6.48 (24)	6.95 (12)	6.85 (27)	8.79 (1)	8.68 (2)	8.84 (1)

Unadjusted

	1980	1985	1990	1995	2000	2005	2008	2009
Summary Rating (Rank) ➤	**5.85** (38)	**5.71** (46)	**5.88** (46)	**6.29** (52)	**6.41** (66)	**7.06** (51)	**6.93** (61)	**6.95** (58)
	Rating Data	Rating Data	Rating Data	Rating Data	Rating Data	Rating Data	Rating Data	Rating Data
1. Size of Government	**5.18**	**5.03**	**4.86**	**6.34**	**6.68**	**6.80**	**6.56**	**6.57**
A. Government consumption	6.10 (19.25)	4.96 (23.15)	5.62 (20.90)	6.56 (17.70)	6.35 (18.42)	6.80 (16.80)	5.98 (19.66)	6.02 (19.53)
B. Transfers and subsidies	9.43 (2.60)	9.16 (3.60)	9.81 (1.20)	9.81 (1.20)	9.69 (1.64)	9.70 (1.60)	9.69 (1.64)	9.69 (1.64)
C. Government enterprises and investment	0.00 (51.00)	2.00 (49.80)	0.00 (55.40)	4.00 (36.10)	4.00 (36.10)	4.00 (36.10)	4.00	4.00
D. Top marginal tax rate		4.00	4.00	5.00				
(i) Top marginal income tax rate		4.00 (50)	4.00 (45)	5.00 (45)				
(ii) Top marginal income and payroll tax rates								
2. Legal Structure and Security of Property Rights				**5.26**	**6.19**	**5.80**	**5.71**	**5.50**
A. Judicial independence								
B. Impartial courts				5.72	6.87	5.60	5.20	4.90
C. Protection of property rights								
D. Military interference in rule of law and politics					7.15	7.10	7.00	6.50
E. Integrity of the legal system								
F. Legal enforcement of contracts						3.30	3.33	3.33
G. Regulatory restrictions on sale of real property						7.30	7.32	7.29
3. Access to Sound Money	**6.18**	**6.56**	**7.01**	**7.16**	**6.65**	**8.30**	**8.18**	**8.32**
A. Money growth	8.50 (7.48)	9.12 (4.39)	9.29 (3.53)	9.83 (−0.84)	8.46 (7.70)	9.70 (−1.30)	9.29 (3.54)	9.14 (4.32)
B. Standard deviation of inflation	8.50 (3.76)	7.50 (6.25)	8.81 (2.98)	9.61 (0.98)	8.28 (4.30)	9.10 (2.31)	9.71 (0.73)	9.35 (1.63)
C. Inflation: most recent year	7.72 (11.40)	9.62 (−1.88)	9.95 (0.26)	9.21 (3.94)	9.88 (0.61)	9.30 (3.64)	8.72 (6.39)	9.78 (−1.08)
D. Freedom to own foreign currency bank accounts	0.00	0.00	0.00	0.00	0.00	5.00	5.00	5.00
4. Freedom to Trade Internationally	**5.19**	**4.46**	**5.16**	**5.72**	**5.68**	**5.50**	**5.45**	**5.45**
A. Taxes on international trade	4.20	4.67	2.80	2.73	5.61	6.20	6.19	6.13
(i) Revenues from trade taxes (% of trade sector)	4.20 (8.70)	2.73 (10.90)	2.80 (10.80)	2.73 (10.90)	5.61 (6.59)	5.60 (6.60)	5.61 (6.59)	5.61 (6.59)
(ii) Mean tariff rate		6.60 (17.00)				7.80 (10.80)	7.84 (10.80)	7.80 (11.00)
(iii) Standard deviation of tariff rates						5.20 (12.10)	5.12 (12.20)	4.98 (12.54)
B. Regulatory trade barriers						7.10	7.09	7.09
(i) Non-tariff trade barriers								
(ii) Compliance cost of importing and exporting						7.10	7.09	7.09
C. Size of trade sector relative to expected	5.34	4.39	4.80	3.27	4.62	3.30	3.94	4.00
D. Black-market exchange rates	3.20	0.00	5.00	9.40	9.20	10.00	10.00	10.00
E. International capital market controls	5.00	5.00	5.00	5.00	0.77	0.80	0.00	0.00
(i) Foreign ownership/investment restrictions								
(ii) Capital controls	5.00	5.00	5.00	5.00	0.77	0.80	0.00	0.00
5. Regulation of Credit, Labor, and Business	**6.87**	**6.78**	**6.48**	**6.95**	**6.85**	**8.90**	**8.77**	**8.90**
A. Credit market regulations	8.11	7.83	9.94	9.48	9.15	9.40	9.37	9.37
(i) Ownership of banks			10.00	10.00	10.00	10.00	10.00	10.00
(ii) Foreign bank competition						9.00	9.00	9.00
(iii) Private sector credit	8.22	7.67	9.82	8.44	8.46	8.50	8.46	8.46
(iv) Interest rate controls/negative real interest rates	8.00	8.00	10.00	10.00	9.00	10.00	10.00	10.00
B. Labor market regulations						9.20	8.89	9.26
(i) Hiring regulations and minimum wage						8.90	7.80	8.90
(ii) Hiring and firing regulations								
(iii) Centralized collective bargaining								
(iv) Hours regulations						10.00	10.00	10.00
(v) Mandated cost of worker dismissal						7.80	7.78	8.15
(vi) Conscription	10.00	10.00	10.00	10.00	10.00	10.00	10.00	10.00
C. Business regulations						8.00	8.06	8.06
(i) Price controls				0.00	6.00	6.00	6.00	6.00
(ii) Administrative requirements								
(iii) Bureaucracy costs								
(iv) Starting a business						8.00	8.06	8.09
(v) Extra payments/bribes/favoritism								
(vi) Licensing restrictions						9.80	9.81	9.81
(vii) Cost of tax compliance						8.40	8.35	8.35

Benin

Chain-Linked

	1980 Rating (Rank)	1985 Rating (Rank)	1990 Rating (Rank)	1995 Rating (Rank)	2000 Rating (Rank)	2005 Rating (Rank)	2008 Rating (Rank)	2009 Rating (Rank)
Summary Rating (Rank) ➤	**5.04** (66)	**4.80** (82)	**5.06** (81)	**4.70** (103)	**5.25** (111)	**5.36** (114)	**5.52** (109)	**5.54** (110)
Area 1. Size of Government	4.67 (65)	3.60 (93)	4.17 (92)	4.04 (102)	4.72 (98)	5.17 (96)	5.81 (81)	5.36 (90)
Area 2. Legal Structure and Security of Property Rights	4.67 (48)	4.25 (72)	4.42 (72)	4.46 (99)	4.33 (94)	4.14 (100)	4.60 (90)	4.58 (90)
Area 3. Access to Sound Money	6.23 (55)	6.40 (70)	6.57 (62)	5.26 (86)	6.62 (95)	6.56 (101)	6.11 (108)	6.72 (102)
Area 4. Freedom to Trade Internationally					5.36 (111)	5.00 (115)	4.95 (114)	4.83 (114)
Area 5. Regulation of Credit, Labor, and Business	4.56 (73)	4.83 (69)	4.96 (73)	4.94 (89)	5.22 (99)	5.79 (97)	5.87 (98)	6.05 (96)

Unadjusted

	1980	1985	1990	1995	2000	2005	2008	2009
Summary Rating (Rank) ➤	**5.15** (66)	**4.83** (82)	**5.03** (83)	**4.60** (106)	**5.25** (111)	**5.82** (115)	**5.95** (114)	**5.96** (117)

	1980 Rating Data	1985 Rating Data	1990 Rating Data	1995 Rating Data	2000 Rating Data	2005 Rating Data	2008 Rating Data	2009 Rating Data
1. Size of Government	**4.67**	**3.60**	**4.17**	**4.04**	**4.72**	**7.00**	**7.62**	**7.03**
A. Government consumption	9.35 (8.22)	7.21 (15.50)	8.34 (11.66)	8.08 (12.53)	7.45 (14.68)	7.00 (16.20)	7.77 (13.59)	7.40 (14.83)
B. Transfers and subsidies						10.00 (0.20)	9.73 (1.49)	9.71 (1.55)
C. Government enterprises and investment	0.00 (53.70)	0.00 (53.50)	0.00 (55.20)	0.00 (60.10)	2.00 (40.31)	4.00 (35.40)	6.00 (28.02)	4.00 (38.37)
D. Top marginal tax rate							7.00	7.00
(i) Top marginal income tax rate							7.00 (35)	7.00 (35)
(ii) Top marginal income and payroll tax rates								
2. Legal Structure and Security of Property Rights	**4.67**	**4.25**	**4.42**	**4.46**	**4.33**	**4.00**	**4.44**	**4.43**
A. Judicial independence						4.60	4.38	3.75
B. Impartial courts				4.81	4.55	4.10	5.43	4.26
C. Protection of property rights						4.40	4.72	6.12
D. Military interference in rule of law and politics				3.82	4.70	7.10	7.20	7.50
E. Integrity of the legal system				5.18	4.00			
F. Legal enforcement of contracts						1.10	1.07	1.07
G. Regulatory restrictions on sale of real property						2.70	3.85	3.85
3. Access to Sound Money	**6.23**	**6.40**	**6.57**	**5.26**	**6.62**	**6.60**	**6.11**	**6.72**
A. Money growth	8.22 (8.91)	9.32 (3.38)	9.18 (4.08)	9.11 (4.44)	8.05 (9.76)	8.40 (−7.90)	7.13 (14.36)	8.30 (8.48)
B. Standard deviation of inflation	8.74 (3.15)	7.24 (6.89)	8.34 (4.16)	4.98 (12.54)	9.26 (1.86)	8.90 (2.79)	8.90 (2.74)	9.01 (2.47)
C. Inflation: most recent year	7.96 (10.19)	9.02 (−4.88)	8.78 (6.11)	6.93 (15.37)	9.17 (4.17)	8.90 (5.36)	8.41 (7.95)	9.57 (2.16)
D. Freedom to own foreign currency bank accounts	0.00	0.00	0.00	0.00	0.00	0.00	0.00	0.00
4. Freedom to Trade Internationally	**5.02**	**5.04**			**5.36**	**5.20**	**5.12**	**5.00**
A. Taxes on international trade	2.93	2.52			7.60	5.90	6.30	6.35
(i) Revenues from trade taxes (% of trade sector)	2.93 (10.60)					3.20 (10.20)	3.98 (9.03)	4.14 (8.79)
(ii) Mean tariff rate		2.52 (37.40)			7.60 (12.00)	7.10 (14.40)	7.62 (11.90)	7.62 (11.90)
(iii) Standard deviation of tariff rates						7.30 (6.80)	7.29 (6.78)	7.29 (6.78)
B. Regulatory trade barriers						5.30	5.80	5.46
(i) Non-tariff trade barriers						5.70	5.95	5.26
(ii) Compliance cost of importing and exporting						4.90	5.65	5.65
C. Size of trade sector relative to expected	4.33	4.68	1.59	3.22	1.01	1.70	0.52	0.10
D. Black-market exchange rates	9.60	9.80	9.20	9.80	10.00	10.00	10.00	10.00
E. International capital market controls	0.00	0.00	0.00	0.00	0.00	3.00	2.99	3.10
(i) Foreign ownership/investment restrictions						6.00	5.20	5.43
(ii) Capital controls	0.00	0.00	0.00	0.00	0.00	0.00	0.77	0.77
5. Regulation of Credit, Labor, and Business	**5.15**	**4.83**	**4.96**	**4.65**	**5.22**	**6.40**	**6.46**	**6.64**
A. Credit market regulations	5.31	5.92	6.25	6.20	9.42	9.10	9.23	9.23
(i) Ownership of banks	0.00	0.00	2.00	10.00	10.00	10.00	10.00	10.00
(ii) Foreign bank competition								
(iii) Private sector credit	9.94	9.76	8.76	6.60	8.84	9.40	9.69	9.69
(iv) Interest rate controls/negative real interest rates	6.00	8.00	8.00	2.00		8.00	8.00	8.00
B. Labor market regulations						5.40	5.48	5.84
(i) Hiring regulations and minimum wage						6.10	6.10	6.10
(ii) Hiring and firing regulations						5.70	5.34	5.78
(iii) Centralized collective bargaining						6.80	7.79	7.10
(iv) Hours regulations						6.00	6.00	8.00
(v) Mandated cost of worker dismissal						6.70	6.66	7.09
(vi) Conscription		1.00	1.00	1.00	1.00	1.00	1.00	1.00
C. Business regulations						4.60	4.67	4.85
(i) Price controls				2.00	2.00	2.00	2.00	2.00
(ii) Administrative requirements						2.40	3.63	4.43
(iii) Bureaucracy costs						6.50	5.97	5.67
(iv) Starting a business						5.60	6.42	6.47
(v) Extra payments/bribes/favoritism						3.80	3.12	3.14
(vi) Licensing restrictions						4.90	4.54	5.25
(vii) Cost of tax compliance						7.00	6.97	6.97

Bolivia

	1980	1985	1990	1995	2000	2005	2008	2009
Chain-Linked	Rating (Rank)	Rating (Rank)	Rating (Rank)	Rating (Rank)	Rating (Rank)	Rating (Rank)	Rating (Rank)	Rating (Rank)
Summary Rating (Rank) ➤	**4.39** (86)	**3.55** (104)	**5.39** (66)	**6.40** (50)	**6.79** (43)	**6.40** (80)	**6.15** (89)	**6.28** (86)
Area 1. Size of Government	4.86 (60)	6.93 (8)	6.81 (22)	6.56 (39)	7.97 (13)	6.14 (78)	6.36 (64)	6.30 (61)
Area 2. Legal Structure and Security of Property Rights	1.83 (88)	1.32 (110)	2.50 (103)	4.28 (104)	3.43 (113)	4.15 (99)	3.77 (106)	3.76 (110)
Area 3. Access to Sound Money	5.38 (85)	0.10 (112)	5.59 (84)	8.10 (39)	9.32 (28)	8.90 (43)	7.97 (67)	8.73 (54)
Area 4. Freedom to Trade Internationally	5.18 (53)	5.60 (50)	6.24 (45)	7.03 (41)	7.23 (48)	7.06 (47)	7.17 (43)	6.85 (50)
Area 5. Regulation of Credit, Labor, and Business			5.75 (48)	5.72 (59)	6.00 (61)	5.80 (96)	5.53 (106)	5.79 (102)

Unadjusted

	1980	1985	1990	1995	2000	2005	2008	2009
Summary Rating (Rank) ➤	**4.34** (88)	**3.60** (105)	**5.65** (55)	**6.73** (39)	**6.79** (43)	**6.39** (87)	**6.16** (102)	**6.27** (99)
	Rating *Data*	Rating *Data*	Rating *Data*	Rating *Data*	Rating *Data*	Rating *Data*	Rating *Data*	Rating *Data*
1. Size of Government	**4.86**	**6.93**	**6.81**	**6.56**	**7.97**	**6.10**	**6.36**	**6.30**
A. Government consumption	6.75 *(17.05)*	8.08 *(12.52)*	7.86 *(13.27)*	7.28 *(15.24)*	7.12 *(15.80)*	6.00 *(19.50)*	6.59 *(17.59)*	6.37 *(18.34)*
B. Transfers and subsidies	9.70 *(1.60)*	9.65 *(1.80)*	9.37 *(2.80)*	9.46 *(2.50)*	8.76 *(5.04)*	8.50 *(5.90)*	8.84 *(4.77)*	8.84 *(4.77)*
C. Government enterprises and investment	0.00 *(50.10)*	2.00 *(42.50)*	0.00 *(60.60)*	0.00 *(51.20)*	6.00 *(28.30)*	0.00 *(50.70)*	0.00 *(56.77)*	0.00 *(59.86)*
D. Top marginal tax rate	3.00	8.00	10.00	9.50	10.00	10.00	10.00	10.00
(i) Top marginal income tax rate	3.00 *(48)*	8.00 *(30)*	10.00 *(10)*	10.00 *(13)*	10.00 *(13)*	10.00 *(13)*	10.00 *(13)*	10.00 *(13)*
(ii) Top marginal income and payroll tax rates			10.00 *(16)*	9.00 *(22)*		10.00 *(13)*	10.00 *(13)*	10.00 *(13)*
2. Legal Structure and Security of Property Rights	**2.32**	**1.67**	**3.17**	**5.43**	**3.43**	**4.20**	**3.77**	**3.76**
A. Judicial independence					2.17	2.50	1.77	2.19
B. Impartial courts				4.93	3.34	2.50	1.97	2.32
C. Protection of property rights					1.65	3.50	1.98	1.99
D. Military interference in rule of law and politics				5.93	5.00	5.00	5.00	5.00
E. Integrity of the legal system				6.96	5.00	5.00	5.00	4.17
F. Legal enforcement of contracts						4.00	3.99	3.99
G. Regulatory restrictions on sale of real property						6.60	6.68	6.68
3. Access to Sound Money	**5.38**	**0.00**	**5.59**	**8.10**	**9.32**	**8.90**	**7.97**	**8.73**
A. Money growth	7.19 *(14.07)*	0.00 *(546.64)*	5.62 *(21.92)*	6.28 *(18.59)*	9.54 *(2.28)*	7.70 *(11.50)*	5.80 *(21.01)*	7.88 *(10.60)*
B. Standard deviation of inflation	3.81 *(15.47)*	0.00 *(4769.22)*	0.00 *(85.90)*	8.42 *(3.95)*	8.66 *(3.36)*	9.00 *(2.50)*	8.90 *(2.75)*	7.72 *(5.70)*
C. Inflation: most recent year	0.54 *(47.30)*	0.00 *(12336.70)*	6.75 *(16.26)*	7.71 *(11.43)*	9.08 *(4.60)*	8.90 *(5.40)*	7.20 *(14.00)*	9.33 *(3.35)*
D. Freedom to own foreign currency bank accounts	10.00	0.00	10.00	10.00	10.00	10.00	10.00	10.00
4. Freedom to Trade Internationally	**5.31**	**5.82**	**6.48**	**7.38**	**7.23**	**7.10**	**7.17**	**6.85**
A. Taxes on international trade	4.80	5.69	7.56	8.74	8.62	8.80	8.79	8.26
(i) Revenues from trade taxes (% of trade sector)	4.80 *(7.80)*	5.33 *(7.00)*	8.47 *(2.30)*	8.60 *(2.10)*	8.41 *(2.38)*	9.20 *(1.30)*	9.24 *(1.14)*	9.24 *(1.14)*
(ii) Mean tariff rate		6.04 *(19.80)*	6.66 *(16.70)*	8.06 *(9.70)*	8.10 *(9.50)*	8.60 *(7.20)*	8.34 *(8.30)*	7.94 *(10.30)*
(iii) Standard deviation of tariff rates				9.56 *(1.10)*	9.36 *(1.60)*	8.80 *(3.00)*	8.80 *(2.99)*	7.61 *(5.97)*
B. Regulatory trade barriers					5.49	4.90	5.35	5.70
(i) Non-tariff trade barriers					4.82	3.90	3.57	4.26
(ii) Compliance cost of importing and exporting					6.16	5.90	7.14	7.14
C. Size of trade sector relative to expected	5.96	5.00	5.23	5.22	4.28	5.60	7.23	5.95
D. Black-market exchange rates	5.60	8.20	9.40	9.80	10.00	10.00	10.00	10.00
E. International capital market controls	2.00	2.00	2.00	5.00	7.78	5.90	4.45	4.32
(i) Foreign ownership / investment restrictions					8.63	4.90	4.29	4.02
(ii) Capital controls	2.00	2.00	2.00	5.00	6.92	6.90	4.62	4.62
5. Regulation of Credit, Labor, and Business	**3.81**		**6.20**	**6.16**	**6.00**	**5.70**	**5.52**	**5.70**
A. Credit market regulations	2.49	0.00	9.33	8.55	7.80	7.80	8.00	8.00
(i) Ownership of banks			10.00	8.00	10.00	8.00	8.00	8.00
(ii) Foreign bank competition					5.07	5.00	5.00	5.00
(iii) Private sector credit	4.97		10.00	9.65	9.63	9.10	10.00	10.00
(iv) Interest rate controls / negative real interest rates	0.00	0.00	8.00	8.00	8.00	9.00	9.00	9.00
B. Labor market regulations					4.73	4.60	3.62	4.60
(i) Hiring regulations and minimum wage					3.09	2.20	2.20	2.23
(ii) Hiring and firing regulations					4.90	5.40	2.46	3.66
(iii) Centralized collective bargaining					7.13	7.50	5.74	6.09
(iv) Hours regulations					5.51	4.70	4.70	8.00
(v) Mandated cost of worker dismissal								
(vi) Conscription	3.00	3.00	3.00	3.00	3.00	3.00	3.00	3.00
C. Business regulations					5.47	4.80	4.93	4.49
(i) Price controls			6.00	8.00	9.00	8.00	8.00	4.00
(ii) Administrative requirements					5.50	2.50	2.93	3.66
(iii) Bureaucracy costs					3.85	4.00	6.75	6.43
(iv) Starting a business					3.87	6.80	7.35	7.33
(v) Extra payments / bribes / favoritism					5.14	4.70	2.83	3.33
(vi) Licensing restrictions						7.50	6.66	6.66
(vii) Cost of tax compliance						0.00	0.00	0.00

Bosnia and Herzegovenia

	1980	1985	1990	1995	2000	2005	2008	2009
Chain-Linked						Rating (Rank)	Rating (Rank)	Rating (Rank)
Summary Rating (Rank) ➤								
Area 1. Size of Government								
Area 2. Legal Structure and Security of Property Rights								
Area 3. Access to Sound Money								
Area 4. Freedom to Trade Internationally								
Area 5. Regulation of Credit, Labor, and Business								

Unadjusted								
Summary Rating (Rank) ➤						**6.11** (104)	**6.03** (111)	**6.23** (100)
						Rating Data	Rating Data	Rating Data
1. Size of Government						**5.50**	**5.59**	**5.49**
A. Government consumption						5.80 (20.40)	6.01 (19.56)	5.62 (20.90)
B. Transfers and subsidies						5.70 (16.50)	5.86 (15.70)	5.86 (15.70)
C. Government enterprises and investment						4.00	4.00	4.00
D. Top marginal tax rate						6.50	6.50	6.50
(i) Top marginal income tax rate						10.00 (15)	10.00 (10)	10.00 (10)
(ii) Top marginal income and payroll tax rates						3.00 (50)	3.00 (47)	3.00 (47)
2. Legal Structure and Security of Property Rights						**3.50**	**3.51**	**3.94**
A. Judicial independence						3.50	1.80	2.62
B. Impartial courts						3.30	1.16	2.23
C. Protection of property rights						3.30	2.96	2.82
D. Military interference in rule of law and politics						4.20	4.80	4.80
E. Integrity of the legal system								
F. Legal enforcement of contracts						3.60	3.65	3.53
G. Regulatory restrictions on sale of real property						3.40	6.70	7.63
3. Access to Sound Money						**8.40**	**7.91**	**8.30**
A. Money growth						9.80 (1.00)	9.11 (4.43)	9.59 (2.06)
B. Standard deviation of inflation						9.30 (1.70)	9.00 (2.50)	8.69 (3.27)
C. Inflation: most recent year						9.60 (2.13)	8.52 (7.41)	9.93 (−0.37)
D. Freedom to own foreign currency bank accounts						5.00	5.00	5.00
4. Freedom to Trade Internationally						**6.30**	**6.17**	**6.53**
A. Taxes on international trade						5.90	8.10	8.34
(i) Revenues from trade taxes (% of trade sector)						3.90 (9.20)	9.99 (0.01)	10.00 (0.00)
(ii) Mean tariff rate						8.60 (7.20)	8.64 (6.80)	8.68 (6.60)
(iii) Standard deviation of tariff rates						5.30 (11.70)	5.68 (10.80)	6.33 (9.17)
B. Regulatory trade barriers						6.20	6.63	6.66
(i) Non-tariff trade barriers						5.70	5.43	5.49
(ii) Compliance cost of importing and exporting						6.80	7.82	7.82
C. Size of trade sector relative to expected						4.60	1.63	3.27
D. Black-market exchange rates						10.00	10.00	10.00
E. International capital market controls						4.50	4.47	4.39
(i) Foreign ownership / investment restrictions						5.30	5.09	4.92
(ii) Capital controls						3.80	3.85	3.85
5. Regulation of Credit, Labor, and Business						**6.80**	**6.97**	**6.91**
A. Credit market regulations						9.50	8.87	8.68
(i) Ownership of banks						8.00	8.00	8.00
(ii) Foreign bank competition						10.00	10.00	10.00
(iii) Private sector credit						10.00	8.47	6.71
(iv) Interest rate controls / negative real interest rates						10.00	9.00	10.00
B. Labor market regulations						6.10	6.71	6.62
(i) Hiring regulations and minimum wage						3.30	4.40	3.33
(ii) Hiring and firing regulations						4.60	7.46	6.69
(iii) Centralized collective bargaining						7.90	7.55	7.40
(iv) Hours regulations						8.70	8.70	10.00
(v) Mandated cost of worker dismissal						7.10	7.13	7.32
(vi) Conscription						5.00	5.00	5.00
C. Business regulations						4.90	5.34	5.43
(i) Price controls							6.00	6.00
(ii) Administrative requirements						2.00	2.64	3.05
(iii) Bureaucracy costs						6.20	6.66	6.27
(iv) Starting a business						7.70	7.82	7.95
(v) Extra payments / bribes / favoritism						5.20	3.23	3.78
(vi) Licensing restrictions						2.40	5.74	5.71
(vii) Cost of tax compliance						5.90	5.27	5.27

Botswana

	1980		1985		1990		1995		2000		2005		2008		2009	
Chain-Linked	Rating	(Rank)	Rating	(Rank)	Rating	(Rank)	Rating	(Rank)	Rating	(Rank)	Rating	(Rank)	Rating	(Rank)	Rating	(Rank)
Summary Rating (Rank) ➤	**5.55**	(51)	**5.80**	(41)	**6.04**	(43)	**6.29**	(54)	**7.10**	(35)	**6.74**	(66)	**6.89**	(54)	**6.64**	(68)
Area 1. Size of Government	3.62	(90)	3.78	(91)	4.74	(82)	4.29	(100)	4.76	(96)	4.54	(110)	5.29	(100)	4.36	(111)
Area 2. Legal Structure and Security of Property Rights			6.31	(33)	6.28	(39)	6.35	(41)	6.77	(36)	6.46	(46)	6.38	(43)	6.42	(41)
Area 3. Access to Sound Money	5.49	(81)	5.46	(90)	5.84	(76)	7.85	(43)	9.09	(37)	8.80	(50)	8.70	(50)	8.42	(63)
Area 4. Freedom to Trade Internationally	7.11	(22)	7.08	(21)	7.34	(23)	6.78	(53)	7.76	(32)	6.87	(56)	7.01	(56)	6.75	(54)
Area 5. Regulation of Credit, Labor, and Business	5.83	(35)	6.33	(23)	6.00	(39)	6.20	(40)	7.10	(18)	6.98	(42)	7.07	(36)	7.19	(31)

Unadjusted

	1980		1985		1990		1995		2000		2005		2008		2009	
Summary Rating (Rank) ➤	**5.66**	(48)	**5.91**	(38)	**6.04**	(42)	**6.29**	(52)	**7.10**	(35)	**6.93**	(61)	**7.09**	(53)	**6.83**	(68)
	Rating	*Data*	Rating	*Data*	Rating	*Data*	Rating	*Data*	Rating	*Data*	Rating	*Data*	Rating	*Data*	Rating	*Data*
1. Size of Government	**3.62**		**3.78**		**4.74**		**4.29**		**4.76**		**4.50**		**5.29**		**4.36**	
A. Government consumption	3.68	*(27.50)*	0.97	*(36.71)*	1.63	*(34.45)*	0.00	*(45.92)*	0.00	*(49.02)*	0.00	*(43.90)*	1.01	*(36.55)*	1.27	*(35.67)*
B. Transfers and subsidies	8.80	*(4.90)*	8.15	*(7.30)*	8.34	*(6.60)*	8.17	*(7.20)*	8.04	*(7.70)*	7.20	*(10.90)*	7.16	*(10.91)*	7.16	*(10.91)*
C. Government enterprises and investment	2.00	*(44.90)*	4.00	*(39.40)*	6.00	*(26.50)*	2.00	*(46.20)*	2.00	*(46.20)*	2.00	*(40.60)*	4.00	*(30.72)*	0.00	*(53.63)*
D. Top marginal tax rate	0.00		2.00		3.00		7.00		9.00		9.00		9.00		9.00	
(i) Top marginal income tax rate	0.00	*(75)*	2.00	*(60)*	3.00	*(50)*	7.00	*(35)*	9.00	*(25)*	9.00	*(25)*	9.00	*(25)*	9.00	*(25)*
(ii) Top marginal income and payroll tax rates					3.00	*(50)*	7.00	*(35)*	9.00	*(25)*	9.00	*(25)*	9.00	*(25)*	9.00	*(25)*
2. Legal Structure and Security of Property Rights			**6.31**		**6.28**		**6.35**		**6.77**		**6.90**		**6.83**		**6.86**	
A. Judicial independence											7.20		7.23		7.00	
B. Impartial courts							6.45		6.76		6.60		5.90		5.94	
C. Protection of property rights											6.40		7.17		7.17	
D. Military interference in rule of law and politics							8.29		10.00		10.00		10.00		10.00	
E. Integrity of the legal system							6.96		6.67		6.70		5.83		5.83	
F. Legal enforcement of contracts											3.30		3.59		4.05	
G. Regulatory restrictions on sale of real property											8.20		8.05		8.05	
3. Access to Sound Money	**5.49**		**5.46**		**5.84**		**7.85**		**9.09**		**8.80**		**8.70**		**8.42**	
A. Money growth	9.32	*(3.41)*	9.91	*(0.44)*	8.00	*(9.98)*	9.98	*(−0.09)*	9.86	*(0.72)*	8.50	*(−7.30)*	8.93	*(5.35)*	8.83	*(5.87)*
B. Standard deviation of inflation	6.44	*(8.90)*	6.46	*(8.86)*	6.55	*(8.62)*	8.28	*(4.30)*	8.24	*(4.40)*	8.40	*(4.01)*	8.39	*(4.01)*	6.47	*(8.82)*
C. Inflation: most recent year	6.18	*(19.08)*	5.47	*(22.67)*	8.79	*(6.03)*	8.14	*(9.31)*	8.28	*(8.60)*	8.30	*(8.61)*	7.46	*(12.70)*	8.39	*(8.03)*
D. Freedom to own foreign currency bank accounts	0.00		0.00		0.00		5.00		10.00		10.00		10.00		10.00	
4. Freedom to Trade Internationally	**7.19**		**7.16**		**7.34**		**6.78**		**7.76**		**6.90**		**7.00**		**6.75**	
A. Taxes on international trade	4.79		7.03		6.29		4.18		6.84		6.30		6.53		6.57	
(i) Revenues from trade taxes (% of trade sector)	1.47	*(12.80)*	5.27	*(7.10)*	5.60	*(6.60)*	5.25	*(7.13)*	5.96	*(6.06)*	6.00	*(6.10)*	5.96	*(6.06)*	5.96	*(6.06)*
(ii) Mean tariff rate	8.12	*(9.40)*	8.80	*(6.00)*	7.80	*(11.00)*	6.06	*(19.70)*	8.56	*(7.20)*	8.00	*(9.90)*	8.44	*(7.80)*	8.46	*(7.70)*
(iii) Standard deviation of tariff rates					5.48	*(11.30)*	1.24	*(21.90)*	6.00	*(10.00)*	4.80	*(13.00)*	5.20	*(12.01)*	5.29	*(11.78)*
B. Regulatory trade barriers											5.50		5.81		5.77	
(i) Non-tariff trade barriers											6.30		6.53		6.27	
(ii) Compliance cost of importing and exporting											4.70		5.09		5.26	
C. Size of trade sector relative to expected	10.00		10.00		8.66		6.93		6.86		5.60		5.60		5.12	
D. Black-market exchange rates	8.00		5.60		8.60		9.60		10.00		10.00		10.00		10.00	
E. International capital market controls	5.00		5.00		5.00		5.00		6.92		6.90		7.06		6.27	
(i) Foreign ownership / investment restrictions											6.90		7.20		7.15	
(ii) Capital controls	5.00		5.00		5.00		5.00		6.92		6.90		6.92		5.38	
5. Regulation of Credit, Labor, and Business	**6.32**		**6.86**		**6.00**		**6.20**		**7.10**		**7.50**		**7.64**		**7.76**	
A. Credit market regulations	6.47		8.07		6.33		7.00		10.00		9.50		9.25		9.50	
(i) Ownership of banks					5.00		5.00		10.00		8.00		8.00		8.00	
(ii) Foreign bank competition											10.00		10.00		10.00	
(iii) Private sector credit	8.95		8.14		10.00		10.00		10.00		10.00		10.00		10.00	
(iv) Interest rate controls / negative real interest rates	4.00		8.00		4.00		6.00		10.00		10.00		9.00		10.00	
B. Labor market regulations											7.10		7.01		7.21	
(i) Hiring regulations and minimum wage											10.00		10.00		10.00	
(ii) Hiring and firing regulations											4.10		4.87		4.88	
(iii) Centralized collective bargaining											6.70		5.54		6.14	
(iv) Hours regulations											10.00		10.00		10.00	
(v) Mandated cost of worker dismissal											1.70		1.66		2.21	
(vi) Conscription	10.00		10.00		10.00		10.00		10.00		10.00		10.00		10.00	
C. Business regulations											6.00		6.66		6.58	
(i) Price controls					6.00		6.00		6.00		6.00		6.00		6.00	
(ii) Administrative requirements											3.60		4.33		4.31	
(iii) Bureaucracy costs											3.40		5.36		5.15	
(iv) Starting a business											6.60		8.02		8.02	
(v) Extra payments / bribes / favoritism											6.90		6.72		6.59	
(vi) Licensing restrictions											7.40		7.75		7.72	
(vii) Cost of tax compliance											8.40		8.43		8.30	

Brazil

	1980	1985	1990	1995	2000	2005	2008	2009
Chain-Linked	Rating (Rank)	Rating (Rank)	Rating (Rank)	Rating (Rank)	Rating (Rank)	Rating (Rank)	Rating (Rank)	Rating (Rank)
Summary Rating (Rank) ➤	**4.45** (83)	**3.87** (101)	**4.54** (97)	**4.58** (107)	**5.85** (91)	**6.25** (88)	**6.25** (86)	**6.20** (91)
Area 1. Size of Government	5.27 (45)	5.08 (56)	6.07 (44)	6.13 (60)	5.98 (71)	6.73 (55)	6.73 (48)	6.67 (47)
Area 2. Legal Structure and Security of Property Rights	6.37 (32)	6.22 (36)	6.73 (34)	5.76 (53)	5.35 (71)	5.19 (78)	5.25 (77)	5.26 (76)
Area 3. Access to Sound Money	1.66 (107)	0.10 (112)	0.10 (118)	0.10 (122)	6.14 (106)	7.64 (76)	7.87 (71)	7.93 (76)
Area 4. Freedom to Trade Internationally	3.56 (80)	3.19 (84)	4.84 (75)	5.85 (86)	6.06 (91)	6.61 (65)	6.39 (79)	5.98 (86)
Area 5. Regulation of Credit, Labor, and Business	5.46 (44)	4.84 (67)	5.02 (70)	5.14 (76)	5.71 (75)	5.09 (114)	5.00 (116)	5.13 (116)

Unadjusted

	1980	1985	1990	1995	2000	2005	2008	2009
Summary Rating (Rank) ➤	**4.43** (84)	**3.62** (104)	**4.29** (100)	**4.51** (110)	**5.85** (91)	**6.25** (97)	**6.25** (97)	**6.19** (102)
	Rating Data	Rating Data	Rating Data	Rating Data	Rating Data	Rating Data	Rating Data	Rating Data
1. Size of Government	**5.27**	**5.08**	**6.07**	**6.13**	**5.98**	**6.70**	**6.73**	**6.67**
A. Government consumption	8.34 (11.65)	7.93 (13.05)	4.55 (24.55)	4.51 (24.66)	4.44 (24.90)	4.40 (24.90)	4.46 (24.82)	4.44 (24.90)
B. Transfers and subsidies	6.76 (12.40)	7.41 (10.00)	7.22 (10.70)	6.52 (13.27)	5.96 (15.33)	9.00 (4.20)	7.95 (8.03)	7.75 (8.76)
C. Government enterprises and investment	2.00 (49.20)	4.00 (36.00)	7.00 (24.90)	8.00 (17.80)	8.00 (17.80)	8.00 (17.80)	8.00	8.00
D. Top marginal tax rate	4.00	1.00	5.50	5.50	5.50	5.50	6.50	6.50
(i) Top marginal income tax rate	4.00 (55)	1.00 (60)	9.00 (25)	8.00 (35)	8.00 (28)	8.00 (28)	8.00 (28)	8.00 (28)
(ii) Top marginal income and payroll tax rates			2.00 (53)	3.00 (60)	3.00 (50)	3.00 (50)	5.00 (36)	5.00 (36)
2. Legal Structure and Security of Property Rights	**5.86**	**5.72**	**6.19**	**5.76**	**5.35**	**5.20**	**5.25**	**5.26**
A. Judicial independence				5.55	5.51	3.00	4.31	4.20
B. Impartial courts				6.67	6.18	3.40	3.68	4.06
C. Protection of property rights				4.15	5.08	6.00	5.63	5.45
D. Military interference in rule of law and politics				5.45	6.67	6.70	6.67	6.67
E. Integrity of the legal system				6.96	3.33	4.20	3.33	3.33
F. Legal enforcement of contracts						4.80	4.82	4.82
G. Regulatory restrictions on sale of real property						8.20	8.32	8.32
3. Access to Sound Money	**1.66**	**0.00**	**0.00**	**0.00**	**6.14**	**7.60**	**7.87**	**7.93**
A. Money growth	3.26 (33.71)	0.00 (111.36)	0.00 (458.38)	0.00 (479.01)	8.07 (9.63)	7.90 (10.40)	8.32 (8.40)	8.27 (8.67)
B. Standard deviation of inflation	3.37 (16.57)	0.00 (53.14)	0.00 (878.93)	0.00 (851.49)	7.88 (5.29)	9.00 (2.45)	9.27 (1.82)	9.44 (1.40)
C. Inflation: most recent year	0.00 (87.47)	0.00 (231.72)	0.00 (2509.47)	0.00 (77.59)	8.59 (7.04)	8.60 (6.87)	8.87 (5.66)	9.02 (4.89)
D. Freedom to own foreign currency bank accounts	0.00	0.00	0.00	0.00	0.00	5.00	5.00	5.00
4. Freedom to Trade Internationally	**4.48**	**2.97**	**4.52**	**5.60**	**6.06**	**6.60**	**6.39**	**5.98**
A. Taxes on international trade	3.33	2.62	4.84	7.66	7.18	7.20	7.32	7.28
(i) Revenues from trade taxes (% of trade sector)	3.33 (10.00)	7.87 (3.20)	7.53 (3.70)	8.13 (2.81)	7.21 (4.18)	7.20 (4.20)	8.61 (2.09)	8.49 (2.27)
(ii) Mean tariff rate		0.00 (55.60)	4.00 (30.00)	7.60 (12.00)	7.12 (14.40)	7.50 (12.30)	7.28 (13.60)	7.28 (13.60)
(iii) Standard deviation of tariff rates		0.00 (26.20)	3.00 (17.50)	7.24 (6.90)	7.20 (7.00)	6.90 (7.90)	6.08 (9.79)	6.08 (9.79)
B. Regulatory trade barriers				5.27	5.34	6.10	6.46	6.39
(i) Non-tariff trade barriers				5.27	4.02	5.10	4.76	4.77
(ii) Compliance cost of importing and exporting					6.66	7.20	8.16	8.01
C. Size of trade sector relative to expected	4.45	3.77	1.51	2.01	3.64	4.50	4.11	2.44
D. Black-market exchange rates	6.40	0.20	8.00	9.40	10.00	9.00	9.27	9.30
E. International capital market controls	0.00	0.00	0.00	3.64	4.17	6.20	4.79	4.48
(i) Foreign ownership/investment restrictions				7.29	7.56	6.20	5.74	5.89
(ii) Capital controls	0.00	0.00	0.00	0.00	0.77	6.20	3.85	3.08
5. Regulation of Credit, Labor, and Business	**4.89**	**4.33**	**4.67**	**5.07**	**5.71**	**5.10**	**5.01**	**5.10**
A. Credit market regulations	5.26	3.43	3.95	4.70	5.77	7.00	7.07	6.65
(i) Ownership of banks	5.00	5.00	5.00	5.00	5.00	5.00	5.00	5.00
(ii) Foreign bank competition				6.47	7.13	8.00	8.00	8.00
(iii) Private sector credit	6.79	5.30	6.85	8.23	5.87	10.00	9.26	7.59
(iv) Interest rate controls/negative real interest rates	4.00	0.00	0.00	0.00	5.00	5.00	6.00	6.00
B. Labor market regulations			4.78	5.30	4.65	3.80	3.91	4.43
(i) Hiring regulations and minimum wage				6.67	3.46	2.20	2.20	2.23
(ii) Hiring and firing regulations			6.18	6.18	5.25	2.90	3.16	3.00
(iii) Centralized collective bargaining	5.18	5.18	5.18	5.18	5.52	5.30	5.39	5.44
(iv) Hours regulations				5.47	6.01	4.00	4.00	6.00
(v) Mandated cost of worker dismissal						5.70	5.74	6.91
(vi) Conscription	3.00	3.00	3.00	3.00	3.00	3.00	3.00	3.00
C. Business regulations				5.21	6.71	4.50	4.04	4.24
(i) Price controls			0.00	6.00	7.00	6.00	7.00	8.00
(ii) Administrative requirements					7.70	1.50	1.41	1.54
(iii) Bureaucracy costs				5.61	7.38	5.30	3.84	3.96
(iv) Starting a business				5.95	5.73	6.60	6.59	6.59
(v) Extra payments/bribes/favoritism				3.27	5.73	6.30	4.50	4.65
(vi) Licensing restrictions						5.70	4.91	4.92
(vii) Cost of tax compliance						0.00	0.00	0.00

Bulgaria

	1980	1985	1990	1995	2000	2005	2008	2009
Chain-Linked		Rating (Rank)	Rating (Rank)	Rating (Rank)	Rating (Rank)	Rating (Rank)	Rating (Rank)	Rating (Rank)
Summary Rating (Rank) ➤		**5.51** (49)	**4.23** (101)	**4.58** (107)	**5.27** (109)	**6.94** (54)	**7.18** (39)	**7.21** (35)
Area 1. Size of Government		4.14 (82)	2.34 (112)	4.03 (104)	4.51 (105)	6.30 (74)	7.46 (27)	7.29 (27)
Area 2. Legal Structure and Security of Property Rights		6.72 (31)	6.72 (35)	5.45 (61)	5.41 (68)	5.47 (69)	5.21 (79)	5.13 (78)
Area 3. Access to Sound Money		8.29 (24)	4.45 (98)	1.99 (112)	3.23 (118)	8.89 (44)	8.74 (48)	9.44 (28)
Area 4. Freedom to Trade Internationally		3.99 (74)	4.21 (88)	6.92 (45)	7.25 (47)	7.16 (42)	7.60 (27)	7.17 (36)
Area 5. Regulation of Credit, Labor, and Business			3.45 (106)	4.45 (104)	5.93 (63)	6.88 (48)	6.92 (44)	7.03 (41)

Unadjusted

	1980	1985	1990	1995	2000	2005	2008	2009
Summary Rating (Rank) ➤		**6.16** (29)	**4.41** (99)	**4.67** (104)	**5.27** (109)	**6.99** (59)	**7.31** (34)	**7.34** (28)
	Rating *Data*	Rating *Data*	Rating *Data*	Rating *Data*	Rating *Data*	Rating *Data*	Rating *Data*	Rating *Data*
1. Size of Government		**6.74**	**2.54**	**4.03**	**4.51**	**6.30**	**7.46**	**7.29**
A. Government consumption	9.04 *(9.26)*	8.12 *(12.40)*	4.91 *(23.31)*	6.54 *(17.77)*	5.24 *(22.20)*	5.60 *(21.00)*	6.10 *(19.27)*	5.96 *(19.75)*
B. Transfers and subsidies		5.37 *(17.50)*	2.72 *(27.20)*	6.59 *(13.00)*	5.81 *(15.90)*	5.60 *(16.60)*	6.25 *(14.28)*	5.69 *(16.32)*
C. Government enterprises and investment			0.00 *(96.40)*	0.00 *(55.60)*	4.00 *(38.95)*	8.00 *(19.00)*	10.00 *(14.24)*	10.00 *(14.24)*
D. Top marginal tax rate				3.00	3.00	6.00	7.50	7.50
(i) Top marginal income tax rate				3.00 *(50)*	5.00 *(38)*	9.00 *(24)*	10.00 *(10)*	10.00 *(10)*
(ii) Top marginal income and payroll tax rates					1.00 *(56)*	3.00 *(50)*	5.00 *(38)*	5.00 *(38)*
2. Legal Structure and Security of Property Rights		**7.25**	**7.25**	**5.88**	**5.41**	**5.50**	**5.21**	**5.13**
A. Judicial independence					4.18	2.50	3.16	3.26
B. Impartial courts				5.29	4.51	2.60	3.02	2.93
C. Protection of property rights					3.35	4.60	4.07	3.72
D. Military interference in rule of law and politics				7.46	8.33	8.30	8.33	8.33
E. Integrity of the legal system				6.96	6.67	6.70	4.17	4.17
F. Legal enforcement of contracts						4.80	4.77	4.77
G. Regulatory restrictions on sale of real property						8.90	8.96	8.73
3. Access to Sound Money		**6.47**	**4.45**	**1.99**	**3.23**	**8.90**	**8.74**	**9.44**
A. Money growth			7.38 *(13.10)*	2.97 *(35.15)*	0.00 *(76.68)*	7.30 *(13.50)*	8.60 *(7.02)*	9.59 *(2.05)*
B. Standard deviation of inflation		9.44 *(1.39)*	5.64 *(10.90)*	0.00 *(66.37)*	0.00 *(409.71)*	9.30 *(1.80)*	8.82 *(2.94)*	8.73 *(3.17)*
C. Inflation: most recent year		9.95 *(0.23)*	4.76 *(26.19)*	0.00 *(62.85)*	7.94 *(10.32)*	9.00 *(5.04)*	7.53 *(12.35)*	9.45 *(2.75)*
D. Freedom to own foreign currency bank accounts	0.00	0.00	0.00	5.00	5.00	10.00	10.00	10.00
4. Freedom to Trade Internationally		**4.20**	**4.28**	**6.88**	**7.25**	**7.20**	**7.60**	**7.17**
A. Taxes on international trade		6.40	8.43	6.37	7.85	7.70	8.03	8.22
(i) Revenues from trade taxes (% of trade sector)		6.40 *(5.40)*	9.13 *(1.30)*	7.87 *(3.20)*	9.53 *(0.71)*	9.60 *(0.60)*	9.61 *(0.59)*	9.44 *(0.84)*
(ii) Mean tariff rate			7.72 *(11.40)*	6.56 *(17.20)*	7.26 *(13.70)*	7.90 *(10.70)*	8.88 *(5.60)*	8.94 *(5.30)*
(iii) Standard deviation of tariff rates				4.68 *(13.30)*	6.76 *(8.11)*	5.80 *(10.50)*	5.61 *(10.98)*	6.29 *(9.28)*
B. Regulatory trade barriers					6.42	5.70	6.16	6.01
(i) Non-tariff trade barriers					4.35	5.00	5.39	5.10
(ii) Compliance cost of importing and exporting					8.50	6.40	6.92	6.92
C. Size of trade sector relative to expected	5.27	6.36	4.76	5.84	6.92	7.40	7.33	5.28
D. Black-market exchange rates	0.00	0.00	0.00	9.00	10.00	10.00	10.00	10.00
E. International capital market controls	0.00	0.00	0.00	5.00	5.04	4.90	6.50	6.36
(i) Foreign ownership / investment restrictions					7.01	5.20	5.31	5.03
(ii) Capital controls	0.00	0.00	0.00	5.00	3.08	4.60	7.69	7.69
5. Regulation of Credit, Labor, and Business			**3.54**	**4.56**	**5.93**	**7.10**	**7.54**	**7.66**
A. Credit market regulations	0.00	0.00	3.52	5.23	7.43	9.80	9.50	9.74
(i) Ownership of banks	0.00	0.00	0.00	2.00	8.00	10.00	10.00	10.00
(ii) Foreign bank competition					5.18	9.00	9.00	9.00
(iii) Private sector credit			6.55	5.70	9.69	10.00	10.00	9.94
(iv) Interest rate controls / negative real interest rates			4.00	8.00	9.00	10.00	9.00	10.00
B. Labor market regulations					4.92	6.40	7.75	7.79
(i) Hiring regulations and minimum wage					2.57	8.30	8.30	6.67
(ii) Hiring and firing regulations					4.33	4.50	5.42	5.43
(iii) Centralized collective bargaining					7.87	7.60	7.59	7.06
(iv) Hours regulations					6.85	6.00	6.00	8.00
(v) Mandated cost of worker dismissal						9.20	9.17	9.60
(vi) Conscription	0.00	0.00	0.00	1.00	3.00	3.00	10.00	10.00
C. Business regulations					5.43	5.20	5.38	5.47
(i) Price controls			0.00	4.00	6.00	3.00	4.00	4.00
(ii) Administrative requirements					6.10	2.70	3.46	3.61
(iii) Bureaucracy costs					5.95	3.40	6.00	6.40
(iv) Starting a business					2.53	8.70	9.34	9.41
(v) Extra payments / bribes / favoritism					6.57	7.40	3.93	3.90
(vi) Licensing restrictions						8.10	7.86	7.85
(vii) Cost of tax compliance						3.10	3.10	3.10

Burkina Faso

	1980	1985	1990	1995	2000	2005	2008	2009
Chain-Linked						Rating (Rank)	Rating (Rank)	Rating (Rank)
Summary Rating (Rank) ➤								
Area 1. Size of Government								
Area 2. Legal Structure and Security of Property Rights								
Area 3. Access to Sound Money								
Area 4. Freedom to Trade Internationally								
Area 5. Regulation of Credit, Labor, and Business								

Unadjusted

	1980	1985	1990	1995	2000	2005	2008	2009
Summary Rating (Rank) ➤						**5.75** (120)	**5.94** (115)	**5.94** (118)
					Rating *Data*	Rating *Data*	Rating *Data*	Rating *Data*
1. Size of Government						**6.10**	**6.24**	**6.42**
A. Government consumption						5.10 *(22.70)*	4.92 *(23.26)*	5.30 *(21.99)*
B. Transfers and subsidies						9.20 *(3.50)*	9.80 *(1.22)*	9.97 *(0.61)*
C. Government enterprises and investment					2.00 *(41.40)*	4.00 *(37.90)*	4.00 *(38.70)*	4.00 *(38.70)*
D. Top marginal tax rate								
(i) Top marginal income tax rate								
(ii) Top marginal income and payroll tax rates								
2. Legal Structure and Security of Property Rights						**3.90**	**4.34**	**4.07**
A. Judicial independence						3.40	3.52	2.43
B. Impartial courts						3.70	4.74	4.02
C. Protection of property rights						5.70	5.49	5.31
D. Military interference in rule of law and politics						5.00	4.17	4.17
E. Integrity of the legal system						5.80	5.83	5.83
F. Legal enforcement of contracts						2.10	2.10	2.14
G. Regulatory restrictions on sale of real property						1.60	4.55	4.58
3. Access to Sound Money						**6.80**	**6.64**	**6.75**
A. Money growth						9.60 *(2.20)*	9.13 *(4.37)*	7.94 *(10.29)*
B. Standard deviation of inflation						9.10 *(2.23)*	9.56 *(1.10)*	9.57 *(1.07)*
C. Inflation: most recent year						8.70 *(6.42)*	7.87 *(10.66)*	9.48 *(2.61)*
D. Freedom to own foreign currency bank accounts						0.00	0.00	0.00
4. Freedom to Trade Internationally						**5.30**	**5.23**	**5.20**
A. Taxes on international trade						7.10	6.93	6.93
(i) Revenues from trade taxes (% of trade sector)						6.50 *(5.20)*	5.89 *(6.16)*	5.89 *(6.16)*
(ii) Mean tariff rate						7.40 *(13.10)*	7.62 *(11.90)*	7.62 *(11.90)*
(iii) Standard deviation of tariff rates						7.30 *(6.80)*	7.29 *(6.78)*	7.29 *(6.78)*
B. Regulatory trade barriers						5.00	4.92	5.06
(i) Non-tariff trade barriers						7.00	6.17	6.45
(ii) Compliance cost of importing and exporting						3.00	3.67	3.67
C. Size of trade sector relative to expected						0.20	1.42	1.28
D. Black-market exchange rates						10.00	10.00	10.00
E. International capital market controls						4.10	2.87	2.72
(i) Foreign ownership / investment restrictions						7.40	4.96	4.66
(ii) Capital controls						0.80	0.77	0.77
5. Regulation of Credit, Labor, and Business						**6.60**	**7.24**	**7.25**
A. Credit market regulations						8.70	8.57	8.51
(i) Ownership of banks						10.00	10.00	10.00
(ii) Foreign bank competition						7.00	7.00	7.00
(iii) Private sector credit						9.60	9.27	9.05
(iv) Interest rate controls / negative real interest rates						8.00	8.00	8.00
B. Labor market regulations						5.90	7.17	7.22
(i) Hiring regulations and minimum wage						1.70	6.70	6.67
(ii) Hiring and firing regulations						4.80	5.16	5.23
(iii) Centralized collective bargaining						6.00	6.33	6.15
(iv) Hours regulations						6.00	8.00	8.00
(v) Mandated cost of worker dismissal						6.80	6.85	7.29
(vi) Conscription						10.00	10.00	10.00
C. Business regulations						5.30	5.98	6.02
(i) Price controls								
(ii) Administrative requirements						4.30	4.22	3.90
(iii) Bureaucracy costs						4.10	5.64	6.26
(iv) Starting a business						6.10	7.62	7.66
(v) Extra payments / bribes / favoritism						5.00	3.96	3.42
(vi) Licensing restrictions						5.40	7.46	7.89
(vii) Cost of tax compliance						7.00	6.97	6.97

Burundi

	1980	1985	1990	1995	2000	2005	2008	2009
Chain-Linked	Rating (Rank)	Rating (Rank)	Rating (Rank)	Rating (Rank)	Rating (Rank)	Rating (Rank)	Rating (Rank)	Rating (Rank)
Summary Rating (Rank) ➤	**4.44** (84)	**4.74** (85)	**4.88** (89)	**4.39** (115)	**4.78** (117)	**4.59** (121)	**4.62** (120)	**4.87** (119)
Area 1. Size of Government	6.50 (18)	6.71 (13)	6.26 (39)	5.78 (70)	5.80 (76)	4.98 (99)	4.94 (106)	4.61 (106)
Area 2. Legal Structure and Security of Property Rights	3.63 (61)	3.31 (86)	3.44 (87)	3.47 (115)	3.26 (117)	2.89 (118)	3.42 (112)	3.42 (115)
Area 3. Access to Sound Money	5.56 (78)	6.27 (78)	6.50 (64)	5.83 (76)	6.19 (104)	6.71 (95)	6.04 (112)	6.78 (98)
Area 4. Freedom to Trade Internationally	2.16 (90)	2.86 (89)	3.68 (97)	2.47 (112)	4.33 (119)	2.49 (121)	2.98 (121)	3.17 (120)
Area 5. Regulation of Credit, Labor, and Business	4.35 (81)	4.70 (73)	4.46 (87)	4.31 (108)	4.31 (115)	5.79 (97)	5.51 (107)	6.12 (89)

Unadjusted

	1980	1985	1990	1995	2000	2005	2008	2009
Summary Rating (Rank) ➤	**4.33** (90)	**4.68** (87)	**4.72** (93)	**4.59** (107)	**4.78** (117)	**4.83** (133)	**4.87** (134)	**5.12** (133)
	Rating *Data*	Rating *Data*	Rating *Data*	Rating *Data*	Rating *Data*	Rating *Data*	Rating *Data*	Rating *Data*
1. Size of Government	**4.53**	**4.68**	**4.37**	**5.78**	**5.80**	**5.00**	**4.94**	**4.61**
A. Government consumption	9.07 *(9.16)*	9.36 *(8.17)*	8.75 *(10.27)*	8.08 *(12.54)*	7.96 *(12.92)*	5.50 *(21.20)*	5.38 *(21.72)*	4.40 *(25.05)*
B. Transfers and subsidies				9.28 *(3.16)*	9.43 *(2.60)*	9.40 *(2.60)*	9.43 *(2.60)*	9.43 *(2.60)*
C. Government enterprises and investment	0.00 *(91.90)*	0.00 *(83.00)*	0.00 *(82.20)*	0.00 *(100.00)*	0.00 *(87.30)*	0.00 *(83.70)*	0.00 *(83.70)*	0.00 *(83.70)*
D. Top marginal tax rate								
(i) Top marginal income tax rate								
(ii) Top marginal income and payroll tax rates								
2. Legal Structure and Security of Property Rights	**4.67**	**4.25**	**4.42**	**4.45**	**3.26**	**2.70**	**3.21**	**3.21**
A. Judicial independence						1.40	1.82	1.56
B. Impartial courts				4.00	3.67	2.50	2.90	2.93
C. Protection of property rights						3.30	3.24	3.27
D. Military interference in rule of law and politics					2.20	1.90	2.50	2.50
E. Integrity of the legal system				5.18				
F. Legal enforcement of contracts						3.90	2.65	2.65
G. Regulatory restrictions on sale of real property						3.20	6.15	6.32
3. Access to Sound Money	**5.56**	**6.27**	**6.50**	**5.83**	**6.19**	**6.70**	**6.04**	**6.78**
A. Money growth	7.91 *(10.45)*	9.05 *(4.74)*	9.97 *(0.15)*	8.29 *(8.56)*	7.67 *(11.66)*	6.80 *(15.90)*	7.36 *(13.20)*	7.56 *(12.20)*
B. Standard deviation of inflation	7.60 *(5.99)*	7.05 *(7.37)*	7.22 *(6.94)*	8.06 *(4.86)*	6.95 *(7.62)*	7.70 *(5.69)*	6.63 *(8.43)*	6.75 *(8.13)*
C. Inflation: most recent year	6.72 *(16.38)*	8.99 *(5.07)*	8.80 *(5.99)*	6.96 *(15.18)*	5.14 *(24.31)*	7.30 *(13.52)*	5.18 *(24.11)*	7.80 *(10.98)*
D. Freedom to own foreign currency bank accounts	0.00	0.00	0.00	0.00	5.00	5.00	5.00	5.00
4. Freedom to Trade Internationally	**2.07**	**2.98**	**3.84**	**2.57**	**4.33**	**3.40**	**4.13**	**4.40**
A. Taxes on international trade	0.00	1.21	1.30	2.11	1.13	4.50	4.94	4.94
(i) Revenues from trade taxes (% of trade sector)	0.00 *(18.10)*	0.00 *(17.00)*	0.00 *(22.90)*	1.60 *(12.60)*	1.13 *(13.31)*	1.10 *(13.30)*	1.13 *(13.31)*	1.13 *(13.31)*
(ii) Mean tariff rate		2.42 *(37.90)*	2.60 *(37.00)*	2.62 *(36.90)*		6.10 *(19.60)*	7.46 *(12.70)*	7.46 *(12.70)*
(iii) Standard deviation of tariff rates						6.20 *(9.40)*	6.24 *(9.40)*	6.24 *(9.40)*
B. Regulatory trade barriers						3.00	2.99	3.04
(i) Non-tariff trade barriers						4.10	4.19	4.29
(ii) Compliance cost of importing and exporting						1.80	1.79	1.79
C. Size of trade sector relative to expected	1.06	0.40	0.83	1.28	0.00	1.00	0.00	1.77
D. Black-market exchange rates	1.00	5.00	8.80	1.20	10.00	4.90	10.00	10.00
E. International capital market controls	0.00	0.00	0.00	0.00	2.31	3.90	2.71	2.25
(i) Foreign ownership / investment restrictions						5.50	3.88	2.96
(ii) Capital controls	0.00	0.00	0.00	0.00	2.31	2.30	1.54	1.54
5. Regulation of Credit, Labor, and Business	**4.84**	**5.23**	**4.46**	**4.31**	**4.31**	**6.30**	**6.04**	**6.63**
A. Credit market regulations	2.94	3.96	3.26	2.07	1.42	6.60	5.81	6.56
(i) Ownership of banks	2.00	2.00	0.00	0.00	0.00	8.00	8.00	8.00
(ii) Foreign bank competition						8.00	8.00	8.00
(iii) Private sector credit	4.81	3.87	5.78	2.21	0.25	0.20	0.25	0.25
(iv) Interest rate controls / negative real interest rates	2.00	6.00	4.00	4.00	4.00	10.00	7.00	10.00
B. Labor market regulations						7.70	7.31	8.21
(i) Hiring regulations and minimum wage						10.00	10.00	10.00
(ii) Hiring and firing regulations						5.80	4.20	4.54
(iii) Centralized collective bargaining						8.10	7.38	7.91
(iv) Hours regulations						4.70	4.70	8.00
(v) Mandated cost of worker dismissal						7.60	7.59	8.79
(vi) Conscription	10.00	10.00	10.00	10.00	10.00	10.00	10.00	10.00
C. Business regulations						4.70	4.99	5.11
(i) Price controls				0.00	2.00	4.00	4.00	4.00
(ii) Administrative requirements						2.80	2.86	3.62
(iii) Bureaucracy costs						4.70	7.12	7.86
(iv) Starting a business						6.60	7.38	7.62
(v) Extra payments / bribes / favoritism						4.00	2.70	2.60
(vi) Licensing restrictions						2.50	2.46	2.46
(vii) Cost of tax compliance						8.40	8.43	7.63

Cameroon

Chain-Linked	1980		1985		1990		1995		2000		2005		2008		2009	
	Rating	(Rank)	Rating	(Rank)	Rating	(Rank)	Rating	(Rank)	Rating	(Rank)	Rating	(Rank)	Rating	(Rank)	Rating	(Rank)
Summary Rating (Rank) ➤	**5.74**	(40)	**5.77**	(43)	**5.70**	(50)	**5.58**	(77)	**5.84**	(92)	**5.94**	(96)	**5.86**	(102)	**6.00**	(97)
Area 1. Size of Government	6.90	(13)	5.53	(39)	5.24	(67)	6.58	(38)	6.89	(37)	7.04	(43)	6.67	(52)	6.79	(43)
Area 2. Legal Structure and Security of Property Rights	5.78	(39)	5.85	(40)	5.79	(47)	4.77	(91)	4.45	(88)	3.67	(108)	3.73	(107)	3.84	(108)
Area 3. Access to Sound Money	5.66	(75)	6.67	(52)	7.01	(45)	5.92	(75)	6.60	(97)	7.21	(84)	6.74	(94)	6.60	(107)
Area 4. Freedom to Trade Internationally	5.44	(48)	6.21	(37)	5.51	(61)	5.52	(93)	5.79	(100)	5.77	(97)	5.96	(94)	6.20	(82)
Area 5. Regulation of Credit, Labor, and Business	4.64	(69)	4.64	(76)	4.94	(75)	5.09	(79)	5.49	(87)	5.98	(90)	6.20	(82)	6.58	(62)

Unadjusted	1980		1985		1990		1995		2000		2005		2008		2009	
Summary Rating (Rank) ➤	**6.05**	(28)	**5.85**	(41)	**5.67**	(53)	**5.50**	(79)	**5.84**	(92)	**5.91**	(113)	**5.83**	(119)	**5.97**	(116)
	Rating	Data	Rating	Data	Rating	Data	Rating	Data	Rating	Data	Rating	Data	Rating	Data	Rating	Data
1. Size of Government	**8.37**		**5.53**		**5.24**		**6.58**		**6.89**		**7.00**		**6.67**		**6.79**	
A. Government consumption	8.18	(12.19)	8.16	(12.27)	7.04	(16.06)	8.61	(10.73)	8.00	(12.80)	8.10	(12.60)	6.62	(17.50)	7.09	(15.88)
B. Transfers and subsidies	9.92	(0.80)	9.97	(0.60)	9.40	(2.70)	9.70	(1.60)	9.57	(2.09)	9.60	(2.10)	9.57	(2.09)	9.57	(2.09)
C. Government enterprises and investment	7.00	(22.20)	2.00	(44.80)	4.00	(31.50)	8.00	(18.10)	10.00	(13.10)	10.00	(14.00)	10.00	(13.95)	10.00	(13.95)
D. Top marginal tax rate			2.00		0.50		0.00		0.00		0.50		0.50		0.50	
(i) Top marginal income tax rate			2.00	(60)	1.00	(60)	0.00	(66)	0.00	(65)	1.00	(60)	1.00	(60)	1.00	(60)
(ii) Top marginal income and payroll tax rates					0.00	(63)	0.00	(69)	0.00	(68)	0.00	(68)	0.00	(68)	0.00	(68)
2. Legal Structure and Security of Property Rights	**5.78**		**5.85**		**5.79**		**4.77**		**4.45**		**3.50**		**3.54**		**3.64**	
A. Judicial independence											2.10		2.36		2.75	
B. Impartial courts							3.76		3.76		2.80		3.68		3.71	
C. Protection of property rights											4.10		4.15		4.48	
D. Military interference in rule of law and politics							4.38		6.67		6.70		5.83		5.83	
E. Integrity of the legal system							6.96		3.33		3.30		3.33		3.33	
F. Legal enforcement of contracts											2.20		2.17		2.17	
G. Regulatory restrictions on sale of real property											3.20		3.24		3.24	
3. Access to Sound Money	**5.66**		**6.67**		**7.01**		**5.92**		**6.60**		**7.20**		**6.74**		**6.60**	
A. Money growth	7.83	(10.86)	9.57	(2.14)	8.98	(−5.10)	9.74	(−1.29)	7.36	(13.21)	9.90	(−0.50)	8.60	(7.02)	8.27	(8.64)
B. Standard deviation of inflation	7.65	(5.88)	9.34	(1.66)	9.38	(1.55)	7.34	(6.64)	9.30	(1.75)	9.30	(1.65)	9.44	(1.39)	8.75	(3.12)
C. Inflation: most recent year	7.15	(14.25)	7.76	(11.19)	9.67	(1.64)	6.59	(17.03)	9.75	(1.23)	9.60	(2.01)	8.93	(5.34)	9.39	(3.04)
D. Freedom to own foreign currency bank accounts	0.00		0.00		0.00		0.00		0.00		0.00		0.00		0.00	
4. Freedom to Trade Internationally	**5.30**		**6.05**		**5.37**		**5.15**		**5.79**		**5.60**		**5.81**		**6.04**	
A. Taxes on international trade	2.67		5.93		6.40		3.71		5.08		5.50		5.50		5.50	
(i) Revenues from trade taxes (% of trade sector)	2.67	(11.00)	5.93	(6.10)	6.40	(5.40)	4.87	(7.70)	3.84	(9.24)	3.80	(9.20)	3.84	(9.24)	3.84	(9.24)
(ii) Mean tariff rate							6.26	(18.70)	6.32	(18.40)	6.30	(18.40)	6.44	(17.80)	6.44	(17.80)
(iii) Standard deviation of tariff rates							0.00	(29.60)			6.30	(9.20)	6.23	(9.43)	6.23	(9.43)
B. Regulatory trade barriers											5.50		6.25		6.68	
(i) Non-tariff trade barriers											5.20		5.88		6.75	
(ii) Compliance cost of importing and exporting											5.80		6.61		6.61	
C. Size of trade sector relative to expected	6.04		6.33		3.04		4.03		4.88		3.50		4.44		4.33	
D. Black-market exchange rates	9.60		9.80		9.20		9.80		10.00		10.00		10.00		10.00	
E. International capital market controls	0.00		0.00		0.00		0.00		0.77		3.60		2.87		3.71	
(i) Foreign ownership / investment restrictions											6.50		5.74		5.88	
(ii) Capital controls	0.00		0.00		0.00		0.00		0.77		0.80		0.00		1.54	
5. Regulation of Credit, Labor, and Business	**5.16**		**5.16**		**4.94**		**5.09**		**5.49**		**6.20**		**6.38**		**6.75**	
A. Credit market regulations	3.00		3.00		4.85		5.33		6.67		8.00		8.00		8.00	
(i) Ownership of banks	0.00		0.00		0.00		2.00		2.00		5.00		5.00		5.00	
(ii) Foreign bank competition																
(iii) Private sector credit					6.54		10.00		10.00		10.00		10.00		10.00	
(iv) Interest rate controls / negative real interest rates	6.00		6.00		8.00		4.00		8.00		9.00		9.00		9.00	
B. Labor market regulations											7.30		7.41		7.57	
(i) Hiring regulations and minimum wage											7.20		7.20		7.23	
(ii) Hiring and firing regulations											5.70		5.40		6.22	
(iii) Centralized collective bargaining											5.90		6.92		6.75	
(iv) Hours regulations											8.00		8.00		8.00	
(v) Mandated cost of worker dismissal											6.90		6.94		7.19	
(vi) Conscription	10.00		10.00		10.00		10.00		10.00		10.00		10.00		10.00	
C. Business regulations											3.20		3.74		4.70	
(i) Price controls					0.00		0.00		0.00		4.00		4.00		4.00	
(ii) Administrative requirements											1.70		2.89		3.16	
(iii) Bureaucracy costs											3.70		6.64		6.41	
(iv) Starting a business											6.50		7.04		8.23	
(v) Extra payments / bribes / favoritism											4.00		2.87		3.20	
(vi) Licensing restrictions											2.70		2.75		5.21	
(vii) Cost of tax compliance											0.00		0.00		2.67	

Canada

	1980	1985	1990	1995	2000	2005	2008	2009
Chain-Linked	Rating *(Rank)*	Rating *(Rank)*	Rating *(Rank)*	Rating *(Rank)*	Rating *(Rank)*	Rating *(Rank)*	Rating *(Rank)*	Rating *(Rank)*
Summary Rating (Rank) ➤	**7.67** (5)	**7.75** (6)	**8.07** (6)	**7.90** (8)	**8.15** (8)	**8.06** (7)	**7.92** (5)	**7.78** (7)
Area 1. Size of Government	5.37 (42)	5.24 (48)	5.81 (53)	5.80 (69)	5.97 (72)	6.88 (49)	6.54 (59)	6.12 (66)
Area 2. Legal Structure and Security of Property Rights	8.46 (16)	9.29 (9)	9.84 (9)	8.95 (11)	9.27 (7)	8.21 (15)	8.28 (12)	8.15 (15)
Area 3. Access to Sound Money	9.09 (6)	8.93 (15)	9.68 (6)	9.63 (12)	9.53 (18)	9.68 (4)	9.54 (7)	9.55 (17)
Area 4. Freedom to Trade Internationally	7.72 (12)	7.70 (13)	7.62 (16)	7.51 (31)	8.31 (15)	7.16 (42)	7.09 (48)	6.95 (45)
Area 5. Regulation of Credit, Labor, and Business	7.67 (4)	7.65 (5)	7.48 (7)	7.60 (7)	7.69 (5)	8.36 (6)	8.16 (10)	8.15 (11)

	1980	1985	1990	1995	2000	2005	2008	2009
Unadjusted								
Summary Rating (Rank) ➤	**7.24** (7)	**7.32** (6)	**7.59** (5)	**7.87** (8)	**8.15** (8)	**8.09** (6)	**7.95** (6)	**7.81** (6)
	Rating *Data*	Rating *Data*	Rating *Data*	Rating *Data*	Rating *Data*	Rating *Data*	Rating *Data*	Rating *Data*
1. Size of Government	**5.37**	**5.24**	**5.81**	**5.80**	**5.97**	**6.90**	**6.54**	**6.12**
A. Government consumption	3.29 *(28.83)*	3.28 *(28.84)*	3.35 *(28.63)*	3.67 *(27.53)*	4.54 *(24.56)*	4.20 *(25.60)*	4.09 *(26.10)*	3.80 *(27.09)*
B. Transfers and subsidies	6.19 *(14.50)*	5.69 *(16.30)*	5.89 *(15.60)*	5.53 *(16.89)*	6.34 *(13.92)*	7.30 *(10.40)*	7.08 *(11.23)*	6.70 *(12.60)*
C. Government enterprises and investment	10.00 *(12.60)*	10.00 *(14.80)*	10.00 *(13.70)*	10.00 *(14.80)*	10.00 *(14.80)*	10.00 *(12.70)*	10.00 *(13.98)*	8.00 *(17.99)*
D. Top marginal tax rate	2.00	2.00	4.00	4.00	3.00	6.00	5.00	6.00
(i) Top marginal income tax rate	2.00 *(60-68)*	2.00 *(50-63)*	4.00 *(44-54)*	4.00 *(44-54)*	3.00 *(44-51)*	6.00 *(39-49)*	5.00 *(39-48)*	6.00 *(39-48)*
(ii) Top marginal income and payroll tax rates			4.00 *(44-54)*	4.00 *(44-54)*	3.00 *(44-51)*	6.00 *(39-49)*	5.00 *(39-48)*	6.00 *(39-48)*
2. Legal Structure and Security of Property Rights	**7.18**	**7.88**	**8.35**	**8.95**	**9.27**	**8.20**	**8.28**	**8.15**
A. Judicial independence				9.52	9.19	7.90	8.68	8.74
B. Impartial courts				8.85	9.19	7.40	6.69	6.81
C. Protection of property rights				7.34	7.98	8.20	8.68	8.43
D. Military interference in rule of law and politics				9.04	10.00	10.00	10.00	10.00
E. Integrity of the legal system				10.00	10.00	10.00	10.00	9.17
F. Legal enforcement of contracts						4.80	4.81	4.81
G. Regulatory restrictions on sale of real property						9.10	9.09	9.09
3. Access to Sound Money	**9.09**	**8.93**	**9.68**	**9.63**	**9.53**	**9.70**	**9.54**	**9.55**
A. Money growth	9.24 *(3.78)*	7.50 *(12.48)*	9.70 *(1.50)*	9.33 *(3.35)*	9.31 *(3.46)*	9.60 *(1.80)*	9.90 *(−0.48)*	9.64 *(1.79)*
B. Standard deviation of inflation	9.32 *(1.70)*	8.71 *(3.22)*	9.65 *(0.88)*	9.72 *(0.69)*	9.34 *(1.65)*	9.50 *(1.15)*	8.74 *(3.15)*	8.62 *(3.45)*
C. Inflation: most recent year	7.80 *(11.00)*	9.52 *(2.42)*	9.38 *(3.11)*	9.46 *(2.69)*	9.45 *(2.75)*	9.60 *(2.21)*	9.53 *(2.37)*	9.94 *(0.30)*
D. Freedom to own foreign currency bank accounts	10.00	10.00	10.00	10.00	10.00	10.00	10.00	10.00
4. Freedom to Trade Internationally	**7.80**	**7.78**	**7.55**	**7.33**	**8.31**	**7.20**	**7.09**	**6.95**
A. Taxes on international trade	8.08	8.38	7.93	5.94	8.78	6.60	6.99	7.19
(i) Revenues from trade taxes (% of trade sector)	8.40 *(2.40)*	8.87 *(1.70)*	9.20 *(1.20)*	9.53 *(0.70)*	9.79 *(0.31)*	9.80 *(0.30)*	9.76 *(0.37)*	9.73 *(0.40)*
(ii) Mean tariff rate	7.76 *(11.20)*	7.90 *(10.50)*	8.12 *(9.40)*	7.98 *(10.10)*	9.22 *(3.90)*	9.10 *(4.50)*	9.06 *(4.70)*	9.10 *(4.50)*
(iii) Standard deviation of tariff rates			6.48 *(8.80)*	0.32 *(24.20)*	7.32 *(6.70)*	1.10 *(22.30)*	2.14 *(19.65)*	2.73 *(18.18)*
B. Regulatory trade barriers				7.20	8.48	7.80	7.70	7.66
(i) Non-tariff trade barriers				7.20	7.45	6.60	6.50	6.42
(ii) Compliance cost of importing and exporting					9.50	8.90	8.89	8.89
C. Size of trade sector relative to expected	4.76	4.35	3.64	5.09	5.65	4.20	3.65	2.75
D. Black-market exchange rates	10.00	10.00	10.00	10.00	10.00	10.00	10.00	10.00
E. International capital market controls	8.00	8.00	8.00	8.39	8.65	7.20	7.14	7.14
(i) Foreign ownership / investment restrictions				8.78	8.83	7.50	7.36	7.35
(ii) Capital controls	8.00	8.00	8.00	8.00	8.46	6.90	6.92	6.92
5. Regulation of Credit, Labor, and Business	**6.76**	**6.75**	**6.54**	**7.66**	**7.69**	**8.50**	**8.30**	**8.28**
A. Credit market regulations	9.72	9.75	9.13	8.19	8.66	9.50	9.48	9.24
(i) Ownership of banks	10.00	10.00	10.00	10.00	10.00	10.00	10.00	10.00
(ii) Foreign bank competition				5.47	5.08	8.00	8.00	8.00
(iii) Private sector credit	9.16	9.25	7.39	7.65	10.00	10.00	9.94	8.96
(iv) Interest rate controls / negative real interest rates	10.00	10.00	10.00	10.00	10.00	10.00	10.00	10.00
B. Labor market regulations	7.33	7.24	7.05	7.13	6.41	8.20	8.33	8.49
(i) Hiring regulations and minimum wage				6.12	4.28	8.90	8.90	8.90
(ii) Hiring and firing regulations			6.47	6.47	5.08	5.40	6.06	6.34
(iii) Centralized collective bargaining	7.24	7.24	7.24	7.24	7.83	7.50	7.61	7.57
(iv) Hours regulations	4.75	4.49	4.49	5.80	4.84	10.00	10.00	10.00
(v) Mandated cost of worker dismissal						7.40	7.40	8.15
(vi) Conscription	10.00	10.00	10.00	10.00	10.00	10.00	10.00	10.00
C. Business regulations				7.67	8.01	7.80	7.08	7.11
(i) Price controls			9.00	7.00	9.00	8.00	7.00	7.00
(ii) Administrative requirements					7.20	3.90	4.26	4.37
(iii) Bureaucracy costs				7.07	7.23	6.40	1.85	1.93
(iv) Starting a business				7.82	7.55	9.90	9.84	9.84
(v) Extra payments / bribes / favoritism				8.82	9.08	8.40	8.47	8.59
(vi) Licensing restrictions						9.50	9.51	9.51
(vii) Cost of tax compliance						8.70	8.67	8.53

Central African Republic

	1980	1985	1990	1995	2000	2005	2008	2009
Chain-Linked	Rating (Rank)	Rating (Rank)	Rating (Rank)	Rating (Rank)	Rating (Rank)	Rating (Rank)	Rating (Rank)	Rating (Rank)
Summary Rating (Rank) ➤		4.70 (86)	5.11 (79)	4.68 (105)	5.09 (113)	4.96 (116)	5.16 (115)	5.26 (116)
Area 1. Size of Government	3.84 (85)	5.58 (36)	4.70 (84)	3.83 (106)	5.28 (86)	4.95 (102)	6.92 (42)	6.98 (35)
Area 2. Legal Structure and Security of Property Rights	4.96 (46)	4.51 (65)	4.69 (66)	5.18 (76)	4.28 (96)	3.76 (106)	2.91 (119)	2.74 (120)
Area 3. Access to Sound Money	5.25 (88)	4.53 (96)	7.08 (40)	5.04 (91)	7.03 (78)	7.04 (88)	6.63 (98)	7.05 (88)
Area 4. Freedom to Trade Internationally		5.19 (57)	4.75 (78)	5.46 (96)	4.76 (117)	3.93 (119)	4.04 (119)	4.44 (118)
Area 5. Regulation of Credit, Labor, and Business		3.72 (93)	4.37 (91)	3.94 (115)	4.11 (119)	4.91 (117)	4.87 (118)	4.68 (121)

Unadjusted

	1980	1985	1990	1995	2000	2005	2008	2009
Summary Rating (Rank) ➤	4.82 (75)	4.70 (85)	5.07 (78)	4.66 (105)	5.09 (113)	4.71 (136)	4.77 (135)	4.88 (136)
	Rating Data	Rating Data	Rating Data	Rating Data	Rating Data	Rating Data	Rating Data	Rating Data
1. Size of Government	3.84	5.58	4.70	3.83	5.28	5.00	6.28	6.33
A. Government consumption	7.67 (13.91)	7.16 (15.66)	7.41 (14.81)	7.65 (13.98)	8.55 (10.92)	7.90 (13.10)	9.84 (6.54)	10.00 (4.54)
B. Transfers and subsidies								
C. Government enterprises and investment	0.00 (53.50)	4.00 (35.70)	2.00 (41.30)	0.00 (74.20)	2.00 (49.16)	2.00 (45.30)	4.00 (38.79)	4.00 (34.84)
D. Top marginal tax rate							5.00	5.00
(i) Top marginal income tax rate							5.00 (39-48)	5.00 (39-48)
(ii) Top marginal income and payroll tax rates								
2. Legal Structure and Security of Property Rights	4.67	4.25	4.42	4.88	4.28	2.80	2.17	2.05
A. Judicial independence								
B. Impartial courts						3.30	3.00	3.20
C. Protection of property rights								
D. Military interference in rule of law and politics					4.70	3.30	1.60	0.90
E. Integrity of the legal system				5.18	4.00			
F. Legal enforcement of contracts						0.50	0.51	0.51
G. Regulatory restrictions on sale of real property						4.10	3.58	3.58
3. Access to Sound Money	5.25	4.53	7.08	5.04	7.03	7.00	6.63	7.05
A. Money growth	7.16 (14.22)	9.29 (3.54)	9.90 (−0.50)	6.81 (15.97)	9.12 (−4.39)	9.70 (1.70)	9.54 (2.31)	9.55 (2.25)
B. Standard deviation of inflation	7.50 (6.24)	5.64 (10.90)	8.86 (2.85)	6.02 (9.94)	9.65 (0.88)	9.10 (2.30)	8.82 (2.94)	9.35 (1.63)
C. Inflation: most recent year	6.35 (18.27)	3.17 (34.15)	9.55 (2.27)	7.32 (13.41)	9.36 (3.20)	9.40 (2.88)	8.15 (9.27)	9.30 (3.52)
D. Freedom to own foreign currency bank accounts	0.00	0.00	0.00	0.00	0.00	0.00	0.00	0.00
4. Freedom to Trade Internationally	5.51	5.35	4.76	5.61	4.76	3.50	3.59	3.95
A. Taxes on international trade	2.93	3.60	2.97	6.22	5.58	6.20	6.17	6.18
(i) Revenues from trade taxes (% of trade sector)	2.93 (10.60)		2.33 (11.50)		4.27 (8.60)	5.90 (6.20)	5.88 (6.18)	5.88 (6.18)
(ii) Mean tariff rate		3.60 (32.00)	3.60 (32.00)	6.28 (18.60)	6.28 (18.60)	6.40 (17.90)	6.42 (17.90)	6.44 (17.80)
(iii) Standard deviation of tariff rates				6.16 (9.60)	6.20 (9.50)	6.30 (9.20)	6.21 (9.49)	6.23 (9.43)
B. Regulatory trade barriers						1.30	1.77	1.77
(i) Non-tariff trade barriers								
(ii) Compliance cost of importing and exporting						1.30	1.77	1.77
C. Size of trade sector relative to expected	6.82	5.12	3.42	3.84	0.00	0.00	0.00	0.26
D. Black-market exchange rates	9.60	9.80	9.20	9.80	10.00	10.00	10.00	10.00
E. International capital market controls	0.00	0.00	0.00	0.00	0.00	0.00	0.00	1.54
(i) Foreign ownership / investment restrictions								
(ii) Capital controls	0.00	0.00	0.00	0.00	0.00	0.00	0.00	1.54
5. Regulation of Credit, Labor, and Business		3.82	4.37	3.94	4.11	5.20	5.18	5.04
A. Credit market regulations	0.00	4.00	6.29	4.87	5.41	7.20	7.10	7.27
(i) Ownership of banks	0.00	0.00	2.00	2.00	2.00	5.00	5.00	5.00
(ii) Foreign bank competition								
(iii) Private sector credit			6.88	6.60	6.24	7.70	7.30	7.81
(iv) Interest rate controls / negative real interest rates		8.00	10.00	6.00	8.00	9.00	9.00	9.00
B. Labor market regulations						4.50	4.47	3.79
(i) Hiring regulations and minimum wage						3.90	3.90	2.77
(ii) Hiring and firing regulations								
(iii) Centralized collective bargaining								
(iv) Hours regulations						6.00	6.00	4.00
(v) Mandated cost of worker dismissal						8.00	7.96	8.39
(vi) Conscription	0.00	0.00	0.00	0.00	0.00	0.00	0.00	0.00
C. Business regulations						4.00	3.98	4.07
(i) Price controls			0.00	0.00	0.00	0.00	0.00	0.00
(ii) Administrative requirements								
(iii) Bureaucracy costs								
(iv) Starting a business						5.20	5.06	5.36
(v) Extra payments / bribes / favoritism								
(vi) Licensing restrictions						6.50	6.52	6.55
(vii) Cost of tax compliance						4.40	4.35	4.35

Chad

Chain-Linked

	1980		1985		1990		1995		2000		2005		2008		2009	
	Rating	(Rank)	Rating	(Rank)	Rating	(Rank)	Rating	(Rank)	Rating	(Rank)	Rating	(Rank)	Rating	(Rank)	Rating	(Rank)
Summary Rating (Rank) ➤			**5.05**	(74)	**5.05**	(83)	**5.02**	(97)	**5.47**	(104)	**5.69**	(107)	**5.28**	(114)	**5.63**	(108)
Area 1. Size of Government			6.14	(24)	6.19	(40)	6.33	(50)	6.45	(52)	7.87	(17)	5.73	(83)	6.94	(37)
Area 2. Legal Structure and Security of Property Rights	4.67	(48)	4.25	(72)	4.42	(72)	4.42	(100)	4.20	(98)	3.39	(112)	3.37	(113)	4.23	(101)
Area 3. Access to Sound Money	6.61	(36)	5.55	(88)	5.68	(82)	5.16	(88)	6.64	(94)	6.03	(111)	5.90	(115)	5.66	(118)
Area 4. Freedom to Trade Internationally											5.75	(103)	6.09	(89)	6.11	(88)	6.40	(72)
Area 5. Regulation of Credit, Labor, and Business			4.69	(74)	4.31	(94)	3.92	(116)	4.29	(116)	4.98	(116)	5.30	(111)	5.18	(115)

Unadjusted

	1980		1985		1990		1995		2000		2005		2008		2009	
Summary Rating (Rank) ➤			**4.56**	(90)	**5.27**	(68)	**5.24**	(89)	**5.47**	(104)	**5.37**	(132)	**4.98**	(132)	**5.32**	(132)
	Rating	Data	Rating	Data	Rating	Data	Rating	Data	Rating	Data	Rating	Data	Rating	Data	Rating	Data
1. Size of Government			4.30		6.19		6.33		6.45		7.90		5.73		6.94	
A. Government consumption	4.12	(26.00)	8.60	(10.75)	8.66	(10.54)	9.08	(9.14)	9.44	(7.90)	9.70	(7.00)	7.26	(15.30)	6.89	(16.58)
B. Transfers and subsidies					9.89	(0.90)	9.92	(0.80)	9.92	(0.80)	9.90	(0.80)	9.92	(0.80)	9.92	(0.80)
C. Government enterprises and investment			0.00	(86.30)	0.00	(94.00)	0.00	(63.30)	0.00	(50.00)	4.00	(36.80)	0.00	(56.03)	4.00	(33.33)
D. Top marginal tax rate																
(i) Top marginal income tax rate																
(ii) Top marginal income and payroll tax rates																
2. Legal Structure and Security of Property Rights	4.67		4.25		4.42		4.42		4.20		2.20		2.18		2.74	
A. Judicial independence											1.30		1.91		2.79	
B. Impartial courts							4.10		4.04		2.00		3.00		3.22	
C. Protection of property rights											2.70		2.51		2.33	
D. Military interference in rule of law and politics							4.35		4.70		2.80		1.20		1.70	
E. Integrity of the legal system							5.18		4.00							
F. Legal enforcement of contracts											0.30		0.30		2.22	
G. Regulatory restrictions on sale of real property											4.20		4.17		4.17	
3. Access to Sound Money	6.61		5.55		5.68		5.16		6.64		6.00		5.90		5.66	
A. Money growth	8.40	(7.98)	6.96	(15.22)	8.81	(−5.93)	9.56	(2.19)	9.67	(−1.66)	9.50	(2.40)	8.68	(6.59)	9.89	(0.56)
B. Standard deviation of inflation	9.76	(0.59)	6.00	(10.00)	6.19	(9.53)	2.84	(17.90)	7.65	(5.87)	6.20	(9.56)	6.99	(7.53)	4.74	(13.15)
C. Inflation: most recent year	8.25	(8.73)	9.25	(3.75)	7.72	(11.41)	8.22	(8.90)	9.24	(3.82)	8.40	(7.89)	7.94	(10.30)	8.01	(9.95)
D. Freedom to own foreign currency bank accounts	0.00		0.00		0.00		0.00		0.00		0.00		0.00		0.00	
4. Freedom to Trade Internationally					5.77		6.39		5.75		5.70		5.71		5.99	
A. Taxes on international trade					7.40		8.53		6.24		6.40		6.31		6.31	
(i) Revenues from trade taxes (% of trade sector)					7.40	(3.90)	8.53	(2.20)								
(ii) Mean tariff rate									6.84	(15.80)	6.60	(17.20)	6.42	(17.90)	6.42	(17.90)
(iii) Standard deviation of tariff rates									5.64	(10.90)	6.30	(9.20)	6.21	(9.49)	6.21	(9.49)
B. Regulatory trade barriers											1.80		1.99		1.96	
(i) Non-tariff trade barriers											3.60		3.99		3.92	
(ii) Compliance cost of importing and exporting											0.00		0.00		0.00	
C. Size of trade sector relative to expected	5.33		4.70		4.07		5.45		4.30		7.90		8.52		9.17	
D. Black-market exchange rates	9.60		9.80		9.20		9.80		10.00		10.00		10.00		10.00	
E. International capital market controls	0.00		0.00		0.00		0.00		0.00		2.30		1.75		2.50	
(i) Foreign ownership/investment restrictions											4.70		3.50		3.47	
(ii) Capital controls	0.00		0.00		0.00		0.00		0.00		0.00		0.00		1.54	
5. Regulation of Credit, Labor, and Business			4.15		4.31		3.92		4.29		5.10		5.39		5.26	
A. Credit market regulations	2.00		5.00		4.76		3.46		4.68		5.70		6.03		6.08	
(i) Ownership of banks	2.00		2.00		0.00		0.00		0.00		2.00		2.00		2.00	
(ii) Foreign bank competition																
(iii) Private sector credit					6.29		6.38		6.04		6.00		7.08		7.24	
(iv) Interest rate controls/negative real interest rates			8.00		8.00		4.00		8.00		9.00		9.00		9.00	
B. Labor market regulations											6.00		5.94		6.03	
(i) Hiring regulations and minimum wage											6.10		6.10		6.10	
(ii) Hiring and firing regulations											4.30		4.72		4.84	
(iii) Centralized collective bargaining											7.70		7.14		6.73	
(iv) Hours regulations											8.00		8.00		8.00	
(v) Mandated cost of worker dismissal											6.70		6.66		7.49	
(vi) Conscription	10.00		0.00		0.00		0.00		0.00		3.00		3.00		3.00	
C. Business regulations											3.50		4.20		3.67	
(i) Price controls					4.00		4.00		4.00		4.00		4.00		4.00	
(ii) Administrative requirements											2.40		3.52		3.16	
(iii) Bureaucracy costs											3.10		6.95		6.99	
(iv) Starting a business											3.90		4.53		3.95	
(v) Extra payments/bribes/favoritism											3.70		2.39		2.52	
(vi) Licensing restrictions											6.00		6.18		3.24	
(vii) Cost of tax compliance											1.80		1.79		1.79	

Chile

	1980	1985	1990	1995	2000	2005	2008	2009
Chain-Linked	Rating (Rank)	Rating (Rank)	Rating (Rank)	Rating (Rank)	Rating (Rank)	Rating (Rank)	Rating (Rank)	Rating (Rank)
Summary Rating (Rank) ➤	**5.56** (50)	**6.18** (31)	**7.02** (25)	**7.47** (14)	**7.28** (28)	**7.94** (9)	**8.08** (4)	**7.83** (6)
Area 1. Size of Government	5.00 (54)	5.71 (34)	6.51 (28)	7.30 (22)	6.12 (64)	7.43 (27)	7.79 (19)	7.65 (21)
Area 2. Legal Structure and Security of Property Rights	7.23 (26)	5.64 (49)	6.95 (31)	6.75 (31)	6.53 (42)	6.79 (32)	7.10 (27)	7.20 (27)
Area 3. Access to Sound Money	2.31 (105)	7.06 (34)	7.65 (37)	8.65 (36)	9.30 (31)	9.34 (34)	9.25 (32)	8.97 (48)
Area 4. Freedom to Trade Internationally	6.91 (24)	5.88 (47)	7.25 (27)	7.59 (28)	7.46 (44)	8.24 (7)	8.61 (4)	7.83 (10)
Area 5. Regulation of Credit, Labor, and Business	6.90 (10)	6.73 (12)	6.82 (12)	7.07 (11)	6.98 (20)	7.89 (18)	7.64 (20)	7.52 (19)

Unadjusted

	1980	1985	1990	1995	2000	2005	2008	2009
Summary Rating (Rank) ➤	**5.25** (60)	**5.87** (40)	**6.67** (27)	**7.47** (16)	**7.28** (28)	**7.87** (11)	**8.02** (5)	**7.77** (7)
	Rating Data	Rating Data	Rating Data	Rating Data	Rating Data	Rating Data	Rating Data	Rating Data
1. Size of Government	**5.00**	**5.71**	**6.51**	**7.30**	**6.12**	**7.40**	**7.79**	**7.65**
A. Government consumption	7.36 (14.98)	6.86 (16.69)	7.76 (13.62)	7.77 (13.58)	7.02 (16.14)	7.10 (15.80)	6.82 (16.80)	6.40 (18.25)
B. Transfers and subsidies	6.62 (12.90)	5.97 (15.30)	7.28 (10.50)	7.42 (9.97)	6.48 (13.42)	7.60 (9.30)	7.34 (10.25)	7.22 (10.70)
C. Government enterprises and investment	4.00 (32.20)	8.00 (16.10)	7.00 (20.50)	8.00 (16.60)	6.00 (28.21)	10.00 (8.70)	10.00 (10.32)	10.00 (13.87)
D. Top marginal tax rate	2.00	2.00	4.00	6.00	5.00	5.00	7.00	7.00
(i) Top marginal income tax rate	2.00 (58)	2.00 (56)	4.00 (50)	6.00 (45)	5.00 (45)	5.00 (40)	7.00 (40)	7.00 (40)
(ii) Top marginal income and payroll tax rates			4.00 (50)	6.00 (45)	5.00 (45)	5.00 (40)	7.00 (40)	7.00 (40)
2. Legal Structure and Security of Property Rights	**6.43**	**5.02**	**6.19**	**6.75**	**6.53**	**6.80**	**7.10**	**7.20**
A. Judicial independence				6.62	5.85	4.80	6.18	7.27
B. Impartial courts				7.07	6.51	6.00	6.07	6.17
C. Protection of property rights				5.60	5.27	7.50	7.51	7.02
D. Military interference in rule of law and politics				7.51	6.67	6.90	7.50	7.50
E. Integrity of the legal system				6.96	8.33	8.30	8.33	8.33
F. Legal enforcement of contracts						5.10	5.11	5.11
G. Regulatory restrictions on sale of real property						9.00	8.99	8.99
3. Access to Sound Money	**2.31**	**7.06**	**7.65**	**8.65**	**9.30**	**9.30**	**9.25**	**8.97**
A. Money growth	0.00 (52.46)	8.21 (8.95)	6.52 (17.40)	8.07 (9.67)	9.58 (2.08)	8.70 (6.40)	8.73 (6.37)	8.44 (7.80)
B. Standard deviation of inflation	0.00 (80.63)	6.17 (9.58)	8.34 (4.15)	8.40 (4.00)	8.40 (4.01)	9.20 (1.92)	8.30 (4.24)	8.29 (4.28)
C. Inflation: most recent year	4.25 (28.76)	3.86 (30.71)	5.75 (21.24)	8.14 (9.32)	9.23 (3.84)	9.40 (3.05)	9.95 (0.23)	9.16 (4.20)
D. Freedom to own foreign currency bank accounts	5.00	10.00	10.00	10.00	10.00	10.00	10.00	10.00
4. Freedom to Trade Internationally	**6.82**	**5.80**	**7.15**	**7.57**	**7.46**	**8.20**	**8.61**	**7.83**
A. Taxes on international trade	8.71	6.73	8.18	8.49	8.91	9.50	9.44	9.48
(i) Revenues from trade taxes (% of trade sector)	8.13 (2.80)	6.20 (5.70)	7.53 (3.70)	7.67 (3.49)	8.53 (2.20)	9.60 (0.60)	9.73 (0.41)	9.83 (0.26)
(ii) Mean tariff rate	8.00 (10.00)	4.00 (30.00)	7.00 (15.00)	7.80 (11.00)	8.20 (9.00)	9.00 (4.90)	8.80 (6.00)	8.80 (6.00)
(iii) Standard deviation of tariff rates	10.00 (0.00)	10.00 (0.00)	10.00 (0.00)	10.00 (0.00)	10.00 (0.00)	9.80 (0.50)	9.78 (0.54)	9.81 (0.48)
B. Regulatory trade barriers				7.05	8.39	7.40	8.02	7.94
(i) Non-tariff trade barriers				7.05	8.28	7.70	8.94	8.80
(ii) Compliance cost of importing and exporting					8.50	7.10	7.09	7.09
C. Size of trade sector relative to expected	6.40	6.49	7.43	6.20	5.68	6.70	7.42	5.90
D. Black-market exchange rates	8.80	5.60	10.00	9.60	10.00	10.00	10.00	10.00
E. International capital market controls	2.00	2.00	2.00	6.49	4.30	7.70	8.17	5.82
(i) Foreign ownership/investment restrictions				7.98	8.61	8.40	7.88	7.80
(ii) Capital controls	2.00	2.00	2.00	5.00	0.00	6.90	8.46	3.85
5. Regulation of Credit, Labor, and Business	**5.70**	**5.74**	**5.84**	**7.06**	**6.98**	**7.60**	**7.33**	**7.20**
A. Credit market regulations	7.54	8.19	8.43	8.60	8.29	9.30	9.25	8.73
(i) Ownership of banks	5.00	8.00	8.00	8.00	8.00	8.00	8.00	8.00
(ii) Foreign bank competition				8.15	5.95	9.00	9.00	9.00
(iii) Private sector credit	9.63	8.56	9.28	9.86	9.68	10.00	10.00	7.93
(iv) Interest rate controls/negative real interest rates	8.00	8.00	8.00	10.00	10.00	10.00	10.00	10.00
B. Labor market regulations			4.95	5.27	4.86	6.00	5.76	5.79
(i) Hiring regulations and minimum wage				5.68	3.36	6.70	6.70	6.67
(ii) Hiring and firing regulations			6.91	6.91	5.57	4.90	3.85	3.77
(iii) Centralized collective bargaining		7.93	7.93	7.93	8.85	8.50	7.82	7.71
(iv) Hours regulations				5.85	6.51	10.00	10.00	10.00
(v) Mandated cost of worker dismissal						5.20	5.18	5.58
(vi) Conscription	3.00	0.00	0.00	0.00	0.00	1.00	1.00	1.00
C. Business regulations				7.32	7.80	7.40	6.99	7.09
(i) Price controls				10.00	9.00	9.00	10.00	10.00
(ii) Administrative requirements					7.88	4.70	4.26	4.31
(iii) Bureaucracy costs				6.18	7.93	6.00	3.51	3.77
(iv) Starting a business				6.52	5.65	9.00	9.06	9.22
(v) Extra payments/bribes/favoritism				6.58	8.53	8.40	7.43	7.66
(vi) Licensing restrictions						8.20	8.21	8.22
(vii) Cost of tax compliance						6.50	6.46	6.46

China

	1980	1985	1990	1995	2000	2005	2008	2009
Chain-Linked	Rating (Rank)	Rating (Rank)	Rating (Rank)	Rating (Rank)	Rating (Rank)	Rating (Rank)	Rating (Rank)	Rating (Rank)
Summary Rating (Rank) ➤	**4.23** (89)	**5.15** (66)	**4.96** (88)	**5.30** (86)	**5.73** (99)	**6.08** (89)	**6.20** (88)	**6.24** (89)
Area 1. Size of Government	3.58 (92)	3.91 (86)	3.65 (99)	4.02 (105)	3.43 (115)	3.31 (121)	3.28 (123)	3.31 (122)
Area 2. Legal Structure and Security of Property Rights		7.30 (28)	6.23 (41)	5.49 (60)	4.95 (78)	5.77 (60)	6.38 (43)	6.35 (44)
Area 3. Access to Sound Money	6.18 (56)	6.19 (80)	6.73 (56)	5.77 (78)	8.12 (56)	8.18 (64)	8.13 (62)	8.05 (73)
Area 4. Freedom to Trade Internationally	3.65 (79)	4.79 (66)	4.55 (81)	6.72 (58)	7.17 (51)	7.55 (25)	7.38 (34)	7.22 (31)
Area 5. Regulation of Credit, Labor, and Business	3.69 (93)	3.69 (95)	3.79 (101)	4.48 (101)	4.99 (102)	5.66 (101)	5.93 (95)	6.35 (78)

	1980	1985	1990	1995	2000	2005	2008	2009
Unadjusted								
Summary Rating (Rank) ➤	**3.99** (96)	**5.07** (73)	**4.85** (89)	**5.20** (94)	**5.73** (99)	**6.28** (95)	**6.40** (93)	**6.43** (92)
	Rating Data	Rating Data	Rating Data	Rating Data	Rating Data	Rating Data	Rating Data	Rating Data
1. Size of Government	**2.63**	**3.91**	**3.65**	**4.02**	**3.43**	**4.50**	**4.51**	**4.55**
A. Government consumption	5.25 (22.14)	5.73 (20.51)	5.94 (19.81)	6.07 (19.38)	4.28 (25.46)	3.90 (26.80)	3.73 (27.31)	3.90 (26.73)
B. Transfers and subsidies						8.30 (6.80)	8.29 (6.76)	8.29 (6.76)
C. Government enterprises and investment	0.00 (56.40)	0.00 (62.90)	0.00 (61.90)	0.00 (77.07)	0.00 (77.97)	0.00 (69.80)	0.00 (53.21)	0.00 (53.21)
D. Top marginal tax rate		6.00	5.00	6.00	6.00	6.00	6.00	6.00
(i) Top marginal income tax rate		6.00 (45)	5.00 (45)	6.00 (45)	6.00 (45)	6.00 (45)	6.00 (45)	6.00 (45)
(ii) Top marginal income and payroll tax rates							6.00 (45)	6.00 (45)
2. Legal Structure and Security of Property Rights		**6.78**	**5.79**	**5.49**	**4.95**	**5.80**	**6.38**	**6.35**
A. Judicial independence				3.80	3.34	3.90	4.91	4.95
B. Impartial courts				4.92	4.18	4.00	4.99	5.16
C. Protection of property rights				4.15	3.22	4.90	7.08	6.85
D. Military interference in rule of law and politics				7.60	7.34	5.00	5.00	5.00
E. Integrity of the legal system				6.96	6.67	7.50	7.50	7.50
F. Legal enforcement of contracts						6.70	6.73	6.73
G. Regulatory restrictions on sale of real property						8.30	8.43	8.27
3. Access to Sound Money	**6.18**	**6.19**	**6.73**	**5.77**	**8.12**	**8.20**	**8.13**	**8.05**
A. Money growth	6.00 (20.00)	8.14 (9.31)	9.18 (4.09)	7.63 (11.83)	8.90 (5.48)	9.00 (4.80)	9.42 (2.91)	8.64 (6.81)
B. Standard deviation of inflation	9.48 (1.31)	8.64 (3.40)	8.86 (2.84)	8.09 (4.77)	8.63 (3.43)	9.00 (2.41)	9.27 (1.83)	8.69 (3.28)
C. Inflation: most recent year	9.24 (3.78)	7.97 (10.14)	8.86 (5.68)	7.36 (13.18)	9.95 (0.26)	9.60 (1.82)	8.83 (5.86)	9.86 (−0.70)
D. Freedom to own foreign currency bank accounts	0.00	0.00	0.00	0.00	5.00	5.00	5.00	5.00
4. Freedom to Trade Internationally	**4.13**	**5.42**	**4.83**	**6.41**	**7.17**	**7.50**	**7.38**	**7.22**
A. Taxes on international trade	3.15	2.72	3.16	3.90	7.11	8.00	8.15	8.15
(i) Revenues from trade taxes (% of trade sector)	6.20 (5.70)	3.33 (10.00)	7.53 (3.70)	9.20 (1.20)	8.86 (1.71)	8.80 (1.80)	9.39 (0.91)	9.39 (0.91)
(ii) Mean tariff rate	0.10 (49.50)	2.10 (39.50)	1.94 (40.30)	2.50 (37.50)	6.74 (16.30)	8.20 (9.20)	8.08 (9.60)	8.08 (9.60)
(iii) Standard deviation of tariff rates			0.00 (32.10)	0.00 (28.00)	5.72 (10.70)	6.90 (7.70)	6.97 (7.58)	6.97 (7.58)
B. Regulatory trade barriers				4.63	6.01	6.00	6.44	6.46
(i) Non-tariff trade barriers				4.63	4.35	5.10	5.97	6.01
(ii) Compliance cost of importing and exporting					7.66	6.90	6.91	6.91
C. Size of trade sector relative to expected	4.26	6.35	7.76	10.00	10.00	10.00	10.00	9.12
D. Black-market exchange rates	5.00	7.80	0.00	8.60	10.00	10.00	10.00	10.00
E. International capital market controls	0.00	2.00	5.00	4.91	2.71	3.70	2.29	2.36
(i) Foreign ownership / investment restrictions				4.82	4.66	6.70	4.59	4.72
(ii) Capital controls	0.00	2.00	5.00	5.00	0.77	0.80	0.00	0.00
5. Regulation of Credit, Labor, and Business	**3.04**	**3.04**	**3.27**	**4.33**	**4.99**	**5.30**	**5.62**	**5.99**
A. Credit market regulations	0.00	0.00	0.00	4.01	4.70	7.40	7.18	7.43
(i) Ownership of banks	0.00	0.00	0.00	0.00	0.00	2.00	2.00	2.00
(ii) Foreign bank competition				4.62	2.30	8.00	8.00	8.00
(iii) Private sector credit				9.81	9.39	9.70	9.73	9.73
(iv) Interest rate controls / negative real interest rates	0.00	0.00	0.00	4.00	10.00	10.00	9.00	10.00
B. Labor market regulations			3.16	4.54	4.66	5.00	4.82	5.51
(i) Hiring regulations and minimum wage				5.80	4.37	8.90	8.90	8.90
(ii) Hiring and firing regulations			4.30	4.30	5.10	5.30	4.63	5.11
(iii) Centralized collective bargaining	4.49	4.49	5.18	6.21	7.67	7.40	7.10	7.10
(iv) Hours regulations				6.42	6.18	6.70	6.70	10.00
(v) Mandated cost of worker dismissal						1.60	1.56	1.97
(vi) Conscription	0.00	0.00	0.00	0.00	0.00	0.00	0.00	0.00
C. Business regulations				4.42	5.60	3.60	4.86	5.04
(i) Price controls				4.00	3.00	2.00	2.00	2.00
(ii) Administrative requirements					7.60	4.00	4.84	4.99
(iii) Bureaucracy costs				4.78	5.40	2.00	4.55	4.65
(iv) Starting a business				6.05	6.52	8.10	8.33	8.35
(v) Extra payments / bribes / favoritism				2.87	5.49	5.50	5.53	5.24
(vi) Licensing restrictions						3.50	4.39	4.49
(vii) Cost of tax compliance						0.20	4.35	5.54

Colombia

	1980	1985	1990	1995	2000	2005	2008	2009
Chain-Linked	Rating (Rank)	Rating (Rank)	Rating (Rank)	Rating (Rank)	Rating (Rank)	Rating (Rank)	Rating (Rank)	Rating (Rank)
Summary Rating (Rank) ➤	**4.83** (73)	**5.19** (62)	**5.12** (77)	**5.45** (80)	**5.31** (107)	**5.87** (101)	**6.14** (91)	**6.27** (87)
Area 1. Size of Government	5.35 (43)	5.94 (30)	7.23 (15)	6.83 (31)	4.64 (99)	4.45 (111)	5.68 (85)	6.01 (70)
Area 2. Legal Structure and Security of Property Rights	3.55 (62)	3.03 (94)	3.04 (92)	2.85 (119)	3.53 (110)	4.39 (94)	4.39 (99)	4.37 (96)
Area 3. Access to Sound Money	4.86 (96)	6.69 (50)	4.90 (91)	5.32 (85)	6.31 (101)	7.81 (73)	7.87 (71)	8.13 (70)
Area 4. Freedom to Trade Internationally	4.69 (62)	4.67 (68)	4.81 (76)	6.56 (66)	6.41 (77)	5.67 (102)	5.69 (103)	5.67 (98)
Area 5. Regulation of Credit, Labor, and Business	5.63 (39)	5.63 (47)	5.63 (51)	5.69 (60)	5.66 (81)	7.01 (40)	7.07 (36)	7.15 (33)

Unadjusted

	1980	1985	1990	1995	2000	2005	2008	2009
Summary Rating (Rank) ➤	**4.81** (77)	**5.17** (69)	**5.19** (71)	**5.35** (85)	**5.31** (107)	**5.81** (116)	**6.09** (107)	**6.21** (101)
	Rating Data	Rating Data	Rating Data	Rating Data	Rating Data	Rating Data	Rating Data	Rating Data
1. Size of Government	**5.35**	**5.94**	**7.23**	**6.83**	**4.64**	**4.40**	**5.68**	**6.01**
A. Government consumption	8.07 (12.57)	7.82 (13.43)	7.78 (13.56)	6.31 (18.54)	4.35 (25.20)	2.70 (30.90)	5.69 (20.64)	5.87 (20.06)
B. Transfers and subsidies	9.35 (2.90)	8.94 (4.40)	9.13 (3.70)	9.02 (4.10)	8.71 (5.24)	7.60 (9.30)	7.53 (9.57)	7.17 (10.89)
C. Government enterprises and investment	2.00 (41.50)	2.00 (49.90)	4.00 (38.50)	4.00 (34.10)	0.00 (51.89)	2.00 (51.90)	4.00	6.00
D. Top marginal tax rate	2.00	5.00	8.00	8.00	5.50	5.50	5.50	5.00
(i) Top marginal income tax rate	2.00 (56)	5.00 (49)	8.00 (30)	8.00 (30)	7.00 (35)	7.00 (35)	7.00 (35)	7.00 (35)
(ii) Top marginal income and payroll tax rates			8.00 (30)	8.00 (30)	4.00 (43)	4.00 (45)	4.00 (45)	3.00 (47)
2. Legal Structure and Security of Property Rights	**3.98**	**3.40**	**3.41**	**2.85**	**3.53**	**4.40**	**4.39**	**4.37**
A. Judicial independence				3.72	3.51	4.40	4.40	4.14
B. Impartial courts				3.52	5.85	4.60	3.98	4.00
C. Protection of property rights				4.13	3.28	6.20	4.94	4.74
D. Military interference in rule of law and politics				2.88	3.33	3.30	3.33	3.33
E. Integrity of the legal system				0.00	1.67	1.70	3.33	3.33
F. Legal enforcement of contracts						1.80	1.80	2.09
G. Regulatory restrictions on sale of real property						8.70	8.96	8.96
3. Access to Sound Money	**4.86**	**6.69**	**4.90**	**5.32**	**6.31**	**7.80**	**7.87**	**8.13**
A. Money growth	6.63 (16.85)	7.40 (12.98)	6.21 (18.97)	6.07 (19.64)	8.28 (8.61)	7.70 (11.50)	8.48 (7.60)	8.94 (5.31)
B. Standard deviation of inflation	8.33 (4.17)	9.33 (1.68)	9.09 (2.27)	9.15 (2.12)	8.81 (2.97)	9.60 (1.09)	9.39 (1.53)	9.42 (1.45)
C. Inflation: most recent year	4.48 (27.61)	5.02 (24.90)	4.29 (28.55)	6.04 (19.79)	8.16 (9.22)	9.00 (5.05)	8.60 (7.00)	9.16 (4.20)
D. Freedom to own foreign currency bank accounts	0.00	5.00	0.00	0.00	0.00	5.00	5.00	5.00
4. Freedom to Trade Internationally	**4.69**	**4.67**	**4.93**	**6.31**	**6.41**	**5.70**	**5.69**	**5.67**
A. Taxes on international trade	4.05	4.14	5.53	7.81	7.85	7.70	7.51	7.52
(i) Revenues from trade taxes (% of trade sector)	4.80 (7.80)	5.00 (7.50)	5.99 (6.01)	8.04 (2.94)	8.37 (2.44)	8.70 (1.90)	8.22 (2.66)	8.21 (2.68)
(ii) Mean tariff rate	3.30 (33.50)	3.28 (33.60)	3.92 (30.40)	7.34 (13.30)	7.66 (11.70)	7.60 (11.90)	7.50 (12.50)	7.50 (12.50)
(iii) Standard deviation of tariff rates			6.68 (8.30)	8.04 (4.90)	7.52 (6.20)	6.80 (8.00)	6.80 (8.00)	6.85 (7.88)
B. Regulatory trade barriers				5.15	6.11	5.00	6.14	6.17
(i) Non-tariff trade barriers				5.15	4.90	4.80	4.16	4.17
(ii) Compliance cost of importing and exporting					7.33	5.10	8.12	8.18
C. Size of trade sector relative to expected	4.36	2.78	4.28	3.97	4.15	3.80	3.40	2.39
D. Black-market exchange rates	6.80	8.20	6.60	8.60	10.00	8.10	8.53	9.26
E. International capital market controls	0.00	0.00	0.00	6.02	3.94	3.80	2.89	3.00
(i) Foreign ownership / investment restrictions				7.04	7.87	6.80	5.02	5.23
(ii) Capital controls	0.00	0.00	0.00	5.00	0.00	0.80	0.77	0.77
5. Regulation of Credit, Labor, and Business	**5.16**	**5.16**	**5.50**	**5.46**	**5.66**	**6.70**	**6.80**	**6.86**
A. Credit market regulations	8.00	8.00	8.20	7.55	7.34	9.00	8.73	8.45
(i) Ownership of banks	8.00	8.00	8.00	8.00	8.00	8.00	8.00	8.00
(ii) Foreign bank competition				7.68	5.58	8.00	8.00	8.00
(iii) Private sector credit			8.61	8.11	8.10	10.00	8.91	7.81
(iv) Interest rate controls / negative real interest rates	8.00	8.00	8.00	8.00	10.00	10.00	10.00	10.00
B. Labor market regulations				4.75	3.89	5.40	5.48	5.92
(i) Hiring regulations and minimum wage				6.83	2.85	7.80	8.90	8.90
(ii) Hiring and firing regulations			5.50	5.50	4.15	5.00	4.50	4.85
(iii) Centralized collective bargaining					5.93	6.80	6.93	7.17
(iv) Hours regulations				5.68	5.51	8.00	8.00	10.00
(v) Mandated cost of worker dismissal						4.50	4.53	4.57
(vi) Conscription	0.00	0.00	0.00	1.00	1.00	0.00	0.00	0.00
C. Business regulations				4.07	5.76	5.90	6.21	6.20
(i) Price controls				5.00	6.00	5.00	5.00	5.00
(ii) Administrative requirements					6.43	2.60	2.82	2.68
(iii) Bureaucracy costs				6.20	6.75	5.80	5.05	5.06
(iv) Starting a business				2.63	3.75	8.40	9.23	9.40
(v) Extra payments / bribes / favoritism				2.44	5.89	6.40	4.41	4.33
(vi) Licensing restrictions						8.10	9.27	9.27
(vii) Cost of tax compliance						4.90	7.67	7.67

Congo, Democratic Republic of

Chain-Linked	1980 Rating (Rank)	1985 Rating (Rank)	1990 Rating (Rank)	1995 Rating (Rank)	2000 Rating (Rank)	2005 Rating (Rank)	2008 Rating (Rank)	2009 Rating (Rank)
Summary Rating (Rank) ➤	3.00 (102)	3.87 (101)	3.39 (110)	3.56 (123)	4.10 (122)	4.66 (119)	4.86 (118)	4.77 (120)
Area 1. Size of Government	4.42 (71)	6.22 (20)	5.74 (57)	5.63 (77)	7.45 (22)	6.91 (47)	5.11 (102)	5.16 (94)
Area 2. Legal Structure and Security of Property Rights	2.37 (80)	2.46 (100)	2.44 (104)	2.22 (122)	2.41 (121)	2.05 (122)	2.14 (123)	2.65 (121)
Area 3. Access to Sound Money	1.10 (110)	1.49 (108)	0.10 (118)	0.10 (122)	1.25 (123)	5.04 (117)	7.63 (79)	6.96 (95)
Area 4. Freedom to Trade Internationally	3.75 (78)	6.09 (42)	5.58 (58)	6.74 (57)	5.02 (116)	6.11 (88)	6.10 (89)	5.19 (111)
Area 5. Regulation of Credit, Labor, and Business	3.05 (98)	3.14 (99)	3.05 (109)	3.10 (120)	4.36 (114)	3.22 (123)	3.32 (122)	3.67 (122)

Unadjusted	1980 Rating Data	1985 Rating Data	1990 Rating Data	1995 Rating Data	2000 Rating Data	2005 Rating Data	2008 Rating Data	2009 Rating Data
Summary Rating (Rank) ➤	3.36 (102)	3.90 (102)	3.56 (108)	3.70 (120)	4.10 (122)	4.74 (134)	4.95 (133)	4.84 (137)
1. Size of Government	5.00	4.71	5.74	5.63	7.45	6.90	5.11	5.16
A. Government consumption	9.04 (9.28)	9.12 (8.98)	8.03 (12.70)	10.00 (5.72)	9.29 (8.41)	9.20 (8.90)	7.94 (13.01)	8.12 (12.38)
B. Transfers and subsidies	9.97 (0.60)		9.92 (0.80)	10.00 (0.49)	10.00 (0.01)	10.00 (0.00)	10.00 (0.00)	10.00 (0.00)
C. Government enterprises and investment	0.00 (58.20)	4.00 (30.50)	4.00 (31.10)	2.00 (45.30)	10.00 (13.10)	6.00 (26.10)	0.00 (52.69)	0.00 (79.69)
D. Top marginal tax rate	1.00	1.00	1.00	0.50	0.50	2.50	2.50	2.50
(i) Top marginal income tax rate	1.00 (60)	1.00 (60)	1.00 (60)	1.00 (60)	1.00 (60)	3.00 (50)	3.00 (50)	3.00 (50)
(ii) Top marginal income and payroll tax rates			1.00 (60)	0.00 (63)	0.00 (63)	2.00 (54)	2.00 (54)	2.00 (54)
2. Legal Structure and Security of Property Rights	2.37	2.46	2.44	2.22	2.41	2.10	2.14	2.65
A. Judicial independence								
B. Impartial courts				3.02	3.59	2.50	2.60	2.50
C. Protection of property rights								
D. Military interference in rule of law and politics				1.45	0.00	0.00	0.00	0.00
E. Integrity of the legal system				0.00	1.67	1.70	1.67	3.33
F. Legal enforcement of contracts						0.30	0.75	0.75
G. Regulatory restrictions on sale of real property						5.80	5.70	6.68
3. Access to Sound Money	1.10	1.49	0.00	0.00	1.25	5.00	7.63	6.96
A. Money growth	4.39 (28.06)	1.12 (44.40)	0.00 (62.92)	0.00 (1631.82)	0.00 (2290.00)	4.40 (27.80)	6.40 (18.02)	6.44 (17.79)
B. Standard deviation of inflation	0.00 (25.49)	0.00 (25.25)	0.00 (30.17)	0.00 (9932.53)	0.00 (248.28)	0.00 (163.85)	7.57 (6.08)	7.44 (6.41)
C. Inflation: most recent year	0.00 (51.40)	4.84 (25.82)	0.00 (108.95)	0.00 (466.40)	0.00 (550.01)	5.70 (21.32)	6.54 (17.30)	3.95 (30.25)
D. Freedom to own foreign currency bank accounts	0.00	0.00	0.00	0.00	5.00	10.00	10.00	10.00
4. Freedom to Trade Internationally	3.88	6.30	5.77	6.74	5.02	5.40	5.43	4.61
A. Taxes on international trade	4.21	4.96	4.90	7.77	8.70	7.30	7.32	7.32
(i) Revenues from trade taxes (% of trade sector)	3.13 (10.30)	4.40 (8.40)	3.93 (9.10)	7.77 (3.34)	8.70 (1.95)	6.80 (4.80)	6.81 (4.78)	6.81 (4.78)
(ii) Mean tariff rate	5.28 (23.60)	5.52 (22.40)	5.86 (20.70)			7.60 (12.00)	7.60 (12.00)	7.60 (12.00)
(iii) Standard deviation of tariff rates						7.60 (6.10)	7.55 (6.12)	7.55 (6.12)
B. Regulatory trade barriers						2.20	2.54	2.54
(i) Non-tariff trade barriers								
(ii) Compliance cost of importing and exporting						2.20	2.54	2.54
C. Size of trade sector relative to expected	4.96	7.53	7.77	6.56	4.46	7.70	6.52	2.44
D. Black-market exchange rates	0.00	8.80	6.00	9.20	1.43	10.00	10.00	10.00
E. International capital market controls	2.00	2.00	2.00	2.00	2.31	0.00	0.77	0.77
(i) Foreign ownership/investment restrictions								
(ii) Capital controls	2.00	2.00	2.00	2.00	2.31	0.00	0.77	0.77
5. Regulation of Credit, Labor, and Business	4.43	4.57	3.85	3.92	4.36	4.30	4.46	4.83
A. Credit market regulations	4.34	4.75	2.88	3.12	5.00	4.30	5.11	4.78
(i) Ownership of banks	0.00	0.00	0.00	0.00	0.00	0.00	0.00	0.00
(ii) Foreign bank competition								
(iii) Private sector credit	8.69	9.50	8.65	9.35		8.00	9.33	9.33
(iv) Interest rate controls/negative real interest rates			0.00	0.00	10.00	5.00	6.00	5.00
B. Labor market regulations						5.10	4.56	5.67
(i) Hiring regulations and minimum wage						5.00	2.80	1.67
(ii) Hiring and firing regulations								
(iii) Centralized collective bargaining								
(iv) Hours regulations						5.30	5.30	8.00
(v) Mandated cost of worker dismissal						7.10	7.13	10.00
(vi) Conscription	3.00	3.00	3.00	3.00	3.00	3.00	3.00	3.00
C. Business regulations						3.40	3.72	4.04
(i) Price controls			2.00	2.00	2.00	2.00	2.00	2.00
(ii) Administrative requirements								
(iii) Bureaucracy costs								
(iv) Starting a business						3.30	3.33	3.98
(v) Extra payments/bribes/favoritism								
(vi) Licensing restrictions						1.50	2.98	3.96
(vii) Cost of tax compliance						6.50	6.55	6.23

Congo, Republic of

Chain-Linked	1980	1985	1990	1995	2000	2005	2008	2009
	Rating (Rank)	Rating (Rank)	Rating (Rank)	Rating (Rank)	Rating (Rank)	Rating (Rank)	Rating (Rank)	Rating (Rank)
Summary Rating (Rank) ➤	**4.63** (78)	**4.43** (90)	**5.12** (77)	**5.24** (92)	**4.50** (121)	**4.66** (119)	**4.77** (119)	**5.06** (118)
Area 1. Size of Government	3.17 (94)	2.63 (107)	5.77 (56)	6.20 (58)	4.54 (104)	4.66 (107)	4.77 (109)	4.99 (99)
Area 2. Legal Structure and Security of Property Rights	4.67 (48)	3.05 (91)	3.02 (94)	3.24 (117)	2.39 (122)	2.35 (121)	2.85 (121)	4.22 (102)
Area 3. Access to Sound Money	5.45 (83)	6.42 (68)	5.96 (73)	5.69 (80)	4.29 (114)	5.33 (115)	4.93 (120)	4.73 (122)
Area 4. Freedom to Trade Internationally			5.68 (55)	6.75 (56)	6.76 (71)	6.28 (83)	6.15 (86)	6.40 (72)
Area 5. Regulation of Credit, Labor, and Business	4.54 (75)	4.83 (69)	5.13 (65)	4.35 (105)	4.53 (110)	4.68 (119)	5.11 (114)	4.95 (117)

Unadjusted

	1980	1985	1990	1995	2000	2005	2008	2009
Summary Rating (Rank) ➤	**5.04** (70)	**4.69** (86)	**4.95** (86)	**5.24** (89)	**4.50** (121)	**4.64** (138)	**4.75** (137)	**5.04** (134)
	Rating Data	Rating Data	Rating Data	Rating Data	Rating Data	Rating Data	Rating Data	Rating Data
1. Size of Government	**2.86**	**2.37**	**4.81**	**6.20**	**4.54**	**4.70**	**4.77**	**4.99**
A. Government consumption	3.72 (27.34)	4.75 (23.86)	6.42 (18.16)	6.50 (17.89)	1.60 (34.55)	2.30 (32.10)	4.27 (25.48)	5.15 (22.49)
B. Transfers and subsidies				9.30 (3.09)	9.55 (2.15)	9.30 (3.00)	9.31 (3.03)	9.31 (3.03)
C. Government enterprises and investment	2.00 (44.20)	0.00 (61.00)	4.00 (32.60)	6.00 (27.00)	4.00 (33.20)	4.00 (33.30)	2.00 (45.96)	2.00 (44.16)
D. Top marginal tax rate			4.00	3.00	3.00	3.00	3.50	3.50
(i) Top marginal income tax rate			4.00 (50)	3.00 (50)	3.00 (50)	3.00 (50)	4.00 (45)	4.00 (45)
(ii) Top marginal income and payroll tax rates							3.00 (49)	3.00 (49)
2. Legal Structure and Security of Property Rights	**4.67**	**3.05**	**3.02**	**3.24**	**2.39**	**2.40**	**2.85**	**4.22**
A. Judicial independence								
B. Impartial courts				1.75	1.86	3.00	3.50	3.50
C. Protection of property rights								
D. Military interference in rule of law and politics				0.00	0.00	0.00	0.00	2.50
E. Integrity of the legal system				6.96	3.33	3.30	3.33	6.67
F. Legal enforcement of contracts						3.00	3.01	3.01
G. Regulatory restrictions on sale of real property						2.40	4.42	5.44
3. Access to Sound Money	**5.45**	**6.42**	**5.96**	**5.69**	**4.29**	**5.30**	**4.93**	**4.73**
A. Money growth	8.78 (6.12)	9.77 (1.16)	9.81 (0.93)	9.40 (2.99)	7.24 (13.81)	8.60 (7.00)	6.87 (15.67)	8.28 (8.61)
B. Standard deviation of inflation	7.04 (7.41)	6.42 (8.96)	4.20 (14.51)	4.04 (14.90)	0.10 (24.75)	3.80 (15.52)	4.30 (14.24)	1.64 (20.91)
C. Inflation: most recent year	5.97 (20.14)	9.50 (2.50)	9.85 (−0.77)	9.32 (3.38)	9.83 (−0.84)	8.90 (5.28)	8.53 (7.33)	8.99 (5.04)
D. Freedom to own foreign currency bank accounts	0.00	0.00	0.00	0.00	0.00	0.00	0.00	0.00
4. Freedom to Trade Internationally	**7.05**	**6.12**	**5.84**	**6.75**	**6.76**	**5.60**	**5.45**	**5.67**
A. Taxes on international trade	7.47	3.60	4.53	6.70	7.43	7.20	7.36	7.36
(i) Revenues from trade taxes (% of trade sector)	7.47 (3.80)		4.53 (8.20)	7.61 (3.58)	9.25 (1.13)	9.20 (1.20)	9.47 (0.80)	9.47 (0.80)
(ii) Mean tariff rate		3.60 (32.00)		6.28 (18.60)	6.48 (17.60)	6.20 (19.10)	6.42 (17.90)	6.42 (17.90)
(iii) Standard deviation of tariff rates				6.20 (9.50)	6.56 (8.60)	6.20 (9.40)	6.21 (9.49)	6.21 (9.49)
B. Regulatory trade barriers						2.10	2.10	2.10
(i) Non-tariff trade barriers								
(ii) Compliance cost of importing and exporting						2.10	2.10	2.10
C. Size of trade sector relative to expected	10.00	9.00	7.25	9.05	8.18	8.50	7.76	7.35
D. Black-market exchange rates	9.60	9.80	9.20	9.80	10.00	10.00	10.00	10.00
E. International capital market controls	0.00	0.00	0.00	0.00	0.00	0.00	0.00	1.54
(i) Foreign ownership/investment restrictions								
(ii) Capital controls	0.00	0.00	0.00	0.00	0.00	0.00	0.00	1.54
5. Regulation of Credit, Labor, and Business	**5.16**	**5.49**	**5.13**	**4.35**	**4.53**	**5.30**	**5.75**	**5.57**
A. Credit market regulations	3.00	4.00	5.45	2.88	3.49	5.30	6.33	6.33
(i) Ownership of banks	0.00	0.00	0.00	0.00	0.00	0.00	0.00	0.00
(ii) Foreign bank competition								
(iii) Private sector credit			6.36	6.64	7.48	10.00	10.00	10.00
(iv) Interest rate controls/negative real interest rates	6.00	8.00	10.00	2.00	3.00	6.00	9.00	9.00
B. Labor market regulations						6.30	6.29	6.37
(i) Hiring regulations and minimum wage						2.20	2.20	2.23
(ii) Hiring and firing regulations								
(iii) Centralized collective bargaining								
(iv) Hours regulations						6.00	6.00	6.00
(v) Mandated cost of worker dismissal						6.90	6.94	7.23
(vi) Conscription	10.00	10.00	10.00	10.00	10.00	10.00	10.00	10.00
C. Business regulations						4.30	4.62	4.00
(i) Price controls			0.00	0.00	0.00	0.00	0.00	0.00
(ii) Administrative requirements								
(iii) Bureaucracy costs								
(iv) Starting a business						6.70	7.59	5.07
(v) Extra payments/bribes/favoritism								
(vi) Licensing restrictions						7.20	7.68	7.73
(vii) Cost of tax compliance						3.20	3.21	3.21

Costa Rica

Chain-Linked	1980 Rating (Rank)	1985 Rating (Rank)	1990 Rating (Rank)	1995 Rating (Rank)	2000 Rating (Rank)	2005 Rating (Rank)	2008 Rating (Rank)	2009 Rating (Rank)
Summary Rating (Rank) ➤	**5.61** (46)	**5.36** (55)	**6.76** (28)	**6.85** (33)	**7.31** (24)	**7.28** (32)	**7.10** (46)	**7.08** (42)
Area 1. Size of Government	5.72 (32)	5.21 (53)	7.20 (16)	6.81 (33)	7.13 (29)	7.57 (23)	7.66 (22)	7.35 (26)
Area 2. Legal Structure and Security of Property Rights	5.27 (43)	5.32 (53)	5.52 (53)	5.87 (48)	6.87 (35)	6.87 (31)	6.57 (34)	6.53 (35)
Area 3. Access to Sound Money	8.04 (20)	5.41 (91)	8.41 (27)	7.87 (42)	7.88 (61)	8.75 (52)	7.41 (83)	7.86 (78)
Area 4. Freedom to Trade Internationally	3.33 (83)	4.68 (67)	6.44 (41)	7.29 (34)	8.00 (26)	7.34 (34)	7.55 (32)	7.26 (28)
Area 5. Regulation of Credit, Labor, and Business	5.86 (34)	6.13 (30)	6.27 (32)	6.39 (30)	6.66 (34)	5.90 (93)	6.31 (79)	6.36 (76)

Unadjusted

	1980 Rating Data	1985 Rating Data	1990 Rating Data	1995 Rating Data	2000 Rating Data	2005 Rating Data	2008 Rating Data	2009 Rating Data
Summary Rating (Rank) ➤	**5.90** (36)	**5.51** (56)	**6.89** (17)	**6.98** (32)	**7.31** (24)	**7.39** (31)	**7.20** (43)	**7.17** (41)
1. Size of Government	**5.72**	**5.21**	**7.20**	**6.81**	**7.13**	**7.60**	**7.66**	**7.35**
A. Government consumption	5.37 (21.75)	5.66 (20.76)	5.04 (22.85)	5.02 (22.93)	6.94 (16.40)	6.70 (17.40)	7.28 (15.26)	5.97 (19.70)
B. Transfers and subsidies	8.50 (6.00)	8.17 (7.20)	8.77 (5.00)	8.23 (7.00)	8.59 (5.66)	8.60 (5.50)	9.35 (2.90)	9.44 (2.54)
C. Government enterprises and investment	4.00 (36.20)	4.00 (34.10)	7.00 (21.00)	6.00 (27.10)	6.00 (27.10)	6.00 (27.10)	6.00	6.00
D. Top marginal tax rate	5.00	3.00	8.00	8.00	7.00	9.00	8.00	8.00
(i) Top marginal income tax rate	5.00 (50)	3.00 (50)	9.00 (25)	9.00 (25)	9.00 (25)	10.00 (15-25)	9.00 (25)	9.00 (25)
(ii) Top marginal income and payroll tax rates			7.00 (33)	7.00 (33)	5.00 (39)	8.00 (24-33)	7.00 (34)	7.00 (34)
2. Legal Structure and Security of Property Rights	**5.21**	**5.25**	**5.46**	**5.80**	**6.87**	**6.90**	**6.57**	**6.53**
A. Judicial independence					6.35	6.90	7.19	7.13
B. Impartial courts				6.54	6.85	6.50	5.11	5.16
C. Protection of property rights					4.50	6.10	5.81	5.59
D. Military interference in rule of law and politics				8.73	10.00	10.00	10.00	10.00
E. Integrity of the legal system				4.11	6.67	6.70	5.83	5.83
F. Legal enforcement of contracts						3.50	3.52	3.52
G. Regulatory restrictions on sale of real property						8.50	8.49	8.49
3. Access to Sound Money	**8.04**	**5.41**	**8.41**	**7.87**	**7.88**	**8.80**	**7.41**	**7.86**
A. Money growth	7.72 (11.41)	5.53 (22.35)	8.66 (6.72)	8.14 (9.28)	5.16 (24.22)	8.40 (8.10)	7.80 (11.00)	8.50 (7.51)
B. Standard deviation of inflation	8.22 (4.46)	0.23 (24.42)	8.68 (3.29)	7.60 (5.99)	8.55 (3.63)	9.40 (1.49)	9.53 (1.18)	9.50 (1.26)
C. Inflation: most recent year	6.23 (18.83)	5.89 (20.53)	6.29 (18.57)	5.73 (21.34)	7.80 (10.99)	7.20 (13.80)	7.32 (13.42)	8.43 (7.84)
D. Freedom to own foreign currency bank accounts	10.00	10.00	10.00	10.00	10.00	10.00	5.00	5.00
4. Freedom to Trade Internationally	**3.62**	**4.90**	**6.75**	**7.64**	**8.00**	**7.30**	**7.55**	**7.26**
A. Taxes on international trade	3.23	1.80	5.63	7.27	8.40	8.10	8.11	8.15
(i) Revenues from trade taxes (% of trade sector)	6.47 (5.30)	5.40 (6.90)	5.33 (7.00)	6.93 (4.60)	9.28 (1.08)	9.20 (1.10)	9.15 (1.28)	9.23 (1.16)
(ii) Mean tariff rate	0.00 (55.00)	0.00 (53.00)	6.72 (16.40)	7.96 (10.20)	8.92 (5.40)	8.60 (7.00)	8.72 (6.40)	8.92 (5.40)
(iii) Standard deviation of tariff rates		0.00 (61.80)	4.84 (12.90)	6.92 (7.70)	7.00 (7.50)	6.40 (9.00)	6.47 (8.83)	6.31 (9.23)
B. Regulatory trade barriers					6.58	4.80	6.78	6.73
(i) Non-tariff trade barriers					5.17	4.70	5.42	5.32
(ii) Compliance cost of importing and exporting					8.00	5.00	8.14	8.14
C. Size of trade sector relative to expected	4.61	4.29	4.96	4.79	5.40	5.40	5.23	4.37
D. Black-market exchange rates	0.00	5.20	10.00	10.00	10.00	10.00	10.00	10.00
E. International capital market controls	2.00	5.00	5.00	8.00	9.63	8.30	7.63	7.05
(i) Foreign ownership/investment restrictions					9.26	7.50	6.79	6.41
(ii) Capital controls	2.00	5.00	5.00	8.00	10.00	9.10	8.46	7.69
5. Regulation of Credit, Labor, and Business	**6.90**	**6.79**	**6.65**	**6.78**	**6.66**	**6.40**	**6.84**	**6.87**
A. Credit market regulations	8.18	8.09	8.50	8.93	7.67	7.60	7.87	7.59
(i) Ownership of banks	10.00	10.00	10.00	10.00	10.00	5.00	5.00	5.00
(ii) Foreign bank competition					6.15	8.00	8.00	8.00
(iii) Private sector credit	6.37	8.28	7.51	8.79	8.64	8.50	9.49	8.35
(iv) Interest rate controls/negative real interest rates		6.00	8.00	8.00	9.00	9.00	9.00	9.00
B. Labor market regulations					5.99	5.90	6.36	6.66
(i) Hiring regulations and minimum wage					3.46	1.10	2.20	2.23
(ii) Hiring and firing regulations					4.97	5.50	5.80	5.41
(iii) Centralized collective bargaining					5.00	5.70	6.84	6.64
(iv) Hours regulations					6.51	6.00	6.00	8.00
(v) Mandated cost of worker dismissal						7.30	7.31	7.67
(vi) Conscription	10.00	10.00	10.00	10.00	10.00	10.00	10.00	10.00
C. Business regulations					6.32	5.70	6.28	6.36
(i) Price controls			6.00	6.00	8.00	8.00	8.00	8.00
(ii) Administrative requirements					6.83	2.60	3.77	3.83
(iii) Bureaucracy costs					6.15	2.30	4.21	4.35
(iv) Starting a business					4.70	7.30	7.87	7.97
(v) Extra payments/bribes/favoritism					5.92	6.90	5.82	5.89
(vi) Licensing restrictions						7.50	7.47	7.49
(vii) Cost of tax compliance						5.50	6.84	6.95

Côte d'Ivoire

	1980	1985	1990	1995	2000	2005	2008	2009
Chain-Linked	Rating (Rank)	Rating (Rank)	Rating (Rank)	Rating (Rank)	Rating (Rank)	Rating (Rank)	Rating (Rank)	Rating (Rank)
Summary Rating (Rank) ➤	**5.59** (47)	**6.15** (35)	**5.60** (54)	**5.24** (92)	**6.07** (82)	**6.03** (91)	**5.67** (104)	**5.88** (103)
Area 1. Size of Government	5.99 (26)	7.20 (5)	5.83 (50)	4.95 (88)	8.41 (8)	8.54 (9)	6.34 (65)	7.01 (33)
Area 2. Legal Structure and Security of Property Rights		5.72 (46)	4.80 (63)	5.44 (63)	3.85 (104)	3.11 (116)	3.19 (117)	3.24 (118)
Area 3. Access to Sound Money	5.00 (93)	6.63 (56)	6.90 (52)	4.87 (96)	6.69 (92)	6.73 (94)	6.40 (102)	6.62 (106)
Area 4. Freedom to Trade Internationally	6.29 (36)	6.47 (32)	5.69 (54)	5.81 (88)	6.01 (93)	5.88 (94)	5.74 (100)	5.60 (100)
Area 5. Regulation of Credit, Labor, and Business	5.52 (42)	5.15 (56)	4.91 (77)	5.12 (77)	5.37 (94)	5.92 (92)	6.73 (51)	7.02 (42)

Unadjusted

	1980	1985	1990	1995	2000	2005	2008	2009
Summary Rating (Rank) ➤	**5.58** (50)	**5.81** (42)	**5.17** (72)	**5.24** (89)	**6.07** (82)	**5.94** (109)	**5.66** (123)	**5.86** (120)
	Rating Data	Rating Data	Rating Data	Rating Data	Rating Data	Rating Data	Rating Data	Rating Data
1. Size of Government	**5.39**	**5.02**	**4.07**	**4.95**	**8.41**	**8.50**	**6.34**	**7.01**
A. Government consumption	5.54 (21.17)	6.06 (19.38)	6.20 (18.93)	7.37 (14.95)	8.18 (12.20)	8.80 (10.00)	8.39 (11.46)	8.67 (10.51)
B. Transfers and subsidies	9.01 (4.15)			9.44 (2.55)	9.48 (2.41)	9.30 (2.90)	9.97 (0.59)	9.85 (1.03)
C. Government enterprises and investment	2.00 (46.80)	4.00 (31.80)	2.00 (42.20)	0.00 (62.70)	6.00 (25.30)	6.00 (28.00)	4.00 (30.06)	6.00 (26.50)
D. Top marginal tax rate	5.00	5.00	4.00	3.00	10.00	10.00	3.00	3.50
(i) Top marginal income tax rate	5.00 (45)	5.00 (45)	4.00 (45)	3.00 (49)	10.00 (10)	10.00 (10)	5.00 (39)	5.00 (39)
(ii) Top marginal income and payroll tax rates							1.00 (57)	2.00 (54)
2. Legal Structure and Security of Property Rights		**5.72**	**4.80**	**5.44**	**3.85**	**3.10**	**3.11**	**3.15**
A. Judicial independence							1.46	1.55
B. Impartial courts				4.97	4.60	3.00	2.89	3.15
C. Protection of property rights							3.99	3.98
D. Military interference in rule of law and politics				5.94	1.67	1.70	2.50	2.50
E. Integrity of the legal system				6.96	5.00	4.20	4.17	4.17
F. Legal enforcement of contracts						2.50	2.47	2.47
G. Regulatory restrictions on sale of real property						4.20	4.26	4.26
3. Access to Sound Money	**5.00**	**6.63**	**6.90**	**4.87**	**6.69**	**6.70**	**6.40**	**6.62**
A. Money growth	8.66 (6.69)	9.00 (5.00)	9.18 (−4.12)	7.60 (12.02)	9.79 (1.06)	8.50 (7.50)	7.99 (10.07)	7.73 (11.37)
B. Standard deviation of inflation	6.18 (9.55)	7.58 (6.05)	9.34 (1.64)	3.57 (16.07)	7.48 (6.29)	9.20 (1.98)	8.87 (2.84)	8.95 (2.63)
C. Inflation: most recent year	5.17 (24.14)	9.93 (0.34)	9.10 (−4.52)	8.30 (8.50)	9.51 (2.46)	9.20 (3.89)	8.74 (6.31)	9.79 (1.03)
D. Freedom to own foreign currency bank accounts	0.00	0.00	0.00	0.00	0.00	0.00	0.00	0.00
4. Freedom to Trade Internationally	**5.74**	**5.90**	**5.19**	**5.81**	**6.01**	**5.90**	**6.39**	**6.24**
A. Taxes on international trade	2.98	3.74	3.07	4.27	5.77	6.50	6.41	6.24
(i) Revenues from trade taxes (% of trade sector)	1.47 (12.80)	2.13 (11.80)	2.73 (10.90)	0.00 (17.32)	3.99 (9.02)	4.80 (7.80)	4.31 (8.53)	3.81 (9.29)
(ii) Mean tariff rate	4.50 (27.50)	5.34 (23.30)	3.40 (33.00)	3.40 (33.00)	7.60 (12.00)	7.50 (12.60)	7.62 (11.90)	7.62 (11.90)
(iii) Standard deviation of tariff rates				9.40 (1.50)	5.72 (10.70)	7.30 (6.80)	7.29 (6.78)	7.29 (6.78)
B. Regulatory trade barriers						5.60	5.79	5.89
(i) Non-tariff trade barriers							5.77	5.95
(ii) Compliance cost of importing and exporting						5.60	5.82	5.82
C. Size of trade sector relative to expected	7.90	7.77	5.45	6.77	6.06	6.40	6.38	5.66
D. Black-market exchange rates	9.60	9.80	9.20	9.80	10.00	10.00	10.00	10.00
E. International capital market controls	0.00	0.00	0.00	0.00	0.00	0.80	3.37	3.39
(i) Foreign ownership/investment restrictions							5.97	6.02
(ii) Capital controls	0.00	0.00	0.00	0.00	0.00	0.80	0.77	0.77
5. Regulation of Credit, Labor, and Business	**6.21**	**5.79**	**4.91**	**5.12**	**5.37**	**5.50**	**6.06**	**6.30**
A. Credit market regulations	6.56	7.12	6.39	6.43	7.26	5.80	7.93	8.00
(i) Ownership of banks	2.00	2.00	2.00	8.00	8.00	8.00	8.00	8.00
(ii) Foreign bank competition								
(iii) Private sector credit	9.67	9.35	9.17	7.29	7.78	3.30	9.78	10.00
(iv) Interest rate controls/negative real interest rates	8.00	10.00	8.00	4.00	6.00	6.00	6.00	6.00
B. Labor market regulations						4.60	5.11	5.67
(i) Hiring regulations and minimum wage						6.70	6.70	6.67
(ii) Hiring and firing regulations							5.12	5.90
(iii) Centralized collective bargaining							7.07	7.38
(iv) Hours regulations						5.30	5.30	6.00
(v) Mandated cost of worker dismissal						5.50	5.46	7.09
(vi) Conscription	10.00	5.00	5.00	5.00	5.00	1.00	1.00	1.00
C. Business regulations						6.00	5.14	5.22
(i) Price controls			0.00	2.00	2.00	6.00	6.00	6.00
(ii) Administrative requirements							2.88	3.08
(iii) Bureaucracy costs							6.19	6.57
(iv) Starting a business						6.40	6.65	6.66
(v) Extra payments/bribes/favoritism							2.74	2.66
(vi) Licensing restrictions						4.50	4.58	4.59
(vii) Cost of tax compliance						7.00	6.97	6.97

Croatia

	1980	1985	1990	1995	2000	2005	2008	2009
Chain-Linked			Rating (Rank)	Rating (Rank)	Rating (Rank)	Rating (Rank)	Rating (Rank)	Rating (Rank)
Summary Rating (Rank) ➤				4.91 (98)	6.10 (79)	6.40 (80)	6.54 (80)	6.49 (78)
Area 1. Size of Government				4.52 (96)	4.03 (108)	4.55 (109)	5.32 (98)	5.13 (95)
Area 2. Legal Structure and Security of Property Rights				6.16 (43)	6.60 (38)	6.13 (56)	6.35 (45)	6.24 (47)
Area 3. Access to Sound Money			1.25 (113)	3.35 (104)	7.88 (61)	8.20 (63)	8.09 (64)	8.49 (61)
Area 4. Freedom to Trade Internationally				6.04 (84)	6.23 (84)	6.57 (67)	6.39 (79)	6.15 (83)
Area 5. Regulation of Credit, Labor, and Business				4.29 (109)	5.79 (70)	6.54 (60)	6.56 (60)	6.47 (66)

Unadjusted								
Summary Rating (Rank) ➤				4.97 (99)	6.10 (79)	6.31 (93)	6.51 (87)	6.46 (89)
	Rating *Data*	Rating *Data*	Rating *Data*	Rating *Data*	Rating *Data*	Rating *Data*	Rating *Data*	Rating *Data*
1. Size of Government				5.28	4.03	4.60	5.32	5.13
A. Government consumption				1.94 *(33.42)*	2.45 *(31.66)*	4.90 *(23.50)*	4.73 *(23.91)*	4.20 *(25.72)*
B. Transfers and subsidies				5.91 *(15.50)*	4.65 *(20.13)*	4.40 *(21.20)*	5.06 *(18.62)*	4.80 *(19.58)*
C. Government enterprises and investment				8.00 *(17.70)*	7.00 *(22.99)*	8.00 *(17.30)*	10.00 *(12.48)*	10.00 *(8.40)*
D. Top marginal tax rate					2.00	1.00	1.50	1.50
(i) Top marginal income tax rate					4.00 *(35-53)*	2.00 *(45-63)*	3.00 *(45-53)*	3.00 *(45-53)*
(ii) Top marginal income and payroll tax rates					0.00 *(55.9-68)*	0.00 *(62-75)*	0.00 *(62-68)*	0.00 *(62-68)*
2. Legal Structure and Security of Property Rights				5.90	6.60	5.40	5.65	5.55
A. Judicial independence						3.70	3.49	3.53
B. Impartial courts				5.82	6.07	4.00	2.67	2.79
C. Protection of property rights						5.00	4.94	4.93
D. Military interference in rule of law and politics				7.39	8.33	8.30	8.33	8.33
E. Integrity of the legal system					8.33	8.30	8.33	7.50
F. Legal enforcement of contracts						5.40	5.40	5.40
G. Regulatory restrictions on sale of real property						3.40	6.39	6.39
3. Access to Sound Money			2.50	3.35	7.88	8.20	8.09	8.49
A. Money growth				0.00 *(62.40)*	8.28 *(8.60)*	8.60 *(6.90)*	9.09 *(4.54)*	9.98 *(−0.09)*
B. Standard deviation of inflation				0.00 *(573.30)*	9.15 *(2.11)*	9.90 *(0.34)*	9.49 *(1.28)*	9.47 *(1.34)*
C. Inflation: most recent year			0.00 *(500.00)*	8.40 *(8.00)*	9.07 *(4.63)*	9.30 *(3.34)*	8.79 *(6.07)*	9.52 *(2.38)*
D. Freedom to own foreign currency bank accounts			5.00	5.00	5.00	5.00	5.00	5.00
4. Freedom to Trade Internationally				6.01	6.23	6.70	6.55	6.30
A. Taxes on international trade				6.97	8.47	8.80	8.71	8.69
(i) Revenues from trade taxes (% of trade sector)				6.97 *(4.55)*	8.29 *(2.57)*	9.60 *(0.70)*	9.60 *(0.60)*	9.55 *(0.68)*
(ii) Mean tariff rate					8.66 *(6.70)*	9.50 *(2.40)*	9.04 *(4.80)*	9.02 *(4.90)*
(iii) Standard deviation of tariff rates						7.40 *(6.60)*	7.48 *(6.29)*	7.49 *(6.27)*
B. Regulatory trade barriers						6.40	6.76	6.77
(i) Non-tariff trade barriers						6.00	6.03	6.05
(ii) Compliance cost of importing and exporting						6.90	7.49	7.49
C. Size of trade sector relative to expected				4.48	4.47	4.50	3.40	1.95
D. Black-market exchange rates			0.00	8.40	10.00	10.00	10.00	10.00
E. International capital market controls			0.00	2.00	0.00	3.90	3.87	4.10
(i) Foreign ownership / investment restrictions						6.20	5.44	5.12
(ii) Capital controls			0.00	2.00	0.00	1.50	2.31	3.08
5. Regulation of Credit, Labor, and Business				4.29	5.79	6.60	6.91	6.82
A. Credit market regulations			0.00	4.34	8.64	9.00	9.37	8.90
(i) Ownership of banks			0.00	0.00	10.00	10.00	10.00	10.00
(ii) Foreign bank competition						8.00	8.00	8.00
(iii) Private sector credit				9.01	6.92	8.80	9.47	8.61
(iv) Interest rate controls / negative real interest rates				4.00	9.00	9.00	10.00	9.00
B. Labor market regulations						5.60	6.31	6.40
(i) Hiring regulations and minimum wage						3.90	3.90	2.23
(ii) Hiring and firing regulations						5.10	4.65	3.90
(iii) Centralized collective bargaining						7.10	6.90	6.70
(iv) Hours regulations						6.00	6.00	8.00
(v) Mandated cost of worker dismissal						6.40	6.38	7.59
(vi) Conscription				3.00	3.00	5.00	10.00	10.00
C. Business regulations						5.30	5.07	5.14
(i) Price controls			0.00	2.00	4.00	3.00	3.00	3.00
(ii) Administrative requirements						3.20	2.53	1.87
(iii) Bureaucracy costs						5.70	4.82	4.80
(iv) Starting a business						9.00	9.16	9.64
(v) Extra payments / bribes / favoritism						5.70	4.78	4.64
(vi) Licensing restrictions						2.50	3.38	4.24
(vii) Cost of tax compliance						7.80	7.80	7.80

Cyprus

	1980	1985	1990	1995	2000	2005	2008	2009
Chain-Linked	Rating (Rank)	Rating (Rank)	Rating (Rank)	Rating (Rank)	Rating (Rank)	Rating (Rank)	Rating (Rank)	Rating (Rank)
Summary Rating (Rank) ➤	**5.57** (48)	**5.51** (49)	**5.98** (45)	**6.16** (57)	**6.17** (76)	**7.34** (30)	**7.50** (21)	**7.48** (15)
Area 1. Size of Government	6.03 (24)	5.85 (31)	5.39 (64)	6.21 (57)	6.19 (58)	7.43 (27)	7.53 (24)	7.28 (28)
Area 2. Legal Structure and Security of Property Rights		3.99 (75)	6.67 (36)	6.30 (42)	6.89 (33)	7.79 (20)	7.79 (18)	7.78 (18)
Area 3. Access to Sound Money	5.69 (74)	6.84 (41)	7.03 (43)	7.25 (49)	6.88 (85)	9.35 (33)	9.30 (29)	9.42 (29)
Area 4. Freedom to Trade Internationally	5.90 (42)	5.90 (45)	5.70 (53)	5.64 (92)	5.78 (102)	6.53 (71)	6.55 (71)	6.21 (80)
Area 5. Regulation of Credit, Labor, and Business	4.56 (73)	4.96 (63)	5.14 (64)	5.37 (67)	5.11 (101)	5.57 (105)	6.26 (81)	6.62 (58)

	1980	1985	1990	1995	2000	2005	2008	2009
Unadjusted								
Summary Rating (Rank) ➤	**5.69** (45)	**5.64** (51)	**5.93** (44)	**6.16** (59)	**6.17** (76)	**7.31** (37)	**7.54** (20)	**7.51** (18)
	Rating Data	Rating Data	Rating Data	Rating Data	Rating Data	Rating Data	Rating Data	Rating Data
1. Size of Government	**6.03**	**5.85**	**5.39**	**6.21**	**6.19**	**7.40**	**7.53**	**7.28**
A. Government consumption	6.77 (16.97)	6.45 (18.06)	5.17 (22.43)	5.53 (21.20)	6.02 (19.53)	5.30 (21.90)	5.45 (21.46)	5.17 (22.41)
B. Transfers and subsidies	8.34 (6.60)	7.93 (8.10)	7.87 (8.30)	7.33 (10.30)	6.73 (12.51)	6.40 (13.70)	6.68 (12.69)	6.46 (13.47)
C. Government enterprises and investment	8.00 (18.10)	8.00 (17.40)	8.00 (17.40)	8.00 (17.40)	8.00 (17.40)	10.00 (3.10)	10.00 (3.07)	10.00 (3.07)
D. Top marginal tax rate	1.00	1.00	0.50	4.00	4.00	8.00	8.00	7.50
(i) Top marginal income tax rate	1.00 (60)	1.00 (60)	1.00 (60)	5.00 (40)	5.00 (40)	8.00 (30)	8.00 (30)	8.00 (30)
(ii) Top marginal income and payroll tax rates			0.00 (62)	3.00 (48)	3.00 (48)	8.00 (30)	8.00 (30)	7.00 (35)
2. Legal Structure and Security of Property Rights		**3.99**	**6.67**	**6.30**	**6.89**	**7.60**	**6.84**	**6.83**
A. Judicial independence						7.00	7.36	7.49
B. Impartial courts				7.20	7.27	6.80	6.19	6.19
C. Protection of property rights						7.50	7.57	7.39
D. Military interference in rule of law and politics				7.32	8.33	8.30	8.33	8.33
E. Integrity of the legal system				6.96	8.33	8.30	8.33	8.33
F. Legal enforcement of contracts							4.00	4.00
G. Regulatory restrictions on sale of real property							6.07	6.07
3. Access to Sound Money	**5.69**	**6.84**	**7.03**	**7.25**	**6.88**	**9.30**	**9.30**	**9.42**
A. Money growth	6.40 (18.00)	9.60 (1.99)	9.45 (2.75)	9.91 (0.45)	8.65 (6.77)	8.50 (7.60)	8.51 (7.45)	8.55 (7.23)
B. Standard deviation of inflation	9.06 (2.36)	8.89 (2.77)	9.71 (0.72)	9.62 (0.94)	9.70 (0.75)	9.40 (1.45)	9.62 (0.95)	9.19 (2.02)
C. Inflation: most recent year	7.30 (13.50)	8.87 (5.67)	8.95 (5.27)	9.48 (2.62)	9.17 (4.14)	9.50 (2.56)	9.07 (4.67)	9.93 (0.37)
D. Freedom to own foreign currency bank accounts	0.00	0.00	0.00	0.00	0.00	10.00	10.00	10.00
4. Freedom to Trade Internationally	**5.90**	**5.90**	**5.41**	**5.64**	**5.78**	**6.90**	**7.08**	**6.71**
A. Taxes on international trade	6.96	6.77	5.47	7.73	7.99	8.40	8.03	8.22
(i) Revenues from trade taxes (% of trade sector)	7.33 (4.00)	7.07 (4.40)	7.20 (4.20)	8.27 (2.60)	9.27 (1.10)	9.60 (0.60)	9.61 (0.59)	9.44 (0.84)
(ii) Mean tariff rate	6.58 (17.10)	6.48 (17.60)	6.70 (16.50)	7.20 (14.00)	6.72 (16.40)	9.50 (2.70)	8.88 (5.60)	8.94 (5.30)
(iii) Standard deviation of tariff rates			2.52 (18.70)			6.10 (9.70)	5.61 (10.98)	6.29 (9.28)
B. Regulatory trade barriers						7.10	8.28	8.21
(i) Non-tariff trade barriers						7.10	7.30	7.15
(ii) Compliance cost of importing and exporting							9.27	9.27
C. Size of trade sector relative to expected	5.14	4.72	4.34	3.26	2.73	2.20	2.57	0.77
D. Black-market exchange rates	9.20	9.80	9.00	9.00	10.00	10.00	10.00	10.00
E. International capital market controls	0.00	0.00	0.00	0.00	0.00	6.80	6.52	6.37
(i) Foreign ownership / investment restrictions						6.70	6.89	6.59
(ii) Capital controls	0.00	0.00	0.00	0.00	0.00	6.90	6.15	6.15
5. Regulation of Credit, Labor, and Business	**5.15**	**5.61**	**5.14**	**5.37**	**5.11**	**5.30**	**6.94**	**7.29**
A. Credit market regulations	7.09	8.30	8.83	8.92	8.08	7.90	9.50	9.50
(i) Ownership of banks	8.00	8.00	8.00	8.00	8.00	10.00	10.00	10.00
(ii) Foreign bank competition						8.00	8.00	8.00
(iii) Private sector credit	9.28	8.90	8.50	8.75	6.23	3.40	10.00	10.00
(iv) Interest rate controls / negative real interest rates	4.00	8.00	10.00	10.00	10.00	10.00	10.00	10.00
B. Labor market regulations						2.90	5.25	6.30
(i) Hiring regulations and minimum wage							6.70	6.67
(ii) Hiring and firing regulations						3.60	4.93	5.15
(iii) Centralized collective bargaining						5.00	5.81	6.00
(iv) Hours regulations							10.00	10.00
(v) Mandated cost of worker dismissal							4.07	10.00
(vi) Conscription	0.00	0.00	0.00	0.00	0.00	0.00	0.00	0.00
C. Business regulations						5.10	6.08	6.08
(i) Price controls			0.00	2.00	2.00	4.00	4.00	4.00
(ii) Administrative requirements						4.20	5.07	4.95
(iii) Bureaucracy costs						5.10	3.40	3.50
(iv) Starting a business							9.60	9.61
(v) Extra payments / bribes / favoritism						7.10	7.22	7.26
(vi) Licensing restrictions							4.91	4.92
(vii) Cost of tax compliance							8.33	8.33

Czech Republic

	1980	1985	1990	1995	2000	2005	2008	2009
Chain-Linked		Rating (Rank)	Rating (Rank)	Rating (Rank)	Rating (Rank)	Rating (Rank)	Rating (Rank)	Rating (Rank)
Summary Rating (Rank) ➤				5.79 (71)	6.48 (63)	6.70 (69)	6.87 (59)	6.82 (58)
Area 1. Size of Government				2.81 (116)	3.13 (118)	3.30 (122)	3.72 (119)	3.62 (118)
Area 2. Legal Structure and Security of Property Rights		7.58 (24)	8.10 (26)	6.55 (37)	6.89 (33)	6.20 (54)	6.43 (40)	6.39 (42)
Area 3. Access to Sound Money				5.95 (74)	8.13 (55)	9.05 (41)	9.14 (35)	9.48 (26)
Area 4. Freedom to Trade Internationally				7.91 (21)	8.37 (13)	7.99 (13)	7.81 (19)	7.59 (21)
Area 5. Regulation of Credit, Labor, and Business			3.70 (102)	5.75 (57)	5.88 (68)	6.97 (43)	7.13 (34)	6.93 (47)

Unadjusted

	1980		1985		1990		1995		2000		2005		2008		2009	
Summary Rating (Rank) ➤							5.74 (73)		6.48 (63)		7.01 (55)		7.19 (45)		7.13 (46)	
	Rating	Data	Rating	Data	Rating	Data	Rating	Data	Rating	Data	Rating	Data	Rating	Data	Rating	Data
1. Size of Government							2.81		3.13		4.50		5.02		4.87	
A. Government consumption							3.04	(29.66)	3.02	(29.73)	2.60	(31.00)	3.20	(29.11)	2.84	(30.35)
B. Transfers and subsidies					0.00	(37.20)	2.40	(28.40)	2.35	(28.56)	3.20	(25.60)	3.37	(24.84)	2.65	(27.47)
C. Government enterprises and investment											8.00	(19.80)	7.00	(20.67)	7.00	(23.35)
D. Top marginal tax rate							3.00		4.00		4.00		6.50		7.00	
(i) Top marginal income tax rate							5.00	(43)	7.00	(32)	7.00	(32)	10.00	(15)	10.00	(15)
(ii) Top marginal income and payroll tax rates							1.00	(64)	1.00	(56)	1.00	(58)	3.00	(46)	4.00	(45)
2. Legal Structure and Security of Property Rights			6.78		7.25		6.55		6.89		6.20		6.43		6.39	
A. Judicial independence							6.17		6.01		4.70		5.01		4.96	
B. Impartial courts							3.58		4.51		4.10		4.05		3.70	
C. Protection of property rights							4.54		5.58		6.00		6.19		5.65	
D. Military interference in rule of law and politics							8.45		10.00		10.00		10.00		10.00	
E. Integrity of the legal system							10.00		8.33		8.30		8.33		8.33	
F. Legal enforcement of contracts											3.50		3.85		3.85	
G. Regulatory restrictions on sale of real property											6.70		7.54		8.20	
3. Access to Sound Money							5.95		8.13		9.00		9.14		9.48	
A. Money growth							6.00	(20.00)	9.87	(0.65)	7.40	(12.80)	8.56	(7.22)	8.70	(6.48)
B. Standard deviation of inflation							4.88	(12.79)	8.43	(3.93)	9.10	(2.23)	9.26	(1.84)	9.41	(1.46)
C. Inflation: most recent year							7.92	(10.41)	9.22	(3.90)	9.60	(1.85)	8.73	(6.36)	9.79	(1.04)
D. Freedom to own foreign currency bank accounts							5.00		5.00		10.00		10.00		10.00	
4. Freedom to Trade Internationally							7.79		8.37		8.00		7.81		7.59	
A. Taxes on international trade							8.45		8.22		8.40		8.03		8.22	
(i) Revenues from trade taxes (% of trade sector)							9.25	(1.13)	9.68	(0.48)	9.60	(0.60)	9.61	(0.59)	9.44	(0.84)
(ii) Mean tariff rate							8.66	(6.70)	8.70	(6.50)	9.50	(2.70)	8.88	(5.60)	8.94	(5.30)
(iii) Standard deviation of tariff rates							7.44	(6.40)	6.28	(9.30)	6.10	(9.70)	5.61	(10.98)	6.29	(9.28)
B. Regulatory trade barriers							7.42		7.88		7.50		7.84		7.67	
(i) Non-tariff trade barriers							7.42		7.27		7.30		8.19		7.84	
(ii) Compliance cost of importing and exporting									8.50		7.70		7.49		7.49	
C. Size of trade sector relative to expected							6.07	7.37		8.73		7.90		7.96		7.03	
D. Black-market exchange rates							10.00		10.00		10.00		10.00		10.00	
E. International capital market controls	0.00		0.00		0.00		5.72		7.03		6.10		5.22		5.04	
(i) Foreign ownership/investment restrictions							6.44		7.92		8.40		7.37		7.01	
(ii) Capital controls	0.00		0.00		0.00		5.00		6.15		3.80		3.08		3.08	
5. Regulation of Credit, Labor, and Business					3.18		5.61		5.88		7.40		7.53		7.33	
A. Credit market regulations	0.00		0.00		0.00		6.37		6.35		9.10		9.33		8.75	
(i) Ownership of banks	0.00		0.00		0.00		5.00		2.00		10.00		10.00		10.00	
(ii) Foreign bank competition							5.07		4.90		8.00		8.00		8.00	
(iii) Private sector credit							9.68		8.56		8.60		9.31		6.99	
(iv) Interest rate controls/negative real interest rates							6.00		10.00		10.00		10.00		10.00	
B. Labor market regulations							5.03		5.22		7.60		7.67		7.60	
(i) Hiring regulations and minimum wage							6.58		5.09		6.70		6.70		6.67	
(ii) Hiring and firing regulations					5.62		5.62		5.30		3.30		3.71		3.36	
(iii) Centralized collective bargaining							5.18		7.70		7.70		7.68		6.81	
(iv) Hours regulations							4.75		5.01		10.00		10.00		10.00	
(v) Mandated cost of worker dismissal											8.00		7.96		8.79	
(vi) Conscription	0.00		0.00		0.00		3.00		3.00		10.00		10.00		10.00	
C. Business regulations							5.44		6.07		5.30		5.60		5.64	
(i) Price controls					0.00		6.00		4.00		7.00		8.00		8.00	
(ii) Administrative requirements									7.80		2.20		2.76		2.78	
(iii) Bureaucracy costs							5.89		8.10		5.50		2.29		2.47	
(iv) Starting a business							5.97		5.53		9.00		9.32		9.16	
(v) Extra payments/bribes/favoritism							3.89		4.92		6.60		5.27		4.88	
(vi) Licensing restrictions											7.10		8.44		8.44	
(vii) Cost of tax compliance											0.00		3.13		3.76	

Denmark

Chain-Linked	1980 Rating (Rank)	1985 Rating (Rank)	1990 Rating (Rank)	1995 Rating (Rank)	2000 Rating (Rank)	2005 Rating (Rank)	2008 Rating (Rank)	2009 Rating (Rank)
Summary Rating (Rank) ➤	**6.53** (21)	**6.68** (23)	**7.41** (15)	**7.46** (15)	**7.65** (14)	**7.72** (12)	**7.70** (11)	**7.54** (12)
Area 1. Size of Government	3.06 (96)	3.14 (99)	3.17 (105)	3.07 (114)	3.48 (114)	4.00 (117)	4.50 (112)	4.14 (113)
Area 2. Legal Structure and Security of Property Rights	8.48 (15)	9.31 (8)	9.86 (8)	9.09 (8)	9.54 (2)	8.94 (5)	8.74 (4)	8.50 (5)
Area 3. Access to Sound Money	6.68 (34)	6.51 (64)	9.46 (13)	9.77 (2)	9.71 (4)	9.49 (24)	9.37 (27)	9.49 (24)
Area 4. Freedom to Trade Internationally	7.37 (16)	7.52 (15)	7.33 (24)	7.93 (20)	8.24 (18)	7.71 (21)	7.70 (20)	7.42 (25)
Area 5. Regulation of Credit, Labor, and Business	7.31 (6)	7.21 (9)	7.30 (9)	7.45 (8)	7.25 (13)	8.45 (5)	8.21 (8)	8.15 (11)

Unadjusted

	1980	1985	1990	1995	2000	2005	2008	2009
Summary Rating (Rank) ➤	**5.95** (31)	**6.09** (33)	**6.78** (20)	**7.46** (17)	**7.65** (14)	**7.70** (15)	**7.69** (12)	**7.52** (15)

	1980 Rating Data	1985 Rating Data	1990 Rating Data	1995 Rating Data	2000 Rating Data	2005 Rating Data	2008 Rating Data	2009 Rating Data
1. Size of Government	**3.06**	**3.14**	**3.17**	**3.07**	**3.48**	**4.00**	**4.50**	**4.14**
A. Government consumption	1.76 *(34.01)*	1.99 *(33.23)*	1.69 *(34.25)*	1.87 *(33.63)*	1.74 *(34.08)*	1.50 *(34.70)*	1.43 *(35.13)*	0.62 *(37.89)*
B. Transfers and subsidies	4.47 *(20.80)*	4.58 *(20.40)*	3.98 *(22.60)*	2.92 *(26.50)*	3.67 *(23.72)*	3.90 *(22.70)*	5.08 *(18.54)*	4.42 *(20.98)*
C. Government enterprises and investment	6.00 *(25.00)*	6.00 *(26.00)*	7.00 *(20.30)*	7.00 *(24.90)*	7.00 *(24.90)*	10.00 *(9.10)*	10.00 *(9.12)*	10.00 *(11.25)*
D. Top marginal tax rate	0.00	0.00	0.00	0.50	1.50	0.50	1.50	1.50
(i) Top marginal income tax rate	0.00 *(66)*	0.00 *(73)*	0.00 *(68)*	1.00 *(64)*	2.00 *(59)*	1.00 *(59)*	2.00 *(59)*	2.00 *(59)*
(ii) Top marginal income and payroll tax rates			0.00 *(69)*	0.00 *(67)*	1.00 *(63)*	0.00 *(63)*	1.00 *(62)*	1.00 *(62)*
2. Legal Structure and Security of Property Rights	**7.18**	**7.88**	**8.35**	**9.09**	**9.54**	**8.90**	**8.74**	**8.50**
A. Judicial independence				8.82	9.35	8.80	9.17	9.00
B. Impartial courts				9.52	9.52	9.30	7.65	7.15
C. Protection of property rights				7.38	8.82	9.30	9.14	8.38
D. Military interference in rule of law and politics				9.73	10.00	10.00	10.00	10.00
E. Integrity of the legal system				10.00	10.00	10.00	10.00	10.00
F. Legal enforcement of contracts						6.20	6.19	5.96
G. Regulatory restrictions on sale of real property						9.00	9.01	9.01
3. Access to Sound Money	**6.68**	**6.51**	**9.46**	**9.77**	**9.71**	**9.50**	**9.37**	**9.49**
A. Money growth	8.70 *(6.51)*	7.86 *(10.71)*	8.80 *(6.01)*	9.75 *(1.27)*	9.75 *(1.27)*	8.60 *(7.20)*	8.58 *(7.11)*	8.83 *(5.83)*
B. Standard deviation of inflation	9.67 *(0.82)*	9.03 *(2.42)*	9.72 *(0.71)*	9.76 *(0.60)*	9.69 *(0.76)*	9.80 *(0.58)*	9.56 *(1.09)*	9.41 *(1.48)*
C. Inflation: most recent year	8.35 *(8.23)*	9.13 *(4.33)*	9.32 *(3.40)*	9.57 *(2.14)*	9.42 *(2.92)*	9.60 *(1.81)*	9.32 *(3.40)*	9.73 *(1.33)*
D. Freedom to own foreign currency bank accounts	0.00	0.00	10.00	10.00	10.00	10.00	10.00	10.00
4. Freedom to Trade Internationally	**7.12**	**7.27**	**6.95**	**7.85**	**8.24**	**7.70**	**7.70**	**7.42**
A. Taxes on international trade	8.95	9.12	8.48	8.70	9.18	8.40	8.03	8.22
(i) Revenues from trade taxes (% of trade sector)	9.67 *(0.50)*	9.73 *(0.40)*	9.80 *(0.30)*	9.80 *(0.30)*	9.78 *(0.33)*	9.60 *(0.60)*	9.61 *(0.59)*	9.44 *(0.84)*
(ii) Mean tariff rate	8.24 *(8.80)*	8.50 *(7.50)*	8.52 *(7.40)*	8.66 *(6.70)*	9.52 *(2.40)*	9.50 *(2.70)*	8.88 *(5.60)*	8.94 *(5.30)*
(iii) Standard deviation of tariff rates				7.12 *(7.20)*	7.64 *(5.90)*	8.24 *(4.40)*	6.10 *(9.70)*	5.61 *(10.98)*	6.29 *(9.28)*
B. Regulatory trade barriers				9.05	9.43	8.40	8.40	8.12
(i) Non-tariff trade barriers				9.05	9.04	7.30	7.36	6.81
(ii) Compliance cost of importing and exporting					9.83	9.40	9.43	9.43
C. Size of trade sector relative to expected	3.89	4.08	3.10	2.74	3.62	3.90	4.41	3.47
D. Black-market exchange rates	9.60	10.00	10.00	10.00	10.00	10.00	10.00	10.00
E. International capital market controls	5.00	5.00	5.00	8.77	8.97	7.90	7.65	7.28
(i) Foreign ownership / investment restrictions				9.54	9.48	8.10	7.60	6.87
(ii) Capital controls	5.00	5.00	5.00	8.00	8.46	7.70	7.69	7.69
5. Regulation of Credit, Labor, and Business	**5.71**	**5.64**	**6.00**	**7.50**	**7.25**	**8.40**	**8.13**	**8.06**
A. Credit market regulations	9.41	9.08	9.34	9.13	9.54	9.50	9.50	9.26
(i) Ownership of banks	10.00	10.00	10.00	10.00	10.00	10.00	10.00	10.00
(ii) Foreign bank competition				8.82	8.23	8.00	8.00	8.00
(iii) Private sector credit	8.24	7.25	8.03	8.16	10.00	10.00	10.00	9.06
(iv) Interest rate controls / negative real interest rates	10.00	10.00	10.00	10.00	10.00	10.00	10.00	10.00
B. Labor market regulations	3.46	3.49	4.66	4.83	4.62	7.40	7.47	7.47
(i) Hiring regulations and minimum wage				3.68	4.76	10.00	10.00	10.00
(ii) Hiring and firing regulations			8.10	8.10	6.47	7.40	8.12	8.00
(iii) Centralized collective bargaining	5.18	5.18	5.18	5.18	4.85	6.20	5.68	5.84
(iv) Hours regulations	2.20	2.29	2.37	4.17	4.01	8.00	8.00	8.00
(v) Mandated cost of worker dismissal						10.00	10.00	10.00
(vi) Conscription	3.00	3.00	3.00	3.00	3.00	3.00	3.00	3.00
C. Business regulations				8.55	7.60	8.20	7.42	7.45
(i) Price controls			7.00	9.00	7.00	7.00	8.00	8.00
(ii) Administrative requirements					7.05	4.60	4.70	4.72
(iii) Bureaucracy costs				8.87	8.23	8.40	1.96	2.32
(iv) Starting a business				6.32	6.45	9.70	9.68	9.72
(v) Extra payments / bribes / favoritism				9.99	9.29	9.50	9.41	9.21
(vi) Licensing restrictions						9.70	9.69	9.68
(vii) Cost of tax compliance						8.50	8.49	8.49

Dominican Republic

	1980	1985	1990	1995	2000	2005	2008	2009
Chain-Linked	Rating (Rank)	Rating (Rank)	Rating (Rank)	Rating (Rank)	Rating (Rank)	Rating (Rank)	Rating (Rank)	Rating (Rank)
Summary Rating (Rank) ➤	**5.33** (59)	**4.98** (76)	**4.60** (96)	**5.86** (68)	**6.54** (58)	**6.30** (85)	**6.25** (86)	**6.58** (72)
Area 1. Size of Government	5.71 (33)	6.20 (21)	6.68 (25)	8.14 (12)	8.88 (3)	8.67 (6)	7.70 (21)	7.68 (19)
Area 2. Legal Structure and Security of Property Rights	5.29 (42)	4.92 (59)	4.85 (62)	4.78 (89)	4.47 (87)	4.72 (90)	4.90 (86)	4.86 (84)
Area 3. Access to Sound Money	7.34 (28)	3.82 (100)	2.05 (112)	4.48 (99)	6.82 (89)	5.87 (112)	5.91 (114)	8.12 (71)
Area 4. Freedom to Trade Internationally	3.51 (81)	4.96 (60)	3.82 (93)	5.32 (98)	5.91 (97)	6.03 (90)	6.41 (77)	6.02 (85)
Area 5. Regulation of Credit, Labor, and Business	5.13 (57)	5.02 (59)	5.44 (54)	6.49 (28)	6.61 (35)	6.24 (72)	6.33 (74)	6.29 (82)

	1980	1985	1990	1995	2000	2005	2008	2009
Unadjusted								
Summary Rating (Rank) ➤	**5.92** (33)	**5.52** (54)	**4.78** (91)	**6.09** (63)	**6.54** (58)	**6.39** (87)	**6.34** (94)	**6.68** (78)
	Rating Data	Rating Data	Rating Data	Rating Data	Rating Data	Rating Data	Rating Data	Rating Data
1. Size of Government	**5.71**	**6.20**	**6.68**	**8.14**	**8.88**	**8.70**	**7.70**	**7.68**
A. Government consumption	9.12 (8.98)	9.35 (8.20)	10.00 (6.00)	9.87 (6.43)	9.03 (9.29)	11.70 (7.50)	9.40 (8.05)	9.29 (8.41)
B. Transfers and subsidies	9.70 (1.60)	9.46 (2.50)	9.73 (1.50)	9.67 (1.70)	9.49 (2.36)	8.00 (7.80)	8.91 (4.50)	8.91 (4.50)
C. Government enterprises and investment	4.00 (31.60)	6.00 (25.10)	7.00 (23.70)	4.00 (33.70)	8.00 (18.00)	7.00 (24.30)	6.00 (25.10)	6.00 (25.10)
D. Top marginal tax rate	0.00	0.00	0.00	9.00	9.00	8.00	6.50	6.50
(i) Top marginal income tax rate	0.00 (73)	0.00 (73)	0.00 (73)	9.00 (25)	9.00 (25)	9.00 (25)	8.00 (30)	9.00 (25)
(ii) Top marginal income and payroll tax rates			0.00 (73)	9.00 (25)	9.00 (25)	7.00 (32)	5.00 (37)	4.00 (41)
2. Legal Structure and Security of Property Rights	**5.78**	**5.38**	**5.30**	**5.22**	**4.47**	**4.60**	**4.79**	**4.75**
A. Judicial independence						4.20	3.83	3.44
B. Impartial courts				6.23	5.57	3.80	3.47	3.53
C. Protection of property rights					2.90	5.30	4.89	4.97
D. Military interference in rule of law and politics				6.63	5.00	5.00	5.00	5.00
E. Integrity of the legal system				4.11	5.00	3.30	4.17	4.17
F. Legal enforcement of contracts						4.50	4.51	4.51
G. Regulatory restrictions on sale of real property						6.30	7.65	7.65
3. Access to Sound Money	**7.34**	**3.82**	**2.05**	**4.48**	**6.82**	**5.90**	**5.91**	**8.12**
A. Money growth	8.96 (5.18)	7.26 (13.69)	4.70 (26.49)	8.44 (7.82)	9.39 (3.06)	7.40 (13.00)	8.81 (5.97)	8.85 (5.75)
B. Standard deviation of inflation	8.14 (4.64)	3.00 (17.49)	3.48 (16.30)	1.99 (20.03)	9.42 (1.45)	1.90 (20.22)	1.97 (20.07)	8.91 (2.72)
C. Inflation: most recent year	7.26 (13.70)	0.00 (50.50)	0.00 (51.05)	7.49 (12.56)	8.46 (7.72)	9.20 (4.19)	7.87 (10.64)	9.71 (1.44)
D. Freedom to own foreign currency bank accounts	5.00	5.00	0.00	0.00	0.00	5.00	5.00	5.00
4. Freedom to Trade Internationally	**3.98**	**5.62**	**4.19**	**5.83**	**5.91**	**6.40**	**6.77**	**6.35**
A. Taxes on international trade	3.47	5.67	5.11	5.00	5.78	7.00	7.80	7.80
(i) Revenues from trade taxes (% of trade sector)	3.47 (9.80)	5.67 (6.50)	5.83 (6.26)	4.01 (8.99)	5.23 (7.16)	6.00 (6.00)	8.38 (2.43)	8.38 (2.43)
(ii) Mean tariff rate			4.40 (28.00)	6.00 (20.00)	6.10 (19.50)	8.20 (9.00)	8.58 (7.10)	8.58 (7.10)
(iii) Standard deviation of tariff rates					6.00 (10.00)	6.90 (7.80)	6.45 (8.88)	6.45 (8.88)
B. Regulatory trade barriers					3.33	6.00	6.80	6.75
(i) Non-tariff trade barriers					3.33	4.40	4.82	4.71
(ii) Compliance cost of importing and exporting						7.70	8.79	8.79
C. Size of trade sector relative to expected	3.60	5.01	5.58	4.33	3.93	2.90	3.17	1.56
D. Black-market exchange rates	2.60	7.20	0.00	9.60	10.00	10.00	10.00	10.00
E. International capital market controls	2.00	2.00	2.00	2.00	6.52	5.80	6.06	5.65
(i) Foreign ownership/investment restrictions					8.42	7.70	6.73	6.68
(ii) Capital controls	2.00	2.00	2.00	2.00	4.62	3.80	5.38	4.62
5. Regulation of Credit, Labor, and Business	**6.76**	**6.61**	**5.69**	**6.79**	**6.61**	**6.40**	**6.53**	**6.50**
A. Credit market regulations	7.79	7.34	5.99	8.97	7.95	7.40	7.45	7.45
(i) Ownership of banks	8.00	8.00	10.00	10.00	10.00	5.00	5.00	5.00
(ii) Foreign bank competition					5.78	6.00	5.78	5.78
(iii) Private sector credit	7.58	6.68	7.97	8.90	9.17	9.60	10.00	10.00
(iv) Interest rate controls/negative real interest rates			0.00	8.00	9.00	9.00	9.00	9.00
B. Labor market regulations					5.92	6.50	6.32	6.25
(i) Hiring regulations and minimum wage					2.93	4.40	5.60	5.57
(ii) Hiring and firing regulations					5.17	7.10	5.00	4.52
(iii) Centralized collective bargaining					5.58	7.50	7.45	7.16
(iv) Hours regulations						8.00	8.00	8.00
(v) Mandated cost of worker dismissal						1.80	1.84	2.25
(vi) Conscription	10.00	10.00	10.00	10.00	10.00	10.00	10.00	10.00
C. Business regulations					5.95	5.50	5.83	5.80
(i) Price controls			4.00	6.00	6.00	4.00	4.00	4.00
(ii) Administrative requirements					7.37	3.60	3.53	3.54
(iii) Bureaucracy costs					5.18	4.40	6.51	6.54
(iv) Starting a business					5.48	7.40	9.21	8.98
(v) Extra payments/bribes/favoritism					5.73	5.10	4.03	3.93
(vi) Licensing restrictions						7.00	7.19	7.20
(vii) Cost of tax compliance						6.80	6.37	6.37

Ecuador

Chain-Linked	1980		1985		1990		1995		2000		2005		2008		2009	
	Rating	(Rank)	Rating	(Rank)	Rating	(Rank)	Rating	(Rank)	Rating	(Rank)	Rating	(Rank)	Rating	(Rank)	Rating	(Rank)
Summary Rating (Rank) ➤	**5.40**	(58)	**4.63**	(88)	**5.31**	(71)	**5.98**	(65)	**5.69**	(100)	**5.79**	(104)	**6.04**	(92)	**6.02**	(95)
Area 1. Size of Government	5.45	(41)	5.09	(55)	8.25	(4)	8.22	(7)	8.93	(2)	8.03	(14)	8.03	(15)	7.89	(14)
Area 2. Legal Structure and Security of Property Rights	5.16	(44)	4.62	(63)	4.59	(68)	3.85	(109)	3.30	(116)	3.99	(104)	4.04	(103)	3.95	(106)
Area 3. Access to Sound Money	8.15	(17)	6.89	(40)	3.98	(101)	6.47	(65)	4.90	(113)	4.73	(121)	6.10	(109)	6.36	(111)
Area 4. Freedom to Trade Internationally	4.64	(63)	3.50	(80)	5.52	(60)	6.36	(74)	7.11	(57)	6.65	(62)	6.49	(74)	6.21	(80)
Area 5. Regulation of Credit, Labor, and Business	3.58	(94)	3.08	(101)	4.06	(99)	4.95	(88)	4.24	(117)	5.56	(106)	5.59	(105)	5.74	(103)

Unadjusted

	1980		1985		1990		1995		2000		2005		2008		2009	
Summary Rating (Rank) ➤	**5.92**	(33)	**5.00**	(78)	**5.57**	(58)	**6.27**	(55)	**5.69**	(100)	**5.80**	(118)	**6.07**	(109)	**6.04**	(112)
	Rating	Data	Rating	Data	Rating	Data	Rating	Data	Rating	Data	Rating	Data	Rating	Data	Rating	Data
1. Size of Government	**5.45**		**5.09**		**8.25**		**8.22**		**8.93**		**8.00**		**8.03**		**7.89**	
A. Government consumption	6.01	(19.57)	7.32	(15.10)	8.48	(11.16)	7.15	(15.68)	7.86	(13.27)	7.50	(14.40)	7.52	(14.42)	6.99	(16.24)
B. Transfers and subsidies	8.80	(4.90)	9.05	(4.00)	9.51	(2.30)	9.73	(1.50)	9.86	(1.02)	9.60	(2.00)	9.59	(2.00)	9.59	(2.00)
C. Government enterprises and investment	2.00	(40.20)	2.00	(41.30)	7.00	(21.70)	8.00	(18.30)	10.00	(3.15)	7.00	(20.10)	7.00	(20.14)	7.00	(20.14)
D. Top marginal tax rate	5.00		2.00		8.00		8.00		8.00		8.00		8.00		8.00	
(i) Top marginal income tax rate	5.00	(50)	2.00	(58)	9.00	(25)	9.00	(25)	9.00	(25)	9.00	(25)	9.00	(25)	9.00	(25)
(ii) Top marginal income and payroll tax rates					7.00	(32)	7.00	(32)	7.00	(32)	7.00	(35)	7.00	(32)	7.00	(32)
2. Legal Structure and Security of Property Rights	**5.86**		**5.25**		**5.21**		**4.38**		**3.30**		**4.00**		**4.04**		**3.95**	
A. Judicial independence									2.67		1.90		1.63		1.66	
B. Impartial courts							4.28		2.51		2.20		2.73		2.37	
C. Protection of property rights									2.98		4.10		3.86		3.63	
D. Military interference in rule of law and politics							5.07		3.33		2.50		2.50		2.50	
E. Integrity of the legal system							4.11		5.00		4.40		4.17		4.17	
F. Legal enforcement of contracts											4.40		4.38		4.38	
G. Regulatory restrictions on sale of real property											8.50		9.01		8.97	
3. Access to Sound Money	**8.15**		**6.89**		**3.98**		**6.47**		**4.90**		**4.70**		**6.10**		**6.36**	
A. Money growth	8.13	(9.33)	7.90	(10.48)	2.62	(36.92)	4.76	(26.19)	4.25	(28.73)	2.70	(36.30)	7.25	(13.76)	7.71	(11.43)
B. Standard deviation of inflation	8.38	(4.06)	5.85	(10.37)	3.29	(16.77)	5.78	(10.54)	5.36	(11.61)	6.70	(8.29)	8.85	(2.88)	8.75	(3.12)
C. Inflation: most recent year	6.10	(19.51)	3.82	(30.90)	0.00	(54.01)	5.35	(23.23)	0.00	(96.09)	9.50	(2.41)	8.32	(8.40)	8.97	(5.16)
D. Freedom to own foreign currency bank accounts	10.00		10.00		10.00		10.00		10.00		0.00		0.00		0.00	
4. Freedom to Trade Internationally	**5.61**		**3.89**		**5.81**		**6.70**		**7.11**		**6.70**		**6.49**		**6.21**	
A. Taxes on international trade	5.20		4.16		3.30		7.66		7.14		7.10		6.78		6.37	
(i) Revenues from trade taxes (% of trade sector)	5.20	(7.20)	5.87	(6.20)	7.33	(4.00)	7.67	(3.50)	6.53	(5.20)	6.50	(5.20)	6.53	(5.20)	6.53	(5.20)
(ii) Mean tariff rate			2.46	(37.70)	2.58	(37.10)	7.54	(12.30)	7.42	(12.90)	7.60	(11.80)	7.74	(11.30)	7.76	(11.20)
(iii) Standard deviation of tariff rates					0.00	(27.00)	7.76	(5.60)	7.48	(6.30)	7.20	(6.90)	6.07	(9.83)	4.80	(12.99)
B. Regulatory trade barriers									4.73		4.70		4.76		4.63	
(i) Non-tariff trade barriers									3.13		3.90		2.84		2.59	
(ii) Compliance cost of importing and exporting									6.33		5.60		6.68		6.68	
C. Size of trade sector relative to expected	5.25		4.64		5.56		5.07		5.97		4.70		5.39		6.09	
D. Black-market exchange rates	7.40		0.40		10.00		7.60		10.00		10.00		10.00		10.00	
E. International capital market controls	2.00		2.00		2.00		5.00		7.69		6.70		5.51		3.95	
(i) Foreign ownership/investment restrictions									9.23		5.00		4.09		4.05	
(ii) Capital controls	2.00		2.00		2.00		5.00		6.15		8.50		6.92		3.85	
5. Regulation of Credit, Labor, and Business	**4.52**		**3.88**		**4.59**		**5.59**		**4.24**		**5.60**		**5.67**		**5.79**	
A. Credit market regulations	5.42		3.74		6.00		8.00		4.45		8.00		7.95		7.95	
(i) Ownership of banks	5.00		5.00		8.00		8.00		2.00		8.00		8.00		8.00	
(ii) Foreign bank competition									3.80		4.00		3.80		3.80	
(iii) Private sector credit	7.27		6.21		10.00		10.00		10.00		10.00		10.00		10.00	
(iv) Interest rate controls/negative real interest rates	4.00		0.00		0.00		6.00		4.00		10.00		10.00		10.00	
B. Labor market regulations									3.57		3.90		3.74		4.09	
(i) Hiring regulations and minimum wage									3.49		5.60		5.60		5.57	
(ii) Hiring and firing regulations									3.43		3.20		2.40		2.45	
(iii) Centralized collective bargaining									4.25		5.70		5.43		5.54	
(iv) Hours regulations									3.67		6.00		6.00		8.00	
(v) Mandated cost of worker dismissal											0.00		0.00		0.00	
(vi) Conscription	0.00		0.00		3.00		3.00		3.00		3.00		3.00		3.00	
C. Business regulations									4.69		5.00		5.31		5.32	
(i) Price controls					0.00		4.00		4.00		6.00		6.00		6.00	
(ii) Administrative requirements									5.33		2.40		3.03		3.22	
(iii) Bureaucracy costs									5.25		3.30		6.07		5.72	
(iv) Starting a business									3.97		7.50		7.52		7.85	
(v) Extra payments/bribes/favoritism									4.87		4.50		3.31		3.80	
(vi) Licensing restrictions											7.80		7.97		8.01	
(vii) Cost of tax compliance											3.30		3.27		2.67	

Egypt

Chain-Linked	1980 Rating (Rank)	1985 Rating (Rank)	1990 Rating (Rank)	1995 Rating (Rank)	2000 Rating (Rank)	2005 Rating (Rank)	2008 Rating (Rank)	2009 Rating (Rank)
Summary Rating (Rank) ➤	4.83 (73)	5.36 (55)	5.01 (87)	5.84 (69)	6.60 (53)	6.63 (71)	6.79 (64)	6.55 (74)
Area 1. Size of Government	3.95 (83)	4.54 (71)	4.37 (88)	4.73 (92)	6.13 (61)	6.69 (59)	7.06 (38)	5.98 (71)
Area 2. Legal Structure and Security of Property Rights	2.89 (71)	5.63 (50)	3.67 (81)	4.88 (82)	5.87 (58)	5.29 (76)	5.44 (71)	5.49 (70)
Area 3. Access to Sound Money	7.70 (23)	8.85 (18)	8.16 (29)	7.61 (45)	9.53 (18)	8.85 (45)	8.26 (59)	8.66 (57)
Area 4. Freedom to Trade Internationally	4.88 (57)	2.97 (87)	3.45 (99)	6.13 (82)	6.09 (90)	6.55 (69)	6.88 (62)	6.40 (72)
Area 5. Regulation of Credit, Labor, and Business	4.61 (70)	5.00 (62)	5.50 (53)	5.91 (52)	5.40 (92)	5.81 (95)	6.33 (74)	6.28 (83)

Unadjusted

	1980 Rating Data	1985 Rating Data	1990 Rating Data	1995 Rating Data	2000 Rating Data	2005 Rating Data	2008 Rating Data	2009 Rating Data
Summary Rating (Rank) ➤	4.85 (74)	5.38 (60)	4.94 (87)	5.77 (70)	6.60 (53)	6.50 (81)	6.65 (82)	6.42 (93)
1. Size of Government	**3.95**	**4.54**	**4.37**	**4.73**	**6.13**	**6.70**	**7.06**	**5.98**
A. Government consumption	6.33 (18.47)	5.83 (20.18)	7.77 (13.60)	8.12 (12.40)	8.29 (11.80)	7.30 (15.10)	7.90 (13.14)	7.94 (13.01)
B. Transfers and subsidies	5.45 (17.20)	6.35 (13.90)	7.71 (8.90)	7.81 (8.53)	9.22 (3.38)	9.40 (2.60)	6.36 (13.87)	6.47 (13.46)
C. Government enterprises and investment	4.00 (39.70)	4.00 (30.70)	0.00 (54.50)	0.00 (76.40)	0.00 (52.10)	0.00 (51.90)	4.00 (35.32)	2.00 (42.41)
D. Top marginal tax rate	0.00	2.00	2.00	3.00	7.00	10.00	10.00	7.50
(i) Top marginal income tax rate	0.00 (80)	2.00 (65)	2.00 (65)	3.00 (50)	7.00 (34)	10.00 (20)	10.00 (20)	10.00 (20)
(ii) Top marginal income and payroll tax rates								5.00 (40)
2. Legal Structure and Security of Property Rights	**2.76**	**5.38**	**3.50**	**4.88**	**5.87**	**5.30**	**5.44**	**5.49**
A. Judicial independence				5.93	6.85	6.40	4.80	4.85
B. Impartial courts				3.33	5.68	5.10	5.00	4.90
C. Protection of property rights				4.90	5.17	6.20	5.71	6.06
D. Military interference in rule of law and politics				6.13	5.00	5.00	5.00	5.00
E. Integrity of the legal system				4.11	6.67	6.70	5.83	5.83
F. Legal enforcement of contracts						3.40	3.41	3.41
G. Regulatory restrictions on sale of real property						4.20	8.34	8.38
3. Access to Sound Money	**7.70**	**8.85**	**8.16**	**7.61**	**9.53**	**8.80**	**8.26**	**8.66**
A. Money growth	6.29 (18.55)	8.57 (7.17)	8.93 (5.33)	9.12 (4.42)	9.46 (2.69)	7.90 (10.30)	7.85 (10.77)	8.13 (9.33)
B. Standard deviation of inflation	8.12 (4.71)	8.63 (3.42)	7.38 (6.56)	8.20 (4.51)	9.20 (2.01)	8.40 (3.94)	8.84 (2.90)	8.88 (2.81)
C. Inflation: most recent year	6.39 (18.03)	8.19 (9.04)	6.31 (18.44)	8.12 (9.41)	9.46 (2.68)	9.00 (4.87)	6.34 (18.32)	7.65 (11.76)
D. Freedom to own foreign currency bank accounts	10.00	10.00	10.00	5.00	10.00	10.00	10.00	10.00
4. Freedom to Trade Internationally	**5.40**	**3.28**	**3.50**	**5.92**	**6.09**	**6.50**	**6.88**	**6.40**
A. Taxes on international trade	0.89	1.69	3.12	3.06	3.74	4.90	5.05	4.98
(i) Revenues from trade taxes (% of trade sector)	1.27 (13.10)	1.93 (12.10)	6.07 (5.90)	4.83 (7.75)	5.33 (7.00)	8.50 (2.30)	8.54 (2.18)	8.41 (2.38)
(ii) Mean tariff rate	0.52 (47.40)	1.44 (42.80)	3.30 (33.50)	4.34 (28.30)	5.90 (20.50)	6.20 (18.90)	6.60 (17.00)	6.54 (17.30)
(iii) Standard deviation of tariff rates			0.00 (425.80)	0.00 (28.90)	0.00 (39.50)	0.00 (141.10)	0.00 (146.71)	0.00 (149.47)
B. Regulatory trade barriers				4.52	5.58	5.70	6.42	6.68
(i) Non-tariff trade barriers				4.52	4.50	4.60	4.79	4.94
(ii) Compliance cost of importing and exporting					6.66	6.90	8.05	8.41
C. Size of trade sector relative to expected	9.71	6.46	6.14	5.51	3.84	6.00	6.71	5.30
D. Black-market exchange rates	8.20	0.00	0.00	9.40	10.00	10.00	10.00	10.00
E. International capital market controls	0.00	0.00	0.00	7.10	7.31	6.00	6.21	5.05
(i) Foreign ownership/investment restrictions				9.21	9.23	5.90	6.27	5.48
(ii) Capital controls	0.00	0.00	0.00	5.00	5.38	6.20	6.15	4.62
5. Regulation of Credit, Labor, and Business	**4.46**	**4.84**	**5.18**	**5.70**	**5.40**	**5.10**	**5.63**	**5.59**
A. Credit market regulations	3.93	5.20	6.79	7.43	7.01	6.30	6.33	6.02
(i) Ownership of banks	5.00	5.00	5.00	5.00	5.00	2.00	2.00	2.00
(ii) Foreign bank competition				6.67	5.83	6.00	6.00	6.00
(iii) Private sector credit	2.80	4.60	9.37	10.00	9.08	7.10	7.31	6.07
(iv) Interest rate controls/negative real interest rates	4.00	6.00	6.00	10.00	10.00	10.00	10.00	10.00
B. Labor market regulations				3.98	5.57	4.01	5.00	4.96	4.97
(i) Hiring regulations and minimum wage					8.33	4.17	10.00	10.00	10.00
(ii) Hiring and firing regulations				4.02	4.02	3.05	3.40	4.71	4.76
(iii) Centralized collective bargaining	7.93	7.93	7.93	7.93	7.50	8.40	7.06	7.06
(iv) Hours regulations				7.55	5.34	8.00	8.00	8.00
(v) Mandated cost of worker dismissal						0.00	0.00	0.00
(vi) Conscription	0.00	0.00	0.00	0.00	0.00	0.00	0.00	0.00
C. Business regulations				4.11	5.18	4.20	5.61	5.77
(i) Price controls			2.00	2.00	4.00	4.00	4.00	4.00
(ii) Administrative requirements					7.50	3.10	3.59	3.53
(iii) Bureaucracy costs				4.70	2.75	1.10	5.83	5.91
(iv) Starting a business				6.02	5.83	6.40	9.61	9.71
(v) Extra payments/bribes/favoritism				3.72	5.80	6.40	4.87	5.28
(vi) Licensing restrictions						5.10	6.76	6.83
(vii) Cost of tax compliance						3.30	4.62	5.15

El Salvador

	1980	1985	1990	1995	2000	2005	2008	2009
Chain-Linked	Rating (Rank)	Rating (Rank)	Rating (Rank)	Rating (Rank)	Rating (Rank)	Rating (Rank)	Rating (Rank)	Rating (Rank)
Summary Rating (Rank) ➤	**4.84** (71)	**4.49** (89)	**4.77** (92)	**7.00** (30)	**7.30** (27)	**7.60** (19)	**7.58** (13)	**7.29** (28)
Area 1. Size of Government	6.59 (17)	6.41 (16)	6.89 (21)	8.59 (5)	8.67 (4)	9.08 (2)	8.96 (3)	8.86 (4)
Area 2. Legal Structure and Security of Property Rights	2.52 (78)	1.98 (108)	1.94 (111)	5.33 (69)	4.51 (86)	4.83 (88)	4.60 (90)	4.37 (96)
Area 3. Access to Sound Money	5.63 (76)	5.48 (89)	5.25 (89)	8.88 (34)	9.42 (26)	9.63 (10)	9.27 (31)	9.28 (33)
Area 4. Freedom to Trade Internationally	3.90 (74)	3.43 (81)	4.60 (80)	6.46 (72)	7.53 (42)	7.05 (48)	7.27 (38)	6.55 (65)
Area 5. Regulation of Credit, Labor, and Business		5.21 (55)	5.21 (62)	5.74 (58)	6.37 (45)	7.47 (25)	7.87 (15)	7.49 (20)

Unadjusted

	1980	1985	1990	1995	2000	2005	2008	2009
Summary Rating (Rank) ➤	**4.61** (80)	**4.59** (89)	**4.81** (90)	**7.04** (27)	**7.30** (27)	**7.48** (25)	**7.44** (27)	**7.15** (43)
	Rating *Data*	Rating *Data*	Rating *Data*	Rating *Data*	Rating *Data*	Rating *Data*	Rating *Data*	Rating *Data*
1. Size of Government	**6.59**	**6.41**	**6.89**	**8.59**	**8.67**	**9.10**	**8.96**	**8.86**
A. Government consumption	6.97 *(16.30)*	7.05 *(16.02)*	8.81 *(10.03)*	9.11 *(9.02)*	8.70 *(10.42)*	9.00 *(9.40)*	9.25 *(8.55)*	8.76 *(10.22)*
B. Transfers and subsidies	9.40 *(2.70)*	9.59 *(2.00)*	9.75 *(1.40)*	9.24 *(3.30)*	10.00 *(0.32)*	9.30 *(3.00)*	9.10 *(3.80)*	9.20 *(3.44)*
C. Government enterprises and investment	7.00 *(20.20)*	6.00 *(28.40)*	7.00 *(20.00)*	8.00 *(19.00)*	8.00 *(19.89)*	10.00 *(1.90)*	10.00 *(1.86)*	10.00 *(1.86)*
D. Top marginal tax rate	3.00	3.00	2.00	8.00	8.00	8.00	7.50	7.50
(i) Top marginal income tax rate	3.00 *(60)*	3.00 *(48)*	2.00 *(60)*	8.00 *(30)*	8.00 *(30)*	8.00 *(30)*	8.00 *(30)*	8.00 *(30)*
(ii) Top marginal income and payroll tax rates							7.00 *(34)*	7.00 *(34)*
2. Legal Structure and Security of Property Rights	**2.54**	**1.99**	**1.95**	**5.37**	**4.51**	**4.80**	**4.60**	**4.37**
A. Judicial independence					4.34	3.10	3.42	3.31
B. Impartial courts				4.40	4.18	3.40	3.93	3.47
C. Protection of property rights					4.05	5.80	5.38	5.12
D. Military interference in rule of law and politics				6.25	5.00	5.00	5.00	4.17
E. Integrity of the legal system				6.96	5.00	4.60	2.50	2.50
F. Legal enforcement of contracts						3.80	3.83	3.83
G. Regulatory restrictions on sale of real property						8.20	8.17	8.17
3. Access to Sound Money	**5.63**	**5.48**	**5.25**	**8.88**	**9.42**	**9.60**	**9.27**	**9.28**
A. Money growth	8.52 *(7.40)*	7.74 *(11.29)*	8.48 *(7.60)*	8.20 *(8.98)*	9.03 *(−4.83)*	10.00 *(0.10)*	8.81 *(5.93)*	8.41 *(7.94)*
B. Standard deviation of inflation	7.39 *(6.53)*	8.23 *(4.43)*	7.02 *(7.45)*	9.39 *(1.52)*	9.09 *(2.29)*	9.50 *(1.29)*	9.60 *(1.01)*	8.90 *(2.75)*
C. Inflation: most recent year	6.61 *(16.95)*	5.97 *(20.17)*	5.51 *(22.47)*	7.91 *(10.44)*	9.55 *(2.27)*	9.10 *(4.69)*	8.66 *(6.71)*	9.79 *(1.06)*
D. Freedom to own foreign currency bank accounts	0.00	0.00	0.00	10.00	10.00	10.00	10.00	10.00
4. Freedom to Trade Internationally	**3.66**	**3.69**	**4.81**	**6.69**	**7.53**	**7.00**	**7.27**	**6.55**
A. Taxes on international trade	3.13	5.27	6.52	7.51	8.02	8.30	8.27	8.17
(i) Revenues from trade taxes (% of trade sector)	5.87 *(6.20)*	5.27 *(7.10)*	7.27 *(4.10)*	7.60 *(3.60)*	8.99 *(1.51)*	9.00 *(1.50)*	9.30 *(1.04)*	9.03 *(1.46)*
(ii) Mean tariff rate	0.40 *(48.00)*		5.78 *(21.10)*	7.96 *(10.20)*	8.52 *(7.40)*	8.70 *(6.40)*	8.82 *(5.90)*	8.82 *(5.90)*
(iii) Standard deviation of tariff rates				6.96 *(7.60)*	6.56 *(8.60)*	7.10 *(7.10)*	6.70 *(8.26)*	6.67 *(8.32)*
B. Regulatory trade barriers					7.11	6.10	7.36	7.34
(i) Non-tariff trade barriers					5.72	5.80	6.34	6.31
(ii) Compliance cost of importing and exporting					8.50	6.40	8.37	8.37
C. Size of trade sector relative to expected	4.91	2.92	2.09	2.98	3.60	3.30	3.34	1.43
D. Black-market exchange rates	0.00	0.00	5.20	9.80	10.00	10.00	10.00	10.00
E. International capital market controls	2.00	2.00	2.00	5.00	8.93	7.50	7.39	5.78
(i) Foreign ownership/investment restrictions					8.62	7.40	7.09	6.95
(ii) Capital controls	2.00	2.00	2.00	5.00	9.23	7.70	7.69	4.62
5. Regulation of Credit, Labor, and Business		**5.38**	**5.15**	**5.68**	**6.37**	**6.80**	**7.08**	**6.72**
A. Credit market regulations	9.85	8.66	8.65	9.74	7.85	8.80	9.75	8.66
(i) Ownership of banks						10.00	10.00	10.00
(ii) Foreign bank competition					4.60	9.00	9.00	9.00
(iii) Private sector credit	9.85	9.32	9.30	9.48	9.39	6.20	10.00	5.62
(iv) Interest rate controls/negative real interest rates		8.00	8.00	10.00	10.00	10.00	10.00	10.00
B. Labor market regulations					4.84	5.40	4.95	4.99
(i) Hiring regulations and minimum wage					3.12	6.70	6.70	6.67
(ii) Hiring and firing regulations					4.85	6.30	6.17	6.51
(iii) Centralized collective bargaining					7.73	8.10	7.80	7.70
(iv) Hours regulations					5.51	6.00	6.00	6.00
(v) Mandated cost of worker dismissal						2.00	2.03	2.05
(vi) Conscription	3.00	0.00	0.00	0.00	3.00	3.00	1.00	1.00
C. Business regulations					6.40	6.30	6.54	6.53
(i) Price controls			4.00	6.00	8.00	8.00	8.00	8.00
(ii) Administrative requirements					7.27	3.80	4.15	4.06
(iii) Bureaucracy costs					5.40	3.00	5.22	5.30
(iv) Starting a business					5.78	8.00	9.04	8.97
(v) Extra payments/bribes/favoritism					5.57	6.90	4.85	4.87
(vi) Licensing restrictions						8.00	8.09	8.08
(vii) Cost of tax compliance						6.40	6.41	6.41

Estonia

	1980	1985	1990	1995	2000	2005	2008	2009
Chain-Linked		Rating (Rank)	Rating (Rank)	Rating (Rank)	Rating (Rank)	Rating (Rank)	Rating (Rank)	Rating (Rank)
Summary Rating (Rank) ➤				**5.70** (76)	**7.36** (23)	**7.84** (11)	**7.55** (16)	**7.45** (19)
Area 1. Size of Government				6.40 (46)	6.43 (54)	6.99 (45)	6.29 (67)	5.51 (86)
Area 2. Legal Structure and Security of Property Rights				5.87 (48)	6.00 (51)	6.69 (36)	6.55 (37)	6.51 (36)
Area 3. Access to Sound Money		6.98 (37)	3.36 (108)	2.30 (111)	8.67 (44)	9.43 (32)	9.08 (38)	9.51 (22)
Area 4. Freedom to Trade Internationally				8.98 (3)	8.83 (7)	8.24 (7)	7.99 (11)	7.83 (10)
Area 5. Regulation of Credit, Labor, and Business			2.68 (115)	5.22 (74)	6.86 (26)	7.83 (19)	7.80 (16)	7.88 (15)

	1980	1985	1990	1995	2000	2005	2008	2009
Unadjusted								
Summary Rating (Rank) ➤				**5.76** (72)	**7.36** (23)	**7.92** (9)	**7.62** (14)	**7.52** (15)
	Rating Data	Rating Data	Rating Data	Rating Data	Rating Data	Rating Data	Rating Data	Rating Data
1. Size of Government				5.22	6.43	7.00	6.29	5.51
A. Government consumption			5.74 (20.48)	3.22 (29.06)	3.73 (27.33)	4.40 (25.10)	4.19 (25.76)	3.01 (29.77)
B. Transfers and subsidies				6.43 (13.60)	5.98 (15.25)	7.10 (11.20)	6.49 (13.40)	5.52 (16.93)
C. Government enterprises and investment					10.00 (14.28)	10.00 (4.80)	8.00 (18.48)	7.00 (23.45)
D. Top marginal tax rate				6.00	6.00	6.50	6.50	6.50
(i) Top marginal income tax rate				8.00 (26)	8.00 (26)	9.00 (24)	9.00 (21)	9.00 (21)
(ii) Top marginal income and payroll tax rates				4.00 (44)	4.00 (44)	4.00 (45)	4.00 (42)	4.00 (42)
2. Legal Structure and Security of Property Rights				6.50	6.00	7.40	7.21	7.17
A. Judicial independence						7.10	7.49	7.43
B. Impartial courts				6.46	6.94	6.80	5.17	5.39
C. Protection of property rights					5.00	7.70	7.66	7.22
D. Military interference in rule of law and politics				8.42	8.33	8.30	8.33	8.33
E. Integrity of the legal system					6.67	6.70	6.67	6.67
F. Legal enforcement of contracts						6.10	5.66	5.66
G. Regulatory restrictions on sale of real property						8.80	9.50	9.50
3. Access to Sound Money		8.77	4.48	2.30	8.67	9.40	9.08	9.51
A. Money growth				0.00 (67.37)	8.32 (8.39)	9.30 (3.30)	9.44 (2.78)	9.56 (−2.19)
B. Standard deviation of inflation		8.65 (3.37)	5.18 (12.06)	0.00 (323.00)	7.15 (7.13)	9.20 (1.99)	8.93 (2.67)	8.49 (3.77)
C. Inflation: most recent year		8.88 (−5.61)	3.27 (33.65)	4.20 (29.00)	9.19 (4.03)	9.20 (4.09)	7.93 (10.37)	9.98 (−0.08)
D. Freedom to own foreign currency bank accounts			5.00	5.00	10.00	10.00	10.00	10.00
4. Freedom to Trade Internationally				8.57	8.83	8.20	7.93	7.76
A. Taxes on international trade			9.77	9.81	9.99	8.40	8.03	8.22
(i) Revenues from trade taxes (% of trade sector)			9.77 (0.34)	9.94 (0.09)	9.99 (0.02)	9.60 (0.60)	9.61 (0.59)	9.44 (0.84)
(ii) Mean tariff rate				9.98 (0.10)		9.50 (2.70)	8.88 (5.60)	8.94 (5.30)
(iii) Standard deviation of tariff rates				9.52 (1.20)		6.10 (9.70)	5.61 (10.98)	6.29 (9.28)
B. Regulatory trade barriers					8.34	8.30	8.67	8.57
(i) Non-tariff trade barriers					8.34	7.20	7.90	7.71
(ii) Compliance cost of importing and exporting						9.40	9.43	9.43
C. Size of trade sector relative to expected				6.91	8.00	6.60	5.62	4.92
D. Black-market exchange rates			0.00	10.00	10.00	10.00	10.00	10.00
E. International capital market controls			0.00	8.00	7.82	7.50	7.31	7.10
(i) Foreign ownership / investment restrictions					9.49	8.00	7.70	7.28
(ii) Capital controls			0.00	8.00	6.15	6.90	6.92	6.92
5. Regulation of Credit, Labor, and Business			2.47	6.22	6.86	7.60	7.62	7.67
A. Credit market regulations			0.00	4.30	8.70	9.80	10.00	9.86
(i) Ownership of banks			0.00	5.00	8.00	10.00	10.00	10.00
(ii) Foreign bank competition					6.63	10.00	10.00	10.00
(iii) Private sector credit				7.90	10.00	10.00	10.00	9.44
(iv) Interest rate controls / negative real interest rates				0.00	10.00	9.00	10.00	10.00
B. Labor market regulations					4.74	5.80	5.56	5.94
(i) Hiring regulations and minimum wage					2.94	6.70	6.70	6.67
(ii) Hiring and firing regulations					4.57	5.30	4.26	5.22
(iii) Centralized collective bargaining					8.45	8.80	8.66	8.37
(iv) Hours regulations						4.00	4.00	4.00
(v) Mandated cost of worker dismissal						6.80	6.76	8.39
(vi) Conscription			0.00	3.00	3.00	3.00	3.00	3.00
C. Business regulations				8.14	7.14	7.40	7.28	7.21
(i) Price controls			0.00	6.00	6.00	6.00	7.00	7.00
(ii) Administrative requirements					7.62	5.30	5.77	5.59
(iii) Bureaucracy costs				8.47	7.15	6.20	3.12	3.15
(iv) Starting a business				8.52	8.03	8.70	9.68	9.67
(v) Extra payments / bribes / favoritism				9.57	6.91	7.50	7.38	7.26
(vi) Licensing restrictions						8.90	8.95	8.68
(vii) Cost of tax compliance						9.10	9.09	9.09

Ethiopia

	1980	1985	1990	1995	2000	2005	2008	2009

Chain-Linked

						2005	2008	2009
						Rating (Rank)	Rating (Rank)	Rating (Rank)
Summary Rating (Rank) ➤								
Area 1. Size of Government								
Area 2. Legal Structure and Security of Property Rights								
Area 3. Access to Sound Money								
Area 4. Freedom to Trade Internationally								
Area 5. Regulation of Credit, Labor, and Business								

Unadjusted

	2005	2008	2009
Summary Rating (Rank) ➤	**5.38** (130)	**5.19** (131)	**5.62** (126)
	Rating *Data*	Rating *Data*	Rating *Data*
1. Size of Government	**5.50**	**5.86**	**5.96**
A. Government consumption	7.40 *(14.90)*	8.79 *(10.11)*	9.18 *(8.79)*
B. Transfers and subsidies	7.70 *(9.10)*	7.65 *(9.11)*	7.65 *(9.11)*
C. Government enterprises and investment	0.00 *(64.00)*	0.00 *(70.40)*	0.00 *(73.76)*
D. Top marginal tax rate	7.00	7.00	7.00
(i) Top marginal income tax rate	7.00 *(35)*	7.00 *(35)*	7.00 *(35)*
(ii) Top marginal income and payroll tax rates			
2. Legal Structure and Security of Property Rights	**4.50**	**5.01**	**5.23**
A. Judicial independence	2.00	3.30	3.76
B. Impartial courts	2.70	3.81	4.34
C. Protection of property rights	4.30	5.45	5.90
D. Military interference in rule of law and politics	1.70	1.67	1.67
E. Integrity of the legal system	8.30	7.50	7.50
F. Legal enforcement of contracts	4.30	4.87	4.87
G. Regulatory restrictions on sale of real property	8.00	8.50	8.53
3. Access to Sound Money	**5.70**	**3.87**	**5.71**
A. Money growth	8.20 *(9.00)*	8.15 *(9.24)*	8.15 *(9.24)*
B. Standard deviation of inflation	6.80 *(8.03)*	6.21 *(9.47)*	6.37 *(9.07)*
C. Inflation: most recent year	7.70 *(11.61)*	1.12 *(44.39)*	8.31 *(8.47)*
D. Freedom to own foreign currency bank accounts	0.00	0.00	0.00
4. Freedom to Trade Internationally	**5.10**	**5.22**	**5.04**
A. Taxes on international trade	4.50	4.49	4.49
(i) Revenues from trade taxes (% of trade sector)	1.60 *(12.70)*	1.56 *(12.66)*	1.56 *(12.66)*
(ii) Mean tariff rate	6.60 *(16.80)*	6.54 *(17.30)*	6.54 *(17.30)*
(iii) Standard deviation of tariff rates	5.40 *(11.40)*	5.36 *(11.59)*	5.36 *(11.59)*
B. Regulatory trade barriers	4.50	4.01	4.37
(i) Non-tariff trade barriers	5.40	4.78	5.08
(ii) Compliance cost of importing and exporting	3.70	3.25	3.67
C. Size of trade sector relative to expected	5.10	4.84	4.37
D. Black-market exchange rates	8.00	10.00	10.00
E. International capital market controls	3.50	2.77	1.98
(i) Foreign ownership/investment restrictions	5.50	4.00	3.96
(ii) Capital controls	1.50	1.54	0.00
5. Regulation of Credit, Labor, and Business	**6.10**	**5.97**	**6.18**
A. Credit market regulations	5.80	4.43	4.43
(i) Ownership of banks	2.00	2.00	2.00
(ii) Foreign bank competition			
(iii) Private sector credit	6.30	6.29	6.29
(iv) Interest rate controls/negative real interest rates	9.00	5.00	5.00
B. Labor market regulations	7.20	7.12	7.60
(i) Hiring regulations and minimum wage	6.70	6.70	6.67
(ii) Hiring and firing regulations	4.60	4.99	4.57
(iii) Centralized collective bargaining	7.40	6.77	7.27
(iv) Hours regulations	8.00	8.00	10.00
(v) Mandated cost of worker dismissal	6.30	6.29	7.09
(vi) Conscription	10.00	10.00	10.00
C. Business regulations	5.40	6.36	6.51
(i) Price controls			
(ii) Administrative requirements	3.30	4.64	4.71
(iii) Bureaucracy costs	3.70	6.12	5.85
(iv) Starting a business	5.70	7.90	8.36
(v) Extra payments/bribes/favoritism	5.20	3.93	4.32
(vi) Licensing restrictions	6.60	7.82	8.07
(vii) Cost of tax compliance	7.80	7.78	7.78

Fiji

	1980	1985	1990	1995	2000	2005	2008	2009
Chain-Linked	Rating (Rank)	Rating (Rank)	Rating (Rank)	Rating (Rank)	Rating (Rank)	Rating (Rank)	Rating (Rank)	Rating (Rank)
Summary Rating (Rank) ➤	**5.70** (42)	**6.03** (37)	**5.90** (47)	**6.09** (61)	**6.23** (73)	**6.48** (76)	**6.57** (76)	**6.56** (73)
Area 1. Size of Government	4.75 (63)	5.22 (51)	4.69 (85)	5.92 (66)	6.56 (50)	6.05 (79)	6.98 (39)	6.98 (35)
Area 2. Legal Structure and Security of Property Rights				5.12 (77)	5.46 (67)	6.34 (49)	5.99 (57)	5.77 (60)
Area 3. Access to Sound Money	6.02 (66)	6.67 (52)	6.53 (63)	6.94 (57)	6.90 (84)	6.56 (101)	6.42 (100)	6.76 (99)
Area 4. Freedom to Trade Internationally	6.49 (34)	6.38 (34)	6.50 (38)	6.53 (67)	6.14 (88)	5.39 (107)	5.24 (108)	5.20 (110)
Area 5. Regulation of Credit, Labor, and Business	5.56 (40)	5.86 (40)	5.90 (45)	5.95 (51)	6.06 (60)	7.93 (16)	8.10 (11)	7.99 (13)

Unadjusted								
Summary Rating (Rank) ➤	**5.72** (44)	**6.04** (34)	**5.89** (45)	**6.08** (64)	**6.23** (73)	**6.61** (78)	**6.71** (79)	**6.71** (77)
	Rating Data	Rating Data	Rating Data	Rating Data	Rating Data	Rating Data	Rating Data	Rating Data
1. Size of Government	**4.75**	**5.22**	**4.69**	**5.92**	**6.56**	**6.10**	**6.98**	**6.98**
A. Government consumption	5.56 (21.09)	4.96 (23.12)	5.90 (19.93)	5.48 (21.38)	5.88 (20.00)	4.60 (24.30)	4.25 (25.54)	4.25 (25.54)
B. Transfers and subsidies	9.46 (2.50)	8.91 (4.50)	9.86 (1.00)	9.18 (3.50)	9.35 (2.90)	8.60 (5.70)	8.69 (5.32)	8.69 (5.32)
C. Government enterprises and investment	2.00 (46.20)	4.00 (32.90)	0.00 (55.40)	2.00 (40.40)	4.00 (33.30)	4.00 (34.80)	8.00 (18.85)	8.00 (18.85)
D. Top marginal tax rate	2.00	3.00	3.00	7.00	7.00	7.00	7.00	7.00
(i) Top marginal income tax rate	2.00 (53)	3.00 (50)	3.00 (50)	7.00 (35)	7.00 (34)	7.00 (31)	7.00 (31)	7.00 (31)
(ii) Top marginal income and payroll tax rates			3.00 (50)	7.00 (35)	7.00 (34)	7.00 (31)	7.00 (31)	7.00 (31)
2. Legal Structure and Security of Property Rights				**5.12**	**5.46**	**6.30**	**5.99**	**5.77**
A. Judicial independence								
B. Impartial courts				4.68	4.63	5.10	4.60	4.20
C. Protection of property rights								
D. Military interference in rule of law and politics				6.34	7.34	7.10	6.20	5.70
E. Integrity of the legal system								
F. Legal enforcement of contracts						5.10	5.11	5.11
G. Regulatory restrictions on sale of real property						8.10	8.06	8.06
3. Access to Sound Money	**6.02**	**6.67**	**6.53**	**6.94**	**6.90**	**6.60**	**6.42**	**6.76**
A. Money growth	9.82 (−0.89)	9.73 (1.34)	8.40 (8.00)	9.02 (4.92)	9.41 (2.93)	7.60 (11.90)	8.19 (9.05)	9.03 (4.86)
B. Standard deviation of inflation	7.72 (5.71)	8.44 (3.89)	9.16 (2.10)	9.06 (2.36)	8.42 (3.95)	9.10 (2.22)	9.02 (2.45)	8.74 (3.15)
C. Inflation: most recent year	6.54 (17.31)	8.50 (7.49)	8.58 (7.10)	9.68 (1.59)	9.78 (1.09)	9.50 (2.37)	8.45 (7.73)	9.26 (3.69)
D. Freedom to own foreign currency bank accounts	0.00	0.00	0.00	0.00	0.00	0.00	0.00	0.00
4. Freedom to Trade Internationally	**6.44**	**6.33**	**6.45**	**6.48**	**6.14**	**5.50**	**5.33**	**5.28**
A. Taxes on international trade	6.13	4.73	5.73	6.60	7.27	5.20	5.13	5.11
(i) Revenues from trade taxes (% of trade sector)	6.13 (5.80)	4.73 (7.90)	5.73 (6.40)	6.60 (5.10)	7.03 (4.46)	7.70 (3.40)	7.73 (3.40)	7.73 (3.40)
(ii) Mean tariff rate					7.52 (12.40)	8.00 (10.20)	7.66 (11.70)	7.60 (12.00)
(iii) Standard deviation of tariff rates						0.00 (43.00)	0.00 (40.37)	0.00 (38.04)
B. Regulatory trade barriers						6.70	6.65	6.88
(i) Non-tariff trade barriers								
(ii) Compliance cost of importing and exporting						6.70	6.65	6.88
C. Size of trade sector relative to expected	6.47	5.31	7.12	5.82	5.86	5.50	4.84	4.43
D. Black-market exchange rates	6.40	8.40	9.20	9.80	9.40	10.00	10.00	10.00
E. International capital market controls	5.00	5.00	2.00	2.00	0.00	0.00	0.00	0.00
(i) Foreign ownership / investment restrictions								
(ii) Capital controls	5.00	5.00	2.00	2.00	0.00	0.00	0.00	0.00
5. Regulation of Credit, Labor, and Business	**5.65**	**5.96**	**5.90**	**5.95**	**6.06**	**8.60**	**8.84**	**8.75**
A. Credit market regulations	5.09	5.91	6.00	6.19	6.56	9.20	10.00	10.00
(i) Ownership of banks	2.00	2.00	2.00	2.00	2.00	10.00	10.00	10.00
(ii) Foreign bank competition						10.00	10.00	10.00
(iii) Private sector credit	7.27	7.73	10.00	8.56	7.67	6.80	10.00	10.00
(iv) Interest rate controls / negative real interest rates	6.00	8.00	6.00	8.00	10.00	10.00	10.00	10.00
B. Labor market regulations						9.40	9.22	8.98
(i) Hiring regulations and minimum wage						7.80	8.90	7.77
(ii) Hiring and firing regulations								
(iii) Centralized collective bargaining								
(iv) Hours regulations						10.00	10.00	10.00
(v) Mandated cost of worker dismissal						9.80	7.96	8.15
(vi) Conscription	10.00	10.00	10.00	10.00	10.00	10.00	10.00	10.00
C. Business regulations						7.30	7.30	7.27
(i) Price controls			6.00	6.00	6.00	4.00	4.00	4.00
(ii) Administrative requirements								
(iii) Bureaucracy costs								
(iv) Starting a business						8.30	8.26	8.28
(v) Extra payments / bribes / favoritism								
(vi) Licensing restrictions						8.60	8.63	8.63
(vii) Cost of tax compliance						8.40	8.32	8.17

Finland

Chain-Linked	1980	1985	1990	1995	2000	2005	2008	2009
	Rating (Rank)	Rating (Rank)	Rating (Rank)	Rating (Rank)	Rating (Rank)	Rating (Rank)	Rating (Rank)	Rating (Rank)
Summary Rating (Rank) ➤	**6.95** (14)	**7.15** (12)	**7.40** (16)	**7.32** (20)	**7.51** (16)	**7.72** (12)	**7.56** (15)	**7.58** (10)
Area 1. Size of Government	4.67 (65)	4.41 (75)	4.15 (93)	2.69 (117)	3.00 (119)	4.97 (100)	5.15 (101)	5.18 (93)
Area 2. Legal Structure and Security of Property Rights	8.09 (20)	9.34 (6)	9.89 (1)	9.28 (1)	9.49 (3)	8.95 (4)	8.66 (5)	8.67 (4)
Area 3. Access to Sound Money	7.78 (22)	7.94 (29)	9.27 (17)	9.55 (18)	9.55 (15)	9.58 (12)	9.47 (18)	9.55 (17)
Area 4. Freedom to Trade Internationally	6.89 (25)	6.80 (29)	6.41 (42)	8.21 (12)	8.33 (14)	7.46 (29)	7.35 (36)	7.17 (36)
Area 5. Regulation of Credit, Labor, and Business	7.29 (7)	7.40 (7)	7.37 (8)	6.88 (15)	7.17 (17)	7.66 (23)	7.15 (33)	7.33 (25)

Unadjusted

	1980	1985	1990	1995	2000	2005	2008	2009
Summary Rating (Rank) ➤	**6.35** (20)	**6.54** (20)	**6.73** (25)	**7.33** (20)	**7.51** (16)	**7.75** (13)	**7.57** (19)	**7.59** (11)
	Rating Data	Rating Data	Rating Data	Rating Data	Rating Data	Rating Data	Rating Data	Rating Data
1. Size of Government	**4.67**	**4.41**	**4.15**	**2.69**	**3.00**	**5.00**	**5.15**	**5.18**
A. Government consumption	4.43 (24.93)	3.82 (27.02)	3.33 (28.69)	3.34 (28.66)	3.08 (29.54)	2.90 (30.00)	2.92 (30.07)	2.54 (31.38)
B. Transfers and subsidies	6.24 (14.30)	5.83 (15.80)	5.78 (16.00)	3.92 (22.80)	4.93 (19.11)	4.40 (20.90)	4.70 (19.96)	4.70 (19.96)
C. Government enterprises and investment	7.00 (23.30)	7.00 (24.20)	6.00 (29.30)	2.00 (42.20)	2.00 (42.20)	10.00 (12.50)	10.00 (11.61)	10.00 (14.49)
D. Top marginal tax rate	1.00	1.00	1.50	1.50	2.00	2.50	3.00	3.50
(i) Top marginal income tax rate	1.00 (65-71)	1.00 (64-70)	2.00 (57-63)	2.00 (54-59)	3.00 (51-57)	3.00 (50-56)	4.00 (48-53)	4.00 (48-53)
(ii) Top marginal income and payroll tax rates			1.00 (61-69)	1.00 (60-66)	1.00 (53.5-60.5)	2.00 (54-60)	2.00 (52-59)	3.00 (52-57)
2. Legal Structure and Security of Property Rights	**6.83**	**7.88**	**8.35**	**9.28**	**9.49**	**9.00**	**8.66**	**8.67**
A. Judicial independence				9.82	9.69	8.60	9.13	8.88
B. Impartial courts				9.35	8.85	8.60	7.03	7.51
C. Protection of property rights				7.23	8.92	9.00	9.09	9.02
D. Military interference in rule of law and politics				10.00	10.00	10.00	10.00	10.00
E. Integrity of the legal system				10.00	10.00	10.00	10.00	10.00
F. Legal enforcement of contracts						8.10	7.01	6.83
G. Regulatory restrictions on sale of real property						8.40	8.39	8.42
3. Access to Sound Money	**7.78**	**7.94**	**9.27**	**9.55**	**9.55**	**9.60**	**9.47**	**9.55**
A. Money growth	8.82 (5.92)	8.58 (7.12)	8.62 (6.91)	8.98 (5.08)	9.48 (2.58)	9.00 (5.00)	9.11 (4.43)	8.64 (6.82)
B. Standard deviation of inflation	9.27 (1.82)	9.26 (1.86)	9.63 (0.92)	9.71 (0.72)	9.38 (1.54)	9.50 (1.31)	9.56 (1.09)	9.58 (1.05)
C. Inflation: most recent year	8.05 (9.75)	8.93 (5.33)	8.84 (5.82)	9.52 (2.42)	9.33 (3.37)	9.80 (0.86)	9.19 (4.07)	10.00 (0.00)
D. Freedom to own foreign currency bank accounts	5.00	5.00	10.00	10.00	10.00	10.00	10.00	10.00
4. Freedom to Trade Internationally	**6.79**	**6.70**	**6.12**	**8.20**	**8.33**	**7.50**	**7.35**	**7.17**
A. Taxes on international trade	8.69	9.17	8.01	8.72	9.18	8.40	8.03	8.22
(i) Revenues from trade taxes (% of trade sector)	9.47 (0.80)	9.73 (0.40)	9.60 (0.60)	9.87 (0.20)	9.78 (0.33)	9.60 (0.60)	9.61 (0.59)	9.44 (0.84)
(ii) Mean tariff rate	7.92 (10.40)	8.60 (7.00)	8.46 (7.70)	8.66 (6.70)	9.52 (2.40)	9.50 (2.70)	8.88 (5.60)	8.94 (5.30)
(iii) Standard deviation of tariff rates			5.96 (10.10)	7.64 (5.90)	8.24 (4.40)	6.10 (9.70)	5.61 (10.98)	6.29 (9.28)
B. Regulatory trade barriers				9.30	9.76	8.90	8.56	8.61
(i) Non-tariff trade barriers				9.30	9.69	8.70	8.13	8.22
(ii) Compliance cost of importing and exporting					9.83	9.00	8.99	8.99
C. Size of trade sector relative to expected	5.27	4.16	2.38	4.28	4.66	4.00	4.44	3.50
D. Black-market exchange rates	9.80	10.00	10.00	10.00	10.00	10.00	10.00	10.00
E. International capital market controls	2.00	2.00	2.00	8.68	8.08	6.00	5.70	5.54
(i) Foreign ownership / investment restrictions				9.36	10.00	8.20	8.32	8.01
(ii) Capital controls	2.00	2.00	2.00	8.00	6.15	3.80	3.08	3.08
5. Regulation of Credit, Labor, and Business	**5.69**	**5.77**	**5.75**	**6.94**	**7.17**	**7.80**	**7.23**	**7.38**
A. Credit market regulations	8.63	9.30	9.32	8.43	9.41	9.80	9.75	9.75
(i) Ownership of banks	8.00	8.00	8.00	8.00	10.00	10.00	10.00	10.00
(ii) Foreign bank competition				8.87	8.13	9.00	9.00	9.00
(iii) Private sector credit	9.89	9.91	9.97	6.54	10.00	10.00	10.00	10.00
(iv) Interest rate controls / negative real interest rates	8.00	10.00	10.00	10.00	10.00	10.00	10.00	10.00
B. Labor market regulations	4.14	3.79	3.71	3.49	3.33	4.80	5.06	5.55
(i) Hiring regulations and minimum wage				4.12	4.72	5.60	5.60	3.90
(ii) Hiring and firing regulations			3.86	3.86	3.23	3.80	4.49	4.83
(iii) Centralized collective bargaining	4.49	4.49	4.49	4.49	2.87	3.10	3.71	3.56
(iv) Hours regulations	4.93	3.87	3.52	2.02	2.84	6.00	6.00	8.00
(v) Mandated cost of worker dismissal						7.60	7.59	10.00
(vi) Conscription	3.00	3.00	3.00	3.00	3.00	3.00	3.00	3.00
C. Business regulations				8.89	8.77	8.70	6.88	6.84
(i) Price controls			6.00	9.00	9.00	9.00	5.00	5.00
(ii) Administrative requirements					7.97	6.40	5.45	5.54
(iii) Bureaucracy costs				8.47	8.48	9.90	1.78	1.73
(iv) Starting a business				8.52	8.80	9.50	9.52	9.51
(v) Extra payments / bribes / favoritism				9.57	9.59	9.40	9.34	9.19
(vi) Licensing restrictions						9.80	9.78	9.60
(vii) Cost of tax compliance						7.00	7.28	7.28

France

	1980	1985	1990	1995	2000	2005	2008	2009
Chain-Linked	Rating (Rank)	Rating (Rank)	Rating (Rank)	Rating (Rank)	Rating (Rank)	Rating (Rank)	Rating (Rank)	Rating (Rank)
Summary Rating (Rank) ➤	**6.22** (24)	**6.13** (36)	**7.07** (23)	**6.80** (34)	**7.06** (37)	**6.97** (53)	**7.20** (37)	**7.05** (44)
Area 1. Size of Government	4.22 (76)	3.13 (100)	3.53 (101)	3.22 (111)	2.56 (123)	4.11 (116)	5.43 (95)	4.72 (105)
Area 2. Legal Structure and Security of Property Rights	7.82 (22)	8.30 (18)	8.86 (20)	7.49 (25)	8.09 (21)	7.20 (26)	7.31 (26)	7.45 (23)
Area 3. Access to Sound Money	6.40 (44)	6.69 (50)	9.69 (5)	9.83 (1)	9.59 (11)	9.58 (12)	9.54 (7)	9.66 (4)
Area 4. Freedom to Trade Internationally	6.83 (27)	6.84 (27)	7.46 (19)	7.44 (32)	8.13 (21)	7.37 (32)	7.27 (38)	7.11 (41)
Area 5. Regulation of Credit, Labor, and Business	5.97 (32)	5.92 (37)	5.94 (43)	5.99 (48)	6.91 (21)	6.59 (57)	6.45 (66)	6.33 (79)

Unadjusted								
Summary Rating (Rank) ➤	**5.96** (30)	**5.88** (39)	**6.76** (23)	**6.78** (37)	**7.06** (37)	**7.09** (48)	**7.31** (34)	**7.16** (42)
	Rating Data	Rating Data	Rating Data	Rating Data	Rating Data	Rating Data	Rating Data	Rating Data
1. Size of Government	**4.22**	**3.13**	**3.53**	**3.22**	**2.56**	**4.10**	**5.43**	**4.72**
A. Government consumption	4.84 (23.55)	4.68 (24.07)	4.85 (23.52)	2.85 (30.29)	1.86 (33.69)	3.10 (29.40)	3.28 (28.84)	3.03 (29.68)
B. Transfers and subsidies	3.02 (26.10)	2.83 (26.80)	3.27 (25.20)	2.53 (27.90)	3.40 (24.71)	3.30 (25.00)	3.42 (24.65)	2.84 (26.78)
C. Government enterprises and investment	6.00 (27.40)	4.00 (33.20)	4.00 (35.00)	4.00 (30.00)	4.00 (30.00)	8.00 (16.50)	10.00 (14.94)	8.00 (16.38)
D. Top marginal tax rate	3.00	1.00	2.00	3.50	1.00	2.00	5.00	5.00
(i) Top marginal income tax rate	3.00 (60)	1.00 (65)	3.00 (53)	4.00 (51)	2.00 (54)	3.00 (52)	6.00 (43)	6.00 (43)
(ii) Top marginal income and payroll tax rates			1.00 (61)	3.00 (60)	0.00 (62-65)	1.00 (62-64)	4.00 (54-56)	4.00 (54-56)
2. Legal Structure and Security of Property Rights	**6.83**	**7.25**	**7.73**	**7.49**	**8.09**	**7.20**	**7.31**	**7.45**
A. Judicial independence				6.62	6.35	6.80	6.26	6.32
B. Impartial courts				5.55	8.02	6.80	6.33	6.51
C. Protection of property rights				7.28	9.40	8.50	8.01	8.06
D. Military interference in rule of law and politics				8.03	8.33	8.80	9.17	9.17
E. Integrity of the legal system				10.00	8.33	8.30	8.33	8.33
F. Legal enforcement of contracts						6.90	6.91	6.91
G. Regulatory restrictions on sale of real property						4.30	6.14	6.88
3. Access to Sound Money	**6.40**	**6.69**	**9.69**	**9.83**	**9.59**	**9.60**	**9.54**	**9.66**
A. Money growth	8.19 (9.06)	8.83 (5.85)	9.72 (1.38)	9.89 (0.57)	8.84 (5.82)	8.80 (6.00)	8.91 (5.46)	8.99 (5.05)
B. Standard deviation of inflation	9.69 (0.77)	9.08 (2.29)	9.64 (0.89)	9.74 (0.65)	9.85 (0.38)	9.90 (0.30)	9.83 (0.42)	9.67 (0.83)
C. Inflation: most recent year	7.72 (11.38)	8.85 (5.76)	9.38 (3.09)	9.69 (1.57)	9.66 (1.69)	9.60 (1.81)	9.44 (2.82)	9.98 (0.08)
D. Freedom to own foreign currency bank accounts	0.00	0.00	10.00	10.00	10.00	10.00	10.00	10.00
4. Freedom to Trade Internationally	**6.64**	**6.66**	**7.12**	**7.37**	**8.13**	**7.40**	**7.27**	**7.11**
A. Taxes on international trade	8.95	9.12	8.46	8.70	9.18	8.40	8.03	8.22
(i) Revenues from trade taxes (% of trade sector)	9.67 (0.50)	9.73 (0.40)	9.73 (0.40)	9.80 (0.30)	9.78 (0.33)	9.60 (0.60)	9.61 (0.59)	9.44 (0.84)
(ii) Mean tariff rate	8.24 (8.80)	8.50 (7.50)	8.52 (7.40)	8.66 (6.70)	9.52 (2.40)	9.50 (2.70)	8.88 (5.60)	8.94 (5.30)
(iii) Standard deviation of tariff rates			7.12 (7.20)	7.64 (5.90)	8.24 (4.40)	6.10 (9.70)	5.61 (10.98)	6.29 (9.28)
B. Regulatory trade barriers				7.70	8.79	7.90	7.93	7.83
(i) Non-tariff trade barriers				7.70	8.42	7.40	7.13	6.94
(ii) Compliance cost of importing and exporting					9.17	8.50	8.72	8.72
C. Size of trade sector relative to expected	4.68	4.78	3.98	3.66	4.66	3.90	3.83	2.87
D. Black-market exchange rates	9.40	9.20	10.00	10.00	10.00	10.00	10.00	10.00
E. International capital market controls	2.00	2.00	5.00	6.81	8.01	6.60	6.57	6.61
(i) Foreign ownership / investment restrictions				8.62	9.09	7.00	6.99	7.07
(ii) Capital controls	2.00	2.00	5.00	5.00	6.92	6.20	6.15	6.15
5. Regulation of Credit, Labor, and Business	**5.70**	**5.65**	**5.71**	**5.96**	**6.91**	**7.20**	**7.01**	**6.86**
A. Credit market regulations	8.91	8.82	9.01	8.40	8.42	9.10	9.22	8.39
(i) Ownership of banks	10.00	10.00	10.00	10.00	10.00	10.00	10.00	10.00
(ii) Foreign bank competition				6.82	6.67	8.00	8.00	8.00
(iii) Private sector credit	8.73	8.46	9.03	8.37	9.23	8.50	8.86	5.57
(iv) Interest rate controls / negative real interest rates	8.00	8.00	8.00	10.00	10.00	10.00	10.00	10.00
B. Labor market regulations	3.93	3.81	3.83	3.35	4.98	5.50	5.62	5.92
(i) Hiring regulations and minimum wage				2.55	4.55	3.30	3.30	3.33
(ii) Hiring and firing regulations			4.16	4.16	1.67	2.40	3.03	3.18
(iii) Centralized collective bargaining	4.49	4.49	4.49	4.49	5.53	6.40	6.33	7.15
(iv) Hours regulations	4.31	3.96	3.69	2.58	3.17	4.00	4.00	4.00
(v) Mandated cost of worker dismissal						7.00	7.03	7.86
(vi) Conscription	3.00	3.00	3.00	3.00	10.00	10.00	10.00	10.00
C. Business regulations				6.12	7.34	6.80	6.19	6.27
(i) Price controls			6.00	8.00	8.00	4.00	5.00	5.00
(ii) Administrative requirements					7.73	2.70	2.22	2.69
(iii) Bureaucracy costs				6.30	8.08	5.90	1.81	1.76
(iv) Starting a business				3.43	5.15	9.80	9.77	9.77
(v) Extra payments / bribes / favoritism				6.76	7.71	8.30	7.34	7.51
(vi) Licensing restrictions						8.60	8.64	8.64
(vii) Cost of tax compliance						8.50	8.52	8.52

Gabon

Chain-Linked	1980 Rating (Rank)	1985 Rating (Rank)	1990 Rating (Rank)	1995 Rating (Rank)	2000 Rating (Rank)	2005 Rating (Rank)	2008 Rating (Rank)	2009 Rating (Rank)
Summary Rating (Rank) ➤	4.55 (80)	5.09 (69)	5.33 (69)	5.26 (90)	5.75 (96)	5.49 (109)	5.64 (106)	5.66 (107)
Area 1. Size of Government	5.47 (40)	4.63 (66)	6.08 (43)	5.54 (79)	7.61 (19)	5.77 (87)	6.18 (72)	6.02 (69)
Area 2. Legal Structure and Security of Property Rights	3.94 (56)	4.46 (67)	4.96 (60)	5.09 (79)	4.29 (95)	4.35 (95)	4.31 (100)	4.35 (99)
Area 3. Access to Sound Money	4.09 (101)	6.20 (79)	5.43 (88)	5.44 (83)	5.81 (109)	5.85 (113)	6.08 (111)	5.68 (117)
Area 4. Freedom to Trade Internationally					5.61 (107)	5.22 (110)	5.28 (107)	5.43 (105)
Area 5. Regulation of Credit, Labor, and Business	4.53 (76)	4.83 (69)	5.12 (67)	5.11 (78)	5.45 (90)	6.25 (69)	6.32 (77)	6.80 (50)

Unadjusted	1980	1985	1990	1995	2000	2005	2008	2009
Summary Rating (Rank) ➤	4.75 (78)	5.66 (50)	5.48 (61)	5.41 (82)	5.75 (96)	5.68 (122)	5.83 (119)	5.82 (122)
	Rating Data	Rating Data	Rating Data	Rating Data	Rating Data	Rating Data	Rating Data	Rating Data
1. Size of Government	4.94	5.93	6.08	5.54	7.61	5.80	6.18	6.02
A. Government consumption	1.88 (33.60)	0.38 (38.72)	5.52 (21.23)	4.33 (25.26)	7.65 (14.00)	4.30 (25.50)	5.90 (19.94)	5.28 (22.06)
B. Transfers and subsidies		9.40 (2.70)	9.81 (1.20)	9.81 (1.20)	9.81 (1.20)	9.80 (1.20)	9.81 (1.20)	9.81 (1.20)
C. Government enterprises and investment	8.00 (19.90)	8.00 (17.30)	8.00 (18.00)	7.00 (24.20)	10.00 (13.30)	8.00 (19.90)	8.00 (18.81)	8.00 (18.34)
D. Top marginal tax rate			1.00	1.00	3.00	1.00	1.00	1.00
(i) Top marginal income tax rate			1.00 (60)	1.00 (60)	3.00 (50)	1.00 (56)	1.00 (56)	1.00 (56)
(ii) Top marginal income and payroll tax rates						1.00 (56)	1.00 (56)	1.00 (56)
2. Legal Structure and Security of Property Rights	3.94	4.46	4.96	5.09	4.29	4.40	4.31	4.35
A. Judicial independence								
B. Impartial courts				4.63	4.78	4.70	4.50	4.70
C. Protection of property rights								
D. Military interference in rule of law and politics				4.82	3.33	3.30	3.33	3.33
E. Integrity of the legal system				6.96	5.00	5.00	5.00	5.00
F. Legal enforcement of contracts						2.90	2.92	2.92
G. Regulatory restrictions on sale of real property						5.80	5.81	5.81
3. Access to Sound Money	4.09	6.20	5.43	5.44	5.81	5.80	6.08	5.68
A. Money growth	8.28 (−8.59)	7.68 (11.59)	9.61 (1.96)	9.97 (0.13)	9.75 (1.27)	6.90 (15.40)	7.49 (12.56)	8.85 (5.76)
B. Standard deviation of inflation	5.43 (11.42)	7.39 (6.53)	5.17 (12.08)	1.88 (20.31)	3.60 (16.00)	6.50 (8.83)	7.89 (5.28)	4.27 (14.33)
C. Inflation: most recent year	2.64 (36.78)	9.74 (−1.28)	6.93 (15.36)	9.89 (−0.54)	9.90 (0.50)	10.00 (−0.01)	8.95 (5.26)	9.62 (1.89)
D. Freedom to own foreign currency bank accounts	0.00	0.00	0.00	0.00	0.00	0.00	0.00	0.00
4. Freedom to Trade Internationally	5.62	6.23	5.83	5.87	5.61	5.60	5.68	5.85
A. Taxes on international trade	3.24	4.91	6.80	5.80	6.00	6.20	6.30	6.30
(i) Revenues from trade taxes (% of trade sector)	5.13 (7.30)	5.73 (6.40)	6.80 (4.80)	5.80 (6.30)				
(ii) Mean tariff rate	1.34 (43.30)	4.08 (29.60)			5.92 (20.40)	6.00 (19.90)	6.44 (17.80)	6.44 (17.80)
(iii) Standard deviation of tariff rates					6.08 (9.80)	6.30 (9.20)	6.16 (9.61)	6.16 (9.61)
B. Regulatory trade barriers						7.20	7.11	7.11
(i) Non-tariff trade barriers								
(ii) Compliance cost of importing and exporting						7.20	7.11	7.11
C. Size of trade sector relative to expected	7.06	8.24	4.95	5.53	3.83	4.70	5.01	4.28
D. Black-market exchange rates	9.60	9.80	9.20	9.80	10.00	10.00	10.00	10.00
E. International capital market controls	0.00	0.00	0.00	0.00	0.00	0.00	0.00	1.54
(i) Foreign ownership / investment restrictions								
(ii) Capital controls	0.00	0.00	0.00	0.00	0.00	0.00	0.00	1.54
5. Regulation of Credit, Labor, and Business	5.16	5.49	5.12	5.11	5.45	6.80	6.90	7.21
A. Credit market regulations	3.00	4.00	5.43	4.73	5.85	7.40	7.56	7.52
(i) Ownership of banks	0.00	0.00	2.00	5.00	5.00	5.00	5.00	5.00
(ii) Foreign bank competition								
(iii) Private sector credit			6.30	5.20	7.56	8.10	8.67	8.57
(iv) Interest rate controls / negative real interest rates	6.00	8.00	8.00	4.00	5.00	9.00	9.00	9.00
B. Labor market regulations						7.10	7.08	8.68
(i) Hiring regulations and minimum wage						8.30	8.30	8.33
(ii) Hiring and firing regulations								
(iii) Centralized collective bargaining								
(iv) Hours regulations						4.00	4.00	8.00
(v) Mandated cost of worker dismissal						6.00	6.01	8.39
(vi) Conscription	10.00	10.00	10.00	10.00	10.00	10.00	10.00	10.00
C. Business regulations						6.00	6.06	5.44
(i) Price controls			0.00	2.00	2.00	2.00	2.00	2.00
(ii) Administrative requirements								
(iii) Bureaucracy costs								
(iv) Starting a business						7.80	7.87	7.81
(v) Extra payments / bribes / favoritism								
(vi) Licensing restrictions						7.40	7.43	7.42
(vii) Cost of tax compliance						7.00	6.95	4.53

Georgia

	1980	1985	1990	1995	2000	2005	2008	2009
Chain-Linked						Rating (Rank)	Rating (Rank)	Rating (Rank)
Summary Rating (Rank) ➤								
Area 1. Size of Government								
Area 2. Legal Structure and Security of Property Rights								
Area 3. Access to Sound Money								
Area 4. Freedom to Trade Internationally								
Area 5. Regulation of Credit, Labor, and Business								

	1980	1985	1990	1995	2000	2005	2008	2009
Unadjusted								
Summary Rating (Rank) ➤						**7.15** (46)	**7.51** (23)	**7.36** (27)
					Rating *Data*	Rating *Data*	Rating *Data*	Rating *Data*
1. Size of Government					**4.70**	**7.20**	**8.05**	**7.81**
A. Government consumption					9.40 *(8.03)*	5.70 *(20.60)*	7.53 *(14.40)*	5.07 *(22.76)*
B. Transfers and subsidies						8.00 *(7.70)*	7.68 *(9.03)*	8.17 *(7.20)*
C. Government enterprises and investment					0.00	6.00	8.00	8.00
D. Top marginal tax rate						9.00	9.00	10.00
(i) Top marginal income tax rate						10.00 *(12)*	9.00 *(25)*	10.00 *(20)*
(ii) Top marginal income and payroll tax rates						8.00 *(27)*	9.00 *(25)*	10.00 *(20)*
2. Legal Structure and Security of Property Rights						**4.80**	**5.07**	**5.13**
A. Judicial independence						1.90	2.79	3.22
B. Impartial courts						2.40	3.42	3.68
C. Protection of property rights						4.20	4.08	3.74
D. Military interference in rule of law and politics						4.20	3.70	3.70
E. Integrity of the legal system								
F. Legal enforcement of contracts						6.50	6.50	6.50
G. Regulatory restrictions on sale of real property						9.70	9.94	9.93
3. Access to Sound Money						**8.60**	**9.08**	**9.24**
A. Money growth					6.24 *(18.80)*	7.00 *(15.00)*	8.66 *(6.68)*	9.30 *(3.51)*
B. Standard deviation of inflation						9.20 *(2.02)*	9.64 *(0.90)*	7.99 *(5.01)*
C. Inflation: most recent year						8.40 *(8.23)*	8.00 *(9.98)*	9.65 *(1.74)*
D. Freedom to own foreign currency bank accounts						10.00	10.00	10.00
4. Freedom to Trade Internationally						**7.30**	**7.73**	**7.41**
A. Taxes on international trade						8.50	8.88	9.10
(i) Revenues from trade taxes (% of trade sector)					9.23 *(1.16)*	9.20 *(1.30)*	9.79 *(0.31)*	9.83 *(0.25)*
(ii) Mean tariff rate						8.60 *(7.00)*	9.72 *(1.40)*	9.74 *(1.30)*
(iii) Standard deviation of tariff rates						7.80 *(5.60)*	7.12 *(7.20)*	7.74 *(5.66)*
B. Regulatory trade barriers						6.80	7.96	7.62
(i) Non-tariff trade barriers						5.20	7.41	6.73
(ii) Compliance cost of importing and exporting						8.30	8.51	8.51
C. Size of trade sector relative to expected						4.30	4.01	3.37
D. Black-market exchange rates						10.00	10.00	10.00
E. International capital market controls						7.10	7.82	6.97
(i) Foreign ownership / investment restrictions						5.80	7.17	6.25
(ii) Capital controls						8.30	8.46	7.69
5. Regulation of Credit, Labor, and Business						**7.80**	**7.62**	**7.23**
A. Credit market regulations						9.30	7.76	6.75
(i) Ownership of banks						10.00	10.00	10.00
(ii) Foreign bank competition						8.00	8.00	8.00
(iii) Private sector credit					9.11	10.00	4.02	0.00
(iv) Interest rate controls / negative real interest rates					10.00	9.00	9.00	9.00
B. Labor market regulations						7.60	7.64	7.54
(i) Hiring regulations and minimum wage						10.00	10.00	10.00
(ii) Hiring and firing regulations						6.80	7.39	6.95
(iii) Centralized collective bargaining						8.30	7.84	7.70
(iv) Hours regulations						8.00	8.00	8.00
(v) Mandated cost of worker dismissal						9.60	9.63	9.60
(vi) Conscription						3.00	3.00	3.00
C. Business regulations						6.40	7.46	7.40
(i) Price controls						8.00	8.00	8.00
(ii) Administrative requirements						4.70	6.39	6.08
(iii) Bureaucracy costs						3.20	6.83	6.65
(iv) Starting a business						9.40	9.87	9.85
(v) Extra payments / bribes / favoritism						5.00	6.21	6.28
(vi) Licensing restrictions						8.80	9.28	9.28
(vii) Cost of tax compliance						5.70	5.66	5.66

Germany

Chain-Linked

	1980	1985	1990	1995	2000	2005	2008	2009
	Rating (Rank)	Rating (Rank)	Rating (Rank)	Rating (Rank)	Rating (Rank)	Rating (Rank)	Rating (Rank)	Rating (Rank)
Summary Rating (Rank) ➤	**7.37** (9)	**7.40** (9)	**7.80** (10)	**7.52** (13)	**7.52** (15)	**7.64** (18)	**7.47** (22)	**7.45** (19)
Area 1. Size of Government	4.34 (74)	4.26 (79)	5.15 (70)	4.36 (99)	3.96 (109)	5.74 (88)	5.64 (87)	5.41 (89)
Area 2. Legal Structure and Security of Property Rights	9.10 (10)	8.85 (14)	9.87 (4)	9.13 (5)	9.14 (10)	8.65 (7)	8.17 (14)	8.16 (14)
Area 3. Access to Sound Money	9.43 (3)	9.47 (6)	9.67 (8)	9.76 (3)	9.55 (15)	9.53 (20)	9.51 (13)	9.53 (20)
Area 4. Freedom to Trade Internationally	7.87 (10)	8.26 (7)	8.18 (9)	8.30 (9)	8.68 (8)	7.77 (18)	7.67 (22)	7.50 (23)
Area 5. Regulation of Credit, Labor, and Business	6.17 (27)	6.17 (29)	6.19 (35)	6.03 (46)	6.28 (49)	6.51 (62)	6.34 (72)	6.66 (57)

Unadjusted

	1980	1985	1990	1995	2000	2005	2008	2009
Summary Rating (Rank) ➤	**6.93** (11)	**6.96** (13)	**7.32** (11)	**7.49** (13)	**7.52** (15)	**7.62** (18)	**7.45** (25)	**7.45** (21)
	Rating Data	Rating Data	Rating Data	Rating Data	Rating Data	Rating Data	Rating Data	Rating Data
1. Size of Government	**4.34**	**4.26**	**5.15**	**4.36**	**3.96**	**5.70**	**5.64**	**5.41**
A. Government consumption	4.03 (26.30)	4.09 (26.10)	4.35 (25.20)	4.19 (25.75)	4.55 (24.52)	4.70 (24.10)	4.61 (24.33)	4.39 (25.07)
B. Transfers and subsidies	5.34 (17.60)	4.96 (19.00)	5.26 (17.90)	4.25 (21.60)	2.29 (28.81)	2.30 (28.80)	2.95 (26.39)	2.26 (28.89)
C. Government enterprises and investment	6.00 (25.70)	7.00 (24.40)	7.00 (24.00)	6.00 (25.50)	6.00 (25.50)	10.00 (7.80)	10.00 (7.79)	10.00 (9.30)
D. Top marginal tax rate	2.00	1.00	4.00	3.00	3.00	6.00	5.00	5.00
(i) Top marginal income tax rate	2.00 (65)	1.00 (65)	4.00 (53)	3.00 (57)	3.00 (56)	6.00 (44)	5.00 (47)	5.00 (47)
(ii) Top marginal income and payroll tax rates			4.00 (53)	3.00 (57)	3.00 (56)	6.00 (44)	5.00 (47)	5.00 (47)
2. Legal Structure and Security of Property Rights	**7.70**	**7.48**	**8.35**	**9.13**	**9.14**	**8.70**	**8.17**	**8.16**
A. Judicial independence				9.27	9.35	9.20	9.01	8.94
B. Impartial courts				8.60	9.19	9.00	6.91	7.12
C. Protection of property rights				7.99	8.84	9.60	8.78	8.54
D. Military interference in rule of law and politics				9.81	10.00	10.00	10.00	10.00
E. Integrity of the legal system				10.00	8.33	8.30	8.33	8.33
F. Legal enforcement of contracts						6.60	6.62	6.62
G. Regulatory restrictions on sale of real property						7.90	7.53	7.57
3. Access to Sound Money	**9.43**	**9.47**	**9.67**	**9.76**	**9.55**	**9.50**	**9.51**	**9.53**
A. Money growth	9.18 (4.10)	8.80 (6.01)	9.68 (1.60)	9.90 (0.48)	8.77 (6.13)	8.60 (6.80)	8.85 (5.77)	8.46 (7.71)
B. Standard deviation of inflation	9.64 (0.89)	9.52 (1.20)	9.52 (1.20)	9.54 (1.16)	9.71 (0.72)	9.90 (0.31)	9.74 (0.65)	9.73 (0.66)
C. Inflation: most recent year	8.90 (5.50)	9.56 (2.18)	9.46 (2.70)	9.58 (2.10)	9.71 (1.47)	9.60 (1.95)	9.47 (2.63)	9.94 (0.31)
D. Freedom to own foreign currency bank accounts	10.00	10.00	10.00	10.00	10.00	10.00	10.00	10.00
4. Freedom to Trade Internationally	**7.96**	**8.35**	**8.15**	**8.21**	**8.68**	**7.80**	**7.67**	**7.50**
A. Taxes on international trade	8.95	9.08	8.44	8.66	9.18	8.40	8.03	8.22
(i) Revenues from trade taxes (% of trade sector)	9.67 (0.50)	9.67 (0.50)	9.67 (0.50)	9.67 (0.50)	9.78 (0.33)	9.60 (0.60)	9.61 (0.59)	9.44 (0.84)
(ii) Mean tariff rate	8.24 (8.80)	8.50 (7.50)	8.52 (7.40)	8.66 (6.70)	9.52 (2.40)	9.50 (2.70)	8.88 (5.60)	8.94 (5.30)
(iii) Standard deviation of tariff rates			7.12 (7.20)	7.64 (5.90)	8.24 (4.40)	6.10 (9.70)	5.61 (10.98)	6.29 (9.28)
B. Regulatory trade barriers				8.28	8.89	8.40	7.99	7.91
(i) Non-tariff trade barriers				8.28	8.45	7.60	6.84	6.68
(ii) Compliance cost of importing and exporting					9.33	9.10	9.14	9.14
C. Size of trade sector relative to expected	4.70	4.54	4.17	4.52	5.86	6.00	6.64	5.75
D. Black-market exchange rates	10.00	10.00	10.00	10.00	10.00	10.00	10.00	10.00
E. International capital market controls	8.00	10.00	10.00	9.61	9.48	6.00	5.70	5.62
(i) Foreign ownership/investment restrictions				9.23	9.72	8.20	7.55	7.39
(ii) Capital controls	8.00	10.00	10.00	10.00	9.23	3.80	3.85	3.85
5. Regulation of Credit, Labor, and Business	**5.22**	**5.22**	**5.27**	**6.00**	**6.28**	**6.40**	**6.25**	**6.62**
A. Credit market regulations	7.61	7.58	7.65	7.42	8.15	8.00	8.22	7.99
(i) Ownership of banks	5.00	5.00	5.00	5.00	5.00	5.00	5.00	5.00
(ii) Foreign bank competition				7.77	7.17	8.00	8.00	8.00
(iii) Private sector credit	7.83	7.74	7.94	5.93	10.00	9.00	9.86	8.98
(iv) Interest rate controls/negative real interest rates	10.00	10.00	10.00	10.00	10.00	10.00	10.00	10.00
B. Labor market regulations	3.29	3.32	3.48	3.56	2.85	3.90	3.94	5.28
(i) Hiring regulations and minimum wage				3.38	4.63	6.70	6.70	6.67
(ii) Hiring and firing regulations			3.94	3.94	1.82	2.40	2.48	2.86
(iii) Centralized collective bargaining	4.49	4.49	4.49	4.49	2.32	3.20	3.13	3.20
(iv) Hours regulations	4.40	4.49	4.49	2.97	2.51	4.70	4.70	8.00
(v) Mandated cost of worker dismissal						3.60	3.60	5.98
(vi) Conscription	1.00	1.00	1.00	3.00	3.00	3.00	3.00	5.00
C. Business regulations				7.03	7.83	7.30	6.61	6.58
(i) Price controls			9.00	9.00	8.00	7.00	7.00	7.00
(ii) Administrative requirements					8.18	3.40	3.38	3.38
(iii) Bureaucracy costs				6.47	8.53	5.80	1.10	1.18
(iv) Starting a business				4.97	6.40	9.00	9.37	9.47
(v) Extra payments/bribes/favoritism				7.68	8.04	9.10	8.43	8.26
(vi) Licensing restrictions						9.20	9.18	9.18
(vii) Cost of tax compliance						7.80	7.80	7.59

Ghana

	1980	1985	1990	1995	2000	2005	2008	2009
Chain-Linked	Rating (Rank)	Rating (Rank)	Rating (Rank)	Rating (Rank)	Rating (Rank)	Rating (Rank)	Rating (Rank)	Rating (Rank)
Summary Rating (Rank) ➤	**3.27** (101)	**3.41** (105)	**5.04** (85)	**5.43** (82)	**5.86** (90)	**6.73** (68)	**7.26** (35)	**7.15** (37)
Area 1. Size of Government	5.70 (34)	5.40 (43)	4.82 (80)	5.61 (78)	6.09 (66)	6.49 (66)	6.58 (55)	6.71 (45)
Area 2. Legal Structure and Security of Property Rights	2.76 (73)	2.69 (98)	5.79 (47)	5.60 (56)	4.45 (88)	5.70 (63)	6.53 (39)	6.63 (32)
Area 3. Access to Sound Money	1.60 (109)	2.38 (107)	4.58 (95)	4.13 (100)	5.82 (108)	7.38 (82)	8.39 (56)	8.24 (67)
Area 4. Freedom to Trade Internationally	2.08 (93)	2.08 (95)	5.04 (69)	5.80 (89)	7.23 (48)	6.92 (55)	7.98 (12)	7.21 (33)
Area 5. Regulation of Credit, Labor, and Business	4.14 (88)	4.40 (83)	4.91 (77)	5.99 (48)	5.73 (74)	7.22 (34)	6.94 (43)	7.11 (36)

Unadjusted

	1980	1985	1990	1995	2000	2005	2008	2009
Summary Rating (Rank) ➤	**3.22** (103)	**3.44** (106)	**4.97** (85)	**5.37** (84)	**5.86** (90)	**6.46** (83)	**6.91** (64)	**6.81** (70)
	Rating Data	Rating Data	Rating Data	Rating Data	Rating Data	Rating Data	Rating Data	Rating Data
1. Size of Government	**5.70**	**5.40**	**4.82**	**5.61**	**6.09**	**6.50**	**6.58**	**6.71**
A. Government consumption	8.31 (11.74)	8.80 (10.07)	8.87 (9.85)	7.72 (13.77)	7.12 (15.80)	7.10 (15.90)	8.34 (11.65)	8.50 (11.09)
B. Transfers and subsidies	9.48 (2.40)	9.78 (1.30)	9.43 (2.60)	9.24 (3.30)	9.24 (3.30)	9.90 (1.00)	8.98 (4.24)	9.34 (2.91)
C. Government enterprises and investment	4.00 (35.40)	2.00 (43.60)	0.00 (51.90)	0.00 (66.50)	2.00 (45.00)	2.00 (40.10)	2.00 (43.59)	2.00 (40.91)
D. Top marginal tax rate	1.00	1.00	1.00	5.50	6.00	7.00	7.00	7.00
(i) Top marginal income tax rate	1.00 (60)	1.00 (60)	2.00 (55)	7.00 (35)	8.00 (30)	9.00 (25)	9.00 (25)	9.00 (25)
(ii) Top marginal income and payroll tax rates			0.00 (62)	4.00 (45)	4.00 (41)	5.00 (37)	5.00 (37)	5.00 (37)
2. Legal Structure and Security of Property Rights	**2.76**	**2.69**	**5.79**	**5.60**	**4.45**	**4.90**	**5.41**	**5.49**
A. Judicial independence							4.61	4.65
B. Impartial courts				5.54	5.42	5.20	4.25	4.85
C. Protection of property rights							5.48	5.34
D. Military interference in rule of law and politics				6.04	5.00	4.40	5.00	5.00
E. Integrity of the legal system				6.96	3.33	3.60	4.17	4.17
F. Legal enforcement of contracts						4.90	5.40	5.40
G. Regulatory restrictions on sale of real property						6.20	9.00	9.03
3. Access to Sound Money	**1.60**	**2.38**	**4.58**	**4.13**	**5.82**	**7.40**	**8.39**	**8.24**
A. Money growth	3.23 (33.84)	3.64 (31.78)	4.46 (27.69)	4.51 (27.44)	7.46 (12.72)	6.10 (19.70)	7.26 (13.68)	7.26 (13.68)
B. Standard deviation of inflation	3.17 (17.07)	0.00 (38.34)	8.00 (4.99)	5.65 (10.88)	5.85 (10.37)	6.50 (8.83)	9.60 (1.01)	9.56 (1.11)
C. Inflation: most recent year	0.00 (51.13)	5.87 (20.65)	5.87 (20.66)	1.37 (43.17)	4.96 (25.19)	7.00 (15.12)	6.70 (16.52)	6.15 (19.25)
D. Freedom to own foreign currency bank accounts	0.00	0.00	0.00	5.00	5.00	10.00	10.00	10.00
4. Freedom to Trade Internationally	**1.66**	**2.06**	**4.99**	**5.80**	**7.23**	**6.20**	**7.60**	**6.86**
A. Taxes on international trade	0.00	2.00	4.38	6.09	6.54	5.50	6.92	7.27
(i) Revenues from trade taxes (% of trade sector)	0.00 (17.30)	0.00 (21.70)	2.27 (11.60)	4.60 (8.10)	6.93 (4.60)	6.90 (4.70)	6.21 (5.69)	7.28 (4.08)
(ii) Mean tariff rate		4.00 (30.00)	6.50 (17.50)	7.00 (15.00)	6.96 (15.20)	7.40 (13.20)	7.40 (13.00)	7.40 (13.00)
(iii) Standard deviation of tariff rates				6.68 (8.30)	5.72 (10.70)	2.20 (19.40)	7.14 (7.15)	7.14 (7.15)
B. Regulatory trade barriers						5.80	6.78	6.67
(i) Non-tariff trade barriers							6.80	6.58
(ii) Compliance cost of importing and exporting						5.80	6.76	6.76
C. Size of trade sector relative to expected	0.00	0.00	3.75	5.09	9.90	7.50	8.80	5.37
D. Black-market exchange rates	0.00	0.00	8.60	9.60	10.00	10.00	10.00	10.00
E. International capital market controls	0.00	0.00	0.00	0.00	1.54	2.30	5.50	5.00
(i) Foreign ownership / investment restrictions							6.38	6.15
(ii) Capital controls	0.00	0.00	0.00	0.00	1.54	2.30	4.62	3.85
5. Regulation of Credit, Labor, and Business	**4.40**	**4.67**	**4.67**	**5.69**	**5.73**	**7.30**	**6.57**	**6.72**
A. Credit market regulations	1.76	2.48	3.93	6.00	4.93	8.60	7.69	7.85
(i) Ownership of banks	2.00	2.00	2.00	5.00	5.00	8.00	8.00	8.00
(ii) Foreign bank competition						7.00	7.00	7.00
(iii) Private sector credit	3.29	5.45	7.79	8.99	4.85	9.30	5.74	6.39
(iv) Interest rate controls / negative real interest rates	0.00	0.00	2.00	4.00		10.00	10.00	10.00
B. Labor market regulations						7.00	6.15	6.23
(i) Hiring regulations and minimum wage						10.00	8.90	8.90
(ii) Hiring and firing regulations							4.66	5.19
(iii) Centralized collective bargaining							5.36	5.28
(iv) Hours regulations						8.00	8.00	8.00
(v) Mandated cost of worker dismissal						0.00	0.00	0.00
(vi) Conscription	10.00	10.00	10.00	10.00	10.00	10.00	10.00	10.00
C. Business regulations						6.50	5.88	6.09
(i) Price controls			0.00	4.00	6.00	6.00	6.00	6.00
(ii) Administrative requirements							3.54	4.23
(iii) Bureaucracy costs							6.20	5.89
(iv) Starting a business						6.80	8.62	9.37
(v) Extra payments / bribes / favoritism							3.97	4.17
(vi) Licensing restrictions						6.40	5.34	5.49
(vii) Cost of tax compliance						6.60	7.49	7.49

Greece

Chain-Linked	1980 Rating (Rank)	1985 Rating (Rank)	1990 Rating (Rank)	1995 Rating (Rank)	2000 Rating (Rank)	2005 Rating (Rank)	2008 Rating (Rank)	2009 Rating (Rank)
Summary Rating (Rank) ➤	**5.97** (32)	**5.38** (54)	**6.04** (43)	**6.18** (56)	**6.66** (48)	**7.00** (50)	**6.82** (63)	**6.53** (75)
Area 1. Size of Government	5.76 (31)	3.74 (92)	4.81 (81)	5.23 (86)	4.95 (92)	6.77 (52)	6.20 (70)	5.95 (72)
Area 2. Legal Structure and Security of Property Rights	6.24 (35)	6.30 (34)	7.59 (27)	6.69 (35)	5.70 (63)	6.55 (42)	6.14 (50)	5.62 (66)
Area 3. Access to Sound Money	7.12 (29)	6.96 (38)	6.89 (53)	7.34 (48)	9.32 (28)	9.56 (16)	9.60 (5)	9.63 (6)
Area 4. Freedom to Trade Internationally	6.11 (39)	5.38 (55)	6.13 (47)	6.69 (59)	7.87 (29)	6.34 (80)	6.36 (82)	6.14 (84)
Area 5. Regulation of Credit, Labor, and Business	4.59 (71)	4.56 (78)	4.87 (80)	4.96 (86)	5.45 (90)	5.78 (99)	5.79 (99)	5.31 (112)

Unadjusted	1980	1985	1990	1995	2000	2005	2008	2009
Summary Rating (Rank) ➤	**5.82** (40)	**5.24** (66)	**5.87** (47)	**6.13** (61)	**6.66** (48)	**7.00** (56)	**6.84** (73)	**6.55** (81)
	Rating Data	Rating Data	Rating Data	Rating Data	Rating Data	Rating Data	Rating Data	Rating Data
1. Size of Government	**5.76**	**3.74**	**4.81**	**5.23**	**4.95**	**6.80**	**6.20**	**5.95**
A. Government consumption	7.44 (14.69)	6.63 (17.46)	6.69 (17.25)	6.95 (16.38)	6.57 (17.67)	6.70 (17.20)	6.14 (19.12)	5.68 (20.67)
B. Transfers and subsidies	8.59 (5.69)	5.31 (17.70)	4.55 (20.50)	4.96 (19.00)	5.23 (18.00)	5.40 (17.60)	4.66 (20.11)	4.12 (22.09)
C. Government enterprises and investment	4.00 (32.00)	2.00 (41.00)	4.00 (37.50)	4.00 (35.80)	4.00 (35.80)	10.00 (13.60)	8.00 (18.85)	8.00 (17.71)
D. Top marginal tax rate	3.00	1.00	4.00	5.00	4.00	5.00	6.00	6.00
(i) Top marginal income tax rate	3.00 (60)	1.00 (63)	4.00 (50)	5.00 (45)	5.00 (42)	5.00 (40)	6.00 (40)	6.00 (40)
(ii) Top marginal income and payroll tax rates			4.00 (50)	5.00 (45)	3.00 (50)	5.00 (40)	6.00 (40)	6.00 (40)
2. Legal Structure and Security of Property Rights	**5.57**	**5.61**	**6.76**	**6.69**	**5.70**	**6.60**	**6.14**	**5.62**
A. Judicial independence				5.45	6.35	5.60	4.47	4.24
B. Impartial courts				5.70	5.68	5.40	3.67	3.57
C. Protection of property rights				5.44	4.83	7.20	6.63	6.19
D. Military interference in rule of law and politics				6.86	6.67	7.60	8.33	8.33
E. Integrity of the legal system				10.00	5.00	7.50	7.50	7.50
F. Legal enforcement of contracts						4.10	4.13	4.13
G. Regulatory restrictions on sale of real property						8.30	8.27	5.41
3. Access to Sound Money	**7.12**	**6.96**	**6.89**	**7.34**	**9.32**	**9.60**	**9.60**	**9.63**
A. Money growth	7.94 (10.30)	7.39 (13.06)	7.05 (14.74)	7.67 (11.66)	8.70 (6.52)	9.10 (4.50)	9.31 (3.43)	9.11 (4.46)
B. Standard deviation of inflation	9.06 (2.35)	9.00 (2.51)	9.05 (2.37)	8.47 (3.82)	9.21 (1.97)	9.90 (0.37)	9.91 (0.22)	9.64 (0.90)
C. Inflation: most recent year	6.46 (17.69)	6.47 (17.67)	6.47 (17.67)	8.22 (8.88)	9.37 (3.17)	9.30 (3.56)	9.17 (4.15)	9.76 (1.21)
D. Freedom to own foreign currency bank accounts	5.00	5.00	5.00	5.00	10.00	10.00	10.00	10.00
4. Freedom to Trade Internationally	**6.20**	**5.45**	**6.09**	**6.56**	**7.87**	**6.30**	**6.36**	**6.14**
A. Taxes on international trade	8.05	9.02	8.41	8.68	9.18	8.40	8.03	8.22
(i) Revenues from trade taxes (% of trade sector)	7.87 (3.20)	9.53 (0.70)	9.60 (0.60)	9.73 (0.40)	9.78 (0.33)	9.60 (0.60)	9.61 (0.59)	9.44 (0.84)
(ii) Mean tariff rate	8.24 (8.80)	8.50 (7.50)	8.52 (7.40)	8.66 (6.70)	9.52 (2.40)	9.50 (2.70)	8.88 (5.60)	8.94 (5.30)
(iii) Standard deviation of tariff rates			7.12 (7.20)	7.64 (5.90)	8.24 (4.40)	6.10 (9.70)	5.61 (10.98)	6.29 (9.28)
B. Regulatory trade barriers				6.25	8.73	7.00	6.89	6.99
(i) Non-tariff trade barriers				6.25	7.95	7.10	6.86	7.06
(ii) Compliance cost of importing and exporting					9.50	6.90	6.93	6.93
C. Size of trade sector relative to expected	4.15	3.04	2.44	1.35	3.13	1.10	1.74	0.51
D. Black-market exchange rates	8.60	5.00	9.40	10.00	10.00	10.00	10.00	10.00
E. International capital market controls	2.00	2.00	2.00	6.52	8.30	5.20	5.15	4.97
(i) Foreign ownership/investment restrictions				8.03	8.91	6.50	6.46	6.10
(ii) Capital controls	2.00	2.00	2.00	5.00	7.69	3.80	3.85	3.85
5. Regulation of Credit, Labor, and Business	**4.45**	**4.42**	**4.82**	**4.85**	**5.45**	**5.80**	**5.91**	**5.42**
A. Credit market regulations	4.24	4.13	5.63	5.89	7.36	7.40	7.57	6.00
(i) Ownership of banks	2.00	2.00	5.00	5.00	5.00	8.00	8.00	8.00
(ii) Foreign bank competition				6.37	7.00	6.00	6.00	6.00
(iii) Private sector credit	4.73	4.38	3.90	4.90	7.08	5.70	6.26	0.00
(iv) Interest rate controls/negative real interest rates	6.00	6.00	8.00	8.00	10.00	10.00	10.00	10.00
B. Labor market regulations	3.61	3.61	3.69	3.99	3.38	4.00	4.43	4.50
(i) Hiring regulations and minimum wage				5.23	4.07	5.60	5.60	5.57
(ii) Hiring and firing regulations			4.81	4.81	2.33	2.90	3.39	3.17
(iii) Centralized collective bargaining	4.49	4.49	4.49	4.49	4.17	3.50	3.53	3.48
(iv) Hours regulations	6.33	6.33	5.45	5.45	6.35	3.30	3.30	4.00
(v) Mandated cost of worker dismissal						7.80	7.78	7.78
(vi) Conscription	0.00	0.00	0.00	0.00	0.00	1.00	3.00	3.00
C. Business regulations				4.68	5.62	6.00	5.74	5.76
(i) Price controls			0.00	6.00	5.00	5.00	4.00	4.00
(ii) Administrative requirements					6.98	2.80	2.37	2.29
(iii) Bureaucracy costs				4.79	6.40	4.50	4.73	5.13
(iv) Starting a business				4.20	4.08	8.20	9.21	9.10
(v) Extra payments/bribes/favoritism				3.71	5.65	6.20	4.33	4.24
(vi) Licensing restrictions						8.00	8.07	8.07
(vii) Cost of tax compliance						7.00	7.49	7.49

Guatemala

Chain-Linked	1980 Rating (Rank)	1985 Rating (Rank)	1990 Rating (Rank)	1995 Rating (Rank)	2000 Rating (Rank)	2005 Rating (Rank)	2008 Rating (Rank)	2009 Rating (Rank)
Summary Rating (Rank) ➤	6.03 (30)	4.90 (80)	5.56 (57)	6.67 (39)	6.38 (68)	7.09 (45)	7.14 (40)	7.10 (39)
Area 1. Size of Government	7.72 (10)	7.07 (6)	8.07 (6)	9.12 (3)	8.53 (5)	7.99 (16)	7.86 (18)	7.76 (17)
Area 2. Legal Structure and Security of Property Rights	2.38 (79)	1.87 (109)	2.28 (106)	4.42 (100)	3.42 (114)	6.53 (43)	5.95 (58)	5.66 (65)
Area 3. Access to Sound Money	8.95 (10)	8.02 (28)	6.83 (54)	8.08 (40)	7.64 (66)	9.17 (39)	8.93 (42)	9.40 (30)
Area 4. Freedom to Trade Internationally	4.72 (60)	2.60 (90)	5.39 (63)	6.34 (75)	6.44 (74)	5.99 (92)	6.91 (60)	6.74 (56)
Area 5. Regulation of Credit, Labor, and Business	6.64 (16)	5.42 (52)	5.28 (59)	5.41 (66)	5.89 (67)	6.37 (64)	6.48 (64)	6.32 (81)

Unadjusted

	1980		1985		1990		1995		2000		2005		2008		2009	
Summary Rating (Rank) ➤	6.38 (18)		5.18 (67)		5.79 (49)		6.95 (34)		6.38 (68)		7.06 (51)		7.11 (50)		7.07 (49)	
	Rating	Data	Rating	Data	Rating	Data	Rating	Data	Rating	Data	Rating	Data	Rating	Data	Rating	Data
1. Size of Government	7.72		7.07		8.07		9.12		8.53		8.00		7.86		7.76	
A. Government consumption	9.07	(9.16)	9.48	(7.77)	9.62	(7.30)	9.99	(6.05)	9.66	(7.14)	9.20	(8.80)	8.99	(9.42)	8.53	(11.00)
B. Transfers and subsidies	9.81	(1.20)	9.78	(1.30)	9.65	(1.80)	10.00	(0.50)	9.47	(2.46)	9.30	(3.10)	8.96	(4.33)	9.02	(4.10)
C. Government enterprises and investment	4.00	(37.40)	4.00	(32.10)	7.00	(21.00)	8.00	(17.30)	8.00	(16.43)	8.00	(16.40)	8.00		8.00	
D. Top marginal tax rate	8.00		5.00		6.00		8.50		7.00		5.50		5.50		5.50	
(i) Top marginal income tax rate	8.00	(40)	5.00	(48)	7.00	(34)	9.00	(25)	7.00	(31)	7.00	(31)	7.00	(31)	7.00	(31)
(ii) Top marginal income and payroll tax rates					5.00	(37)	8.00	(28)	7.00	(34)	4.00	(42)	4.00	(42)	4.00	(42)
2. Legal Structure and Security of Property Rights	2.54		1.99		2.44		4.72		3.42		5.40		4.88		4.64	
A. Judicial independence											3.80		3.34		2.87	
B. Impartial courts							3.60		3.79		3.80		3.46		3.39	
C. Protection of property rights									2.18		5.30		4.80		4.43	
D. Military interference in rule of law and politics							4.31		3.33		8.30		8.33		6.67	
E. Integrity of the legal system							6.96		3.33		3.90		1.67		2.50	
F. Legal enforcement of contracts											3.40		3.39		3.39	
G. Regulatory restrictions on sale of real property											8.90		9.16		9.24	
3. Access to Sound Money	8.95		8.02		6.83		8.08		7.64		9.20		8.93		9.40	
A. Money growth	9.26	(3.72)	7.97	(10.14)	7.15	(14.24)	7.69	(11.54)	7.47	(12.64)	8.60	(6.80)	8.64	(6.79)	8.93	(5.35)
B. Standard deviation of inflation	8.56	(3.61)	7.88	(5.31)	3.94	(15.15)	6.37	(9.07)	9.28	(1.79)	9.70	(0.68)	9.60	(1.00)	9.05	(2.37)
C. Inflation: most recent year	8.00	(10.00)	6.24	(18.78)	6.24	(18.78)	8.27	(8.67)	8.80	(5.98)	8.30	(8.42)	7.47	(12.64)	9.63	(1.86)
D. Freedom to own foreign currency bank accounts	10.00		10.00		10.00		10.00		5.00		10.00		10.00		10.00	
4. Freedom to Trade Internationally	5.72		3.15		6.11		7.18		6.44		6.40		7.36		7.18	
A. Taxes on international trade	3.40		2.50		4.33		7.36		7.93		6.70		8.50		8.51	
(i) Revenues from trade taxes (% of trade sector)	6.80	(4.80)	5.00	(7.50)	7.60	(3.60)	7.07	(4.40)	8.36	(2.46)	8.20	(2.70)	9.07	(1.40)	9.09	(1.37)
(ii) Mean tariff rate	0.00	(50.00)	0.00	(50.00)	5.40	(23.00)	7.96	(10.20)	8.56	(7.20)	9.50	(2.70)	8.88	(5.60)	8.88	(5.60)
(iii) Standard deviation of tariff rates					0.00	(26.70)	7.04	(7.40)	6.88	(7.80)	2.60	(18.60)	7.56	(6.10)	7.56	(6.10)
B. Regulatory trade barriers									4.13		6.10		6.87		6.85	
(i) Non-tariff trade barriers									4.13		5.60		6.07		6.03	
(ii) Compliance cost of importing and exporting											6.70		7.68		7.68	
C. Size of trade sector relative to expected	3.99		0.00		3.00		2.38		2.66		1.40		3.67		2.82	
D. Black-market exchange rates	8.00		0.00		10.00		10.00		10.00		10.00		10.00		10.00	
E. International capital market controls	5.00		5.00		5.00		8.00		7.46		7.60		7.76		7.72	
(i) Foreign ownership/investment restrictions									7.23		6.80		7.06		6.98	
(ii) Capital controls	5.00		5.00		5.00		8.00		7.69		8.50		8.46		8.46	
5. Regulation of Credit, Labor, and Business	6.95		5.67		5.51		5.65		5.89		6.40		6.53		6.38	
A. Credit market regulations	8.53		8.46		8.07		8.53		7.16		9.00		8.97		8.61	
(i) Ownership of banks	8.00		8.00		8.00		8.00		8.00		10.00		10.00		10.00	
(ii) Foreign bank competition									5.60		8.00		8.00		8.00	
(iii) Private sector credit	9.58		9.38		8.22		9.58		8.56		8.90		8.88		7.45	
(iv) Interest rate controls/negative real interest rates	8.00		8.00		8.00		8.00		9.00		9.00		9.00		9.00	
B. Labor market regulations									4.77		4.70		4.67		4.55	
(i) Hiring regulations and minimum wage									4.62		5.60		5.60		5.57	
(ii) Hiring and firing regulations									5.25		5.90		5.28		5.00	
(iii) Centralized collective bargaining									6.22		6.80		7.51		7.10	
(iv) Hours regulations											6.00		6.00		6.00	
(v) Mandated cost of worker dismissal											0.60		0.64		0.63	
(vi) Conscription	10.00		0.00		0.00		0.00		3.00		3.00		3.00		3.00	
C. Business regulations									5.74		5.60		5.94		5.97	
(i) Price controls					6.00		6.00		8.00		6.00		6.00		6.00	
(ii) Administrative requirements									6.10		3.90		4.46		4.30	
(iii) Bureaucracy costs									4.53		4.60		5.41		5.68	
(iv) Starting a business									5.12		8.40		8.52		8.22	
(v) Extra payments/bribes/favoritism									4.94		6.00		4.97		4.49	
(vi) Licensing restrictions											4.20		6.06		6.93	
(vii) Cost of tax compliance											6.10		6.14		6.14	

Guinea-Bissau

	1980	1985	1990	1995	2000	2005	2008	2009
Chain-Linked	Rating (Rank)	Rating (Rank)	Rating (Rank)	Rating (Rank)	Rating (Rank)	Rating (Rank)	Rating (Rank)	Rating (Rank)
Summary Rating (Rank) ➤			**3.15** (111)	**3.71** (122)	**4.51** (120)	**4.78** (117)	**4.89** (117)	**5.16** (117)
Area 1. Size of Government			4.32 (89)	4.95 (88)	4.56 (103)	2.87 (123)	3.74 (117)	4.25 (112)
Area 2. Legal Structure and Security of Property Rights		1.99 (107)	2.93 (97)	2.54 (121)	3.04 (119)	3.17 (113)	3.27 (115)	3.28 (117)
Area 3. Access to Sound Money	4.07 (102)	1.47 (109)	0.88 (115)	1.82 (115)	3.26 (117)	6.59 (100)	5.74 (117)	6.26 (112)
Area 4. Freedom to Trade Internationally					5.94 (94)	4.80 (116)	5.13 (109)	4.67 (115)
Area 5. Regulation of Credit, Labor, and Business			3.45 (106)	4.35 (105)	5.75 (73)	6.56 (59)	6.67 (55)	7.55 (18)

	1980	1985	1990	1995	2000	2005	2008	2009
Unadjusted								
Summary Rating (Rank) ➤			**2.90** (113)	**3.42** (123)	**4.51** (120)	**4.66** (137)	**4.77** (135)	**5.03** (135)
	Rating Data	Rating Data	Rating Data	Rating Data	Rating Data	Rating Data	Rating Data	Rating Data
1. Size of Government			**4.32**	**4.95**	**4.56**	**2.90**	**3.74**	**4.25**
A. Government consumption		7.46 (14.64)	8.65 (10.59)	9.90 (6.33)	9.11 (9.02)	5.70 (20.50)	7.48 (14.57)	8.50 (11.10)
B. Transfers and subsidies								
C. Government enterprises and investment			0.00 (91.40)	0.00 (67.60)	0.00 (88.30)	0.00 (54.60)	0.00 (55.61)	0.00 (55.61)
D. Top marginal tax rate								
(i) Top marginal income tax rate								
(ii) Top marginal income and payroll tax rates								
2. Legal Structure and Security of Property Rights		**1.99**	**2.93**	**2.54**	**3.04**	**3.20**	**3.27**	**3.28**
A. Judicial independence								
B. Impartial courts				2.70	2.90	3.20	2.70	3.10
C. Protection of property rights								
D. Military interference in rule of law and politics				3.11	3.33	2.50	2.50	1.67
E. Integrity of the legal system				0.00	1.67	5.00	4.17	4.17
F. Legal enforcement of contracts						3.50	3.48	3.48
G. Regulatory restrictions on sale of real property						1.70	3.51	4.01
3. Access to Sound Money	**5.43**	**1.96**	**0.88**	**1.82**	**3.26**	**6.60**	**5.74**	**6.26**
A. Money growth			0.00 (105.63)	2.67 (36.64)	1.65 (41.76)	9.10 (−4.50)	7.05 (14.75)	7.44 (12.79)
B. Standard deviation of inflation	8.61 (3.48)	2.33 (19.18)	0.00 (28.57)	3.58 (16.06)	3.10 (17.24)	7.90 (5.17)	7.98 (5.04)	7.95 (5.14)
C. Inflation: most recent year	7.67 (11.63)	3.54 (32.31)	3.54 (32.31)	1.05 (44.74)	8.27 (8.64)	9.30 (3.33)	7.91 (10.46)	9.67 (−1.65)
D. Freedom to own foreign currency bank accounts	0.00	0.00	0.00	0.00	0.00	0.00	0.00	0.00
4. Freedom to Trade Internationally		**4.13**			**5.94**	**5.20**	**5.50**	**5.02**
A. Taxes on international trade		4.84			7.60	8.40	7.45	7.45
(i) Revenues from trade taxes (% of trade sector)		4.84 (7.74)						
(ii) Mean tariff rate					7.60 (12.00)	7.20 (13.90)	7.62 (11.90)	7.62 (11.90)
(iii) Standard deviation of tariff rates						9.70 (0.80)	7.29 (6.78)	7.29 (6.78)
B. Regulatory trade barriers						6.60	6.86	6.86
(i) Non-tariff trade barriers								
(ii) Compliance cost of importing and exporting						6.60	6.86	6.86
C. Size of trade sector relative to expected	2.30	3.35	0.00	0.00	3.92	0.00	2.43	0.00
D. Black-market exchange rates		4.20	8.20	9.60	10.00	10.00	10.00	10.00
E. International capital market controls	0.00	0.00	5.00	5.00	0.00	0.80	0.77	0.77
(i) Foreign ownership/investment restrictions								
(ii) Capital controls	0.00	0.00	5.00	5.00	0.00	0.80	0.77	0.77
5. Regulation of Credit, Labor, and Business			**3.45**	**4.35**	**5.75**	**5.50**	**5.61**	**6.31**
A. Credit market regulations			3.87	4.46	10.01	9.10	8.95	9.29
(i) Ownership of banks						10.00	10.00	10.00
(ii) Foreign bank competition								
(iii) Private sector credit			7.75	8.92	10.01	7.20	6.86	7.87
(iv) Interest rate controls/negative real interest rates			0.00	0.00	10.00	10.00	10.00	10.00
B. Labor market regulations						3.10	3.13	3.82
(i) Hiring regulations and minimum wage						3.30	3.30	3.33
(ii) Hiring and firing regulations								
(iii) Centralized collective bargaining								
(iv) Hours regulations						7.30	7.30	10.00
(v) Mandated cost of worker dismissal						1.90	1.93	1.97
(vi) Conscription		0.00	0.00	0.00	0.00	0.00	0.00	0.00
C. Business regulations						4.30	4.75	5.82
(i) Price controls			0.00	6.00	6.00	6.00	6.00	6.00
(ii) Administrative requirements								
(iii) Bureaucracy costs								
(iv) Starting a business						0.00	0.78	3.38
(v) Extra payments/bribes/favoritism								
(vi) Licensing restrictions						3.60	4.54	6.25
(vii) Cost of tax compliance						7.70	7.67	7.67

Guyana

	1980	1985	1990	1995	2000	2005	2008	2009
Chain-Linked	Rating (Rank)	Rating (Rank)	Rating (Rank)	Rating (Rank)	Rating (Rank)	Rating (Rank)	Rating (Rank)	Rating (Rank)
Summary Rating (Rank) ➤				5.27 (89)	6.66 (48)	6.66 (70)	6.74 (67)	6.59 (71)
Area 1. Size of Government		3.08 (101)	4.04 (94)	4.38 (98)	3.85 (111)	3.79 (119)	4.19 (114)	3.77 (116)
Area 2. Legal Structure and Security of Property Rights	2.23 (84)	2.11 (106)	3.41 (88)	4.80 (88)	6.54 (40)	5.65 (64)	5.65 (66)	5.80 (59)
Area 3. Access to Sound Money	5.82 (71)	5.24 (92)	2.19 (111)	4.94 (94)	7.87 (63)	7.72 (75)	7.75 (74)	7.94 (75)
Area 4. Freedom to Trade Internationally					8.13 (21)	8.45 (4)	8.09 (9)	7.22 (31)
Area 5. Regulation of Credit, Labor, and Business				5.79 (55)	6.91 (21)	7.90 (17)	8.24 (7)	8.47 (5)

	1980	1985	1990	1995	2000	2005	2008	2009
Unadjusted								
Summary Rating (Rank) ➤		3.83 (103)		4.98 (98)	6.66 (48)	6.17 (101)	6.25 (97)	6.10 (110)
	Rating Data	Rating Data	Rating Data	Rating Data	Rating Data	Rating Data	Rating Data	Rating Data
1. Size of Government		3.48	4.04	4.38	3.85	3.80	4.19	3.77
A. Government consumption	2.82 (30.41)	4.96 (23.14)	7.11 (15.83)	5.64 (20.81)	5.54 (21.15)	3.90 (26.80)	5.08 (22.72)	3.82 (27.00)
B. Transfers and subsidies								
C. Government enterprises and investment		2.00 (49.30)	2.00 (47.90)	2.00 (48.90)	0.00 (58.07)	2.00 (41.20)	2.00 (44.62)	2.00 (48.15)
D. Top marginal tax rate			3.00	5.50	6.00	5.50	5.50	5.50
(i) Top marginal income tax rate			3.00 (50)	7.00 (33)	7.00 (33)	7.00 (33)	7.00 (33)	7.00 (33)
(ii) Top marginal income and payroll tax rates			3.00 (50)	4.00 (41)	5.00 (39)	4.00 (41)	4.00 (41)	4.00 (41)
2. Legal Structure and Security of Property Rights	2.23	2.11	3.41	4.80	6.54	4.70	4.66	4.78
A. Judicial independence						3.00	3.75	3.96
B. Impartial courts				5.31	5.79	2.40	2.81	3.32
C. Protection of property rights						3.90	4.43	4.55
D. Military interference in rule of law and politics				5.79	10.00	6.70	6.67	6.67
E. Integrity of the legal system				4.11	6.67	4.20	2.50	2.50
F. Legal enforcement of contracts						4.60	4.55	4.55
G. Regulatory restrictions on sale of real property						7.80	7.88	7.88
3. Access to Sound Money	5.82	5.24	2.19	4.94	7.87	7.70	7.75	7.94
A. Money growth	8.55 (7.26)	6.21 (18.95)	1.87 (40.67)	6.98 (15.12)	9.25 (3.74)	8.50 (7.60)	8.48 (7.62)	8.59 (7.07)
B. Standard deviation of inflation	7.07 (7.32)	7.66 (5.86)	0.00 (53.12)	0.00 (48.31)	8.47 (3.83)	8.80 (3.01)	9.16 (2.10)	8.77 (3.07)
C. Inflation: most recent year	7.64 (11.78)	7.10 (14.51)	6.90 (15.51)	7.77 (11.17)	8.77 (6.15)	8.60 (6.93)	8.38 (8.10)	9.42 (2.91)
D. Freedom to own foreign currency bank accounts	0.00	0.00	0.00	5.00	5.00	5.00	5.00	5.00
4. Freedom to Trade Internationally	5.40	4.49			8.13	7.70	7.42	6.62
A. Taxes on international trade	8.80	7.01			6.60	6.50	6.47	6.47
(i) Revenues from trade taxes (% of trade sector)	8.80 (1.80)	7.41 (3.88)						
(ii) Mean tariff rate		6.60 (17.00)			6.60 (17.00)	7.80 (11.10)	7.82 (10.90)	7.82 (10.90)
(iii) Standard deviation of tariff rates						5.20 (12.00)	5.12 (12.21)	5.12 (12.21)
B. Regulatory trade barriers						6.40	6.61	6.47
(i) Non-tariff trade barriers						6.00	6.23	5.73
(ii) Compliance cost of importing and exporting						6.80	6.99	7.20
C. Size of trade sector relative to expected	10.00	7.22	8.64	10.00	10.00	10.00	7.76	4.23
D. Black-market exchange rates	0.00	0.00	8.20	9.20	9.00	9.50	10.00	10.00
E. International capital market controls	0.00	0.00	5.00	5.00	6.92	6.40	6.26	5.95
(i) Foreign ownership / investment restrictions						5.80	5.85	5.22
(ii) Capital controls	0.00	0.00	5.00	5.00	6.92	6.90	6.67	6.67
5. Regulation of Credit, Labor, and Business				5.79	6.91	6.90	7.20	7.37
A. Credit market regulations	3.02	2.38	4.61	4.90	8.21	7.90	8.08	8.07
(i) Ownership of banks						10.00	10.00	10.00
(ii) Foreign bank competition						7.00	7.00	7.00
(iii) Private sector credit	3.02	2.38	4.61	5.80	7.42	5.60	6.30	6.27
(iv) Interest rate controls / negative real interest rates				4.00	9.00	9.00	9.00	9.00
B. Labor market regulations						7.10	7.34	7.82
(i) Hiring regulations and minimum wage						6.70	7.80	8.90
(ii) Hiring and firing regulations						6.00	5.86	6.08
(iii) Centralized collective bargaining						6.50	6.86	6.76
(iv) Hours regulations						8.70	8.70	10.00
(v) Mandated cost of worker dismissal						4.80	4.81	5.18
(vi) Conscription			10.00	10.00	10.00	10.00	10.00	10.00
C. Business regulations						5.80	6.20	6.23
(i) Price controls						6.00	6.00	6.00
(ii) Administrative requirements						2.50	4.22	4.21
(iii) Bureaucracy costs						5.20	5.80	5.62
(iv) Starting a business						7.50	8.57	8.84
(v) Extra payments / bribes / favoritism						4.30	3.68	3.67
(vi) Licensing restrictions						8.10	8.34	8.51
(vii) Cost of tax compliance						6.80	6.77	6.77

Haiti

	1980		1985		1990		1995		2000		2005		2008		2009	
Chain-Linked	Rating	(Rank)	Rating	(Rank)	Rating	(Rank)	Rating	(Rank)	Rating	(Rank)	Rating	(Rank)	Rating	(Rank)	Rating	(Rank)
Summary Rating (Rank) ➤	**6.29**	(22)	**5.66**	(47)	**5.36**	(68)	**5.29**	(88)	**6.54**	(58)	**6.61**	(72)	**6.66**	(72)	**6.84**	(55)
Area 1. Size of Government	9.13	(4)	5.66	(35)	6.37	(34)	6.49	(43)	8.34	(9)	9.20	(1)	8.89	(4)	8.79	(5)
Area 2. Legal Structure and Security of Property Rights	2.23	(84)	2.93	(95)	1.95	(110)	3.94	(108)	3.86	(103)	3.65	(109)	3.70	(109)	3.48	(114)
Area 3. Access to Sound Money	7.70	(23)	8.92	(17)	8.46	(26)	6.34	(68)	8.37	(49)	7.99	(69)	8.13	(62)	8.65	(58)
Area 4. Freedom to Trade Internationally									5.79	(100)	6.33	(81)	6.45	(75)	6.66	(60)
Area 5. Regulation of Credit, Labor, and Business			5.23	(61)	4.99	(85)	6.36	(46)	5.97	(91)	6.20	(82)	6.56	(64)

	1980		1985		1990		1995		2000		2005		2008		2009	
Unadjusted																
Summary Rating (Rank) ➤	**5.64**	(49)	**5.33**	(63)	**5.05**	(81)	**5.29**	(87)	**6.54**	(58)	**6.63**	(77)	**6.68**	(80)	**6.84**	(67)
	Rating	Data	Rating	Data	Rating	Data	Rating	Data	Rating	Data	Rating	Data	Rating	Data	Rating	Data
1. Size of Government	**8.27**		**6.14**		**6.85**		**5.88**		**8.34**		**8.90**		**8.60**		**8.51**	
A. Government consumption	8.54	(10.96)	8.26	(11.92)	9.54	(7.58)	9.76	(6.82)	5.10	(22.65)	9.70	(7.10)	9.46	(7.82)	9.10	(9.05)
B. Transfers and subsidies			8.15	(7.30)					9.92	(0.81)	9.90	(0.80)	9.92	(0.81)	9.92	(0.81)
C. Government enterprises and investment	8.00	(19.00)	2.00	(48.80)	2.00	(42.00)	2.00	(47.00)	10.00	(11.50)	8.00	(18.70)	7.00	(24.90)	7.00	(24.90)
D. Top marginal tax rate					9.00						8.00		8.00		8.00	
(i) Top marginal income tax rate					9.00	(30)					8.00	(30)	8.00	(30)	8.00	(30)
(ii) Top marginal income and payroll tax rates																
2. Legal Structure and Security of Property Rights	**2.23**		**2.93**		**1.95**		**3.94**		**3.86**		**2.70**		**2.70**		**2.54**	
A. Judicial independence																
B. Impartial courts							2.91		2.99		2.70		3.20		3.20	
C. Protection of property rights																
D. Military interference in rule of law and politics							1.76		5.00		0.00		0.00		0.00	
E. Integrity of the legal system							6.96		3.33		3.80		3.33		2.50	
F. Legal enforcement of contracts											4.00		4.05		4.05	
G. Regulatory restrictions on sale of real property											2.80		2.90		2.93	
3. Access to Sound Money	**7.70**		**8.92**		**8.46**		**6.34**		**8.37**		**8.00**		**8.13**		**8.65**	
A. Money growth	8.40	(7.99)	9.02	(4.91)	8.94	(5.30)	5.26	(23.72)	7.87	(10.67)	7.10	(14.60)	7.20	(14.01)	7.42	(12.91)
B. Standard deviation of inflation	6.67	(8.33)	8.75	(3.13)	7.00	(7.50)	6.32	(9.19)	8.38	(4.06)	8.00	(4.88)	8.43	(3.92)	7.18	(7.05)
C. Inflation: most recent year	5.72	(21.39)	7.92	(10.41)	7.92	(10.41)	3.80	(31.00)	7.26	(13.71)	6.90	(15.73)	6.90	(15.52)	10.00	(−0.01)
D. Freedom to own foreign currency bank accounts	10.00		10.00		10.00		10.00		10.00		10.00		10.00		10.00	
4. Freedom to Trade Internationally	**4.37**		**3.33**		**2.76**				**5.79**		**6.50**		**6.64**		**6.86**	
A. Taxes on international trade	3.93		6.17		5.53				8.00		8.80		8.80		8.79	
(i) Revenues from trade taxes (% of trade sector)	3.40	(9.90)	4.67	(8.00)	5.53	(6.70)										
(ii) Mean tariff rate	4.46	(27.70)	7.68	(11.60)					8.00	(10.00)	9.40	(2.80)	9.44	(2.80)	9.44	(2.80)
(iii) Standard deviation of tariff rates											8.20	(4.60)	8.15	(4.62)	8.14	(4.65)
B. Regulatory trade barriers											3.40		5.17		5.17	
(i) Non-tariff trade barriers																
(ii) Compliance cost of importing and exporting											3.40		5.17		5.17	
C. Size of trade sector relative to expected	3.70		2.21		0.00		0.11		0.73		1.30		0.12		1.89	
D. Black-market exchange rates	6.00		0.00		0.00		0.60		10.00		10.00		10.00		10.00	
E. International capital market controls	0.00		0.00		0.00		2.00		2.00		9.10		9.09		8.46	
(i) Foreign ownership/investment restrictions																
(ii) Capital controls	0.00		0.00		0.00		2.00		2.00		9.10		9.09		8.46	
5. Regulation of Credit, Labor, and Business					**5.23**		**4.99**		**6.36**		**7.10**		**7.33**		**7.65**	
A. Credit market regulations	10.00		9.71		4.97		4.99		9.44		8.30		8.56		8.56	
(i) Ownership of banks																
(ii) Foreign bank competition																
(iii) Private sector credit	10.00		9.71		9.94		9.99		9.88		8.60		9.12		9.12	
(iv) Interest rate controls/negative real interest rates					0.00		0.00		9.00		8.00		8.00		8.00	
B. Labor market regulations											8.60		8.83		9.73	
(i) Hiring regulations and minimum wage											7.80		8.90		8.90	
(ii) Hiring and firing regulations																
(iii) Centralized collective bargaining																
(iv) Hours regulations											8.00		8.00		10.00	
(v) Mandated cost of worker dismissal											8.40		8.42		10.00	
(vi) Conscription	10.00		10.00		10.00		10.00		10.00		10.00		10.00		10.00	
C. Business regulations											4.40		4.59		4.66	
(i) Price controls					2.00		0.00		2.00		2.00		2.00		2.00	
(ii) Administrative requirements																
(iii) Bureaucracy costs																
(iv) Starting a business											3.90		4.20		4.37	
(v) Extra payments/bribes/favoritism																
(vi) Licensing restrictions											3.60		3.97		4.05	
(vii) Cost of tax compliance											8.20		8.21		8.21	

Honduras

	1980	1985	1990	1995	2000	2005	2008	2009
Chain-Linked	Rating (Rank)	Rating (Rank)	Rating (Rank)	Rating (Rank)	Rating (Rank)	Rating (Rank)	Rating (Rank)	Rating (Rank)
Summary Rating (Rank) ➤	**6.06** (29)	**5.46** (52)	**5.52** (58)	**6.07** (63)	**6.51** (61)	**6.85** (58)	**7.14** (40)	**6.92** (50)
Area 1. Size of Government	8.52 (5)	5.48 (40)	6.38 (33)	6.51 (42)	8.12 (10)	8.46 (10)	8.87 (5)	8.16 (8)
Area 2. Legal Structure and Security of Property Rights	2.55 (75)	2.82 (97)	3.24 (89)	4.69 (95)	3.72 (109)	4.91 (84)	5.54 (69)	5.31 (75)
Area 3. Access to Sound Money	8.76 (11)	9.51 (5)	8.38 (28)	7.17 (51)	8.22 (53)	8.85 (45)	8.88 (44)	9.24 (38)
Area 4. Freedom to Trade Internationally			5.45 (62)	6.83 (49)	6.80 (69)	6.75 (60)	7.10 (47)	6.75 (54)
Area 5. Regulation of Credit, Labor, and Business	5.20 (54)	4.24 (85)	4.26 (95)	5.03 (82)	5.71 (75)	5.62 (104)	5.76 (101)	5.56 (108)

Unadjusted								
Summary Rating (Rank) ➤	**5.80** (42)	**5.77** (44)	**5.83** (48)	**6.39** (49)	**6.51** (61)	**6.98** (60)	**7.28** (37)	**7.06** (51)
	Rating *Data*	Rating *Data*	Rating *Data*	Rating *Data*	Rating *Data*	Rating *Data*	Rating *Data*	Rating *Data*
1. Size of Government	**6.43**	**5.48**	**6.38**	**6.51**	**8.12**	**8.50**	**8.87**	**8.16**
A. Government consumption	7.28 *(15.25)*	7.40 *(14.83)*	7.00 *(16.21)*	8.00 *(12.80)*	7.43 *(14.75)*	7.30 *(15.10)*	6.97 *(16.30)*	6.15 *(19.09)*
B. Transfers and subsidies		9.51 *(2.30)*	9.54 *(2.20)*	9.05 *(4.00)*	9.05 *(4.00)*	10.00 *(0.50)*	10.00 *(0.50)*	10.00 *(0.35)*
C. Government enterprises and investment	4.00 *(37.90)*	0.00 *(52.40)*	4.00 *(32.50)*	2.00 *(41.80)*	7.00 *(21.30)*	8.00 *(17.90)*	10.00 *(13.08)*	8.00 *(15.54)*
D. Top marginal tax rate	8.00	5.00	5.00	7.00	9.00	8.50	8.50	8.50
(i) Top marginal income tax rate	8.00 *(40)*	5.00 *(46)*	5.00 *(46)*	7.00 *(40)*	9.00 *(25)*	9.00 *(25)*	9.00 *(25)*	9.00 *(25)*
(ii) Top marginal income and payroll tax rates			5.00 *(46)*	7.00 *(40)*	9.00 *(25)*	8.00 *(28)*	8.00 *(28)*	8.00 *(28)*
2. Legal Structure and Security of Property Rights	**2.76**	**3.05**	**3.50**	**5.07**	**3.72**	**4.00**	**4.51**	**4.31**
A. Judicial independence						2.40	3.30	3.53
B. Impartial courts				3.98	3.68	3.00	3.52	3.86
C. Protection of property rights					2.30	4.10	4.94	4.70
D. Military interference in rule of law and politics				5.42	5.00	5.60	6.67	5.00
E. Integrity of the legal system				6.96	3.33	2.50	2.50	2.50
F. Legal enforcement of contracts						2.90	2.86	2.86
G. Regulatory restrictions on sale of real property						7.40	7.76	7.76
3. Access to Sound Money	**8.76**	**9.51**	**8.38**	**7.17**	**8.22**	**8.80**	**8.88**	**9.24**
A. Money growth	8.89 *(5.56)*	9.67 *(1.66)*	7.23 *(13.85)*	7.09 *(14.57)*	7.66 *(11.70)*	7.70 *(11.30)*	8.67 *(6.67)*	9.12 *(4.41)*
B. Standard deviation of inflation	8.81 *(2.97)*	9.42 *(1.45)*	7.34 *(6.64)*	6.88 *(7.81)*	7.42 *(6.44)*	9.40 *(1.49)*	9.14 *(2.15)*	8.93 *(2.69)*
C. Inflation: most recent year	7.35 *(13.27)*	8.95 *(5.25)*	8.95 *(5.25)*	4.73 *(26.34)*	7.79 *(11.06)*	8.20 *(8.81)*	7.72 *(11.41)*	8.90 *(5.49)*
D. Freedom to own foreign currency bank accounts	10.00	10.00	10.00	10.00	10.00	10.00	10.00	10.00
4. Freedom to Trade Internationally	**4.87**		**5.93**	**7.38**	**6.80**	**7.10**	**7.45**	**7.08**
A. Taxes on international trade	3.67		6.00	7.69	7.83	8.50	8.47	8.48
(i) Revenues from trade taxes (% of trade sector)	5.53 *(6.70)*				8.07 *(2.90)*	9.40 *(0.90)*	9.43 *(0.85)*	9.51 *(0.74)*
(ii) Mean tariff rate	1.80 *(41.00)*		6.00 *(20.00)*	7.98 *(10.10)*	8.42 *(7.90)*	8.70 *(6.70)*	8.88 *(5.60)*	8.88 *(5.60)*
(iii) Standard deviation of tariff rates				7.40 *(6.50)*	7.00 *(7.50)*	7.50 *(6.30)*	7.09 *(7.28)*	7.04 *(7.39)*
B. Regulatory trade barriers					3.35	5.80	6.61	6.43
(i) Non-tariff trade barriers					3.35	4.50	6.17	5.72
(ii) Compliance cost of importing and exporting						7.10	7.05	7.14
C. Size of trade sector relative to expected	6.45	3.92	5.48	6.27	6.26	6.10	7.41	5.88
D. Black-market exchange rates	6.00	0.00	10.00	9.80	10.00	10.00	10.00	10.00
E. International capital market controls	0.00	0.00	0.00	5.00	6.57	5.00	4.76	4.61
(i) Foreign ownership / investment restrictions					8.53	6.20	6.43	6.15
(ii) Capital controls	0.00	0.00	0.00	5.00	4.61	3.80	3.08	3.08
5. Regulation of Credit, Labor, and Business	**6.20**	**5.06**	**4.93**	**5.82**	**5.71**	**6.50**	**6.71**	**6.49**
A. Credit market regulations	6.10	7.70	7.77	6.30	7.01	8.90	8.72	8.04
(i) Ownership of banks						10.00	10.00	10.00
(ii) Foreign bank competition					4.70	6.00	6.00	6.00
(iii) Private sector credit	8.20	7.41	7.54	8.60	9.86	9.70	9.90	7.17
(iv) Interest rate controls / negative real interest rates	4.00	8.00	8.00	4.00	9.00	10.00	9.00	9.00
B. Labor market regulations					5.72	5.40	4.96	5.00
(i) Hiring regulations and minimum wage					2.72	0.00	0.00	0.00
(ii) Hiring and firing regulations					4.50	5.10	4.34	4.24
(iii) Centralized collective bargaining					5.67	6.30	6.24	5.80
(iv) Hours regulations						8.00	8.00	8.00
(v) Mandated cost of worker dismissal						3.10	1.19	1.97
(vi) Conscription	10.00	0.00	0.00	10.00	10.00	10.00	10.00	10.00
C. Business regulations					4.39	5.20	6.45	6.44
(i) Price controls			4.00	4.00	4.00	6.00	6.00	6.00
(ii) Administrative requirements					5.80	3.00	4.52	4.43
(iii) Bureaucracy costs					4.88	3.30	5.83	5.91
(iv) Starting a business					2.85	7.90	9.00	9.00
(v) Extra payments / bribes / favoritism					4.42	4.60	3.96	3.93
(vi) Licensing restrictions						6.70	8.35	8.34
(vii) Cost of tax compliance						5.20	7.49	7.49

Hong Kong

	1980	1985	1990	1995	2000	2005	2008	2009
Chain-Linked	Rating (Rank)	Rating (Rank)	Rating (Rank)	Rating (Rank)	Rating (Rank)	Rating (Rank)	Rating (Rank)	Rating (Rank)
Summary Rating (Rank) ➤	**9.21** (1)	**8.81** (1)	**8.76** (1)	**9.11** (1)	**8.82** (1)	**8.94** (1)	**9.04** (1)	**8.98** (1)
Area 1. Size of Government	9.75 (2)	8.89 (1)	9.31 (1)	9.47 (1)	9.35 (1)	9.08 (2)	9.41 (1)	9.38 (1)
Area 2. Legal Structure and Security of Property Rights	9.45 (6)	7.34 (27)	6.91 (32)	8.17 (18)	7.23 (26)	8.04 (16)	8.10 (16)	8.20 (12)
Area 3. Access to Sound Money	8.51 (12)	9.33 (12)	9.02 (19)	9.44 (26)	9.11 (36)	9.48 (26)	9.54 (7)	9.28 (33)
Area 4. Freedom to Trade Internationally	9.75 (1)	9.75 (1)	9.76 (1)	9.77 (1)	9.78 (1)	9.53 (1)	9.55 (1)	9.34 (2)
Area 5. Regulation of Credit, Labor, and Business	8.73 (1)	8.73 (1)	8.73 (1)	8.72 (1)	8.64 (1)	8.59 (4)	8.61 (3)	8.68 (3)

	1980	1985	1990	1995	2000	2005	2008	2009
Unadjusted								
Summary Rating (Rank) ➤	**8.64** (1)	**8.27** (1)	**8.22** (1)	**9.08** (1)	**8.82** (1)	**8.98** (1)	**9.08** (1)	**9.01** (1)
	Rating Data	Rating Data	Rating Data	Rating Data	Rating Data	Rating Data	Rating Data	Rating Data
1. Size of Government	**9.75**	**8.89**	**9.31**	**9.47**	**9.35**	**9.10**	**9.41**	**9.38**
A. Government consumption	9.02 (9.34)	8.66 (10.57)	8.36 (11.58)	8.03 (12.70)	7.58 (14.22)	7.90 (13.10)	8.21 (12.09)	8.10 (12.45)
B. Transfers and subsidies	9.97 (0.60)	9.89 (0.90)	9.89 (0.90)	9.84 (1.10)	9.84 (1.10)	8.40 (6.30)	9.43 (2.58)	9.43 (2.58)
C. Government enterprises and investment	10.00 (14.80)	8.00 (15.20)	10.00 (12.70)	10.00 (14.00)	10.00 (14.00)	10.00 (1.40)	10.00 (10.70)	10.00 (12.70)
D. Top marginal tax rate	10.00	9.00	9.00	10.00	10.00	10.00	10.00	10.00
(i) Top marginal income tax rate	10.00 (15)	9.00 (25c)	9.00 (25)	10.00 (20)	10.00 (17)	10.00 (20)	10.00 (17)	10.00 (17)
(ii) Top marginal income and payroll tax rates			9.00 (25)	10.00 (20)	10.00 (17)	10.00 (20)	10.00 (17)	10.00 (17)
2. Legal Structure and Security of Property Rights	**8.13**	**6.31**	**5.94**	**8.17**	**7.23**	**8.00**	**8.10**	**8.20**
A. Judicial independence				8.07	7.68	8.20	8.39	8.58
B. Impartial courts				7.93	8.85	8.30	8.16	8.23
C. Protection of property rights				6.07	6.30	8.70	8.81	8.82
D. Military interference in rule of law and politics				8.76	5.00	8.30	8.33	8.33
E. Integrity of the legal system				10.00	8.33	7.70	8.33	8.33
F. Legal enforcement of contracts						7.70	7.17	7.17
G. Regulatory restrictions on sale of real property						7.30	7.51	7.94
3. Access to Sound Money	**8.51**	**9.33**	**9.02**	**9.44**	**9.11**	**9.50**	**9.54**	**9.28**
A. Money growth	9.04 (4.80)	9.48 (2.60)	8.36 (8.20)	9.33 (3.37)	9.46 (−2.71)	9.00 (5.10)	9.97 (−0.16)	7.75 (11.25)
B. Standard deviation of inflation	7.99 (5.03)	8.97 (2.57)	8.86 (2.85)	8.96 (2.59)	7.73 (5.68)	9.10 (2.25)	9.04 (2.41)	9.47 (1.32)
C. Inflation: most recent year	7.01 (14.96)	8.86 (5.71)	8.86 (5.71)	9.49 (2.56)	9.25 (−3.76)	9.80 (0.91)	9.14 (4.31)	9.89 (0.55)
D. Freedom to own foreign currency bank accounts	10.00	10.00	10.00	10.00	10.00	10.00	10.00	10.00
4. Freedom to Trade Internationally	**9.59**	**9.58**	**9.60**	**9.68**	**9.78**	**9.50**	**9.55**	**9.34**
A. Taxes on international trade	9.83	9.80	9.91	9.93	9.93	10.00	10.00	10.00
(i) Revenues from trade taxes (% of trade sector)	9.67 (0.50)	9.60 (0.60)	9.73 (0.40)	9.80 (0.30)	9.80 (0.30)	10.00 (0.00)	10.00 (0.00)	10.00 (0.00)
(ii) Mean tariff rate	10.00 (0.00)	10.00 (0.00)	10.00 (0.00)	10.00 (0.00)	10.00 (0.00)	10.00 (0.00)	10.00 (0.00)	10.00 (0.00)
(iii) Standard deviation of tariff rates			10.00 (0.00)	10.00 (0.00)	10.00 (0.00)	10.00 (0.00)	10.00 (0.00)	10.00 (0.00)
B. Regulatory trade barriers				8.75	9.38	8.90	9.27	9.12
(i) Non-tariff trade barriers				8.75	8.94	8.60	9.19	8.89
(ii) Compliance cost of importing and exporting					9.83	9.30	9.35	9.35
C. Size of trade sector relative to expected	10.00	10.00	10.00	10.00	10.00	10.00	10.00	10.00
D. Black-market exchange rates	10.00	10.00	10.00	10.00	10.00	10.00	10.00	10.00
E. International capital market controls	10.00	10.00	10.00	9.70	9.57	8.70	8.47	7.56
(i) Foreign ownership/investment restrictions				9.40	9.92	9.00	9.25	8.96
(ii) Capital controls	10.00	10.00	10.00	10.00	9.23	8.50	7.69	6.15
5. Regulation of Credit, Labor, and Business	**7.25**	**7.25**	**7.22**	**8.66**	**8.64**	**8.80**	**8.78**	**8.85**
A. Credit market regulations	10.00	10.00	9.94	9.10	8.83	9.20	9.28	9.28
(i) Ownership of banks	10.00	10.00	10.00	10.00	10.00	10.00	10.00	10.00
(ii) Foreign bank competition				8.58	7.32	8.00	8.00	8.00
(iii) Private sector credit			9.82	9.68	9.10	8.90	9.12	9.12
(iv) Interest rate controls/negative real interest rates	10.00	10.00	10.00	10.00	10.00	10.00	10.00	10.00
B. Labor market regulations			8.92	8.14	8.55	9.10	9.31	9.46
(i) Hiring regulations and minimum wage				7.40		10.00	10.00	10.00
(ii) Hiring and firing regulations			8.83	8.83	7.55	6.90	7.94	8.28
(iii) Centralized collective bargaining	7.93	7.93	7.93	7.94	8.99	8.90	8.86	9.00
(iv) Hours regulations				6.53	7.68	10.00	10.00	10.00
(v) Mandated cost of worker dismissal						9.10	9.07	9.46
(vi) Conscription	10.00	10.00	10.00	10.00	10.00	10.00	10.00	10.00
C. Business regulations				8.73	8.52	8.00	7.76	7.81
(i) Price controls			10.00	9.00	9.00	9.00	7.00	7.00
(ii) Administrative requirements					8.54	6.40	6.94	6.91
(iii) Bureaucracy costs				9.55	7.25	4.60	3.16	3.21
(iv) Starting a business				9.08	9.02	9.60	9.79	9.79
(v) Extra payments/bribes/favoritism				7.27	8.81	8.80	8.52	8.86
(vi) Licensing restrictions						8.30	9.79	9.79
(vii) Cost of tax compliance						9.10	9.10	9.10

Hungary

	1980		1985		1990		1995		2000		2005		2008		2009	
Chain-Linked	Rating	(Rank)	Rating	(Rank)	Rating	(Rank)	Rating	(Rank)	Rating	(Rank)	Rating	(Rank)	Rating	(Rank)	Rating	(Rank)
Summary Rating (Rank) ➤	**4.63**	(78)	**5.24**	(60)	**5.39**	(66)	**6.14**	(59)	**6.55**	(56)	**7.39**	(25)	**7.38**	(27)	**7.47**	(17)
Area 1. Size of Government	2.58	(100)	2.64	(106)	2.94	(108)	3.73	(109)	3.85	(111)	5.84	(85)	6.28	(68)	6.20	(65)
Area 2. Legal Structure and Security of Property Rights			7.79	(22)	8.32	(23)	7.60	(22)	7.01	(29)	6.70	(35)	6.28	(47)	6.48	(39)
Area 3. Access to Sound Money	6.48	(41)	6.82	(43)	5.75	(81)	6.24	(70)	7.16	(74)	9.44	(30)	9.25	(32)	9.53	(20)
Area 4. Freedom to Trade Internationally	4.40	(68)	4.51	(70)	5.00	(73)	7.14	(36)	7.69	(36)	7.95	(14)	8.04	(10)	7.95	(7)
Area 5. Regulation of Credit, Labor, and Business	4.32	(86)	4.46	(82)	5.10	(68)	6.00	(47)	7.05	(19)	7.03	(38)	7.05	(39)	7.18	(32)

Unadjusted																
Summary Rating (Rank) ➤	**4.60**	(81)	**4.87**	(80)	**5.08**	(75)	**6.13**	(61)	**6.55**	(56)	**7.44**	(28)	**7.43**	(28)	**7.52**	(15)
	Rating	Data	Rating	Data	Rating	Data	Rating	Data	Rating	Data	Rating	Data	Rating	Data	Rating	Data
1. Size of Government	**3.77**		**2.92**		**2.94**		**3.73**		**3.85**		**5.80**		**6.28**		**6.20**	
A. Government consumption	7.53	(14.40)	7.69	(13.87)	7.43	(14.75)	7.58	(14.23)	7.86	(13.27)	8.00	(12.80)	8.05	(12.63)	7.90	(13.14)
B. Transfers and subsidies			1.06	(33.30)	2.32	(28.70)	3.32	(25.00)	5.04	(18.71)	4.90	(19.40)	4.57	(20.43)	4.40	(21.06)
C. Government enterprises and investment	0.00	(92.60)	0.00	(83.50)	0.00	(68.50)	0.00	(68.50)	0.00	(68.50)	8.00	(17.20)	10.00	(13.42)	10.00	(14.74)
D. Top marginal tax rate					2.00		4.00		2.50		2.50		2.50		2.50	
(i) Top marginal income tax rate					3.00	(50)	4.00	(44)	5.00	(40)	5.00	(38)	5.00	(40)	5.00	(40)
(ii) Top marginal income and payroll tax rates					1.00	(60)	4.00	(44)	0.00	(62)	0.00	(64)	0.00	(63)	0.00	(63)
2. Legal Structure and Security of Property Rights			**6.78**		**7.25**		**7.60**		**7.01**		**6.70**		**6.28**		**6.48**	
A. Judicial independence							6.68		6.51		5.40		5.20		5.06	
B. Impartial courts							6.77		6.35		5.40		3.33		3.45	
C. Protection of property rights							4.93		5.53		7.40		6.04		5.59	
D. Military interference in rule of law and politics							9.62		10.00		10.00		10.00		10.00	
E. Integrity of the legal system							10.00		6.67		6.70		6.67		6.67	
F. Legal enforcement of contracts											7.20		6.70		6.58	
G. Regulatory restrictions on sale of real property											4.90		6.06		8.04	
3. Access to Sound Money	**6.48**		**6.82**		**5.75**		**6.24**		**7.16**		**9.40**		**9.25**		**9.53**	
A. Money growth	8.26	(8.70)	8.66	(6.70)	7.33	(13.34)	7.67	(11.67)	7.62	(11.91)	9.50	(2.50)	8.70	(6.52)	9.49	(2.54)
B. Standard deviation of inflation	8.87	(2.82)	9.80	(0.50)	6.87	(7.83)	7.64	(5.90)	7.97	(5.08)	9.00	(2.54)	9.50	(1.25)	9.49	(1.28)
C. Inflation: most recent year	8.79	(6.03)	8.82	(5.91)	8.82	(5.91)	4.65	(26.73)	8.04	(9.80)	9.30	(3.55)	8.79	(6.07)	9.16	(4.21)
D. Freedom to own foreign currency bank accounts	0.00		0.00		0.00		5.00		5.00		10.00		10.00		10.00	
4. Freedom to Trade Internationally	**4.34**		**4.45**		**4.83**		**7.09**		**7.69**		**8.00**		**8.04**		**7.95**	
A. Taxes on international trade	6.67		7.53		6.09		6.67		7.31		8.40		8.03		8.22	
(i) Revenues from trade taxes (% of trade sector)	6.67	(5.00)	7.53	(3.70)	6.57	(5.14)	6.09	(5.86)	9.45	(0.83)	9.60	(0.60)	9.61	(0.59)	9.44	(0.84)
(ii) Mean tariff rate							7.80	(11.00)	8.36	(8.20)	9.50	(2.70)	8.88	(5.60)	8.94	(5.30)
(iii) Standard deviation of tariff rates					5.60	(11.00)	6.12	(9.70)	4.12	(14.70)	6.10	(9.70)	5.61	(10.98)	6.29	(9.28)
B. Regulatory trade barriers							7.13		8.52		7.40		7.46		7.65	
(i) Non-tariff trade barriers							7.13		8.20		7.30		7.32		7.71	
(ii) Compliance cost of importing and exporting									8.83		7.60		7.59		7.59	
C. Size of trade sector relative to expected	6.77		6.47		4.26		5.25		8.11		8.10		8.96		8.17	
D. Black-market exchange rates	0.00		0.00		5.60		10.00		10.00		10.00		10.00		10.00	
E. International capital market controls	0.00		0.00		0.00		6.38		4.53		5.90		5.73		5.69	
(i) Foreign ownership/investment restrictions							7.76		8.29		7.90		7.61		7.53	
(ii) Capital controls	0.00		0.00		0.00		5.00		0.77		3.80		3.85		3.85	
5. Regulation of Credit, Labor, and Business	**3.82**		**3.37**		**4.61**		**5.99**		**7.05**		**7.30**		**7.30**		**7.41**	
A. Credit market regulations	3.56		2.66		4.40		6.60		8.29		8.50		8.84		8.84	
(i) Ownership of banks	0.00		0.00		2.00		8.00		8.00		10.00		10.00		10.00	
(ii) Foreign bank competition							7.30		6.85		8.00		8.00		8.00	
(iii) Private sector credit	4.68		5.33		5.21		5.28		8.62		5.90		7.34		7.34	
(iv) Interest rate controls/negative real interest rates	6.00				6.00		6.00		10.00		10.00		10.00		10.00	
B. Labor market regulations							5.41		5.59		6.80		7.08		7.31	
(i) Hiring regulations and minimum wage							6.67		4.65		8.90		10.00		7.23	
(ii) Hiring and firing regulations					7.07		7.07		5.50		4.60		4.91		5.14	
(iii) Centralized collective bargaining							5.18		6.97		7.50		7.50		7.51	
(iv) Hours regulations							5.15		5.85		3.30		3.30		6.00	
(v) Mandated cost of worker dismissal											6.80		6.76		7.99	
(vi) Conscription	0.00		0.00		1.00		3.00		5.00		10.00		10.00		10.00	
C. Business regulations							5.97		7.26		6.50		5.98		6.09	
(i) Price controls							8.00		8.00		7.00		8.00		8.00	
(ii) Administrative requirements									7.42		3.00		1.88		2.00	
(iii) Bureaucracy costs							6.14		6.18		6.60		3.21		3.12	
(iv) Starting a business							6.40		7.37		8.30		9.75		9.75	
(v) Extra payments/bribes/favoritism							3.32		7.35		7.30		5.16		5.07	
(vi) Licensing restrictions											7.40		7.57		7.82	
(vii) Cost of tax compliance											6.20		6.30		6.90	

Iceland

Chain-Linked	1980 Rating (Rank)	1985 Rating (Rank)	1990 Rating (Rank)	1995 Rating (Rank)	2000 Rating (Rank)	2005 Rating (Rank)	2008 Rating (Rank)	2009 Rating (Rank)
Summary Rating (Rank) ➤	**5.43** (55)	**5.75** (44)	**7.03** (24)	**7.40** (16)	**7.76** (12)	**7.71** (14)	**6.89** (54)	**6.72** (63)
Area 1. Size of Government	5.12 (50)	5.35 (46)	6.03 (45)	5.72 (72)	6.07 (69)	6.91 (47)	6.12 (75)	5.01 (98)
Area 2. Legal Structure and Security of Property Rights	7.96 (21)	9.18 (12)	9.73 (13)	8.30 (17)	9.03 (12)	9.01 (2)	8.43 (8)	8.31 (8)
Area 3. Access to Sound Money	2.62 (103)	2.84 (104)	7.08 (40)	9.45 (25)	9.18 (34)	8.75 (52)	7.69 (75)	7.78 (79)
Area 4. Freedom to Trade Internationally	5.56 (45)	5.57 (51)	5.91 (50)	6.60 (63)	6.86 (65)	5.72 (101)	5.74 (100)	5.40 (106)
Area 5. Regulation of Credit, Labor, and Business	6.29 (22)	6.30 (26)	6.66 (17)	6.91 (13)	7.63 (6)	8.14 (12)	6.50 (62)	7.10 (37)

Unadjusted

	1980	1985	1990	1995	2000	2005	2008	2009
Summary Rating (Rank) ➤	**5.14** (67)	**5.44** (58)	**6.62** (28)	**7.40** (18)	**7.76** (12)	**7.81** (12)	**6.99** (59)	**6.81** (70)
	Rating Data	Rating Data	Rating Data	Rating Data	Rating Data	Rating Data	Rating Data	Rating Data
1. Size of Government	**5.12**	**5.35**	**6.03**	**5.72**	**6.07**	**6.90**	**6.12**	**5.01**
A. Government consumption	5.23 (22.21)	5.45 (21.48)	4.74 (23.87)	4.22 (25.65)	3.44 (28.31)	3.20 (29.00)	2.59 (31.20)	1.72 (34.15)
B. Transfers and subsidies	7.25 (10.60)	6.95 (11.70)	7.38 (10.10)	7.65 (9.12)	8.34 (6.60)	7.90 (8.20)	7.91 (8.17)	7.32 (10.35)
C. Government enterprises and investment	8.00 (15.30)	8.00 (16.10)	7.00 (22.20)	7.00 (24.80)	7.00 (24.80)	10.00 (10.90)	8.00 (18.13)	7.00 (24.96)
D. Top marginal tax rate	0.00	1.00	5.00	4.00	5.50	6.50	6.00	4.00
(i) Top marginal income tax rate	0.00 (63)	1.00 (56)	5.00 (40)	4.00 (47)	6.00 (45)	7.00 (39)	7.00 (36)	5.00 (40)
(ii) Top marginal income and payroll tax rates					5.00 (48)	6.00 (42)	5.00 (46)	3.00 (50)
2. Legal Structure and Security of Property Rights	**6.83**	**7.88**	**8.35**	**8.30**	**9.03**	**9.00**	**8.43**	**8.31**
A. Judicial independence				7.78	8.52	8.40	8.06	8.18
B. Impartial courts				8.28	9.02	8.90	6.61	6.73
C. Protection of property rights				5.80	7.62	9.40	8.28	7.30
D. Military interference in rule of law and politics				9.64	10.00	10.00	10.00	10.00
E. Integrity of the legal system				10.00	10.00	10.00	10.00	10.00
F. Legal enforcement of contracts						7.10	6.95	6.82
G. Regulatory restrictions on sale of real property						9.10	9.14	9.14
3. Access to Sound Money	**2.62**	**2.84**	**7.08**	**9.45**	**9.18**	**8.70**	**7.69**	**7.78**
A. Money growth	3.57 (32.16)	4.81 (25.96)	5.77 (21.13)	9.18 (4.12)	8.16 (9.21)	7.10 (14.70)	4.92 (25.38)	4.92 (25.38)
B. Standard deviation of inflation	6.92 (7.70)	2.82 (17.95)	8.81 (2.97)	9.16 (2.09)	9.61 (0.97)	8.80 (3.11)	8.35 (4.12)	8.58 (3.54)
C. Inflation: most recent year	0.00 (52.48)	3.74 (31.30)	3.74 (31.30)	9.45 (2.75)	8.97 (5.16)	9.20 (4.16)	7.46 (12.68)	7.60 (12.00)
D. Freedom to own foreign currency bank accounts	0.00	0.00	10.00	10.00	10.00	10.00	10.00	10.00
4. Freedom to Trade Internationally	**5.61**	**5.62**	**5.89**	**6.52**	**6.86**	**5.70**	**5.74**	**5.40**
A. Taxes on international trade	6.87	7.80	7.86	8.65	8.02	6.10	6.08	6.34
(i) Revenues from trade taxes (% of trade sector)	5.67 (6.50)	6.93 (4.60)	7.34 (3.99)	9.61 (0.58)	9.65 (0.53)	9.70 (0.50)	9.71 (0.43)	9.76 (0.36)
(ii) Mean tariff rate	8.08 (9.60)	8.66 (6.70)	9.24 (3.80)	9.26 (3.70)	9.62 (1.90)	8.50 (7.70)	8.54 (7.30)	8.84 (5.80)
(iii) Standard deviation of tariff rates			7.00 (7.50)	7.08 (7.30)	4.80 (13.00)	0.00 (38.70)	0.00 (32.05)	0.42 (23.95)
B. Regulatory trade barriers				6.62	8.71	6.90	6.48	6.51
(i) Non-tariff trade barriers				6.62	8.25	5.90	5.27	5.33
(ii) Compliance cost of importing and exporting					9.17	8.00	7.70	7.70
C. Size of trade sector relative to expected	2.79	3.30	1.37	1.03	1.34	0.60	1.95	2.39
D. Black-market exchange rates	8.20	6.80	10.00	10.00	10.00	10.00	10.00	10.00
E. International capital market controls	2.00	2.00	2.00	6.28	6.25	5.00	4.18	1.76
(i) Foreign ownership / investment restrictions				7.56	8.65	6.10	4.52	2.75
(ii) Capital controls	2.00	2.00	2.00	5.00	3.85	3.80	3.85	0.77
5. Regulation of Credit, Labor, and Business	**5.50**	**5.51**	**5.76**	**7.01**	**7.63**	**8.70**	**6.96**	**7.57**
A. Credit market regulations	5.20	5.23	6.28	6.86	7.91	9.30	5.50	7.26
(i) Ownership of banks	2.00	2.00	2.00	2.00	5.00	10.00	10.00	10.00
(ii) Foreign bank competition				5.83	8.10	8.00	8.00	8.00
(iii) Private sector credit	9.61	9.69	8.83	9.42	10.00	10.00	0.00	2.03
(iv) Interest rate controls / negative real interest rates	4.00	4.00	8.00	10.00	9.00	9.00	4.00	9.00
B. Labor market regulations			6.80	6.38	6.66	8.00	7.65	7.84
(i) Hiring regulations and minimum wage				6.20	4.76	6.70	5.60	5.57
(ii) Hiring and firing regulations			5.92	5.92	6.03	7.70	7.41	7.51
(iii) Centralized collective bargaining	4.49	4.49	4.49	4.49	5.48	6.70	6.12	5.94
(iv) Hours regulations				5.28	7.01	8.00	8.00	8.00
(v) Mandated cost of worker dismissal						8.80	8.79	10.00
(vi) Conscription	10.00	10.00	10.00	10.00	10.00	10.00	10.00	10.00
C. Business regulations				7.81	8.33	8.80	7.72	7.62
(i) Price controls				6.00	8.00	8.00	8.00	8.00
(ii) Administrative requirements					6.98	7.20	6.13	5.49
(iii) Bureaucracy costs				8.06	8.43	8.60	2.79	3.01
(iv) Starting a business				7.67	8.25	9.80	9.76	9.78
(v) Extra payments / bribes / favoritism				9.50	9.99	9.70	9.28	8.97
(vi) Licensing restrictions						9.60	9.66	9.66
(vii) Cost of tax compliance						8.40	8.43	8.43

India

	1980	1985	1990	1995	2000	2005	2008	2009
Chain-Linked	Rating (Rank)	Rating (Rank)	Rating (Rank)	Rating (Rank)	Rating (Rank)	Rating (Rank)	Rating (Rank)	Rating (Rank)
Summary Rating (Rank) ➤	**5.41** (57)	**5.08** (71)	**5.13** (75)	**5.76** (72)	**6.27** (72)	**6.55** (74)	**6.45** (83)	**6.38** (85)
Area 1. Size of Government	5.00 (54)	4.50 (72)	4.88 (76)	6.26 (54)	6.83 (41)	6.67 (60)	6.67 (52)	6.69 (46)
Area 2. Legal Structure and Security of Property Rights	6.32 (34)	5.38 (52)	4.79 (64)	5.87 (48)	5.99 (52)	6.44 (47)	5.93 (61)	5.72 (64)
Area 3. Access to Sound Money	6.29 (51)	6.61 (57)	6.63 (60)	6.50 (64)	6.88 (85)	6.84 (91)	6.69 (96)	6.55 (108)
Area 4. Freedom to Trade Internationally	4.32 (69)	3.68 (77)	4.02 (90)	4.67 (104)	5.54 (108)	6.45 (73)	6.82 (63)	6.54 (68)
Area 5. Regulation of Credit, Labor, and Business	5.22 (52)	5.24 (53)	5.29 (58)	5.52 (65)	6.09 (59)	6.36 (66)	6.16 (85)	6.39 (74)

Unadjusted								
Summary Rating (Rank) ➤	**5.39** (56)	**5.06** (74)	**5.04** (82)	**5.73** (74)	**6.27** (72)	**6.58** (80)	**6.48** (90)	**6.40** (94)
	Rating Data	Rating Data	Rating Data	Rating Data	Rating Data	Rating Data	Rating Data	Rating Data
1. Size of Government	**5.00**	**4.50**	**4.88**	**6.26**	**6.83**	**6.70**	**6.67**	**6.69**
A. Government consumption	8.34 (11.65)	7.62 (14.11)	7.15 (15.68)	7.31 (15.16)	6.74 (17.10)	6.90 (16.40)	6.63 (17.46)	6.72 (17.14)
B. Transfers and subsidies	8.66 (5.40)	8.37 (6.50)	8.37 (6.50)	8.72 (5.20)	8.59 (5.66)	8.70 (5.10)	8.04 (7.68)	8.04 (7.68)
C. Government enterprises and investment	2.00 (46.70)	2.00 (49.50)	2.00 (42.30)	4.00 (31.40)	4.00 (31.40)	4.00 (31.40)	4.00	4.00
D. Top marginal tax rate	1.00	0.00	2.00	5.00	8.00	7.00	8.00	8.00
(i) Top marginal income tax rate	1.00 (60)	0.00 (62)	2.00 (53)	5.00 (40)	8.00 (30)	7.00 (34)	8.00 (34)	8.00 (34)
(ii) Top marginal income and payroll tax rates			2.00 (53)	5.00 (40)	8.00 (30)	7.00 (34)	8.00 (34)	8.00 (34)
2. Legal Structure and Security of Property Rights	**5.78**	**4.92**	**4.39**	**5.87**	**5.99**	**6.40**	**5.93**	**5.72**
A. Judicial independence				7.33	7.01	8.20	6.60	6.28
B. Impartial courts				7.60	8.02	6.90	5.91	5.24
C. Protection of property rights				4.10	3.27	7.90	6.30	5.90
D. Military interference in rule of law and politics				6.21	5.00	6.70	6.67	6.67
E. Integrity of the legal system				4.11	6.67	6.70	6.67	6.67
F. Legal enforcement of contracts						2.60	2.59	2.59
G. Regulatory restrictions on sale of real property						6.30	6.74	6.74
3. Access to Sound Money	**6.29**	**6.61**	**6.63**	**6.50**	**6.88**	**6.80**	**6.69**	**6.55**
A. Money growth	9.36 (3.22)	8.38 (8.10)	8.58 (7.08)	8.56 (7.22)	9.03 (4.86)	8.40 (8.00)	8.77 (6.15)	8.87 (5.65)
B. Standard deviation of inflation	8.10 (4.76)	9.56 (1.11)	9.42 (1.45)	9.06 (2.34)	9.29 (1.77)	9.80 (0.53)	9.66 (0.85)	9.52 (1.21)
C. Inflation: most recent year	7.69 (11.54)	8.50 (7.52)	8.50 (7.52)	8.37 (8.16)	9.20 (4.01)	9.20 (4.25)	8.33 (8.35)	7.82 (10.88)
D. Freedom to own foreign currency bank accounts	0.00	0.00	0.00	0.00	0.00	0.00	0.00	0.00
4. Freedom to Trade Internationally	**4.19**	**3.56**	**3.89**	**4.62**	**5.54**	**6.50**	**6.82**	**6.54**
A. Taxes on international trade	0.00	0.00	0.00	0.91	4.34	5.60	6.15	6.26
(i) Revenues from trade taxes (% of trade sector)	0.00 (15.50)	0.00 (24.20)	0.00 (21.10)	2.16 (11.76)	4.49 (8.26)	7.20 (4.30)	7.54 (3.69)	7.71 (3.43)
(ii) Mean tariff rate	0.00 (74.30)	0.00 (98.80)	0.00 (79.20)	0.00 (55.20)	3.50 (32.50)	6.60 (17.00)	7.40 (13.00)	7.42 (12.90)
(iii) Standard deviation of tariff rates			0.00 (45.20)	0.56 (23.60)	5.04 (12.40)	3.00 (17.50)	3.50 (16.25)	3.65 (15.87)
B. Regulatory trade barriers				6.35	5.67	6.10	6.59	6.43
(i) Non-tariff trade barriers				6.35	5.35	6.90	5.68	5.37
(ii) Compliance cost of importing and exporting					5.99	5.30	7.49	7.49
C. Size of trade sector relative to expected	3.70	2.36	3.22	5.10	5.67	6.90	8.29	7.10
D. Black-market exchange rates	9.00	7.20	8.00	8.40	10.00	10.00	10.00	10.00
E. International capital market controls	0.00	0.00	0.00	2.33	2.02	3.70	3.08	2.90
(i) Foreign ownership / investment restrictions				4.67	4.05	7.40	6.16	5.81
(ii) Capital controls	0.00	0.00	0.00	0.00	0.00	0.00	0.00	0.00
5. Regulation of Credit, Labor, and Business	**5.68**	**5.70**	**5.43**	**5.40**	**6.09**	**6.50**	**6.31**	**6.50**
A. Credit market regulations	5.22	5.28	5.49	5.74	6.35	6.80	6.89	6.65
(i) Ownership of banks	0.00	0.00	0.00	2.00	2.00	2.00	2.00	2.00
(ii) Foreign bank competition				5.27	6.35	6.00	6.00	6.00
(iii) Private sector credit	7.67	7.84	8.46	9.17	8.45	9.00	9.58	8.60
(iv) Interest rate controls / negative real interest rates	8.00	8.00	8.00	8.00	10.00	10.00	10.00	10.00
B. Labor market regulations			6.26	6.11	6.05	7.30	7.29	7.93
(i) Hiring regulations and minimum wage				6.23	4.35	10.00	10.00	10.00
(ii) Hiring and firing regulations			2.56	2.56	1.70	3.30	3.71	4.49
(iii) Centralized collective bargaining	6.21	6.21	6.21	6.21	7.72	7.50	7.22	7.05
(iv) Hours regulations				5.55	6.50	8.00	8.00	10.00
(v) Mandated cost of worker dismissal						4.80	4.81	6.03
(vi) Conscription	10.00	10.00	10.00	10.00	10.00	10.00	10.00	10.00
C. Business regulations				4.36	5.85	5.50	4.75	4.93
(i) Price controls			3.00	4.00	4.00	3.00	3.00	3.00
(ii) Administrative requirements					7.37	3.20	3.14	3.31
(iii) Bureaucracy costs				6.06	7.40	5.20	4.41	4.92
(iv) Starting a business				4.95	5.93	7.00	7.65	7.86
(v) Extra payments / bribes / favoritism				2.42	4.57	6.60	4.70	4.47
(vi) Licensing restrictions						6.60	3.40	3.86
(vii) Cost of tax compliance						7.00	6.96	7.11

Indonesia

Chain-Linked

	1980		1985		1990		1995		2000		2005		2008		2009	
	Rating	(Rank)	Rating	(Rank)	Rating	(Rank)	Rating	(Rank)	Rating	(Rank)	Rating	(Rank)	Rating	(Rank)	Rating	(Rank)
Summary Rating (Rank) ➤	**5.24**	(60)	**6.16**	(33)	**6.53**	(32)	**6.57**	(40)	**6.04**	(83)	**6.41**	(78)	**6.56**	(78)	**6.53**	(75)
Area 1. Size of Government	5.27	(45)	6.35	(18)	7.13	(17)	7.96	(14)	7.57	(21)	7.18	(34)	7.45	(28)	7.58	(22)
Area 2. Legal Structure and Security of Property Rights	3.27	(66)	4.27	(70)	4.52	(69)	3.55	(113)	3.36	(115)	3.95	(105)	4.44	(97)	4.40	(95)
Area 3. Access to Sound Money	6.54	(38)	9.27	(14)	8.76	(23)	9.09	(32)	6.20	(103)	7.39	(80)	7.55	(81)	7.71	(80)
Area 4. Freedom to Trade Internationally	6.62	(31)	6.21	(37)	6.46	(40)	6.59	(64)	7.67	(37)	7.45	(30)	7.05	(52)	6.72	(57)
Area 5. Regulation of Credit, Labor, and Business	4.36	(80)	4.51	(80)	5.65	(50)	5.56	(62)	5.40	(92)	6.12	(80)	6.31	(79)	6.28	(83)

Unadjusted

	1980		1985		1990		1995		2000		2005		2008		2009	
Summary Rating (Rank) ➤	**5.20**	(61)	**6.12**	(30)	**6.46**	(32)	**6.42**	(45)	**6.04**	(83)	**6.37**	(91)	**6.51**	(87)	**6.50**	(84)
	Rating	Data	Rating	Data	Rating	Data	Rating	Data	Rating	Data	Rating	Data	Rating	Data	Rating	Data
1. Size of Government	**5.27**		**6.35**		**7.13**		**7.96**		**7.57**		**7.20**		**7.45**		**7.58**	
A. Government consumption	6.84	(16.75)	6.95	(16.36)	7.93	(13.04)	8.45	(11.28)	8.98	(9.47)	8.50	(11.20)	8.20	(12.13)	7.50	(14.52)
B. Transfers and subsidies	9.24	(3.30)	9.46	(2.50)	9.59	(2.00)	9.89	(0.90)	8.30	(6.73)	7.20	(10.70)	8.60	(5.64)	9.34	(2.92)
C. Government enterprises and investment	2.00	(49.50)	2.00	(43.00)	4.00	(32.50)	7.00	(20.70)	7.00	(20.70)	7.00	(20.70)	7.00		7.00	
D. Top marginal tax rate	3.00		7.00		7.00		6.50		6.00		6.00		6.00		6.50	
(i) Top marginal income tax rate	3.00	(50)	7.00	(35)	7.00	(35)	8.00	(30)	7.00	(35)	7.00	(35)	7.00	(35)	8.00	(30)
(ii) Top marginal income and payroll tax rates					7.00	(35)	5.00	(40)	5.00	(40)	5.00	(40)	5.00	(40)	5.00	(37)
2. Legal Structure and Security of Property Rights	**3.41**		**4.46**		**4.72**		**3.55**		**3.36**		**4.00**		**4.44**		**4.40**	
A. Judicial independence							2.33		3.01		3.00		4.72		4.66	
B. Impartial courts							4.22		4.01		3.90		4.79		4.72	
C. Protection of property rights							4.20		3.13		4.60		5.18		5.07	
D. Military interference in rule of law and politics							2.88		3.33		4.20		4.17		4.17	
E. Integrity of the legal system							4.11		3.33		5.00		5.00		5.00	
F. Legal enforcement of contracts											1.20		1.17		1.17	
G. Regulatory restrictions on sale of real property											5.80		6.07		6.00	
3. Access to Sound Money	**6.54**		**9.27**		**8.76**		**9.09**		**6.20**		**7.40**		**7.55**		**7.71**	
A. Money growth	6.30	(18.49)	9.36	(3.20)	8.03	(9.87)	8.97	(5.17)	5.56	(22.19)	8.40	(7.80)	8.67	(6.67)	8.57	(7.14)
B. Standard deviation of inflation	6.07	(9.82)	8.59	(3.52)	7.86	(5.35)	9.38	(1.54)	0.00	(27.72)	8.20	(4.48)	8.54	(3.64)	8.53	(3.67)
C. Inflation: most recent year	3.80	(30.99)	9.14	(4.28)	9.14	(4.28)	8.02	(9.89)	9.26	(3.72)	7.90	(10.45)	7.98	(10.10)	8.72	(6.38)
D. Freedom to own foreign currency bank accounts	10.00		10.00		10.00		10.00		10.00		5.00		5.00		5.00	
4. Freedom to Trade Internationally	**6.74**		**6.32**		**6.32**		**6.23**		**7.67**		**7.50**		**7.05**		**6.72**	
A. Taxes on international trade	6.13		7.66		5.88		6.43		7.88		7.90		7.87		7.90	
(i) Revenues from trade taxes (% of trade sector)	8.07	(2.90)	8.93	(1.60)	8.39	(2.41)	9.13	(1.31)	9.65	(0.53)	9.40	(0.90)	9.48	(0.79)	9.53	(0.71)
(ii) Mean tariff rate	4.20	(29.00)	6.38	(18.10)	5.94	(20.30)	6.60	(17.00)	8.32	(8.40)	8.70	(6.50)	8.62	(6.90)	8.64	(6.80)
(iii) Standard deviation of tariff rates					3.32	(16.70)	3.56	(16.10)	5.68	(10.80)	5.70	(10.70)	5.53	(11.18)	5.54	(11.15)
B. Regulatory trade barriers							3.33		5.91		6.30		6.70		6.48	
(i) Non-tariff trade barriers							3.33		3.82		6.40		6.69		6.16	
(ii) Compliance cost of importing and exporting									8.00		6.20		6.72		6.80	
C. Size of trade sector relative to expected	9.77		7.17		7.55		7.64		9.72		8.10		6.73		5.24	
D. Black-market exchange rates	9.60		8.60		10.00		10.00		10.00		10.00		10.00		10.00	
E. International capital market controls	0.00		0.00		0.00		3.76		4.83		4.90		3.92		3.99	
(i) Foreign ownership / investment restrictions							7.53		8.12		8.40		7.08		6.45	
(ii) Capital controls	0.00		0.00		0.00		0.00		1.54		1.50		0.77		1.54	
5. Regulation of Credit, Labor, and Business	**4.05**		**4.18**		**5.37**		**5.27**		**5.40**		**5.90**		**6.08**		**6.07**	
A. Credit market regulations	3.18		4.53		7.33		7.22		6.46		8.10		7.84		8.07	
(i) Ownership of banks	0.00		2.00		2.00		5.00		5.00		5.00		5.00		5.00	
(ii) Foreign bank competition							5.88		4.58		8.00		8.00		8.00	
(iii) Private sector credit	7.53		7.58		10.00		10.00		8.13		9.30		9.34		9.28	
(iv) Interest rate controls / negative real interest rates	2.00		4.00		10.00		10.00		10.00		10.00		9.00		10.00	
B. Labor market regulations							4.22		4.97		4.90		5.11		4.81	
(i) Hiring regulations and minimum wage							5.12		4.62		2.80		3.90		2.23	
(ii) Hiring and firing regulations					5.56		5.56		3.20		4.50		5.54		5.64	
(iii) Centralized collective bargaining									6.18		7.30		6.20		5.98	
(iv) Hours regulations							6.22		5.85		10.00		10.00		10.00	
(v) Mandated cost of worker dismissal											0.00		0.00		0.00	
(vi) Conscription	3.00		0.00		0.00		0.00		5.00		5.00		5.00		5.00	
C. Business regulations							4.36		4.76		4.70		5.29		5.32	
(i) Price controls					7.00		3.00		2.00		1.00		1.00		1.00	
(ii) Administrative requirements									6.95		6.30		4.79		4.42	
(iii) Bureaucracy costs							6.30		5.30		5.90		4.57		4.68	
(iv) Starting a business							5.22		5.63		5.80		7.61		8.09	
(v) Extra payments / bribes / favoritism							2.91		3.91		3.10		4.10		4.07	
(vi) Licensing restrictions											7.20		7.96		8.00	
(vii) Cost of tax compliance											3.50		7.02		7.02	

Iran

Chain-Linked	1980		1985		1990		1995		2000		2005		2008		2009	
	Rating	(Rank)	Rating	(Rank)	Rating	(Rank)	Rating	(Rank)	Rating	(Rank)	Rating	(Rank)	Rating	(Rank)	Rating	(Rank)
Summary Rating (Rank) ➤	**3.75**	(97)	**4.07**	(93)	**4.77**	(92)	**4.50**	(111)	**5.76**	(95)	**6.30**	(85)	**6.15**	(89)	**6.22**	(90)
Area 1. Size of Government	3.42	(93)	4.33	(76)	5.06	(72)	5.35	(82)	4.92	(93)	6.32	(73)	6.26	(69)	6.47	(55)
Area 2. Legal Structure and Security of Property Rights	1.76	(89)	2.26	(105)	2.20	(109)	5.60	(56)	5.91	(57)	6.11	(57)	6.12	(51)	6.01	(54)
Area 3. Access to Sound Money	6.90	(30)	8.10	(26)	8.99	(21)	3.87	(102)	8.00	(59)	8.06	(68)	7.88	(68)	8.18	(69)
Area 4. Freedom to Trade Internationally	3.03	(86)	2.30	(93)	4.00	(91)	4.00	(107)	5.88	(98)	5.74	(99)	5.03	(111)	4.93	(113)
Area 5. Regulation of Credit, Labor, and Business	3.82	(91)	3.35	(98)	3.62	(103)	3.68	(117)	4.08	(120)	5.16	(110)	5.29	(112)	5.35	(111)

Unadjusted

	1980		1985		1990		1995		2000		2005		2008		2009	
Summary Rating (Rank) ➤	**4.02**	(94)	**4.07**	(95)	**4.77**	(92)	**4.50**	(111)	**5.76**	(95)	**6.29**	(94)	**6.15**	(104)	**6.16**	(105)
	Rating	Data	Rating	Data	Rating	Data	Rating	Data	Rating	Data	Rating	Data	Rating	Data	Rating	Data
1. Size of Government	**4.56**		**4.33**		**5.06**		**5.35**		**4.92**		**6.30**		**6.26**		**6.47**	
A. Government consumption	3.44	(28.29)	6.00	(19.59)	7.30	(15.17)	6.12	(19.19)	4.68	(24.10)	5.50	(21.30)	5.93	(19.85)	6.83	(16.78)
B. Transfers and subsidies	8.23	(7.00)	9.32	(3.00)	8.94	(4.40)	9.29	(3.10)	9.52	(2.26)	8.30	(6.90)	8.11	(7.42)	8.04	(7.70)
C. Government enterprises and investment	2.00	(44.50)	2.00	(40.40)	4.00	(32.50)	2.00	(49.70)	4.00	(33.60)	4.00	(33.70)	4.00	(35.30)	4.00	(35.30)
D. Top marginal tax rate			0.00		0.00		4.00		1.50		7.50		7.00		7.00	
(i) Top marginal income tax rate			0.00	(90)	0.00	(75)	4.00	(54)	2.00	(54)	8.00	(35)	7.00	(35)	7.00	(35)
(ii) Top marginal income and payroll tax rates					0.00	(75)	4.00	(54)	1.00	(57)	7.00	(37)	7.00	(37)	7.00	(37)
2. Legal Structure and Security of Property Rights	**1.76**		**2.26**		**2.20**		**5.60**		**5.91**		**6.10**		**6.12**		**5.76**	
A. Judicial independence															4.73	
B. Impartial courts							4.92		4.86		4.20		4.20		3.57	
C. Protection of property rights															5.48	
D. Military interference in rule of law and politics							6.67		8.33		8.30		8.33		8.33	
E. Integrity of the legal system							6.96		6.67		6.70		6.67		6.67	
F. Legal enforcement of contracts											5.50		5.51		5.63	
G. Regulatory restrictions on sale of real property											5.80		5.87		5.87	
3. Access to Sound Money	**6.90**		**8.10**		**8.99**		**3.87**		**8.00**		**8.10**		**7.88**		**8.18**	
A. Money growth	4.64	(26.80)	5.94	(20.30)	8.19	(9.07)	6.09	(19.57)	7.15	(14.27)	7.70	(11.60)	8.18	(9.12)	8.58	(7.08)
B. Standard deviation of inflation	7.66	(5.85)	7.40	(6.51)	8.73	(3.17)	7.31	(6.72)	7.73	(5.67)	7.20	(6.93)	8.45	(3.88)	6.83	(7.92)
C. Inflation: most recent year	5.32	(23.41)	9.05	(4.73)	9.05	(4.73)	2.10	(39.50)	7.10	(14.48)	7.30	(13.43)	4.89	(25.55)	7.30	(13.50)
D. Freedom to own foreign currency bank accounts	10.00		10.00		10.00		0.00		10.00		10.00		10.00		10.00	
4. Freedom to Trade Internationally	**3.03**		**2.30**		**4.00**		**4.00**		**5.88**		**5.60**		**4.99**		**4.98**	
A. Taxes on international trade	2.93		3.20		6.15		7.30		8.34		6.90		4.17		4.17	
(i) Revenues from trade taxes (% of trade sector)	0.00	(17.00)	0.53	(14.20)	6.43	(5.35)	8.74	(1.89)	7.67	(3.49)	7.60	(3.60)	7.72	(3.42)	7.72	(3.42)
(ii) Mean tariff rate	5.86	(20.70)	5.86	(20.70)	5.86	(20.70)	5.86	(20.70)	9.02	(4.90)	6.30	(18.70)	4.80	(26.00)	4.80	(26.00)
(iii) Standard deviation of tariff rates									8.32	(4.20)			0.00	(28.08)	0.00	(28.08)
B. Regulatory trade barriers											5.50		5.70		5.02	
(i) Non-tariff trade barriers															3.97	
(ii) Compliance cost of importing and exporting											5.50		5.70		6.07	
C. Size of trade sector relative to expected	3.95		0.00		5.59		4.46		3.98		5.60		5.08		4.21	
D. Black-market exchange rates	0.00		0.00		0.00		0.00		8.86		10.00		10.00		10.00	
E. International capital market controls	0.00		0.00		0.00		0.00		0.00		0.00		0.00		1.51	
(i) Foreign ownership / investment restrictions															3.03	
(ii) Capital controls	0.00		0.00		0.00		0.00		0.00		0.00		0.00		0.00	
5. Regulation of Credit, Labor, and Business	**3.86**		**3.38**		**3.62**		**3.68**		**4.08**		**5.40**		**5.52**		**5.42**	
A. Credit market regulations	2.68		2.40		3.13		3.33		4.67		6.30		6.33		6.67	
(i) Ownership of banks	0.00		0.00		0.00		0.00		0.00		0.00		0.00		0.00	
(ii) Foreign bank competition																
(iii) Private sector credit	8.03		7.19		9.38		10.00		10.00		10.00		10.00		10.00	
(iv) Interest rate controls / negative real interest rates	0.00		0.00		0.00		0.00		4.00		9.00		9.00		10.00	
B. Labor market regulations											4.50		4.53		4.38	
(i) Hiring regulations and minimum wage											8.90		8.90		7.77	
(ii) Hiring and firing regulations															4.36	
(iii) Centralized collective bargaining															4.22	
(iv) Hours regulations											7.30		7.30		8.00	
(v) Mandated cost of worker dismissal											1.90		1.93		1.97	
(vi) Conscription	3.00		0.00		0.00		0.00		0.00		0.00		0.00		0.00	
C. Business regulations											5.20		5.70		5.20	
(i) Price controls					2.00		2.00		2.00		2.00		2.00		2.00	
(ii) Administrative requirements															3.18	
(iii) Bureaucracy costs															5.60	
(iv) Starting a business											9.00		9.67		9.70	
(v) Extra payments / bribes / favoritism															4.81	
(vi) Licensing restrictions											3.80		5.00		4.97	
(vii) Cost of tax compliance											6.10		6.14		6.14	

Ireland

	1980	1985	1990	1995	2000	2005	2008	2009
Chain-Linked	Rating (Rank)	Rating (Rank)	Rating (Rank)	Rating (Rank)	Rating (Rank)	Rating (Rank)	Rating (Rank)	Rating (Rank)
Summary Rating (Rank) ➤	**6.73** (17)	**6.75** (19)	**7.32** (18)	**8.20** (5)	**8.16** (7)	**8.07** (4)	**7.71** (10)	**7.32** (26)
Area 1. Size of Government	4.67 (65)	4.26 (79)	5.56 (61)	5.76 (71)	6.13 (61)	6.64 (62)	5.43 (95)	4.59 (107)
Area 2. Legal Structure and Security of Property Rights	8.37 (17)	7.86 (20)	9.14 (16)	9.09 (8)	8.97 (14)	7.93 (17)	7.92 (17)	7.85 (17)
Area 3. Access to Sound Money	5.93 (69)	6.65 (55)	6.80 (55)	9.60 (15)	9.43 (25)	9.65 (7)	9.48 (14)	9.12 (43)
Area 4. Freedom to Trade Internationally	7.82 (11)	7.74 (12)	7.70 (15)	8.75 (4)	9.05 (3)	8.43 (5)	8.20 (7)	8.33 (4)
Area 5. Regulation of Credit, Labor, and Business	7.15 (9)	7.49 (6)	7.67 (6)	7.77 (6)	7.20 (14)	7.68 (22)	7.51 (22)	6.73 (53)

Unadjusted

	1980	1985	1990	1995	2000	2005	2008	2009
Summary Rating (Rank) ➤	**6.24** (23)	**6.26** (24)	**6.75** (24)	**8.18** (5)	**8.16** (7)	**8.13** (5)	**7.77** (11)	**7.38** (25)
	Rating Data	Rating Data	Rating Data	Rating Data	Rating Data	Rating Data	Rating Data	Rating Data
1. Size of Government	**4.67**	**4.26**	**5.56**	**5.76**	**6.13**	**6.60**	**5.43**	**4.59**
A. Government consumption	5.31 (21.96)	5.15 (22.49)	5.80 (20.27)	5.44 (21.52)	5.33 (21.88)	5.10 (22.60)	3.99 (26.43)	3.60 (27.75)
B. Transfers and subsidies	5.37 (17.50)	4.88 (19.30)	5.42 (17.30)	5.10 (18.50)	4.20 (21.78)	6.90 (11.70)	6.23 (14.33)	5.26 (17.91)
C. Government enterprises and investment	7.00 (24.60)	7.00 (24.70)	10.00 (11.10)	10.00 (14.30)	10.00 (14.30)	10.00 (13.30)	7.00 (23.84)	6.00 (26.86)
D. Top marginal tax rate	1.00	0.00	1.00	2.50	5.00	4.50	4.50	3.50
(i) Top marginal income tax rate	1.00 (60)	0.00 (65)	1.00 (56)	3.00 (48)	5.00 (42)	5.00 (42)	5.00 (42)	5.00 (41)
(ii) Top marginal income and payroll tax rates			1.00 (57)	2.00 (51)	5.00 (42)	4.00 (49)	4.00 (48)	2.00 (56)
2. Legal Structure and Security of Property Rights	**7.08**	**6.65**	**7.73**	**9.09**	**8.97**	**7.90**	**7.92**	**7.85**
A. Judicial independence				9.30	8.68	8.60	8.90	8.75
B. Impartial courts				8.88	9.19	7.10	6.04	5.88
C. Protection of property rights				7.29	7.00	9.00	8.44	8.15
D. Military interference in rule of law and politics				10.00	10.00	10.00	10.00	10.00
E. Integrity of the legal system				10.00	10.00	10.00	10.00	10.00
F. Legal enforcement of contracts						4.90	4.95	4.95
G. Regulatory restrictions on sale of real property						5.90	7.08	7.21
3. Access to Sound Money	**5.93**	**6.65**	**6.80**	**9.60**	**9.43**	**9.70**	**9.48**	**9.12**
A. Money growth	8.07 (9.64)	9.56 (2.19)	9.25 (3.75)	9.03 (4.87)	9.39 (−3.05)	9.70 (1.30)	9.47 (2.63)	8.55 (7.26)
B. Standard deviation of inflation	8.61 (3.48)	8.09 (4.78)	8.97 (2.57)	9.47 (1.32)	9.42 (1.44)	9.40 (1.57)	9.27 (1.83)	8.84 (2.91)
C. Inflation: most recent year	7.06 (14.71)	8.96 (5.18)	8.96 (5.18)	9.91 (0.43)	8.89 (5.56)	9.50 (2.43)	9.19 (4.05)	9.10 (−4.48)
D. Freedom to own foreign currency bank accounts	0.00	0.00	0.00	10.00	10.00	10.00	10.00	10.00
4. Freedom to Trade Internationally	**7.55**	**7.47**	**7.36**	**8.60**	**9.05**	**8.40**	**8.20**	**8.33**
A. Taxes on international trade	7.95	8.25	7.88	8.37	9.18	8.40	8.03	8.22
(i) Revenues from trade taxes (% of trade sector)	7.67 (3.50)	8.00 (3.00)	8.00 (3.00)	8.80 (1.80)	9.78 (0.33)	9.60 (0.60)	9.61 (0.59)	9.44 (0.84)
(ii) Mean tariff rate	8.24 (8.80)	8.50 (7.50)	8.52 (7.40)	8.66 (6.70)	9.52 (2.40)	9.50 (2.70)	8.88 (5.60)	8.94 (5.30)
(iii) Standard deviation of tariff rates			7.12 (7.20)	7.64 (5.90)	8.24 (4.40)	6.10 (9.70)	5.61 (10.98)	6.29 (9.28)
B. Regulatory trade barriers				8.88	8.93	8.50	8.32	8.25
(i) Non-tariff trade barriers				8.88	8.18	8.20	7.82	7.67
(ii) Compliance cost of importing and exporting					9.67	8.80	8.83	8.83
C. Size of trade sector relative to expected	6.64	6.56	5.95	7.31	8.54	6.50	6.49	7.03
D. Black-market exchange rates	10.00	9.40	9.80	10.00	10.00	10.00	10.00	10.00
E. International capital market controls	5.00	5.00	5.00	8.46	8.61	8.80	8.14	8.14
(i) Foreign ownership / investment restrictions				8.91	8.76	9.10	7.94	7.81
(ii) Capital controls	5.00	5.00	5.00	8.00	8.46	8.50	8.33	8.46
5. Regulation of Credit, Labor, and Business	**5.97**	**6.26**	**6.32**	**7.82**	**7.20**	**8.00**	**7.81**	**7.01**
A. Credit market regulations	7.35	8.46	8.77	8.51	8.39	9.00	9.00	6.50
(i) Ownership of banks	8.00	8.00	8.00	8.00	8.00	8.00	8.00	8.00
(ii) Foreign bank competition				8.05	6.95	8.00	8.00	8.00
(iii) Private sector credit	8.04	7.37	8.32	9.01	10.00	10.00	10.00	0.00
(iv) Interest rate controls / negative real interest rates	6.00	10.00	10.00	10.00	9.00	10.00	10.00	10.00
B. Labor market regulations	6.55	6.58	6.53	6.68	5.35	7.50	7.58	7.77
(i) Hiring regulations and minimum wage				6.95	4.69	8.90	8.90	8.90
(ii) Hiring and firing regulations			5.52	5.52	3.77	4.00	4.66	4.55
(iii) Centralized collective bargaining	5.18	5.18	6.21	6.21	2.93	4.20	3.60	4.06
(iv) Hours regulations	4.49	4.57	4.40	4.72	5.34	10.00	10.00	10.00
(v) Mandated cost of worker dismissal						7.80	8.33	9.09
(vi) Conscription	10.00	10.00	10.00	10.00	10.00	10.00	10.00	10.00
C. Business regulations				8.28	7.84	7.50	6.86	6.76
(i) Price controls			7.00	9.00	9.00	6.00	7.00	7.00
(ii) Administrative requirements					7.20	4.80	3.56	3.44
(iii) Bureaucracy costs				7.61	7.93	6.70	2.38	2.23
(iv) Starting a business				7.63	6.92	9.60	9.58	9.58
(v) Extra payments / bribes / favoritism				8.87	8.17	8.40	8.52	8.26
(vi) Licensing restrictions						7.90	7.82	7.68
(vii) Cost of tax compliance						9.10	9.15	9.15

Israel

Chain-Linked	1980		1985		1990		1995		2000		2005		2008		2009	
	Rating	(Rank)	Rating	(Rank)	Rating	(Rank)	Rating	(Rank)	Rating	(Rank)	Rating	(Rank)	Rating	(Rank)	Rating	(Rank)
Summary Rating (Rank) ➤	3.79	(95)	4.34	(92)	4.79	(90)	5.87	(67)	6.55	(56)	7.03	(48)	6.55	(79)	6.43	(81)
Area 1. Size of Government	1.82	(105)	2.74	(104)	3.72	(98)	3.10	(113)	2.87	(121)	4.45	(111)	3.68	(120)	3.48	(120)
Area 2. Legal Structure and Security of Property Rights	4.59	(52)	7.67	(23)	4.96	(60)	6.98	(28)	8.01	(22)	6.39	(48)	5.90	(62)	5.97	(55)
Area 3. Access to Sound Money	2.03	(106)	1.25	(110)	3.95	(102)	7.43	(47)	8.09	(57)	9.34	(34)	9.07	(39)	8.84	(52)
Area 4. Freedom to Trade Internationally	6.65	(30)	6.61	(30)	6.64	(36)	6.79	(52)	7.87	(29)	8.07	(10)	7.59	(28)	7.37	(26)
Area 5. Regulation of Credit, Labor, and Business	3.91	(90)	3.71	(94)	4.60	(83)	5.03	(82)	5.90	(65)	6.93	(44)	6.72	(52)	6.72	(56)

Unadjusted

	1980		1985		1990		1995		2000		2005		2008		2009	
Summary Rating (Rank) ➤	3.63	(101)	4.15	(93)	4.61	(97)	5.77	(70)	6.55	(56)	6.87	(68)	6.67	(81)	6.53	(83)
	Rating	Data	Rating	Data	Rating	Data	Rating	Data	Rating	Data	Rating	Data	Rating	Data	Rating	Data
1. Size of Government	**1.82**		**2.74**		**3.72**		**3.10**		**2.87**		**4.50**		**4.83**		**4.56**	
A. Government consumption	0.00	(43.15)	0.45	(38.48)	2.09	(32.90)	2.24	(32.38)	2.18	(32.58)	2.10	(32.80)	2.97	(29.90)	3.01	(29.76)
B. Transfers and subsidies	4.47	(20.80)	4.77	(19.70)	5.59	(16.70)	5.07	(18.60)	3.92	(22.80)	7.30	(10.60)	7.37	(10.16)	7.24	(10.61)
C. Government enterprises and investment													4.00	(9.85)	4.00	(10.57)
D. Top marginal tax rate	1.00		3.00		3.50		2.00		2.50		4.00		5.00		4.00	
(i) Top marginal income tax rate	1.00	(66)	3.00	(60)	5.00	(48)	4.00	(50)	4.00	(50)	4.00	(49)	5.00	(46)	5.00	(46)
(ii) Top marginal income and payroll tax rates					2.00	(64)	0.00	(66)	1.00	(62)	4.00	(49)	5.00	(46)	3.00	(60)
2. Legal Structure and Security of Property Rights	**4.06**		**6.78**		**4.39**		**6.98**		**8.01**		**6.40**		**5.90**		**5.97**	
A. Judicial independence							8.68		9.19		8.90		8.38		8.68	
B. Impartial courts							7.02		9.35		7.10		5.59		5.28	
C. Protection of property rights							7.15		6.53		7.90		5.75		6.25	
D. Military interference in rule of law and politics							5.10		6.67		4.20		4.17		4.17	
E. Integrity of the legal system							6.96		8.33		8.30		8.33		8.33	
F. Legal enforcement of contracts											3.50		3.46		3.46	
G. Regulatory restrictions on sale of real property											4.80		5.63		5.63	
3. Access to Sound Money	**2.03**		**1.25**		**3.95**		**7.43**		**8.09**		**9.30**		**9.07**		**8.84**	
A. Money growth	3.13	(34.36)	0.00	(136.22)	5.48	(22.59)	7.80	(10.98)	9.07	(4.64)	8.40	(7.80)	7.64	(11.79)	6.86	(15.71)
B. Standard deviation of inflation	0.00	(37.42)	0.00	(103.70)	5.32	(11.71)	8.59	(3.53)	8.50	(3.74)	9.20	(2.08)	9.56	(1.09)	9.18	(2.04)
C. Inflation: most recent year	0.00	(134.74)	0.00	(260.00)	0.00	(260.00)	8.33	(8.36)	9.77	(1.14)	9.70	(1.33)	9.08	(4.60)	9.34	(3.33)
D. Freedom to own foreign currency bank accounts	5.00		5.00		5.00		5.00		5.00		10.00		10.00		10.00	
4. Freedom to Trade Internationally	**6.71**		**6.66**		**6.69**		**6.35**		**7.87**		**7.70**		**7.26**		**7.05**	
A. Taxes on international trade	6.60		8.07		9.39		7.95		9.68		7.90		7.16		7.39	
(i) Revenues from trade taxes (% of trade sector)	6.60	(5.10)	8.07	(2.90)	9.39	(0.92)	9.84	(0.24)	9.75	(0.37)	9.80	(0.30)	9.73	(0.40)	9.69	(0.47)
(ii) Mean tariff rate							8.34	(8.30)	9.60	(2.00)	9.50	(2.70)	8.64	(6.80)	8.70	(6.50)
(iii) Standard deviation of tariff rates							5.68	(10.80)			4.40	(14.10)	3.12	(17.20)	3.79	(15.54)
B. Regulatory trade barriers							5.38		8.11		7.80		7.89		8.05	
(i) Non-tariff trade barriers							5.38		6.88		7.30		7.38		7.49	
(ii) Compliance cost of importing and exporting									9.33		8.40		8.41		8.62	
C. Size of trade sector relative to expected	6.95		6.47		4.69		4.20		4.55		4.50		3.46		2.05	
D. Black-market exchange rates	9.80		8.60		9.20		10.00		10.00		10.00		10.00		10.00	
E. International capital market controls	2.00		2.00		2.00		4.21		7.02		8.40		7.78		7.77	
(i) Foreign ownership/investment restrictions							6.42		9.42		7.70		6.40		6.38	
(ii) Capital controls	2.00		2.00		2.00		2.00		4.61		9.20		9.17		9.17	
5. Regulation of Credit, Labor, and Business	**3.52**		**3.34**		**4.27**		**4.97**		**5.90**		**6.50**		**6.27**		**6.24**	
A. Credit market regulations	1.75		1.14		3.81		4.88		6.04		7.50		7.50		6.97	
(i) Ownership of banks	0.00		0.00		0.00		0.00		0.00		5.00		5.00		5.00	
(ii) Foreign bank competition							4.23		5.43		6.00		6.00		6.00	
(iii) Private sector credit	5.25		3.43		5.43		8.14		8.89		9.10		9.02		7.87	
(iv) Interest rate controls/negative real interest rates	0.00		0.00		6.00		8.00		10.00		10.00		10.00		9.00	
B. Labor market regulations					3.35		3.84		4.26		4.90		4.83		5.32	
(i) Hiring regulations and minimum wage							4.75		4.20		8.90		8.90		8.90	
(ii) Hiring and firing regulations					4.87		4.87		5.43		5.70		5.33		5.41	
(iii) Centralized collective bargaining	5.18		5.18		5.18		5.18		6.17		7.00		7.18		7.67	
(iv) Hours regulations							4.38		5.51		6.00		6.00		8.00	
(v) Mandated cost of worker dismissal											1.60		1.56		1.97	
(vi) Conscription	0.00		0.00		0.00		0.00		0.00		0.00		0.00		0.00	
C. Business regulations							6.20		7.41		7.00		6.48		6.42	
(i) Price controls							5.00		5.00		6.00		6.00		6.00	
(ii) Administrative requirements							8.18		4.40		3.55		3.45			
(iii) Bureaucracy costs							6.34		7.73		7.30		4.76		4.23	
(iv) Starting a business							5.77		7.68		8.90		8.87		8.87	
(v) Extra payments/bribes/favoritism							7.69		8.44		8.40		7.83		8.15	
(vi) Licensing restrictions											6.80		6.89		6.90	
(vii) Cost of tax compliance											7.40		7.42		7.37	

Italy

Chain-Linked	1980	1985	1990	1995	2000	2005	2008	2009
	Rating (Rank)	Rating (Rank)	Rating (Rank)	Rating (Rank)	Rating (Rank)	Rating (Rank)	Rating (Rank)	Rating (Rank)
Summary Rating (Rank) ➤	**5.53** (52)	**5.68** (46)	**6.59** (29)	**6.50** (43)	**7.11** (34)	**7.01** (49)	**6.75** (66)	**6.67** (66)
Area 1. Size of Government	4.10 (78)	2.96 (103)	3.33 (103)	3.75 (108)	4.62 (100)	5.92 (83)	5.71 (84)	5.27 (91)
Area 2. Legal Structure and Security of Property Rights	6.35 (33)	7.56 (25)	8.62 (21)	6.47 (40)	7.66 (23)	6.27 (51)	5.67 (65)	5.76 (61)
Area 3. Access to Sound Money	5.55 (79)	6.29 (75)	9.28 (16)	9.58 (17)	9.47 (21)	9.52 (23)	9.48 (14)	9.58 (12)
Area 4. Freedom to Trade Internationally	7.28 (18)	7.23 (18)	6.99 (29)	7.83 (24)	8.17 (20)	7.25 (36)	7.09 (48)	6.88 (47)
Area 5. Regulation of Credit, Labor, and Business	4.39 (79)	4.52 (79)	4.97 (72)	4.87 (92)	5.64 (82)	6.07 (85)	5.77 (100)	5.83 (101)

Unadjusted

	1980	1985	1990	1995	2000	2005	2008	2009
Summary Rating (Rank) ➤	**5.52** (53)	**5.68** (48)	**6.54** (30)	**6.46** (43)	**7.11** (34)	**7.16** (44)	**6.90** (65)	**6.81** (70)
	Rating Data	Rating Data	Rating Data	Rating Data	Rating Data	Rating Data	Rating Data	Rating Data
1. Size of Government	**4.10**	**2.96**	**3.33**	**3.75**	**4.62**	**5.90**	**5.71**	**5.27**
A. Government consumption	5.96 (19.75)	5.48 (21.37)	5.22 (22.26)	5.67 (20.71)	4.84 (23.54)	4.20 (25.70)	4.26 (25.51)	3.99 (26.45)
B. Transfers and subsidies	4.44 (20.90)	2.37 (28.50)	3.11 (25.80)	2.32 (28.70)	4.64 (20.17)	4.50 (20.80)	4.08 (22.22)	3.59 (24.02)
C. Government enterprises and investment	6.00 (25.90)	4.00 (33.20)	4.00 (30.30)	6.00 (28.30)	6.00 (28.30)	10.00 (11.40)	10.00 (10.65)	10.00 (13.14)
D. Top marginal tax rate	0.00	0.00	1.00	1.00	3.00	5.00	4.50	3.50
(i) Top marginal income tax rate	0.00 (72)	0.00 (81)	1.00 (66)	1.00 (67)	3.00 (51)	6.00 (43-45)	5.00 (43-45)	5.00 (43-45)
(ii) Top marginal income and payroll tax rates			1.00 (66)	1.00 (67)	3.00 (52)	4.00 (51)	4.00 (48-50)	2.00 (59-61)
2. Legal Structure and Security of Property Rights	**5.70**	**6.78**	**7.73**	**6.47**	**7.66**	**6.30**	**5.67**	**5.76**
A. Judicial independence				5.12	4.84	4.30	3.56	4.13
B. Impartial courts				5.43	5.68	3.70	2.60	2.82
C. Protection of property rights				5.43	7.80	6.80	5.69	5.50
D. Military interference in rule of law and politics				9.39	10.00	10.00	10.00	10.00
E. Integrity of the legal system				6.96	10.00	6.70	6.67	6.67
F. Legal enforcement of contracts						3.20	3.18	3.18
G. Regulatory restrictions on sale of real property						9.30	7.98	8.01
3. Access to Sound Money	**5.55**	**6.29**	**9.28**	**9.58**	**9.47**	**9.50**	**9.48**	**9.58**
A. Money growth	7.33 (13.36)	8.40 (7.99)	9.20 (4.00)	9.89 (0.56)	8.94 (5.29)	8.60 (6.80)	8.77 (6.13)	8.64 (6.79)
B. Standard deviation of inflation	9.04 (2.41)	8.54 (3.65)	9.72 (0.69)	9.43 (1.42)	9.43 (1.43)	9.80 (0.41)	9.81 (0.47)	9.85 (0.38)
C. Inflation: most recent year	5.82 (20.91)	8.20 (9.01)	8.20 (9.01)	8.99 (5.06)	9.49 (2.54)	9.60 (1.99)	9.33 (3.35)	9.85 (0.77)
D. Freedom to own foreign currency bank accounts	0.00	0.00	10.00	10.00	10.00	10.00	10.00	10.00
4. Freedom to Trade Internationally	**7.49**	**7.44**	**7.06**	**7.67**	**8.17**	**7.20**	**7.09**	**6.88**
A. Taxes on international trade	8.99	9.15	8.48	8.70	9.18	8.40	8.03	8.22
(i) Revenues from trade taxes (% of trade sector)	9.73 (0.40)	9.80 (0.30)	9.80 (0.30)	9.80 (0.30)	9.78 (0.33)	9.60 (0.60)	9.61 (0.59)	9.44 (0.84)
(ii) Mean tariff rate	8.24 (8.80)	8.50 (7.50)	8.52 (7.40)	8.66 (6.70)	9.52 (2.40)	9.50 (2.70)	8.88 (5.60)	8.94 (5.30)
(iii) Standard deviation of tariff rates			7.12 (7.20)	7.64 (5.90)	8.24 (4.40)	6.10 (9.70)	5.61 (10.98)	6.29 (9.28)
B. Regulatory trade barriers				6.98	8.51	7.20	6.84	6.94
(i) Non-tariff trade barriers				6.98	7.68	7.00	6.31	6.53
(ii) Compliance cost of importing and exporting					9.33	7.40	7.36	7.36
C. Size of trade sector relative to expected	5.32	4.89	3.66	4.68	4.82	4.00	4.27	3.09
D. Black-market exchange rates	10.00	10.00	10.00	10.00	10.00	10.00	10.00	10.00
E. International capital market controls	5.00	5.00	5.00	8.00	8.36	6.60	6.29	6.12
(i) Foreign ownership/investment restrictions				8.00	9.04	5.60	4.89	5.32
(ii) Capital controls	5.00	5.00	5.00	8.00	7.69	7.70	7.69	6.92
5. Regulation of Credit, Labor, and Business	**4.77**	**4.91**	**5.27**	**4.83**	**5.64**	**6.80**	**6.54**	**6.58**
A. Credit market regulations	5.02	5.58	6.93	6.56	7.11	8.10	7.91	7.49
(i) Ownership of banks	5.00	5.00	5.00	5.00	5.00	8.00	8.00	8.00
(ii) Foreign bank competition				4.78	5.70	6.00	6.00	6.00
(iii) Private sector credit	6.06	5.73	5.80	6.55	9.65	8.20	8.64	6.95
(iv) Interest rate controls/negative real interest rates	4.00	6.00	10.00	10.00	10.00	10.00	9.00	9.00
B. Labor market regulations	4.12	4.12	4.20	3.49	3.53	6.50	6.30	6.76
(i) Hiring regulations and minimum wage				3.40	4.01	6.70	6.70	5.57
(ii) Hiring and firing regulations			2.62	2.62	2.10	2.80	2.45	3.09
(iii) Centralized collective bargaining	4.49	4.49	4.49	4.49	3.68	3.60	3.68	3.88
(iv) Hours regulations	6.86	6.86	6.69	3.95	4.84	6.00	6.00	8.00
(v) Mandated cost of worker dismissal						9.80	8.98	10.00
(vi) Conscription	1.00	1.00	3.00	3.00	3.00	10.00	10.00	10.00
C. Business regulations				4.43	6.27	6.00	5.40	5.48
(i) Price controls			5.00	6.00	6.00	5.00	5.00	5.00
(ii) Administrative requirements					6.85	1.70	1.94	2.03
(iii) Bureaucracy costs				4.71	6.05	6.10	3.91	3.76
(iv) Starting a business				4.10	5.08	9.30	9.46	9.58
(v) Extra payments/bribes/favoritism				2.91	7.39	7.40	4.77	4.74
(vi) Licensing restrictions						6.50	6.48	6.47
(vii) Cost of tax compliance						6.00	6.26	6.81

Jamaica

	1980		1985		1990		1995		2000		2005		2008		2009	
Chain-Linked	Rating	(Rank)	Rating	(Rank)	Rating	(Rank)	Rating	(Rank)	Rating	(Rank)	Rating	(Rank)	Rating	(Rank)	Rating	(Rank)
Summary Rating (Rank) ➤	4.22	(90)	5.03	(75)	5.59	(55)	6.43	(47)	7.23	(31)	7.26	(34)	6.89	(54)	6.86	(54)
Area 1. Size of Government	2.62	(99)	6.91	(9)	7.49	(10)	7.86	(15)	8.52	(6)	8.66	(7)	8.81	(6)	8.70	(6)
Area 2. Legal Structure and Security of Property Rights	3.07	(69)	3.30	(87)	3.96	(80)	4.81	(86)	5.17	(74)	5.11	(81)	5.09	(81)	5.01	(82)
Area 3. Access to Sound Money	5.19	(90)	4.10	(99)	4.96	(90)	6.10	(71)	8.72	(42)	8.64	(57)	7.66	(78)	8.22	(68)
Area 4. Freedom to Trade Internationally	4.45	(67)	5.65	(49)	5.04	(69)	7.09	(39)	7.17	(51)	6.63	(63)	6.42	(76)	5.85	(91)
Area 5. Regulation of Credit, Labor, and Business	5.25	(51)	5.23	(54)	6.54	(20)	6.25	(37)	6.55	(38)	7.29	(32)	6.49	(63)	6.56	(64)

Unadjusted

	1980		1985		1990		1995		2000		2005		2008		2009	
Summary Rating (Rank) ➤	4.29	(91)	5.28	(64)	5.71	(52)	6.56	(42)	7.23	(31)	7.48	(25)	7.10	(52)	7.07	(49)
	Rating	Data	Rating	Data	Rating	Data	Rating	Data	Rating	Data	Rating	Data	Rating	Data	Rating	Data
1. Size of Government	2.23		6.91		7.49		7.86		8.52		8.70		8.81		8.70	
A. Government consumption	4.68	(24.08)	6.64	(17.41)	6.35	(18.40)	6.37	(18.33)	6.09	(19.30)	6.70	(17.20)	7.47	(14.60)	7.02	(16.12)
B. Transfers and subsidies			10.00	(0.50)	9.59	(2.00)	9.07	(3.90)	10.00	(0.00)	9.90	(0.80)	9.78	(1.31)	9.79	(1.27)
C. Government enterprises and investment	2.00	(46.50)	10.00	(13.40)	8.00	(16.50)	8.00	(17.00)	10.00	(10.30)	10.00	(6.10)	10.00	(6.10)	10.00	(6.10)
D. Top marginal tax rate	0.00		1.00		6.00		8.00		8.00		8.00		8.00		8.00	
(i) Top marginal income tax rate	0.00	(80)	1.00	(58)	7.00	(33)	9.00	(25)	9.00	(25)	9.00	(25)	9.00	(25)	9.00	(25)
(ii) Top marginal income and payroll tax rates					5.00	(37)	7.00	(31)	7.00	(31)	7.00	(33)	7.00	(33)	7.00	(33)
2. Legal Structure and Security of Property Rights	3.28		3.52		4.23		5.14		5.17		5.50		5.52		5.43	
A. Judicial independence											5.40		6.08		5.76	
B. Impartial courts							4.27		4.90		4.70		3.90		3.91	
C. Protection of property rights									4.10		6.60		5.91		5.45	
D. Military interference in rule of law and politics							5.39		10.00		10.00		10.00		10.00	
E. Integrity of the legal system							6.96		3.33		4.20		4.17		3.33	
F. Legal enforcement of contracts											3.40		2.76		2.76	
G. Regulatory restrictions on sale of real property											4.50		5.84		6.84	
3. Access to Sound Money	5.19		4.10		4.96		6.10		8.72		8.60		7.66		8.22	
A. Money growth	6.54	(17.28)	6.93	(15.34)	7.76	(11.21)	4.67	(26.67)	8.62	(6.89)	8.40	(8.10)	8.53	(7.37)	8.60	(7.00)
B. Standard deviation of inflation	7.88	(5.29)	5.61	(10.97)	8.20	(4.49)	5.31	(11.73)	7.90	(5.26)	9.20	(1.89)	6.52	(8.70)	6.18	(9.55)
C. Inflation: most recent year	6.33	(18.34)	3.86	(30.69)	3.86	(30.69)	4.41	(27.93)	8.37	(8.17)	6.90	(15.30)	5.60	(22.02)	8.09	(9.57)
D. Freedom to own foreign currency bank accounts	0.00		0.00		0.00		10.00		10.00		10.00		10.00		10.00	
4. Freedom to Trade Internationally	4.91		6.23		5.36		7.47		7.17		6.90		6.69		6.10	
A. Taxes on international trade	8.05		7.73		6.60		6.92		7.28		7.30		7.64		7.59	
(i) Revenues from trade taxes (% of trade sector)	9.40	(0.90)	8.87	(1.70)			8.55	(2.18)	8.49	(2.27)	7.70	(3.50)	8.68	(1.98)	8.52	(2.22)
(ii) Mean tariff rate	6.70	(16.50)	6.60	(17.00)	6.60	(17.00)	7.20	(14.00)	7.88	(10.60)	8.50	(7.30)	8.50	(7.50)	8.50	(7.50)
(iii) Standard deviation of tariff rates							5.00	(12.50)	5.48	(11.30)	5.80	(10.50)	5.74	(10.65)	5.74	(10.65)
B. Regulatory trade barriers									5.73		6.40		6.96		6.58	
(i) Non-tariff trade barriers									5.73		5.90		6.88		6.13	
(ii) Compliance cost of importing and exporting											7.00		7.03		7.03	
C. Size of trade sector relative to expected	6.26		7.01		5.37		5.70		4.66		4.30		3.85		3.05	
D. Black-market exchange rates	0.00		6.20		4.60		8.60		10.00		10.00		10.00		10.00	
E. International capital market controls	2.00		2.00		2.00		8.00		8.18		6.50		5.01		3.29	
(i) Foreign ownership / investment restrictions									8.67		7.60		6.94		6.59	
(ii) Capital controls	2.00		2.00		2.00		8.00		7.69		5.40		3.08		0.00	
5. Regulation of Credit, Labor, and Business	5.85		5.62		6.52		6.23		6.55		7.60		6.83		6.88	
A. Credit market regulations	5.06		5.00		8.72		7.76		7.26		9.60		7.40		7.25	
(i) Ownership of banks			5.00		10.00		10.00		10.00		10.00		10.00		10.00	
(ii) Foreign bank competition									5.70		10.00		10.00		10.00	
(iii) Private sector credit	6.13		5.99		8.17		7.29		7.27		9.50		1.59		0.00	
(iv) Interest rate controls / negative real interest rates	4.00		4.00		8.00		6.00		9.00		9.00		8.00		9.00	
B. Labor market regulations									6.45		7.60		7.53		7.74	
(i) Hiring regulations and minimum wage									3.98		8.90		8.90		8.90	
(ii) Hiring and firing regulations									4.77		5.30		5.13		5.15	
(iii) Centralized collective bargaining									7.07		7.30		6.90		7.00	
(iv) Hours regulations											10.00		10.00		10.00	
(v) Mandated cost of worker dismissal											4.30		4.25		5.36	
(vi) Conscription	10.00		10.00		10.00		10.00		10.00		10.00		10.00		10.00	
C. Business regulations									5.94		5.70		5.55		5.66	
(i) Price controls					4.00		4.00		4.00		4.00		4.00		4.00	
(ii) Administrative requirements									6.83		2.90		2.51		2.84	
(iii) Bureaucracy costs									6.88		5.40		4.69		5.11	
(iv) Starting a business									5.70		9.60		9.69		9.69	
(v) Extra payments / bribes / favoritism									6.28		6.10		4.71		4.72	
(vi) Licensing restrictions											6.20		7.89		7.91	
(vii) Cost of tax compliance											5.40		5.36		5.36	

Japan

Chain-Linked	1980 Rating (Rank)	1985 Rating (Rank)	1990 Rating (Rank)	1995 Rating (Rank)	2000 Rating (Rank)	2005 Rating (Rank)	2008 Rating (Rank)	2009 Rating (Rank)
Summary Rating (Rank) ➤	**7.08** (12)	**7.12** (13)	**7.47** (14)	**7.11** (27)	**7.45** (17)	**7.47** (21)	**7.46** (23)	**7.37** (23)
Area 1. Size of Government	5.80 (30)	5.95 (29)	5.83 (50)	4.95 (88)	5.71 (79)	5.72 (90)	6.59 (54)	6.46 (56)
Area 2. Legal Structure and Security of Property Rights	9.19 (9)	8.42 (17)	8.98 (18)	8.13 (19)	8.18 (19)	7.82 (19)	7.49 (23)	7.47 (22)
Area 3. Access to Sound Money	8.28 (15)	8.54 (20)	9.80 (1)	9.72 (8)	9.65 (8)	9.66 (6)	9.77 (1)	9.77 (1)
Area 4. Freedom to Trade Internationally	5.97 (41)	6.34 (35)	6.41 (42)	6.26 (77)	6.84 (67)	6.38 (77)	6.10 (89)	5.77 (94)
Area 5. Regulation of Credit, Labor, and Business	6.31 (21)	6.33 (23)	6.40 (28)	6.46 (29)	6.85 (27)	7.75 (21)	7.34 (25)	7.36 (24)

Unadjusted

	1980 Rating Data	1985 Rating Data	1990 Rating Data	1995 Rating Data	2000 Rating Data	2005 Rating Data	2008 Rating Data	2009 Rating Data
Summary Rating (Rank) ➤	**7.03** (10)	**7.07** (11)	**7.35** (9)	**7.04** (27)	**7.45** (17)	**7.54** (21)	**7.54** (20)	**7.44** (22)
1. Size of Government	**5.80**	**5.95**	**5.83**	**4.95**	**5.71**	**5.70**	**6.59**	**6.46**
A. Government consumption	7.56 (14.29)	7.65 (13.98)	7.80 (13.47)	5.50 (21.32)	5.04 (22.85)	4.80 (23.80)	4.62 (24.28)	4.45 (24.88)
B. Transfers and subsidies	7.63 (9.20)	7.17 (10.90)	7.00 (11.50)	6.81 (12.20)	6.81 (12.20)	5.10 (18.50)	6.72 (12.54)	6.38 (13.78)
C. Government enterprises and investment	8.00 (19.60)	8.00 (17.90)	7.00 (20.40)	6.00 (28.50)	6.00 (28.50)	8.00 (15.30)	10.00 (12.86)	10.00 (12.86)
D. Top marginal tax rate	0.00	1.00	1.50	1.50	5.00	5.00	5.00	5.00
(i) Top marginal income tax rate	0.00 (75)	1.00 (70)	2.00 (65)	2.00 (65)	5.00 (50)	5.00 (50)	5.00 (50)	5.00 (50)
(ii) Top marginal income and payroll tax rates			1.00 (69)	1.00 (69)	5.00 (50)	5.00 (50)	5.00 (50)	5.00 (50)
2. Legal Structure and Security of Property Rights	**7.91**	**7.25**	**7.73**	**8.13**	**8.18**	**7.80**	**7.49**	**7.47**
A. Judicial independence				8.33	8.02	7.60	7.49	7.83
B. Impartial courts				6.13	7.01	7.30	5.67	5.87
C. Protection of property rights				6.83	7.55	8.70	8.16	7.64
D. Military interference in rule of law and politics				9.38	10.00	8.30	8.33	8.33
E. Integrity of the legal system				10.00	8.33	8.30	8.33	8.33
F. Legal enforcement of contracts						6.40	6.37	6.37
G. Regulatory restrictions on sale of real property						8.10	8.09	7.93
3. Access to Sound Money	**8.28**	**8.54**	**9.80**	**9.72**	**9.65**	**9.70**	**9.77**	**9.77**
A. Money growth	9.92 (0.39)	9.93 (−0.37)	9.96 (0.22)	9.46 (2.70)	9.09 (4.56)	8.80 (6.00)	9.45 (2.74)	9.46 (2.72)
B. Standard deviation of inflation	9.28 (1.80)	9.65 (0.87)	9.66 (0.84)	9.53 (1.17)	9.65 (0.89)	9.90 (0.22)	9.91 (0.23)	9.91 (0.22)
C. Inflation: most recent year	8.91 (5.44)	9.58 (2.12)	9.58 (2.12)	9.87 (−0.64)	9.86 (−0.71)	9.90 (−0.27)	9.72 (1.38)	9.73 (−1.35)
D. Freedom to own foreign currency bank accounts	5.00	5.00	10.00	10.00	10.00	10.00	10.00	10.00
4. Freedom to Trade Internationally	**6.69**	**7.10**	**7.02**	**5.90**	**6.84**	**6.40**	**6.10**	**5.77**
A. Taxes on international trade	8.75	9.06	8.23	8.10	8.43	6.10	6.27	6.82
(i) Revenues from trade taxes (% of trade sector)	9.40 (0.90)	9.47 (0.80)	9.40 (0.90)	8.93 (1.60)	9.00 (1.50)	9.00 (1.50)	9.67 (0.50)	9.67 (0.50)
(ii) Mean tariff rate	8.10 (9.50)	8.66 (6.70)	8.62 (6.90)	8.74 (6.30)	9.10 (4.50)	9.30 (3.30)	8.92 (5.40)	9.02 (4.90)
(iii) Standard deviation of tariff rates			6.68 (8.30)	6.64 (8.40)	7.20 (7.00)	0.00 (25.60)	0.24 (24.41)	1.77 (20.58)
B. Regulatory trade barriers				3.68	7.37	7.30	7.01	7.12
(i) Non-tariff trade barriers				3.68	5.42	6.00	5.38	5.61
(ii) Compliance cost of importing and exporting					9.33	8.60	8.64	8.64
C. Size of trade sector relative to expected	4.52	3.27	0.69	0.00	0.00	1.10	2.29	0.00
D. Black-market exchange rates	10.00	10.00	10.00	10.00	10.00	10.00	10.00	10.00
E. International capital market controls	2.00	5.00	8.00	7.70	8.40	7.40	4.94	4.93
(i) Foreign ownership / investment restrictions				7.40	9.11	6.30	6.03	6.01
(ii) Capital controls	2.00	5.00	8.00	8.00	7.69	8.50	3.85	3.85
5. Regulation of Credit, Labor, and Business	**6.46**	**6.48**	**6.35**	**6.51**	**6.85**	**8.10**	**7.73**	**7.74**
A. Credit market regulations	7.82	7.88	8.22	7.03	6.88	8.90	8.91	8.91
(i) Ownership of banks	5.00	5.00	5.00	5.00	5.00	8.00	8.00	8.00
(ii) Foreign bank competition				4.92	4.18	8.00	8.00	8.00
(iii) Private sector credit	8.45	8.65	9.65	9.65	9.65	9.70	9.65	9.65
(iv) Interest rate controls / negative real interest rates	10.00	10.00	10.00	10.00	10.00	10.00	10.00	10.00
B. Labor market regulations	8.03	8.06	7.20	7.46	6.48	8.50	8.19	8.35
(i) Hiring regulations and minimum wage				7.55	3.99	8.90	8.90	8.90
(ii) Hiring and firing regulations			4.82	4.82	4.18	4.60	3.28	3.29
(iii) Centralized collective bargaining	7.93	7.93	7.93	7.93	7.40	8.40	8.02	7.93
(iv) Hours regulations	6.16	6.25	6.07	6.98	6.85	9.30	9.30	10.00
(v) Mandated cost of worker dismissal						9.60	9.63	10.00
(vi) Conscription	10.00	10.00	10.00	10.00	10.00	10.00	10.00	10.00
C. Business regulations				5.04	7.20	7.10	6.10	5.95
(i) Price controls			6.00	5.00	6.00	5.00	5.00	5.00
(ii) Administrative requirements					6.50	4.30	4.84	3.80
(iii) Bureaucracy costs				5.86	9.13	7.10	1.72	1.50
(iv) Starting a business				4.72	5.85	9.20	9.18	9.18
(v) Extra payments / bribes / favoritism				4.60	8.50	8.90	8.14	8.33
(vi) Licensing restrictions						8.70	7.83	7.83
(vii) Cost of tax compliance						6.10	6.02	6.02

Jordan

	1980		1985		1990		1995		2000		2005		2008		2009	
Chain-Linked	Rating	(Rank)	Rating	(Rank)	Rating	(Rank)	Rating	(Rank)	Rating	(Rank)	Rating	(Rank)	Rating	(Rank)	Rating	(Rank)
Summary Rating (Rank) ➤	**5.50**	(54)	**5.84**	(40)	**6.05**	(42)	**6.42**	(48)	**7.24**	(30)	**7.38**	(26)	**7.14**	(40)	**6.84**	(55)
Area 1. Size of Government	5.33	(44)	5.14	(54)	7.27	(14)	6.38	(48)	6.08	(67)	6.27	(76)	5.64	(87)	4.37	(109)
Area 2. Legal Structure and Security of Property Rights	2.54	(76)	3.86	(79)	4.37	(74)	5.95	(45)	7.22	(27)	6.31	(50)	6.56	(35)	6.31	(45)
Area 3. Access to Sound Money	6.82	(32)	7.74	(30)	6.20	(69)	7.15	(53)	9.67	(7)	9.21	(37)	8.35	(58)	9.27	(35)
Area 4. Freedom to Trade Internationally	6.52	(33)	6.32	(36)	6.56	(37)	6.47	(70)	7.02	(63)	7.74	(20)	7.67	(22)	7.18	(34)
Area 5. Regulation of Credit, Labor, and Business	6.08	(30)	6.01	(35)	5.98	(40)	6.24	(39)	6.22	(53)	7.35	(29)	7.45	(24)	7.04	(39)

Unadjusted																
Summary Rating (Rank) ➤	**5.43**	(54)	**5.79**	(43)	**5.73**	(51)	**6.33**	(51)	**7.24**	(30)	**7.45**	(27)	**7.20**	(43)	**6.90**	(62)
	Rating	Data	Rating	Data	Rating	Data	Rating	Data	Rating	Data	Rating	Data	Rating	Data	Rating	Data
1. Size of Government	**4.77**		**4.60**		**6.12**		**5.71**		**6.08**		**6.30**		**5.64**		**4.37**	
A. Government consumption	3.89	(26.78)	5.04	(22.85)	4.37	(25.14)	3.72	(27.36)	4.75	(23.84)	6.70	(17.30)	4.77	(23.78)	5.28	(22.04)
B. Transfers and subsidies	8.42	(6.30)	8.75	(5.10)	9.13	(3.70)	9.40	(2.70)	9.56	(2.13)	6.40	(13.60)	6.78	(12.31)	7.21	(10.72)
C. Government enterprises and investment	2.00	(48.70)	0.00	(56.20)	6.00	(27.60)	4.00	(30.50)	2.00	(43.60)	7.00	(23.90)	6.00	(25.52)	0.00	(56.80)
D. Top marginal tax rate							5.00				8.00		5.00		5.00	
(i) Top marginal income tax rate							5.00	(45)			8.00	(30)	7.00	(35)	7.00	(35)	7.00	(35)
(ii) Top marginal income and payroll tax rates											3.00	(46)	3.00	(46)	3.00	(46)
2. Legal Structure and Security of Property Rights	**2.32**		**3.52**		**3.99**		**5.95**		**7.22**		**6.30**		**6.56**		**6.31**	
A. Judicial independence							6.45		8.18		6.50		6.61		6.02	
B. Impartial courts							5.85		6.85		6.30		5.86		5.28	
C. Protection of property rights							4.33		6.05		6.60		7.92		7.33	
D. Military interference in rule of law and politics							6.16		8.33		8.30		8.33		8.33	
E. Integrity of the legal system							6.96		6.67		6.70		6.67		6.67	
F. Legal enforcement of contracts											3.40		3.38		3.38	
G. Regulatory restrictions on sale of real property											6.30		7.14		7.14	
3. Access to Sound Money	**6.82**		**7.74**		**6.20**		**7.15**		**9.67**		**9.20**		**8.35**		**9.27**	
A. Money growth	5.86	(20.70)	9.17	(−4.13)	8.36	(8.18)	9.77	(−1.14)	9.85	(0.75)	8.00	(9.90)	8.44	(7.80)	9.15	(4.23)
B. Standard deviation of inflation	6.64	(8.40)	7.09	(7.27)	6.74	(8.14)	9.52	(1.21)	8.97	(2.57)	9.50	(1.23)	7.93	(5.17)	8.06	(4.85)
C. Inflation: most recent year	9.78	(1.10)	9.71	(−1.45)	9.71	(−1.45)	9.32	(3.39)	9.87	(0.67)	9.30	(3.49)	7.01	(14.93)	9.86	(−0.68)
D. Freedom to own foreign currency bank accounts	5.00		5.00		0.00		0.00		10.00		10.00		10.00		10.00	
4. Freedom to Trade Internationally	**6.76**		**6.68**		**6.40**		**6.77**		**7.02**		**7.70**		**7.67**		**7.18**	
A. Taxes on international trade	5.27		6.59		4.63		6.20		4.35		6.50		7.03		6.86	
(i) Revenues from trade taxes (% of trade sector)	5.27	(7.10)	5.93	(6.10)	6.67	(5.00)	6.20	(5.70)	6.98	(4.53)	8.20	(2.70)	9.09	(1.37)	9.00	(1.50)
(ii) Mean tariff rate			7.24	(13.80)					5.20	(24.00)	7.50	(12.40)	7.84	(10.80)	7.96	(10.20)
(iii) Standard deviation of tariff rates					2.60	(18.50)			0.88	(22.80)	3.90	(15.30)	4.17	(14.58)	3.64	(15.91)
B. Regulatory trade barriers							5.08		6.34		6.70		6.79		6.77	
(i) Non-tariff trade barriers							5.08		5.35		6.30		6.02		5.68	
(ii) Compliance cost of importing and exporting									7.33		7.20		7.55		7.87	
C. Size of trade sector relative to expected	8.35		7.25		9.38		7.34		6.21		7.70		7.54		5.51	
D. Black-market exchange rates	10.00		9.40		7.80		9.80		10.00		10.00		10.00		10.00	
E. International capital market controls	2.00		2.00		2.00		5.43		8.20		7.80		7.00		6.76	
(i) Foreign ownership/investment restrictions							8.85		8.71		7.80		7.08		6.60	
(ii) Capital controls	2.00		2.00		2.00		2.00		7.69		7.70		6.92		6.92	
5. Regulation of Credit, Labor, and Business	**6.49**		**6.42**		**5.94**		**6.06**		**6.22**		**7.70**		**7.80**		**7.37**	
A. Credit market regulations	7.01		6.70		5.72		6.22		6.81		9.00		8.57		7.34	
(i) Ownership of banks	5.00		5.00		5.00		5.00		5.00		10.00		10.00		10.00	
(ii) Foreign bank competition							6.10		5.88		8.00		8.00		8.00	
(iii) Private sector credit	9.02		8.40		8.16		9.31		8.38		8.10		9.26		1.35	
(iv) Interest rate controls/negative real interest rates					4.00		6.00		10.00		10.00		7.00		10.00	
B. Labor market regulations					8.07		7.34		6.50		8.40		8.38		8.44	
(i) Hiring regulations and minimum wage							6.62		3.75		8.90		8.90		8.90	
(ii) Hiring and firing regulations					6.27		6.27		4.45		3.90		3.98		4.21	
(iii) Centralized collective bargaining	7.93		7.93		7.93		7.93		7.80		7.90		7.79		7.51	
(iv) Hours regulations							5.88		6.51		10.00		10.00		10.00	
(v) Mandated cost of worker dismissal											9.60		9.63		10.00	
(vi) Conscription	10.00		10.00		10.00		10.00		10.00		10.00		10.00		10.00	
C. Business regulations							4.62		5.36		5.70		6.45		6.34	
(i) Price controls					2.00		2.00		2.00		3.00		3.00		3.00	
(ii) Administrative requirements							7.55		4.30		5.02		4.13	
(iii) Bureaucracy costs							5.40		4.60		3.10		4.08		4.77	
(iv) Starting a business							6.57		6.27		5.90		9.00		9.06	
(v) Extra payments/bribes/favoritism							4.50		6.37		7.10		6.92		6.22	
(vi) Licensing restrictions											7.30		8.24		8.35	
(vii) Cost of tax compliance											8.90		8.87		8.87	

Kazakhstan

	1980	1985	1990	1995	2000	2005	2008	2009
Chain-Linked						Rating (Rank)	Rating (Rank)	Rating (Rank)
Summary Rating (Rank) ➤								
Area 1. Size of Government								
Area 2. Legal Structure and Security of Property Rights								
Area 3. Access to Sound Money								
Area 4. Freedom to Trade Internationally								
Area 5. Regulation of Credit, Labor, and Business								

Unadjusted

						2005	2008	2009
Summary Rating (Rank) ➤						**6.88** (65)	**7.04** (57)	**6.97** (56)
					Rating *Data*	Rating *Data*	Rating *Data*	Rating *Data*
1. Size of Government						**7.20**	**6.83**	**6.83**
A. Government consumption						6.40 *(18.30)*	5.33 *(21.88)*	5.56 *(21.10)*
B. Transfers and subsidies						8.80 *(5.10)*	9.00 *(4.19)*	8.78 *(4.98)*
C. Government enterprises and investment						4.00	4.00	4.00
D. Top marginal tax rate						9.50	9.00	9.00
(i) Top marginal income tax rate						10.00 *(20)*	10.00 *(10)*	10.00 *(10)*
(ii) Top marginal income and payroll tax rates						9.00 *(25)*	8.00 *(30)*	8.00 *(30)*
2. Legal Structure and Security of Property Rights						**6.00**	**6.03**	**5.92**
A. Judicial independence						2.90	3.50	3.10
B. Impartial courts						4.10	3.95	3.85
C. Protection of property rights						4.90	4.36	4.11
D. Military interference in rule of law and politics						8.30	8.33	8.33
E. Integrity of the legal system						6.70	6.67	6.67
F. Legal enforcement of contracts						6.20	6.19	6.19
G. Regulatory restrictions on sale of real property						8.60	9.21	9.21
3. Access to Sound Money						**6.90**	**8.48**	**8.29**
A. Money growth						5.90 *(20.70)*	8.47 *(7.65)*	7.37 *(13.15)*
B. Standard deviation of inflation						8.10 *(4.82)*	8.89 *(2.77)*	7.26 *(6.85)*
C. Inflation: most recent year						8.50 *(7.58)*	6.57 *(17.15)*	8.54 *(7.31)*
D. Freedom to own foreign currency bank accounts						5.00	10.00	10.00
4. Freedom to Trade Internationally						**7.10**	**6.36**	**6.25**
A. Taxes on international trade						9.50	7.74	8.34
(i) Revenues from trade taxes (% of trade sector)					9.56 *(0.66)*	9.40 *(0.90)*	8.14 *(2.79)*	9.21 *(1.19)*
(ii) Mean tariff rate						9.50 *(2.30)*	8.80 *(6.00)*	8.82 *(5.90)*
(iii) Standard deviation of tariff rates							6.28 *(9.30)*	7.00 *(7.49)*
B. Regulatory trade barriers						2.40	2.40	2.83
(i) Non-tariff trade barriers						4.60	4.54	4.84
(ii) Compliance cost of importing and exporting						0.30	0.25	0.82
C. Size of trade sector relative to expected						9.70	8.60	6.87
D. Black-market exchange rates						10.00	10.00	10.00
E. International capital market controls						3.80	3.08	3.19
(i) Foreign ownership / investment restrictions						6.10	4.62	4.85
(ii) Capital controls						1.50	1.54	1.54
5. Regulation of Credit, Labor, and Business						**7.40**	**7.47**	**7.53**
A. Credit market regulations						9.50	9.50	9.32
(i) Ownership of banks						10.00	10.00	10.00
(ii) Foreign bank competition						8.00	8.00	8.00
(iii) Private sector credit					10.00	10.00	10.00	9.29
(iv) Interest rate controls / negative real interest rates						10.00	10.00	10.00
B. Labor market regulations						7.20	6.87	7.17
(i) Hiring regulations and minimum wage						10.00	10.00	10.00
(ii) Hiring and firing regulations						7.60	6.68	5.84
(iii) Centralized collective bargaining						8.30	7.39	7.58
(iv) Hours regulations						8.00	8.00	10.00
(v) Mandated cost of worker dismissal						9.20	9.17	9.60
(vi) Conscription						0.00	0.00	0.00
C. Business regulations						5.40	6.05	6.11
(i) Price controls							6.00	6.00
(ii) Administrative requirements						3.40	3.33	3.70
(iii) Bureaucracy costs						4.20	5.34	5.50
(iv) Starting a business						9.20	9.27	9.38
(v) Extra payments / bribes / favoritism						5.50	4.16	4.09
(vi) Licensing restrictions						2.90	7.26	7.13
(vii) Cost of tax compliance						7.00	6.96	6.96

Kenya

Chain-Linked	1980		1985		1990		1995		2000		2005		2008		2009	
	Rating	(Rank)	Rating	(Rank)	Rating	(Rank)	Rating	(Rank)	Rating	(Rank)	Rating	(Rank)	Rating	(Rank)	Rating	(Rank)
Summary Rating (Rank) ➤	5.04	(66)	5.41	(53)	5.58	(56)	5.88	(66)	6.68	(46)	7.28	(32)	6.99	(51)	7.17	(36)
Area 1. Size of Government	3.79	(87)	3.94	(85)	4.83	(79)	5.70	(73)	7.09	(30)	7.82	(19)	7.77	(20)	7.66	(20)
Area 2. Legal Structure and Security of Property Rights	4.20	(55)	5.25	(54)	5.30	(54)	3.76	(111)	3.97	(101)	5.73	(62)	5.35	(74)	5.35	(73)
Area 3. Access to Sound Money	6.17	(59)	6.84	(41)	6.66	(58)	6.81	(58)	8.76	(41)	8.62	(58)	7.68	(76)	8.65	(58)
Area 4. Freedom to Trade Internationally	5.52	(47)	5.33	(56)	5.21	(65)	7.56	(29)	7.07	(60)	7.02	(49)	7.16	(44)	7.14	(39)
Area 5. Regulation of Credit, Labor, and Business	5.50	(43)	5.67	(46)	5.89	(46)	5.57	(61)	6.50	(41)	7.44	(26)	7.20	(29)	7.21	(30)

Unadjusted

	1980		1985		1990		1995		2000		2005		2008		2009	
Summary Rating (Rank) ➤	5.18	(64)	5.55	(53)	5.58	(57)	5.88	(67)	6.68	(46)	7.09	(48)	6.81	(76)	6.97	(56)
	Rating	Data	Rating	Data	Rating	Data	Rating	Data	Rating	Data	Rating	Data	Rating	Data	Rating	Data
1. Size of Government	3.79		3.94		4.83		5.70		7.09		7.80		7.77		7.66	
A. Government consumption	4.65	(24.20)	4.92	(23.26)	4.96	(23.14)	6.58	(17.63)	6.15	(19.10)	6.40	(18.40)	6.28	(18.65)	6.81	(16.85)
B. Transfers and subsidies	9.51	(2.30)	8.86	(4.70)	9.37	(2.80)	9.22	(3.35)	9.21	(3.40)	9.90	(0.80)	9.80	(1.25)	9.81	(1.18)
C. Government enterprises and investment	0.00	(55.10)	2.00	(49.50)	2.00	(47.10)	4.00	(36.80)	6.00	(27.30)	7.00	(20.50)	7.00	(24.66)	6.00	(27.67)
D. Top marginal tax rate	1.00		0.00		3.00		3.00		7.00		8.00		8.00		8.00	
(i) Top marginal income tax rate	1.00	(65)	0.00	(65)	3.00	(50)	3.00	(50)	7.00	(32)	8.00	(30)	8.00	(30)	8.00	(30)
(ii) Top marginal income and payroll tax rates					3.00	(50)	3.00	(50)	7.00	(32)	8.00	(30)	8.00	(30)	8.00	(30)
2. Legal Structure and Security of Property Rights	4.20		5.25		5.30		3.76		3.97		4.90		4.57		4.57	
A. Judicial independence											3.30		2.90		2.63	
B. Impartial courts							3.40		3.43		3.30		2.93		3.42	
C. Protection of property rights											4.90		4.65		4.42	
D. Military interference in rule of law and politics							3.39		5.00		6.70		6.67		6.67	
E. Integrity of the legal system							4.11		3.33		3.90		3.33		3.33	
F. Legal enforcement of contracts											4.90		4.09		4.09	
G. Regulatory restrictions on sale of real property											7.30		7.41		7.41	
3. Access to Sound Money	6.17		6.84		6.66		6.81		8.76		8.60		7.68		8.65	
A. Money growth	9.07	(4.63)	9.53	(2.37)	8.85	(5.77)	7.18	(14.09)	8.60	(6.99)	7.80	(11.00)	7.26	(13.72)	7.73	(11.37)
B. Standard deviation of inflation	7.53	(6.18)	9.48	(1.31)	9.44	(1.39)	7.32	(6.71)	8.44	(3.89)	8.80	(3.12)	8.72	(3.19)	8.71	(3.23)
C. Inflation: most recent year	8.09	(9.55)	8.35	(8.23)	8.35	(8.23)	7.74	(11.31)	8.00	(9.98)	7.90	(10.31)	4.75	(26.24)	8.15	(9.23)
D. Freedom to own foreign currency bank accounts	0.00		0.00		0.00		5.00		10.00		10.00		10.00		10.00	
4. Freedom to Trade Internationally	5.67		5.48		5.21		7.56		7.07		6.60		6.73		6.72	
A. Taxes on international trade	3.94		3.61		2.81		4.72		5.79		6.90		6.86		6.83	
(i) Revenues from trade taxes (% of trade sector)	5.93	(6.10)	5.07	(7.40)	5.80	(6.30)	6.27	(5.59)	6.31	(5.54)	7.70	(3.40)	7.83	(3.26)	7.73	(3.40)
(ii) Mean tariff rate	1.94	(40.30)	2.16	(39.20)	1.26	(43.70)	3.20	(34.00)	6.14	(19.30)	7.60	(12.10)	7.48	(12.60)	7.48	(12.60)
(iii) Standard deviation of tariff rates					1.36	(21.60)	4.68	(13.30)	4.92	(12.70)	5.30	(11.70)	5.26	(11.84)	5.26	(11.84)
B. Regulatory trade barriers											4.80		5.55		6.03	
(i) Non-tariff trade barriers											4.10		4.76		5.58	
(ii) Compliance cost of importing and exporting											5.40		6.34		6.49	
C. Size of trade sector relative to expected	8.23		5.98		6.21		7.35		6.03		5.80		5.98		5.54	
D. Black-market exchange rates	8.00		9.60		8.80		9.60		10.00		10.00		10.00		10.00	
E. International capital market controls	0.00		0.00		0.00		8.00		5.38		5.60		5.28		5.18	
(i) Foreign ownership/investment restrictions											6.50		5.94		5.75	
(ii) Capital controls	0.00		0.00		0.00		8.00		5.38		4.60		4.62		4.62	
5. Regulation of Credit, Labor, and Business	6.06		6.26		5.89		5.57		6.50		7.50		7.29		7.28	
A. Credit market regulations	6.17		6.69		7.33		5.60		8.00		9.50		8.47		8.35	
(i) Ownership of banks	2.00		2.00		5.00		5.00		5.00		10.00		10.00		10.00	
(ii) Foreign bank competition											8.00		8.00		8.00	
(iii) Private sector credit	8.52		8.06		6.99		7.81		10.00		10.00		6.88		6.41	
(iv) Interest rate controls/negative real interest rates	8.00		10.00		10.00		4.00		9.00		10.00		9.00		9.00	
B. Labor market regulations											7.60		7.67		7.82	
(i) Hiring regulations and minimum wage											6.70		7.80		7.77	
(ii) Hiring and firing regulations											5.90		5.95		6.53	
(iii) Centralized collective bargaining											7.10		6.61		6.63	
(iv) Hours regulations											10.00		10.00		10.00	
(v) Mandated cost of worker dismissal											5.60		5.64		6.03	
(vi) Conscription	10.00		10.00		10.00		10.00		10.00		10.00		10.00		10.00	
C. Business regulations											5.50		5.72		5.67	
(i) Price controls					2.00		4.00		6.00		6.00		6.00		6.00	
(ii) Administrative requirements											2.90		3.51		3.06	
(iii) Bureaucracy costs											4.30		4.70		5.06	
(iv) Starting a business											7.80		8.53		8.54	
(v) Extra payments/bribes/favoritism											4.40		3.34		2.75	
(vi) Licensing restrictions											8.20		8.67		8.66	
(vii) Cost of tax compliance											5.20		5.33		5.59	

Korea, South

	1980	1985	1990	1995	2000	2005	2008	2009
Chain-Linked	Rating (Rank)	Rating (Rank)	Rating (Rank)	Rating (Rank)	Rating (Rank)	Rating (Rank)	Rating (Rank)	Rating (Rank)
Summary Rating (Rank) ➤	**5.71** (41)	**5.65** (48)	**6.19** (39)	**6.42** (48)	**6.58** (54)	**7.36** (27)	**7.39** (26)	**7.37** (23)
Area 1. Size of Government	5.97 (27)	6.24 (19)	6.49 (29)	6.42 (45)	6.26 (57)	6.66 (61)	6.92 (42)	6.82 (42)
Area 2. Legal Structure and Security of Property Rights	7.06 (27)	4.50 (66)	5.90 (45)	5.62 (55)	5.97 (54)	7.01 (28)	6.76 (31)	6.61 (33)
Area 3. Access to Sound Money	5.29 (86)	6.41 (69)	6.59 (61)	8.05 (41)	8.27 (51)	9.53 (20)	9.47 (18)	9.49 (24)
Area 4. Freedom to Trade Internationally	6.07 (40)	6.12 (40)	7.08 (28)	7.13 (38)	7.09 (58)	6.51 (72)	7.14 (45)	7.12 (40)
Area 5. Regulation of Credit, Labor, and Business	4.33 (83)	4.84 (67)	4.90 (79)	4.90 (90)	5.31 (97)	7.06 (37)	6.65 (57)	6.81 (49)

	1980	1985	1990	1995	2000	2005	2008	2009
Unadjusted								
Summary Rating (Rank) ➤	**5.81** (41)	**5.74** (45)	**6.24** (36)	**6.34** (50)	**6.58** (54)	**7.30** (39)	**7.35** (33)	**7.32** (30)
	Rating Data	Rating Data	Rating Data	Rating Data	Rating Data	Rating Data	Rating Data	Rating Data
1. Size of Government	**5.97**	**6.24**	**6.49**	**6.42**	**6.26**	**6.70**	**6.92**	**6.82**
A. Government consumption	7.29 (15.23)	7.43 (14.74)	7.10 (15.87)	6.99 (16.22)	6.37 (18.33)	5.50 (21.10)	5.32 (21.90)	5.07 (22.77)
B. Transfers and subsidies	9.59 (2.00)	9.54 (2.20)	9.35 (2.90)	7.68 (9.01)	7.68 (9.01)	7.10 (11.10)	8.37 (6.48)	8.22 (7.02)
C. Government enterprises and investment	7.00 (22.60)	6.00 (25.40)	8.00 (19.20)	6.00 (25.50)	6.00 (25.50)	8.00 (18.80)	8.00 (17.18)	8.00 (17.18)
D. Top marginal tax rate	0.00	2.00	1.50	5.00	5.00	6.00	6.00	6.00
(i) Top marginal income tax rate	0.00 (89)	2.00 (65)	2.00 (64)	5.00 (48)	5.00 (44)	6.00 (39)	6.00 (39)	6.00 (39)
(ii) Top marginal income and payroll tax rates			1.00 (66)	5.00 (48)	5.00 (44)	6.00 (39)	6.00 (39)	6.00 (39)
2. Legal Structure and Security of Property Rights	**6.52**	**4.16**	**5.45**	**5.62**	**5.97**	**7.00**	**6.76**	**6.61**
A. Judicial independence				4.87	4.68	5.20	5.13	4.98
B. Impartial courts				5.25	5.18	5.30	4.37	3.91
C. Protection of property rights				4.26	5.00	7.40	6.61	6.18
D. Military interference in rule of law and politics				6.75	8.33	6.70	6.67	5.00
E. Integrity of the legal system				6.96	6.67	8.30	8.33	10.00
F. Legal enforcement of contracts						8.10	8.11	8.11
G. Regulatory restrictions on sale of real property						8.10	8.12	8.12
3. Access to Sound Money	**5.29**	**6.41**	**6.59**	**8.05**	**8.27**	**9.50**	**9.47**	**9.49**
A. Money growth	7.32 (13.39)	8.53 (7.37)	9.11 (4.47)	9.06 (4.68)	9.68 (−1.62)	9.20 (3.90)	9.42 (2.92)	9.19 (4.03)
B. Standard deviation of inflation	8.79 (3.02)	8.04 (4.89)	9.22 (1.94)	9.26 (1.85)	8.87 (2.83)	9.40 (1.45)	9.40 (1.50)	9.33 (1.68)
C. Inflation: most recent year	5.03 (24.87)	9.07 (4.64)	8.02 (9.91)	8.88 (5.60)	9.55 (2.27)	9.40 (2.75)	9.06 (4.68)	9.43 (2.83)
D. Freedom to own foreign currency bank accounts	0.00	0.00	0.00	5.00	5.00	10.00	10.00	10.00
4. Freedom to Trade Internationally	**6.20**	**6.26**	**7.22**	**6.79**	**7.09**	**6.50**	**7.14**	**7.12**
A. Taxes on international trade	6.59	6.50	7.46	7.91	8.35	5.90	5.68	5.66
(i) Revenues from trade taxes (% of trade sector)	7.27 (4.10)	7.60 (3.60)	7.73 (3.40)	8.67 (2.00)	9.15 (1.28)	9.40 (0.90)	9.47 (0.79)	9.40 (0.90)
(ii) Mean tariff rate	5.92 (20.40)	5.40 (23.00)	7.34 (13.30)	7.70 (11.50)	8.26 (8.70)	8.20 (9.00)	7.56 (12.20)	7.58 (12.10)
(iii) Standard deviation of tariff rates			7.32 (6.70)	7.36 (6.60)	7.64 (5.90)	0.00 (49.40)	0.00 (49.90)	0.00 (49.25)
B. Regulatory trade barriers				5.97	6.84	7.20	7.43	7.02
(i) Non-tariff trade barriers				5.97	5.18	6.00	5.86	4.98
(ii) Compliance cost of importing and exporting					8.50	8.40	8.99	9.06
C. Size of trade sector relative to expected	8.40	6.79	5.65	5.26	6.69	5.80	7.19	6.44
D. Black-market exchange rates	7.80	7.80	9.80	10.00	10.00	10.00	10.00	10.00
E. International capital market controls	0.00	2.00	5.00	4.83	3.58	3.70	5.38	6.46
(i) Foreign ownership/investment restrictions				4.66	7.16	5.80	6.14	5.23
(ii) Capital controls	0.00	2.00	5.00	5.00	0.00	1.50	4.62	7.69
5. Regulation of Credit, Labor, and Business	**5.05**	**5.65**	**5.47**	**4.80**	**5.31**	**6.80**	**6.44**	**6.58**
A. Credit market regulations	6.13	8.11	8.33	6.90	6.53	9.30	9.25	9.25
(i) Ownership of banks	5.00	5.00	5.00	5.00	5.00	8.00	8.00	8.00
(ii) Foreign bank competition				4.93	3.17	9.00	9.00	9.00
(iii) Private sector credit	9.40	9.32	10.00	10.00	10.00	10.00	10.00	10.00
(iv) Interest rate controls/negative real interest rates	4.00	10.00	10.00	10.00	10.00	10.00	10.00	10.00
B. Labor market regulations			3.59	4.43	4.20	4.80	4.02	4.44
(i) Hiring regulations and minimum wage				5.83	4.14	8.90	5.60	5.57
(ii) Hiring and firing regulations			3.53	3.53	4.70	4.70	3.55	3.66
(iii) Centralized collective bargaining	7.24	7.24	7.24	7.24	6.17	7.90	7.43	7.46
(iv) Hours regulations				5.53	6.01	6.00	6.00	8.00
(v) Mandated cost of worker dismissal						1.60	1.56	1.97
(vi) Conscription	0.00	0.00	0.00	0.00	0.00	0.00	0.00	0.00
C. Business regulations				3.08	5.19	6.30	6.06	6.04
(i) Price controls			0.00	0.00	1.00	3.00	3.00	3.00
(ii) Administrative requirements					6.52	3.50	3.04	3.01
(iii) Bureaucracy costs				5.38	7.65	6.30	3.99	4.06
(iv) Starting a business				3.65	5.38	8.30	9.40	9.40
(v) Extra payments/bribes/favoritism				3.28	5.40	6.50	6.01	5.84
(vi) Licensing restrictions						9.80	9.75	9.76
(vii) Cost of tax compliance						6.70	7.20	7.20

Kuwait

	1980	1985	1990	1995	2000	2005	2008	2009
Chain-Linked	Rating (Rank)	Rating (Rank)	Rating (Rank)	Rating (Rank)	Rating (Rank)	Rating (Rank)	Rating (Rank)	Rating (Rank)
Summary Rating (Rank) ➤	**5.01** (68)	**6.88** (16)	**5.47** (61)	**6.69** (38)	**6.72** (44)	**7.25** (35)	**7.55** (16)	**7.13** (38)
Area 1. Size of Government	10.00 (1)	4.63 (66)	3.89 (96)	5.97 (63)	6.37 (55)	6.72 (56)	6.98 (39)	5.12 (96)
Area 2. Legal Structure and Security of Property Rights	1.84 (87)	5.85 (40)	2.73 (99)	6.49 (39)	6.95 (30)	7.60 (22)	7.36 (25)	7.36 (25)
Area 3. Access to Sound Money	5.19 (90)	8.93 (15)	7.84 (35)	8.89 (33)	8.09 (57)	7.84 (72)	8.80 (46)	9.26 (37)
Area 4. Freedom to Trade Internationally			6.98 (30)	6.81 (50)	7.20 (50)	7.22 (37)	7.11 (46)	6.51 (69)
Area 5. Regulation of Credit, Labor, and Business	6.12 (29)	5.75 (44)	5.95 (41)	5.23 (73)	4.99 (102)	6.93 (44)	7.46 (23)	7.37 (22)

Unadjusted

	1980	1985	1990	1995	2000	2005	2008	2009
Summary Rating (Rank) ➤	**3.78** (98)	**5.68** (48)	**5.07** (78)	**6.45** (44)	**6.72** (44)	**7.21** (43)	**7.51** (23)	**7.10** (47)
	Rating *Data*	Rating *Data*	Rating *Data*	Rating *Data*	Rating *Data*	Rating *Data*	Rating *Data*	Rating *Data*
1. Size of Government	**2.97**	**1.19**	**3.15**	**4.83**	**6.37**	**6.70**	**6.98**	**5.12**
A. Government consumption	3.95 *(26.58)*	2.38 *(31.90)*	0.00 *(40.57)*	0.00 *(44.39)*	1.41 *(35.21)*	2.10 *(33.00)*	2.58 *(31.23)*	1.31 *(35.55)*
B. Transfers and subsidies			7.46 *(9.83)*	7.50 *(9.66)*	7.08 *(11.22)*	7.80 *(8.50)*	8.35 *(6.57)*	2.16 *(29.26)*
C. Government enterprises and investment	2.00 *(43.50)*	0.00 *(61.30)*	2.00 *(46.00)*	7.00 *(21.80)*	7.00 *(21.80)*	7.00 *(21.80)*	7.00	7.00
D. Top marginal tax rate					10.00	10.00	10.00	10.00
(i) Top marginal income tax rate					10.00 *(0)*	10.00 *(0)*	10.00 *(0)*	10.00 *(0)*
(ii) Top marginal income and payroll tax rates					10.00 *(0)*	10.00 *(0)*	10.00 *(0)*	10.00 *(0)*
2. Legal Structure and Security of Property Rights	**1.84**	**5.85**	**2.73**	**6.49**	**6.95**	**7.20**	**7.01**	**7.01**
A. Judicial independence						7.00	6.06	6.55
B. Impartial courts				7.17	7.51	6.80	5.60	5.44
C. Protection of property rights						6.30	6.86	6.53
D. Military interference in rule of law and politics				8.13	8.33	8.30	8.33	8.33
E. Integrity of the legal system				6.96	8.33	8.30	8.33	8.33
F. Legal enforcement of contracts						5.10	5.06	5.06
G. Regulatory restrictions on sale of real property						8.80	8.80	8.80
3. Access to Sound Money	**5.18**	**8.92**	**7.51**	**8.89**	**8.09**	**7.80**	**8.80**	**9.26**
A. Money growth	7.16 *(14.18)*	9.63 *(−1.85)*	9.95 *(−0.24)*	9.29 *(−3.57)*	9.89 *(−0.55)*	7.10 *(14.40)*	8.75 *(6.26)*	9.04 *(4.82)*
B. Standard deviation of inflation	2.07 *(19.83)*	7.03 *(7.43)*	4.55 *(13.62)*	7.54 *(6.16)*	2.98 *(17.55)*	5.10 *(12.36)*	8.59 *(3.53)*	8.80 *(3.00)*
C. Inflation: most recent year	1.49 *(42.57)*	9.03 *(4.86)*	8.03 *(9.83)*	8.74 *(6.29)*	9.50 *(2.51)*	9.20 *(4.12)*	7.88 *(10.58)*	9.21 *(3.97)*
D. Freedom to own foreign currency bank accounts	10.00	10.00		10.00	10.00	10.00	10.00	10.00
4. Freedom to Trade Internationally		**6.96**	**6.98**	**6.81**	**7.20**	**6.80**	**6.72**	**6.15**
A. Taxes on international trade		9.20	9.20	9.40	9.27	8.80	8.86	8.86
(i) Revenues from trade taxes (% of trade sector)			9.20 *(1.20)*	9.40 *(0.90)*	9.27 *(1.09)*	9.50 *(0.80)*	9.59 *(0.61)*	9.59 *(0.61)*
(ii) Mean tariff rate		9.20 *(4.00)*				9.10 *(4.70)*	9.06 *(4.70)*	9.06 *(4.70)*
(iii) Standard deviation of tariff rates						7.90 *(5.10)*	7.93 *(5.17)*	7.93 *(5.17)*
B. Regulatory trade barriers						7.30	6.73	7.09
(i) Non-tariff trade barriers						7.30	5.92	6.63
(ii) Compliance cost of importing and exporting						7.20	7.55	7.55
C. Size of trade sector relative to expected	6.66	5.45	5.51	4.47	3.95	3.90	3.53	0.49
D. Black-market exchange rates	10.00	10.00	10.00	10.00	10.00	10.00	10.00	10.00
E. International capital market controls	2.00	2.00	2.00	2.00	4.61	4.20	4.47	4.32
(i) Foreign ownership / investment restrictions						3.70	4.76	4.46
(ii) Capital controls	2.00	2.00	2.00	2.00	4.61	4.60	4.17	4.17
5. Regulation of Credit, Labor, and Business	**5.13**	**5.49**	**4.99**	**5.23**	**4.99**	**7.50**	**8.03**	**7.95**
A. Credit market regulations	7.41	7.66	7.50	7.13	6.33	8.30	10.00	10.00
(i) Ownership of banks	5.00	5.00	5.00	5.00	5.00	10.00	10.00	10.00
(ii) Foreign bank competition								
(iii) Private sector credit	9.83	7.98	10.00	6.40	6.99	10.00	10.00	10.00
(iv) Interest rate controls / negative real interest rates		10.00		10.00	7.00	5.00	10.00	10.00
B. Labor market regulations						7.80	7.57	7.30
(i) Hiring regulations and minimum wage						10.00	10.00	10.00
(ii) Hiring and firing regulations						5.50	5.14	4.95
(iii) Centralized collective bargaining						8.40	7.53	7.91
(iv) Hours regulations						10.00	10.00	8.00
(v) Mandated cost of worker dismissal						2.80	2.77	2.97
(vi) Conscription	1.00	1.00	0.00	0.00	0.00	10.00	10.00	10.00
C. Business regulations						6.30	6.53	6.56
(i) Price controls				6.00	6.00	6.00	6.00	6.00
(ii) Administrative requirements						3.20	2.72	2.80
(iii) Bureaucracy costs						1.60	5.13	5.25
(iv) Starting a business						8.50	8.67	8.59
(v) Extra payments / bribes / favoritism						7.10	5.49	5.68
(vi) Licensing restrictions						8.70	9.00	8.91
(vii) Cost of tax compliance						8.70	8.68	8.68

Kyrgyz Republic

	1980	1985	1990	1995	2000	2005	2008	2009
Chain-Linked						Rating (Rank)	Rating (Rank)	Rating (Rank)
Summary Rating (Rank) ➤								
Area 1. Size of Government								
Area 2. Legal Structure and Security of Property Rights								
Area 3. Access to Sound Money								
Area 4. Freedom to Trade Internationally								
Area 5. Regulation of Credit, Labor, and Business								

Unadjusted

	1980	1985	1990	1995	2000	2005	2008	2009
Summary Rating (Rank) ➤						**6.75** (74)	**6.93** (61)	**6.81** (70)
				Rating *Data*	Rating *Data*	Rating *Data*	Rating *Data*	Rating *Data*
1. Size of Government						**7.30**	**7.82**	**7.07**
A. Government consumption						6.40 *(18.10)*	9.44 *(7.92)*	6.05 *(19.44)*
B. Transfers and subsidies						9.40 *(2.60)*	9.35 *(2.87)*	9.25 *(3.25)*
C. Government enterprises and investment						6.00	4.00	4.00
D. Top marginal tax rate							8.50	9.00
(i) Top marginal income tax rate							10.00 *(10)*	10.00 *(10)*
(ii) Top marginal income and payroll tax rates							7.00 *(31)*	8.00 *(30)*
2. Legal Structure and Security of Property Rights						**4.40**	**4.70**	**4.72**
A. Judicial independence						1.60	2.19	1.77
B. Impartial courts						2.40	2.57	2.78
C. Protection of property rights						3.30	3.22	2.96
D. Military interference in rule of law and politics						3.10	4.50	4.90
E. Integrity of the legal system								
F. Legal enforcement of contracts						6.70	6.74	6.74
G. Regulatory restrictions on sale of real property						9.20	8.99	9.15
3. Access to Sound Money						**8.60**	**7.40**	**8.20**
A. Money growth						6.30 *(18.30)*	7.05 *(14.75)*	7.05 *(14.75)*
B. Standard deviation of inflation						9.10 *(2.22)*	7.45 *(6.37)*	7.13 *(7.18)*
C. Inflation: most recent year						9.10 *(4.35)*	5.10 *(24.52)*	8.63 *(6.86)*
D. Freedom to own foreign currency bank accounts						10.00	10.00	10.00
4. Freedom to Trade Internationally						**6.60**	**7.39**	**6.69**
A. Taxes on international trade						8.80	8.62	8.67
(i) Revenues from trade taxes (% of trade sector)					9.69 *(0.47)*	9.60 *(0.60)*	8.89 *(1.67)*	8.92 *(1.61)*
(ii) Mean tariff rate						9.00 *(4.80)*	9.06 *(4.70)*	9.08 *(4.60)*
(iii) Standard deviation of tariff rates						7.70 *(5.70)*	7.91 *(5.22)*	8.01 *(4.97)*
B. Regulatory trade barriers						2.20	2.54	2.40
(i) Non-tariff trade barriers						4.00	4.57	4.29
(ii) Compliance cost of importing and exporting						0.30	0.50	0.50
C. Size of trade sector relative to expected						6.80	10.00	8.87
D. Black-market exchange rates						10.00	10.00	10.00
E. International capital market controls						5.10	5.81	3.50
(i) Foreign ownership / investment restrictions						4.90	4.69	3.92
(ii) Capital controls						5.40	6.92	3.08
5. Regulation of Credit, Labor, and Business						**6.80**	**7.35**	**7.37**
A. Credit market regulations						9.10	9.24	9.01
(i) Ownership of banks						10.00	10.00	10.00
(ii) Foreign bank competition						9.00	9.00	9.00
(iii) Private sector credit				0.00	8.05	9.60	9.97	9.03
(iv) Interest rate controls / negative real interest rates						8.00	8.00	8.00
B. Labor market regulations						6.50	6.18	6.44
(i) Hiring regulations and minimum wage						6.70	6.70	5.00
(ii) Hiring and firing regulations						7.40	5.93	5.93
(iii) Centralized collective bargaining						7.60	7.04	7.88
(iv) Hours regulations						8.00	8.00	10.00
(v) Mandated cost of worker dismissal						8.40	8.42	8.79
(vi) Conscription						1.00	1.00	1.00
C. Business regulations						4.90	6.62	6.68
(i) Price controls							8.00	8.00
(ii) Administrative requirements						1.80	3.10	3.46
(iii) Bureaucracy costs						3.00	6.63	6.81
(iv) Starting a business						9.20	9.59	9.64
(v) Extra payments / bribes / favoritism						3.50	2.87	2.83
(vi) Licensing restrictions						4.00	8.39	8.31
(vii) Cost of tax compliance						7.70	7.74	7.74

Latvia

	1980	1985	1990	1995	2000	2005	2008	2009
Chain-Linked			Rating (Rank)	Rating (Rank)	Rating (Rank)	Rating (Rank)	Rating (Rank)	Rating (Rank)
Summary Rating (Rank) ➤				**5.19** (94)	**6.62** (52)	**7.18** (39)	**6.88** (57)	**6.73** (62)
Area 1. Size of Government				5.03 (87)	5.18 (89)	6.35 (71)	5.10 (103)	4.84 (103)
Area 2. Legal Structure and Security of Property Rights				5.56 (58)	5.95 (55)	6.68 (37)	6.40 (42)	6.24 (47)
Area 3. Access to Sound Money			4.86 (93)	2.98 (109)	8.55 (46)	8.68 (55)	8.90 (43)	8.90 (50)
Area 4. Freedom to Trade Internationally				7.28 (35)	7.17 (51)	7.20 (39)	7.02 (55)	6.80 (52)
Area 5. Regulation of Credit, Labor, and Business				4.83 (95)	6.24 (52)	6.99 (41)	6.96 (42)	6.86 (48)

	1980	1985	1990	1995	2000	2005	2008	2009
Unadjusted								
Summary Rating (Rank) ➤				**5.40** (83)	**6.62** (52)	**7.31** (37)	**7.08** (55)	**6.92** (60)
	Rating *Data*	Rating *Data*	Rating *Data*	Rating *Data*	Rating *Data*	Rating *Data*	Rating *Data*	Rating *Data*
1. Size of Government				**5.41**	**5.18**	**6.30**	**5.10**	**4.84**
A. Government consumption			7.65 *(13.99)*	4.06 *(26.19)*	4.94 *(23.22)*	5.30 *(22.10)*	4.26 *(25.51)*	4.66 *(24.17)*
B. Transfers and subsidies				5.18 *(18.20)*	5.80 *(15.91)*	7.60 *(9.20)*	5.65 *(16.45)*	4.19 *(21.84)*
C. Government enterprises and investment				4.00	6.00	4.00	4.00	
D. Top marginal tax rate				7.00	6.00	6.50	6.50	6.50
(i) Top marginal income tax rate				7.00 *(35)*	9.00 *(25)*	9.00 *(25)*	9.00 *(25)*	9.00 *(23)*
(ii) Top marginal income and payroll tax rates					3.00 *(48)*	4.00 *(45)*	4.00 *(45)*	4.00 *(44)*
2. Legal Structure and Security of Property Rights				**5.96**	**5.95**	**6.90**	**6.59**	**6.42**
A. Judicial independence					4.60	4.54	4.44	
B. Impartial courts				5.83	6.20	4.60	3.28	3.07
C. Protection of property rights				3.82	6.50	6.40	5.45	
D. Military interference in rule of law and politics				7.53	8.33	8.30	8.33	8.33
E. Integrity of the legal system				8.33	8.30	8.33	8.33	
F. Legal enforcement of contracts					7.40	6.73	6.73	
G. Regulatory restrictions on sale of real property					8.30	8.49	8.55	
3. Access to Sound Money			**6.43**	**2.98**	**8.55**	**8.70**	**8.90**	**8.90**
A. Money growth				0.10 *(49.50)*	6.81 *(15.97)*	7.40 *(12.90)*	9.93 *(−0.33)*	8.77 *(−6.15)*
B. Standard deviation of inflation	8.91 *(2.73)*		7.44 *(6.39)*	0.00 *(365.31)*	7.93 *(5.17)*	8.70 *(3.37)*	8.76 *(3.11)*	7.52 *(6.20)*
C. Inflation: most recent year			6.85 *(15.74)*	6.80 *(16.00)*	9.47 *(2.65)*	8.60 *(6.76)*	6.92 *(15.40)*	9.29 *(3.53)*
D. Freedom to own foreign currency bank accounts			5.00	5.00	10.00	10.00	10.00	10.00
4. Freedom to Trade Internationally				**8.02**	**7.17**	**7.50**	**7.30**	**7.06**
A. Taxes on international trade				9.46	8.33	8.40	8.03	8.22
(i) Revenues from trade taxes (% of trade sector)				9.46 *(0.81)*	9.78 *(0.33)*	9.60 *(0.60)*	9.61 *(0.59)*	9.44 *(0.84)*
(ii) Mean tariff rate					8.88 *(5.60)*	9.50 *(2.70)*	8.88 *(5.60)*	8.94 *(5.30)*
(iii) Standard deviation of tariff rates					6.32 *(9.20)*	6.10 *(9.70)*	5.61 *(10.98)*	6.29 *(9.28)*
B. Regulatory trade barriers					5.30	7.50	7.93	7.78
(i) Non-tariff trade barriers					5.30	6.40	7.53	6.92
(ii) Compliance cost of importing and exporting						8.50	8.33	8.64
C. Size of trade sector relative to expected				5.20	4.87	4.64	4.70	3.59	2.74
D. Black-market exchange rates				0.00	9.60	10.00	10.00	10.00	10.00
E. International capital market controls				0.00	8.00	7.60	6.90	6.93	6.56
(i) Foreign ownership/investment restrictions						8.28	6.90	6.94	6.20
(ii) Capital controls				0.00	8.00	6.92	6.90	6.92	6.92
5. Regulation of Credit, Labor, and Business				**4.62**	**6.24**	**7.20**	**7.49**	**7.39**
A. Credit market regulations				5.03	8.44	9.40	9.20	8.94
(i) Ownership of banks					10.00	10.00	10.00	10.00
(ii) Foreign bank competition					5.12	9.00	9.00	9.00
(iii) Private sector credit				8.05	8.82	9.60	8.79	7.77
(iv) Interest rate controls/negative real interest rates				2.00	10.00	9.00	9.00	9.00
B. Labor market regulations					4.53	5.70	7.13	7.16
(i) Hiring regulations and minimum wage					3.33	3.30	5.00	3.33
(ii) Hiring and firing regulations					3.93	5.30	5.19	5.39
(iii) Centralized collective bargaining					7.85	8.30	8.15	7.82
(iv) Hours regulations						6.00	6.00	8.00
(v) Mandated cost of worker dismissal						8.40	8.42	8.39
(vi) Conscription				0.00	1.00	3.00	3.00	10.00	10.00
C. Business regulations					5.75	6.30	6.14	6.06
(i) Price controls				0.00	6.00	6.00	6.00	6.00	6.00
(ii) Administrative requirements					7.18	3.90	3.59	3.44
(iii) Bureaucracy costs					4.73	4.50	4.09	4.27
(iv) Starting a business					5.00	9.40	9.42	9.42
(v) Extra payments/bribes/favoritism					5.84	6.40	5.14	4.70
(vi) Licensing restrictions						7.80	7.84	7.85
(vii) Cost of tax compliance						6.40	6.87	6.72

Lesotho

	1980	1985	1990	1995	2000	2005	2008	2009
Chain-Linked						Rating (Rank)	Rating (Rank)	Rating (Rank)
Summary Rating (Rank) ➤								
Area 1. Size of Government								
Area 2. Legal Structure and Security of Property Rights								
Area 3. Access to Sound Money								
Area 4. Freedom to Trade Internationally								
Area 5. Regulation of Credit, Labor, and Business								

Unadjusted

	1980	1985	1990	1995	2000	2005	2008	2009
Summary Rating (Rank) ➤						**6.19** (100)	**6.08** (108)	**6.11** (109)
			Rating Data	Rating Data	Rating Data	Rating Data	Rating Data	Rating Data
1. Size of Government						**4.60**	**4.83**	**4.44**
A. Government consumption						2.70 (30.70)	1.30 (35.59)	0.13 (39.56)
B. Transfers and subsidies						7.20 (10.90)	9.20 (3.45)	9.20 (3.45)
C. Government enterprises and investment						4.00 (31.66)	4.00 (38.16)	4.00 (38.16)
D. Top marginal tax rate								
(i) Top marginal income tax rate								
(ii) Top marginal income and payroll tax rates								
2. Legal Structure and Security of Property Rights						**5.00**	**4.55**	**4.64**
A. Judicial independence						5.00	4.10	3.73
B. Impartial courts						4.70	2.71	3.07
C. Protection of property rights						4.00	4.82	4.44
D. Military interference in rule of law and politics						7.10	6.20	7.30
E. Integrity of the legal system								
F. Legal enforcement of contracts						4.00	4.04	3.82
G. Regulatory restrictions on sale of real property						5.40	5.46	5.46
3. Access to Sound Money						**8.10**	**7.40**	**7.65**
A. Money growth						8.90 (5.40)	7.77 (11.15)	8.10 (9.48)
B. Standard deviation of inflation						9.10 (2.24)	8.99 (2.53)	8.95 (2.64)
C. Inflation: most recent year						9.30 (3.44)	7.86 (10.72)	8.57 (7.16)
D. Freedom to own foreign currency bank accounts						5.00	5.00	5.00
4. Freedom to Trade Internationally						**6.30**	**6.23**	**6.43**
A. Taxes on international trade						4.60	4.71	4.66
(i) Revenues from trade taxes (% of trade sector)					0.00 (15.81)	0.00 (17.40)	0.00 (23.76)	0.00 (23.76)
(ii) Mean tariff rate						8.00 (9.90)	8.44 (7.80)	8.46 (7.70)
(iii) Standard deviation of tariff rates						5.70 (10.70)	5.70 (10.76)	5.53 (11.17)
B. Regulatory trade barriers						4.30	4.15	5.14
(i) Non-tariff trade barriers						5.10	4.89	4.90
(ii) Compliance cost of importing and exporting						3.40	3.42	5.38
C. Size of trade sector relative to expected						8.10	8.27	8.49
D. Black-market exchange rates						10.00	10.00	10.00
E. International capital market controls						4.50	4.01	3.88
(i) Foreign ownership / investment restrictions						6.70	5.70	5.45
(ii) Capital controls						2.30	2.31	2.31
5. Regulation of Credit, Labor, and Business						**6.90**	**7.37**	**7.38**
A. Credit market regulations						10.00	9.75	9.75
(i) Ownership of banks						10.00	10.00	10.00
(ii) Foreign bank competition						10.00	10.00	10.00
(iii) Private sector credit			9.92	10.00	10.00	10.00	10.00	10.00
(iv) Interest rate controls / negative real interest rates						10.00	9.00	9.00
B. Labor market regulations						6.80	6.93	7.12
(i) Hiring regulations and minimum wage						7.80	7.80	7.77
(ii) Hiring and firing regulations						4.50	4.88	4.87
(iii) Centralized collective bargaining						4.40	4.97	5.78
(iv) Hours regulations						8.00	8.00	8.00
(v) Mandated cost of worker dismissal						5.90	5.92	6.29
(vi) Conscription						10.00	10.00	10.00
C. Business regulations						3.90	5.44	5.27
(i) Price controls								
(ii) Administrative requirements						2.50	4.19	3.98
(iii) Bureaucracy costs						1.30	6.00	6.41
(iv) Starting a business						7.20	8.40	8.41
(v) Extra payments / bribes / favoritism						5.30	3.91	3.80
(vi) Licensing restrictions						3.40	3.79	2.66
(vii) Cost of tax compliance						3.70	6.37	6.37

Lithuania

	1980	1985	1990	1995	2000	2005	2008	2009
Chain-Linked			Rating (Rank)	Rating (Rank)	Rating (Rank)	Rating (Rank)	Rating (Rank)	Rating (Rank)
Summary Rating (Rank) ➤				**5.10** (96)	**6.28** (70)	**7.11** (41)	**7.08** (47)	**7.02** (45)
Area 1. Size of Government				5.64 (76)	5.45 (82)	5.61 (92)	5.79 (82)	5.56 (83)
Area 2. Legal Structure and Security of Property Rights				5.39 (66)	5.81 (61)	6.71 (33)	6.59 (33)	6.49 (38)
Area 3. Access to Sound Money			3.74 (106)	1.85 (114)	7.09 (76)	8.83 (48)	8.81 (45)	9.16 (42)
Area 4. Freedom to Trade Internationally				7.61 (27)	7.26 (46)	7.13 (45)	7.08 (50)	6.61 (63)
Area 5. Regulation of Credit, Labor, and Business			2.68 (115)	4.86 (94)	5.78 (71)	7.34 (30)	7.16 (31)	7.37 (22)

Unadjusted

	1980	1985	1990	1995	2000	2005	2008	2009
Summary Rating (Rank) ➤				**5.21** (93)	**6.28** (70)	**7.43** (29)	**7.39** (31)	**7.40** (24)
			Rating *Data*	Rating *Data*	Rating *Data*	Rating *Data*	Rating *Data*	Rating *Data*
1. Size of Government				**5.64**	**5.45**	**6.80**	**7.00**	**6.73**
A. Government consumption			4.34 *(25.25)*	5.11 *(22.62)*	4.44 *(24.90)*	5.80 *(20.40)*	5.40 *(21.64)*	4.66 *(24.17)*
B. Transfers and subsidies				7.30 *(10.40)*	6.92 *(11.82)*	6.80 *(12.10)*	6.10 *(14.81)*	4.75 *(19.77)*
C. Government enterprises and investment						10.00 *(5.60)*	10.00 *(5.58)*	10.00 *(5.58)*
D. Top marginal tax rate				4.50	5.00	4.50	6.50	7.50
(i) Top marginal income tax rate				7.00 *(35)*	7.00 *(33)*	7.00 *(33)*	9.00 *(24)*	10.00 *(15)*
(ii) Top marginal income and payroll tax rates				2.00 *(51)*	3.00 *(50)*	2.00 *(51)*	4.00 *(44)*	5.00 *(37)*
2. Legal Structure and Security of Property Rights				**5.87**	**5.81**	**6.70**	**6.58**	**6.48**
A. Judicial independence						4.00	4.56	4.32
B. Impartial courts				5.88	6.07	4.30	3.90	3.86
C. Protection of property rights					3.20	6.50	5.88	5.56
D. Military interference in rule of law and politics				7.23	8.33	8.30	8.33	8.33
E. Integrity of the legal system					8.33	6.70	6.67	6.67
F. Legal enforcement of contracts						7.40	6.96	6.96
G. Regulatory restrictions on sale of real property						9.70	9.78	9.68
3. Access to Sound Money			**7.49**	**1.85**	**7.09**	**8.80**	**8.81**	**9.16**
A. Money growth				0.00 *(53.00)*	7.47 *(12.63)*	7.00 *(15.20)*	8.10 *(9.50)*	9.42 *(−2.88)*
B. Standard deviation of inflation				0.00 *(329.24)*	6.09 *(9.77)*	8.90 *(2.73)*	8.84 *(2.90)*	8.09 *(4.79)*
C. Inflation: most recent year			9.97 *(−0.15)*	2.39 *(38.05)*	9.80 *(1.01)*	9.50 *(2.66)*	8.30 *(8.50)*	9.11 *(4.45)*
D. Freedom to own foreign currency bank accounts			5.00	5.00	5.00	10.00	10.00	10.00
4. Freedom to Trade Internationally				**8.16**	**7.26**	**7.50**	**7.43**	**6.94**
A. Taxes on international trade				8.35	8.50	8.40	8.03	8.22
(i) Revenues from trade taxes (% of trade sector)				9.56 *(0.66)*	9.78 *(0.33)*	9.60 *(0.60)*	9.61 *(0.59)*	9.44 *(0.84)*
(ii) Mean tariff rate				9.10 *(4.50)*	8.92 *(5.40)*	9.50 *(2.70)*	8.88 *(5.60)*	8.94 *(5.30)*
(iii) Standard deviation of tariff rates				6.40 *(9.00)*	6.80 *(8.00)*	6.10 *(9.70)*	5.61 *(10.98)*	6.29 *(9.28)*
B. Regulatory trade barriers					5.20	7.40	7.50	7.40
(i) Non-tariff trade barriers					5.20	6.10	6.35	6.11
(ii) Compliance cost of importing and exporting						8.60	8.64	8.70
C. Size of trade sector relative to expected			6.34	6.32	4.81	5.60	5.54	4.62
D. Black-market exchange rates			0.00	10.00	10.00	10.00	10.00	10.00
E. International capital market controls			0.00	8.00	7.81	6.10	6.11	4.44
(i) Foreign ownership/investment restrictions					8.12	6.00	6.06	5.81
(ii) Capital controls			0.00	8.00	7.50	6.20	6.15	3.08
5. Regulation of Credit, Labor, and Business			**2.47**	**4.52**	**5.78**	**7.30**	**7.13**	**7.71**
A. Credit market regulations			0.00	4.44	6.87	9.90	9.23	9.48
(i) Ownership of banks			0.00	5.00	5.00	10.00	10.00	10.00
(ii) Foreign bank competition					5.18	10.00	10.00	10.00
(iii) Private sector credit				8.32	7.89	9.70	7.92	7.92
(iv) Interest rate controls/negative real interest rates				0.00	9.00	10.00	9.00	10.00
B. Labor market regulations					4.23	5.50	5.59	7.11
(i) Hiring regulations and minimum wage					3.01	6.70	6.70	5.00
(ii) Hiring and firing regulations					2.75	3.50	4.43	3.86
(iii) Centralized collective bargaining					8.17	8.30	8.20	8.19
(iv) Hours regulations						4.00	4.00	8.00
(v) Mandated cost of worker dismissal						7.20	7.22	7.59
(vi) Conscription			0.00	3.00	3.00	3.00	3.00	10.00
C. Business regulations					6.25	6.60	6.58	6.55
(i) Price controls			0.00	4.00	4.00	6.00	8.00	8.00
(ii) Administrative requirements					7.28	3.30	3.12	2.81
(iii) Bureaucracy costs					7.48	4.80	4.00	4.03
(iv) Starting a business					4.18	9.00	9.04	9.15
(v) Extra payments/bribes/favoritism					8.29	6.90	5.64	5.67
(vi) Licensing restrictions						8.00	8.10	8.15
(vii) Cost of tax compliance						8.10	8.14	8.04

Luxembourg

	1980	1985	1990	1995	2000	2005	2008	2009
Chain-Linked	Rating (Rank)	Rating (Rank)	Rating (Rank)	Rating (Rank)	Rating (Rank)	Rating (Rank)	Rating (Rank)	Rating (Rank)
Summary Rating (Rank) ➤	**7.58** (6)	**7.94** (5)	**7.88** (8)	**7.70** (11)	**7.87** (11)	**7.47** (21)	**7.52** (20)	**7.42** (21)
Area 1. Size of Government	4.41 (72)	4.81 (63)	4.73 (83)	4.40 (97)	4.78 (95)	4.35 (114)	4.79 (108)	4.37 (109)
Area 2. Legal Structure and Security of Property Rights	9.25 (8)	9.87 (1)	9.87 (4)	9.10 (7)	8.62 (16)	8.74 (6)	8.92 (2)	8.83 (1)
Area 3. Access to Sound Money	9.05 (7)	9.58 (3)	9.53 (11)	9.73 (6)	9.75 (3)	9.47 (27)	9.43 (21)	9.55 (17)
Area 4. Freedom to Trade Internationally	8.67 (3)	8.85 (4)	8.70 (4)	8.62 (7)	9.01 (4)	8.03 (12)	8.10 (8)	7.95 (7)
Area 5. Regulation of Credit, Labor, and Business	6.63 (17)	6.63 (16)	6.63 (18)	6.63 (23)	7.20 (14)	6.77 (50)	6.41 (68)	6.45 (68)

	1980	1985	1990	1995	2000	2005	2008	2009
Unadjusted								
Summary Rating (Rank) ➤	**7.84** (2)	**8.21** (2)	**7.55** (7)	**7.69** (11)	**7.87** (11)	**7.53** (22)	**7.59** (16)	**7.49** (20)
	Rating Data	Rating Data	Rating Data	Rating Data	Rating Data	Rating Data	Rating Data	Rating Data
1. Size of Government	**6.77**	**7.39**	**4.73**	**4.40**	**4.78**	**4.40**	**4.79**	**4.37**
A. Government consumption	6.54 (17.75)	6.79 (16.92)	6.54 (17.77)	3.84 (26.95)	3.15 (29.30)	2.40 (31.80)	2.39 (31.86)	2.09 (32.89)
B. Transfers and subsidies			2.89 (26.60)	3.27 (25.20)	4.47 (20.81)	4.00 (22.50)	3.78 (23.31)	3.39 (24.76)
C. Government enterprises and investment	7.00 (22.00)	8.00 (18.20)	8.00 (19.20)	8.00 (19.20)	8.00 (19.20)	7.00 (21.90)	8.00 (15.75)	7.00 (21.25)
D. Top marginal tax rate			1.50	2.50	3.50	4.00	5.00	5.00
(i) Top marginal income tax rate			1.00 (56)	3.00 (50)	4.00 (48)	5.00 (39)	6.00 (39)	6.00 (39)
(ii) Top marginal income and payroll tax rates			2.00 (58)	2.00 (60)	3.00 (54)	3.00 (46)	4.00 (46)	4.00 (46)
2. Legal Structure and Security of Property Rights	**7.83**	**8.35**	**8.35**	**9.10**	**8.62**	**8.20**	**8.35**	**8.27**
A. Judicial independence				9.45	7.30	7.40	8.31	8.11
B. Impartial courts				8.62	8.20	7.40	7.76	7.50
C. Protection of property rights				7.39	7.60	8.80	8.86	8.73
D. Military interference in rule of law and politics				10.03	10.00	10.00	10.00	10.00
E. Integrity of the legal system				10.00	10.00	10.00	10.00	10.00
F. Legal enforcement of contracts						7.50	7.46	7.46
G. Regulatory restrictions on sale of real property						6.10	6.07	6.10
3. Access to Sound Money	**9.05**	**9.58**	**9.53**	**9.73**	**9.75**	**9.50**	**9.43**	**9.55**
A. Money growth	9.22 (3.88)	9.98 (0.10)	9.27 (3.64)	9.82 (0.92)	9.81 (0.95)	9.20 (4.00)	9.20 (4.02)	9.28 (3.62)
B. Standard deviation of inflation	8.56 (3.60)	8.93 (2.68)	9.52 (1.20)	9.23 (1.93)	9.84 (0.41)	9.20 (2.05)	9.22 (1.94)	9.01 (2.47)
C. Inflation: most recent year	8.42 (7.92)	9.40 (2.98)	9.32 (3.42)	9.86 (0.71)	9.37 (3.15)	9.50 (2.49)	9.32 (3.40)	9.93 (0.37)
D. Freedom to own foreign currency bank accounts	10.00	10.00	10.00	10.00	10.00	10.00	10.00	10.00
4. Freedom to Trade Internationally	**8.64**	**8.82**	**8.53**	**8.45**	**9.01**	**8.00**	**8.09**	**7.95**
A. Taxes on international trade	9.09	9.22	8.52	8.74	9.18	8.40	8.03	8.22
(i) Revenues from trade taxes (% of trade sector)	9.93 (0.10)	9.93 (0.10)	9.93 (0.10)	9.93 (0.10)	9.78 (0.33)	9.60 (0.60)	9.61 (0.59)	9.44 (0.84)
(ii) Mean tariff rate	8.24 (8.80)	8.50 (7.50)	8.52 (7.40)	8.66 (6.70)	9.52 (2.40)	9.50 (2.70)	8.88 (5.60)	8.94 (5.30)
(iii) Standard deviation of tariff rates			7.12 (7.20)	7.64 (5.90)	8.24 (4.40)	6.10 (9.70)	5.61 (10.98)	6.29 (9.28)
B. Regulatory trade barriers				8.67	9.10	8.70	8.79	8.88
(i) Non-tariff trade barriers				8.67	8.20	8.10	8.30	8.47
(ii) Compliance cost of importing and exporting					10.00	9.30	9.29	9.29
C. Size of trade sector relative to expected	5.96	6.76	6.01	5.39	7.20	6.10	7.23	6.69
D. Black-market exchange rates	10.00	10.00	10.00	10.00	10.00	10.00	10.00	10.00
E. International capital market controls	10.00	10.00	10.00	9.45	9.56	7.00	6.42	5.98
(i) Foreign ownership / investment restrictions				8.90	9.90	8.60	8.23	8.11
(ii) Capital controls	10.00	10.00	10.00	10.00	9.23	5.40	4.62	3.85
5. Regulation of Credit, Labor, and Business	**6.90**	**6.90**	**6.62**	**6.78**	**7.20**	**7.60**	**7.27**	**7.30**
A. Credit market regulations	10.00	10.00	10.00	8.37	10.00	9.50	9.50	9.41
(i) Ownership of banks	10.00	10.00	10.00	10.00	10.00	8.00	8.00	8.00
(ii) Foreign bank competition				8.62		10.00	10.00	10.00
(iii) Private sector credit				6.28	10.00	10.00	10.00	9.62
(iv) Interest rate controls / negative real interest rates	10.00	10.00	10.00	10.00	10.00	10.00	10.00	10.00
B. Labor market regulations			6.48	5.45		5.80	5.29	5.52
(i) Hiring regulations and minimum wage				3.62		3.30	3.30	2.23
(ii) Hiring and firing regulations			4.28	4.28		4.60	3.46	3.74
(iii) Centralized collective bargaining	5.18	5.18	5.18	5.18		6.50	5.77	5.56
(iv) Hours regulations				4.17		4.00	4.00	4.00
(v) Mandated cost of worker dismissal						6.40	5.18	7.59
(vi) Conscription	10.00	10.00	10.00	10.00	10.00	10.00	10.00	10.00
C. Business regulations				6.52		7.60	7.04	6.99
(i) Price controls			2.00	5.00	7.00	7.00	7.00	7.00
(ii) Administrative requirements						4.90	5.30	4.97
(iii) Bureaucracy costs				7.24		6.80	2.11	2.06
(iv) Starting a business				6.95		9.00	9.15	9.29
(v) Extra payments / bribes / favoritism				6.87		8.80	9.03	8.92
(vi) Licensing restrictions						7.30	7.34	7.34
(vii) Cost of tax compliance						9.30	9.34	9.34

Macedonia

	1980	1985	1990	1995	2000	2005	2008	2009
Chain-Linked						Rating (Rank)	Rating (Rank)	Rating (Rank)
Summary Rating (Rank) ➤								
Area 1. Size of Government								
Area 2. Legal Structure and Security of Property Rights								
Area 3. Access to Sound Money								
Area 4. Freedom to Trade Internationally								
Area 5. Regulation of Credit, Labor, and Business								

	1980	1985	1990	1995	2000	2005	2008	2009
Unadjusted								
Summary Rating (Rank) ➤						**6.24** (98)	**6.84** (73)	**6.88** (64)
					Rating *Data*	Rating *Data*	Rating *Data*	Rating *Data*
1. Size of Government						**5.70**	**6.88**	**6.88**
A. Government consumption					6.94 *(16.42)*	6.00 *(19.50)*	6.08 *(19.33)*	6.08 *(19.33)*
B. Transfers and subsidies						6.80 *(12.20)*	5.95 *(15.37)*	5.95 *(15.37)*
C. Government enterprises and investment						4.00 *(34.00)*	8.00 *(19.40)*	8.00 *(19.40)*
D. Top marginal tax rate						6.00	7.50	7.50
(i) Top marginal income tax rate						9.00 *(24)*	10.00 *(10)*	10.00 *(10)*
(ii) Top marginal income and payroll tax rates						3.00 *(47)*	5.00 *(39)*	5.00 *(36)*
2. Legal Structure and Security of Property Rights						**4.30**	**5.08**	**5.05**
A. Judicial independence						2.40	3.25	3.24
B. Impartial courts						3.20	3.47	3.42
C. Protection of property rights						4.10	4.73	4.42
D. Military interference in rule of law and politics						3.50	5.50	5.70
E. Integrity of the legal system								
F. Legal enforcement of contracts						5.60	5.66	5.66
G. Regulatory restrictions on sale of real property						7.00	7.85	7.85
3. Access to Sound Money						**7.60**	**7.56**	**7.96**
A. Money growth					7.20 *(13.98)*	6.00 *(19.90)*	7.57 *(12.16)*	7.62 *(11.88)*
B. Standard deviation of inflation						9.40 *(1.59)*	9.11 *(2.23)*	9.25 *(1.87)*
C. Inflation: most recent year						10.00 *(0.04)*	8.56 *(7.22)*	9.95 *(−0.27)*
D. Freedom to own foreign currency bank accounts						5.00	5.00	5.00
4. Freedom to Trade Internationally						**6.50**	**6.75**	**6.66**
A. Taxes on international trade						9.00	8.00	8.00
(i) Revenues from trade taxes (% of trade sector)						8.80 *(1.80)*	9.20 *(1.20)*	9.20 *(1.20)*
(ii) Mean tariff rate						9.20 *(4.10)*	8.46 *(7.70)*	8.46 *(7.70)*
(iii) Standard deviation of tariff rates							6.34 *(9.16)*	6.34 *(9.16)*
B. Regulatory trade barriers						6.00	7.25	7.11
(i) Non-tariff trade barriers						5.60	6.03	5.75
(ii) Compliance cost of importing and exporting						6.30	8.47	8.47
C. Size of trade sector relative to expected						4.80	5.63	4.75
D. Black-market exchange rates						10.00	10.00	10.00
E. International capital market controls						2.90	2.87	3.44
(i) Foreign ownership/investment restrictions						5.00	4.97	4.57
(ii) Capital controls						0.80	0.77	2.31
5. Regulation of Credit, Labor, and Business						**7.10**	**7.95**	**7.86**
A. Credit market regulations						9.30	9.13	9.13
(i) Ownership of banks						10.00	10.00	10.00
(ii) Foreign bank competition						7.00	7.00	7.00
(iii) Private sector credit						10.00	9.51	9.51
(iv) Interest rate controls/negative real interest rates					10.00	10.00	10.00	10.00
B. Labor market regulations						5.90	7.95	7.86
(i) Hiring regulations and minimum wage						3.90	8.90	7.23
(ii) Hiring and firing regulations						5.10	5.09	5.58
(iii) Centralized collective bargaining						7.80	8.13	8.35
(iv) Hours regulations						6.00	8.00	8.00
(v) Mandated cost of worker dismissal						7.60	7.59	7.99
(vi) Conscription						5.00	10.00	10.00
C. Business regulations						6.10	6.76	6.60
(i) Price controls						8.00	8.00	8.00
(ii) Administrative requirements						3.20	3.78	3.42
(iii) Bureaucracy costs						5.30	5.63	5.23
(iv) Starting a business						9.00	9.85	9.88
(v) Extra payments/bribes/favoritism						4.90	5.27	5.36
(vi) Licensing restrictions						3.70	5.63	5.64
(vii) Cost of tax compliance						8.90	9.16	8.67

Madagascar

Chain-Linked	1980 Rating (Rank)	1985 Rating (Rank)	1990 Rating (Rank)	1995 Rating (Rank)	2000 Rating (Rank)	2005 Rating (Rank)	2008 Rating (Rank)	2009 Rating (Rank)
Summary Rating (Rank) ➤	4.55 (80)	4.79 (84)	4.68 (94)	4.67 (106)	5.94 (88)	5.94 (96)	6.28 (85)	6.40 (83)
Area 1. Size of Government	5.65 (36)	6.06 (26)	6.34 (35)	6.52 (41)	7.21 (25)	7.66 (21)	8.12 (11)	9.09 (2)
Area 2. Legal Structure and Security of Property Rights		4.32 (69)	3.09 (91)	4.81 (86)	4.59 (84)	3.49 (111)	3.93 (104)	3.74 (111)
Area 3. Access to Sound Money	5.82 (71)	5.99 (85)	5.79 (79)	2.82 (110)	7.17 (73)	7.02 (89)	7.67 (77)	7.55 (81)
Area 4. Freedom to Trade Internationally	3.28 (84)	3.91 (75)	4.65 (79)	5.50 (94)	6.29 (82)	6.40 (75)	6.59 (70)	6.30 (79)
Area 5. Regulation of Credit, Labor, and Business	3.51 (95)	3.57 (96)	3.51 (105)	3.68 (117)	4.45 (111)	5.15 (111)	5.18 (113)	5.39 (110)

Unadjusted

	1980 Rating Data	1985 Rating Data	1990 Rating Data	1995 Rating Data	2000 Rating Data	2005 Rating Data	2008 Rating Data	2009 Rating Data
Summary Rating (Rank) ➤	4.40 (85)	4.62 (88)	4.67 (95)	4.70 (102)	5.94 (88)	5.89 (114)	6.18 (101)	6.29 (96)
1. Size of Government	**4.13**	**4.43**	**6.34**	**6.52**	**7.21**	**7.70**	**7.84**	**8.78**
A. Government consumption	8.25 (11.94)	8.86 (9.89)	9.25 (8.54)	9.73 (6.90)	9.75 (6.83)	9.20 (8.60)	8.36 (11.59)	8.13 (12.37)
B. Transfers and subsidies			9.75 (1.40)	9.84 (1.10)	9.86 (1.00)	9.80 (1.40)	10.00 (0.00)	10.00 (0.00)
C. Government enterprises and investment	0.00 (65.40)	0.00 (69.80)	0.00 (53.50)	0.00 (52.90)	2.00 (44.73)	4.00 (39.20)	6.00 (27.45)	10.00 (9.58)
D. Top marginal tax rate						7.00	7.00	
(i) Top marginal income tax rate						9.00 (23)	9.00 (23)	
(ii) Top marginal income and payroll tax rates						5.00 (36)	5.00 (36)	
2. Legal Structure and Security of Property Rights		**4.32**	**3.09**	**4.81**	**4.59**	**3.00**	**3.40**	**3.24**
A. Judicial independence						3.30	3.00	2.50
B. Impartial courts				4.10	4.35	3.70	3.20	3.19
C. Protection of property rights						4.30	3.97	3.34
D. Military interference in rule of law and politics				4.22	5.00	1.70	1.67	1.67
E. Integrity of the legal system				6.96	5.00	2.10	4.17	4.17
F. Legal enforcement of contracts						2.40	2.42	2.42
G. Regulatory restrictions on sale of real property						3.70	5.41	5.38
3. Access to Sound Money	**5.82**	**5.99**	**5.79**	**2.82**	**7.17**	**7.00**	**7.67**	**7.55**
A. Money growth	7.38 (13.08)	9.18 (4.09)	7.37 (13.13)	6.26 (18.68)	7.85 (10.74)	9.30 (3.40)	8.96 (5.20)	8.57 (7.14)
B. Standard deviation of inflation	8.89 (2.77)	6.87 (7.82)	8.08 (4.81)	4.05 (14.88)	8.22 (4.44)	7.40 (6.39)	8.55 (3.64)	8.42 (3.96)
C. Inflation: most recent year	7.00 (14.99)	7.92 (10.42)	7.71 (11.46)	0.97 (45.17)	7.59 (12.03)	6.30 (18.51)	8.16 (9.22)	8.21 (8.96)
D. Freedom to own foreign currency bank accounts	0.00	0.00	0.00	0.00	5.00	5.00	5.00	5.00
4. Freedom to Trade Internationally	**3.47**	**4.06**	**4.62**	**5.65**	**6.29**	**6.40**	**6.61**	**6.32**
A. Taxes on international trade	4.02	0.80	1.73	5.08	4.11	6.90	6.67	6.65
(i) Revenues from trade taxes (% of trade sector)	4.33 (8.50)		0.67 (14.00)	4.33 (8.50)	4.11 (8.83)	5.20 (7.20)	5.00 (7.50)	5.00 (7.50)
(ii) Mean tariff rate	3.70 (31.50)	0.80 (46.00)	2.80 (36.00)	4.00 (30.00)		7.70 (11.60)	7.50 (12.50)	7.64 (11.80)
(iii) Standard deviation of tariff rates				6.92 (7.70)		7.70 (5.90)	7.50 (6.25)	7.31 (6.73)
B. Regulatory trade barriers						4.30	6.10	6.31
(i) Non-tariff trade barriers						5.50	5.42	5.72
(ii) Compliance cost of importing and exporting						3.10	6.78	6.91
C. Size of trade sector relative to expected	5.08	3.07	4.55	5.36	6.17	6.40	6.35	6.53
D. Black-market exchange rates	0.00	8.20	8.60	9.60	10.00	10.00	10.00	10.00
E. International capital market controls	0.00	0.00	0.00	0.00	3.00	4.50	3.92	2.09
(i) Foreign ownership/investment restrictions						6.00	4.84	4.18
(ii) Capital controls	0.00	0.00	0.00	0.00	3.00	3.00	3.00	0.00
5. Regulation of Credit, Labor, and Business	**4.20**	**4.28**	**3.51**	**3.68**	**4.45**	**5.40**	**5.39**	**5.57**
A. Credit market regulations	4.63	4.87	3.09	3.67	6.23	6.60	5.61	5.61
(i) Ownership of banks	0.00	0.00	0.00	2.00	2.00	5.00	5.00	5.00
(ii) Foreign bank competition								
(iii) Private sector credit	9.27	9.75	9.26	9.00	7.68	5.80	5.84	5.84
(iv) Interest rate controls/negative real interest rates			0.00	0.00	9.00	9.00	6.00	6.00
B. Labor market regulations						4.60	4.61	5.25
(i) Hiring regulations and minimum wage						1.10	1.10	2.23
(ii) Hiring and firing regulations						5.30	5.46	5.82
(iii) Centralized collective bargaining						6.90	6.87	6.86
(iv) Hours regulations						6.00	6.00	8.00
(v) Mandated cost of worker dismissal						7.20	7.22	7.59
(vi) Conscription	1.00	1.00	1.00	1.00	1.00	1.00	1.00	1.00
C. Business regulations						4.90	5.95	5.85
(i) Price controls			0.00	0.00	0.00	4.00	4.00	4.00
(ii) Administrative requirements						2.70	3.28	3.34
(iii) Bureaucracy costs						4.10	6.58	6.84
(iv) Starting a business						7.70	9.70	8.83
(v) Extra payments/bribes/favoritism						4.10	3.50	3.38
(vi) Licensing restrictions						4.80	6.87	6.83
(vii) Cost of tax compliance						6.60	7.75	7.75

Malawi

	1980	1985	1990	1995	2000	2005	2008	2009
Chain-Linked	Rating (Rank)	Rating (Rank)	Rating (Rank)	Rating (Rank)	Rating (Rank)	Rating (Rank)	Rating (Rank)	Rating (Rank)
Summary Rating (Rank) ➤	**4.94** (69)	**5.16** (64)	**5.48** (59)	**4.69** (104)	**5.01** (114)	**5.46** (110)	**5.95** (97)	**6.00** (97)
Area 1. Size of Government	5.05 (52)	4.87 (61)	6.15 (42)	5.83 (68)	5.33 (83)	6.44 (69)	6.15 (73)	5.71 (76)
Area 2. Legal Structure and Security of Property Rights	3.88 (58)	4.27 (70)	4.79 (64)	5.36 (67)	5.53 (66)	5.17 (79)	5.34 (75)	5.50 (69)
Area 3. Access to Sound Money	6.05 (64)	6.55 (61)	5.59 (84)	1.21 (118)	2.88 (120)	4.44 (122)	6.89 (90)	6.97 (94)
Area 4. Freedom to Trade Internationally	4.77 (59)	4.93 (61)	5.78 (51)	6.25 (78)	5.84 (99)	5.36 (108)	5.08 (110)	5.48 (104)
Area 5. Regulation of Credit, Labor, and Business	4.86 (66)	5.08 (57)	5.10 (68)	5.04 (81)	5.48 (88)	5.87 (94)	6.34 (72)	6.38 (75)

Unadjusted

	1980	1985	1990	1995	2000	2005	2008	2009
Summary Rating (Rank) ➤	**4.90** (73)	**5.17** (69)	**5.36** (65)	**4.43** (114)	**5.01** (114)	**5.58** (126)	**6.12** (106)	**6.17** (103)
	Rating *Data*	Rating *Data*	Rating *Data*	Rating *Data*	Rating *Data*	Rating *Data*	Rating *Data*	Rating *Data*
1. Size of Government	**4.75**	**4.58**	**5.78**	**4.32**	**5.33**	**6.40**	**6.15**	**5.71**
A. Government consumption	5.41 *(21.62)*	5.79 *(20.30)*	6.65 *(17.39)*	5.95 *(19.77)*	6.82 *(16.80)*	7.30 *(15.20)*	6.11 *(19.21)*	4.34 *(25.23)*
B. Transfers and subsidies	9.59 *(2.00)*	9.51 *(2.30)*	9.48 *(2.40)*		9.48 *(2.40)*	9.50 *(2.40)*	9.48 *(2.40)*	9.48 *(2.40)*
C. Government enterprises and investment	0.00 *(78.60)*	0.00 *(62.00)*	4.00 *(38.30)*	0.00 *(65.10)*	0.00 *(81.30)*	4.00 *(32.50)*	4.00 *(35.14)*	4.00 *(35.14)*
D. Top marginal tax rate	4.00	3.00	3.00	7.00	5.00	5.00	5.00	5.00
(i) Top marginal income tax rate	4.00 *(45)*	3.00 *(50)*	3.00 *(50)*	7.00 *(35)*	5.00 *(38)*	5.00 *(38)*	5.00 *(38)*	5.00 *(38)*
(ii) Top marginal income and payroll tax rates			3.00 *(50)*	7.00 *(35)*	5.00 *(38)*	5.00 *(38)*	5.00 *(38)*	5.00 *(38)*
2. Legal Structure and Security of Property Rights	**3.62**	**3.99**	**4.48**	**5.36**	**5.53**	**5.20**	**5.42**	**5.58**
A. Judicial independence				6.67	6.18	5.90	6.54	6.08
B. Impartial courts				4.84	4.91	4.40	4.80	4.89
C. Protection of property rights				4.77	3.23	5.30	5.42	5.31
D. Military interference in rule of law and politics				6.41	6.67	6.70	6.67	6.67
E. Integrity of the legal system				4.11	6.67	5.00	5.00	5.00
F. Legal enforcement of contracts						2.20	2.21	3.11
G. Regulatory restrictions on sale of real property						7.20	7.28	8.02
3. Access to Sound Money	**6.05**	**6.55**	**5.59**	**1.21**	**2.88**	**4.40**	**6.89**	**6.97**
A. Money growth	9.73 *(1.36)*	9.04 *(4.82)*	7.17 *(14.15)*	4.85 *(25.73)*	5.05 *(24.75)*	5.90 *(20.70)*	6.15 *(19.26)*	6.50 *(17.51)*
B. Standard deviation of inflation	7.64 *(5.89)*	8.94 *(2.66)*	7.35 *(6.63)*	0.00 *(28.51)*	2.37 *(19.06)*	0.00 *(26.01)*	8.16 *(4.61)*	8.05 *(4.88)*
C. Inflation: most recent year	6.84 *(15.79)*	8.21 *(8.93)*	7.83 *(10.85)*	0.00 *(90.42)*	4.08 *(29.58)*	6.90 *(15.41)*	8.26 *(8.71)*	8.32 *(8.42)*
D. Freedom to own foreign currency bank accounts	0.00	0.00	0.00	0.00	0.00	5.00	5.00	5.00
4. Freedom to Trade Internationally	**4.59**	**4.99**	**5.86**	**6.25**	**5.84**	**5.60**	**5.30**	**5.71**
A. Taxes on international trade	5.60	5.40	6.58	4.61	4.96	4.00	6.07	6.02
(i) Revenues from trade taxes (% of trade sector)	5.60 *(6.60)*	4.13 *(8.80)*	6.20 *(5.70)*	6.20 *(5.70)*	4.60 *(8.10)*	4.60 *(8.10)*	4.60 *(8.10)*	4.60 *(8.10)*
(ii) Mean tariff rate		6.66 *(16.70)*	6.96 *(15.20)*	3.84 *(30.80)*	6.08 *(19.60)*	7.30 *(13.50)*	7.40 *(13.00)*	7.40 *(13.00)*
(iii) Standard deviation of tariff rates				3.80 *(15.50)*	4.20 *(14.50)*	0.00 *(34.30)*	6.20 *(9.49)*	6.05 *(9.88)*
B. Regulatory trade barriers						3.90	4.32	4.13
(i) Non-tariff trade barriers						4.80	5.09	4.72
(ii) Compliance cost of importing and exporting						3.00	3.54	3.54
C. Size of trade sector relative to expected	6.71	5.36	5.31	6.63	5.23	6.80	2.91	4.95
D. Black-market exchange rates	0.40	4.00	7.20	9.80	10.00	10.00	10.00	10.00
E. International capital market controls	2.00	2.00	2.00	2.00	0.83	3.30	3.19	3.46
(i) Foreign ownership / investment restrictions						6.60	5.54	5.39
(ii) Capital controls	2.00	2.00	2.00	2.00	0.83	0.00	0.83	1.54
5. Regulation of Credit, Labor, and Business	**5.49**	**5.74**	**5.10**	**5.04**	**5.48**	**6.20**	**6.86**	**6.89**
A. Credit market regulations	4.65	5.32	5.35	3.82	5.30	7.50	7.67	7.84
(i) Ownership of banks	2.00	2.00	2.00	2.00	2.00	10.00	10.00	10.00
(ii) Foreign bank competition						6.00	6.00	6.00
(iii) Private sector credit	7.95	5.96	8.05	5.47	5.91	5.80	6.68	7.36
(iv) Interest rate controls / negative real interest rates	4.00	8.00	6.00	4.00	8.00	8.00	8.00	8.00
B. Labor market regulations						6.60	6.74	6.99
(i) Hiring regulations and minimum wage						5.60	5.60	5.57
(ii) Hiring and firing regulations						4.60	4.95	5.79
(iii) Centralized collective bargaining						7.10	7.66	8.00
(iv) Hours regulations						10.00	10.00	10.00
(v) Mandated cost of worker dismissal						2.20	2.21	2.58
(vi) Conscription	10.00	10.00	10.00	10.00	10.00	10.00	10.00	10.00
C. Business regulations						4.60	6.17	5.83
(i) Price controls			0.00	4.00	4.00	6.00	6.00	6.00
(ii) Administrative requirements						4.00	4.71	4.42
(iii) Bureaucracy costs						1.10	5.53	5.15
(iv) Starting a business						6.50	7.62	7.61
(v) Extra payments / bribes / favoritism						5.50	5.63	5.21
(vi) Licensing restrictions						3.00	5.46	4.16
(vii) Cost of tax compliance						5.90	8.24	8.24

Malaysia

	1980		1985		1990		1995		2000		2005		2008		2009	
Chain-Linked	Rating	(Rank)	Rating	(Rank)	Rating	(Rank)	Rating	(Rank)	Rating	(Rank)	Rating	(Rank)	Rating	(Rank)	Rating	(Rank)
Summary Rating (Rank) ➤	**7.07**	(13)	**7.12**	(13)	**7.49**	(13)	**7.55**	(12)	**6.72**	(44)	**6.89**	(57)	**6.71**	(70)	**6.68**	(64)
Area 1. Size of Government	4.84	(61)	5.56	(38)	6.27	(38)	6.92	(27)	6.08	(67)	5.86	(84)	5.96	(79)	5.55	(85)
Area 2. Legal Structure and Security of Property Rights	7.39	(24)	7.07	(29)	7.30	(28)	6.63	(36)	5.62	(64)	6.90	(30)	6.24	(48)	6.54	(34)
Area 3. Access to Sound Money	9.05	(7)	8.38	(21)	9.00	(20)	9.11	(31)	8.15	(54)	6.60	(98)	6.58	(99)	6.50	(109)
Area 4. Freedom to Trade Internationally	7.95	(9)	8.02	(9)	8.20	(8)	8.24	(11)	7.50	(43)	7.50	(27)	7.27	(38)	7.23	(29)
Area 5. Regulation of Credit, Labor, and Business	6.24	(24)	6.67	(15)	6.77	(15)	6.85	(17)	6.27	(50)	7.59	(24)	7.52	(21)	7.58	(17)

Unadjusted

	1980		1985		1990		1995		2000		2005		2008		2009	
Summary Rating (Rank) ➤	**6.91**	(12)	**6.97**	(12)	**7.26**	(15)	**7.48**	(14)	**6.72**	(44)	**6.89**	(63)	**6.72**	(78)	**6.68**	(78)
	Rating	Data	Rating	Data	Rating	Data	Rating	Data	Rating	Data	Rating	Data	Rating	Data	Rating	Data
1. Size of Government	**4.84**		**5.56**		**6.27**		**6.92**		**6.08**		**5.90**		**5.96**		**5.55**	
A. Government consumption	4.52	(24.64)	5.08	(22.72)	5.58	(21.02)	5.62	(20.88)	5.87	(20.05)	5.00	(22.90)	5.39	(21.69)	5.28	(22.06)
B. Transfers and subsidies	8.83	(4.80)	9.16	(3.60)	9.48	(2.40)	9.05	(4.00)	8.45	(6.20)	8.40	(6.40)	8.47	(6.12)	8.90	(4.52)
C. Government enterprises and investment	4.00	(37.30)	2.00	(46.80)	4.00	(33.80)	6.00	(28.40)	2.00	(47.00)	2.00	(49.90)	2.00	(46.50)	0.00	(52.38)
D. Top marginal tax rate	2.00		6.00		6.00		7.00		8.00		8.00		8.00		8.00	
(i) Top marginal income tax rate	2.00	(60)	6.00	(45)	6.00	(45)	7.00	(32)	8.00	(29)	8.00	(28)	8.00	(28)	8.00	(26)
(ii) Top marginal income and payroll tax rates					6.00	(45)	7.00	(32)	8.00	(29)	8.00	(28)	8.00	(28)	8.00	(26)
2. Legal Structure and Security of Property Rights	**6.59**		**6.31**		**6.52**		**6.63**		**5.62**		**6.90**		**6.24**		**6.54**	
A. Judicial independence							6.22		4.51		7.20		5.34		5.56	
B. Impartial courts							6.05		6.01		7.30		5.49		5.86	
C. Protection of property rights							6.14		4.23		7.90		7.02		6.82	
D. Military interference in rule of law and politics							7.78		8.33		8.30		8.33		8.33	
E. Integrity of the legal system							6.96		5.00		6.70		6.67		6.67	
F. Legal enforcement of contracts											4.30		4.38		4.38	
G. Regulatory restrictions on sale of real property											6.50		6.42		8.12	
3. Access to Sound Money	**9.05**		**8.38**		**9.00**		**9.11**		**8.15**		**6.60**		**6.58**		**6.50**	
A. Money growth	8.81	(5.94)	9.89	(−0.53)	8.69	(6.57)	8.03	(9.86)	9.12	(−4.39)	9.20	(4.20)	8.93	(5.36)	8.60	(7.00)
B. Standard deviation of inflation	8.78	(3.06)	8.95	(2.63)	7.92	(5.20)	9.41	(1.48)	8.79	(3.04)	7.80	(5.40)	8.48	(3.79)	7.52	(6.19)
C. Inflation: most recent year	8.63	(6.87)	9.70	(−1.51)	9.41	(2.95)	9.00	(5.02)	9.69	(1.53)	9.40	(2.96)	8.91	(5.44)	9.88	(0.58)
D. Freedom to own foreign currency bank accounts	10.00		5.00		10.00		10.00		5.00		0.00		0.00		0.00	
4. Freedom to Trade Internationally	**7.90**		**7.98**		**7.98**		**7.96**		**7.50**		**7.50**		**7.27**		**7.23**	
A. Taxes on international trade	6.37		6.74		6.76		6.92		5.92		6.60		6.11		6.04	
(i) Revenues from trade taxes (% of trade sector)	4.87	(7.70)	6.20	(5.70)	7.87	(3.20)	8.93	(1.60)	9.59	(0.62)	9.60	(0.60)	9.74	(0.39)	9.81	(0.28)
(ii) Mean tariff rate	7.88	(10.60)	7.28	(13.60)	7.40	(13.00)	7.44	(12.80)	8.16	(9.20)	8.50	(7.50)	8.24	(8.80)	8.32	(8.40)
(iii) Standard deviation of tariff rates					5.00	(12.50)	4.40	(14.00)	0.00	(33.30)	1.80	(20.50)	0.36	(24.11)	0.00	(27.22)
B. Regulatory trade barriers							6.73		7.92		7.00		6.67		6.65	
(i) Non-tariff trade barriers							6.73		6.67		6.30		5.57		5.52	
(ii) Compliance cost of importing and exporting									9.17		7.80		7.78		7.78	
C. Size of trade sector relative to expected	10.00		10.00		10.00		10.00		10.00		10.00		10.00		10.00	
D. Black-market exchange rates	10.00		10.00		10.00		10.00		10.00		10.00		10.00		10.00	
E. International capital market controls	5.00		5.00		5.00		6.15		3.69		3.80		3.57		3.43	
(i) Foreign ownership / investment restrictions							7.31		6.61		7.70		6.37		6.10	
(ii) Capital controls	5.00		5.00		5.00		5.00		0.77		0.00		0.77		0.77	
5. Regulation of Credit, Labor, and Business	**6.18**		**6.60**		**6.55**		**6.77**		**6.27**		**7.60**		**7.55**		**7.61**	
A. Credit market regulations	6.30		7.68		8.02		6.59		5.99		9.20		8.96		8.98	
(i) Ownership of banks	5.00		5.00		5.00		5.00		5.00		10.00		10.00		10.00	
(ii) Foreign bank competition							3.22		2.07		8.00		8.00		8.00	
(iii) Private sector credit	7.90		8.04		9.06		10.00		9.16		8.80		8.84		7.92	
(iv) Interest rate controls / negative real interest rates	6.00		10.00		10.00		10.00		10.00		10.00		9.00		10.00	
B. Labor market regulations							8.19		7.55		6.60		7.70		7.57		7.75	
(i) Hiring regulations and minimum wage							6.73		4.47		10.00		10.00		10.00	
(ii) Hiring and firing regulations					6.65		6.65		4.00		5.00		5.28		5.35	
(iii) Centralized collective bargaining	7.93		7.93		7.93		7.93		7.53		7.90		7.10		7.35	
(iv) Hours regulations							6.45		7.01		10.00		10.00		10.00	
(v) Mandated cost of worker dismissal											3.00		3.05		3.82	
(vi) Conscription	10.00		10.00		10.00		10.00		10.00		10.00		10.00		10.00	
C. Business regulations							6.15		6.20		6.00		6.13		6.08	
(i) Price controls					5.00		4.00		3.00		2.00		4.00		4.00	
(ii) Administrative requirements									7.13		6.00		5.08		5.07	
(iii) Bureaucracy costs							8.08		8.43		3.50		3.58		3.55	
(iv) Starting a business							7.17		6.33		8.80		9.52		9.27	
(v) Extra payments / bribes / favoritism							5.36		6.11		7.40		5.73		5.66	
(vi) Licensing restrictions											6.30		6.65		6.65	
(vii) Cost of tax compliance											7.90		8.37		8.37	

Mali

	1980	1985	1990	1995	2000	2005	2008	2009
Chain-Linked	Rating (Rank)	Rating (Rank)	Rating (Rank)	Rating (Rank)	Rating (Rank)	Rating (Rank)	Rating (Rank)	Rating (Rank)
Summary Rating (Rank) ➤	**5.78** (37)	**4.93** (77)	**5.16** (73)	**5.26** (90)	**6.23** (73)	**6.03** (91)	5.98 (94)	**6.03** (94)
Area 1. Size of Government	7.98 (7)	5.24 (48)	5.80 (55)	5.27 (84)	7.15 (27)	7.49 (26)	6.47 (62)	6.43 (58)
Area 2. Legal Structure and Security of Property Rights	4.23 (54)	3.05 (91)	3.02 (94)	5.29 (71)	5.00 (77)	4.87 (86)	4.98 (83)	4.85 (85)
Area 3. Access to Sound Money	6.04 (65)	6.39 (71)	6.98 (47)	5.14 (89)	8.40 (47)	6.12 (109)	6.28 (105)	6.76 (99)
Area 4. Freedom to Trade Internationally	5.56 (45)	5.97 (44)	5.77 (52)	6.12 (83)	6.39 (79)	5.88 (94)	5.99 (93)	5.86 (89)
Area 5. Regulation of Credit, Labor, and Business	4.89 (65)	4.01 (91)	4.22 (96)	4.32 (107)	4.22 (118)	5.66 (101)	6.01 (91)	6.07 (94)

Unadjusted								
Summary Rating (Rank) ➤	**6.08** (27)	**5.18** (67)	**5.33** (66)	**5.04** (96)	**6.23** (73)	**5.98** (107)	5.93 (116)	**5.98** (115)
	Rating *Data*	Rating *Data*	Rating *Data*	Rating *Data*	Rating *Data*	Rating *Data*	Rating *Data*	Rating *Data*
1. Size of Government	**8.84**	**5.81**	**6.43**	**4.23**	**7.15**	**7.50**	**6.47**	**6.43**
A. Government consumption	10.00 *(4.86)*	7.92 *(13.08)*	7.31 *(15.13)*	6.46 *(18.03)*	7.47 *(14.60)*	8.50 *(11.20)*	5.41 *(21.61)*	5.30 *(21.97)*
B. Transfers and subsidies	9.51 *(2.30)*	9.51 *(2.30)*	9.97 *(0.60)*		9.97 *(0.60)*	10.00 *(0.00)*	10.00 *(0.00)*	10.00 *(0.00)*
C. Government enterprises and investment	7.00 *(21.40)*	0.00 *(57.10)*	2.00 *(45.90)*	2.00 *(41.10)*	4.00 *(35.07)*	4.00 *(33.90)*	4.00 *(37.60)*	4.00 *(37.60)*
D. Top marginal tax rate								
(i) Top marginal income tax rate								
(ii) Top marginal income and payroll tax rates								
2. Legal Structure and Security of Property Rights	**4.23**	**3.05**	**3.02**	**5.29**	**5.00**	**4.40**	**4.47**	**4.36**
A. Judicial independence						4.40	4.26	3.08
B. Impartial courts				4.74	4.38	3.90	4.40	4.19
C. Protection of property rights						5.10	4.75	4.22
D. Military interference in rule of law and politics				5.55	6.67	5.80	5.83	5.83
E. Integrity of the legal system				6.96	5.00	5.00	5.00	5.00
F. Legal enforcement of contracts						2.00	2.59	2.63
G. Regulatory restrictions on sale of real property						4.40	4.45	5.54
3. Access to Sound Money	**6.04**	**6.39**	**6.98**	**5.14**	**8.40**	**6.10**	**6.28**	**6.76**
A. Money growth	8.58 *(7.09)*	7.51 *(12.44)*	9.10 *(−4.52)*	7.89 *(10.55)*	10.00 *(−0.02)*	8.60 *(7.20)*	9.09 *(4.56)*	9.25 *(3.74)*
B. Standard deviation of inflation	8.83 *(2.93)*	8.30 *(4.26)*	9.36 *(1.59)*	5.18 *(12.04)*	8.72 *(3.20)*	7.20 *(6.97)*	7.88 *(5.31)*	8.22 *(4.45)*
C. Inflation: most recent year	6.74 *(16.31)*	9.73 *(1.33)*	9.45 *(2.73)*	7.50 *(12.49)*	9.86 *(−0.68)*	8.70 *(6.40)*	8.17 *(9.17)*	9.56 *(2.20)*
D. Freedom to own foreign currency bank accounts	0.00	0.00	0.00	0.00	5.00	0.00	0.00	0.00
4. Freedom to Trade Internationally	**5.56**	**5.97**	**5.77**	**6.00**	**6.39**	**5.90**	**6.00**	**5.87**
A. Taxes on international trade	5.23	4.83	5.97	6.17	7.73	7.30	7.65	7.65
(i) Revenues from trade taxes (% of trade sector)	7.47 *(3.80)*	6.67 *(5.00)*	6.93 *(4.60)*	6.80 *(4.80)*	7.87 *(3.20)*	7.10 *(4.30)*	8.03 *(2.95)*	8.03 *(2.95)*
(ii) Mean tariff rate	3.00 *(35.00)*	3.00 *(35.00)*	5.00 *(25.00)*	6.74 *(16.30)*	7.60 *(12.00)*	7.50 *(12.40)*	7.62 *(11.90)*	7.62 *(11.90)*
(iii) Standard deviation of tariff rates				4.96 *(12.60)*		7.30 *(6.80)*	7.29 *(6.78)*	7.29 *(6.78)*
B. Regulatory trade barriers						3.70	4.89	5.55
(i) Non-tariff trade barriers						5.00	4.62	5.05
(ii) Compliance cost of importing and exporting						2.40	5.17	6.05
C. Size of trade sector relative to expected	5.38	6.99	5.51	5.85	6.03	5.10	4.82	3.83
D. Black-market exchange rates	9.00	9.80	9.20	9.80	10.00	10.00	10.00	10.00
E. International capital market controls	0.00	0.00	0.00	0.00	0.00	3.40	2.66	2.33
(i) Foreign ownership/investment restrictions						6.80	4.56	3.90
(ii) Capital controls	0.00	0.00	0.00	0.00	0.00	0.00	0.77	0.77
5. Regulation of Credit, Labor, and Business	**5.73**	**4.70**	**4.44**	**4.56**	**4.22**	**6.00**	**6.42**	**6.48**
A. Credit market regulations	5.29	5.90	6.52	5.57	4.94	7.90	8.00	8.00
(i) Ownership of banks	2.00	2.00	2.00	2.00	2.00	8.00	8.00	8.00
(ii) Foreign bank competition								
(iii) Private sector credit	9.88	9.70	9.57	8.71	7.89	7.80	8.00	8.00
(iv) Interest rate controls/negative real interest rates	4.00	6.00	8.00	6.00		8.00	8.00	8.00
B. Labor market regulations						5.60	5.47	5.54
(i) Hiring regulations and minimum wage						6.70	6.70	6.67
(ii) Hiring and firing regulations						5.60	5.56	5.18
(iii) Centralized collective bargaining						6.10	5.42	5.92
(iv) Hours regulations						8.00	8.00	8.00
(v) Mandated cost of worker dismissal						7.10	7.13	7.49
(vi) Conscription	10.00	0.00	0.00	0.00	0.00	0.00	0.00	0.00
C. Business regulations						4.50	5.80	5.89
(i) Price controls				0.00	4.00	4.00	6.00	6.00	6.00
(ii) Administrative requirements						3.30	4.18	4.07
(iii) Bureaucracy costs						1.70	6.47	6.51
(iv) Starting a business						4.90	7.49	7.90
(v) Extra payments/bribes/favoritism						4.10	3.05	2.50
(vi) Licensing restrictions						4.80	6.42	7.27
(vii) Cost of tax compliance						7.00	6.97	6.97

Malta

Chain-Linked	1980 Rating (Rank)	1985 Rating (Rank)	1990 Rating (Rank)	1995 Rating (Rank)	2000 Rating (Rank)	2005 Rating (Rank)	2008 Rating (Rank)	2009 Rating (Rank)
Summary Rating (Rank) ➤	**5.57** (48)	**5.23** (61)	**5.42** (63)	**6.56** (41)	**6.45** (65)	**7.10** (43)	**7.02** (50)	**6.98** (46)
Area 1. Size of Government	4.67 (65)	4.67 (65)	4.30 (90)	5.97 (63)	6.00 (70)	5.83 (86)	5.58 (90)	5.76 (74)
Area 2. Legal Structure and Security of Property Rights		3.52 (82)	4.48 (70)	7.60 (22)	7.17 (28)	7.58 (23)	7.45 (24)	7.39 (24)
Area 3. Access to Sound Money	6.50 (40)	7.01 (36)	7.27 (38)	7.07 (54)	7.00 (80)	8.99 (42)	9.46 (20)	9.46 (27)
Area 4. Freedom to Trade Internationally	5.89 (43)	5.89 (46)	6.10 (48)	6.58 (65)	6.40 (78)	7.08 (46)	6.77 (64)	6.63 (62)
Area 5. Regulation of Credit, Labor, and Business	5.05 (61)	5.01 (61)	4.93 (76)	5.56 (62)	5.68 (79)	6.08 (84)	5.93 (95)	5.73 (104)

Unadjusted

	1980	1985	1990	1995	2000	2005	2008	2009
Summary Rating (Rank) ➤	**5.73** (43)	**5.39** (59)	**5.46** (62)	**6.60** (41)	**6.45** (65)	**7.38** (32)	**7.30** (36)	**7.31** (33)
	Rating Data	Rating Data	Rating Data	Rating Data	Rating Data	Rating Data	Rating Data	Rating Data
1. Size of Government	**4.67**	**4.67**	**4.30**	**5.97**	**6.00**	**5.80**	**5.58**	**5.76**
A. Government consumption	5.88 (20.01)	5.83 (20.19)	5.33 (21.89)	4.38 (25.11)	5.10 (22.67)	4.60 (24.40)	4.31 (25.33)	4.26 (25.53)
B. Transfers and subsidies	6.81 (12.20)	5.86 (15.70)	5.89 (15.60)	6.49 (13.38)	5.92 (15.49)	5.70 (16.20)	5.00 (18.86)	5.79 (15.95)
C. Government enterprises and investment	6.00 (28.60)	7.00 (20.00)	6.00 (28.80)	6.00 (28.80)	6.00 (28.80)	6.00	6.00	6.00
D. Top marginal tax rate	0.00	0.00	0.00	7.00	7.00	7.00	7.00	7.00
(i) Top marginal income tax rate	0.00 (65)	0.00 (65)	0.00 (65)	7.00 (35)	7.00 (35)	7.00 (35)	7.00 (35)	7.00 (35)
(ii) Top marginal income and payroll tax rates			0.00 (65)	7.00 (35)	7.00 (35)	7.00 (35)	7.00 (35)	7.00 (35)
2. Legal Structure and Security of Property Rights		**3.52**	**4.48**	**7.60**	**7.17**	**7.70**	**7.55**	**7.49**
A. Judicial independence						7.20	6.78	6.73
B. Impartial courts				7.09	6.77	5.90	5.16	5.18
C. Protection of property rights						6.90	7.46	7.19
D. Military interference in rule of law and politics				9.82	10.00	10.00	10.00	10.00
E. Integrity of the legal system				10.00	8.33	8.30	8.33	8.33
F. Legal enforcement of contracts								
G. Regulatory restrictions on sale of real property								
3. Access to Sound Money	**6.50**	**7.01**	**7.27**	**7.07**	**7.00**	**9.00**	**9.46**	**9.46**
A. Money growth	9.68 (1.60)	9.39 (−3.03)	10.00 (−0.02)	9.75 (−1.24)	9.94 (−0.28)	6.80 (15.90)	8.88 (5.58)	8.41 (7.97)
B. Standard deviation of inflation	8.80 (3.00)	8.77 (3.07)	9.74 (0.64)	9.63 (0.93)	8.51 (3.72)	9.70 (0.63)	9.80 (0.51)	9.86 (0.36)
C. Inflation: most recent year	7.52 (12.40)	9.87 (0.63)	9.36 (3.21)	8.89 (5.56)	9.53 (2.37)	9.40 (3.01)	9.15 (4.26)	9.58 (2.09)
D. Freedom to own foreign currency bank accounts	0.00	0.00	0.00	0.00	0.00	10.00	10.00	10.00
4. Freedom to Trade Internationally	**6.09**	**6.09**	**6.30**	**6.80**	**6.40**	**7.40**	**7.11**	**6.96**
A. Taxes on international trade	6.73	7.00	6.73	9.50	8.51	9.30	8.03	8.22
(i) Revenues from trade taxes (% of trade sector)	6.73 (4.90)	7.00 (4.50)	6.73 (4.90)	9.50 (0.75)	9.58 (0.63)	9.60 (0.60)	9.61 (0.59)	9.44 (0.84)
(ii) Mean tariff rate					8.24 (8.80)	9.50 (2.70)	8.88 (5.60)	8.94 (5.30)
(iii) Standard deviation of tariff rates					7.72 (5.70)	8.80 (3.00)	5.61 (10.98)	6.29 (9.28)
B. Regulatory trade barriers						7.50	7.34	7.45
(i) Non-tariff trade barriers						7.50	7.34	7.45
(ii) Compliance cost of importing and exporting								
C. Size of trade sector relative to expected	5.92	4.63	4.97	5.13	5.13	2.50	2.84	1.99
D. Black-market exchange rates	7.60	8.60	9.60	9.20	9.40	10.00	10.00	10.00
E. International capital market controls	2.00	2.00	2.00	2.00	0.77	8.00	7.35	7.13
(i) Foreign ownership / investment restrictions						7.50	7.00	6.58
(ii) Capital controls	2.00	2.00	2.00	2.00	0.77	8.50	7.69	7.69
5. Regulation of Credit, Labor, and Business	**5.68**	**5.64**	**4.93**	**5.56**	**5.68**	**7.00**	**6.83**	**6.89**
A. Credit market regulations	5.15	5.06	4.81	6.22	6.62	9.10	8.86	8.49
(i) Ownership of banks	0.00	0.00	0.00	0.00	2.00	10.00	10.00	10.00
(ii) Foreign bank competition						9.00	9.00	9.00
(iii) Private sector credit	9.45	9.17	8.43	8.65	7.86	7.20	6.43	4.94
(iv) Interest rate controls / negative real interest rates	6.00	6.00	6.00	10.00	10.00	10.00	10.00	10.00
B. Labor market regulations						7.10	7.01	7.69
(i) Hiring regulations and minimum wage								
(ii) Hiring and firing regulations						4.10	3.91	4.20
(iii) Centralized collective bargaining						7.10	7.11	6.55
(iv) Hours regulations								10.00
(v) Mandated cost of worker dismissal								
(vi) Conscription	10.00	10.00	10.00	10.00	10.00	10.00	10.00	10.00
C. Business regulations						4.80	4.62	4.49
(i) Price controls			0.00	2.00	2.00	4.00	4.00	4.00
(ii) Administrative requirements						3.00	3.31	3.26
(iii) Bureaucracy costs						4.80	4.71	4.51
(iv) Starting a business								
(v) Extra payments / bribes / favoritism						7.30	6.48	6.20
(vi) Licensing restrictions								
(vii) Cost of tax compliance								

Mauritania

	1980	1985	1990	1995	2000	2005	2008	2009
Chain-Linked						Rating (Rank)	Rating (Rank)	Rating (Rank)
Summary Rating (Rank) ➤								
Area 1. Size of Government								
Area 2. Legal Structure and Security of Property Rights								
Area 3. Access to Sound Money								
Area 4. Freedom to Trade Internationally								
Area 5. Regulation of Credit, Labor, and Business								

Unadjusted								
Summary Rating (Rank) ➤						**6.44** (84)	**6.16** (102)	**6.05** (111)
						Rating *Data*	Rating *Data*	Rating *Data*
1. Size of Government						**7.00**	**6.47**	**6.47**
A. Government consumption						6.00 *(19.60)*	4.94 *(23.19)*	4.94 *(23.19)*
B. Transfers and subsidies								
C. Government enterprises and investment						8.00 *(18.17)*	8.00 *(18.10)*	8.00 *(18.10)*
D. Top marginal tax rate								
(i) Top marginal income tax rate								
(ii) Top marginal income and payroll tax rates								
2. Legal Structure and Security of Property Rights						**5.60**	**4.65**	**4.54**
A. Judicial independence						4.70	3.20	2.31
B. Impartial courts						5.10	3.32	3.88
C. Protection of property rights						4.60	3.97	4.23
D. Military interference in rule of law and politics						5.50	3.80	3.20
E. Integrity of the legal system								
F. Legal enforcement of contracts						6.00	6.27	6.27
G. Regulatory restrictions on sale of real property						7.40	7.36	7.36
3. Access to Sound Money						**6.10**	**5.67**	**5.61**
A. Money growth						9.20 *(4.20)*	8.83 *(5.83)*	8.83 *(5.83)*
B. Standard deviation of inflation						7.70 *(5.72)*	5.32 *(11.70)*	4.07 *(14.83)*
C. Inflation: most recent year						7.60 *(12.13)*	8.53 *(7.35)*	9.56 *(2.22)*
D. Freedom to own foreign currency bank accounts						0.00	0.00	0.00
4. Freedom to Trade Internationally						**6.70**	**6.80**	**6.37**
A. Taxes on international trade						7.50	7.41	7.41
(i) Revenues from trade taxes (% of trade sector)								
(ii) Mean tariff rate						7.90 *(10.70)*	7.62 *(11.90)*	7.62 *(11.90)*
(iii) Standard deviation of tariff rates						7.10 *(7.20)*	7.19 *(7.02)*	7.19 *(7.02)*
B. Regulatory trade barriers						4.00	5.35	4.84
(i) Non-tariff trade barriers						3.40	6.44	5.40
(ii) Compliance cost of importing and exporting						4.60	4.27	4.27
C. Size of trade sector relative to expected						8.50	8.51	7.35
D. Black-market exchange rates						10.00	10.00	10.00
E. International capital market controls						3.60	2.73	2.27
(i) Foreign ownership / investment restrictions						6.40	4.46	3.54
(ii) Capital controls						0.80	1.00	1.00
5. Regulation of Credit, Labor, and Business						**6.80**	**7.20**	**7.23**
A. Credit market regulations						9.20	9.22	9.22
(i) Ownership of banks								
(ii) Foreign bank competition								
(iii) Private sector credit						9.40	9.44	9.44
(iv) Interest rate controls / negative real interest rates						9.00	9.00	9.00
B. Labor market regulations						7.00	6.99	7.06
(i) Hiring regulations and minimum wage						3.30	4.40	4.43
(ii) Hiring and firing regulations						7.80	5.40	5.40
(iii) Centralized collective bargaining						5.90	7.02	7.03
(iv) Hours regulations						8.00	8.00	8.00
(v) Mandated cost of worker dismissal						7.10	7.13	7.49
(vi) Conscription						10.00	10.00	10.00
C. Business regulations						4.20	5.38	5.40
(i) Price controls								
(ii) Administrative requirements						6.00	5.66	5.55
(iii) Bureaucracy costs						2.70	6.84	7.49
(iv) Starting a business						4.00	7.55	7.69
(v) Extra payments / bribes / favoritism						3.80	3.30	2.70
(vi) Licensing restrictions						6.40	6.72	6.80
(vii) Cost of tax compliance						2.20	2.20	2.20

Mauritius

	1980	1985	1990	1995	2000	2005	2008	2009
Chain-Linked	Rating (Rank)	Rating (Rank)	Rating (Rank)	Rating (Rank)	Rating (Rank)	Rating (Rank)	Rating (Rank)	Rating (Rank)
Summary Rating (Rank) ➤	**5.16** (61)	**6.25** (27)	**6.23** (37)	**7.29** (22)	**7.39** (20)	**7.17** (40)	**7.61** (12)	**7.47** (17)
Area 1. Size of Government	5.63 (38)	6.79 (11)	6.81 (22)	6.89 (28)	7.37 (24)	7.19 (33)	8.37 (8)	7.76 (17)
Area 2. Legal Structure and Security of Property Rights		6.41 (32)	6.37 (38)	7.04 (27)	6.94 (31)	5.80 (59)	6.55 (37)	6.51 (36)
Area 3. Access to Sound Money	4.92 (94)	6.81 (44)	6.20 (69)	9.51 (21)	9.58 (12)	9.49 (24)	9.00 (41)	9.20 (41)
Area 4. Freedom to Trade Internationally	4.07 (72)	5.47 (53)	5.67 (56)	6.86 (48)	6.80 (69)	7.16 (42)	7.38 (34)	7.18 (34)
Area 5. Regulation of Credit, Labor, and Business	5.64 (38)	5.76 (43)	6.03 (38)	6.17 (41)	6.26 (51)	6.15 (77)	6.71 (53)	6.61 (61)

Unadjusted								
Summary Rating (Rank) ➤	**5.35** (57)	**6.51** (21)	**6.32** (33)	**7.48** (14)	**7.39** (20)	**7.37** (33)	**7.82** (9)	**7.67** (9)
	Rating Data	Rating Data	Rating Data	Rating Data	Rating Data	Rating Data	Rating Data	Rating Data
1. Size of Government	**5.63**	**6.79**	**6.81**	**6.89**	**7.37**	**7.20**	**8.37**	**7.76**
A. Government consumption	7.14 (15.72)	7.44 (14.69)	7.24 (15.40)	7.13 (15.75)	7.00 (16.19)	6.60 (17.50)	7.34 (15.06)	6.95 (16.39)
B. Transfers and subsidies	8.37 (6.50)	8.72 (5.20)	8.99 (4.20)	8.94 (4.40)	8.49 (6.06)	8.60 (5.60)	8.63 (5.52)	8.61 (5.62)
C. Government enterprises and investment	4.00 (36.00)	4.00 (32.26)	4.00 (37.32)	4.00 (34.43)	6.00 (28.01)	6.00 (29.60)	8.00 (17.13)	6.00 (25.64)
D. Top marginal tax rate	3.00	7.00	7.00	7.50	8.00	7.50	9.50	9.50
(i) Top marginal income tax rate	3.00 (50)	7.00 (35)	7.00 (35)	8.00 (30)	9.00 (25)	8.00 (30)	10.00 (15)	10.00 (15)
(ii) Top marginal income and payroll tax rates			7.00 (35)	7.00 (32)	7.00 (33)	7.00 (31)	9.00 (25)	9.00 (25)
2. Legal Structure and Security of Property Rights		**6.31**	**6.28**	**6.94**	**6.94**	**5.60**	**6.36**	**6.32**
A. Judicial independence					6.18	6.10	6.73	6.38
B. Impartial courts				7.82	7.01	6.40	5.61	5.94
C. Protection of property rights					4.80	7.60	7.36	7.16
D. Military interference in rule of law and politics				9.35	10.00	8.70	8.50	7.90
E. Integrity of the legal system				6.96	6.70			
F. Legal enforcement of contracts						3.90	3.98	4.55
G. Regulatory restrictions on sale of real property						1.00	5.99	6.02
3. Access to Sound Money	**4.92**	**6.81**	**6.20**	**9.51**	**9.58**	**9.50**	**9.00**	**9.20**
A. Money growth	9.21 (3.95)	9.35 (3.26)	7.47 (12.64)	9.54 (2.30)	9.64 (−1.81)	9.40 (3.20)	8.53 (7.35)	8.29 (8.57)
B. Standard deviation of inflation	5.80 (10.50)	9.54 (1.14)	9.37 (1.58)	9.46 (1.36)	9.51 (1.21)	9.60 (1.03)	9.41 (1.47)	9.02 (2.46)
C. Inflation: most recent year	4.69 (26.57)	8.36 (8.20)	7.98 (10.12)	9.06 (4.69)	9.16 (4.20)	9.00 (4.91)	8.05 (9.73)	9.49 (2.55)
D. Freedom to own foreign currency bank accounts	0.00	0.00	0.00	10.00	10.00	10.00	10.00	10.00
4. Freedom to Trade Internationally	**4.26**	**5.73**	**5.63**	**7.17**	**6.80**	**7.20**	**7.38**	**7.18**
A. Taxes on international trade	3.31	3.31	3.14	4.41	3.54	7.40	8.06	9.15
(i) Revenues from trade taxes (% of trade sector)	3.60 (9.60)	3.60 (9.60)	4.93 (7.60)	6.05 (5.92)	6.81 (4.78)	7.60 (3.60)	8.62 (2.08)	9.66 (0.51)
(ii) Mean tariff rate	3.02 (34.90)	3.02 (34.90)	4.48 (27.60)	2.76 (36.20)	3.80 (31.00)	8.30 (8.50)	9.42 (2.90)	9.72 (1.40)
(iii) Standard deviation of tariff rates			0.00 (91.50)		0.00 (27.80)	6.40 (8.90)	6.14 (9.66)	8.06 (4.86)
B. Regulatory trade barriers					7.44	7.00	7.47	7.44
(i) Non-tariff trade barriers					7.88	6.20	6.83	6.61
(ii) Compliance cost of importing and exporting					6.99	7.80	8.12	8.26
C. Size of trade sector relative to expected	5.75	5.32	6.39	5.30	5.19	4.60	4.18	3.50
D. Black-market exchange rates	2.00	9.80	8.40	10.00	10.00	10.00	10.00	10.00
E. International capital market controls	2.00	2.00	2.00	8.00	7.84	6.70	7.18	5.81
(i) Foreign ownership/investment restrictions					8.75	6.60	7.68	7.01
(ii) Capital controls	2.00	2.00	2.00	8.00	6.92	6.90	6.67	4.62
5. Regulation of Credit, Labor, and Business	**6.59**	**6.93**	**6.70**	**6.85**	**6.26**	**7.40**	**7.98**	**7.88**
A. Credit market regulations	7.28	8.47	9.33	9.84	7.72	9.20	9.50	9.50
(i) Ownership of banks	8.00	8.00	10.00	10.00	10.00	10.00	10.00	10.00
(ii) Foreign bank competition					4.27	9.00	9.00	9.00
(iii) Private sector credit	6.56	7.42	10.00	9.52	9.59	8.80	10.00	10.00
(iv) Interest rate controls/negative real interest rates		10.00	8.00	10.00	9.00	9.00	9.00	9.00
B. Labor market regulations					4.90	6.90	7.70	7.46
(i) Hiring regulations and minimum wage					3.12	10.00	10.00	10.00
(ii) Hiring and firing regulations					1.98	2.60	4.20	4.77
(iii) Centralized collective bargaining					3.55	3.50	5.68	5.97
(iv) Hours regulations					5.85	8.70	6.70	8.00
(v) Mandated cost of worker dismissal						6.80	9.63	6.03
(vi) Conscription	10.00	10.00	10.00	10.00	10.00	10.00	10.00	10.00
C. Business regulations					6.17	6.00	6.73	6.68
(i) Price controls			4.00	4.00	6.00	4.00	4.00	4.00
(ii) Administrative requirements					5.93	2.20	4.58	4.61
(iii) Bureaucracy costs					7.50	4.40	5.09	4.88
(iv) Starting a business					5.42	8.40	9.76	9.77
(v) Extra payments/bribes/favoritism					6.01	6.60	6.38	6.17
(vi) Licensing restrictions						8.30	9.11	9.12
(vii) Cost of tax compliance						8.20	8.20	8.20

Mexico

Chain-Linked	1980	1985	1990	1995	2000	2005	2008	2009
	Rating (Rank)	Rating (Rank)	Rating (Rank)	Rating (Rank)	Rating (Rank)	Rating (Rank)	Rating (Rank)	Rating (Rank)
Summary Rating (Rank) ➤	**5.69** (43)	**4.91** (79)	**6.28** (36)	**6.46** (45)	**6.39** (67)	**7.00** (50)	**6.87** (59)	**6.75** (60)
Area 1. Size of Government	5.69 (35)	6.19 (22)	7.96 (8)	7.47 (18)	7.14 (28)	7.11 (41)	7.17 (34)	6.84 (41)
Area 2. Legal Structure and Security of Property Rights	6.72 (30)	5.74 (45)	7.22 (29)	5.30 (70)	4.25 (97)	5.59 (67)	5.42 (72)	5.06 (80)
Area 3. Access to Sound Money	7.70 (23)	3.67 (102)	3.59 (107)	5.50 (82)	6.85 (88)	8.08 (67)	7.98 (66)	7.97 (74)
Area 4. Freedom to Trade Internationally	3.10 (85)	4.97 (59)	7.36 (22)	7.89 (22)	7.54 (41)	7.21 (38)	6.89 (61)	6.88 (47)
Area 5. Regulation of Credit, Labor, and Business	5.39 (47)	4.06 (89)	5.37 (56)	6.16 (42)	6.15 (56)	7.03 (38)	6.88 (46)	6.97 (45)

Unadjusted

	1980	1985	1990	1995	2000	2005	2008	2009
Summary Rating (Rank) ➤	**5.55** (52)	**4.79** (83)	**6.15** (41)	**6.41** (46)	**6.39** (67)	**7.00** (56)	**6.87** (68)	**6.74** (75)
	Rating Data	Rating Data	Rating Data	Rating Data	Rating Data	Rating Data	Rating Data	Rating Data
1. Size of Government	**5.69**	**6.19**	**7.96**	**7.47**	**7.14**	**7.10**	**7.17**	**6.84**
A. Government consumption	7.83 (13.36)	8.08 (12.52)	8.60 (10.75)	7.80 (13.48)	7.65 (13.98)	7.50 (14.50)	7.76 (13.60)	7.44 (14.72)
B. Transfers and subsidies	8.94 (4.40)	8.66 (5.40)	9.25 (3.24)	8.09 (7.50)	7.92 (8.13)	7.90 (8.10)	7.92 (8.13)	7.92 (8.13)
C. Government enterprises and investment	2.00 (43.00)	4.00 (34.80)	7.00 (23.90)	7.00 (23.20)	8.00 (16.80)	7.00 (22.40)	7.00 (24.85)	6.00 (26.62)
D. Top marginal tax rate	4.00	4.00	7.00	7.00	5.00	6.00	6.00	6.00
(i) Top marginal income tax rate	4.00 (55)	4.00 (55)	7.00 (40)	7.00 (35)	7.00 (40)	8.00 (30)	8.00 (28)	8.00 (28)
(ii) Top marginal income and payroll tax rates					3.00 (47)	4.00 (42)	4.00 (41)	4.00 (41)
2. Legal Structure and Security of Property Rights	**6.29**	**5.38**	**6.76**	**5.30**	**4.25**	**5.60**	**5.42**	**5.06**
A. Judicial independence				3.88	3.34	4.40	3.73	3.69
B. Impartial courts				5.05	5.18	3.80	3.70	3.74
C. Protection of property rights				5.22	4.38	6.10	4.92	4.88
D. Military interference in rule of law and politics				5.37	5.00	7.50	7.50	7.50
E. Integrity of the legal system				6.96	3.33	5.00	5.83	3.33
F. Legal enforcement of contracts						5.40	5.39	5.39
G. Regulatory restrictions on sale of real property						6.90	6.89	6.89
3. Access to Sound Money	**7.70**	**3.67**	**3.59**	**5.50**	**6.85**	**8.10**	**7.98**	**7.97**
A. Money growth	6.27 (18.66)	2.80 (36.00)	0.00 (51.34)	8.95 (5.23)	7.22 (13.89)	8.60 (7.00)	8.44 (7.81)	8.29 (8.55)
B. Standard deviation of inflation	9.08 (2.29)	1.90 (20.26)	0.00 (43.89)	5.62 (10.95)	7.09 (7.27)	9.50 (1.22)	9.51 (1.22)	9.64 (0.90)
C. Inflation: most recent year	5.44 (22.80)	0.00 (54.01)	4.37 (28.13)	2.43 (37.85)	8.10 (9.50)	9.20 (3.99)	8.97 (5.13)	8.94 (5.30)
D. Freedom to own foreign currency bank accounts	10.00	10.00	10.00	5.00	5.00	5.00	5.00	5.00
4. Freedom to Trade Internationally	**3.10**	**4.96**	**7.28**	**7.71**	**7.54**	**7.20**	**6.89**	**6.88**
A. Taxes on international trade	1.91	6.13	7.88	8.21	7.48	7.60	6.62	6.66
(i) Revenues from trade taxes (% of trade sector)	0.00 (17.60)	8.27 (2.60)	8.67 (2.00)	9.30 (1.05)	9.37 (0.94)	9.40 (0.90)	9.37 (0.94)	9.37 (0.94)
(ii) Mean tariff rate	3.82 (30.90)	4.00 (30.00)	7.78 (11.10)	7.48 (12.60)	6.76 (16.20)	8.20 (9.20)	7.48 (12.60)	7.70 (11.50)
(iii) Standard deviation of tariff rates			7.20 (7.00)	7.84 (5.40)	6.32 (9.20)	5.10 (12.20)	3.00 (17.51)	2.92 (17.71)
B. Regulatory trade barriers				6.30	7.28	7.00	7.17	7.33
(i) Non-tariff trade barriers				6.30	6.40	6.10	6.41	6.25
(ii) Compliance cost of importing and exporting					8.16	7.90	7.93	8.41
C. Size of trade sector relative to expected	3.30	3.45	5.35	7.64	7.83	6.90	6.31	6.13
D. Black-market exchange rates	0.00	5.00	10.00	10.00	10.00	10.00	10.00	10.00
E. International capital market controls	2.00	2.00	5.00	6.39	5.12	4.50	4.35	4.28
(i) Foreign ownership / investment restrictions				7.77	8.70	7.50	7.15	7.02
(ii) Capital controls	2.00	2.00	5.00	5.00	1.54	1.50	1.54	1.54
5. Regulation of Credit, Labor, and Business	**4.97**	**3.74**	**5.16**	**6.09**	**6.15**	**7.00**	**6.87**	**6.96**
A. Credit market regulations	5.62	2.36	5.58	7.74	8.16	9.90	9.86	9.86
(i) Ownership of banks	8.00	0.00	0.00	8.00	10.00	10.00	10.00	10.00
(ii) Foreign bank competition				7.28	5.87	10.00	10.00	10.00
(iii) Private sector credit	4.87	3.08	8.74	9.68	9.43	9.40	9.43	9.43
(iv) Interest rate controls / negative real interest rates	4.00	4.00	8.00	8.00	9.00	10.00	10.00	10.00
B. Labor market regulations			5.08	5.87	4.40	5.70	5.47	5.47
(i) Hiring regulations and minimum wage				7.92	2.75	6.70	6.70	6.67
(ii) Hiring and firing regulations			5.00	5.00	4.10	4.70	3.63	3.32
(iii) Centralized collective bargaining			7.24	7.24	5.65	6.90	6.32	6.18
(iv) Hours regulations				6.18	6.51	8.00	8.00	8.00
(v) Mandated cost of worker dismissal						5.20	5.18	5.63
(vi) Conscription	3.00	3.00	3.00	3.00	3.00	3.00	3.00	3.00
C. Business regulations				4.65	5.90	5.40	5.28	5.57
(i) Price controls			0.00	5.00	7.00	4.00	3.00	3.00
(ii) Administrative requirements					6.73	2.70	2.64	2.80
(iii) Bureaucracy costs				6.09	6.33	3.80	4.90	4.89
(iv) Starting a business				4.15	3.70	8.90	9.43	9.55
(v) Extra payments / bribes / favoritism				3.36	5.73	6.20	4.34	4.26
(vi) Licensing restrictions						8.50	8.46	9.00
(vii) Cost of tax compliance						3.80	4.20	5.47

Moldova

	1980	1985	1990	1995	2000	2005	2008	2009
Chain-Linked						Rating (Rank)	Rating (Rank)	Rating (Rank)
Summary Rating (Rank) ➤								
Area 1. Size of Government								
Area 2. Legal Structure and Security of Property Rights								
Area 3. Access to Sound Money								
Area 4. Freedom to Trade Internationally								
Area 5. Regulation of Credit, Labor, and Business								

	1980	1985	1990	1995	2000	2005	2008	2009
Unadjusted								
Summary Rating (Rank) ➤						**6.37** (91)	**6.51** (87)	**6.29** (96)
					Rating *Data*	Rating *Data*	Rating *Data*	Rating *Data*
1. Size of Government						**6.00**	**5.87**	**5.61**
A. Government consumption						7.60 *(14.30)*	6.40 *(18.24)*	5.78 *(20.34)*
B. Transfers and subsidies						6.60 *(13.10)*	6.10 *(14.82)*	5.64 *(16.51)*
C. Government enterprises and investment						4.00	4.00	4.00
D. Top marginal tax rate							7.00	7.00
(i) Top marginal income tax rate							10.00 *(18)*	10.00 *(18)*
(ii) Top marginal income and payroll tax rates							4.00 *(41)*	4.00 *(41)*
2. Legal Structure and Security of Property Rights						**5.60**	**6.38**	**5.65**
A. Judicial independence						2.00	5.59	2.12
B. Impartial courts						2.60	3.16	3.35
C. Protection of property rights						4.20	4.86	3.86
D. Military interference in rule of law and politics						6.70	6.67	6.67
E. Integrity of the legal system						8.30	8.33	7.50
F. Legal enforcement of contracts						6.70	6.44	6.44
G. Regulatory restrictions on sale of real property						8.70	9.61	9.61
3. Access to Sound Money						**6.60**	**7.22**	**7.74**
A. Money growth						5.30 *(23.50)*	7.69 *(11.57)*	8.01 *(9.93)*
B. Standard deviation of inflation						8.90 *(2.70)*	8.76 *(3.11)*	7.97 *(5.09)*
C. Inflation: most recent year						7.40 *(13.11)*	7.45 *(12.77)*	9.99 *(−0.05)*
D. Freedom to own foreign currency bank accounts						5.00	5.00	5.00
4. Freedom to Trade Internationally						**6.80**	**6.82**	**6.32**
A. Taxes on international trade						8.50	8.47	8.64
(i) Revenues from trade taxes (% of trade sector)					9.23 *(1.15)*	9.20 *(1.30)*	9.08 *(1.38)*	9.09 *(1.37)*
(ii) Mean tariff rate						9.00 *(5.20)*	9.06 *(4.70)*	9.08 *(4.60)*
(iii) Standard deviation of tariff rates						7.40 *(6.60)*	7.27 *(6.82)*	7.76 *(5.61)*
B. Regulatory trade barriers						5.50	6.20	5.45
(i) Non-tariff trade barriers						5.70	7.10	5.61
(ii) Compliance cost of importing and exporting						5.30	5.30	5.30
C. Size of trade sector relative to expected						7.40	6.21	5.14
D. Black-market exchange rates						10.00	10.00	10.00
E. International capital market controls						2.50	3.24	2.38
(i) Foreign ownership / investment restrictions						5.00	5.70	4.76
(ii) Capital controls						0.00	0.77	0.00
5. Regulation of Credit, Labor, and Business						**6.80**	**6.26**	**6.14**
A. Credit market regulations						8.50	8.46	7.74
(i) Ownership of banks						8.00	8.00	8.00
(ii) Foreign bank competition						6.00	6.00	6.00
(iii) Private sector credit					9.09	10.00	9.82	6.97
(iv) Interest rate controls / negative real interest rates						10.00	10.00	10.00
B. Labor market regulations						6.00	4.95	5.38
(i) Hiring regulations and minimum wage						6.70	5.60	4.43
(ii) Hiring and firing regulations						5.70	3.27	4.05
(iii) Centralized collective bargaining						7.50	5.25	7.43
(iv) Hours regulations						6.00	6.00	6.00
(v) Mandated cost of worker dismissal						7.30	6.57	7.34
(vi) Conscription						3.00	3.00	3.00
C. Business regulations						5.80	5.37	5.30
(i) Price controls							2.00	2.00
(ii) Administrative requirements						2.60	2.94	3.08
(iii) Bureaucracy costs						3.50	5.11	5.36
(iv) Starting a business						8.80	9.57	9.53
(v) Extra payments / bribes / favoritism						6.80	4.60	3.72
(vi) Licensing restrictions						5.80	5.94	5.94
(vii) Cost of tax compliance						7.40	7.44	7.44

Mongolia

	1980	1985	1990	1995	2000	2005	2008	2009
Chain-Linked						Rating (Rank)	Rating (Rank)	Rating (Rank)
Summary Rating (Rank) ➤								
Area 1. Size of Government								
Area 2. Legal Structure and Security of Property Rights								
Area 3. Access to Sound Money								
Area 4. Freedom to Trade Internationally								
Area 5. Regulation of Credit, Labor, and Business								

Unadjusted								
Summary Rating (Rank) ➤						**7.35** (35)	**7.05** (56)	**7.29** (36)
				Rating *Data*	Rating *Data*	Rating *Data*	Rating *Data*	Rating *Data*
1. Size of Government						**7.60**	**7.71**	**7.65**
A. Government consumption						6.40 *(18.20)*	4.92 *(23.26)*	4.96 *(23.13)*
B. Transfers and subsidies						7.90 *(8.20)*	6.91 *(11.83)*	6.62 *(12.89)*
C. Government enterprises and investment						10.00 *(7.70)*	10.00 *(9.53)*	10.00 *(6.42)*
D. Top marginal tax rate						6.00	9.00	9.00
(i) Top marginal income tax rate						8.00 *(30)*	10.00 *(10)*	10.00 *(10)*
(ii) Top marginal income and payroll tax rates						4.00 *(49)*	8.00 *(29)*	8.00 *(29)*
2. Legal Structure and Security of Property Rights						**5.70**	**5.71**	**5.70**
A. Judicial independence						2.60	2.56	2.64
B. Impartial courts						2.50	3.06	3.04
C. Protection of property rights						5.00	4.01	3.94
D. Military interference in rule of law and politics						8.80	8.33	8.33
E. Integrity of the legal system							6.67	6.67
F. Legal enforcement of contracts						6.20	6.24	6.24
G. Regulatory restrictions on sale of real property						9.10	9.10	9.07
3. Access to Sound Money						**8.30**	**7.45**	**7.98**
A. Money growth						8.50 *(7.60)*	6.60 *(17.02)*	7.02 *(14.91)*
B. Standard deviation of inflation						7.30 *(6.74)*	8.23 *(4.43)*	6.15 *(9.62)*
C. Inflation: most recent year						7.50 *(12.72)*	4.99 *(25.06)*	8.74 *(6.28)*
D. Freedom to own foreign currency bank accounts						10.00	10.00	10.00
4. Freedom to Trade Internationally						**7.70**	**7.16**	**7.55**
A. Taxes on international trade						9.20	9.14	9.21
(i) Revenues from trade taxes (% of trade sector)						9.00 *(1.50)*	8.73 *(1.91)*	8.92 *(1.62)*
(ii) Mean tariff rate						9.20 *(4.20)*	9.00 *(5.00)*	9.00 *(5.00)*
(iii) Standard deviation of tariff rates						9.40 *(1.60)*	9.70 *(0.75)*	9.72 *(0.70)*
B. Regulatory trade barriers						4.60	4.31	4.60
(i) Non-tariff trade barriers						3.90	5.25	5.82
(ii) Compliance cost of importing and exporting						5.30	3.37	3.37
C. Size of trade sector relative to expected						10.00	8.67	7.93
D. Black-market exchange rates						10.00	10.00	10.00
E. International capital market controls						4.90	3.67	5.99
(i) Foreign ownership / investment restrictions						6.70	5.81	5.62
(ii) Capital controls						3.10	1.54	6.36
5. Regulation of Credit, Labor, and Business						**7.40**	**7.23**	**7.57**
A. Credit market regulations						9.10	8.32	8.97
(i) Ownership of banks								
(ii) Foreign bank competition								
(iii) Private sector credit				10.00	10.00	9.30	8.65	8.95
(iv) Interest rate controls / negative real interest rates						9.00	8.00	9.00
B. Labor market regulations						7.10	6.86	7.24
(i) Hiring regulations and minimum wage						8.90	8.90	8.90
(ii) Hiring and firing regulations						7.00	6.16	5.96
(iii) Centralized collective bargaining						8.30	7.92	7.97
(iv) Hours regulations						6.00	6.00	8.00
(v) Mandated cost of worker dismissal						9.20	9.17	9.60
(vi) Conscription						3.00	3.00	3.00
C. Business regulations						6.10	6.51	6.49
(i) Price controls						8.00	8.00	8.00
(ii) Administrative requirements						2.90	2.81	2.83
(iii) Bureaucracy costs						3.40	6.98	6.88
(iv) Starting a business						9.10	9.41	9.40
(v) Extra payments / bribes / favoritism						4.70	3.20	3.19
(vi) Licensing restrictions						7.10	7.30	7.29
(vii) Cost of tax compliance						7.70	7.85	7.85

Montenegro

	1980	1985	1990	1995	2000	2005	2008	2009
Chain-Linked						Rating (Rank)	Rating (Rank)	Rating (Rank)
Summary Rating (Rank) ➤								
Area 1. Size of Government								
Area 2. Legal Structure and Security of Property Rights								
Area 3. Access to Sound Money								
Area 4. Freedom to Trade Internationally								
Area 5. Regulation of Credit, Labor, and Business								

	1980	1985	1990	1995	2000	2005	2008	2009
Unadjusted								
Summary Rating (Rank) ➤						**6.64** (76)	**7.15** (47)	**7.27** (37)
						Rating *Data*	Rating *Data*	Rating *Data*
1. Size of Government						**5.60**	**5.84**	**5.96**
A. Government consumption						3.80 *(27.00)*	6.52 *(17.82)*	6.89 *(16.57)*
B. Transfers and subsidies								
C. Government enterprises and investment						6.00 *(25.80)*	4.00 *(33.61)*	4.00 *(31.43)*
D. Top marginal tax rate						7.00	7.00	7.00
(i) Top marginal income tax rate						9.00 *(23)*	10.00 *(17)*	10.00 *(14)*
(ii) Top marginal income and payroll tax rates							3.00 *(46)*	4.00 *(43)*
2. Legal Structure and Security of Property Rights						**5.70**	**5.94**	**6.13**
A. Judicial independence						3.50	4.66	5.16
B. Impartial courts						3.50	4.89	5.21
C. Protection of property rights						4.50	6.13	6.25
D. Military interference in rule of law and politics						10.00	7.90	7.80
E. Integrity of the legal system								
F. Legal enforcement of contracts						4.80	4.80	4.80
G. Regulatory restrictions on sale of real property						7.70	7.29	7.57
3. Access to Sound Money						**8.80**	**9.00**	**9.49**
A. Money growth							8.91 *(5.46)*	9.73 *(1.35)*
B. Standard deviation of inflation						7.20 *(6.90)*	9.08 *(2.31)*	8.74 *(3.16)*
C. Inflation: most recent year						9.10 *(4.32)*	8.00 *(10.01)*	9.51 *(2.45)*
D. Freedom to own foreign currency bank accounts						10.00	10.00	10.00
4. Freedom to Trade Internationally						**6.70**	**7.19**	**6.75**
A. Taxes on international trade						7.50	8.10	8.12
(i) Revenues from trade taxes (% of trade sector)						7.80 *(3.30)*	7.80 *(3.30)*	7.80 *(3.30)*
(ii) Mean tariff rate						8.70 *(6.60)*	9.02 *(4.90)*	9.02 *(4.90)*
(iii) Standard deviation of tariff rates						6.10 *(9.90)*	7.49 *(6.27)*	7.55 *(6.13)*
B. Regulatory trade barriers						6.30	7.45	7.38
(i) Non-tariff trade barriers						4.50	6.77	6.65
(ii) Compliance cost of importing and exporting						8.10	8.12	8.12
C. Size of trade sector relative to expected						3.00	2.60	1.41
D. Black-market exchange rates						10.00	10.00	10.00
E. International capital market controls							7.81	6.84
(i) Foreign ownership / investment restrictions							7.16	6.75
(ii) Capital controls							8.46	6.92
5. Regulation of Credit, Labor, and Business						**6.40**	**7.80**	**8.01**
A. Credit market regulations						9.40	9.59	9.80
(i) Ownership of banks						10.00	10.00	10.00
(ii) Foreign bank competition								
(iii) Private sector credit						8.30	9.77	9.39
(iv) Interest rate controls / negative real interest rates						10.00	9.00	10.00
B. Labor market regulations						4.80	7.91	8.29
(i) Hiring regulations and minimum wage						6.70	10.00	10.00
(ii) Hiring and firing regulations						2.00	5.24	5.46
(iii) Centralized collective bargaining						2.50	6.82	6.68
(iv) Hours regulations						8.00	8.00	10.00
(v) Mandated cost of worker dismissal						6.40	7.40	7.59
(vi) Conscription						3.00	10.00	10.00
C. Business regulations						5.10	5.90	5.95
(i) Price controls						6.00	6.00	6.00
(ii) Administrative requirements						4.00	3.79	4.49
(iii) Bureaucracy costs						3.00	5.49	5.05
(iv) Starting a business						9.20	9.56	9.66
(v) Extra payments / bribes / favoritism						3.00	5.45	5.64
(vi) Licensing restrictions						4.60	5.20	4.97
(vii) Cost of tax compliance						5.80	5.83	5.83

Morocco

Chain-Linked	1980 Rating (Rank)	1985 Rating (Rank)	1990 Rating (Rank)	1995 Rating (Rank)	2000 Rating (Rank)	2005 Rating (Rank)	2008 Rating (Rank)	2009 Rating (Rank)
Summary Rating (Rank) ➤	4.54 (82)	5.25 (59)	5.27 (72)	6.15 (58)	6.12 (78)	6.31 (84)	6.29 (84)	6.25 (88)
Area 1. Size of Government	4.63 (69)	5.23 (50)	5.91 (47)	6.27 (53)	6.32 (56)	6.71 (58)	6.73 (48)	6.33 (59)
Area 2. Legal Structure and Security of Property Rights	2.24 (83)	3.99 (75)	3.99 (78)	6.74 (32)	6.67 (37)	6.51 (44)	6.43 (40)	6.38 (43)
Area 3. Access to Sound Money	6.26 (52)	6.81 (44)	6.50 (64)	6.69 (59)	6.96 (83)	7.10 (86)	6.72 (95)	7.02 (91)
Area 4. Freedom to Trade Internationally	5.21 (51)	6.01 (43)	5.55 (59)	6.14 (81)	5.44 (110)	5.81 (96)	6.07 (91)	5.86 (89)
Area 5. Regulation of Credit, Labor, and Business	4.34 (82)	4.24 (85)	4.41 (90)	4.90 (90)	5.19 (100)	5.40 (107)	5.48 (108)	5.66 (105)

Unadjusted

	1980 Rating Data	1985 Rating Data	1990 Rating Data	1995 Rating Data	2000 Rating Data	2005 Rating Data	2008 Rating Data	2009 Rating Data
Summary Rating (Rank) ➤	4.59 (82)	5.36 (62)	5.28 (67)	6.15 (60)	6.12 (78)	6.22 (99)	6.20 (100)	6.16 (105)
1. Size of Government	4.63	5.23	5.91	6.27	6.32	6.70	6.73	6.33
A. Government consumption	5.51 (21.26)	6.06 (19.41)	6.12 (19.18)	6.01 (19.57)	5.10 (22.65)	4.50 (24.80)	5.22 (22.25)	4.71 (23.98)
B. Transfers and subsidies	9.02 (4.10)	8.88 (4.60)	9.51 (2.30)	9.07 (3.92)	8.16 (7.25)	8.40 (6.50)	7.71 (8.89)	8.63 (5.54)
C. Government enterprises and investment	2.00 (46.80)	6.00 (27.90)	8.00 (19.80)	7.00 (21.90)	8.00 (18.10)	10.00 (13.60)	10.00 (14.18)	8.00 (19.33)
D. Top marginal tax rate	2.00	0.00	0.00	3.00	4.00	4.00	4.00	4.00
(i) Top marginal income tax rate	2.00 (64)	0.00 (87)	0.00 (87)	3.00 (46)	4.00 (44)	4.00 (44)	4.00 (44)	4.00 (44)
(ii) Top marginal income and payroll tax rates								
2. Legal Structure and Security of Property Rights	2.24	3.99	3.99	6.74	6.67	6.00	5.97	5.93
A. Judicial independence						4.10	4.20	4.14
B. Impartial courts				6.76	6.37	5.10	4.86	4.84
C. Protection of property rights						6.30	5.97	5.70
D. Military interference in rule of law and politics				6.55	6.67	6.70	6.67	6.67
E. Integrity of the legal system				10.00	10.00	8.30	8.33	8.33
F. Legal enforcement of contracts						4.30	4.30	4.30
G. Regulatory restrictions on sale of real property						7.60	7.50	7.50
3. Access to Sound Money	6.26	6.81	6.50	6.69	6.96	7.10	6.72	7.02
A. Money growth	8.75 (6.25)	9.30 (3.48)	8.09 (9.57)	9.25 (3.73)	8.63 (6.84)	8.90 (5.30)	8.55 (7.24)	8.97 (5.16)
B. Standard deviation of inflation	8.19 (4.52)	9.64 (0.91)	9.06 (2.36)	9.11 (2.22)	9.60 (0.99)	9.70 (0.86)	9.07 (2.32)	9.30 (1.75)
C. Inflation: most recent year	8.11 (9.46)	8.32 (8.42)	8.87 (5.66)	8.41 (7.96)	9.62 (1.89)	9.80 (0.98)	9.26 (3.71)	9.80 (1.00)
D. Freedom to own foreign currency bank accounts	0.00	0.00	0.00	0.00	0.00	0.00	0.00	0.00
4. Freedom to Trade Internationally	5.25	6.06	5.59	6.14	5.44	5.90	6.17	5.95
A. Taxes on international trade	1.43	5.52	4.78	5.20	3.19	4.70	5.26	5.41
(i) Revenues from trade taxes (% of trade sector)	2.87 (10.70)	5.73 (6.40)	4.27 (8.60)	5.45 (6.82)	5.09 (7.36)	7.50 (3.70)	8.37 (2.45)	8.03 (2.95)
(ii) Mean tariff rate	0.00 (54.00)	5.30 (23.50)	5.30 (23.50)	5.44 (22.80)	3.28 (33.60)	6.10 (19.40)	5.72 (21.40)	6.38 (18.10)
(iii) Standard deviation of tariff rates				4.72 (13.20)	1.20 (22.00)	0.60 (23.50)	1.70 (20.76)	1.82 (20.45)
B. Regulatory trade barriers						5.90	6.54	6.59
(i) Non-tariff trade barriers						5.00	5.15	5.25
(ii) Compliance cost of importing and exporting						6.80	7.93	7.93
C. Size of trade sector relative to expected	4.79	5.98	5.56	5.53	5.79	5.60	6.51	5.10
D. Black-market exchange rates	9.80	8.60	7.40	9.80	10.00	9.40	10.00	10.00
E. International capital market controls	2.00	2.00	2.00	2.00	0.00	3.90	2.53	2.67
(i) Foreign ownership/investment restrictions						7.10	5.05	5.35
(ii) Capital controls	2.00	2.00	2.00	2.00	0.00	0.80	0.00	0.00
5. Regulation of Credit, Labor, and Business	4.55	4.70	4.41	4.90	5.19	5.30	5.42	5.57
A. Credit market regulations	5.69	5.57	6.09	6.39	7.32	6.60	6.75	6.75
(i) Ownership of banks	5.00	5.00	5.00	5.00	5.00	5.00	5.00	5.00
(ii) Foreign bank competition						3.00	3.00	3.00
(iii) Private sector credit	6.38	5.72	5.26	6.16	7.95	9.20	10.00	10.00
(iv) Interest rate controls/negative real interest rates		6.00	8.00	8.00	9.00	9.00	9.00	9.00
B. Labor market regulations						3.70	3.65	4.12
(i) Hiring regulations and minimum wage						0.00	1.10	1.10
(ii) Hiring and firing regulations						5.30	4.86	4.92
(iii) Centralized collective bargaining						7.50	6.82	6.77
(iv) Hours regulations						6.00	6.00	8.00
(v) Mandated cost of worker dismissal						2.10	2.12	2.92
(vi) Conscription	1.00	1.00	1.00	1.00	1.00	1.00	1.00	1.00
C. Business regulations						5.80	5.87	5.85
(i) Price controls				0.00	4.00	4.00	4.00	4.00
(ii) Administrative requirements						3.60	3.99	3.99
(iii) Bureaucracy costs						5.40	5.46	5.18
(iv) Starting a business						9.30	9.41	9.41
(v) Extra payments/bribes/favoritism						5.10	4.43	4.60
(vi) Licensing restrictions						7.40	7.78	7.81
(vii) Cost of tax compliance						6.00	5.99	5.99

Mozambique

	1980	1985	1990	1995	2000	2005	2008	2009
Chain-Linked						Rating (Rank)	Rating (Rank)	Rating (Rank)
Summary Rating (Rank) ➤								
Area 1. Size of Government								
Area 2. Legal Structure and Security of Property Rights								
Area 3. Access to Sound Money								
Area 4. Freedom to Trade Internationally								
Area 5. Regulation of Credit, Labor, and Business								

	1980	1985	1990	1995	2000	2005	2008	2009
Unadjusted								
Summary Rating (Rank) ➤						**5.56** (127)	**5.77** (121)	**5.53** (128)
			Rating *Data*	Rating *Data*	Rating *Data*	Rating *Data*	Rating *Data*	Rating *Data*
1. Size of Government						**5.50**	**4.82**	**4.74**
A. Government consumption					8.08 *(12.51)*	8.40 *(11.40)*	7.97 *(12.91)*	7.73 *(13.73)*
B. Transfers and subsidies								
C. Government enterprises and investment						2.00 *(45.70)*	0.00 *(62.65)*	0.00 *(62.38)*
D. Top marginal tax rate						6.00	6.50	6.50
(i) Top marginal income tax rate						7.00 *(32)*	7.00 *(32)*	7.00 *(32)*
(ii) Top marginal income and payroll tax rates						5.00 *(37)*	6.00 *(37)*	6.00 *(38)*
2. Legal Structure and Security of Property Rights						**3.30**	**4.02**	**4.11**
A. Judicial independence						2.50	3.27	3.22
B. Impartial courts						2.70	4.00	4.02
C. Protection of property rights						4.80	3.72	3.89
D. Military interference in rule of law and politics						3.60	6.67	6.67
E. Integrity of the legal system						5.00	5.00	5.00
F. Legal enforcement of contracts						0.00	0.00	0.00
G. Regulatory restrictions on sale of real property						4.50	5.49	5.95
3. Access to Sound Money						**7.60**	**7.63**	**6.53**
A. Money growth			2.88 *(35.58)*	3.91 *(30.43)*	7.63 *(11.85)*	8.40 *(7.80)*	8.07 *(9.65)*	7.62 *(11.88)*
B. Standard deviation of inflation						8.60 *(3.59)*	9.54 *(1.16)*	9.16 *(2.09)*
C. Inflation: most recent year						8.60 *(7.17)*	7.93 *(10.33)*	9.35 *(3.25)*
D. Freedom to own foreign currency bank accounts						5.00	5.00	0.00
4. Freedom to Trade Internationally						**6.20**	**6.44**	**6.29**
A. Taxes on international trade						6.80	7.54	7.51
(i) Revenues from trade taxes (% of trade sector)								
(ii) Mean tariff rate						7.40 *(13.10)*	7.98 *(10.10)*	7.94 *(10.30)*
(iii) Standard deviation of tariff rates						6.10 *(9.70)*	7.09 *(7.27)*	7.07 *(7.31)*
B. Regulatory trade barriers						5.10	5.72	5.58
(i) Non-tariff trade barriers						4.70	5.08	4.80
(ii) Compliance cost of importing and exporting						5.50	6.36	6.36
C. Size of trade sector relative to expected						6.00	6.64	5.79
D. Black-market exchange rates						10.00	10.00	10.00
E. International capital market controls						3.30	2.31	2.55
(i) Foreign ownership / investment restrictions						6.70	4.62	5.10
(ii) Capital controls						0.00	0.00	0.00
5. Regulation of Credit, Labor, and Business						**5.10**	**5.95**	**6.00**
A. Credit market regulations						8.10	8.91	8.97
(i) Ownership of banks								
(ii) Foreign bank competition						10.00	10.00	10.00
(iii) Private sector credit						5.30	6.73	6.90
(iv) Interest rate controls / negative real interest rates					10.00	9.00	10.00	10.00
B. Labor market regulations						3.00	3.19	3.06
(i) Hiring regulations and minimum wage						2.80	3.30	3.33
(ii) Hiring and firing regulations						3.00	3.97	3.84
(iii) Centralized collective bargaining						5.20	5.20	5.20
(iv) Hours regulations						6.70	6.70	6.00
(v) Mandated cost of worker dismissal						0.00	0.00	0.00
(vi) Conscription						0.00	0.00	0.00
C. Business regulations						4.30	5.74	5.98
(i) Price controls								
(ii) Administrative requirements						2.00	3.58	4.02
(iii) Bureaucracy costs						2.30	6.70	6.61
(iv) Starting a business						5.70	8.96	9.44
(v) Extra payments / bribes / favoritism						5.10	3.92	4.35
(vi) Licensing restrictions						3.50	3.86	4.04
(vii) Cost of tax compliance						7.40	7.42	7.42

Myanmar

	1980	1985	1990	1995	2000	2005	2008	2009
Chain-Linked	Rating (Rank)	Rating (Rank)	Rating (Rank)	Rating (Rank)	Rating (Rank)	Rating (Rank)	Rating (Rank)	Rating (Rank)
Summary Rating (Rank) ➤	**4.84** (71)	**4.42** (91)	**3.46** (109)	**4.02** (118)	**4.00** (123)	**3.67** (122)	**3.49** (123)	**3.59** (123)
Area 1. Size of Government					5.76 (78)	6.33 (72)	6.33 (66)	6.33 (59)
Area 2. Legal Structure and Security of Property Rights	5.35 (41)	3.99 (75)	3.50 (83)	4.69 (95)	3.25 (118)	2.60 (119)	3.19 (117)	3.19 (119)
Area 3. Access to Sound Money	6.90 (30)	7.31 (33)	4.23 (99)	4.84 (97)	5.53 (111)	4.96 (118)	4.46 (122)	5.65 (119)
Area 4. Freedom to Trade Internationally	2.12 (91)	1.66 (98)	1.66 (103)	1.66 (113)	1.66 (122)	0.74 (122)	0.73 (122)	0.73 (122)
Area 5. Regulation of Credit, Labor, and Business	2.91 (99)	2.82 (104)	2.93 (111)	3.10 (120)	3.81 (121)	4.16 (122)	3.24 (123)	2.71 (123)

Unadjusted

	1980	1985	1990	1995	2000	2005	2008	2009
Summary Rating (Rank) ➤	**4.35** (86)	**3.97** (100)	**3.08** (110)	**3.57** (121)	**4.00** (123)	**4.01** (139)	**3.81** (141)	**4.16** (140)
	Rating Data	Rating Data	Rating Data	Rating Data	Rating Data	Rating Data	Rating Data	Rating Data
1. Size of Government					5.76	6.30	6.33	6.33
A. Government consumption					8.28 (11.86)	10.00 (4.10)	10.00 (4.49)	10.00 (5.16)
B. Transfers and subsidies								
C. Government enterprises and investment			2.00 (45.00)	2.00 (47.65)	4.00 (34.36)	4.00 (34.40)	4.00	4.00
D. Top marginal tax rate					5.00	5.00	5.00	5.00
(i) Top marginal income tax rate					5.00 (40)	5.00 (40)	5.00 (40)	5.00 (40)
(ii) Top marginal income and payroll tax rates					5.00 (40)	5.00 (40)	5.00 (40)	5.00 (40)
2. Legal Structure and Security of Property Rights	5.35	3.99	3.50	4.69	3.25	2.60	3.19	3.19
A. Judicial independence								
B. Impartial courts				4.08	3.76	2.80	2.90	2.90
C. Protection of property rights								
D. Military interference in rule of law and politics				3.74	0.00	0.00	1.67	1.67
E. Integrity of the legal system				6.96	5.00	5.00	5.00	5.00
F. Legal enforcement of contracts								
G. Regulatory restrictions on sale of real property								
3. Access to Sound Money	6.90	7.31	4.23	4.84	5.53	5.00	4.46	5.65
A. Money growth	9.26 (3.69)	9.98 (−0.10)	7.46 (12.70)	5.64 (21.82)	6.93 (15.36)	7.10 (14.50)	8.16 (9.19)	8.26 (8.70)
B. Standard deviation of inflation	8.59 (3.53)	9.59 (1.03)	3.16 (17.09)	7.62 (5.96)	5.22 (11.96)	4.60 (13.49)	5.02 (12.46)	4.64 (13.39)
C. Inflation: most recent year	9.75 (1.24)	9.69 (1.57)	6.29 (18.54)	6.11 (19.44)	9.98 (−0.11)	8.10 (9.37)	4.64 (26.80)	9.71 (1.47)
D. Freedom to own foreign currency bank accounts	0.00	0.00	0.00	0.00	0.00	0.00	0.00	0.00
4. Freedom to Trade Internationally	2.12	1.66	1.66	1.66	1.66	1.40	1.34	1.34
A. Taxes on international trade	0.53	0.00	0.00	0.00	0.00	5.40	5.35	5.35
(i) Revenues from trade taxes (% of trade sector)	0.53 (14.20)	0.00 (17.60)	0.00 (19.35)	0.00 (24.66)	0.00 (19.80)	0.00 (57.20)	0.00 (57.21)	0.00 (57.21)
(ii) Mean tariff rate						9.10 (4.50)	8.88 (5.60)	8.88 (5.60)
(iii) Standard deviation of tariff rates						7.20 (7.10)	7.16 (7.11)	7.16 (7.11)
B. Regulatory trade barriers								
(i) Non-tariff trade barriers								
(ii) Compliance cost of importing and exporting								
C. Size of trade sector relative to expected	1.79	0.00	0.00	0.00	0.00	0.00	0.00	0.00
D. Black-market exchange rates	0.00	0.00	0.00	0.00	0.00	0.00	0.00	0.00
E. International capital market controls	0.00	0.00	0.00	0.00	0.00	0.00	0.00	0.00
(i) Foreign ownership / investment restrictions								
(ii) Capital controls	0.00	0.00	0.00	0.00	0.00	0.00	0.00	0.00
5. Regulation of Credit, Labor, and Business	3.03	2.93	2.93	3.10	3.81	4.80	3.73	4.27
A. Credit market regulations	0.47	0.20	0.50	1.08	3.42	5.20	3.91	3.91
(i) Ownership of banks	0.00	0.00	0.00	0.00	0.00	0.00	0.00	0.00
(ii) Foreign bank competition						9.00	9.00	9.00
(iii) Private sector credit	1.40	0.61	1.49	3.25	3.26	2.00	1.66	1.62
(iv) Interest rate controls / negative real interest rates	0.00	0.00	0.00	0.00	7.00	10.00	5.00	5.00
B. Labor market regulations								
(i) Hiring regulations and minimum wage								
(ii) Hiring and firing regulations								
(iii) Centralized collective bargaining								
(iv) Hours regulations							10.00	
(v) Mandated cost of worker dismissal								
(vi) Conscription	3.00	3.00	3.00	3.00	3.00	3.00	3.00	0.00
C. Business regulations								
(i) Price controls				0.00	0.00	0.00	0.00	0.00
(ii) Administrative requirements								
(iii) Bureaucracy costs								
(iv) Starting a business								
(v) Extra payments / bribes / favoritism								
(vi) Licensing restrictions								
(vii) Cost of tax compliance								

Namibia

Chain-Linked

	1980		1985		1990		1995		2000		2005		2008		2009	
	Rating	(Rank)	Rating	(Rank)	Rating	(Rank)	Rating	(Rank)	Rating	(Rank)	Rating	(Rank)	Rating	(Rank)	Rating	(Rank)
Summary Rating (Rank) ➤					5.33	(69)	6.28	(55)	6.47	(64)	6.56	(73)	6.63	(73)	6.63	(70)
Area 1. Size of Government	3.02	(97)	1.16	(111)	4.88	(76)	4.72	(93)	5.14	(90)	6.21	(77)	6.53	(60)	6.53	(52)
Area 2. Legal Structure and Security of Property Rights					2.69	(100)	7.83	(21)	8.15	(20)	7.33	(25)	7.58	(21)	7.52	(20)
Area 3. Access to Sound Money			4.28	(98)	5.82	(77)	6.03	(72)	6.07	(107)	6.48	(103)	6.12	(107)	6.09	(115)
Area 4. Freedom to Trade Internationally					6.72	(35)	6.41	(73)	6.18	(86)	5.89	(93)	5.89	(97)	5.91	(88)
Area 5. Regulation of Credit, Labor, and Business					6.06	(36)	6.39	(30)	6.84	(29)	6.93	(44)	7.07	(36)	7.13	(35)

Unadjusted

	1980		1985		1990		1995		2000		2005		2008		2009	
Summary Rating (Rank) ➤					5.07	(78)	6.25	(56)	6.47	(64)	6.79	(71)	6.87	(68)	6.86	(66)
	Rating	Data	Rating	Data	Rating	Data	Rating	Data	Rating	Data	Rating	Data	Rating	Data	Rating	Data
1. Size of Government	1.70		0.65		4.92		4.77		5.14		6.20		6.53		6.53	
A. Government consumption	3.40	(28.44)	1.31	(35.55)	1.50	(34.91)	1.09	(36.28)	2.24	(32.40)	4.40	(25.00)	4.85	(23.52)	3.85	(26.89)
B. Transfers and subsidies					9.26	(3.20)	9.21	(3.40)	9.33	(2.96)	9.40	(2.70)	9.26	(3.20)	9.26	(3.20)
C. Government enterprises and investment	0.00	(57.90)	0.00	(64.30)	4.00	(38.60)	4.00	(31.90)	4.00	(32.26)	4.00	(34.30)	6.00	(28.09)	7.00	(21.44)
D. Top marginal tax rate									5.00		7.00		6.00		6.00	
(i) Top marginal income tax rate									5.00	(36)	7.00	(35)	6.00	(37)	6.00	(37)
(ii) Top marginal income and payroll tax rates									5.00	(36)	7.00	(35)	6.00	(37)	6.00	(37)
2. Legal Structure and Security of Property Rights					2.33		7.83		8.15		7.30		7.58		7.52	
A. Judicial independence							7.17		7.18		7.10		7.79		7.43	
B. Impartial courts							7.25		7.75		5.90		6.24		6.50	
C. Protection of property rights							6.53		5.82		7.50		8.06		7.74	
D. Military interference in rule of law and politics							8.21		10.00		10.00		10.00		10.00	
E. Integrity of the legal system							10.00		10.00		8.30		8.33		8.33	
F. Legal enforcement of contracts											6.30		6.25		6.25	
G. Regulatory restrictions on sale of real property											6.30		6.41		6.41	
3. Access to Sound Money			4.00		5.44		6.03		6.07		6.50		6.12		6.09	
A. Money growth							7.21	(13.96)	7.57	(12.15)	9.00	(5.20)	8.78	(6.10)	8.12	(9.42)
B. Standard deviation of inflation			6.96	(7.61)	7.99	(5.03)	8.34	(4.16)	8.70	(3.25)	7.40	(6.49)	7.77	(5.56)	8.02	(4.95)
C. Inflation: most recent year			5.04	(24.82)	8.33	(8.34)	8.56	(7.18)	8.00	(10.02)	9.50	(2.26)	7.93	(10.35)	8.24	(8.78)
D. Freedom to own foreign currency bank accounts			0.00		0.00		0.00		0.00		0.00		0.00		0.00	
4. Freedom to Trade Internationally					6.72		6.41		6.18		6.20		6.21		6.24	
A. Taxes on international trade	8.12		8.80		6.14		3.86		5.40		5.70		5.06		5.10	
(i) Revenues from trade taxes (% of trade sector)					5.13	(7.30)	4.29	(8.56)	1.63	(12.55)	3.00	(10.40)	1.55	(12.67)	1.55	(12.67)
(ii) Mean tariff rate	8.12	(9.40)	8.80	(6.00)	7.80	(11.00)	6.06	(19.70)	8.56	(7.20)	8.90	(5.60)	8.44	(7.80)	8.46	(7.70)
(iii) Standard deviation of tariff rates					5.48	(11.30)	1.24	(21.90)	6.00	(10.00)	5.20	(12.10)	5.20	(12.01)	5.29	(11.78)
B. Regulatory trade barriers											5.70		6.22		6.02	
(i) Non-tariff trade barriers											5.20		6.20		5.80	
(ii) Compliance cost of importing and exporting											6.20		6.23		6.23	
C. Size of trade sector relative to expected	10.00		9.44		7.86		8.02		7.29		6.30		6.40		6.62	
D. Black-market exchange rates			5.00		9.40		10.00		10.00		10.00		10.00		10.00	
E. International capital market controls					2.00		2.00		0.00		3.30		3.40		3.46	
(i) Foreign ownership / investment restrictions											6.60		6.03		6.15	
(ii) Capital controls					2.00		2.00		0.00		0.00		0.77		0.77	
5. Regulation of Credit, Labor, and Business					5.92		6.23		6.84		7.70		7.88		7.93	
A. Credit market regulations					7.68		7.94		9.79		10.00		10.00		10.00	
(i) Ownership of banks									10.00		10.00		10.00		10.00	
(ii) Foreign bank competition																
(iii) Private sector credit					9.37		7.88		9.36		10.00		10.00		10.00	
(iv) Interest rate controls / negative real interest rates					6.00		8.00		10.00		10.00		10.00		10.00	
B. Labor market regulations											7.60		7.45		7.66	
(i) Hiring regulations and minimum wage											10.00		10.00		10.00	
(ii) Hiring and firing regulations											3.70		2.38		3.20	
(iii) Centralized collective bargaining											6.20		6.53		6.60	
(iv) Hours regulations											8.00		8.00		8.00	
(v) Mandated cost of worker dismissal											7.80		7.78		8.15	
(vi) Conscription					10.00		10.00		10.00		10.00		10.00		10.00	
C. Business regulations											5.50		6.20		6.14	
(i) Price controls					2.00		4.00		4.00		6.00		6.00		6.00	
(ii) Administrative requirements											2.90		4.52		4.40	
(iii) Bureaucracy costs											3.50		4.49		4.41	
(iv) Starting a business											6.80		7.67		7.69	
(v) Extra payments / bribes / favoritism											5.80		6.47		6.23	
(vi) Licensing restrictions											8.10		8.43		8.45	
(vii) Cost of tax compliance											5.80		5.80		5.80	

Nepal

	1980	1985	1990	1995	2000	2005	2008	2009
Chain-Linked	Rating (Rank)	Rating (Rank)	Rating (Rank)	Rating (Rank)	Rating (Rank)	Rating (Rank)	Rating (Rank)	Rating (Rank)
Summary Rating (Rank) ➤	**5.75** (39)	**5.31** (57)	**5.42** (63)	**5.37** (85)	**5.75** (96)	**5.38** (113)	**5.44** (110)	**5.40** (113)
Area 1. Size of Government	6.77 (16)	5.29 (47)	5.50 (62)	5.33 (83)	5.30 (85)	5.23 (94)	6.20 (70)	6.10 (67)
Area 2. Legal Structure and Security of Property Rights				4.88 (82)	4.76 (80)	3.69 (107)	3.51 (111)	3.41 (116)
Area 3. Access to Sound Money	6.10 (60)	6.28 (77)	6.26 (68)	6.26 (69)	6.97 (82)	6.60 (98)	6.36 (104)	6.13 (114)
Area 4. Freedom to Trade Internationally	5.03 (56)	4.60 (69)	4.22 (87)	5.08 (101)	6.16 (87)	5.32 (109)	5.00 (112)	5.32 (109)
Area 5. Regulation of Credit, Labor, and Business	4.82 (67)	4.76 (72)	5.36 (57)	5.35 (68)	5.57 (84)	6.07 (85)	6.16 (85)	6.06 (95)

Unadjusted

	1980	1985	1990	1995	2000	2005	2008	2009
Summary Rating (Rank) ➤	**5.83** (39)	**5.38** (60)	**5.37** (64)	**5.29** (87)	**5.75** (96)	**5.48** (129)	**5.54** (128)	**5.50** (129)
	Rating Data	Rating Data	Rating Data	Rating Data	Rating Data	Rating Data	Rating Data	Rating Data
1. Size of Government	**6.77**	**5.29**	**5.50**	**5.33**	**5.30**	**5.20**	**6.20**	**6.10**
A. Government consumption	9.55 (7.54)	8.58 (10.83)	9.00 (9.40)	8.65 (10.57)	8.60 (10.77)	8.50 (11.30)	8.40 (11.43)	8.20 (12.12)
B. Transfers and subsidies								
C. Government enterprises and investment	4.00 (37.30)	2.00 (45.80)	2.00 (43.20)	2.00 (43.20)	2.00 (43.20)	2.00	4.00	4.00
D. Top marginal tax rate								
(i) Top marginal income tax rate								
(ii) Top marginal income and payroll tax rates								
2. Legal Structure and Security of Property Rights				**4.44**	**4.76**	**4.20**	**3.96**	**3.86**
A. Judicial independence						5.20	3.83	3.68
B. Impartial courts				4.57	4.42	3.60	2.78	2.84
C. Protection of property rights						5.10	3.68	3.41
D. Military interference in rule of law and politics					5.61	0.00	1.80	1.50
E. Integrity of the legal system								
F. Legal enforcement of contracts						3.40	3.37	3.37
G. Regulatory restrictions on sale of real property						7.80	8.33	8.33
3. Access to Sound Money	**6.10**	**6.28**	**6.26**	**6.26**	**6.97**	**6.60**	**6.36**	**6.13**
A. Money growth	8.07 (9.66)	8.26 (8.71)	7.71 (11.47)	8.13 (9.35)	9.19 (−4.05)	8.90 (−5.50)	8.14 (9.32)	7.77 (11.14)
B. Standard deviation of inflation	7.86 (5.36)	9.13 (2.18)	9.48 (1.29)	8.16 (4.60)	9.19 (2.03)	8.90 (2.86)	9.47 (1.31)	9.05 (2.37)
C. Inflation: most recent year	8.48 (7.61)	7.72 (11.42)	7.86 (10.71)	8.74 (6.30)	9.50 (2.48)	8.60 (6.84)	7.82 (10.91)	7.68 (11.61)
D. Freedom to own foreign currency bank accounts	0.00	0.00	0.00	0.00	0.00	0.00	0.00	0.00
4. Freedom to Trade Internationally	**5.22**	**4.77**	**4.38**	**5.08**	**6.16**	**5.40**	**5.11**	**5.43**
A. Taxes on international trade	4.92	5.17	4.81	5.60	6.10	6.10	6.32	6.62
(i) Revenues from trade taxes (% of trade sector)	4.27 (8.60)	4.87 (7.70)	4.13 (8.80)	6.37 (5.44)	6.59 (5.11)	6.00 (6.10)	6.16 (5.75)	6.50 (5.26)
(ii) Mean tariff rate	5.58 (22.10)	5.48 (22.60)	5.48 (22.60)	6.78 (16.10)	7.06 (14.70)	7.10 (14.70)	7.46 (12.70)	7.52 (12.40)
(iii) Standard deviation of tariff rates				3.64 (15.90)	4.64 (13.40)	5.40 (11.50)	5.33 (11.68)	5.83 (10.42)
B. Regulatory trade barriers						4.60	4.61	4.81
(i) Non-tariff trade barriers						4.80	4.68	5.08
(ii) Compliance cost of importing and exporting						4.40	4.54	4.54
C. Size of trade sector relative to expected	2.97	2.67	2.05	5.38	4.71	2.80	2.67	3.80
D. Black-market exchange rates	10.00	7.80	6.80	6.20	10.00	10.00	10.00	10.00
E. International capital market controls	0.00	0.00	0.00	0.00	1.82	3.70	1.93	1.92
(i) Foreign ownership/investment restrictions						4.80	3.87	3.85
(ii) Capital controls	0.00	0.00	0.00	0.00	1.82	2.50	0.00	0.00
5. Regulation of Credit, Labor, and Business	**5.24**	**5.18**	**5.36**	**5.35**	**5.57**	**6.00**	**6.07**	**5.97**
A. Credit market regulations	4.00	3.84	5.56	5.52	6.25	7.20	7.23	6.89
(i) Ownership of banks	0.00	0.00	0.00	0.00	0.00	2.00	2.00	2.00
(ii) Foreign bank competition								
(iii) Private sector credit	6.00	5.53	6.68	8.55	8.76	9.70	9.68	9.68
(iv) Interest rate controls/negative real interest rates	6.00	6.00	10.00	8.00	10.00	10.00	10.00	9.00
B. Labor market regulations						5.90	5.77	5.85
(i) Hiring regulations and minimum wage						4.40	3.30	3.33
(ii) Hiring and firing regulations						3.60	3.77	4.09
(iii) Centralized collective bargaining						5.90	5.92	5.65
(iv) Hours regulations						10.00	10.00	10.00
(v) Mandated cost of worker dismissal						1.70	1.66	2.05
(vi) Conscription	10.00	10.00	10.00	10.00	10.00	10.00	10.00	10.00
C. Business regulations						4.80	5.20	5.16
(i) Price controls			2.00	2.00	2.00	4.00	4.00	4.00
(ii) Administrative requirements						3.10	3.22	2.81
(iii) Bureaucracy costs						4.20	6.94	7.06
(iv) Starting a business						8.20	8.44	8.52
(v) Extra payments/bribes/favoritism						4.20	3.02	2.89
(vi) Licensing restrictions						4.40	4.60	4.65
(vii) Cost of tax compliance						5.40	6.21	6.21

Netherlands

	1980		1985		1990		1995		2000		2005		2008		2009	
Chain-Linked	Rating	(Rank)	Rating	(Rank)	Rating	(Rank)	Rating	(Rank)	Rating	(Rank)	Rating	(Rank)	Rating	(Rank)	Rating	(Rank)
Summary Rating (Rank) ➤	**7.51**	(7)	**7.65**	(8)	**7.82**	(9)	**7.80**	(9)	**8.05**	(9)	**7.59**	(20)	**7.45**	(24)	**7.25**	(31)
Area 1. Size of Government	4.34	(74)	4.28	(77)	4.94	(74)	4.78	(91)	4.46	(106)	4.40	(113)	4.09	(116)	3.45	(121)
Area 2. Legal Structure and Security of Property Rights	8.84	(12)	9.87	(1)	9.87	(4)	9.11	(6)	9.62	(1)	8.60	(11)	8.22	(13)	8.13	(16)
Area 3. Access to Sound Money	9.43	(3)	9.44	(8)	9.64	(9)	9.70	(9)	9.57	(14)	9.46	(28)	9.52	(12)	9.50	(23)
Area 4. Freedom to Trade Internationally	8.33	(5)	8.46	(5)	8.21	(7)	8.65	(6)	8.97	(5)	8.13	(9)	8.23	(6)	8.12	(5)
Area 5. Regulation of Credit, Labor, and Business	6.67	(15)	6.31	(25)	6.52	(23)	6.74	(20)	7.63	(6)	7.34	(30)	7.17	(30)	7.04	(39)

	1980		1985		1990		1995		2000		2005		2008		2009	
Unadjusted																
Summary Rating (Rank) ➤	**7.04**	(9)	**7.17**	(7)	**7.31**	(12)	**7.79**	(9)	**8.05**	(9)	**7.66**	(16)	**7.52**	(22)	**7.32**	(30)
	Rating	Data	Rating	Data	Rating	Data	Rating	Data	Rating	Data	Rating	Data	Rating	Data	Rating	Data
1. Size of Government	**4.34**		**4.28**		**4.94**		**4.78**		**4.46**		**4.40**		**4.09**		**3.45**	
A. Government consumption	5.23	(22.22)	5.60	(20.96)	5.93	(19.85)	6.08	(19.34)	2.54	(31.37)	2.10	(33.00)	1.43	(35.15)	0.51	(38.25)
B. Transfers and subsidies	2.13	(29.40)	1.53	(31.60)	2.32	(28.70)	2.04	(29.70)	2.79	(26.97)	4.50	(20.50)	3.92	(22.82)	3.27	(25.20)
C. Government enterprises and investment	10.00	(14.80)	10.00	(14.70)	10.00	(12.70)	10.00	(13.80)	10.00	(13.80)	8.00	(17.40)	8.00	(16.93)	7.00	(20.29)
D. Top marginal tax rate	0.00		0.00		1.50		1.00		2.50		3.00		3.00		3.00	
(i) Top marginal income tax rate	0.00	(72)	0.00	(72)	3.00	(60)	2.00	(60)	3.00	(52)	3.00	(52)	3.00	(52)	3.00	(52)
(ii) Top marginal income and payroll tax rates					0.00	(63)	0.00	(63)	2.00	(54)	3.00	(52)	3.00	(52)	3.00	(52)
2. Legal Structure and Security of Property Rights	**7.48**		**8.35**		**8.35**		**9.11**		**9.62**		**8.60**		**8.22**		**8.13**	
A. Judicial independence							9.37		9.52		9.00		8.94		8.71	
B. Impartial courts							8.73		9.52		8.90		7.13		7.16	
C. Protection of property rights							7.46		9.09		9.20		8.51		8.07	
D. Military interference in rule of law and politics							10.00		10.00		10.00		10.00		10.00	
E. Integrity of the legal system							10.00		10.00		10.00		10.00		10.00	
F. Legal enforcement of contracts											5.10		5.11		5.11	
G. Regulatory restrictions on sale of real property											7.90		7.87		7.86	
3. Access to Sound Money	**9.43**		**9.44**		**9.64**		**9.70**		**9.57**		**9.50**		**9.52**		**9.50**	
A. Money growth	9.47	(2.64)	8.84	(5.79)	9.45	(2.74)	9.27	(3.65)	9.26	(3.70)	8.90	(5.60)	8.89	(5.57)	8.69	(6.57)
B. Standard deviation of inflation	9.35	(1.63)	9.28	(1.79)	9.58	(1.04)	9.85	(0.37)	9.54	(1.15)	9.30	(1.75)	9.71	(0.72)	9.56	(1.09)
C. Inflation: most recent year	8.90	(5.52)	9.65	(1.76)	9.54	(2.31)	9.67	(1.63)	9.50	(2.52)	9.70	(1.70)	9.50	(2.48)	9.76	(1.19)
D. Freedom to own foreign currency bank accounts	10.00		10.00		10.00		10.00		10.00		10.00		10.00		10.00	
4. Freedom to Trade Internationally	**8.35**		**8.48**		**8.10**		**8.60**		**8.97**		**8.10**		**8.23**		**8.12**	
A. Taxes on international trade	8.99		9.12		8.44		8.66		9.18		8.40		8.03		8.22	
(i) Revenues from trade taxes (% of trade sector)	9.73	(0.40)	9.73	(0.40)	9.67	(0.50)	9.67	(0.50)	9.78	(0.33)	9.60	(0.60)	9.61	(0.59)	9.44	(0.84)
(ii) Mean tariff rate	8.24	(8.80)	8.50	(7.50)	8.52	(7.40)	8.66	(6.70)	9.52	(2.40)	9.50	(2.70)	8.88	(5.60)	8.94	(5.30)
(iii) Standard deviation of tariff rates					7.12	(7.20)	7.64	(5.90)	8.24	(4.40)	6.10	(9.70)	5.61	(10.98)	6.29	(9.28)
B. Regulatory trade barriers							8.88		9.54		8.10		8.31		8.28	
(i) Non-tariff trade barriers							8.88		9.25		7.00		7.34		7.27	
(ii) Compliance cost of importing and exporting									9.83		9.30		9.29		9.29	
C. Size of trade sector relative to expected	6.63		7.14		5.93		5.90		6.57		5.90		6.43		5.81	
D. Black-market exchange rates	10.00		10.00		10.00		10.00		10.00		10.00		10.00		10.00	
E. International capital market controls	8.00		8.00		8.00		9.55		9.54		8.20		8.36		8.27	
(i) Foreign ownership/investment restrictions							9.10		9.85		7.90		7.56		7.38	
(ii) Capital controls	8.00		8.00		8.00		10.00		9.23		8.50		9.17		9.17	
5. Regulation of Credit, Labor, and Business	**5.60**		**5.29**		**5.52**		**6.78**		**7.63**		**7.70**		**7.55**		**7.41**	
A. Credit market regulations	9.44		8.59		9.26		8.65		9.42		9.50		9.50		8.96	
(i) Ownership of banks	10.00		8.00		10.00		10.00		10.00		10.00		10.00		10.00	
(ii) Foreign bank competition							8.17		8.18		8.00		8.00		8.00	
(iii) Private sector credit	8.33		7.77		7.78		6.54		10.00		10.00		10.00		7.83	
(iv) Interest rate controls/negative real interest rates	10.00		10.00		10.00		10.00		10.00		10.00		10.00		10.00	
B. Labor market regulations	2.97		2.62		2.83		4.09		5.19		6.70		6.70		6.74	
(i) Hiring regulations and minimum wage							4.52		4.47		8.30		8.30		6.67	
(ii) Hiring and firing regulations					3.38		3.38		2.58		3.20		3.30		3.71	
(iii) Centralized collective bargaining	5.18		4.49		4.49		4.49		4.40		4.10		4.18		4.06	
(iv) Hours regulations	2.73		2.37		2.46		5.08		4.51		6.00		6.00		6.00	
(v) Mandated cost of worker dismissal											8.40		8.42		10.00	
(vi) Conscription	1.00		1.00		1.00		3.00		10.00		10.00		10.00		10.00	
C. Business regulations							7.59		8.26		7.00		6.45		6.53	
(i) Price controls					7.00		7.00		8.00		7.00		7.00		7.00	
(ii) Administrative requirements									7.73		3.60		3.23		3.55	
(iii) Bureaucracy costs							7.37		9.10		6.00		1.61		1.64	
(iv) Starting a business							7.53		7.58		9.40		9.46		9.51	
(v) Extra payments/bribes/favoritism							8.46		8.88		8.90		8.70		8.55	
(vi) Licensing restrictions											7.00		6.97		6.96	
(vii) Cost of tax compliance											7.20		8.16		8.50	

New Zealand

	1980	1985	1990	1995	2000	2005	2008	2009
Chain-Linked	Rating (Rank)	Rating (Rank)	Rating (Rank)	Rating (Rank)	Rating (Rank)	Rating (Rank)	Rating (Rank)	Rating (Rank)
Summary Rating (Rank) ➤	**6.73** (17)	**6.57** (25)	**7.95** (7)	**8.64** (3)	**8.35** (5)	**8.37** (3)	**8.22** (3)	**8.15** (3)
Area 1. Size of Government	3.82 (86)	3.54 (96)	5.30 (66)	7.46 (20)	6.68 (47)	6.74 (54)	6.11 (76)	6.08 (68)
Area 2. Legal Structure and Security of Property Rights	9.52 (3)	9.32 (7)	9.88 (2)	9.17 (3)	9.10 (11)	8.96 (3)	8.98 (1)	8.80 (2)
Area 3. Access to Sound Money	6.31 (50)	6.17 (81)	8.64 (25)	9.75 (5)	9.54 (17)	9.65 (7)	9.61 (4)	9.70 (2)
Area 4. Freedom to Trade Internationally	7.22 (20)	7.00 (23)	7.92 (12)	8.14 (14)	8.51 (10)	7.85 (17)	7.91 (15)	7.71 (13)
Area 5. Regulation of Credit, Labor, and Business	7.22 (8)	7.34 (8)	8.29 (3)	8.66 (2)	7.89 (4)	8.65 (3)	8.50 (4)	8.45 (6)

Unadjusted								
Summary Rating (Rank) ➤	**6.26** (22)	**6.11** (31)	**7.35** (9)	**8.64** (3)	**8.35** (5)	**8.42** (3)	**8.27** (3)	**8.20** (3)
	Rating Data	Rating Data	Rating Data	Rating Data	Rating Data	Rating Data	Rating Data	Rating Data
1. Size of Government	**3.82**	**3.54**	**5.30**	**7.46**	**6.68**	**6.70**	**6.11**	**6.08**
A. Government consumption	5.12 (22.59)	5.63 (20.86)	5.54 (21.17)	6.21 (18.89)	4.84 (23.56)	4.90 (23.50)	4.31 (25.34)	4.17 (25.84)
B. Transfers and subsidies	4.17 (21.90)	4.52 (20.60)	2.64 (27.50)	6.65 (12.80)	6.90 (11.87)	7.10 (11.20)	7.15 (10.97)	7.15 (10.97)
C. Government enterprises and investment	4.00 (30.80)	4.00 (31.40)	6.00 (25.30)	10.00 (12.00)	10.00 (12.00)	10.00 (13.50)	8.00 (17.42)	8.00 (19.36)
D. Top marginal tax rate	2.00	0.00	7.00	7.00	5.00	5.00	5.00	5.00
(i) Top marginal income tax rate	2.00 (62)	0.00 (66)	7.00 (33)	7.00 (33)	5.00 (39)	5.00 (39)	5.00 (39)	5.00 (38)
(ii) Top marginal income and payroll tax rates			7.00 (33)	7.00 (33)	5.00 (40)	5.00 (40)	5.00 (40)	5.00 (40)
2. Legal Structure and Security of Property Rights	**8.04**	**7.88**	**8.35**	**9.17**	**9.10**	**9.00**	**8.98**	**8.80**
A. Judicial independence				9.47	9.19	8.90	9.56	9.60
B. Impartial courts				9.08	9.19	8.10	7.98	7.54
C. Protection of property rights				7.29	7.15	8.70	8.75	7.88
D. Military interference in rule of law and politics				10.00	10.00	10.00	10.00	10.00
E. Integrity of the legal system				10.00	10.00	9.70	9.17	9.17
F. Legal enforcement of contracts						7.50	7.48	7.48
G. Regulatory restrictions on sale of real property						9.90	9.93	9.93
3. Access to Sound Money	**6.31**	**6.17**	**8.64**	**9.75**	**9.54**	**9.60**	**9.61**	**9.70**
A. Money growth	9.11 (4.46)	8.84 (5.80)	7.25 (13.76)	9.58 (2.09)	9.19 (4.06)	9.70 (1.40)	9.73 (1.37)	9.76 (1.21)
B. Standard deviation of inflation	9.20 (2.00)	8.68 (3.29)	7.84 (5.39)	9.87 (0.33)	9.48 (1.29)	9.50 (1.33)	9.48 (1.30)	9.41 (1.48)
C. Inflation: most recent year	6.93 (15.36)	7.16 (14.19)	9.46 (2.70)	9.55 (2.27)	9.48 (2.62)	9.40 (3.04)	9.23 (3.85)	9.62 (1.89)
D. Freedom to own foreign currency bank accounts	0.00	0.00	10.00	10.00	10.00	10.00	10.00	10.00
4. Freedom to Trade Internationally	**7.44**	**7.20**	**7.87**	**8.09**	**8.51**	**7.80**	**7.91**	**7.71**
A. Taxes on international trade	7.87	7.73	6.56	7.74	9.01	8.90	9.04	9.09
(i) Revenues from trade taxes (% of trade sector)	8.33 (2.50)	8.67 (2.00)	8.87 (1.70)	9.07 (1.40)	9.47 (0.79)	9.30 (1.00)	8.77 (1.85)	8.77 (1.85)
(ii) Mean tariff rate	7.40 (13.00)	6.80 (16.00)	7.10 (14.50)	8.30 (8.50)	9.32 (3.40)	9.00 (5.00)	9.56 (2.20)	9.58 (2.10)
(iii) Standard deviation of tariff rates			3.72 (15.70)	5.84 (10.40)	8.24 (4.40)	8.30 (4.20)	8.80 (2.99)	8.92 (2.69)
B. Regulatory trade barriers				8.52	9.38	8.90	8.75	8.78
(i) Non-tariff trade barriers				8.52	9.09	9.00	8.74	8.80
(ii) Compliance cost of importing and exporting					9.67	8.80	8.76	8.76
C. Size of trade sector relative to expected	6.16	5.92	4.66	4.59	5.28	3.70	4.04	3.00
D. Black-market exchange rates	10.00	9.20	10.00	10.00	10.00	10.00	10.00	10.00
E. International capital market controls	5.00	5.00	10.00	9.59	8.89	7.80	7.71	7.68
(i) Foreign ownership / investment restrictions				9.18	9.32	7.80	7.92	7.87
(ii) Capital controls	5.00	5.00	10.00	10.00	8.46	7.70	7.50	7.50
5. Regulation of Credit, Labor, and Business	**5.68**	**5.78**	**6.59**	**8.76**	**7.89**	**8.90**	**8.76**	**8.71**
A. Credit market regulations	6.18	6.64	9.59	9.37	9.29	10.00	10.00	10.00
(i) Ownership of banks	5.00	5.00	10.00	10.00	10.00	10.00	10.00	10.00
(ii) Foreign bank competition				9.08	7.85	10.00	10.00	10.00
(iii) Private sector credit	7.54	6.91	8.77	9.58	9.49	10.00	10.00	10.00
(iv) Interest rate controls/negative real interest rates	6.00	8.00	10.00	10.00	10.00	10.00	10.00	10.00
B. Labor market regulations	6.58	6.50	6.78	7.46	5.92	8.50	8.48	8.51
(i) Hiring regulations and minimum wage				6.52	3.62	8.90	8.90	8.90
(ii) Hiring and firing regulations			7.62	7.62	3.07	4.50	4.14	4.59
(iii) Centralized collective bargaining	5.18	5.18	5.18	7.93	8.05	7.70	7.82	7.58
(iv) Hours regulations	4.57	4.31	4.31	5.25	4.84	10.00	10.00	10.00
(v) Mandated cost of worker dismissal						10.00	10.00	10.00
(vi) Conscription	10.00	10.00	10.00	10.00	10.00	10.00	10.00	10.00
C. Business regulations				9.44	8.47	8.20	7.79	7.61
(i) Price controls			9.00	10.00	10.00	9.00	9.00	9.00
(ii) Administrative requirements				7.47	4.10	4.54	4.75
(iii) Bureaucracy costs				9.35	7.80	6.10	2.40	2.31
(iv) Starting a business				8.47	7.85	9.60	9.96	9.96
(v) Extra payments/bribes/favoritism				9.94	9.23	9.60	9.62	9.58
(vi) Licensing restrictions						9.80	9.79	9.80
(vii) Cost of tax compliance						9.20	9.22	7.85

Nicaragua

	1980	1985	1990	1995	2000	2005	2008	2009
Chain-Linked	Rating (Rank)	Rating (Rank)	Rating (Rank)	Rating (Rank)	Rating (Rank)	Rating (Rank)	Rating (Rank)	Rating (Rank)
Summary Rating (Rank) ➤	4.17 (92)	2.11 (109)	2.96 (113)	5.38 (83)	6.50 (62)	6.82 (61)	6.83 (61)	6.76 (59)
Area 1. Size of Government	4.08 (80)	2.73 (105)	3.32 (104)	6.63 (37)	6.81 (42)	7.32 (29)	7.47 (26)	7.00 (34)
Area 2. Legal Structure and Security of Property Rights	2.31 (82)	2.32 (101)	3.57 (82)	4.00 (106)	4.07 (100)	4.81 (89)	5.20 (80)	5.13 (78)
Area 3. Access to Sound Money	5.78 (73)	0.10 (112)	0.10 (118)	5.20 (87)	8.66 (45)	8.85 (45)	8.03 (65)	8.71 (55)
Area 4. Freedom to Trade Internationally	2.90 (88)	2.15 (94)	5.04 (69)	5.82 (87)	7.04 (62)	6.44 (74)	6.73 (68)	6.55 (65)
Area 5. Regulation of Credit, Labor, and Business		3.13 (100)	2.41 (118)	5.16 (75)	5.92 (64)	6.86 (49)	6.90 (45)	6.62 (58)

Unadjusted

	1980	1985	1990	1995	2000	2005	2008	2009
Summary Rating (Rank) ➤	4.13 (92)	2.30 (110)	3.07 (111)	5.62 (77)	6.50 (62)	6.88 (65)	6.88 (67)	6.82 (69)
	Rating Data	Rating Data	Rating Data	Rating Data	Rating Data	Rating Data	Rating Data	Rating Data
1. Size of Government	5.03	3.36	3.43	6.63	6.81	7.30	7.47	7.00
A. Government consumption	6.09 (19.29)	0.00 (42.59)	0.00 (42.57)	8.03 (12.71)	6.72 (17.14)	8.50 (11.20)	5.99 (19.65)	6.17 (19.03)
B. Transfers and subsidies	9.02 (4.10)	8.45 (6.20)	8.28 (6.80)	8.50 (6.00)	8.53 (5.88)	7.80 (8.60)	9.90 (0.86)	9.82 (1.17)
C. Government enterprises and investment	0.00 (71.90)	0.00 (62.18)	2.00 (45.30)	4.00 (38.30)	6.00 (25.50)	7.00 (24.30)	8.00 (17.10)	6.00 (26.10)
D. Top marginal tax rate	5.00	5.00		6.00	6.00	6.00	6.00	6.00
(i) Top marginal income tax rate	5.00 (50)	5.00 (50)		8.00 (30)	8.00 (30)	8.00 (30)	8.00 (30)	8.00 (30)
(ii) Top marginal income and payroll tax rates				4.00 (41)	4.00 (44)	4.00 (44)	4.00 (45)	4.00 (45)
2. Legal Structure and Security of Property Rights	2.58	2.59	3.99	4.47	4.07	4.10	4.42	4.36
A. Judicial independence						0.80	1.96	1.81
B. Impartial courts				4.28	4.16	1.90	2.75	2.42
C. Protection of property rights					2.08	4.10	3.37	3.47
D. Military interference in rule of law and politics				5.45	3.33	3.90	5.00	5.00
E. Integrity of the legal system				4.11	6.67	6.70	6.67	6.67
F. Legal enforcement of contracts						4.80	4.77	4.77
G. Regulatory restrictions on sale of real property						6.50	6.41	6.37
3. Access to Sound Money	5.78	0.00	0.00	5.20	8.66	8.80	8.03	8.71
A. Money growth	5.91 (20.47)	0.00 (62.40)	0.00 (1589.23)	7.76 (11.22)	7.58 (12.11)	8.30 (8.30)	7.39 (13.07)	7.09 (14.55)
B. Standard deviation of inflation	4.56 (13.61)	0.00 (60.08)	0.00 (4792.48)	0.00 (1852.08)	9.26 (1.85)	9.00 (2.59)	8.68 (3.30)	8.47 (3.82)
C. Inflation: most recent year	2.68 (36.62)	0.00 (168.07)	0.00 (5012.69)	8.04 (9.79)	7.81 (10.94)	8.10 (9.60)	6.03 (19.83)	9.26 (3.69)
D. Freedom to own foreign currency bank accounts	10.00	0.00	0.00	5.00	10.00	10.00	10.00	10.00
4. Freedom to Trade Internationally	3.14	2.33	5.46	6.50	7.04	6.90	7.22	7.03
A. Taxes on international trade	2.10	2.53	6.09	7.88	8.77	8.30	8.45	8.44
(i) Revenues from trade taxes (% of trade sector)	4.20 (8.70)	5.07 (7.40)	7.13 (4.30)	6.07 (5.90)	8.84 (1.74)	9.20 (1.30)	9.41 (0.89)	9.46 (0.81)
(ii) Mean tariff rate	0.00 (54.00)	0.00 (54.00)	5.04 (24.80)	7.86 (10.70)	9.36 (3.20)	8.60 (6.80)	8.88 (5.60)	8.88 (5.60)
(iii) Standard deviation of tariff rates				9.72 (25.70)	8.12 (4.70)	7.10 (7.20)	7.06 (7.34)	6.98 (7.56)
B. Regulatory trade barriers					3.78	4.20	5.15	5.65
(i) Non-tariff trade barriers					3.78	3.70	4.38	4.95
(ii) Compliance cost of importing and exporting						4.80	5.92	6.36
C. Size of trade sector relative to expected	5.35	0.85	5.02	3.01	4.64	5.00	6.09	5.41
D. Black-market exchange rates	0.00	0.00	8.00	8.40	10.00	10.00	10.00	10.00
E. International capital market controls	0.00	0.00	0.00	5.00	7.99	7.00	6.41	5.62
(i) Foreign ownership / investment restrictions					8.30	6.40	5.89	5.85
(ii) Capital controls	0.00	0.00	0.00	5.00	7.69	7.70	6.92	5.38
5. Regulation of Credit, Labor, and Business		3.21	2.47	5.29	5.92	7.20	7.28	7.00
A. Credit market regulations	0.00	2.20	0.00	4.21	6.40	8.90	8.97	8.44
(i) Ownership of banks						10.00	10.00	10.00
(ii) Foreign bank competition					5.52	8.00	8.00	8.00
(iii) Private sector credit		4.40	0.00	2.42	5.60	8.80	8.87	7.75
(iv) Interest rate controls / negative real interest rates	0.00	0.00	0.00	6.00	9.00	9.00	9.00	8.00
B. Labor market regulations					6.60	7.20	7.00	6.77
(i) Hiring regulations and minimum wage					3.63	7.80	7.80	6.67
(ii) Hiring and firing regulations					6.12	5.70	5.49	5.40
(iii) Centralized collective bargaining					6.65	7.60	6.77	6.55
(iv) Hours regulations						4.00	4.00	4.00
(v) Mandated cost of worker dismissal						8.00	7.96	7.99
(vi) Conscription	5.00	0.00	0.00	10.00	10.00	10.00	10.00	10.00
C. Business regulations					4.75	5.50	5.86	5.80
(i) Price controls			0.00	4.00	4.00	6.00	6.00	6.00
(ii) Administrative requirements					6.03	3.20	3.86	3.94
(iii) Bureaucracy costs					5.18	4.60	6.44	6.01
(iv) Starting a business					4.10	7.40	7.58	7.51
(v) Extra payments / bribes / favoritism					4.45	4.80	3.78	3.68
(vi) Licensing restrictions						5.40	6.05	5.96
(vii) Cost of tax compliance						7.30	7.31	7.51

Niger

Chain-Linked	1980		1985		1990		1995		2000		2005		2008		2009	
	Rating	(Rank)	Rating	(Rank)	Rating	(Rank)	Rating	(Rank)	Rating	(Rank)	Rating	(Rank)	Rating	(Rank)	Rating	(Rank)
Summary Rating (Rank) ➤	4.69	(75)	5.06	(73)	5.06	(81)	4.43	(114)	5.42	(106)	5.40	(112)	5.35	(112)	5.47	(111)
Area 1. Size of Government	4.10	(78)	4.28	(77)	3.81	(97)	3.81	(107)	3.96	(109)	6.02	(81)	5.56	(93)	5.49	(87)
Area 2. Legal Structure and Security of Property Rights	4.67	(48)	4.78	(62)	5.30	(54)	3.02	(118)	4.38	(92)	4.11	(101)	4.18	(102)	4.24	(100)
Area 3. Access to Sound Money	4.90	(95)	6.53	(62)	7.08	(40)	5.71	(79)	8.25	(52)	6.47	(104)	6.20	(106)	6.50	(109)
Area 4. Freedom to Trade Internationally									5.93	(96)	5.13	(112)	5.52	(104)	5.68	(97)
Area 5. Regulation of Credit, Labor, and Business			4.30	(84)	4.32	(93)	4.76	(96)	4.59	(109)	5.25	(109)	5.42	(109)	5.61	(106)

Unadjusted

	1980		1985		1990		1995		2000		2005		2008		2009	
Summary Rating (Rank) ➤	5.20	(61)	5.06	(74)	5.08	(75)	4.45	(113)	5.42	(106)	5.38	(130)	5.33	(129)	5.44	(130)
	Rating	Data	Rating	Data	Rating	Data	Rating	Data	Rating	Data	Rating	Data	Rating	Data	Rating	Data
1. Size of Government	5.88		4.28		3.81		3.81		3.96		7.30		6.78		6.69	
A. Government consumption	8.19	(12.15)	8.56	(10.90)	7.63	(14.06)	7.62	(14.10)	7.91	(13.10)	8.00	(12.70)	6.51	(17.87)	6.24	(18.77)
B. Transfers and subsidies	9.46	(2.50)									10.00	(0.40)	9.84	(1.09)	9.84	(1.09)
C. Government enterprises and investment	0.00	(79.90)	0.00	(79.90)	0.00	(64.80)	0.00	(74.30)	0.00	(58.50)	4.00	(33.80)	4.00	(33.80)	4.00	(33.80)
D. Top marginal tax rate																
(i) Top marginal income tax rate																
(ii) Top marginal income and payroll tax rates																
2. Legal Structure and Security of Property Rights	4.67		4.78		5.30		3.02		4.38		4.10		4.18		4.24	
A. Judicial independence																
B. Impartial courts							3.54		3.49		4.10		4.10		4.40	
C. Protection of property rights																
D. Military interference in rule of law and politics							4.28		6.67		5.00		5.00		5.00	
E. Integrity of the legal system							0.00		3.33		3.30		3.33		3.33	
F. Legal enforcement of contracts											2.70		2.74		2.74	
G. Regulatory restrictions on sale of real property											5.40		5.72		5.72	
3. Access to Sound Money	4.90		6.53		7.08		5.71		8.25		6.50		6.20		6.50	
A. Money growth	5.92	(20.42)	9.92	(0.40)	9.78	(−1.10)	9.28	(3.62)	9.04	(−4.78)	9.00	(−5.10)	8.79	(6.05)	8.15	(9.26)
B. Standard deviation of inflation	7.86	(5.35)	7.36	(6.60)	8.86	(2.85)	4.64	(13.40)	9.54	(1.14)	8.50	(3.85)	8.27	(4.32)	8.73	(3.19)
C. Inflation: most recent year	5.84	(20.82)	8.82	(−5.90)	9.68	(−1.60)	8.92	(5.38)	9.42	(2.90)	8.40	(7.80)	7.74	(11.31)	9.14	(4.31)
D. Freedom to own foreign currency bank accounts	0.00		0.00		0.00		0.00		5.00		0.00		0.00		0.00	
4. Freedom to Trade Internationally	5.92		5.53		4.89		4.96		5.93		4.10		4.36		4.49	
A. Taxes on international trade	4.40		3.67		3.47		2.80		7.60		5.20		6.24		6.24	
(i) Revenues from trade taxes (% of trade sector)	4.40	(8.40)	3.67	(9.50)	3.47	(9.80)	2.80	(10.80)			0.90	(13.70)	3.82	(9.27)	3.82	(9.27)
(ii) Mean tariff rate									7.60	(12.00)	7.50	(12.70)	7.62	(11.90)	7.62	(11.90)
(iii) Standard deviation of tariff rates											7.30	(6.80)	7.29	(6.78)	7.29	(6.78)
B. Regulatory trade barriers											1.20		1.22		1.22	
(i) Non-tariff trade barriers																
(ii) Compliance cost of importing and exporting											1.20		1.22		1.22	
C. Size of trade sector relative to expected	7.42		5.97		3.57		3.96		3.85		3.80		4.35		4.98	
D. Black-market exchange rates	9.60		9.80		9.20		9.80		10.00		10.00		10.00		10.00	
E. International capital market controls	0.00		0.00		0.00		0.00		0.00		0.00		0.00		0.00	
(i) Foreign ownership / investment restrictions																
(ii) Capital controls	0.00		0.00		0.00		0.00		0.00		0.00		0.00		0.00	
5. Regulation of Credit, Labor, and Business	4.64		4.19		4.32		4.76		4.59		4.90		5.15		5.29	
A. Credit market regulations	4.30		5.12		6.13		6.24		5.67		7.70		7.70		7.70	
(i) Ownership of banks	2.00		2.00		2.00		5.00		5.00		10.00		10.00		10.00	
(ii) Foreign bank competition																
(iii) Private sector credit	8.91		8.24		8.38		7.73		8.01		9.10		9.09		9.09	
(iv) Interest rate controls / negative real interest rates	2.00				8.00		6.00		4.00		4.00		4.00		4.00	
B. Labor market regulations											3.10		2.86		3.30	
(i) Hiring regulations and minimum wage											1.10		0.00		0.00	
(ii) Hiring and firing regulations																
(iii) Centralized collective bargaining																
(iv) Hours regulations											4.70		4.70		6.00	
(v) Mandated cost of worker dismissal											6.80		6.76		7.19	
(vi) Conscription			0.00		0.00		0.00		0.00		0.00		0.00		0.00	
C. Business regulations											4.00		4.88		4.88	
(i) Price controls					0.00		4.00		4.00		4.00		4.00		4.00	
(ii) Administrative requirements																
(iii) Bureaucracy costs																
(iv) Starting a business											3.30		6.20		6.20	
(v) Extra payments / bribes / favoritism																
(vi) Licensing restrictions											1.60		2.33		2.34	
(vii) Cost of tax compliance											7.00		6.97		6.97	

Nigeria

	1980	1985	1990	1995	2000	2005	2008	2009
Chain-Linked	Rating (Rank)	Rating (Rank)	Rating (Rank)	Rating (Rank)	Rating (Rank)	Rating (Rank)	Rating (Rank)	Rating (Rank)
Summary Rating (Rank) ➤	**3.76** (96)	**4.04** (96)	**3.73** (107)	**4.20** (117)	**5.52** (103)	**6.01** (94)	**5.96** (96)	**5.84** (104)
Area 1. Size of Government	2.19 (103)	4.07 (83)	2.49 (111)	6.26 (54)	6.19 (58)	6.72 (56)	6.06 (77)	6.27 (62)
Area 2. Legal Structure and Security of Property Rights	2.86 (72)	2.30 (103)	2.74 (98)	4.23 (105)	3.74 (107)	4.06 (102)	4.49 (94)	4.18 (104)
Area 3. Access to Sound Money	5.91 (70)	6.32 (72)	4.14 (100)	1.27 (116)	5.37 (112)	6.41 (105)	6.04 (112)	6.16 (113)
Area 4. Freedom to Trade Internationally	2.96 (87)	2.53 (92)	4.32 (86)	3.95 (108)	5.94 (94)	6.21 (86)	6.32 (83)	5.71 (95)
Area 5. Regulation of Credit, Labor, and Business	5.32 (48)	5.69 (45)	4.95 (74)	5.28 (71)	6.36 (46)	6.72 (54)	6.99 (41)	6.99 (43)

Unadjusted								
Summary Rating (Rank) ➤	**3.98** (97)	**4.56** (90)	**3.90** (105)	**4.30** (116)	**5.52** (103)	**6.14** (102)	**6.24** (99)	**6.12** (107)
	Rating Data	Rating Data	Rating Data	Rating Data	Rating Data	Rating Data	Rating Data	Rating Data
1. Size of Government	**2.19**	**5.50**	**2.49**	**6.26**	**6.19**	**6.70**	**6.82**	**7.05**
A. Government consumption	6.58 (17.64)	7.21 (15.49)	5.48 (21.37)	7.78 (13.56)	7.56 (14.28)	9.10 (8.90)	8.66 (10.57)	9.59 (7.41)
B. Transfers and subsidies		9.78 (1.30)					9.62 (1.91)	9.62 (1.91)
C. Government enterprises and investment	0.00 (50.90)	2.00 (49.80)	0.00 (88.10)	4.00 (32.14)	2.00 (47.28)	2.00 (45.30)	2.00 (46.82)	2.00 (46.82)
D. Top marginal tax rate	0.00	3.00	2.00	7.00	9.00	9.00	7.00	7.00
(i) Top marginal income tax rate	0.00 (70)	3.00 (55)	2.00 (55)	7.00 (35)	9.00 (25)	9.00 (25)	9.00 (25)	9.00 (25)
(ii) Top marginal income and payroll tax rates					9.00 (25)	9.00 (25)	5.00 (37)	5.00 (37)
2. Legal Structure and Security of Property Rights	**3.06**	**2.46**	**2.93**	**4.53**	**3.74**	**3.80**	**4.20**	**3.92**
A. Judicial independence						3.60	5.13	4.14
B. Impartial courts				3.62	3.56	3.70	4.29	4.20
C. Protection of property rights					2.52	4.70	4.82	3.88
D. Military interference in rule of law and politics				3.51	3.33	3.30	3.33	3.33
E. Integrity of the legal system				6.96	5.00	2.80	3.33	3.33
F. Legal enforcement of contracts						5.10	5.08	5.08
G. Regulatory restrictions on sale of real property						3.50	3.45	3.45
3. Access to Sound Money	**5.91**	**6.32**	**4.14**	**1.27**	**5.37**	**6.40**	**6.04**	**6.16**
A. Money growth	6.70 (16.51)	8.64 (6.79)	6.06 (19.72)	4.00 (29.98)	5.93 (20.35)	7.70 (11.30)	4.96 (25.18)	5.96 (20.19)
B. Standard deviation of inflation	9.44 (1.39)	7.39 (6.52)	1.93 (20.18)	1.06 (22.35)	1.95 (20.12)	6.50 (8.86)	6.50 (8.75)	6.00 (10.01)
C. Inflation: most recent year	7.52 (12.42)	9.26 (3.69)	8.57 (7.16)	0.00 (55.83)	8.61 (6.93)	6.40 (17.86)	7.68 (11.58)	7.69 (11.54)
D. Freedom to own foreign currency bank accounts	0.00	0.00	0.00	0.00	5.00	5.00	5.00	5.00
4. Freedom to Trade Internationally	**3.93**	**3.37**	**5.39**	**4.58**	**5.94**	**6.80**	**6.95**	**6.27**
A. Taxes on international trade	3.91	4.60	3.49	4.68	3.76	7.00	6.95	7.22
(i) Revenues from trade taxes (% of trade sector)	4.33 (8.50)	6.60 (5.10)	7.33 (4.00)					
(ii) Mean tariff rate	3.48 (32.60)	2.60 (37.00)	3.14 (34.30)	5.64 (21.80)		7.70 (11.60)	7.60 (12.00)	7.76 (11.20)
(iii) Standard deviation of tariff rates			0.00 (30.80)	3.72 (15.70)	3.76 (15.60)	6.40 (9.00)	6.30 (9.24)	6.68 (8.29)
B. Regulatory trade barriers					3.20	4.80	5.27	5.04
(i) Non-tariff trade barriers					3.20	4.50	5.03	4.36
(ii) Compliance cost of importing and exporting						5.10	5.51	5.72
C. Size of trade sector relative to expected	7.51	3.97	9.85	10.00	10.00	8.30	7.15	6.80
D. Black-market exchange rates	0.00	0.00	5.40	0.00	5.68	7.90	10.00	7.06
E. International capital market controls	0.00	0.00	0.00	0.00	7.04	6.20	5.36	5.24
(i) Foreign ownership/investment restrictions					8.69	6.90	5.72	5.48
(ii) Capital controls	0.00	0.00	0.00	0.00	5.38	5.40	5.00	5.00
5. Regulation of Credit, Labor, and Business	**4.82**	**5.16**	**4.56**	**4.86**	**6.36**	**7.00**	**7.21**	**7.21**
A. Credit market regulations	2.00	3.00	3.56	4.57	6.67	8.70	8.97	8.95
(i) Ownership of banks	2.00	2.00	2.00	5.00	5.00	10.00	10.00	10.00
(ii) Foreign bank competition					7.57	8.00	7.57	7.57
(iii) Private sector credit			8.69	8.71	6.60	7.40	8.31	8.23
(iv) Interest rate controls/negative real interest rates	2.00	4.00	0.00	0.00	8.00	10.00	10.00	10.00
B. Labor market regulations					7.22	8.10	8.33	8.35
(i) Hiring regulations and minimum wage					4.79	10.00	10.00	10.00
(ii) Hiring and firing regulations					7.15	6.60	7.26	6.95
(iii) Centralized collective bargaining					6.93	6.70	7.36	7.40
(iv) Hours regulations						10.00	10.00	10.00
(v) Mandated cost of worker dismissal						5.40	5.36	5.76
(vi) Conscription	10.00	10.00	10.00	10.00	10.00	10.00	10.00	10.00
C. Business regulations					5.20	4.00	4.34	4.33
(i) Price controls			0.00	0.00	4.00	6.00	6.00	6.00
(ii) Administrative requirements					7.83	3.70	3.55	3.44
(iii) Bureaucracy costs					6.03	3.20	4.87	5.32
(iv) Starting a business					5.12	8.10	8.20	8.18
(v) Extra payments/bribes/favoritism					3.03	3.90	3.57	3.24
(vi) Licensing restrictions						3.20	4.17	4.13
(vii) Cost of tax compliance						0.00	0.00	0.00

Norway

	1980	1985	1990	1995	2000	2005	2008	2009
Chain-Linked	Rating (Rank)	Rating (Rank)	Rating (Rank)	Rating (Rank)	Rating (Rank)	Rating (Rank)	Rating (Rank)	Rating (Rank)
Summary Rating (Rank) ➤	**6.17** (27)	**6.70** (21)	**7.26** (19)	**7.34** (18)	**7.04** (38)	**7.47** (21)	**7.36** (30)	**7.24** (32)
Area 1. Size of Government	2.87 (98)	3.25 (97)	2.94 (108)	3.17 (112)	3.25 (116)	5.69 (91)	5.55 (94)	4.92 (100)
Area 2. Legal Structure and Security of Property Rights	8.34 (18)	9.60 (5)	9.88 (2)	9.19 (2)	8.85 (15)	9.03 (1)	8.80 (3)	8.79 (3)
Area 3. Access to Sound Money	6.43 (43)	6.45 (67)	8.73 (24)	9.47 (23)	9.03 (38)	9.20 (38)	9.30 (29)	9.24 (38)
Area 4. Freedom to Trade Internationally	7.21 (21)	7.86 (10)	8.35 (6)	8.10 (16)	7.58 (40)	6.55 (69)	6.54 (72)	6.49 (71)
Area 5. Regulation of Credit, Labor, and Business	6.22 (25)	6.62 (17)	6.53 (22)	6.79 (19)	6.50 (41)	6.90 (47)	6.65 (57)	6.78 (52)

Unadjusted								
Summary Rating (Rank) ➤	**5.69** (45)	**6.17** (28)	**6.69** (26)	**7.35** (19)	**7.04** (38)	**7.53** (22)	**7.42** (30)	**7.30** (35)
	Rating *Data*	Rating *Data*	Rating *Data*	Rating *Data*	Rating *Data*	Rating *Data*	Rating *Data*	Rating *Data*
1. Size of Government	**2.87**	**3.25**	**2.94**	**3.17**	**3.25**	**5.70**	**5.55**	**4.92**
A. Government consumption	3.36 *(28.57)*	3.69 *(27.46)*	3.06 *(29.59)*	3.00 *(29.79)*	2.76 *(30.62)*	2.10 *(32.80)*	2.03 *(33.09)*	1.64 *(34.43)*
B. Transfers and subsidies	4.11 *(22.10)*	4.31 *(21.40)*	2.70 *(27.30)*	4.20 *(21.80)*	4.76 *(19.72)*	5.10 *(18.40)*	5.67 *(16.40)*	5.55 *(16.84)*
C. Government enterprises and investment	4.00 *(35.90)*	4.00 *(34.20)*	4.00 *(37.40)*	2.00 *(43.10)*	2.00 *(43.10)*	10.00 *(14.50)*	10.00 *(14.22)*	8.00 *(16.48)*
D. Top marginal tax rate	0.00	1.00	2.00	3.50	3.50	5.50	4.50	4.50
(i) Top marginal income tax rate	0.00 *(75)*	1.00 *(64)*	3.00 *(51)*	5.00 *(42)*	5.00 *(48)*	7.00 *(40)*	6.00 *(40)*	6.00 *(40)*
(ii) Top marginal income and payroll tax rates			1.00 *(64)*	2.00 *(56)*	2.00 *(64)*	4.00 *(54)*	3.00 *(54)*	3.00 *(54)*
2. Legal Structure and Security of Property Rights	**7.05**	**8.11**	**8.35**	**9.19**	**8.85**	**9.00**	**8.80**	**8.79**
A. Judicial independence				9.45	8.35	8.90	8.61	8.71
B. Impartial courts				8.88	8.68	8.80	7.37	7.51
C. Protection of property rights				7.61	7.20	8.80	8.78	8.44
D. Military interference in rule of law and politics				10.00	10.00	10.00	10.00	10.00
E. Integrity of the legal system				10.00	10.00	10.00	10.00	10.00
F. Legal enforcement of contracts						7.50	7.75	7.75
G. Regulatory restrictions on sale of real property						9.20	9.12	9.12
3. Access to Sound Money	**6.43**	**6.45**	**8.73**	**9.47**	**9.03**	**9.20**	**9.30**	**9.24**
A. Money growth	9.41 *(2.93)*	7.97 *(10.15)*	6.77 *(16.13)*	9.06 *(4.69)*	9.17 *(4.17)*	8.60 *(6.80)*	9.20 *(3.98)*	9.67 *(1.64)*
B. Standard deviation of inflation	8.95 *(2.63)*	8.86 *(2.84)*	8.91 *(2.72)*	9.43 *(1.43)*	7.55 *(6.11)*	8.50 *(3.87)*	8.74 *(3.16)*	7.70 *(5.74)*
C. Inflation: most recent year	7.38 *(13.12)*	8.96 *(5.21)*	9.23 *(3.87)*	9.38 *(3.09)*	9.38 *(3.09)*	9.70 *(1.52)*	9.25 *(3.77)*	9.57 *(2.17)*
D. Freedom to own foreign currency bank accounts	0.00	0.00	10.00	10.00	10.00	10.00	10.00	10.00
4. Freedom to Trade Internationally	**6.94**	**7.57**	**7.90**	**7.99**	**7.58**	**6.60**	**6.54**	**6.49**
A. Taxes on international trade	9.28	9.33	8.63	8.09	7.55	6.10	6.09	6.23
(i) Revenues from trade taxes (% of trade sector)	9.80 *(0.30)*	9.80 *(0.30)*	9.80 *(0.30)*	9.73 *(0.40)*	9.88 *(0.17)*	9.90 *(0.10)*	9.92 *(0.13)*	9.90 *(0.15)*
(ii) Mean tariff rate	8.76 *(6.20)*	8.86 *(5.70)*	8.86 *(5.70)*	8.82 *(5.90)*	9.42 *(2.90)*	8.30 *(8.60)*	8.36 *(8.20)*	8.78 *(6.10)*
(iii) Standard deviation of tariff rates			7.24 *(6.90)*	5.72 *(10.70)*	3.36 *(16.60)*	0.00 *(37.40)*	0.00 *(36.16)*	0.00 *(27.51)*
B. Regulatory trade barriers				9.17	8.32	7.00	7.12	7.23
(i) Non-tariff trade barriers				9.17	7.80	4.90	5.10	5.33
(ii) Compliance cost of importing and exporting					8.83	9.10	9.14	9.14
C. Size of trade sector relative to expected	5.85	5.34	4.72	4.05	4.17	3.30	3.35	2.65
D. Black-market exchange rates	9.40	10.00	10.00	10.00	10.00	10.00	10.00	10.00
E. International capital market controls	2.00	5.00	8.00	8.64	7.84	6.40	6.15	6.33
(i) Foreign ownership / investment restrictions				9.28	8.76	7.40	6.91	7.28
(ii) Capital controls	2.00	5.00	8.00	8.00	6.92	5.40	5.38	5.38
5. Regulation of Credit, Labor, and Business	**5.17**	**5.50**	**5.53**	**6.93**	**6.50**	**7.20**	**6.92**	**7.06**
A. Credit market regulations	7.19	8.80	8.51	8.61	8.06	9.30	9.25	9.50
(i) Ownership of banks	10.00	10.00	8.00	8.00	10.00	10.00	10.00	10.00
(ii) Foreign bank competition				8.33	6.23	8.00	8.00	8.00
(iii) Private sector credit	5.56	6.39	7.53	8.12	10.00	10.00	10.00	10.00
(iv) Interest rate controls / negative real interest rates	6.00	10.00	10.00	10.00	7.00	9.00	9.00	10.00
B. Labor market regulations	3.52	3.23	3.64	4.33	3.79	4.90	4.93	5.07
(i) Hiring regulations and minimum wage				4.45	5.00	3.90	3.90	3.90
(ii) Hiring and firing regulations			4.88	4.88	2.05	2.80	3.21	3.21
(iii) Centralized collective bargaining	5.18	5.18	5.18	5.18	4.03	4.60	4.65	4.29
(iv) Hours regulations	4.40	3.52	3.52	4.17	4.84	6.00	6.00	6.00
(v) Mandated cost of worker dismissal						8.80	8.79	10.00
(vi) Conscription	1.00	1.00	1.00	3.00	3.00	3.00	3.00	3.00
C. Business regulations				7.83	7.67	7.50	6.60	6.62
(i) Price controls			6.00	7.00	8.00	6.00	6.00	6.00
(ii) Administrative requirements					6.08	4.70	4.14	4.01
(iii) Bureaucracy costs				8.11	8.70	7.10	1.61	1.80
(iv) Starting a business				7.22	6.83	9.70	9.69	9.69
(v) Extra payments / bribes / favoritism				9.01	8.73	9.30	8.97	9.06
(vi) Licensing restrictions						6.70	6.73	6.73
(vii) Cost of tax compliance						9.00	9.02	9.02

Oman

Chain-Linked

	1980		1985		1990		1995		2000		2005		2008		2009	
	Rating	(Rank)	Rating	(Rank)	Rating	(Rank)	Rating	(Rank)	Rating	(Rank)	Rating	(Rank)	Rating	(Rank)	Rating	(Rank)
Summary Rating (Rank) ➤			**6.70**	(21)	**6.23**	(37)	**6.73**	(37)	**7.03**	(39)	**7.33**	(31)	**7.40**	(25)	**7.64**	(9)
Area 1. Size of Government	4.90	(58)	4.82	(62)	4.84	(78)	5.24	(85)	5.31	(84)	4.94	(103)	5.57	(92)	5.58	(82)
Area 2. Legal Structure and Security of Property Rights			5.85	(40)	5.21	(57)	6.71	(34)	6.93	(32)	7.46	(24)	7.72	(19)	7.71	(19)
Area 3. Access to Sound Money	5.40	(84)	9.45	(7)	7.67	(36)	9.15	(30)	8.31	(50)	8.68	(55)	7.88	(68)	8.87	(51)
Area 4. Freedom to Trade Internationally			6.81	(28)	6.74	(32)	6.77	(54)	7.86	(31)	7.47	(28)	7.85	(17)	7.62	(19)
Area 5. Regulation of Credit, Labor, and Business	6.71	(12)	6.60	(19)	6.69	(16)	5.80	(54)	6.75	(32)	8.07	(14)	8.01	(13)	8.39	(7)

Unadjusted

	1980		1985		1990		1995		2000		2005		2008		2009	
Summary Rating (Rank) ➤			**6.87**	(15)	**6.27**	(35)	**6.73**	(39)	**7.03**	(39)	**7.30**	(39)	**7.12**	(49)	**7.34**	(28)
	Rating	Data	Rating	Data	Rating	Data	Rating	Data	Rating	Data	Rating	Data	Rating	Data	Rating	Data
1. Size of Government	**4.90**		**4.82**		**4.84**		**5.24**		**5.31**		**4.90**		**5.57**		**5.58**	
A. Government consumption	0.00	(47.45)	0.00	(45.46)	0.00	(58.84)	1.18	(36.00)	1.65	(34.40)	0.30	(38.80)	2.86	(30.27)	2.91	(30.10)
B. Transfers and subsidies	9.59	(2.00)	9.29	(3.10)	9.35	(2.90)	9.78	(1.30)	9.61	(1.92)	9.40	(2.70)	9.40	(2.69)	9.40	(2.69)
C. Government enterprises and investment	0.00	(58.80)	0.00	(58.80)	0.00	(59.19)	0.00	(65.23)	0.00	(62.99)	0.00	(65.30)	0.00		0.00	
D. Top marginal tax rate	10.00		10.00		10.00		10.00		10.00		10.00		10.00		10.00	
(i) Top marginal income tax rate	10.00	(0)	10.00	(0)	10.00	(0)	10.00	(0)	10.00	(0)	10.00	(0)	10.00	(0)	10.00	(0)
(ii) Top marginal income and payroll tax rates					10.00	(0)	10.00	(0)	10.00	(0)	10.00	(0)	10.00	(0)	10.00	(0)
2. Legal Structure and Security of Property Rights			**5.85**		**5.21**		**6.71**		**6.93**		**7.50**		**7.36**		**7.35**	
A. Judicial independence													7.02		6.84	
B. Impartial courts							7.47		7.43		6.80		6.29		6.60	
C. Protection of property rights													7.69		7.52	
D. Military interference in rule of law and politics							8.74		8.33		8.30		8.33		8.33	
E. Integrity of the legal system							6.96		8.33		8.30		8.33		8.33	
F. Legal enforcement of contracts											5.10		5.14		5.14	
G. Regulatory restrictions on sale of real property											8.70		8.71		8.71	
3. Access to Sound Money	**5.40**		**9.45**		**7.67**		**9.15**		**8.31**		**8.70**		**7.88**		**8.87**	
A. Money growth	9.35	(3.25)	9.80	(0.98)	9.47	(−2.67)	9.76	(−1.20)	9.62	(−1.92)	8.80	(6.20)	7.71	(11.43)	7.88	(10.60)
B. Standard deviation of inflation	2.24	(19.39)	8.09	(4.78)	4.54	(13.65)	7.56	(6.11)	3.88	(15.31)	6.30	(9.19)	6.21	(9.48)	8.39	(4.02)
C. Inflation: most recent year	0.00	(51.11)	9.90	(−0.51)	6.68	(16.62)	9.26	(3.68)	9.75	(−1.27)	9.60	(1.86)	7.58	(12.09)	9.21	(3.94)
D. Freedom to own foreign currency bank accounts	10.00		10.00		10.00		10.00		10.00		10.00		10.00		10.00	
4. Freedom to Trade Internationally			**7.07**		**6.96**		**6.77**		**7.86**		**7.30**		**7.38**		**7.16**	
A. Taxes on international trade			9.23		9.33		8.15		9.38		7.70		7.80		7.92	
(i) Revenues from trade taxes (% of trade sector)			9.07	(1.40)	9.33	(1.00)	9.27	(1.10)	9.55	(0.67)	9.50	(0.80)	9.45	(0.82)	9.45	(0.82)
(ii) Mean tariff rate			9.40	(3.00)			8.86	(5.70)	9.06	(4.70)	9.20	(3.80)	8.86	(5.70)	8.86	(5.70)
(iii) Standard deviation of tariff rates							6.32	(9.20)	9.52	(1.20)	4.40	(14.00)	5.10	(12.26)	5.44	(11.40)
B. Regulatory trade barriers											6.70		7.00		7.43	
(i) Non-tariff trade barriers													7.31		6.94	
(ii) Compliance cost of importing and exporting											6.70		6.70		7.93	
C. Size of trade sector relative to expected	7.23		5.93		5.28		5.52		5.09		5.20		5.39		4.36	
D. Black-market exchange rates	10.00		10.00		10.00		10.00		10.00		10.00		10.00		10.00	
E. International capital market controls	2.00		2.00		2.00		2.00		6.67		6.70		6.69		6.09	
(i) Foreign ownership / investment restrictions													6.72		6.35	
(ii) Capital controls	2.00		2.00		2.00		2.00		6.67		6.70		6.67		5.83	
5. Regulation of Credit, Labor, and Business	**7.14**		**7.14**		**6.69**		**5.80**		**6.75**		**8.20**		**7.44**		**7.74**	
A. Credit market regulations	8.89		9.04		9.28		6.36		9.49		8.70		7.44		7.44	
(i) Ownership of banks	8.00		8.00		8.00		8.00		10.00		10.00		10.00		10.00	
(ii) Foreign bank competition											6.00		6.00		6.00	
(iii) Private sector credit	9.79		9.12		9.85		1.09		8.47		8.80		8.76		8.76	
(iv) Interest rate controls / negative real interest rates			10.00		10.00		10.00		10.00		10.00		5.00		5.00	
B. Labor market regulations											8.90		8.12		8.85	
(i) Hiring regulations and minimum wage											10.00		10.00		10.00	
(ii) Hiring and firing regulations													5.41		5.62	
(iii) Centralized collective bargaining													7.70		7.47	
(iv) Hours regulations											6.00		6.00		10.00	
(v) Mandated cost of worker dismissal											9.60		9.63		10.00	
(vi) Conscription	10.00		10.00		10.00		10.00		10.00		10.00		10.00		10.00	
C. Business regulations											6.90		6.75		6.93	
(i) Price controls					4.00		4.00		4.00		6.00		6.00		6.00	
(ii) Administrative requirements													5.93		5.57	
(iii) Bureaucracy costs													3.35		3.32	
(iv) Starting a business											7.00		8.70		8.64	
(v) Extra payments / bribes / favoritism													7.80		7.96	
(vi) Licensing restrictions											5.40		6.20		7.69	
(vii) Cost of tax compliance											9.40		9.31		9.31	

Pakistan

	1980		1985		1990		1995		2000		2005		2008		2009	
Chain-Linked	Rating	(Rank)	Rating	(Rank)	Rating	(Rank)	Rating	(Rank)	Rating	(Rank)	Rating	(Rank)	Rating	(Rank)	Rating	(Rank)
Summary Rating (Rank) ➤	**4.65**	(76)	**5.09**	(69)	**5.13**	(75)	**5.73**	(74)	**5.55**	(102)	**5.90**	(99)	**5.83**	(103)	**6.00**	(97)
Area 1. Size of Government	5.03	(53)	4.73	(64)	5.14	(71)	5.84	(67)	7.19	(26)	7.26	(31)	7.65	(23)	7.99	(13)
Area 2. Legal Structure and Security of Property Rights	2.54	(76)	3.52	(82)	2.68	(101)	4.93	(80)	4.63	(82)	4.48	(93)	4.58	(92)	4.59	(89)
Area 3. Access to Sound Money	6.39	(45)	6.78	(46)	7.87	(34)	7.60	(46)	6.15	(105)	6.04	(110)	5.67	(118)	5.98	(116)
Area 4. Freedom to Trade Internationally	4.09	(71)	4.85	(64)	4.51	(82)	5.05	(102)	4.08	(120)	5.62	(103)	5.29	(106)	5.36	(108)
Area 5. Regulation of Credit, Labor, and Business	5.17	(56)	5.54	(49)	5.41	(55)	5.24	(72)	5.69	(77)	6.25	(69)	6.12	(88)	6.26	(85)

Unadjusted																
Summary Rating (Rank) ➤	**4.68**	(79)	**5.12**	(71)	**5.16**	(73)	**5.73**	(74)	**5.55**	(102)	**5.93**	(111)	**5.86**	(118)	**6.03**	(114)
	Rating	Data	Rating	Data	Rating	Data	Rating	Data	Rating	Data	Rating	Data	Rating	Data	Rating	Data
1. Size of Government	**5.03**		**4.73**		**5.14**		**5.84**		**7.19**		**7.30**		**7.65**		**7.99**	
A. Government consumption	8.60	(10.77)	7.97	(12.91)	6.62	(17.49)	7.70	(13.81)	7.91	(13.12)	9.10	(9.00)	7.86	(13.28)	8.78	(10.15)
B. Transfers and subsidies	9.54	(2.20)	9.95	(0.70)	8.94	(4.40)	9.66	(1.75)	9.85	(1.05)	8.90	(4.40)	8.75	(5.07)	9.18	(3.51)
C. Government enterprises and investment	0.00	(65.30)	0.00	(53.90)	2.00	(49.40)	2.00	(46.80)	4.00	(35.29)	4.00	(30.90)	4.00	(30.89)	4.00	(30.89)
D. Top marginal tax rate	2.00		1.00		3.00		4.00		7.00		7.00		10.00		10.00	
(i) Top marginal income tax rate	2.00	(55)	1.00	(60)	3.00	(50)	4.00	(45)	7.00	(35)	7.00	(35)	10.00	(20)	10.00	(20)
(ii) Top marginal income and payroll tax rates					3.00	(50)	4.00	(45)	7.00	(35)	7.00	(35)	10.00	(20)	10.00	(20)
2. Legal Structure and Security of Property Rights	**2.54**		**3.52**		**2.68**		**4.93**		**4.63**		**3.90**		**4.04**		**4.04**	
A. Judicial independence											3.80		3.52		4.26	
B. Impartial courts							4.21		4.26		3.40		3.21		3.51	
C. Protection of property rights											4.50		4.63		4.28	
D. Military interference in rule of law and politics							4.57		5.28		0.40		1.67		1.67	
E. Integrity of the legal system							6.96		5.00		5.00		5.00		5.00	
F. Legal enforcement of contracts											3.60		3.55		3.55	
G. Regulatory restrictions on sale of real property											7.00		6.69		6.03	
3. Access to Sound Money	**6.39**		**6.78**		**7.87**		**7.60**		**6.15**		**6.00**		**5.67**		**5.98**	
A. Money growth	8.05	(9.75)	8.94	(5.28)	8.72	(6.40)	8.97	(5.17)	8.55	(7.27)	6.90	(15.40)	8.24	(8.82)	8.94	(5.29)
B. Standard deviation of inflation	9.33	(1.67)	9.06	(2.34)	9.05	(2.38)	9.21	(1.97)	6.91	(7.73)	9.00	(2.38)	8.49	(3.78)	7.71	(5.72)
C. Inflation: most recent year	8.19	(9.06)	9.09	(4.53)	8.71	(6.45)	7.24	(13.79)	9.13	(4.37)	8.20	(9.06)	5.94	(20.29)	7.27	(13.65)
D. Freedom to own foreign currency bank accounts	0.00		0.00		5.00		5.00		0.00		0.00		0.00		0.00	
4. Freedom to Trade Internationally	**4.09**		**4.85**		**4.51**		**5.05**		**4.08**		**6.00**		**5.66**		**5.73**	
A. Taxes on international trade	0.00		0.10		0.00		1.27		2.79		6.40		6.43		6.77	
(i) Revenues from trade taxes (% of trade sector)	0.00	(15.30)	0.20	(14.70)	0.00	(15.21)	2.58	(11.13)	6.18	(5.73)	6.60	(5.10)	6.37	(5.44)	7.72	(3.43)
(ii) Mean tariff rate	0.00	(77.60)	0.00	(78.00)	0.00	(58.80)	0.00	(61.10)	0.68	(46.60)	7.10	(14.60)	7.30	(13.50)	7.22	(13.90)
(iii) Standard deviation of tariff rates					0.00	(34.00)	1.24	(21.90)	1.52	(21.20)	5.60	(11.00)	5.62	(10.94)	5.39	(11.54)
B. Regulatory trade barriers											6.30		6.12		6.22	
(i) Non-tariff trade barriers											5.60		5.05		5.15	
(ii) Compliance cost of importing and exporting											7.10		7.20		7.28	
C. Size of trade sector relative to expected	5.62		4.73		5.14		4.36		3.62		4.60		3.33		2.65	
D. Black-market exchange rates	4.60		9.20		7.20		9.40		5.00		8.90		9.25		10.00	
E. International capital market controls	2.00		2.00		2.00		2.00		0.77		3.70		3.17		3.01	
(i) Foreign ownership/investment restrictions											6.70		5.57		5.24	
(ii) Capital controls	2.00		2.00		2.00		2.00		0.77		0.80		0.77		0.77	
5. Regulation of Credit, Labor, and Business	**5.35**		**5.74**		**5.61**		**5.24**		**5.69**		**6.40**		**6.29**		**6.42**	
A. Credit market regulations	4.29		5.31		4.97		4.49		6.00		8.90		8.06		8.46	
(i) Ownership of banks	0.00		0.00		0.00		0.00		0.00		8.00		8.00		8.00	
(ii) Foreign bank competition											9.00		9.00		9.00	
(iii) Private sector credit	6.87		7.93		8.90		7.46		7.99		8.70		6.24		7.84	
(iv) Interest rate controls/negative real interest rates	6.00		8.00		6.00		6.00		10.00		10.00		9.00		9.00	
B. Labor market regulations											5.70		5.58		5.59	
(i) Hiring regulations and minimum wage											2.20		2.20		2.23	
(ii) Hiring and firing regulations											6.00		5.46		5.35	
(iii) Centralized collective bargaining											6.60		6.19		5.87	
(iv) Hours regulations											8.00		8.00		8.00	
(v) Mandated cost of worker dismissal											1.70		1.66		2.05	
(vi) Conscription	10.00		10.00		10.00		10.00		10.00		10.00		10.00		10.00	
C. Business regulations											4.60		5.24		5.22	
(i) Price controls							4.00		4.00		4.00		4.00		4.00	
(ii) Administrative requirements											3.40		3.81		3.73	
(iii) Bureaucracy costs											1.90		6.14		6.25	
(iv) Starting a business											9.00		9.30		9.22	
(v) Extra payments/bribes/favoritism											4.50		3.69		3.40	
(vi) Licensing restrictions											5.30		5.99		6.24	
(vii) Cost of tax compliance											3.70		3.72		3.72	

Panama

	1980	1985	1990	1995	2000	2005	2008	2009
Chain-Linked	Rating (Rank)	Rating (Rank)	Rating (Rank)	Rating (Rank)	Rating (Rank)	Rating (Rank)	Rating (Rank)	Rating (Rank)
Summary Rating (Rank) ➤	**5.66** (44)	**6.22** (29)	**6.53** (32)	**7.36** (17)	**7.41** (19)	**7.47** (21)	**7.32** (32)	**7.30** (27)
Area 1. Size of Government	4.82 (62)	5.00 (58)	5.57 (59)	7.36 (21)	7.81 (15)	8.30 (11)	8.05 (14)	7.78 (15)
Area 2. Legal Structure and Security of Property Rights	2.97 (70)	3.28 (89)	3.49 (86)	5.21 (73)	5.24 (72)	5.41 (72)	5.65 (66)	5.36 (72)
Area 3. Access to Sound Money	6.78 (33)	9.68 (1)	9.79 (2)	9.50 (22)	9.58 (12)	9.55 (17)	8.74 (48)	9.09 (45)
Area 4. Freedom to Trade Internationally	7.36 (17)	7.06 (22)	7.50 (18)	8.21 (12)	7.94 (27)	7.92 (15)	7.88 (16)	7.93 (9)
Area 5. Regulation of Credit, Labor, and Business	6.15 (28)	6.11 (32)	6.30 (31)	6.50 (27)	6.46 (43)	6.19 (74)	6.32 (77)	6.36 (76)

Unadjusted

	1980	1985	1990	1995	2000	2005	2008	2009
Summary Rating (Rank) ➤	**6.12** (24)	**6.72** (18)	**6.78** (20)	**7.65** (12)	**7.41** (19)	**7.58** (20)	**7.43** (28)	**7.41** (23)
	Rating Data	Rating Data	Rating Data	Rating Data	Rating Data	Rating Data	Rating Data	Rating Data
1. Size of Government	**4.82**	**5.00**	**5.57**	**7.36**	**7.81**	**8.30**	**8.05**	**7.78**
A. Government consumption	3.48 (28.18)	4.16 (25.84)	4.66 (24.15)	5.14 (22.51)	5.26 (22.10)	6.60 (17.40)	7.63 (14.05)	6.56 (17.69)
B. Transfers and subsidies	8.80 (4.90)	8.83 (4.80)	8.12 (7.40)	8.31 (6.70)	8.48 (6.06)	8.60 (5.80)	8.56 (5.80)	8.56 (5.80)
C. Government enterprises and investment	4.00 (39.90)	4.00 (31.40)	7.00 (22.10)	8.00 (16.10)	10.00 (11.86)	10.00 (11.90)	10.00	10.00
D. Top marginal tax rate	3.00	3.00	2.50	8.00	7.50	8.00	6.00	6.00
(i) Top marginal income tax rate	3.00 (56)	3.00 (56)	3.00 (56)	9.00 (30)	8.00 (31)	9.00 (30)	8.00 (27)	8.00 (27)
(ii) Top marginal income and payroll tax rates			2.00 (64)	7.00 (38)	7.00 (38)	7.00 (36)	4.00 (43)	4.00 (43)
2. Legal Structure and Security of Property Rights	**3.19**	**3.52**	**3.75**	**5.60**	**5.24**	**5.20**	**5.39**	**5.11**
A. Judicial independence						2.40	3.27	2.52
B. Impartial courts				4.87	5.35	3.10	3.84	3.82
C. Protection of property rights					4.07	6.70	6.42	6.24
D. Military interference in rule of law and politics				6.71	8.33	8.30	8.33	8.33
E. Integrity of the legal system				6.96	5.00	5.00	5.00	5.00
F. Legal enforcement of contracts						2.30	2.26	2.26
G. Regulatory restrictions on sale of real property						8.40	8.61	7.62
3. Access to Sound Money	**6.78**	**9.68**	**9.79**	**9.50**	**9.58**	**9.50**	**8.74**	**9.09**
A. Money growth	8.23 (8.85)	9.86 (−0.71)	9.75 (−1.23)	8.82 (5.90)	9.32 (3.39)	9.00 (4.80)	7.88 (10.58)	7.95 (10.23)
B. Standard deviation of inflation	5.62 (10.96)	9.04 (2.39)	9.54 (1.16)	9.26 (1.85)	9.28 (1.80)	9.80 (0.49)	8.84 (2.90)	8.88 (2.80)
C. Inflation: most recent year	3.26 (33.69)	9.84 (0.81)	9.89 (0.57)	9.91 (0.47)	9.70 (1.50)	9.30 (3.26)	8.25 (8.76)	9.52 (2.41)
D. Freedom to own foreign currency bank accounts	10.00	10.00	10.00	10.00	10.00	10.00	10.00	10.00
4. Freedom to Trade Internationally	**8.81**	**8.46**	**8.31**	**9.09**	**7.94**	**8.20**	**8.18**	**8.23**
A. Taxes on international trade	7.93	7.27	5.40	7.33	7.49	7.90	7.86	7.88
(i) Revenues from trade taxes (% of trade sector)	7.93 (3.10)	7.27 (4.10)	8.80 (1.80)	9.07 (1.40)	7.33 (4.00)	8.90 (1.60)	8.94 (1.59)	8.94 (1.59)
(ii) Mean tariff rate			2.00 (40.00)	5.60 (22.00)	8.10 (9.50)	8.50 (7.40)	8.56 (7.20)	8.58 (7.10)
(iii) Standard deviation of tariff rates					7.04 (7.40)	6.40 (9.10)	6.08 (9.79)	6.14 (9.66)
B. Regulatory trade barriers					4.95	7.00	7.22	7.56
(i) Non-tariff trade barriers					4.95	5.10	5.59	6.27
(ii) Compliance cost of importing and exporting						8.80	8.85	8.85
C. Size of trade sector relative to expected	10.00	8.88	10.00	10.00	8.13	7.60	7.59	7.07
D. Black-market exchange rates	10.00	10.00	10.00	10.00	10.00	10.00	10.00	10.00
E. International capital market controls	8.00	8.00	8.00	10.00	9.12	8.60	8.23	8.66
(i) Foreign ownership/investment restrictions					8.24	7.10	7.23	7.33
(ii) Capital controls	8.00	8.00	8.00	10.00	10.00	10.00	9.23	10.00
5. Regulation of Credit, Labor, and Business	**6.99**	**6.95**	**6.50**	**6.70**	**6.46**	**6.70**	**6.78**	**6.82**
A. Credit market regulations	8.47	8.33	9.33	9.33	8.31	9.30	9.00	9.25
(i) Ownership of banks	8.00	8.00	8.00	8.00	8.00	8.00	8.00	8.00
(ii) Foreign bank competition					7.05	9.00	9.00	9.00
(iii) Private sector credit	8.95	8.67	10.00	10.00	9.64	10.00	10.00	10.00
(iv) Interest rate controls/negative real interest rates			10.00	10.00	10.00	10.00	9.00	10.00
B. Labor market regulations					5.94	5.20	5.39	5.32
(i) Hiring regulations and minimum wage					3.76	1.10	2.20	2.23
(ii) Hiring and firing regulations					4.15	3.40	3.55	3.42
(iii) Centralized collective bargaining					5.85	6.60	6.69	6.35
(iv) Hours regulations						4.00	4.00	4.00
(v) Mandated cost of worker dismissal						5.90	5.92	5.92
(vi) Conscription	10.00	10.00	10.00	10.00	10.00	10.00	10.00	10.00
C. Business regulations					5.13	5.50	5.94	5.88
(i) Price controls			2.00	4.00	4.00	4.00	4.00	4.00
(ii) Administrative requirements					6.93	3.10	4.51	4.37
(iii) Bureaucracy costs					3.90	4.70	4.94	4.91
(iv) Starting a business					5.53	9.20	9.51	9.60
(v) Extra payments/bribes/favoritism					5.30	5.80	5.20	4.81
(vi) Licensing restrictions						8.40	8.83	8.85
(vii) Cost of tax compliance						3.70	4.60	4.60

Papua New Guinea

Chain-Linked

	1980 Rating (Rank)	1985 Rating (Rank)	1990 Rating (Rank)	1995 Rating (Rank)	2000 Rating (Rank)	2005 Rating (Rank)	2008 Rating (Rank)	2009 Rating (Rank)
Summary Rating (Rank) ➤		**6.16** (33)	**6.31** (35)	**6.53** (42)	**5.96** (86)	**6.51** (75)	**6.94** (52)	**6.98** (46)
Area 1. Size of Government	3.64 (88)	5.39 (44)	5.87 (49)	9.19 (2)	6.18 (60)	6.75 (53)	7.14 (35)	7.23 (29)
Area 2. Legal Structure and Security of Property Rights		5.72 (46)	6.28 (39)	5.28 (72)	4.36 (93)	4.21 (98)	4.71 (87)	4.69 (88)
Area 3. Access to Sound Money	6.06 (63)	6.57 (59)	6.65 (59)	5.56 (81)	6.27 (102)	7.08 (87)	6.65 (97)	7.04 (89)
Area 4. Freedom to Trade Internationally		6.59 (31)	6.18 (46)	6.47 (70)	6.20 (85)	6.35 (79)	7.98 (12)	7.70 (14)
Area 5. Regulation of Credit, Labor, and Business	6.25 (23)	6.42 (21)	6.42 (26)	6.61 (24)	6.80 (31)	8.15 (11)	8.17 (9)	8.19 (10)

Unadjusted

	1980 Rating Data	1985 Rating Data	1990 Rating Data	1995 Rating Data	2000 Rating Data	2005 Rating Data	2008 Rating Data	2009 Rating Data
Summary Rating (Rank) ➤		**6.27** (23)	**6.30** (34)	**6.23** (57)	**5.96** (86)	**6.44** (84)	**6.87** (68)	**6.91** (61)
1. Size of Government	**2.75**	**5.86**	**5.79**	**7.33**	**6.18**	**6.70**	**7.14**	**7.23**
A. Government consumption	3.50 (28.12)	4.13 (25.95)	3.06 (29.61)	6.00 (19.59)	3.80 (27.08)	6.90 (16.60)	7.45 (14.66)	7.80 (13.49)
B. Transfers and subsidies		9.46 (2.50)	9.10 (3.80)		9.92 (0.79)	9.10 (3.70)	9.12 (3.74)	9.12 (3.74)
C. Government enterprises and investment	2.00 (41.40)	4.00 (34.20)	7.00 (20.40)	8.00 (18.70)	8.00 (18.70)	8.00 (18.70)	8.00	8.00
D. Top marginal tax rate			4.00	8.00	3.00	3.00	4.00	4.00
(i) Top marginal income tax rate			4.00 (45)	8.00 (28)	3.00 (47)	3.00 (47)	5.00 (42)	5.00 (42)
(ii) Top marginal income and payroll tax rates			4.00 (45)	8.00 (28)	3.00 (47)	3.00 (47)	3.00 (47)	3.00 (47)
2. Legal Structure and Security of Property Rights		**5.72**	**6.28**	**5.28**	**4.36**	**4.20**	**4.71**	**4.69**
A. Judicial independence								
B. Impartial courts				5.02	5.06	3.90	3.90	3.80
C. Protection of property rights								
D. Military interference in rule of law and politics				5.25	5.00	5.40	7.50	7.50
E. Integrity of the legal system				6.96	3.33	3.80	4.17	4.17
F. Legal enforcement of contracts						1.00	1.01	1.01
G. Regulatory restrictions on sale of real property						7.00	6.96	6.96
3. Access to Sound Money	**6.06**	**6.57**	**6.65**	**5.56**	**6.27**	**7.10**	**6.65**	**7.04**
A. Money growth	8.71 (6.47)	9.38 (3.12)	9.05 (4.73)	8.68 (6.60)	9.73 (1.36)	6.60 (17.10)	6.82 (15.91)	7.80 (11.00)
B. Standard deviation of inflation	6.95 (7.63)	7.23 (6.93)	8.39 (4.02)	7.52 (6.19)	8.49 (3.78)	7.10 (7.30)	6.94 (7.64)	6.73 (8.18)
C. Inflation: most recent year	8.58 (7.09)	9.68 (1.62)	9.17 (4.13)	6.05 (19.73)	6.88 (15.60)	9.70 (1.70)	7.85 (10.76)	8.62 (6.92)
D. Freedom to own foreign currency bank accounts	0.00	0.00	0.00	0.00	0.00	5.00	5.00	5.00
4. Freedom to Trade Internationally		**6.73**	**6.32**	**6.37**	**6.20**	**6.40**	**7.99**	**7.71**
A. Taxes on international trade	7.80	7.33	6.93	6.50	4.80	6.10	7.04	6.83
(i) Revenues from trade taxes (% of trade sector)	7.80 (3.30)	6.07 (5.90)	5.27 (7.10)	5.99 (6.01)	6.03 (5.96)	6.60 (5.10)	6.61 (5.08)	6.61 (5.08)
(ii) Mean tariff rate		8.60 (7.00)	8.60 (7.00)		5.78 (21.10)	8.80 (6.10)	9.02 (4.90)	9.00 (5.00)
(iii) Standard deviation of tariff rates				7.00 (7.50)	2.60 (18.50)	3.00 (17.40)	5.49 (11.27)	4.88 (12.80)
B. Regulatory trade barriers						6.20	6.17	6.17
(i) Non-tariff trade barriers								
(ii) Compliance cost of importing and exporting						6.20	6.17	6.17
C. Size of trade sector relative to expected	9.85	8.96	7.88	8.57	6.48	9.50	9.04	7.88
D. Black-market exchange rates		9.20	8.60	8.60	10.00	10.00	10.00	10.00
E. International capital market controls	0.00	0.00	0.00	0.00	1.54	0.00	7.69	7.69
(i) Foreign ownership / investment restrictions								
(ii) Capital controls	0.00	0.00	0.00	0.00	1.54	0.00	7.69	7.69
5. Regulation of Credit, Labor, and Business	**6.29**	**6.46**	**6.45**	**6.61**	**6.80**	**7.80**	**7.84**	**7.88**
A. Credit market regulations	6.37	6.88	6.87	7.62	8.14	7.90	7.93	8.18
(i) Ownership of banks	5.00	5.00	5.00	5.00	5.00	10.00	10.00	10.00
(ii) Foreign bank competition						4.00	4.00	4.00
(iii) Private sector credit	7.75	8.76	8.73	9.87	9.42	8.70	8.70	8.70
(iv) Interest rate controls / negative real interest rates				8.00	10.00	9.00	9.00	10.00
B. Labor market regulations						8.80	8.82	8.64
(i) Hiring regulations and minimum wage						8.90	8.90	7.77
(ii) Hiring and firing regulations								
(iii) Centralized collective bargaining								
(iv) Hours regulations						10.00	10.00	10.00
(v) Mandated cost of worker dismissal						6.40	6.38	6.79
(vi) Conscription	10.00	10.00	10.00	10.00	10.00	10.00	10.00	10.00
C. Business regulations						6.70	6.76	6.81
(i) Price controls						4.00	4.00	4.00
(ii) Administrative requirements								
(iii) Bureaucracy costs								
(iv) Starting a business						7.90	7.99	8.18
(v) Extra payments / bribes / favoritism								
(vi) Licensing restrictions						7.20	7.23	7.24
(vii) Cost of tax compliance						7.70	7.83	7.83

Paraguay

Chain-Linked	1980		1985		1990		1995		2000		2005		2008		2009	
	Rating	(Rank)	Rating	(Rank)	Rating	(Rank)	Rating	(Rank)	Rating	(Rank)	Rating	(Rank)	Rating	(Rank)	Rating	(Rank)
Summary Rating (Rank) ➤	**5.76**	(38)	**5.12**	(67)	**5.78**	(49)	**6.50**	(43)	**6.28**	(70)	**6.46**	(77)	**6.62**	(74)	**6.65**	(67)
Area 1. Size of Government	9.16	(3)	7.75	(3)	9.31	(1)	8.69	(4)	7.58	(20)	7.62	(22)	7.48	(25)	7.41	(24)
Area 2. Legal Structure and Security of Property Rights	3.41	(63)	3.66	(81)	4.11	(76)	3.97	(107)	3.79	(105)	4.23	(97)	4.23	(101)	4.37	(96)
Area 3. Access to Sound Money	7.87	(21)	7.48	(32)	6.50	(64)	8.20	(38)	8.72	(42)	8.37	(60)	8.58	(51)	8.70	(56)
Area 4. Freedom to Trade Internationally	4.71	(61)	3.58	(78)	5.16	(66)	6.76	(55)	6.36	(80)	6.94	(53)	7.29	(37)	6.94	(46)
Area 5. Regulation of Credit, Labor, and Business					3.99	(100)	4.87	(92)	4.95	(105)	5.27	(108)	5.64	(104)	5.94	(98)

Unadjusted	1980		1985		1990		1995		2000		2005		2008		2009	
Summary Rating (Rank) ➤	**6.64**	(14)	**5.93**	(37)	**6.21**	(39)	**6.99**	(30)	**6.28**	(70)	**6.40**	(86)	**6.56**	(85)	**6.57**	(80)
	Rating	Data	Rating	Data	Rating	Data	Rating	Data	Rating	Data	Rating	Data	Rating	Data	Rating	Data
1. Size of Government	**9.06**		**7.75**		**9.31**		**8.69**		**7.58**		**7.60**		**7.48**		**7.41**	
A. Government consumption	9.60	(7.36)	9.45	(7.87)	9.57	(7.45)	8.46	(11.23)	7.04	(16.07)	8.30	(12.00)	8.06	(12.58)	7.88	(13.20)
B. Transfers and subsidies	9.59	(2.00)	9.56	(2.10)	9.65	(1.80)	9.32	(3.00)	9.26	(3.21)	9.20	(3.40)	9.37	(2.80)	9.25	(3.24)
C. Government enterprises and investment	8.00	(17.80)	4.00	(31.40)	10.00	(13.30)	7.00	(23.20)	4.00	(35.71)	4.00	(35.70)	4.00		4.00	
D. Top marginal tax rate			8.00		8.00		10.00		10.00		9.00		8.50		8.50	
(i) Top marginal income tax rate			8.00	(30)	8.00	(30)	10.00	(0)	10.00	(0)	10.00	(0)	10.00	(8)	10.00	(8)
(ii) Top marginal income and payroll tax rates											8.00	(27)	7.00	(33)	7.00	(33)
2. Legal Structure and Security of Property Rights	**3.71**		**3.99**		**4.48**		**4.32**		**3.79**		**3.50**		**3.53**		**3.64**	
A. Judicial independence											1.10		0.96		1.17	
B. Impartial courts							4.33		4.08		1.80		2.49		2.57	
C. Protection of property rights									2.27		3.40		3.23		3.22	
D. Military interference in rule of law and politics							4.79		3.33		2.50		2.50		2.50	
E. Integrity of the legal system							4.11		5.00		3.30		3.33		3.33	
F. Legal enforcement of contracts											4.20		4.19		4.19	
G. Regulatory restrictions on sale of real property											8.50		7.98		8.51	
3. Access to Sound Money	**7.87**		**7.48**		**6.50**		**8.20**		**8.72**		**8.40**		**8.58**		**8.70**	
A. Money growth	6.93	(15.33)	8.12	(9.39)	4.67	(26.66)	7.09	(14.57)	8.66	(6.72)	7.10	(14.50)	7.34	(13.28)	7.06	(14.68)
B. Standard deviation of inflation	7.91	(5.23)	6.84	(7.91)	8.58	(3.55)	8.29	(4.27)	8.02	(4.94)	7.80	(5.62)	8.99	(2.51)	8.26	(4.36)
C. Inflation: most recent year	6.66	(16.71)	4.95	(25.24)	2.74	(36.28)	7.40	(12.99)	8.20	(8.98)	8.60	(6.79)	7.97	(10.15)	9.48	(2.59)
D. Freedom to own foreign currency bank accounts	10.00		10.00		10.00		10.00		10.00		10.00		10.00		10.00	
4. Freedom to Trade Internationally	**5.91**		**4.49**		**6.31**		**8.27**		**6.36**		**7.20**		**7.57**		**7.21**	
A. Taxes on international trade	3.00		4.27		6.51		7.99		7.63		7.90		7.90		7.90	
(i) Revenues from trade taxes (% of trade sector)	6.00	(6.00)	8.53	(2.20)	7.80	(3.30)	8.60	(2.10)	7.76	(3.37)	8.90	(1.70)	9.09	(1.36)	9.06	(1.41)
(ii) Mean tariff rate	0.00	(71.00)	0.00	(71.70)	6.80	(16.00)	8.14	(9.30)	7.82	(10.90)	8.30	(8.30)	7.68	(11.60)	7.94	(10.30)
(iii) Standard deviation of tariff rates					4.92	(12.70)	7.24	(6.90)	7.32	(6.70)	6.60	(8.50)	6.94	(7.66)	6.70	(8.24)
B. Regulatory trade barriers									2.43		5.10		5.45		5.51	
(i) Non-tariff trade barriers									2.43		5.00		5.57		5.68	
(ii) Compliance cost of importing and exporting											5.20		5.34		5.34	
C. Size of trade sector relative to expected	4.76		4.97		7.05		7.83		4.69		5.90		8.51		7.43	
D. Black-market exchange rates	8.60		0.00		4.80		7.40		10.00		10.00		10.00		10.00	
E. International capital market controls	5.00		5.00		5.00		10.00		7.06		7.20		6.01		5.22	
(i) Foreign ownership/investment restrictions									5.67		5.10		5.86		5.82	
(ii) Capital controls	5.00		5.00		5.00		10.00		8.46		9.20		6.15		4.62	
5. Regulation of Credit, Labor, and Business					**4.48**		**5.46**		**4.95**		**5.30**		**5.62**		**5.87**	
A. Credit market regulations					5.97		8.88		6.93		7.30		7.52		7.27	
(i) Ownership of banks									8.00		8.00		8.00		8.00	
(ii) Foreign bank competition									4.08		4.00		4.08		4.08	
(iii) Private sector credit					9.95		9.76		9.47		10.00		10.00		10.00	
(iv) Interest rate controls/negative real interest rates					2.00		8.00		9.00		7.00		8.00		7.00	
B. Labor market regulations									3.33		3.30		3.59		4.34	
(i) Hiring regulations and minimum wage									4.67		4.40		4.40		4.43	
(ii) Hiring and firing regulations									4.72		3.30		3.94		3.97	
(iii) Centralized collective bargaining									3.95		5.70		6.70		6.58	
(iv) Hours regulations											4.70		4.70		8.00	
(v) Mandated cost of worker dismissal											0.80		0.82		2.05	
(vi) Conscription	1.00		0.00		0.00		0.00		0.00		1.00		1.00		1.00	
C. Business regulations									4.57		5.20		5.73		6.00	
(i) Price controls					4.00		6.00		6.00		6.00		6.00		6.00	
(ii) Administrative requirements									4.87		2.90		4.09		4.02	
(iii) Bureaucracy costs									4.95		5.10		6.90		6.73	
(iv) Starting a business									3.98		6.20		8.28		8.30	
(v) Extra payments/bribes/favoritism									3.07		4.30		2.88		2.99	
(vi) Licensing restrictions											5.40		5.63		7.46	
(vii) Cost of tax compliance											6.30		6.32		6.51	

Peru

	1980	1985	1990	1995	2000	2005	2008	2009
Chain-Linked	Rating (Rank)	Rating (Rank)	Rating (Rank)	Rating (Rank)	Rating (Rank)	Rating (Rank)	Rating (Rank)	Rating (Rank)
Summary Rating (Rank) ➤	**4.27** (88)	**3.11** (107)	**4.13** (102)	**6.31** (53)	**7.07** (36)	**7.19** (38)	**7.36** (30)	**7.29** (28)
Area 1. Size of Government	6.47 (20)	5.42 (42)	7.13 (17)	8.21 (9)	8.07 (11)	7.78 (20)	7.90 (17)	7.56 (23)
Area 2. Legal Structure and Security of Property Rights	3.92 (57)	2.32 (101)	3.04 (92)	4.76 (92)	3.94 (102)	4.96 (83)	5.49 (70)	5.43 (71)
Area 3. Access to Sound Money	1.62 (108)	0.10 (112)	1.25 (113)	5.13 (90)	8.79 (40)	9.68 (4)	9.02 (40)	9.23 (40)
Area 4. Freedom to Trade Internationally	4.47 (65)	3.30 (83)	4.48 (83)	6.88 (46)	7.29 (45)	7.18 (40)	7.64 (25)	7.48 (24)
Area 5. Regulation of Credit, Labor, and Business	5.02 (62)	4.91 (64)	4.82 (82)	6.59 (25)	7.27 (11)	6.37 (64)	6.76 (50)	6.73 (53)

Unadjusted								
Summary Rating (Rank) ➤	**4.02** (94)	**2.90** (109)	**3.97** (103)	**6.29** (52)	**7.07** (36)	**7.23** (41)	**7.39** (31)	**7.31** (33)
	Rating Data	Rating Data	Rating Data	Rating Data	Rating Data	Rating Data	Rating Data	Rating Data
1. Size of Government	**6.47**	**5.42**	**7.13**	**8.21**	**8.07**	**7.80**	**7.90**	**7.56**
A. Government consumption	7.26 (15.33)	8.04 (12.67)	8.69 (10.46)	8.77 (10.17)	7.73 (13.72)	7.90 (13.30)	8.10 (12.45)	7.75 (13.64)
B. Transfers and subsidies	9.62 (1.90)	9.65 (1.80)	9.32 (3.00)	9.07 (3.90)	9.04 (4.02)	9.30 (3.20)	9.51 (2.30)	9.49 (2.35)
C. Government enterprises and investment	7.00 (24.30)	4.00 (33.90)	7.00 (20.00)	8.00 (19.50)	8.00 (19.61)	8.00 (15.60)	8.00 (16.63)	7.00 (24.34)
D. Top marginal tax rate	2.00	0.00	3.50	7.00	7.50	6.00	6.00	6.00
(i) Top marginal income tax rate	2.00 (65)	0.00 (65)	4.00 (45)	8.00 (30)	10.00 (20)	8.00 (30)	8.00 (30)	8.00 (30)
(ii) Top marginal income and payroll tax rates			3.00 (48)	6.00 (39)	5.00 (41)	4.00 (48)	4.00 (48)	4.00 (48)
2. Legal Structure and Security of Property Rights	**3.77**	**2.23**	**2.93**	**4.76**	**3.94**	**5.00**	**5.49**	**5.43**
A. Judicial independence				2.75	1.50	1.60	3.09	2.69
B. Impartial courts				4.33	3.17	2.60	3.38	3.44
C. Protection of property rights				4.83	3.33	4.10	4.92	4.71
D. Military interference in rule of law and politics				4.90	6.67	8.30	8.33	7.50
E. Integrity of the legal system				6.96	5.00	5.00	5.00	5.83
F. Legal enforcement of contracts						4.80	5.07	5.07
G. Regulatory restrictions on sale of real property						8.30	8.65	8.78
3. Access to Sound Money	**1.62**	**0.00**	**1.25**	**5.13**	**8.79**	**9.70**	**9.02**	**9.23**
A. Money growth	3.38 (33.12)	0.00 (83.59)	0.00 (597.16)	2.94 (35.32)	7.03 (14.85)	9.80 (1.10)	8.13 (9.35)	8.38 (8.10)
B. Standard deviation of inflation	3.10 (17.26)	0.00 (37.94)	0.00 (2341.35)	0.00 (127.50)	8.87 (2.83)	9.30 (1.87)	9.09 (2.28)	9.14 (2.15)
C. Inflation: most recent year	0.00 (65.92)	0.00 (167.75)	0.00 (6134.79)	7.56 (12.18)	9.25 (3.76)	9.70 (1.62)	8.84 (5.79)	9.41 (2.94)
D. Freedom to own foreign currency bank accounts	0.00	0.00	5.00	10.00	10.00	10.00	10.00	10.00
4. Freedom to Trade Internationally	**4.77**	**3.45**	**4.70**	**6.89**	**7.29**	**7.20**	**7.64**	**7.48**
A. Taxes on international trade	1.47	1.89	3.40	7.02	7.80	8.10	8.50	8.59
(i) Revenues from trade taxes (% of trade sector)	2.93 (10.60)	4.47 (8.30)	7.40 (3.90)	6.33 (5.50)	7.23 (4.16)	8.50 (2.30)	9.37 (0.94)	9.41 (0.88)
(ii) Mean tariff rate	0.00 (57.00)	0.00 (64.00)	2.80 (36.00)	6.48 (17.60)	7.32 (13.40)	8.20 (9.20)	8.78 (6.10)	8.90 (5.50)
(iii) Standard deviation of tariff rates		1.20 (22.00)	0.00 (25.00)	8.24 (4.40)	8.84 (2.90)	7.60 (6.00)	7.34 (6.65)	7.45 (6.38)
B. Regulatory trade barriers				5.98	6.71	5.70	6.63	7.41
(i) Non-tariff trade barriers				5.98	6.75	5.20	6.52	6.71
(ii) Compliance cost of importing and exporting					6.66	6.20	6.74	8.10
C. Size of trade sector relative to expected	5.75	5.10	3.05	2.84	3.05	4.20	5.03	3.85
D. Black-market exchange rates	6.40	0.00	6.80	10.00	10.00	10.00	10.00	10.00
E. International capital market controls	2.00	2.00	2.00	8.61	8.88	7.90	8.06	7.57
(i) Foreign ownership/investment restrictions				9.22	9.30	7.30	7.65	7.45
(ii) Capital controls	2.00	2.00	2.00	8.00	8.46	8.50	8.46	7.69
5. Regulation of Credit, Labor, and Business	**3.46**	**3.39**	**3.87**	**6.46**	**7.27**	**6.60**	**6.88**	**6.86**
A. Credit market regulations	2.95	2.72	2.54	7.91	8.53	7.60	7.50	7.34
(i) Ownership of banks					10.00	8.00	8.00	8.00
(ii) Foreign bank competition				8.12	6.58	4.00	4.00	4.00
(iii) Private sector credit	5.90	5.44	5.08	9.18	8.81	9.60	10.00	9.35
(iv) Interest rate controls/negative real interest rates	0.00	0.00	0.00	6.00	9.00	9.00	8.00	8.00
B. Labor market regulations				5.36	6.75	6.50	7.37	7.31
(i) Hiring regulations and minimum wage				6.45	3.08	5.60	5.60	3.90
(ii) Hiring and firing regulations			6.75	6.75	7.20	3.70	4.10	3.98
(iii) Centralized collective bargaining				7.93	7.93	7.80	7.41	7.58
(iv) Hours regulations				5.68	5.51	6.70	8.70	10.00
(v) Mandated cost of worker dismissal						5.20	8.42	8.41
(vi) Conscription	0.00	0.00	0.00	0.00	10.00	10.00	10.00	10.00
C. Business regulations				6.11	6.52	5.50	5.76	5.92
(i) Price controls			2.00	6.00	8.00	6.00	6.00	6.00
(ii) Administrative requirements				6.75	2.20	2.54	2.76	
(iii) Bureaucracy costs				7.00	7.50	4.20	5.10	5.23
(iv) Starting a business				6.43	3.57	7.40	8.43	8.99
(v) Extra payments/bribes/favoritism				5.02	6.78	6.40	5.20	5.09
(vi) Licensing restrictions						7.20	7.34	7.62
(vii) Cost of tax compliance						5.20	5.74	5.74

Philippines

Chain-Linked	1980		1985		1990		1995		2000		2005		2008		2009	
	Rating	(Rank)	Rating	(Rank)	Rating	(Rank)	Rating	(Rank)	Rating	(Rank)	Rating	(Rank)	Rating	(Rank)	Rating	(Rank)
Summary Rating (Rank) ➤	**5.42**	(56)	**5.11**	(68)	**5.85**	(48)	**7.24**	(24)	**6.98**	(41)	**7.09**	(45)	**6.77**	(65)	**6.45**	(80)
Area 1. Size of Government	6.49	(19)	6.75	(12)	8.00	(7)	8.20	(10)	6.87	(38)	8.61	(8)	8.06	(13)	7.77	(16)
Area 2. Legal Structure and Security of Property Rights	3.19	(68)	2.57	(99)	2.55	(102)	4.82	(85)	4.65	(81)	4.89	(85)	4.64	(89)	4.57	(91)
Area 3. Access to Sound Money	6.10	(60)	4.59	(95)	5.76	(80)	8.80	(35)	9.23	(33)	7.94	(71)	7.78	(73)	6.79	(97)
Area 4. Freedom to Trade Internationally	6.29	(36)	6.11	(41)	6.40	(44)	7.66	(25)	7.61	(39)	7.37	(32)	6.70	(69)	6.55	(65)
Area 5. Regulation of Credit, Labor, and Business	5.07	(60)	5.51	(50)	6.48	(24)	6.73	(21)	6.55	(38)	6.63	(56)	6.66	(56)	6.62	(58)

Unadjusted																
Summary Rating (Rank) ➤	**5.41**	(55)	**5.10**	(72)	**5.77**	(50)	**7.13**	(25)	**6.98**	(41)	**7.09**	(48)	**6.78**	(77)	**6.46**	(89)
	Rating	Data	Rating	Data	Rating	Data	Rating	Data	Rating	Data	Rating	Data	Rating	Data	Rating	Data
1. Size of Government	**6.49**		**6.75**		**8.00**		**8.20**		**6.87**		**8.60**		**8.06**		**7.77**	
A. Government consumption	8.13	(12.35)	9.01	(9.37)	8.11	(12.43)	7.85	(13.32)	7.26	(15.31)	8.20	(12.20)	8.25	(11.95)	8.09	(12.49)
B. Transfers and subsidies	9.84	(1.10)	10.00	(0.20)	9.89	(0.90)	9.95	(0.70)	9.21	(3.40)	9.30	(3.10)	10.00	(0.28)	10.00	(0.23)
C. Government enterprises and investment	7.00	(20.10)	7.00	(23.70)	7.00	(23.30)	8.00	(17.50)	4.00	(31.10)	10.00	(14.90)	7.00	(22.53)	6.00	(27.61)
D. Top marginal tax rate	1.00		1.00		7.00		7.00		7.00		7.00		7.00		7.00	
(i) Top marginal income tax rate	1.00	(70)	1.00	(60)	7.00	(35)	7.00	(35)	7.00	(32)	7.00	(32)	7.00	(32)	7.00	(32)
(ii) Top marginal income and payroll tax rates					7.00	(35)	7.00	(35)	7.00	(32)	7.00	(32)	7.00	(32)	7.00	(32)
2. Legal Structure and Security of Property Rights	**3.06**		**2.46**		**2.44**		**4.82**		**4.65**		**4.90**		**4.64**		**4.57**	
A. Judicial independence							3.72		4.51		3.90		3.56		3.07	
B. Impartial courts							5.27		5.51		3.60		2.85		3.06	
C. Protection of property rights							3.96		3.22		5.70		4.69		4.45	
D. Military interference in rule of law and politics							7.04		6.67		5.80		5.83		5.83	
E. Integrity of the legal system							4.11		3.33		3.80		4.17		4.17	
F. Legal enforcement of contracts											3.40		3.42		3.42	
G. Regulatory restrictions on sale of real property											8.00		7.96		7.96	
3. Access to Sound Money	**6.10**		**4.59**		**5.76**		**8.80**		**9.23**		**7.90**		**7.78**		**6.79**	
A. Money growth	8.41	(7.94)	8.43	(7.87)	6.95	(15.23)	8.11	(9.47)	8.41	(7.96)	8.80	(6.10)	8.69	(6.57)	8.69	(6.57)
B. Standard deviation of inflation	8.83	(2.92)	3.45	(16.37)	8.69	(3.27)	8.58	(3.54)	9.32	(1.71)	9.50	(1.22)	9.29	(1.78)	9.12	(2.20)
C. Inflation: most recent year	7.15	(14.25)	6.47	(17.63)	7.41	(12.97)	8.49	(7.55)	9.21	(3.95)	8.50	(7.63)	8.14	(9.31)	9.35	(3.23)
D. Freedom to own foreign currency bank accounts	0.00		0.00		0.00		10.00		10.00		5.00		5.00		0.00	
4. Freedom to Trade Internationally	**6.04**		**5.88**		**6.21**		**7.27**		**7.61**		**7.40**		**6.70**		**6.55**	
A. Taxes on international trade	3.93		5.17		5.69		6.08		7.86		8.10		7.59		7.63	
(i) Revenues from trade taxes (% of trade sector)	5.47	(6.80)	5.87	(6.20)	5.60	(6.60)	5.73	(6.40)	8.26	(2.61)	8.20	(2.60)	6.91	(4.64)	6.94	(4.59)
(ii) Mean tariff rate	2.40	(38.00)	4.48	(27.60)	5.14	(24.30)	4.48	(27.60)	8.48	(7.60)	8.90	(5.40)	8.74	(6.30)	8.74	(6.30)
(iii) Standard deviation of tariff rates					6.32	(9.20)	8.04	(4.90)	6.84	(7.90)	7.30	(6.90)	7.13	(7.18)	7.20	(6.99)
B. Regulatory trade barriers							5.72		5.89		6.80		6.57		6.76	
(i) Non-tariff trade barriers							5.72		3.95		6.00		5.31		5.50	
(ii) Compliance cost of importing and exporting									7.83		7.60		7.82		8.03	
C. Size of trade sector relative to expected	6.68		5.41		6.59		7.92		9.68		8.40		6.15		5.09	
D. Black-market exchange rates	9.40		8.60		8.60		10.00		10.00		10.00		10.00		10.00	
E. International capital market controls	2.00		2.00		2.00		6.61		4.60		3.50		3.22		3.25	
(i) Foreign ownership / investment restrictions							8.21		8.44		6.20		5.67		5.73	
(ii) Capital controls	2.00		2.00		2.00		5.00		0.77		0.80		0.77		0.77	
5. Regulation of Credit, Labor, and Business	**5.34**		**5.81**		**6.46**		**6.59**		**6.55**		**6.70**		**6.69**		**6.64**	
A. Credit market regulations	6.60		5.50		8.19		8.48		8.01		8.80		8.91		8.75	
(i) Ownership of banks	5.00		5.00		8.00		8.00		8.00		8.00		8.00		8.00	
(ii) Foreign bank competition							7.47		5.67		8.00		8.00		8.00	
(iii) Private sector credit	6.79		7.51		8.56		9.58		8.94		9.00		9.63		9.02	
(iv) Interest rate controls / negative real interest rates	8.00		4.00		8.00		10.00		10.00		10.00		10.00		10.00	
B. Labor market regulations							7.65		6.82		6.06		6.00		5.93		6.02	
(i) Hiring regulations and minimum wage							5.05		4.38		4.40		4.40		4.43	
(ii) Hiring and firing regulations							5.70		5.70		3.30		4.30		3.53		3.62	
(iii) Centralized collective bargaining							7.24		7.24		6.92		5.50		6.06		6.08	
(iv) Hours regulations									6.10		5.68		10.00		10.00		10.00	
(v) Mandated cost of worker dismissal											1.60		1.56		1.97	
(vi) Conscription	3.00		10.00		10.00		10.00		10.00		10.00		10.00		10.00	
C. Business regulations							4.47		5.57		5.30		5.24		5.16	
(i) Price controls							4.00		4.00		3.00		2.00		2.00	
(ii) Administrative requirements									7.20		2.40		2.78		2.56	
(iii) Bureaucracy costs							5.48		6.68		4.10		5.63		5.65	
(iv) Starting a business							6.08		5.63		7.90		8.02		8.45	
(v) Extra payments / bribes / favoritism							2.32		4.35		4.20		2.99		2.88	
(vi) Licensing restrictions											7.40		7.46		6.75	
(vii) Cost of tax compliance											7.80		7.81		7.81	

Poland

Chain-Linked

	1980	1985	1990	1995	2000	2005	2008	2009
	Rating (Rank)	Rating (Rank)	Rating (Rank)	Rating (Rank)	Rating (Rank)	Rating (Rank)	Rating (Rank)	Rating (Rank)
Summary Rating (Rank) ➤		4.07 (93)	4.00 (104)	5.30 (86)	6.19 (75)	6.78 (63)	6.88 (57)	6.90 (52)
Area 1. Size of Government	4.00 (82)	3.90 (87)	1.85 (113)	2.62 (119)	4.25 (107)	5.40 (93)	5.59 (89)	5.63 (79)
Area 2. Legal Structure and Security of Property Rights		5.39 (51)	6.97 (30)	6.84 (30)	6.50 (43)	5.75 (61)	5.94 (59)	6.25 (46)
Area 3. Access to Sound Money	8.34 (14)	4.43 (97)	2.50 (109)	6.03 (72)	7.49 (68)	9.27 (36)	9.21 (34)	9.32 (31)
Area 4. Freedom to Trade Internationally		3.19 (84)	5.32 (64)	6.48 (69)	6.84 (67)	6.73 (61)	7.03 (54)	6.84 (51)
Area 5. Regulation of Credit, Labor, and Business	3.35 (96)	3.39 (97)	3.56 (104)	4.54 (100)	5.86 (69)	6.74 (51)	6.63 (59)	6.47 (66)

Unadjusted

	1980	1985	1990	1995	2000	2005	2008	2009
Summary Rating (Rank) ➤		3.98 (99)	3.94 (104)	5.24 (89)	6.19 (75)	6.79 (71)	6.90 (65)	7.00 (53)
	Rating Data	Rating Data	Rating Data	Rating Data	Rating Data	Rating Data	Rating Data	Rating Data
1. Size of Government	5.10	4.21	2.00	2.62	4.25	5.40	5.59	5.63
A. Government consumption	8.21 (12.09)	7.95 (12.97)	3.33 (28.69)	4.99 (23.02)	5.00 (23.00)	5.10 (22.50)	4.61 (24.34)	4.94 (23.19)
B. Transfers and subsidies		2.67 (27.40)	2.67 (27.40)	3.49 (24.40)	4.50 (20.69)	5.00 (19.00)	5.24 (17.97)	5.06 (18.65)
C. Government enterprises and investment	2.00 (40.70)	2.00 (40.70)	0.00 (58.80)	0.00 (55.80)	4.00 (36.62)	8.00 (18.70)	7.00 (20.59)	7.00 (24.56)
D. Top marginal tax rate				2.00	3.50	3.50	5.50	5.50
(i) Top marginal income tax rate				4.00 (45)	5.00 (40)	5.00 (40)	7.00 (32)	7.00 (32)
(ii) Top marginal income and payroll tax rates				0.00 (63)	2.00 (53)	2.00 (55)	4.00 (44)	4.00 (44)
2. Legal Structure and Security of Property Rights		4.78	6.19	6.84	6.50	5.70	5.94	6.25
A. Judicial independence				6.47	5.34	4.20	5.24	5.56
B. Impartial courts				5.60	5.85	4.40	3.02	3.48
C. Protection of property rights				3.58	4.63	4.60	5.42	5.98
D. Military interference in rule of law and politics				8.54	10.00	10.00	10.00	10.00
E. Integrity of the legal system				10.00	6.67	7.10	7.50	7.50
F. Legal enforcement of contracts						4.30	4.27	4.27
G. Regulatory restrictions on sale of real property						5.80	6.11	7.00
3. Access to Sound Money	7.42	4.43	2.50	6.03	7.49	9.30	9.21	9.32
A. Money growth		5.90 (20.50)	0.00 (110.44)	3.83 (30.87)	8.97 (5.14)	8.10 (9.70)	8.19 (9.06)	8.48 (7.61)
B. Standard deviation of inflation	9.21 (1.97)	0.00 (37.35)	0.00 (167.57)	5.91 (10.22)	8.00 (5.00)	9.40 (1.41)	9.54 (1.16)	9.58 (1.05)
C. Inflation: most recent year	8.04 (9.80)	6.83 (15.83)	0.00 (435.66)	4.37 (28.17)	7.99 (10.06)	9.60 (2.11)	9.13 (4.35)	9.23 (3.83)
D. Freedom to own foreign currency bank accounts	5.00	5.00	10.00	10.00	5.00	10.00	10.00	10.00
4. Freedom to Trade Internationally		3.32	5.50	6.25	6.84	6.70	7.03	6.84
A. Taxes on international trade		5.77	6.70	6.38	7.76	8.40	8.03	8.22
(i) Revenues from trade taxes (% of trade sector)		4.27 (8.60)	6.00 (6.00)	5.95 (6.08)	9.20 (1.20)	9.60 (0.60)	9.61 (0.59)	9.44 (0.84)
(ii) Mean tariff rate		7.28 (13.60)	7.66 (11.70)	6.32 (18.40)	8.00 (10.00)	9.50 (2.70)	8.88 (5.60)	8.94 (5.30)
(iii) Standard deviation of tariff rates			6.44 (8.90)	6.88 (7.80)	6.08 (9.80)	6.10 (9.70)	5.61 (10.98)	6.29 (9.28)
B. Regulatory trade barriers				5.70	7.45	6.20	6.78	6.79
(i) Non-tariff trade barriers				5.70	6.23	5.20	6.38	6.40
(ii) Compliance cost of importing and exporting					8.66	7.20	7.18	7.18
C. Size of trade sector relative to expected	6.10	2.57	4.41	3.95	5.22	5.50	5.75	5.36
D. Black-market exchange rates	0.00	0.00	8.20	10.00	10.00	10.00	10.00	10.00
E. International capital market controls	0.00	0.00	0.00	5.21	3.78	3.60	4.59	3.81
(i) Foreign ownership/investment restrictions				5.41	6.78	5.60	6.88	6.09
(ii) Capital controls	0.00	0.00	0.00	5.00	0.77	1.50	2.31	1.54
5. Regulation of Credit, Labor, and Business	3.10	3.13	3.49	4.46	5.86	6.80	6.72	6.95
A. Credit market regulations	0.24	0.38	0.44	3.99	7.15	8.70	8.75	8.43
(i) Ownership of banks	0.00	0.00	0.00	2.00	5.00	8.00	8.00	8.00
(ii) Foreign bank competition				4.20	6.67	9.00	9.00	9.00
(iii) Private sector credit	0.48	0.76	1.31	3.82	7.84	7.80	7.99	6.71
(iv) Interest rate controls/negative real interest rates			0.00	6.00	10.00	10.00	10.00	10.00
B. Labor market regulations			3.62	4.45	4.20	6.60	6.52	7.45
(i) Hiring regulations and minimum wage				5.38	3.39	10.00	8.90	5.57
(ii) Hiring and firing regulations			5.67	5.67	2.72	4.80	4.08	3.86
(iii) Centralized collective bargaining	4.49	4.49	5.18	5.18	7.03	6.10	7.63	7.30
(iv) Hours regulations				5.00	4.84	6.70	6.70	8.00
(v) Mandated cost of worker dismissal						8.80	8.79	10.00
(vi) Conscription	0.00	0.00	0.00	1.00	3.00	3.00	3.00	10.00
C. Business regulations				4.95	6.22	5.20	4.89	4.97
(i) Price controls				7.00	4.00	2.00	1.00	1.00
(ii) Administrative requirements					7.40	3.40	2.79	2.86
(iii) Bureaucracy costs				5.14	7.13	6.50	4.08	3.84
(iv) Starting a business				4.37	6.98	8.10	8.74	8.74
(v) Extra payments/bribes/favoritism				3.30	5.60	5.50	6.39	6.35
(vi) Licensing restrictions						5.60	5.67	5.63
(vii) Cost of tax compliance						5.30	5.57	6.36

Portugal

	1980		1985		1990		1995		2000		2005		2008		2009	
Chain-Linked	Rating	(Rank)	Rating	(Rank)	Rating	(Rank)	Rating	(Rank)	Rating	(Rank)	Rating	(Rank)	Rating	(Rank)	Rating	(Rank)
Summary Rating (Rank) ➤	**5.99**	(31)	**5.74**	(45)	**6.54**	(30)	**7.32**	(20)	**7.37**	(21)	**7.11**	(41)	**7.07**	(48)	**6.90**	(52)
Area 1. Size of Government	3.63	(89)	3.86	(88)	5.22	(68)	5.49	(80)	5.26	(88)	5.73	(89)	5.67	(86)	5.56	(83)
Area 2. Legal Structure and Security of Property Rights	9.27	(7)	7.05	(30)	8.97	(19)	8.04	(20)	7.64	(24)	7.16	(27)	6.81	(30)	6.68	(30)
Area 3. Access to Sound Money	5.61	(77)	5.61	(87)	6.05	(72)	9.18	(29)	9.51	(20)	9.54	(19)	9.55	(6)	9.61	(10)
Area 4. Freedom to Trade Internationally	6.73	(28)	6.91	(24)	7.44	(20)	8.11	(15)	8.10	(23)	7.02	(49)	7.20	(42)	7.05	(42)
Area 5. Regulation of Credit, Labor, and Business	5.09	(59)	5.49	(51)	5.26	(60)	5.79	(55)	6.32	(48)	6.09	(83)	6.13	(87)	5.61	(106)

Unadjusted

	1980		1985		1990		1995		2000		2005		2008		2009	
Summary Rating (Rank) ➤	**5.69**	(45)	**5.46**	(57)	**6.19**	(40)	**7.27**	(21)	**7.37**	(21)	**7.13**	(47)	**7.09**	(53)	**6.93**	(59)
	Rating	Data	Rating	Data	Rating	Data	Rating	Data	Rating	Data	Rating	Data	Rating	Data	Rating	Data
1. Size of Government	**3.63**		**3.86**		**5.22**		**5.49**		**5.26**		**5.70**		**5.67**		**5.56**	
A. Government consumption	6.83	(16.76)	6.60	(17.57)	5.95	(19.76)	5.47	(21.41)	4.18	(25.80)	4.60	(24.30)	4.79	(23.71)	4.70	(24.03)
B. Transfers and subsidies	5.69	(16.30)	4.82	(19.50)	5.91	(15.50)	6.49	(13.40)	5.88	(15.64)	4.80	(19.50)	4.38	(21.11)	4.04	(22.37)
C. Government enterprises and investment	2.00	(42.20)	4.00	(30.50)	6.00	(29.90)	7.00	(23.20)	7.00	(23.20)	10.00	(13.20)	10.00	(12.73)	10.00	(14.78)
D. Top marginal tax rate	0.00		0.00		3.00		3.00		4.00		3.50		3.50		3.50	
(i) Top marginal income tax rate	0.00	(84)	0.00	(69)	5.00	(40)	5.00	(40)	6.00	(40)	5.00	(42)	5.00	(42)	5.00	(42)
(ii) Top marginal income and payroll tax rates					1.00	(57)	1.00	(57)	2.00	(57)	2.00	(58)	2.00	(58)	2.00	(58)
2. Legal Structure and Security of Property Rights	**8.00**		**6.08**		**7.73**		**8.04**		**7.64**		**7.20**		**6.81**		**6.68**	
A. Judicial independence							8.15		7.01		7.80		6.16		5.48	
B. Impartial courts							6.97		6.35		5.30		3.32		3.14	
C. Protection of property rights							5.10		6.48		7.40		6.99		6.73	
D. Military interference in rule of law and politics							9.99		10.00		10.00		10.00		10.00	
E. Integrity of the legal system							10.00		8.33		8.30		8.33		8.33	
F. Legal enforcement of contracts											5.30		5.55		5.55	
G. Regulatory restrictions on sale of real property											6.00		7.34		7.55	
3. Access to Sound Money	**5.61**		**5.61**		**6.05**		**9.18**		**9.51**		**9.50**		**9.55**		**9.61**	
A. Money growth	7.96	(10.18)	7.84	(10.78)	8.23	(8.87)	8.80	(5.98)	8.77	(6.14)	8.80	(5.80)	8.89	(5.54)	9.08	(4.60)
B. Standard deviation of inflation	8.66	(3.34)	8.94	(2.64)	8.54	(3.66)	8.95	(2.62)	9.85	(0.39)	9.80	(0.55)	9.83	(0.42)	9.51	(1.21)
C. Inflation: most recent year	5.82	(20.90)	5.65	(21.73)	7.45	(12.77)	8.97	(5.16)	9.43	(2.85)	9.50	(2.29)	9.48	(2.59)	9.84	(−0.83)
D. Freedom to own foreign currency bank accounts	0.00		0.00		0.00		10.00		10.00		10.00		10.00		10.00	
4. Freedom to Trade Internationally	**6.69**		**6.87**		**7.21**		**7.94**		**8.10**		**7.00**		**7.20**		**7.05**	
A. Taxes on international trade	8.60		9.20		8.26		8.70		9.18		8.40		8.03		8.22	
(i) Revenues from trade taxes (% of trade sector)	8.60	(2.10)	9.20	(1.20)	9.13	(1.30)	9.80	(0.30)	9.78	(0.33)	9.60	(0.60)	9.61	(0.59)	9.44	(0.84)
(ii) Mean tariff rate					8.52	(7.40)	8.66	(6.70)	9.52	(2.40)	9.50	(2.70)	8.88	(5.60)	8.94	(5.30)
(iii) Standard deviation of tariff rates					7.12	(7.20)	7.64	(5.90)	8.24	(4.40)	6.10	(9.70)	5.61	(10.98)	6.29	(9.28)
B. Regulatory trade barriers							8.18		8.62		7.80		7.69		7.81	
(i) Non-tariff trade barriers							8.18		7.73		7.80		7.50		7.74	
(ii) Compliance cost of importing and exporting									9.50		7.80		7.89		7.89	
C. Size of trade sector relative to expected	5.05		5.35		5.24		4.47		4.70		3.50		3.94		2.82	
D. Black-market exchange rates	9.60		9.60		9.40		10.00		10.00		10.00		10.00		10.00	
E. International capital market controls	2.00		2.00		5.00		8.32		7.99		5.40		6.36		6.41	
(i) Foreign ownership/investment restrictions							8.64		9.05		7.70		6.56		6.67	
(ii) Capital controls	2.00		2.00		5.00		8.00		6.92		3.10		6.15		6.15	
5. Regulation of Credit, Labor, and Business	**4.54**		**4.89**		**4.71**		**5.72**		**6.32**		**6.20**		**6.24**		**5.73**	
A. Credit market regulations	4.42		6.17		5.76		7.12		7.82		7.20		7.60		6.08	
(i) Ownership of banks	0.00		0.00		2.00		2.00		5.00		5.00		5.00		5.00	
(ii) Foreign bank competition							7.87		7.27		8.00		8.00		8.00	
(iii) Private sector credit	9.27		8.50		7.29		7.78		8.51		5.70		7.39		1.32	
(iv) Interest rate controls/negative real interest rates	4.00		10.00		8.00		10.00		10.00		10.00		10.00		10.00	
B. Labor market regulations	3.78		3.46		3.13		4.64		4.46		5.30		5.18		5.16	
(i) Hiring regulations and minimum wage							6.42		4.05		6.70		6.70		5.57	
(ii) Hiring and firing regulations					3.40		3.40		2.83		2.90		2.44		2.18	
(iii) Centralized collective bargaining	5.18		5.18		5.18		5.18		4.88		5.50		5.62		5.28	
(iv) Hours regulations	6.16		5.19		3.96		5.22		5.51		5.30		5.30		6.00	
(v) Mandated cost of worker dismissal											1.20		1.01		1.97	
(vi) Conscription	0.00		0.00		0.00		3.00		5.00		10.00		10.00		10.00	
C. Business regulations							5.41		6.70		6.10		5.93		5.94	
(i) Price controls					5.00		6.00		6.00		6.00		6.00		6.00	
(ii) Administrative requirements									7.58		3.70		3.03		2.54	
(iii) Bureaucracy costs							5.53		7.20		3.60		3.50		3.54	
(iv) Starting a business							4.32		5.65		9.50		9.63		9.63	
(v) Extra payments/bribes/favoritism							5.79		7.04		8.30		6.89		6.83	
(vi) Licensing restrictions											5.50		6.14		6.39	
(vii) Cost of tax compliance											6.30		6.32		6.66	

Romania

Chain-Linked

	1980 Rating (Rank)	1985 Rating (Rank)	1990 Rating (Rank)	1995 Rating (Rank)	2000 Rating (Rank)	2005 Rating (Rank)	2008 Rating (Rank)	2009 Rating (Rank)
Summary Rating (Rank) ➤		4.64 (87)	4.54 (97)	3.90 (119)	5.19 (112)	6.82 (61)	6.72 (68)	6.93 (49)
Area 1. Size of Government	4.08 (80)	4.63 (66)	3.09 (107)	3.37 (110)	5.02 (91)	6.86 (50)	6.14 (74)	6.27 (62)
Area 2. Legal Structure and Security of Property Rights		3.67 (80)	5.77 (50)	5.19 (74)	5.58 (65)	5.90 (58)	6.07 (53)	6.09 (52)
Area 3. Access to Sound Money	6.61 (36)	6.95 (39)	7.18 (39)	0.74 (119)	2.71 (121)	8.30 (61)	8.24 (60)	9.03 (46)
Area 4. Freedom to Trade Internationally				3.97 (92)	5.78 (90)	6.42 (76)	6.93 (54)	7.05 (52)	7.04 (43)
Area 5. Regulation of Credit, Labor, and Business	3.29 (97)	3.08 (101)	3.08 (108)	4.21 (111)	6.22 (53)	6.18 (75)	6.20 (82)	6.33 (79)

Unadjusted

	1980	1985	1990	1995	2000	2005	2008	2009
Summary Rating (Rank) ➤		5.58 (52)	5.22 (70)	3.81 (119)	5.19 (112)	6.89 (63)	6.87 (68)	7.08 (48)
	Rating Data	Rating Data	Rating Data	Rating Data	Rating Data	Rating Data	Rating Data	Rating Data
1. Size of Government	**7.85**	**8.92**	**5.94**	**3.37**	**5.02**	**6.90**	**6.14**	**6.27**
A. Government consumption	9.41 (8.01)	9.85 (6.51)	6.82 (16.82)	6.81 (16.84)	7.50 (14.48)	8.40 (11.30)	5.54 (21.18)	6.09 (19.31)
B. Transfers and subsidies	6.29 (14.10)	7.98 (7.90)	5.07 (18.60)	6.16 (14.59)	6.09 (14.84)	7.00 (11.50)	6.52 (13.28)	6.50 (13.33)
C. Government enterprises and investment				0.00 (60.70)	4.00 (60.70)	6.00 (60.70)	6.00	6.00
D. Top marginal tax rate				0.50	2.50	6.00	6.50	6.50
(i) Top marginal income tax rate				1.00 (60)	5.00 (40)	10.00 (16)	10.00 (16)	10.00 (16)
(ii) Top marginal income and payroll tax rates				0.00 (72)	0.00 (68)	2.00 (54)	3.00 (50)	3.00 (50)
2. Legal Structure and Security of Property Rights		**3.99**	**6.28**	**5.64**	**5.58**	**5.70**	**5.86**	**5.87**
A. Judicial independence						3.10	4.09	4.12
B. Impartial courts				5.40	5.52	3.50	3.25	3.20
C. Protection of property rights					4.10	5.10	5.16	5.29
D. Military interference in rule of law and politics				6.37	8.33	8.30	8.33	8.33
E. Integrity of the legal system				6.96	6.67	6.70	6.67	6.67
F. Legal enforcement of contracts						5.20	4.85	4.85
G. Regulatory restrictions on sale of real property						8.00	8.67	8.67
3. Access to Sound Money	**6.61**	**6.95**	**7.18**	**0.74**	**2.71**	**8.30**	**8.24**	**9.03**
A. Money growth	7.76 (11.20)	9.75 (−1.25)	8.57 (7.13)	0.00 (58.13)	9.98 (−0.12)	8.90 (−5.40)	5.30 (23.50)	8.15 (9.25)
B. Standard deviation of inflation	8.78 (3.05)	8.11 (4.73)	7.87 (5.32)	0.00 (68.32)	0.00 (44.43)	6.10 (9.82)	9.24 (1.90)	9.10 (2.24)
C. Inflation: most recent year	9.88 (0.59)	9.93 (0.37)	7.26 (13.72)	2.94 (35.30)	0.87 (45.67)	8.20 (8.99)	8.43 (7.85)	8.88 (5.59)
D. Freedom to own foreign currency bank accounts	0.00	0.00	5.00	0.00	0.00	10.00	10.00	10.00
4. Freedom to Trade Internationally				**4.22**	**5.94**	**6.42**	**7.30**	**7.41**	**7.40**
A. Taxes on international trade				9.73	7.22	6.76	7.70	8.03	8.22
(i) Revenues from trade taxes (% of trade sector)				9.73 (0.40)	8.20 (2.70)	8.95 (1.58)	9.60 (0.60)	9.61 (0.59)	9.44 (0.84)
(ii) Mean tariff rate					6.24 (18.80)	6.96 (15.20)	8.70 (6.60)	8.88 (5.60)	8.94 (5.30)
(iii) Standard deviation of tariff rates						4.36 (14.10)	5.00 (12.60)	5.61 (10.98)	6.29 (9.28)
B. Regulatory trade barriers						5.48	6.90	7.34	7.43
(i) Non-tariff trade barriers						5.48	5.40	6.33	6.51
(ii) Compliance cost of importing and exporting							8.30	8.35	8.35
C. Size of trade sector relative to expected	7.35	3.41	3.11	4.86	5.30	5.20	4.42	4.66
D. Black-market exchange rates	0.00	0.00	0.00	9.40	10.00	10.00	10.00	10.00
E. International capital market controls	0.00	0.00	0.00	0.00	4.54	6.60	7.24	6.69
(i) Foreign ownership / investment restrictions					7.55	6.20	6.02	5.70
(ii) Capital controls	0.00	0.00	0.00	0.00	1.54	6.90	8.46	7.69
5. Regulation of Credit, Labor, and Business	**2.64**	**2.47**	**2.47**	**3.38**	**6.22**	**6.30**	**6.72**	**6.83**
A. Credit market regulations	0.00	0.00	0.00	0.67	6.58	7.60	7.53	7.53
(i) Ownership of banks	0.00	0.00	0.00	2.00		5.00	5.00	5.00
(ii) Foreign bank competition					8.07	7.00	7.00	7.00
(iii) Private sector credit	0.00	0.00	0.00	0.00	6.02	9.40	8.14	8.14
(iv) Interest rate controls / negative real interest rates			0.00	0.00	10.00	9.00	10.00	10.00
B. Labor market regulations					6.28	5.60	6.69	7.05
(i) Hiring regulations and minimum wage					4.66	3.30	3.30	3.33
(ii) Hiring and firing regulations					8.80	4.20	5.20	4.73
(iii) Centralized collective bargaining					8.67	7.90	6.39	6.62
(iv) Hours regulations						6.00	6.00	8.00
(v) Mandated cost of worker dismissal						9.40	9.26	9.60
(vi) Conscription	1.00	0.00	0.00	1.00	3.00	3.00	10.00	10.00
C. Business regulations					5.78	5.70	5.95	5.91
(i) Price controls				0.00	6.00	6.00	0.00	3.00	3.00
(ii) Administrative requirements					6.63	3.50	3.32	3.20
(iii) Bureaucracy costs					7.50	7.00	5.22	5.56
(iv) Starting a business					3.60	9.60	9.65	9.65
(v) Extra payments / bribes / favoritism					5.18	5.20	5.91	5.40
(vi) Licensing restrictions						6.70	6.80	7.07
(vii) Cost of tax compliance						7.80	7.74	7.51

Russia

Chain-Linked	1980 Rating (Rank)	1985 Rating (Rank)	1990 Rating (Rank)	1995 Rating (Rank)	2000 Rating (Rank)	2005 Rating (Rank)	2008 Rating (Rank)	2009 Rating (Rank)
Summary Rating (Rank) ➤				4.49 (112)	5.27 (109)	6.37 (82)	6.57 (76)	6.50 (77)
Area 1. Size of Government	1.25 (108)	1.15 (112)	1.24 (114)	6.78 (35)	6.77 (44)	7.24 (32)	7.27 (33)	6.78 (44)
Area 2. Legal Structure and Security of Property Rights				3.54 (114)	4.45 (88)	5.60 (66)	5.73 (64)	5.73 (63)
Area 3. Access to Sound Money	6.38 (46)	6.52 (63)	5.95 (74)	1.25 (117)	3.66 (115)	6.69 (96)	8.43 (55)	8.30 (66)
Area 4. Freedom to Trade Internationally				6.69 (59)	6.85 (66)	6.20 (87)	5.77 (99)	5.82 (92)
Area 5. Regulation of Credit, Labor, and Business	2.82 (100)	2.82 (104)	2.82 (112)	4.20 (112)	4.63 (108)	6.12 (80)	5.69 (103)	5.89 (99)

Unadjusted

	1980 Rating Data	1985 Rating Data	1990 Rating Data	1995 Rating Data	2000 Rating Data	2005 Rating Data	2008 Rating Data	2009 Rating Data
Summary Rating (Rank) ➤				4.40 (115)	5.27 (109)	6.38 (89)	6.62 (84)	6.55 (81)
1. Size of Government	**1.66**	**1.54**	**1.24**	**6.78**	**6.77**	**7.20**	**7.27**	**6.78**
A. Government consumption	3.03 (29.70)	2.65 (31.00)	2.99 (29.84)	3.74 (27.30)	5.01 (22.96)	4.40 (25.10)	4.21 (25.69)	3.83 (26.96)
B. Transfers and subsidies	1.96 (30.00)	1.96 (30.00)	1.96 (30.00)	7.90 (8.20)	6.56 (13.11)	7.00 (11.30)	6.36 (13.85)	4.80 (19.58)
C. Government enterprises and investment			0.00 (90.00)	10.00 (11.10)	10.00 (10.30)	10.00 (14.50)	10.00 (14.61)	10.00 (14.95)
D. Top marginal tax rate	0.00	0.00	0.00	5.50	5.50	7.50	8.50	8.50
(i) Top marginal income tax rate	0.00 (100)	0.00 (100)	0.00 (80)	8.00 (30)	8.00 (30)	10.00 (13)	10.00 (13)	10.00 (13)
(ii) Top marginal income and payroll tax rates				3.00 (51)	3.00 (50)	5.00 (39)	7.00 (35)	7.00 (35)
2. Legal Structure and Security of Property Rights				**3.43**	**4.45**	**5.60**	**5.73**	**5.73**
A. Judicial independence				3.48	3.51	2.10	2.82	2.87
B. Impartial courts				4.20	5.18	2.80	2.98	3.13
C. Protection of property rights				1.56	1.88	3.60	3.45	3.23
D. Military interference in rule of law and politics				4.49	6.67	7.50	7.50	7.50
E. Integrity of the legal system					5.00	6.70	6.67	6.67
F. Legal enforcement of contracts						7.50	7.53	7.53
G. Regulatory restrictions on sale of real property						8.90	9.15	9.15
3. Access to Sound Money	**5.72**	**6.52**	**5.95**	**1.25**	**3.66**	**6.70**	**8.43**	**8.30**
A. Money growth	7.88 (10.60)	8.08 (9.60)	8.06 (9.70)	0.00 (401.40)	2.19 (39.06)	5.30 (23.40)	7.65 (11.74)	8.28 (8.60)
B. Standard deviation of inflation	9.28 (1.80)	9.44 (1.40)	8.92 (2.70)	0.00 (522.92)	1.61 (20.98)	9.00 (2.57)	8.90 (2.75)	7.23 (6.92)
C. Inflation: most recent year		8.54 (7.30)	6.82 (15.90)	0.00 (170.74)	5.84 (20.78)	7.50 (12.68)	7.18 (14.11)	7.67 (11.65)
D. Freedom to own foreign currency bank accounts	0.00	0.00	0.00	5.00	5.00	5.00	10.00	10.00
4. Freedom to Trade Internationally				**6.44**	**6.85**	**6.20**	**5.77**	**5.82**
A. Taxes on international trade				6.60	7.00	5.10	4.26	4.31
(i) Revenues from trade taxes (% of trade sector)				7.07 (4.40)	6.92 (4.62)	1.20 (13.20)	0.00 (16.16)	0.79 (13.82)
(ii) Mean tariff rate				7.70 (11.50)	7.48 (12.60)	8.10 (9.60)	7.84 (10.80)	7.90 (10.50)
(iii) Standard deviation of tariff rates				5.04 (12.40)	6.60 (8.50)	6.00 (10.00)	4.94 (12.64)	4.25 (14.39)
B. Regulatory trade barriers				4.32	5.06	4.80	4.61	4.54
(i) Non-tariff trade barriers				4.32	3.78	4.80	4.33	4.17
(ii) Compliance cost of importing and exporting					6.33	4.90	4.90	4.90
C. Size of trade sector relative to expected			5.79	7.73	9.35	7.10	6.23	5.65
D. Black-market exchange rates	0.00	0.00	0.00	10.00	10.00	10.00	10.00	10.00
E. International capital market controls	0.00	0.00	0.00	3.54	2.86	4.00	3.73	4.61
(i) Foreign ownership/investment restrictions				5.08	5.71	4.20	4.12	4.21
(ii) Capital controls	0.00	0.00	0.00	2.00	0.00	3.80	3.33	5.00
5. Regulation of Credit, Labor, and Business	**2.47**	**2.47**	**2.98**	**4.12**	**4.63**	**6.20**	**5.91**	**6.11**
A. Credit market regulations	0.00	0.00	0.17	4.67	4.28	8.00	7.50	8.25
(i) Ownership of banks	0.00	0.00	0.00	2.00	2.00	5.00	5.00	5.00
(ii) Foreign bank competition				3.93	4.32	8.00	8.00	8.00
(iii) Private sector credit			0.50	5.05	5.88	10.00	10.00	10.00
(iv) Interest rate controls/negative real interest rates	0.00	0.00	0.00	8.00	5.00	9.00	7.00	10.00
B. Labor market regulations			1.84	4.00	4.50	6.00	6.07	6.10
(i) Hiring regulations and minimum wage				6.00	2.58	6.70	6.70	5.00
(ii) Hiring and firing regulations			1.03	1.03	6.08	6.80	5.39	4.76
(iii) Centralized collective bargaining			4.49	7.24	8.30	8.00	6.93	6.67
(iv) Hours regulations				5.72	5.51	6.00	6.00	8.00
(v) Mandated cost of worker dismissal						8.40	8.42	9.20
(vi) Conscription	0.00	0.00	0.00	0.00	0.00	0.00	3.00	3.00
C. Business regulations				3.68	5.12	4.50	4.14	3.98
(i) Price controls			0.00	5.00	5.00	2.00	1.00	1.00
(ii) Administrative requirements				6.22	2.10	2.39	2.45	
(iii) Bureaucracy costs				4.79	5.00	3.60	5.40	5.50
(iv) Starting a business				3.52	4.00	9.00	9.01	9.00
(v) Extra payments/bribes/favoritism				1.40	5.36	5.60	3.66	3.53
(vi) Licensing restrictions						4.40	1.13	0.00
(vii) Cost of tax compliance						5.00	6.41	6.41

Rwanda

	1980	1985	1990	1995	2000	2005	2008	2009
Chain-Linked	Rating (Rank)	Rating (Rank)	Rating (Rank)	Rating (Rank)	Rating (Rank)	Rating (Rank)	Rating (Rank)	Rating (Rank)
Summary Rating (Rank) ➤			5.08 (80)	3.89 (120)	5.45 (105)	5.70 (105)	6.61 (75)	6.43 (81)
Area 1. Size of Government	4.94 (57)	5.08 (56)	6.59 (27)	6.32 (51)	7.39 (23)	6.50 (65)	6.69 (50)	5.60 (81)
Area 2. Legal Structure and Security of Property Rights				1.97 (123)	1.98 (123)	1.86 (123)	3.56 (110)	3.65 (112)
Area 3. Access to Sound Money	6.45 (42)	6.76 (47)	6.06 (71)	3.17 (107)	7.44 (70)	7.75 (74)	7.29 (86)	7.55 (81)
Area 4. Freedom to Trade Internationally								
Area 5. Regulation of Credit, Labor, and Business	4.99 (64)	5.07 (58)	5.01 (71)	3.99 (114)	4.99 (102)	6.53 (61)	7.65 (19)	7.75 (16)

Unadjusted								
Summary Rating (Rank) ➤	5.13 (68)		5.08 (75)	3.92 (118)	5.45 (105)	5.60 (125)	6.44 (91)	6.29 (96)
	Rating Data	Rating Data	Rating Data	Rating Data	Rating Data	Rating Data	Rating Data	Rating Data
1. Size of Government	5.95	4.08	6.59	6.32	7.39	6.50	6.69	5.60
A. Government consumption	7.93 (13.04)	8.15 (12.28)	8.59 (10.81)	9.42 (7.98)	8.63 (10.66)	8.00 (12.90)	8.52 (11.02)	7.27 (15.29)
B. Transfers and subsidies	9.92 (0.80)		9.18 (3.50)	9.54 (2.20)	9.54 (2.20)	9.50 (2.20)	9.54 (2.20)	9.54 (2.20)
C. Government enterprises and investment	0.00 (100.00)	0.00 (100.00)	2.00 (40.46)	0.00 (60.25)	4.00 (33.90)	2.00 (42.20)	2.00 (45.61)	0.00 (51.17)
D. Top marginal tax rate								
(i) Top marginal income tax rate								
(ii) Top marginal income and payroll tax rates								
2. Legal Structure and Security of Property Rights				2.38	1.98	3.00	5.78	6.19
A. Judicial independence								6.80
B. Impartial courts				3.43	3.48	3.80	4.70	5.54
C. Protection of property rights								6.59
D. Military interference in rule of law and politics					0.00	3.10	6.00	5.40
E. Integrity of the legal system				0.00	0.00			
F. Legal enforcement of contracts						3.30	3.72	3.95
G. Regulatory restrictions on sale of real property						1.80	8.70	8.83
3. Access to Sound Money	6.45	6.76	6.06	3.17	7.44	7.70	7.29	7.55
A. Money growth	8.44 (7.78)	10.00 (0.01)	9.59 (−2.07)	4.43 (27.87)	8.62 (6.88)	9.90 (0.30)	8.86 (5.71)	8.86 (5.71)
B. Standard deviation of inflation	7.99 (5.03)	7.97 (5.07)	7.34 (6.65)	3.27 (16.82)	6.98 (7.56)	7.90 (5.35)	8.38 (4.04)	8.40 (3.99)
C. Inflation: most recent year	9.39 (3.06)	9.09 (4.56)	7.31 (13.46)	0.00 (54.20)	9.14 (4.29)	8.20 (9.01)	6.91 (15.44)	7.93 (10.36)
D. Freedom to own foreign currency bank accounts	0.00	0.00	0.00	5.00	5.00	5.00	5.00	5.00
4. Freedom to Trade Internationally	2.50		2.64	3.75		4.10	5.03	5.01
A. Taxes on international trade	1.13		0.53	1.10		6.30	6.17	6.15
(i) Revenues from trade taxes (% of trade sector)	1.13 (13.30)		0.53 (14.20)	0.27 (14.60)				
(ii) Mean tariff rate					3.04 (34.80)	6.60 (17.20)	6.28 (18.60)	6.26 (18.70)
(iii) Standard deviation of tariff rates					0.00 (33.10)	6.00 (9.90)	6.06 (9.86)	6.04 (9.91)
B. Regulatory trade barriers						0.10	4.79	4.72
(i) Non-tariff trade barriers								4.33
(ii) Compliance cost of importing and exporting						0.10	4.79	5.11
C. Size of trade sector relative to expected	3.10	0.24	0.00	0.00	0.00	0.50	1.10	0.00
D. Black-market exchange rates	0.00	0.20	4.40	9.40	10.00	10.00	10.00	10.00
E. International capital market controls	0.00	0.00	0.00	0.00	1.54	3.80	3.08	4.17
(i) Foreign ownership / investment restrictions								6.03
(ii) Capital controls	0.00	0.00	0.00	0.00	1.54	3.80	3.08	2.31
5. Regulation of Credit, Labor, and Business	5.62	5.72	5.01	3.99	4.99	6.60	7.43	7.09
A. Credit market regulations	5.01	5.26	5.08	1.68	5.01	6.30	6.01	6.01
(i) Ownership of banks	0.00	0.00	0.00	0.00	0.00	8.00	8.00	8.00
(ii) Foreign bank competition						3.00	3.00	3.00
(iii) Private sector credit	9.03	7.79	5.24	5.04	5.04	5.00	5.04	5.04
(iv) Interest rate controls / negative real interest rates	6.00	8.00	10.00	0.00	10.00	9.00	8.00	8.00
B. Labor market regulations						7.30	9.12	8.47
(i) Hiring regulations and minimum wage						5.60	8.90	8.90
(ii) Hiring and firing regulations								5.93
(iii) Centralized collective bargaining								7.99
(iv) Hours regulations						6.00	10.00	10.00
(v) Mandated cost of worker dismissal						7.60	7.59	7.99
(vi) Conscription	10.00	10.00	10.00	10.00	10.00	10.00	10.00	10.00
C. Business regulations						6.10	7.17	6.79
(i) Price controls			0.00	0.00	0.00	4.00	4.00	4.00
(ii) Administrative requirements								6.72
(iii) Bureaucracy costs								4.08
(iv) Starting a business						7.50	9.80	9.81
(v) Extra payments / bribes / favoritism								7.46
(vi) Licensing restrictions						4.90	6.67	7.10
(vii) Cost of tax compliance						8.10	8.21	8.34

Senegal

	1980	1985	1990	1995	2000	2005	2008	2009
Chain-Linked	Rating (Rank)	Rating (Rank)	Rating (Rank)	Rating (Rank)	Rating (Rank)	Rating (Rank)	Rating (Rank)	Rating (Rank)
Summary Rating (Rank) ➤	**4.65** (76)	**5.31** (57)	**5.41** (65)	**4.83** (101)	**5.90** (89)	**5.70** (105)	**5.56** (108)	**5.67** (106)
Area 1. Size of Government	4.15 (77)	6.17 (23)	6.96 (20)	5.67 (75)	7.08 (31)	6.05 (79)	5.32 (98)	5.42 (88)
Area 2. Legal Structure and Security of Property Rights	3.41 (63)	3.99 (75)	3.99 (78)	3.40 (116)	4.43 (91)	4.05 (103)	3.90 (105)	4.01 (105)
Area 3. Access to Sound Money	6.36 (47)	6.76 (47)	6.93 (51)	5.80 (77)	7.28 (72)	7.11 (85)	6.83 (91)	7.02 (91)
Area 4. Freedom to Trade Internationally	5.13 (54)	5.50 (52)	4.90 (74)	5.20 (100)	6.32 (81)	5.61 (104)	5.73 (102)	5.69 (96)
Area 5. Regulation of Credit, Labor, and Business	4.33 (83)	4.13 (88)	4.35 (92)	4.05 (113)	4.41 (113)	5.64 (103)	5.89 (97)	6.11 (90)

	1980	1985	1990	1995	2000	2005	2008	2009
Unadjusted								
Summary Rating (Rank) ➤	**5.27** (59)	**5.25** (65)	**5.25** (69)	**4.69** (103)	**5.90** (89)	**5.66** (123)	**5.62** (124)	**5.73** (124)
	Rating Data	Rating Data	Rating Data	Rating Data	Rating Data	Rating Data	Rating Data	Rating Data
1. Size of Government	**6.36**	**5.32**	**6.01**	**4.89**	**7.08**	**6.00**	**5.32**	**5.42**
A. Government consumption	6.08 (19.34)	6.97 (16.31)	7.02 (16.13)	7.68 (13.90)	8.32 (11.70)	8.50 (11.20)	8.58 (10.84)	8.98 (9.45)
B. Transfers and subsidies	8.99 (4.20)				10.00 (0.43)	8.70 (5.20)	8.71 (5.24)	8.71 (5.24)
C. Government enterprises and investment	4.00 (32.20)	8.00 (18.20)	7.00 (22.60)	7.00 (21.50)	7.00 (20.10)	4.00 (33.60)	4.00 (33.11)	4.00 (36.20)
D. Top marginal tax rate		1.00	4.00	0.00	3.00	3.00	0.00	0.00
(i) Top marginal income tax rate		1.00 (65)	4.00 (48)	0.00 (64)	3.00 (50)	3.00 (50)	0.00 (61)	0.00 (61)
(ii) Top marginal income and payroll tax rates			4.00 (48)	0.00 (64)	3.00 (50)	3.00 (50)	0.00 (61)	0.00 (61)
2. Legal Structure and Security of Property Rights	**3.41**	**3.99**	**3.99**	**3.40**	**4.43**	**3.80**	**3.76**	**3.87**
A. Judicial independence							2.90	3.49
B. Impartial courts				5.39	5.33	5.10	3.62	4.08
C. Protection of property rights							5.40	5.07
D. Military interference in rule of law and politics				3.99	3.33	3.30	3.33	3.33
E. Integrity of the legal system				0.00	5.00	5.00	5.00	5.00
F. Legal enforcement of contracts						3.40	3.39	3.39
G. Regulatory restrictions on sale of real property						2.30	2.66	2.69
3. Access to Sound Money	**6.36**	**6.76**	**6.93**	**5.80**	**7.28**	**7.10**	**6.83**	**7.02**
A. Money growth	8.79 (6.05)	9.54 (2.30)	8.94 (−5.32)	8.73 (6.34)	9.45 (2.74)	9.40 (2.90)	9.41 (2.93)	9.32 (3.41)
B. Standard deviation of inflation	8.95 (2.63)	9.38 (1.55)	9.01 (2.47)	5.65 (10.87)	9.82 (0.44)	9.30 (1.64)	9.07 (2.33)	8.98 (2.54)
C. Inflation: most recent year	7.69 (11.53)	8.14 (9.30)	9.76 (1.19)	8.82 (5.92)	9.85 (0.73)	9.70 (1.70)	8.85 (5.77)	9.79 (−1.05)
D. Freedom to own foreign currency bank accounts	0.00	0.00	0.00	0.00	0.00	0.00	0.00	0.00
4. Freedom to Trade Internationally	**5.34**	**5.50**	**4.90**	**5.20**	**6.32**	**5.70**	**6.22**	**6.18**
A. Taxes on international trade	2.40	3.33	2.57	2.25	6.02	6.10	6.25	6.25
(i) Revenues from trade taxes (% of trade sector)	2.40 (11.40)	4.47 (8.30)	2.13 (11.80)	1.33 (13.00)	4.44 (8.34)	3.80 (9.30)	3.83 (9.25)	3.83 (9.25)
(ii) Mean tariff rate		2.20 (39.00)	3.00 (35.00)	3.16 (34.20)	7.60 (12.00)	7.20 (14.00)	7.62 (11.90)	7.62 (11.90)
(iii) Standard deviation of tariff rates						7.30 (6.80)	7.29 (6.78)	7.29 (6.78)
B. Regulatory trade barriers						6.90	6.93	7.11
(i) Non-tariff trade barriers						5.49	5.49	5.86
(ii) Compliance cost of importing and exporting						6.90	8.37	8.37
C. Size of trade sector relative to expected	6.50	6.13	4.51	5.76	5.09	4.70	4.72	4.39
D. Black-market exchange rates	9.60	9.80	9.20	9.80	10.00	10.00	10.00	10.00
E. International capital market controls	0.00	0.00	0.00	0.00	2.31	0.80	3.21	3.13
(i) Foreign ownership/investment restrictions							5.65	5.50
(ii) Capital controls	0.00	0.00	0.00	0.00	2.31	0.80	0.77	0.77
5. Regulation of Credit, Labor, and Business	**4.91**	**4.68**	**4.45**	**4.14**	**4.41**	**5.70**	**5.97**	**6.17**
A. Credit market regulations	6.46	5.86	6.53	4.84	5.68	8.80	8.84	8.84
(i) Ownership of banks	2.00	2.00	2.00	2.00	2.00	10.00	10.00	10.00
(ii) Foreign bank competition								
(iii) Private sector credit	9.37	9.57	9.60	8.53	9.37	8.50	8.52	8.52
(iv) Interest rate controls/negative real interest rates	8.00	6.00	8.00	4.00		8.00	8.00	8.00
B. Labor market regulations						3.50	4.16	4.59
(i) Hiring regulations and minimum wage						2.80	2.80	3.90
(ii) Hiring and firing regulations							5.13	4.85
(iii) Centralized collective bargaining							5.84	5.93
(iv) Hours regulations						4.70	4.70	6.00
(v) Mandated cost of worker dismissal						6.50	6.48	6.89
(vi) Conscription	0.00	0.00	0.00	0.00	0.00	0.00	0.00	0.00
C. Business regulations						4.60	4.91	5.08
(i) Price controls				0.00	2.00	4.00	4.00	4.00	4.00
(ii) Administrative requirements							3.64	4.03
(iii) Bureaucracy costs							5.76	5.55
(iv) Starting a business						6.10	8.40	8.41
(v) Extra payments/bribes/favoritism							3.56	4.36
(vi) Licensing restrictions						6.20	6.49	6.66
(vii) Cost of tax compliance						2.20	2.53	2.53

Serbia

	1980	1985	1990	1995	2000	2005	2008	2009
Chain-Linked						Rating (Rank)	Rating (Rank)	Rating (Rank)
Summary Rating (Rank) ➤								
Area 1. Size of Government								
Area 2. Legal Structure and Security of Property Rights								
Area 3. Access to Sound Money								
Area 4. Freedom to Trade Internationally								
Area 5. Regulation of Credit, Labor, and Business								

Unadjusted

	1980	1985	1990	1995	2000	2005	2008	2009
Summary Rating (Rank) ➤						**5.75** (120)	**6.32** (96)	**6.44** (91)
						Rating *Data*	Rating *Data*	Rating *Data*
1. Size of Government						**6.50**	**6.34**	**6.85**
A. Government consumption						5.60 *(21.00)*	5.46 *(21.43)*	5.76 *(20.42)*
B. Transfers and subsidies						4.30 *(21.60)*	4.38 *(21.11)*	4.14 *(21.99)*
C. Government enterprises and investment						10.00 *(14.90)*	8.00 *(18.14)*	10.00 *(13.16)*
D. Top marginal tax rate						6.00	7.50	7.50
(i) Top marginal income tax rate						10.00 *(15)*	10.00 *(15)*	10.00 *(15)*
(ii) Top marginal income and payroll tax rates						2.00 *(53)*	5.00 *(37)*	5.00 *(37)*
2. Legal Structure and Security of Property Rights						**4.70**	**4.74**	**4.68**
A. Judicial independence						2.50	3.04	2.55
B. Impartial courts						2.90	2.72	2.71
C. Protection of property rights						4.60	4.03	3.68
D. Military interference in rule of law and politics						6.70	6.67	6.67
E. Integrity of the legal system						5.80	5.83	5.83
F. Legal enforcement of contracts						4.00	3.92	3.92
G. Regulatory restrictions on sale of real property						6.10	6.98	7.39
3. Access to Sound Money						**4.50**	**7.34**	**7.72**
A. Money growth						6.40 *(18.00)*	8.33 *(8.36)*	8.91 *(5.44)*
B. Standard deviation of inflation						0.00 *(32.54)*	8.60 *(3.51)*	8.52 *(3.69)*
C. Inflation: most recent year						6.80 *(16.10)*	7.43 *(12.87)*	8.44 *(7.78)*
D. Freedom to own foreign currency bank accounts						5.00	5.00	5.00
4. Freedom to Trade Internationally						**6.40**	**6.68**	**6.30**
A. Taxes on international trade						7.80	7.92	8.05
(i) Revenues from trade taxes (% of trade sector)						7.50 *(3.80)*	8.11 *(2.83)*	8.46 *(2.32)*
(ii) Mean tariff rate						8.40 *(8.20)*	8.52 *(7.40)*	8.54 *(7.30)*
(iii) Standard deviation of tariff rates						7.40 *(6.40)*	7.13 *(7.18)*	7.17 *(7.08)*
B. Regulatory trade barriers						6.80	6.92	6.99
(i) Non-tariff trade barriers						5.40	5.56	5.70
(ii) Compliance cost of importing and exporting						8.30	8.28	8.28
C. Size of trade sector relative to expected						4.30	4.36	3.46
D. Black-market exchange rates						10.00	10.00	10.00
E. International capital market controls						3.10	4.21	3.01
(i) Foreign ownership / investment restrictions						5.40	5.08	5.24
(ii) Capital controls						0.80	3.33	0.77
5. Regulation of Credit, Labor, and Business						**6.70**	**6.49**	**6.64**
A. Credit market regulations						9.00	8.68	9.12
(i) Ownership of banks						10.00	10.00	10.00
(ii) Foreign bank competition						8.00	8.00	8.00
(iii) Private sector credit						9.20	7.71	8.49
(iv) Interest rate controls / negative real interest rates						9.00	9.00	10.00
B. Labor market regulations						5.90	5.72	5.71
(i) Hiring regulations and minimum wage						3.30	2.20	2.23
(ii) Hiring and firing regulations						5.00	5.25	4.61
(iii) Centralized collective bargaining						7.10	6.90	6.79
(iv) Hours regulations						9.30	9.30	10.00
(v) Mandated cost of worker dismissal						7.70	7.68	7.66
(vi) Conscription						3.00	3.00	3.00
C. Business regulations						5.20	5.08	5.09
(i) Price controls							4.00	4.00
(ii) Administrative requirements						1.70	1.93	2.22
(iii) Bureaucracy costs						5.10	5.67	5.76
(iv) Starting a business						9.10	9.49	9.48
(v) Extra payments / bribes / favoritism						5.70	4.70	4.20
(vi) Licensing restrictions						2.60	2.92	3.07
(vii) Cost of tax compliance						6.90	6.87	6.87

Sierra Leone

	1980	1985	1990	1995	2000	2005	2008	2009
Chain-Linked	Rating (Rank)	Rating (Rank)	Rating (Rank)	Rating (Rank)	Rating (Rank)	Rating (Rank)	Rating (Rank)	Rating (Rank)
Summary Rating (Rank) ➤	**5.51** (53)	**3.89** (100)	**4.04** (103)	**4.47** (113)	**5.31** (107)	**5.35** (115)	**5.42** (111)	**5.44** (112)
Area 1. Size of Government	7.79 (9)	7.71 (4)	6.67 (26)	6.23 (56)	5.83 (75)	7.12 (39)	6.68 (51)	5.87 (73)
Area 2. Legal Structure and Security of Property Rights		5.25 (54)	5.30 (54)	2.64 (120)	3.52 (111)	3.15 (115)	3.35 (114)	3.95 (106)
Area 3. Access to Sound Money	6.02 (66)	0.42 (111)	0.06 (121)	3.81 (103)	6.47 (99)	6.32 (106)	7.32 (85)	7.54 (83)
Area 4. Freedom to Trade Internationally	2.85 (89)	2.07 (96)	3.58 (98)	4.59 (106)	4.64 (118)	5.05 (113)	4.46 (117)	4.53 (116)
Area 5. Regulation of Credit, Labor, and Business	5.19 (55)	4.04 (90)	4.57 (85)	5.07 (80)	6.10 (58)	5.13 (112)	5.36 (110)	5.40 (109)

	1980	1985	1990	1995	2000	2005	2008	2009
Unadjusted								
Summary Rating (Rank) ➤	**5.35** (57)	**4.00** (97)	**4.04** (102)	**4.48** (112)	**5.31** (107)	**5.52** (128)	**5.59** (126)	**5.62** (126)
	Rating Data	Rating Data	Rating Data	Rating Data	Rating Data	Rating Data	Rating Data	Rating Data
1. Size of Government	**6.65**	**7.71**	**6.67**	**6.23**	**5.83**	**7.10**	**6.68**	**5.87**
A. Government consumption	9.29 (8.40)	9.15 (8.90)	8.30 (11.78)	7.72 (13.75)	7.79 (13.50)	7.80 (13.40)	8.03 (12.70)	7.62 (14.09)
B. Transfers and subsidies		9.97 (0.60)	9.70 (1.60)	8.96 (4.30)	9.71 (1.57)	9.50 (2.30)	10.00 (0.00)	10.00 (0.00)
C. Government enterprises and investment	4.00 (35.80)	4.00 (31.00)	2.00 (40.40)	2.00 (46.43)	0.00 (75.30)	4.00 (33.40)	2.00 (41.86)	0.00 (50.79)
D. Top marginal tax rate								
(i) Top marginal income tax rate								
(ii) Top marginal income and payroll tax rates								
2. Legal Structure and Security of Property Rights		**5.25**	**5.30**	**2.64**	**3.52**	**3.10**	**3.35**	**3.95**
A. Judicial independence								
B. Impartial courts				3.96	4.89	3.60	3.70	3.80
C. Protection of property rights								
D. Military interference in rule of law and politics				2.27	0.00	4.20	4.17	4.17
E. Integrity of the legal system				0.00	5.00	5.80	5.83	5.83
F. Legal enforcement of contracts						1.60	1.58	1.58
G. Regulatory restrictions on sale of real property						0.60	1.46	4.36
3. Access to Sound Money	**6.02**	**0.42**	**0.06**	**3.81**	**6.47**	**6.30**	**7.32**	**7.54**
A. Money growth	7.16 (14.22)	1.69 (41.56)	0.24 (48.82)	6.93 (15.37)	4.37 (28.16)	5.90 (20.40)	8.15 (9.23)	8.22 (8.92)
B. Standard deviation of inflation	8.90 (2.76)	0.00 (26.10)	0.00 (29.16)	0.00 (26.09)	6.67 (8.33)	6.80 (8.04)	9.09 (2.28)	8.80 (3.01)
C. Inflation: most recent year	8.02 (9.90)	0.00 (85.08)	0.00 (89.15)	3.30 (33.49)	9.83 (−0.84)	7.60 (12.05)	7.03 (14.83)	8.15 (9.25)
D. Freedom to own foreign currency bank accounts	0.00	0.00	0.00	5.00	5.00	5.00	5.00	5.00
4. Freedom to Trade Internationally	**3.23**	**2.35**	**3.58**	**4.67**	**4.64**	**5.60**	**4.93**	**5.00**
A. Taxes on international trade	2.99	3.45	7.37	4.48	3.37	5.60	5.26	6.46
(i) Revenues from trade taxes (% of trade sector)	1.13 (13.30)	2.07 (11.90)	7.37 (3.95)	4.11 (8.83)	3.37 (9.95)	3.30 (10.00)	2.19 (11.71)	5.80 (6.30)
(ii) Mean tariff rate	4.84 (25.80)	4.84 (25.80)		4.84 (25.80)		7.30 (13.60)	7.28 (13.60)	7.28 (13.60)
(iii) Standard deviation of tariff rates						6.30 (9.20)	6.30 (9.25)	6.30 (9.25)
B. Regulatory trade barriers						5.40	6.05	6.05
(i) Non-tariff trade barriers								
(ii) Compliance cost of importing and exporting						5.40	6.05	6.05
C. Size of trade sector relative to expected	4.88	0.00	2.28	1.02	1.97	2.90	0.00	0.00
D. Black-market exchange rates	0.00	0.00	0.00	9.60	5.00	10.00	10.00	10.00
E. International capital market controls	0.00	0.00	0.00	0.00	4.61	3.80	3.33	2.50
(i) Foreign ownership / investment restrictions								
(ii) Capital controls	0.00	0.00	0.00	0.00	4.61	3.80	3.33	2.50
5. Regulation of Credit, Labor, and Business	**5.49**	**4.29**	**4.57**	**5.07**	**6.10**	**5.40**	**5.66**	**5.74**
A. Credit market regulations	4.67	1.47	2.94	3.25	6.67	5.30	5.31	5.66
(i) Ownership of banks	2.00	2.00	2.00	2.00	2.00	2.00	2.00	2.00
(ii) Foreign bank competition								
(iii) Private sector credit	6.02	2.40	6.82	5.76	10.00	4.90	4.94	5.98
(iv) Interest rate controls / negative real interest rates	6.00	0.00	0.00	2.00	8.00	9.00	9.00	9.00
B. Labor market regulations						5.70	5.68	5.39
(i) Hiring regulations and minimum wage						6.70	6.70	5.57
(ii) Hiring and firing regulations								
(iii) Centralized collective bargaining								
(iv) Hours regulations						6.00	6.00	6.00
(v) Mandated cost of worker dismissal						0.00	0.00	0.00
(vi) Conscription	10.00	10.00	10.00	10.00	10.00	10.00	10.00	10.00
C. Business regulations						5.30	6.00	6.16
(i) Price controls			2.00	6.00	6.00	4.00	4.00	4.00
(ii) Administrative requirements								
(iii) Bureaucracy costs								
(iv) Starting a business						5.80	8.37	8.45
(v) Extra payments / bribes / favoritism								
(vi) Licensing restrictions						6.00	5.64	6.19
(vii) Cost of tax compliance						5.50	6.00	6.00

Singapore

	1980		1985		1990		1995		2000		2005		2008		2009	
Chain-Linked	Rating	(Rank)	Rating	(Rank)	Rating	(Rank)	Rating	(Rank)	Rating	(Rank)	Rating	(Rank)	Rating	(Rank)	Rating	(Rank)
Summary Rating (Rank) ➤	**7.93**	(4)	**8.13**	(4)	**8.73**	(2)	**8.81**	(2)	**8.53**	(2)	**8.82**	(2)	**8.75**	(2)	**8.73**	(2)
Area 1. Size of Government	6.98	(12)	6.59	(15)	8.22	(5)	8.39	(6)	7.97	(13)	8.00	(15)	8.17	(10)	8.11	(11)
Area 2. Legal Structure and Security of Property Rights	9.48	(4)	8.45	(16)	8.45	(22)	8.31	(16)	8.53	(17)	8.28	(14)	8.38	(10)	8.30	(9)
Area 3. Access to Sound Money	6.51	(39)	8.29	(24)	9.34	(15)	9.69	(10)	9.46	(22)	9.71	(2)	9.10	(36)	9.12	(43)
Area 4. Freedom to Trade Internationally	9.29	(2)	9.70	(2)	9.71	(2)	9.68	(2)	9.32	(2)	9.34	(2)	9.34	(2)	9.36	(1)
Area 5. Regulation of Credit, Labor, and Business	7.83	(3)	7.84	(4)	7.97	(5)	7.97	(5)	7.39	(9)	8.75	(2)	8.72	(1)	8.74	(2)

Unadjusted																
Summary Rating (Rank) ➤	**7.40**	(6)	**7.58**	(5)	**8.15**	(2)	**8.80**	(2)	**8.53**	(2)	**8.77**	(2)	**8.70**	(2)	**8.68**	(2)
	Rating	Data	Rating	Data	Rating	Data	Rating	Data	Rating	Data	Rating	Data	Rating	Data	Rating	Data
1. Size of Government	**6.98**		**6.59**		**8.22**		**8.39**		**7.97**		**8.00**		**8.17**		**8.11**	
A. Government consumption	7.08	(15.93)	4.70	(24.02)	6.45	(18.06)	6.92	(16.47)	5.65	(20.80)	5.80	(20.20)	5.68	(20.68)	5.42	(21.56)
B. Transfers and subsidies	9.84	(1.10)	9.65	(1.80)	9.43	(2.60)	9.65	(1.80)	9.23	(3.32)	9.20	(3.50)	10.00	(0.05)	10.00	(0.05)
C. Government enterprises and investment	7.00	(24.20)	4.00	(34.70)	8.00	(18.60)	8.00	(18.60)	8.00	(18.60)	7.00	(21.30)	7.00	(21.30)	7.00	
D. Top marginal tax rate	4.00		8.00		9.00		9.00		9.00		10.00		10.00		10.00	
(i) Top marginal income tax rate	4.00	(55)	8.00	(40)	9.00	(33)	9.00	(30)	9.00	(28)	10.00	(21)	10.00	(20)	10.00	(20)
(ii) Top marginal income and payroll tax rates					9.00	(33)	9.00	(30)	9.00	(28)	10.00	(21)	10.00	(20)	10.00	(20)
2. Legal Structure and Security of Property Rights	**8.13**		**7.25**		**7.25**		**8.31**		**8.53**		**8.30**		**8.38**		**8.30**	
A. Judicial independence							7.17		7.35		7.00		7.99		7.73	
B. Impartial courts							7.05		7.68		8.00		8.21		8.03	
C. Protection of property rights							7.33		7.62		8.90		9.02		8.90	
D. Military interference in rule of law and politics							10.00		10.00		8.30		8.33		8.33	
E. Integrity of the legal system							10.00		10.00		8.30		8.33		8.33	
F. Legal enforcement of contracts											8.50		7.77		7.77	
G. Regulatory restrictions on sale of real property											8.90		8.99		8.99	
3. Access to Sound Money	**6.51**		**8.29**		**9.34**		**9.69**		**9.46**		**9.70**		**9.10**		**9.12**	
A. Money growth	9.76	(1.21)	9.47	(−2.66)	9.42	(2.90)	9.89	(0.55)	9.42	(−2.88)	9.80	(0.90)	8.44	(7.79)	7.45	(12.77)
B. Standard deviation of inflation	8.57	(3.57)	8.90	(2.76)	8.91	(2.73)	9.39	(1.53)	8.70	(3.24)	9.10	(2.21)	9.26	(1.85)	9.15	(2.13)
C. Inflation: most recent year	7.71	(11.47)	9.78	(−1.10)	9.02	(4.92)	9.47	(2.66)	9.73	(1.36)	9.90	(0.43)	8.70	(6.52)	9.88	(0.60)
D. Freedom to own foreign currency bank accounts	0.00		5.00		10.00		10.00		10.00		10.00		10.00		10.00	
4. Freedom to Trade Internationally	**9.19**		**9.60**		**9.56**		**9.56**		**9.32**		**9.30**		**9.34**		**9.36**	
A. Taxes on international trade	9.84		9.87		9.70		9.59		9.95		10.00		10.00		10.00	
(i) Revenues from trade taxes (% of trade sector)	9.73	(0.40)	9.80	(0.30)	9.91	(0.14)	9.93	(0.10)	9.93	(0.11)	10.00	(0.00)	10.00	(0.00)	10.00	(0.00)
(ii) Mean tariff rate	9.94	(0.30)	9.94	(0.30)	9.92	(0.40)	9.92	(0.40)	9.92	(0.40)	10.00	(0.10)	10.00	(0.00)	10.00	(0.00)
(iii) Standard deviation of tariff rates					9.28	(1.80)	8.92	(2.70)	10.00	(0.00)	10.00	(0.00)	10.00	(0.00)	10.00	(0.00)
B. Regulatory trade barriers							8.85		9.39		9.10		9.24		9.11	
(i) Non-tariff trade barriers							8.85		8.79		8.60		8.92		8.73	
(ii) Compliance cost of importing and exporting									10.00		9.60		9.56		9.50	
C. Size of trade sector relative to expected	10.00		10.00		10.00		10.00		10.00		10.00		10.00		10.00	
D. Black-market exchange rates	10.00		10.00		10.00		10.00		10.00		10.00		10.00		10.00	
E. International capital market controls	8.00		10.00		10.00		9.34		7.25		7.60		7.46		7.71	
(i) Foreign ownership/investment restrictions							8.68		9.12		9.10		8.76		8.49	
(ii) Capital controls	8.00		10.00		10.00		10.00		5.38		6.20		6.15		6.92	
5. Regulation of Credit, Labor, and Business	**6.18**		**6.19**		**6.37**		**8.03**		**7.39**		**8.50**		**8.50**		**8.51**	
A. Credit market regulations	9.64		9.67		10.00		8.56		8.27		9.80		9.75		9.75	
(i) Ownership of banks	10.00		10.00		10.00		10.00		10.00		10.00		10.00		10.00	
(ii) Foreign bank competition							6.05		4.55		9.00		9.00		9.00	
(iii) Private sector credit	8.91		9.00		10.00		10.00		10.00		10.00		10.00		10.00	
(iv) Interest rate controls/negative real interest rates	10.00		10.00		10.00		10.00		10.00		10.00		10.00		10.00	
B. Labor market regulations							5.48		6.16		5.52		7.70		7.74		7.78	
(i) Hiring regulations and minimum wage							7.13		4.56		10.00		10.00		10.00	
(ii) Hiring and firing regulations					8.50		8.50		7.17		8.10		8.14		8.20	
(iii) Centralized collective bargaining	7.93		7.93		7.93		7.93		8.37		8.10		8.66		8.46	
(iv) Hours regulations							7.25		7.52		10.00		10.00		10.00	
(v) Mandated cost of worker dismissal											9.60		9.63		10.00	
(vi) Conscription	0.00		0.00		0.00		0.00		0.00		0.00		0.00		0.00	
C. Business regulations							9.38		8.38		8.20		8.01		8.01	
(i) Price controls					8.00		9.00		9.00		6.00		8.00		8.00	
(ii) Administrative requirements							7.68		6.80		7.62		7.56	
(iii) Bureaucracy costs							9.73		8.05		6.40		2.18		2.25	
(iv) Starting a business							9.07		8.02		9.80		9.90		9.90	
(v) Extra payments/bribes/favoritism							9.72		9.15		9.60		9.34		9.37	
(vi) Licensing restrictions											9.20		9.96		9.96	
(vii) Cost of tax compliance											9.50		9.06		9.06	

Slovak Republic

	1980	1985	1990	1995	2000	2005	2008	2009
Chain-Linked			Rating (Rank)	Rating (Rank)	Rating (Rank)	Rating (Rank)	Rating (Rank)	Rating (Rank)
Summary Rating (Rank) ➤				**5.54** (78)	**6.16** (77)	**7.67** (17)	**7.55** (16)	**7.53** (14)
Area 1. Size of Government				2.66 (118)	2.98 (120)	6.48 (67)	6.57 (57)	6.44 (57)
Area 2. Legal Structure and Security of Property Rights				6.50 (38)	6.30 (47)	6.61 (40)	6.24 (48)	5.96 (57)
Area 3. Access to Sound Money			8.16 (29)	6.69 (59)	7.90 (60)	9.15 (40)	9.48 (14)	9.69 (3)
Area 4. Freedom to Trade Internationally				6.88 (46)	7.91 (28)	8.30 (6)	8.25 (5)	8.57 (3)
Area 5. Regulation of Credit, Labor, and Business				4.96 (86)	5.69 (77)	7.78 (20)	7.22 (28)	6.98 (44)

Unadjusted

	1980	1985	1990	1995	2000	2005	2008	2009
Summary Rating (Rank) ➤				**5.42** (81)	**6.16** (77)	**7.63** (17)	**7.58** (18)	**7.56** (13)
			Rating Data	Rating Data	Rating Data	Rating Data	Rating Data	Rating Data
1. Size of Government				**2.39**	**2.98**	**6.50**	**6.57**	**6.44**
A. Government consumption			3.27 (28.89)	3.18 (29.20)	4.04 (26.26)	4.60 (24.40)	4.87 (23.44)	5.04 (22.85)
B. Transfers and subsidies					3.88 (22.95)	4.80 (19.50)	4.91 (19.18)	4.23 (21.68)
C. Government enterprises and investment				0.00 (75.10)	0.00 (75.10)	10.00 (7.90)	10.00 (7.86)	10.00 (11.26)
D. Top marginal tax rate				4.00	4.00	6.50	6.50	6.50
(i) Top marginal income tax rate				4.00 (42)	4.00 (42)	10.00 (19)	10.00 (19)	10.00 (19)
(ii) Top marginal income and payroll tax rates				4.00 (42)	4.00 (44)	3.00 (48)	3.00 (48)	3.00 (48)
2. Legal Structure and Security of Property Rights				**6.50**	**6.30**	**6.60**	**6.24**	**5.96**
A. Judicial independence				5.08	5.01	4.30	4.18	3.17
B. Impartial courts				5.43	5.18	4.40	2.92	2.43
C. Protection of property rights				3.97	4.67	6.70	5.92	5.41
D. Military interference in rule of law and politics				8.04	10.00	10.00	10.00	10.00
E. Integrity of the legal system				10.00	6.67	6.70	6.67	6.67
F. Legal enforcement of contracts						4.60	4.38	4.38
G. Regulatory restrictions on sale of real property						9.60	9.65	9.68
3. Access to Sound Money			8.81	**6.69**	**7.90**	**9.10**	**9.48**	**9.69**
A. Money growth				7.32 (13.40)	9.81 (−0.94)	7.70 (11.70)	9.56 (2.20)	9.56 (2.20)
B. Standard deviation of inflation			8.99 (2.52)	6.39 (9.03)	9.20 (2.01)	9.50 (1.34)	9.28 (1.81)	9.52 (1.21)
C. Inflation: most recent year			8.63 (6.86)	8.05 (9.73)	7.59 (12.04)	9.50 (2.71)	9.08 (4.60)	9.68 (1.62)
D. Freedom to own foreign currency bank accounts				5.00	5.00	10.00	10.00	10.00
4. Freedom to Trade Internationally				**6.75**	**7.91**	**8.10**	**8.03**	**8.34**
A. Taxes on international trade				8.78	9.07	8.40	8.03	8.22
(i) Revenues from trade taxes (% of trade sector)					9.34 (0.99)	9.60 (0.60)	9.61 (0.59)	9.44 (0.84)
(ii) Mean tariff rate				8.78 (6.10)	8.80 (6.00)	9.50 (2.70)	8.88 (5.60)	8.94 (5.30)
(iii) Standard deviation of tariff rates						6.10 (9.70)	5.61 (10.98)	6.29 (9.28)
B. Regulatory trade barriers				4.83	7.17	7.30	7.47	7.52
(i) Non-tariff trade barriers				4.83	6.67	7.90	8.02	7.48
(ii) Compliance cost of importing and exporting					7.66	6.80	6.93	7.55
C. Size of trade sector relative to expected				6.50	7.85	7.60	7.88	9.44
D. Black-market exchange rates				10.00	10.00	10.00	10.00	10.00
E. International capital market controls				3.65	5.46	7.10	6.75	6.52
(i) Foreign ownership/investment restrictions				5.29	7.83	8.80	8.13	7.66
(ii) Capital controls				2.00	3.08	5.40	5.38	5.38
5. Regulation of Credit, Labor, and Business				**4.75**	**5.69**	**7.80**	**7.57**	**7.34**
A. Credit market regulations				5.71	7.35	9.70	9.75	9.37
(i) Ownership of banks				5.00	5.00	10.00	10.00	10.00
(ii) Foreign bank competition				6.12	5.33	10.00	10.00	10.00
(iii) Private sector credit				5.31	8.10	8.70	9.00	7.48
(iv) Interest rate controls/negative real interest rates				6.00	10.00	10.00	10.00	10.00
B. Labor market regulations				4.38	4.54	7.50	7.65	7.44
(i) Hiring regulations and minimum wage				6.12	4.17	8.30	8.30	6.67
(ii) Hiring and firing regulations			4.92	4.92	3.00	6.80	4.38	3.97
(iii) Centralized collective bargaining				5.18	7.67	8.30	7.64	7.18
(iv) Hours regulations				4.68	4.84	8.00	8.00	8.00
(v) Mandated cost of worker dismissal						8.80	7.59	8.79
(vi) Conscription				1.00	3.00	5.00	10.00	10.00
C. Business regulations				4.17	5.19	6.30	5.31	5.22
(i) Price controls				4.00	4.00	7.00	3.00	3.00
(ii) Administrative requirements					8.00	3.50	3.24	3.07
(iii) Bureaucracy costs				4.70	4.50	5.20	3.01	2.75
(iv) Starting a business				4.28	3.00	9.00	9.39	9.39
(v) Extra payments/bribes/favoritism				3.70	6.47	6.60	5.19	4.96
(vi) Licensing restrictions						6.20	6.21	6.21
(vii) Cost of tax compliance						6.40	7.12	7.12

Slovenia

	1980	1985	1990	1995	2000	2005	2008	2009
Chain-Linked				Rating (Rank)	Rating (Rank)	Rating (Rank)	Rating (Rank)	Rating (Rank)
Summary Rating (Rank) ➤				**4.76** (102)	**6.36** (69)	**6.41** (78)	**6.52** (82)	**6.46** (79)
Area 1. Size of Government				1.46 (121)	4.92 (93)	4.91 (104)	4.73 (110)	4.57 (108)
Area 2. Legal Structure and Security of Property Rights				6.94 (29)	6.40 (45)	5.30 (75)	5.37 (73)	5.54 (68)
Area 3. Access to Sound Money				3.12 (108)	7.49 (68)	8.79 (51)	9.42 (23)	9.63 (6)
Area 4. Freedom to Trade Internationally				6.93 (44)	7.09 (58)	7.02 (49)	7.06 (51)	6.56 (64)
Area 5. Regulation of Credit, Labor, and Business				5.55 (64)	5.90 (65)	6.11 (82)	6.11 (89)	6.08 (92)

	1980	1985	1990	1995	2000	2005	2008	2009
Unadjusted								
Summary Rating (Rank) ➤				**5.02** (97)	**6.36** (69)	**6.73** (75)	**6.85** (72)	**6.78** (74)
	Rating *Data*	Rating *Data*	Rating *Data*	Rating *Data*	Rating *Data*	Rating *Data*	Rating *Data*	Rating *Data*
1. Size of Government				**1.75**	**4.92**	**4.90**	**4.73**	**4.57**
A. Government consumption			4.15 *(25.90)*	4.17 *(25.83)*	3.67 *(27.51)*	4.00 *(26.30)*	4.29 *(25.40)*	3.84 *(26.95)*
B. Transfers and subsidies				1.09 *(33.20)*	4.02 *(22.44)*	4.10 *(22.20)*	4.63 *(20.21)*	3.95 *(22.72)*
C. Government enterprises and investment				0.00 *(75.10)*	10.00 *(4.60)*	10.00 *(8.70)*	8.00 *(15.27)*	8.00 *(19.04)*
D. Top marginal tax rate					2.00	1.50	2.00	2.50
(i) Top marginal income tax rate					4.00 *(50)*	3.00 *(50)*	4.00 *(41)*	4.00 *(41)*
(ii) Top marginal income and payroll tax rates					0.00 *(70)*	0.00 *(70)*	0.00 *(63)*	1.00 *(60)*
2. Legal Structure and Security of Property Rights				**7.44**	**6.40**	**6.00**	**6.02**	**6.21**
A. Judicial independence						5.90	5.75	5.41
B. Impartial courts				7.02	7.14	5.30	4.74	3.96
C. Protection of property rights					5.37	6.50	6.41	6.04
D. Military interference in rule of law and politics				9.22	8.33	8.30	9.17	9.17
E. Integrity of the legal system				10.00	8.33	7.50	7.50	7.50
F. Legal enforcement of contracts						3.90	4.23	4.23
G. Regulatory restrictions on sale of real property						4.30	4.34	7.17
3. Access to Sound Money				**3.12**	**7.49**	**8.80**	**9.42**	**9.63**
A. Money growth				0.00 *(57.50)*	7.62 *(11.91)*	6.90 *(15.60)*	9.28 *(3.59)*	9.19 *(4.03)*
B. Standard deviation of inflation				0.00 *(79.63)*	9.12 *(2.19)*	8.80 *(3.04)*	9.54 *(1.14)*	9.51 *(1.23)*
C. Inflation: most recent year				7.48 *(12.60)*	8.22 *(8.88)*	9.50 *(2.48)*	8.87 *(5.65)*	9.83 *(0.86)*
D. Freedom to own foreign currency bank accounts			5.00	5.00	5.00	10.00	10.00	10.00
4. Freedom to Trade Internationally				**7.08**	**7.09**	**7.20**	**7.25**	**6.74**
A. Taxes on international trade				7.53	8.05	8.50	8.11	8.36
(i) Revenues from trade taxes (% of trade sector)				7.53 *(3.70)*	9.48 *(0.78)*	9.80 *(0.20)*	9.84 *(0.24)*	9.84 *(0.24)*
(ii) Mean tariff rate					7.64 *(11.80)*	9.50 *(2.70)*	8.88 *(5.60)*	8.94 *(5.30)*
(iii) Standard deviation of tariff rates					7.04 *(7.40)*	6.10 *(9.70)*	5.61 *(10.98)*	6.29 *(9.28)*
B. Regulatory trade barriers				7.38	7.20	7.10	7.17
(i) Non-tariff trade barriers				7.38	7.30	7.03	6.83
(ii) Compliance cost of importing and exporting						7.20	7.18	7.51
C. Size of trade sector relative to expected				4.68	4.73	4.60	4.73	3.68
D. Black-market exchange rates			0.00	10.00	10.00	10.00	10.00	10.00
E. International capital market controls	0.00	0.00	0.00	5.00	5.30	5.70	6.32	4.48
(i) Foreign ownership/investment restrictions					6.76	5.30	5.72	5.12
(ii) Capital controls	0.00	0.00	0.00	5.00	3.85	6.20	6.92	3.85
5. Regulation of Credit, Labor, and Business				**5.69**	**5.90**	**6.80**	**6.81**	**6.73**
A. Credit market regulations				7.65	7.09	8.90	8.98	8.38
(i) Ownership of banks				5.00	5.00	8.00	8.00	8.00
(ii) Foreign bank competition					4.78	8.00	8.00	8.00
(iii) Private sector credit				9.94	9.55	9.40	9.93	7.51
(iv) Interest rate controls/negative real interest rates				8.00	10.00	10.00	10.00	10.00
B. Labor market regulations					3.60	5.60	5.43	5.97
(i) Hiring regulations and minimum wage					4.02	3.90	2.20	2.23
(ii) Hiring and firing regulations					2.32	2.90	3.39	2.91
(iii) Centralized collective bargaining					5.05	5.50	5.74	5.38
(iv) Hours regulations						4.70	4.70	8.00
(v) Mandated cost of worker dismissal						6.30	6.57	7.32
(vi) Conscription				3.00	3.00	10.00	10.00	10.00
C. Business regulations					7.01	6.00	6.01	5.85
(i) Price controls				6.00	8.00	3.00	3.00	3.00
(ii) Administrative requirements					6.95	3.20	4.72	4.11
(iii) Bureaucracy costs					7.80	5.40	2.90	2.83
(iv) Starting a business					5.73	7.80	9.67	9.66
(v) Extra payments/bribes/favoritism					6.58	8.30	7.17	6.77
(vi) Licensing restrictions						7.10	7.56	7.52
(vii) Cost of tax compliance						7.10	7.09	7.09

South Africa

	1980	1985	1990	1995	2000	2005	2008	2009
Chain-Linked	Rating (Rank)	Rating (Rank)	Rating (Rank)	Rating (Rank)	Rating (Rank)	Rating (Rank)	Rating (Rank)	Rating (Rank)
Summary Rating (Rank) ➤	**6.12** (28)	**5.78** (42)	**5.62** (53)	**6.44** (46)	**6.96** (42)	**6.77** (64)	**6.53** (81)	**6.39** (84)
Area 1. Size of Government	5.97 (27)	6.10 (25)	6.32 (36)	6.30 (52)	6.45 (52)	5.99 (82)	5.33 (97)	5.02 (97)
Area 2. Legal Structure and Security of Property Rights	6.81 (29)	4.91 (60)	3.22 (90)	6.11 (44)	6.54 (40)	6.61 (40)	6.33 (46)	6.16 (51)
Area 3. Access to Sound Money	5.29 (86)	5.63 (86)	5.81 (78)	6.44 (66)	7.85 (64)	7.98 (70)	7.52 (82)	7.92 (77)
Area 4. Freedom to Trade Internationally	7.46 (15)	6.39 (33)	6.74 (32)	6.49 (68)	7.15 (54)	6.56 (68)	6.76 (65)	6.40 (72)
Area 5. Regulation of Credit, Labor, and Business	5.22 (52)	5.82 (41)	5.82 (47)	6.85 (17)	6.84 (29)	6.68 (55)	6.70 (54)	6.42 (70)

Unadjusted

	1980	1985	1990	1995	2000	2005	2008	2009
Summary Rating (Rank) ➤	**6.03** (29)	**5.69** (47)	**5.46** (62)	**6.40** (48)	**6.96** (42)	**6.88** (65)	**6.64** (83)	**6.49** (87)
	Rating Data	Rating Data	Rating Data	Rating Data	Rating Data	Rating Data	Rating Data	Rating Data
1. Size of Government	**5.97**	**6.10**	**6.32**	**6.30**	**6.45**	**6.00**	**5.33**	**5.02**
A. Government consumption	5.61 (20.94)	4.58 (24.43)	4.46 (24.83)	4.50 (24.69)	5.17 (22.42)	4.80 (23.80)	4.37 (25.13)	4.26 (25.53)
B. Transfers and subsidies	9.26 (3.20)	8.83 (4.80)	8.83 (4.80)	8.69 (5.30)	8.62 (5.55)	8.70 (5.30)	8.46 (6.16)	8.34 (6.59)
C. Government enterprises and investment	7.00 (24.60)	7.00 (24.60)	7.00 (20.30)	8.00 (15.10)	8.00 (17.80)	6.00 (25.60)	4.00 (32.10)	2.00 (40.63)
D. Top marginal tax rate	2.00	4.00	5.00	4.00	4.00	4.50	4.50	5.50
(i) Top marginal income tax rate	2.00 (60)	4.00 (50)	5.00 (45)	4.00 (43)	4.00 (45)	5.00 (40)	5.00 (40)	6.00 (40)
(ii) Top marginal income and payroll tax rates			5.00 (45)	4.00 (43)	4.00 (45)	4.00 (41)	4.00 (41)	5.00 (41)
2. Legal Structure and Security of Property Rights	**6.18**	**4.46**	**2.93**	**6.11**	**6.54**	**6.60**	**6.33**	**6.16**
A. Judicial independence				7.17	7.18	7.60	6.60	6.16
B. Impartial courts				7.85	8.02	7.60	6.48	6.54
C. Protection of property rights				6.53	5.82	8.00	8.11	7.34
D. Military interference in rule of law and politics				4.91	8.33	8.30	8.33	8.33
E. Integrity of the legal system				4.11	3.33	4.20	4.17	4.17
F. Legal enforcement of contracts						3.90	3.93	3.93
G. Regulatory restrictions on sale of real property						6.60	6.69	6.65
3. Access to Sound Money	**5.29**	**5.63**	**5.81**	**6.44**	**7.85**	**8.00**	**7.52**	**7.92**
A. Money growth	7.86 (10.69)	7.60 (12.01)	6.75 (16.24)	8.22 (8.89)	7.87 (10.66)	8.60 (7.00)	8.36 (8.21)	9.01 (4.94)
B. Standard deviation of inflation	8.12 (4.71)	8.54 (3.66)	9.49 (1.27)	9.29 (1.78)	9.60 (0.99)	9.00 (2.48)	9.02 (2.46)	9.08 (2.29)
C. Inflation: most recent year	5.18 (24.12)	6.39 (18.06)	6.98 (15.09)	8.25 (8.76)	8.93 (5.34)	9.30 (3.40)	7.69 (11.54)	8.58 (7.13)
D. Freedom to own foreign currency bank accounts	0.00	0.00	0.00	0.00	5.00	5.00	5.00	5.00
4. Freedom to Trade Internationally	**7.42**	**6.36**	**6.52**	**6.32**	**7.15**	**6.60**	**6.76**	**6.40**
A. Taxes on international trade	8.66	8.93	7.27	5.54	7.74	6.80	7.04	7.15
(i) Revenues from trade taxes (% of trade sector)	9.20 (1.20)	9.07 (1.40)	8.53 (2.20)	9.33 (1.00)	9.01 (1.48)	8.60 (2.10)	9.11 (1.33)	9.06 (1.41)
(ii) Mean tariff rate	8.12 (9.40)	8.80 (6.00)	7.80 (11.00)	6.06 (19.70)	8.30 (8.50)	8.30 (8.50)	8.44 (7.80)	8.46 (7.70)
(iii) Standard deviation of tariff rates			5.48 (11.30)	1.24 (21.90)	5.92 (10.20)	3.60 (15.90)	3.57 (16.07)	3.93 (15.17)
B. Regulatory trade barriers				6.40	7.56	6.10	5.84	5.80
(i) Non-tariff trade barriers				6.40	6.62	6.70	6.22	6.13
(ii) Compliance cost of importing and exporting					8.50	5.50	5.46	5.46
C. Size of trade sector relative to expected	9.48	7.65	5.77	5.65	6.34	6.00	7.64	5.73
D. Black-market exchange rates	8.80	5.00	9.40	10.00	10.00	10.00	10.00	10.00
E. International capital market controls	2.00	2.00	2.00	3.98	4.12	3.90	3.27	3.33
(i) Foreign ownership/investment restrictions				5.97	7.46	7.00	5.78	5.88
(ii) Capital controls	2.00	2.00	2.00	2.00	0.77	0.80	0.77	0.77
5. Regulation of Credit, Labor, and Business	**5.30**	**5.90**	**5.74**	**6.82**	**6.84**	**7.20**	**7.25**	**6.96**
A. Credit market regulations	7.48	9.08	9.07	8.50	8.42	9.50	9.44	8.70
(i) Ownership of banks	10.00	10.00	10.00	10.00	10.00	10.00	10.00	10.00
(ii) Foreign bank competition				7.93	6.78	8.00	8.00	8.00
(iii) Private sector credit	8.43	9.25	9.22	9.30	8.76	9.90	9.74	6.81
(iv) Interest rate controls/negative real interest rates	4.00	8.00	8.00	10.00	10.00	10.00	10.00	10.00
B. Labor market regulations			3.92	6.11	5.47	6.10	6.09	6.11
(i) Hiring regulations and minimum wage				2.87	4.61	4.40	4.40	4.43
(ii) Hiring and firing regulations			5.55	5.55	2.05	2.40	2.48	2.49
(iii) Centralized collective bargaining			6.21	6.21	4.52	3.80	3.87	3.58
(iv) Hours regulations			5.90	5.90	6.18	8.00	8.00	8.00
(v) Mandated cost of worker dismissal						7.80	7.78	8.15
(vi) Conscription	0.00	0.00	0.00	10.00	10.00	10.00	10.00	10.00
C. Business regulations				5.85	6.62	6.20	6.23	6.07
(i) Price controls				6.00	7.00	5.00	5.00	5.00
(ii) Administrative requirements					6.92	3.30	3.72	3.33
(iii) Bureaucracy costs				6.38	6.53	4.50	3.39	3.10
(iv) Starting a business				6.43	5.88	8.80	9.23	9.23
(v) Extra payments/bribes/favoritism				4.60	6.77	7.50	6.48	6.00
(vi) Licensing restrictions						8.00	8.04	8.04
(vii) Cost of tax compliance						6.10	7.76	7.76

Spain

Chain-Linked	1980		1985		1990		1995		2000		2005		2008		2009	
	Rating	(Rank)	Rating	(Rank)	Rating	(Rank)	Rating	(Rank)	Rating	(Rank)	Rating	(Rank)	Rating	(Rank)	Rating	(Rank)
Summary Rating (Rank) ➤	**6.19**	(25)	**6.18**	(31)	**6.51**	(34)	**7.04**	(28)	**7.31**	(24)	**7.35**	(28)	**7.19**	(38)	**6.92**	(50)
Area 1. Size of Government	5.18	(48)	4.20	(81)	4.67	(86)	4.16	(101)	4.75	(97)	6.57	(64)	6.48	(61)	5.64	(78)
Area 2. Legal Structure and Security of Property Rights	7.26	(25)	7.35	(26)	8.19	(24)	7.46	(26)	7.54	(25)	6.71	(33)	6.56	(35)	6.45	(40)
Area 3. Access to Sound Money	6.07	(62)	6.61	(57)	6.36	(67)	9.61	(14)	9.44	(24)	9.58	(12)	9.53	(11)	9.57	(15)
Area 4. Freedom to Trade Internationally	6.97	(23)	7.13	(20)	7.57	(17)	7.97	(19)	8.27	(17)	7.17	(41)	6.99	(57)	6.87	(49)
Area 5. Regulation of Credit, Labor, and Business	5.56	(40)	5.77	(42)	5.94	(43)	5.97	(50)	6.55	(38)	6.73	(53)	6.39	(70)	6.08	(92)

Unadjusted

	1980		1985		1990		1995		2000		2005		2008		2009	
Summary Rating (Rank) ➤	**5.95**	(31)	**5.95**	(36)	**6.22**	(38)	**6.99**	(30)	**7.31**	(24)	**7.42**	(30)	**7.26**	(39)	**6.99**	(54)
	Rating	Data	Rating	Data	Rating	Data	Rating	Data	Rating	Data	Rating	Data	Rating	Data	Rating	Data
1. Size of Government	**5.18**		**4.20**		**4.67**		**4.16**		**4.75**		**6.60**		**6.48**		**5.64**	
A. Government consumption	6.93	(16.45)	6.27	(18.67)	5.89	(19.98)	5.53	(21.18)	5.22	(22.25)	4.80	(23.70)	4.40	(25.05)	3.77	(27.19)
B. Transfers and subsidies	6.78	(12.30)	5.53	(16.90)	5.78	(16.00)	5.10	(18.47)	5.76	(16.05)	6.00	(15.20)	5.52	(16.95)	4.78	(19.65)
C. Government enterprises and investment	6.00	(27.10)	4.00	(30.20)	4.00	(33.50)	4.00	(33.50)	4.00	(33.50)	10.00	(12.10)	10.00	(13.70)	8.00	(18.21)
D. Top marginal tax rate	1.00		1.00		3.00		2.00		4.00		5.50		6.00		6.00	
(i) Top marginal income tax rate	1.00	(66)	1.00	(66)	3.00	(56)	2.00	(56)	4.00	(48)	6.00	(35-45)	6.00	(35-43)	6.00	(35-43)
(ii) Top marginal income and payroll tax rates					3.00	(56)	2.00	(56)	4.00	(48)	5.00	(45)	6.00	(35-43)	6.00	(35-43)
2. Legal Structure and Security of Property Rights	**6.35**		**6.42**		**7.16**		**7.46**		**7.54**		**6.70**		**6.56**		**6.45**	
A. Judicial independence							6.75		7.52		4.50		5.11		4.70	
B. Impartial courts							6.63		8.02		5.30		4.39		4.39	
C. Protection of property rights							6.09		7.15		7.70		6.91		6.54	
D. Military interference in rule of law and politics							7.85		8.33		8.30		8.33		8.33	
E. Integrity of the legal system							10.00		6.67		8.30		8.33		8.33	
F. Legal enforcement of contracts											5.50		5.54		5.54	
G. Regulatory restrictions on sale of real property											7.30		7.29		7.33	
3. Access to Sound Money	**6.07**		**6.61**		**6.36**		**9.61**		**9.44**		**9.60**		**9.53**		**9.57**	
A. Money growth	8.36	(8.21)	8.80	(5.98)	7.70	(11.50)	9.93	(−0.35)	8.66	(6.70)	9.00	(4.90)	9.13	(4.37)	8.98	(5.08)
B. Standard deviation of inflation	8.60	(3.49)	9.16	(2.09)	9.22	(1.95)	9.48	(1.31)	9.77	(0.57)	10.00	(0.12)	9.80	(0.51)	9.38	(1.54)
C. Inflation: most recent year	7.33	(13.35)	8.46	(7.69)	8.54	(7.31)	9.04	(4.81)	9.31	(3.43)	9.30	(3.37)	9.19	(4.07)	9.92	(−0.40)
D. Freedom to own foreign currency bank accounts	0.00		0.00		0.00		10.00		10.00		10.00		10.00		10.00	
4. Freedom to Trade Internationally	**6.92**		**7.09**		**7.41**		**7.76**		**8.27**		**7.20**		**6.99**		**6.87**	
A. Taxes on international trade	8.22		8.25		8.21		8.72		9.18		8.40		8.03		8.22	
(i) Revenues from trade taxes (% of trade sector)	8.20	(2.70)	8.00	(3.00)	9.00	(1.50)	9.87	(0.20)	9.78	(0.33)	9.60	(0.60)	9.61	(0.59)	9.44	(0.84)
(ii) Mean tariff rate	8.24	(8.80)	8.50	(7.50)	8.52	(7.40)	8.66	(6.70)	9.52	(2.40)	9.50	(2.70)	8.88	(5.60)	8.94	(5.30)
(iii) Standard deviation of tariff rates					7.12	(7.20)	7.64	(5.90)	8.24	(4.40)	6.10	(9.70)	5.61	(10.98)	6.29	(9.28)
B. Regulatory trade barriers							7.63		8.73		7.80		7.67		7.75	
(i) Non-tariff trade barriers							7.63		7.62		6.70		6.56		6.71	
(ii) Compliance cost of importing and exporting									9.83		8.80		8.79		8.79	
C. Size of trade sector relative to expected	3.21		4.41		3.09		4.16		5.43		4.50		4.47		3.38	
D. Black-market exchange rates	10.00		9.60		9.60		10.00		10.00		10.00		10.00		10.00	
E. International capital market controls	5.00		5.00		8.00		8.28		8.02		5.20		4.79		4.98	
(i) Foreign ownership/investment restrictions							8.57		9.11		7.40		6.51		6.89	
(ii) Capital controls	5.00		5.00		8.00		8.00		6.92		3.10		3.08		3.08	
5. Regulation of Credit, Labor, and Business	**5.22**		**5.42**		**5.49**		**5.94**		**6.55**		**7.10**		**6.73**		**6.43**	
A. Credit market regulations	7.37		8.27		8.27		8.06		8.81		9.50		9.25		8.40	
(i) Ownership of banks	8.00		8.00		8.00		8.00		10.00		10.00		10.00		10.00	
(ii) Foreign bank competition							7.67		6.12		8.00		8.00		8.00	
(iii) Private sector credit	8.11		6.80		6.82		7.36		9.79		10.00		9.01		5.60	
(iv) Interest rate controls/negative real interest rates	6.00		10.00		10.00		10.00		10.00		10.00		10.00		10.00	
B. Labor market regulations	3.55		3.44		3.71		4.07		3.92		5.30		5.14		5.05	
(i) Hiring regulations and minimum wage							5.78		3.06		2.20		2.20		2.23	
(ii) Hiring and firing regulations					2.62		2.62		3.67		2.80		2.85		2.40	
(iii) Centralized collective bargaining	5.18		5.18		5.18		5.18		4.85		6.10		4.97		4.48	
(iv) Hours regulations	4.49		4.13		4.05		3.75		5.01		6.00		6.00		6.00	
(v) Mandated cost of worker dismissal											4.80		4.81		5.18	
(vi) Conscription	1.00		1.00		3.00		3.00		3.00		10.00		10.00		10.00	
C. Business regulations							5.69		6.92		6.40		5.79		5.83	
(i) Price controls					7.00		6.00		6.00		5.00		5.00		5.00	
(ii) Administrative requirements									7.40		3.20		2.85		2.93	
(iii) Bureaucracy costs							6.37		7.90		6.30		3.16		3.24	
(iv) Starting a business							5.32		5.67		8.30		8.30		8.29	
(v) Extra payments/bribes/favoritism							5.06		7.63		8.00		6.59		6.56	
(vi) Licensing restrictions											7.00		7.01		7.03	
(vii) Cost of tax compliance											6.70		7.61		7.79	

Sri Lanka

	1980	1985	1990	1995	2000	2005	2008	2009
Chain-Linked	Rating (Rank)	Rating (Rank)	Rating (Rank)	Rating (Rank)	Rating (Rank)	Rating (Rank)	Rating (Rank)	Rating (Rank)
Summary Rating (Rank) ➤	**5.10** (62)	**5.17** (63)	**5.02** (86)	**6.02** (64)	**6.10** (79)	**5.97** (95)	**5.90** (100)	**5.98** (100)
Area 1. Size of Government	5.64 (37)	5.77 (32)	7.03 (19)	6.83 (31)	7.02 (35)	7.09 (42)	6.85 (46)	6.66 (49)
Area 2. Legal Structure and Security of Property Rights	3.83 (59)	3.26 (90)	2.22 (108)	4.30 (103)	4.18 (99)	4.24 (96)	4.48 (95)	4.56 (93)
Area 3. Access to Sound Money	5.47 (82)	6.29 (75)	5.50 (87)	6.69 (59)	6.74 (90)	6.13 (108)	5.86 (116)	6.69 (103)
Area 4. Freedom to Trade Internationally	5.09 (55)	4.45 (71)	4.40 (84)	6.17 (59)	6.43 (75)	6.22 (85)	5.90 (96)	5.60 (100)
Area 5. Regulation of Credit, Labor, and Business	5.46 (44)	6.13 (30)	6.05 (37)	6.14 (45)	6.13 (57)	6.22 (73)	6.41 (68)	6.40 (73)

Unadjusted

	1980	1985	1990	1995	2000	2005	2008	2009
Summary Rating (Rank) ➤	**4.96** (72)	**5.03** (77)	**5.03** (83)	**6.05** (65)	**6.10** (79)	**6.12** (103)	**6.04** (110)	**6.12** (107)
	Rating Data	Rating Data	Rating Data	Rating Data	Rating Data	Rating Data	Rating Data	Rating Data
1. Size of Government	**4.20**	**4.29**	**6.97**	**6.83**	**7.02**	**7.10**	**6.85**	**6.66**
A. Government consumption	8.93 (9.62)	8.42 (11.39)	8.41 (11.39)	7.78 (13.54)	8.04 (12.68)	8.80 (10.00)	6.22 (18.85)	5.43 (21.53)
B. Transfers and subsidies	7.85 (8.40)	8.75 (5.10)	8.50 (6.00)	8.53 (5.90)	9.03 (4.05)	8.50 (5.90)	9.19 (3.47)	9.19 (3.47)
C. Government enterprises and investment	0.00 (53.50)	0.00 (54.30)	4.00 (39.20)	4.00 (39.20)	4.00 (39.20)	4.00	6.00	6.00
D. Top marginal tax rate	0.00	0.00		7.00	7.00	7.00	6.00	6.00
(i) Top marginal income tax rate	0.00 (60)	0.00 (60)		7.00 (35)	7.00 (35)	7.00 (35)	7.00 (35)	7.00 (35)
(ii) Top marginal income and payroll tax rates				7.00 (35)	7.00 (35)	7.00 (35)	5.00 (38)	5.00 (38)
2. Legal Structure and Security of Property Rights	**3.98**	**3.40**	**2.31**	**4.47**	**4.18**	**4.80**	**5.02**	**5.11**
A. Judicial independence						4.20	5.87	6.09
B. Impartial courts				4.92	5.01	4.40	4.84	5.26
C. Protection of property rights					3.50	6.00	5.70	5.70
D. Military interference in rule of law and politics				1.98	3.33	3.30	3.33	3.33
E. Integrity of the legal system				6.96	5.00	5.00	5.00	5.00
F. Legal enforcement of contracts						3.60	3.61	3.61
G. Regulatory restrictions on sale of real property						6.80	6.75	6.75
3. Access to Sound Money	**5.47**	**6.29**	**5.50**	**6.69**	**6.74**	**6.10**	**5.86**	**6.69**
A. Money growth	7.31 (13.43)	8.27 (8.64)	8.03 (9.85)	8.78 (6.08)	9.22 (3.92)	8.10 (9.40)	9.14 (4.29)	9.12 (4.41)
B. Standard deviation of inflation	8.57 (3.57)	7.01 (7.47)	8.01 (4.97)	9.82 (0.45)	8.99 (2.52)	8.70 (3.13)	8.78 (3.05)	8.36 (4.10)
C. Inflation: most recent year	6.00 (19.98)	9.88 (0.58)	5.94 (20.29)	8.14 (9.30)	8.76 (6.18)	7.70 (11.64)	5.51 (22.46)	9.30 (3.51)
D. Freedom to own foreign currency bank accounts	0.00	0.00	0.00	0.00	0.00	0.00	0.00	0.00
4. Freedom to Trade Internationally	**5.49**	**4.80**	**4.46**	**6.25**	**6.43**	**6.30**	**5.96**	**5.65**
A. Taxes on international trade	1.97	3.57	2.92	4.85	7.62	6.90	6.73	6.81
(i) Revenues from trade taxes (% of trade sector)	2.20 (11.70)	2.93 (10.60)	4.13 (8.80)	7.00 (4.50)	8.57 (2.15)	7.90 (3.10)	7.66 (3.51)	7.66 (3.51)
(ii) Mean tariff rate	1.74 (41.30)	4.20 (29.00)	4.62 (26.90)	4.78 (26.10)	8.02 (9.90)	7.70 (11.30)	7.76 (11.20)	7.76 (11.20)
(iii) Standard deviation of tariff rates			0.00 (25.50)	2.76 (18.10)	6.28 (9.30)	4.90 (12.80)	4.76 (13.10)	5.03 (12.43)
B. Regulatory trade barriers					4.75	5.80	6.13	6.24
(i) Non-tariff trade barriers					4.75	5.20	5.10	5.25
(ii) Compliance cost of importing and exporting						6.40	7.16	7.22
C. Size of trade sector relative to expected	9.06	6.21	5.93	6.59	6.77	5.20	3.96	2.25
D. Black-market exchange rates	8.20	6.00	5.20	9.60	10.00	10.00	10.00	10.00
E. International capital market controls	0.00	0.00	0.00	2.00	3.02	3.50	3.01	2.97
(i) Foreign ownership/investment restrictions					6.04	7.00	6.01	5.94
(ii) Capital controls	0.00	0.00	0.00	2.00	0.00	0.00	0.00	0.00
5. Regulation of Credit, Labor, and Business	**5.67**	**6.36**	**5.92**	**6.01**	**6.13**	**6.30**	**6.50**	**6.51**
A. Credit market regulations	5.13	6.97	6.76	7.06	6.49	7.50	7.29	7.54
(i) Ownership of banks	5.00	5.00	5.00	5.00	5.00	5.00	5.00	5.00
(ii) Foreign bank competition					6.07	8.00	8.00	8.00
(iii) Private sector credit	6.39	7.92	7.27	6.19	6.12	7.00	7.16	7.16
(iv) Interest rate controls/negative real interest rates	4.00	8.00	8.00	10.00	10.00	10.00	9.00	10.00
B. Labor market regulations					5.87	6.60	6.82	6.49
(i) Hiring regulations and minimum wage					4.06	10.00	10.00	10.00
(ii) Hiring and firing regulations					2.88	3.40	4.27	4.17
(iii) Centralized collective bargaining					6.53	6.20	6.66	6.77
(iv) Hours regulations						10.00	10.00	8.00
(v) Mandated cost of worker dismissal						0.00	0.00	0.00
(vi) Conscription	10.00	10.00	10.00	10.00	10.00	10.00	10.00	10.00
C. Business regulations					6.04	4.90	5.37	5.50
(i) Price controls			4.00	4.00	4.00	4.00	4.00	4.00
(ii) Administrative requirements					7.27	2.80	3.49	3.88
(iii) Bureaucracy costs					7.15	3.70	4.48	4.48
(iv) Starting a business					6.48	8.30	8.72	8.82
(v) Extra payments/bribes/favoritism					5.30	4.70	5.00	5.19
(vi) Licensing restrictions						3.50	4.79	5.01
(vii) Cost of tax compliance						7.10	7.13	7.13

Sweden

Chain-Linked	1980 Rating (Rank)	1985 Rating (Rank)	1990 Rating (Rank)	1995 Rating (Rank)	2000 Rating (Rank)	2005 Rating (Rank)	2008 Rating (Rank)	2009 Rating (Rank)
Summary Rating (Rank) ➤	**5.95** (33)	**6.66** (24)	**7.08** (22)	**7.14** (26)	**7.44** (18)	**7.35** (28)	**7.26** (35)	**7.22** (34)
Area 1. Size of Government	1.63 (106)	2.61 (108)	2.62 (110)	2.60 (120)	3.17 (117)	3.67 (120)	3.61 (121)	3.25 (123)
Area 2. Legal Structure and Security of Property Rights	7.78 (23)	8.72 (15)	9.83 (10)	8.85 (12)	9.02 (13)	8.31 (13)	8.47 (6)	8.45 (6)
Area 3. Access to Sound Money	7.56 (26)	8.10 (26)	8.03 (31)	9.54 (20)	9.84 (1)	9.71 (2)	9.37 (27)	9.57 (15)
Area 4. Freedom to Trade Internationally	6.72 (29)	7.63 (14)	8.43 (5)	8.55 (8)	8.29 (16)	7.67 (22)	7.67 (22)	7.60 (20)
Area 5. Regulation of Credit, Labor, and Business	6.32 (20)	6.42 (21)	6.78 (14)	6.15 (44)	6.90 (23)	7.39 (28)	7.16 (31)	7.24 (28)

Unadjusted

	1980 Rating Data	1985 Rating Data	1990 Rating Data	1995 Rating Data	2000 Rating Data	2005 Rating Data	2008 Rating Data	2009 Rating Data
Summary Rating (Rank) ➤	**5.58** (50)	**6.25** (25)	**6.62** (28)	**7.14** (24)	**7.44** (18)	**7.37** (33)	**7.27** (38)	**7.24** (39)
1. Size of Government	**1.63**	**2.61**	**2.62**	**2.60**	**3.17**	**3.70**	**3.61**	**3.25**
A. Government consumption	1.10 (36.25)	1.39 (35.27)	1.49 (34.95)	2.05 (33.02)	1.68 (34.28)	1.20 (36.00)	1.10 (36.26)	1.09 (36.30)
B. Transfers and subsidies	3.41 (24.70)	3.05 (26.00)	1.99 (29.90)	0.84 (34.10)	3.98 (22.59)	4.00 (22.50)	4.35 (21.24)	3.91 (22.86)
C. Government enterprises and investment	2.00 (41.20)	6.00 (28.00)	7.00 (22.80)	6.00 (28.30)	6.00 (28.30)	8.00 (17.10)	8.00 (16.42)	7.00 (20.05)
D. Top marginal tax rate	0.00	0.00	0.00	1.50	1.00	1.50	1.00	1.00
(i) Top marginal income tax rate	0.00 (87)	0.00 (80)	0.00 (61-68)	3.00 (46-53)	2.00 (51-58)	3.00 (52-59)	2.00 (52-59)	2.00 (52-59)
(ii) Top marginal income and payroll tax rates			0.00 (79-86)	0.00 (66-73)	0.00 (68.4-75.4)	0.00 (66)	0.00 (64-69)	0.00 (63-69)
2. Legal Structure and Security of Property Rights	**6.61**	**7.41**	**8.35**	**8.85**	**9.02**	**8.30**	**8.47**	**8.45**
A. Judicial independence				8.82	8.68	8.10	9.35	9.26
B. Impartial courts				8.88	8.35	8.70	8.26	8.27
C. Protection of property rights				6.57	8.08	8.70	9.01	8.80
D. Military interference in rule of law and politics				10.00	10.00	9.20	9.17	9.17
E. Integrity of the legal system				10.00	10.00	10.00	10.00	10.00
F. Legal enforcement of contracts						4.70	4.74	4.74
G. Regulatory restrictions on sale of real property						8.70	8.73	8.88
3. Access to Sound Money	**7.56**	**8.10**	**8.03**	**9.54**	**9.84**	**9.70**	**9.37**	**9.57**
A. Money growth	8.18 (9.11)	9.23 (3.86)	9.44 (2.78)	9.81 (0.97)	9.71 (1.47)	9.20 (3.80)	8.67 (6.66)	8.69 (6.56)
B. Standard deviation of inflation	9.41 (1.47)	9.50 (1.26)	9.44 (1.40)	9.10 (2.24)	9.83 (0.44)	9.70 (0.79)	9.48 (1.29)	9.65 (0.87)
C. Inflation: most recent year	7.66 (11.72)	8.67 (6.63)	8.23 (8.84)	9.27 (3.67)	9.82 (0.90)	9.90 (0.45)	9.31 (3.44)	9.94 (−0.28)
D. Freedom to own foreign currency bank accounts	5.00	5.00	5.00	10.00	10.00	10.00	10.00	10.00
4. Freedom to Trade Internationally	**6.69**	**7.60**	**8.30**	**8.48**	**8.29**	**7.70**	**7.67**	**7.60**
A. Taxes on international trade	9.02	9.49	8.96	8.68	9.18	8.40	8.03	8.22
(i) Revenues from trade taxes (% of trade sector)	9.53 (0.70)	9.80 (0.30)	9.73 (0.40)	9.73 (0.40)	9.78 (0.33)	9.60 (0.60)	9.61 (0.59)	9.44 (0.84)
(ii) Mean tariff rate	8.50 (7.50)	9.18 (4.10)	9.06 (4.70)	8.66 (6.70)	9.52 (2.40)	9.50 (2.70)	8.88 (5.60)	8.94 (5.30)
(iii) Standard deviation of tariff rates			8.08 (4.80)	7.64 (5.90)	8.24 (4.40)	6.10 (9.70)	5.61 (10.98)	6.29 (9.28)
B. Regulatory trade barriers				9.13	9.15	8.70	8.73	8.87
(i) Non-tariff trade barriers				9.13	8.80	8.30	8.34	8.61
(ii) Compliance cost of importing and exporting					9.50	9.10	9.12	9.12
C. Size of trade sector relative to expected	5.24	5.53	4.40	5.29	5.89	5.60	5.84	5.21
D. Black-market exchange rates	9.00	9.80	10.00	10.00	10.00	10.00	10.00	10.00
E. International capital market controls	2.00	5.00	10.00	9.30	7.22	5.70	5.77	5.72
(i) Foreign ownership / investment restrictions				8.59	9.05	8.20	8.47	8.36
(ii) Capital controls	2.00	5.00	10.00	10.00	5.38	3.10	3.08	3.08
5. Regulation of Credit, Labor, and Business	**5.42**	**5.51**	**5.82**	**6.23**	**6.90**	**7.50**	**7.24**	**7.31**
A. Credit market regulations	7.59	8.07	9.33	8.00	9.01	9.50	9.50	9.50
(i) Ownership of banks	8.00	8.00	8.00	8.00	10.00	10.00	10.00	10.00
(ii) Foreign bank competition				8.33	6.48	8.00	8.00	8.00
(iii) Private sector credit	6.76	6.22	10.00	5.43	10.00	10.00	10.00	10.00
(iv) Interest rate controls / negative real interest rates	8.00	10.00	10.00	10.00	10.00	10.00	10.00	10.00
B. Labor market regulations	4.11	3.99	3.95	3.03	3.38	5.10	5.13	5.37
(i) Hiring regulations and minimum wage				1.83	4.41	8.30	6.70	6.67
(ii) Hiring and firing regulations			3.93	3.93	2.18	1.90	3.74	3.11
(iii) Centralized collective bargaining	4.49	4.49	4.49	4.49	3.78	3.60	3.76	3.43
(iv) Hours regulations	4.84	4.49	4.40	1.90	3.51	6.00	6.00	6.00
(v) Mandated cost of worker dismissal						7.60	7.59	10.00
(vi) Conscription	3.00	3.00	3.00	3.00	3.00	3.00	3.00	3.00
C. Business regulations				7.66	8.31	7.90	7.10	7.08
(i) Price controls			6.00	8.00	9.00	7.00	7.00	7.00
(ii) Administrative requirements				7.27		3.70	4.99	5.07
(iii) Bureaucracy costs				8.28	8.30	8.30	1.35	1.11
(iv) Starting a business				5.08	7.87	9.40	9.42	9.47
(v) Extra payments / bribes / favoritism				9.29	9.12	9.30	9.45	9.41
(vi) Licensing restrictions						8.80	8.84	8.83
(vii) Cost of tax compliance						8.60	8.63	8.63

Switzerland

Chain-Linked

	1980 Rating (Rank)	1985 Rating (Rank)	1990 Rating (Rank)	1995 Rating (Rank)	2000 Rating (Rank)	2005 Rating (Rank)	2008 Rating (Rank)	2009 Rating (Rank)
Summary Rating (Rank) ➤	**8.18** (2)	**8.28** (2)	**8.22** (4)	**7.96** (7)	**8.39** (4)	**8.07** (4)	**7.91** (6)	**7.93** (4)
Area 1. Size of Government	6.78 (15)	6.69 (14)	6.43 (30)	6.37 (49)	7.00 (36)	7.16 (36)	6.90 (44)	6.94 (37)
Area 2. Legal Structure and Security of Property Rights	9.62 (2)	9.87 (1)	9.87 (4)	9.14 (4)	9.27 (7)	8.64 (8)	8.44 (7)	8.44 (7)
Area 3. Access to Sound Money	9.59 (1)	9.66 (2)	9.72 (4)	9.63 (12)	9.70 (6)	9.61 (11)	9.40 (25)	9.29 (32)
Area 4. Freedom to Trade Internationally	8.11 (7)	8.11 (8)	8.01 (11)	7.55 (30)	8.52 (9)	6.82 (57)	6.75 (67)	6.64 (61)
Area 5. Regulation of Credit, Labor, and Business	6.69 (14)	7.05 (10)	7.07 (11)	7.10 (10)	7.46 (8)	8.10 (13)	8.07 (12)	8.29 (9)

Unadjusted

	1980 Rating (Data)	1985 Rating (Data)	1990 Rating (Data)	1995 Rating (Data)	2000 Rating (Data)	2005 Rating (Data)	2008 Rating (Data)	2009 Rating (Data)
Summary Rating (Rank) ➤	**7.66** (3)	**7.75** (3)	**7.74** (4)	**7.94** (7)	**8.39** (4)	**8.19** (4)	**8.03** (4)	**8.03** (4)
1. Size of Government	**6.78**	**6.69**	**6.43**	**6.37**	**7.00**	**7.90**	**7.59**	**7.64**
A. Government consumption	6.86 (16.68)	6.54 (17.77)	6.01 (19.55)	6.12 (19.19)	7.16 (15.64)	7.10 (15.90)	6.78 (16.96)	6.96 (16.34)
B. Transfers and subsidies	6.49 (13.40)	6.54 (13.20)	5.78 (16.00)	4.99 (18.90)	5.85 (15.75)	6.40 (13.70)	5.59 (16.67)	5.59 (16.67)
C. Government enterprises and investment						10.00 (10.30)	10.00 (8.90)	10.00 (9.74)
D. Top marginal tax rate	7.00	7.00	7.50	8.00	8.00	8.00	8.00	8.00
(i) Top marginal income tax rate	7.00 (31-44)	7.00 (33-46)	8.00 (33-43)	8.00 (35-39)	9.00 (31-40)	9.00 (26-42)	9.00 (26-42)	9.00 (26-42)
(ii) Top marginal income and payroll tax rates			7.00 (36-46)	8.00 (38-42)	7.00 (39-48)	7.00 (34-50)	7.00 (35-49)	7.00 (35-49)
2. Legal Structure and Security of Property Rights	**8.13**	**8.35**	**8.35**	**9.14**	**9.27**	**8.60**	**8.44**	**8.44**
A. Judicial independence				9.35	8.68	8.60	8.95	8.98
B. Impartial courts				7.92	8.52	8.60	7.13	7.35
C. Protection of property rights				8.44	9.17	9.30	9.25	9.02
D. Military interference in rule of law and politics				10.00	10.00	10.00	10.00	10.00
E. Integrity of the legal system				10.00	10.00	8.30	8.33	8.33
F. Legal enforcement of contracts						6.00	5.86	5.86
G. Regulatory restrictions on sale of real property						9.60	9.57	9.57
3. Access to Sound Money	**9.59**	**9.66**	**9.72**	**9.63**	**9.70**	**9.60**	**9.40**	**9.29**
A. Money growth	9.35 (3.25)	9.81 (0.94)	9.93 (0.33)	9.44 (2.82)	9.28 (3.60)	8.90 (5.30)	8.43 (7.83)	7.63 (11.84)
B. Standard deviation of inflation	9.55 (1.13)	9.30 (1.75)	9.78 (0.55)	9.32 (1.70)	9.83 (0.42)	9.70 (0.63)	9.65 (0.88)	9.63 (0.93)
C. Inflation: most recent year	9.46 (2.71)	9.53 (2.37)	9.15 (4.27)	9.77 (1.13)	9.69 (1.54)	9.80 (1.17)	9.51 (2.43)	9.90 (−0.48)
D. Freedom to own foreign currency bank accounts	10.00	10.00	10.00	10.00	10.00	10.00	10.00	10.00
4. Freedom to Trade Internationally	**8.36**	**8.36**	**8.32**	**7.42**	**8.52**	**6.80**	**6.75**	**6.64**
A. Taxes on international trade	8.74	8.89	9.28	7.70	9.92	6.40	5.90	5.98
(i) Revenues from trade taxes (% of trade sector)	8.40 (2.40)	8.67 (2.00)	8.73 (1.90)	8.47 (2.30)	9.79 (0.31)	9.80 (0.20)	9.25 (1.13)	9.25 (1.13)
(ii) Mean tariff rate	9.08 (4.60)	9.12 (4.40)	9.12 (4.40)	9.28 (3.60)	10.00 (0.00)	9.50 (2.70)	8.46 (7.70)	8.70 (6.50)
(iii) Standard deviation of tariff rates			10.00 (0.00)	5.36 (11.60)	9.96 (0.10)	0.00 (30.50)	0.00 (33.42)	0.00 (29.45)
B. Regulatory trade barriers				6.40	8.94	7.00	7.16	7.17
(i) Non-tariff trade barriers				6.40	8.22	5.10	5.39	5.41
(ii) Compliance cost of importing and exporting					9.67	8.90	8.93	8.93
C. Size of trade sector relative to expected	4.93	4.76	4.19	3.37	4.64	4.80	4.71	4.12
D. Black-market exchange rates	10.00	10.00	10.00	10.00	10.00	10.00	10.00	10.00
E. International capital market controls	10.00	10.00	10.00	9.62	9.08	5.90	5.99	5.94
(i) Foreign ownership / investment restrictions				9.25	9.70	8.00	8.14	8.03
(ii) Capital controls	10.00	10.00	10.00	10.00	8.46	3.80	3.85	3.85
5. Regulation of Credit, Labor, and Business	**5.42**	**5.71**	**5.90**	**7.14**	**7.46**	**8.00**	**7.95**	**8.14**
A. Credit market regulations	6.69	8.08	8.15	8.25	8.83	9.00	9.00	9.00
(i) Ownership of banks	5.00	5.00	5.00	5.00	8.00	8.00	8.00	8.00
(ii) Foreign bank competition				7.80	7.00	8.00	8.00	8.00
(iii) Private sector credit	9.07	9.25	9.46	9.81	10.00	9.90	10.00	10.00
(iv) Interest rate controls / negative real interest rates	6.00	10.00	10.00	10.00	10.00	10.00	10.00	10.00
B. Labor market regulations	5.01	4.77	5.48	5.79	5.70	7.60	7.88	8.45
(i) Hiring regulations and minimum wage				7.05	4.56	10.00	10.00	10.00
(ii) Hiring and firing regulations			7.71	7.71	5.62	7.80	7.63	7.91
(iii) Centralized collective bargaining	6.21	6.21	6.21	6.21	7.80	8.10	7.83	7.80
(iv) Hours regulations	5.81	5.10	5.01	5.00	5.51	6.00	8.00	10.00
(v) Mandated cost of worker dismissal						8.80	8.79	10.00
(vi) Conscription	3.00	3.00	3.00	3.00	5.00	5.00	5.00	5.00
C. Business regulations				7.38	7.85	7.40	6.97	6.95
(i) Price controls			7.00	6.00	7.00	5.00	6.00	6.00
(ii) Administrative requirements					7.30	5.10	5.46	5.35
(iii) Bureaucracy costs				8.31	9.08	6.00	1.67	1.67
(iv) Starting a business				6.58	7.67	9.30	9.25	9.25
(v) Extra payments / bribes / favoritism				8.62	8.18	8.90	8.77	8.80
(vi) Licensing restrictions						8.30	8.32	8.31
(vii) Cost of tax compliance						9.30	9.29	9.29

Syria

	1980	1985	1990	1995	2000	2005	2008	2009
Chain-Linked	Rating (Rank)	Rating (Rank)	Rating (Rank)	Rating (Rank)	Rating (Rank)	Rating (Rank)	Rating (Rank)	Rating (Rank)
Summary Rating (Rank) ➤	**3.67** (98)	**3.36** (106)	**3.87** (106)	**4.53** (109)	**4.91** (116)	**5.46** (110)	**5.08** (116)	**5.31** (115)
Area 1. Size of Government	2.09 (104)	1.95 (110)	4.38 (87)	4.57 (94)	3.75 (113)	3.90 (118)	3.73 (118)	3.67 (117)
Area 2. Legal Structure and Security of Property Rights	1.76 (89)	3.05 (91)	3.02 (94)	4.91 (81)	5.06 (75)	4.84 (87)	4.41 (98)	4.19 (103)
Area 3. Access to Sound Money	8.18 (16)	6.10 (83)	5.58 (86)	6.59 (62)	6.46 (100)	7.39 (80)	6.93 (88)	7.30 (85)
Area 4. Freedom to Trade Internationally	3.77 (77)	2.99 (86)	3.70 (95)	3.88 (110)	5.65 (106)	6.38 (77)	6.07 (91)	6.39 (78)
Area 5. Regulation of Credit, Labor, and Business	2.59 (101)	2.74 (106)	2.71 (114)	2.75 (123)	3.62 (123)	4.66 (120)	4.13 (121)	4.94 (118)

Unadjusted								
Summary Rating (Rank) ➤	**4.10** (93)	**3.41** (107)	**3.83** (107)	**4.59** (107)	**4.91** (116)	**5.77** (119)	**5.59** (126)	**5.83** (121)
	Rating Data	Rating Data	Rating Data	Rating Data	Rating Data	Rating Data	Rating Data	Rating Data
1. Size of Government	**3.84**	**1.95**	**4.38**	**4.57**	**3.75**	**5.70**	**6.34**	**6.24**
A. Government consumption	4.17 (25.82)	3.89 (26.76)	6.76 (17.03)	7.14 (15.72)	7.50 (14.51)	7.20 (15.70)	6.78 (16.96)	6.85 (16.71)
B. Transfers and subsidies	7.36 (10.20)						9.09 (3.82)	9.09 (3.82)
C. Government enterprises and investment	0.00 (59.50)	0.00 (62.50)	2.00 (45.00)	2.00 (43.75)	0.00 (63.64)	2.00 (46.40)	2.00 (45.20)	2.00 (46.55)
D. Top marginal tax rate						8.00	7.50	7.00
(i) Top marginal income tax rate						8.00 (28)	10.00 (20)	9.00 (22)
(ii) Top marginal income and payroll tax rates							5.00 (38)	5.00 (39)
2. Legal Structure and Security of Property Rights	**1.76**	**3.05**	**3.02**	**4.91**	**5.06**	**4.80**	**4.72**	**4.49**
A. Judicial independence							3.87	3.13
B. Impartial courts				5.05	4.64	4.80	3.00	3.03
C. Protection of property rights							6.67	5.72
D. Military interference in rule of law and politics				6.53	3.33	3.30	3.33	3.33
E. Integrity of the legal system				4.11	8.33	8.30	8.33	8.33
F. Legal enforcement of contracts						3.20	3.22	3.22
G. Regulatory restrictions on sale of real property						4.50	4.64	4.64
3. Access to Sound Money	**8.18**	**6.10**	**5.58**	**6.59**	**6.46**	**7.40**	**6.93**	**7.30**
A. Money growth	7.66 (11.72)	7.29 (13.53)	7.42 (12.90)	8.83 (5.83)	9.16 (4.20)	8.00 (9.90)	8.42 (7.91)	9.00 (5.02)
B. Standard deviation of inflation	8.56 (3.60)	7.91 (5.22)	8.75 (3.13)	8.62 (3.46)	7.47 (6.33)	8.00 (4.99)	7.46 (6.36)	5.79 (10.54)
C. Inflation: most recent year	6.51 (17.47)	9.18 (4.10)	6.13 (19.33)	8.92 (5.38)	9.23 (−3.85)	8.60 (7.24)	6.85 (15.75)	9.42 (2.92)
D. Freedom to own foreign currency bank accounts	10.00	0.00	0.00	0.00	0.00	5.00	5.00	5.00
4. Freedom to Trade Internationally	**3.99**	**3.16**	**3.45**	**4.10**	**5.65**	**5.70**	**5.48**	**5.78**
A. Taxes on international trade	3.90	5.43	4.66	7.09	5.17	5.20	5.17	5.97
(i) Revenues from trade taxes (% of trade sector)	5.27 (7.10)	6.27 (5.60)	8.07 (2.90)	7.15 (4.28)	7.55 (3.67)	7.60 (3.70)	7.55 (3.67)	7.55 (3.67)
(ii) Mean tariff rate	2.54 (37.30)	4.60 (27.00)	5.92 (20.40)	7.04 (14.80)	6.08 (19.60)	6.10 (19.60)	6.08 (19.60)	7.16 (14.20)
(iii) Standard deviation of tariff rates			0.00 (27.70)		1.89 (20.28)	1.90 (20.30)	1.89 (20.28)	3.18 (17.04)
B. Regulatory trade barriers						7.10	6.42	6.19
(i) Non-tariff trade barriers							5.24	4.78
(ii) Compliance cost of importing and exporting						7.10	7.60	7.60
C. Size of trade sector relative to expected	4.81	2.10	4.33	5.19	4.87	5.40	3.87	4.47
D. Black-market exchange rates	3.00	0.00	0.00	0.00	10.00	10.00	10.00	10.00
E. International capital market controls	0.00	0.00	0.00	0.00	0.00	1.00	1.96	2.26
(i) Foreign ownership/investment restrictions							3.93	3.68
(ii) Capital controls	0.00	0.00	0.00	0.00	0.00	1.00	0.00	0.83
5. Regulation of Credit, Labor, and Business	**2.75**	**2.80**	**2.71**	**2.75**	**3.62**	**5.20**	**4.47**	**5.37**
A. Credit market regulations	0.82	0.85	0.78	0.92	3.79	4.40	3.01	4.84
(i) Ownership of banks	0.00	0.00	0.00	0.00	0.00	0.00	0.00	0.00
(ii) Foreign bank competition								
(iii) Private sector credit	1.63	2.56	2.33	2.75	2.38	4.20	4.04	4.51
(iv) Interest rate controls/negative real interest rates		0.00	0.00	0.00	9.00	9.00	5.00	10.00
B. Labor market regulations						5.60	5.37	6.08
(i) Hiring regulations and minimum wage						10.00	8.90	7.23
(ii) Hiring and firing regulations							3.61	4.08
(iii) Centralized collective bargaining							7.14	7.15
(iv) Hours regulations						10.00	10.00	8.00
(v) Mandated cost of worker dismissal						2.60	2.58	10.00
(vi) Conscription	0.00	0.00	0.00	0.00	0.00	0.00	0.00	0.00
C. Business regulations						5.40	5.01	5.19
(i) Price controls			0.00	0.00	0.00	2.00	2.00	2.00
(ii) Administrative requirements							3.14	2.22
(iii) Bureaucracy costs							6.23	6.56
(iv) Starting a business						5.10	5.84	8.02
(v) Extra payments/bribes/favoritism							3.79	3.51
(vi) Licensing restrictions						8.40	7.85	7.80
(vii) Cost of tax compliance						6.20	6.23	6.23

Taiwan

	1980		1985		1990		1995		2000		2005		2008		2009	
Chain-Linked	Rating	(Rank)	Rating	(Rank)	Rating	(Rank)	Rating	(Rank)	Rating	(Rank)	Rating	(Rank)	Rating	(Rank)	Rating	(Rank)
Summary Rating (Rank) ➤	**6.92**	(15)	**7.10**	(15)	**7.39**	(17)	**7.33**	(19)	**7.31**	(24)	**7.69**	(16)	**7.54**	(19)	**7.42**	(21)
Area 1. Size of Government	4.96	(56)	4.91	(60)	5.40	(63)	6.10	(62)	6.73	(45)	7.15	(37)	6.96	(41)	6.92	(39)
Area 2. Legal Structure and Security of Property Rights	8.79	(13)	8.14	(19)	8.14	(25)	6.74	(32)	6.08	(50)	6.62	(39)	6.69	(32)	6.75	(29)
Area 3. Access to Sound Money	8.05	(19)	9.33	(12)	9.42	(14)	9.69	(10)	9.46	(22)	9.58	(12)	9.66	(3)	9.27	(35)
Area 4. Freedom to Trade Internationally	7.66	(14)	7.30	(17)	7.86	(14)	7.84	(23)	8.08	(24)	7.92	(15)	7.57	(29)	7.23	(29)
Area 5. Regulation of Credit, Labor, and Business	5.32	(48)	5.99	(36)	6.25	(33)	6.25	(37)	6.17	(55)	7.17	(36)	6.80	(48)	6.96	(46)

Unadjusted

	1980		1985		1990		1995		2000		2005		2008		2009	
Summary Rating (Rank) ➤	**6.56**	(17)	**6.73**	(17)	**7.05**	(16)	**7.27**	(21)	**7.31**	(24)	**7.60**	(19)	**7.45**	(25)	**7.37**	(26)
	Rating	Data	Rating	Data	Rating	Data	Rating	Data	Rating	Data	Rating	Data	Rating	Data	Rating	Data
1. Size of Government	**4.96**		**4.91**		**5.40**		**6.10**		**6.73**		**7.20**		**6.96**		**6.92**	
A. Government consumption	4.82	(23.60)	4.71	(24.00)	4.74	(23.90)	6.03	(19.50)	6.69	(17.25)	6.50	(17.80)	6.76	(17.02)	6.59	(17.59)
B. Transfers and subsidies	10.00	(0.35)	9.95	(0.67)	9.87	(0.99)	9.37	(2.80)	9.21	(3.40)	9.10	(3.90)	9.08	(3.89)	9.08	(3.89)
C. Government enterprises and investment	2.00	(44.30)	2.00	(43.00)	2.00	(44.30)	2.00	(47.20)	4.00	(30.23)	6.00	(25.50)	7.00	(22.98)	7.00	(22.98)
D. Top marginal tax rate	3.00		3.00		5.00		7.00		7.00		7.00		5.00		5.00	
(i) Top marginal income tax rate	3.00	(60)	3.00	(60)	5.00	(50)	7.00	(40)	7.00	(40)	7.00	(40)	5.00	(40)	5.00	(40)
(ii) Top marginal income and payroll tax rates					5.00	(50)	7.00	(40)	7.00	(40)	7.00	(40)	5.00	(40)	5.00	(40)
2. Legal Structure and Security of Property Rights	**7.83**		**7.25**		**7.25**		**6.74**		**6.08**		**6.60**		**6.69**		**6.75**	
A. Judicial independence							5.53		5.34		5.10		6.02		6.00	
B. Impartial courts							6.47		5.68		5.70		5.03		5.08	
C. Protection of property rights							5.92		6.07		7.20		7.39		7.75	
D. Military interference in rule of law and politics							8.81		6.67		6.70		6.67		6.67	
E. Integrity of the legal system							6.96		6.67		8.30		8.33		8.33	
F. Legal enforcement of contracts											5.50		5.55		5.55	
G. Regulatory restrictions on sale of real property											7.90		7.87		7.87	
3. Access to Sound Money	**8.05**		**9.33**		**9.42**		**9.69**		**9.46**		**9.60**		**9.66**		**9.27**	
A. Money growth	8.24	(8.79)	9.84	(−0.81)	9.18	(4.09)	9.56	(−2.21)	9.50	(−2.52)	8.90	(5.30)	9.81	(−0.95)	9.27	(3.66)
B. Standard deviation of inflation	7.76	(5.60)	7.52	(6.21)	9.32	(1.71)	9.80	(0.51)	9.09	(2.28)	9.60	(0.90)	9.55	(1.14)	9.50	(1.24)
C. Inflation: most recent year	6.20	(19.00)	9.96	(−0.20)	9.18	(4.10)	9.40	(3.00)	9.27	(3.67)	9.70	(1.26)	9.29	(3.53)	8.32	(−8.38)
D. Freedom to own foreign currency bank accounts	10.00		10.00		10.00		10.00		10.00		10.00		10.00		10.00	
4. Freedom to Trade Internationally	**7.51**		**7.16**		**7.66**		**7.61**		**8.08**		**7.90**		**7.57**		**7.23**	
A. Taxes on international trade	7.60		8.13		8.33		8.63		7.98		7.40		7.55		7.50	
(i) Revenues from trade taxes (% of trade sector)	7.60	(3.60)	8.13	(2.80)	8.60	(2.10)	8.87	(1.70)	8.98	(1.52)	9.60	(0.60)	9.70	(0.45)	9.68	(0.47)
(ii) Mean tariff rate					8.06	(9.70)	8.40	(8.00)	8.24	(8.80)	8.70	(6.40)	8.78	(6.10)	8.78	(6.10)
(iii) Standard deviation of tariff rates									6.72	(8.20)	3.90	(15.30)	4.17	(14.58)	4.05	(14.88)
B. Regulatory trade barriers							7.30		8.23		7.70		7.30		7.28	
(i) Non-tariff trade barriers							7.30		7.13		7.00		6.27		6.14	
(ii) Compliance cost of importing and exporting									9.33		8.30		8.33		8.41	
C. Size of trade sector relative to expected	9.99		8.08		6.79		6.41		6.56		7.10		6.88		5.45	
D. Black-market exchange rates	9.80		9.40		10.00		10.00		10.00		10.00		10.00		10.00	
E. International capital market controls	2.00		2.00		5.00		5.71		7.63		7.40		6.13		5.92	
(i) Foreign ownership / investment restrictions							6.43		7.63		7.40		6.13		5.92	
(ii) Capital controls	2.00		2.00		5.00		5.00									
5. Regulation of Credit, Labor, and Business	**4.46**		**5.02**		**5.51**		**6.23**		**6.17**		**6.70**		**6.37**		**6.67**	
A. Credit market regulations	5.26		6.74		7.33		7.25		6.68		9.00		8.53		8.49	
(i) Ownership of banks	0.00		2.00		2.00		2.00		2.00		8.00		8.00		8.00	
(ii) Foreign bank competition							7.33		5.57		8.00		8.00		8.00	
(iii) Private sector credit	7.79		8.23		10.00		10.00		10.00		10.00		8.10		7.97	
(iv) Interest rate controls / negative real interest rates	8.00		10.00		10.00		10.00		10.00		10.00		10.00		10.00	
B. Labor market regulations							4.73		5.22		4.51		4.30		4.36		5.17	
(i) Hiring regulations and minimum wage							6.50		3.78		2.20		2.20		2.23	
(ii) Hiring and firing regulations					6.26		6.26		4.60		5.90		6.37		5.92	
(iii) Centralized collective bargaining					7.93		7.93		7.98		8.40		8.02		7.88	
(iv) Hours regulations							5.43		6.18		8.00		8.00		10.00	
(v) Mandated cost of worker dismissal											1.60		1.56		1.97	
(vi) Conscription	0.00		0.00		0.00		0.00		0.00		0.00		0.00		3.00	
C. Business regulations							6.21		7.33		6.90		6.23		6.36	
(i) Price controls					6.00		6.00		6.00		6.00		5.00		5.00	
(ii) Administrative requirements									7.63		5.20		4.48		4.53	
(iii) Bureaucracy costs							6.88		7.35		6.50		3.12		3.38	
(iv) Starting a business							7.50		7.58		7.80		9.22		9.48	
(v) Extra payments / bribes / favoritism							4.46		8.09		7.90		6.49		6.73	
(vi) Licensing restrictions											8.40		8.43		8.42	
(vii) Cost of tax compliance											6.20		6.85		6.98	

Tanzania

Chain-Linked	1980 Rating (Rank)	1985 Rating (Rank)	1990 Rating (Rank)	1995 Rating (Rank)	2000 Rating (Rank)	2005 Rating (Rank)	2008 Rating (Rank)	2009 Rating (Rank)
Summary Rating (Rank) ➤	4.06 (93)	3.73 (103)	4.24 (99)	5.53 (79)	5.95 (87)	6.02 (93)	5.89 (101)	6.02 (95)
Area 1. Size of Government	2.48 (102)	2.15 (109)	3.58 (100)	7.01 (24)	5.77 (77)	4.60 (108)	4.10 (115)	4.73 (104)
Area 2. Legal Structure and Security of Property Rights	6.13 (36)	5.85 (40)	5.21 (57)	5.41 (64)	6.15 (49)	6.15 (55)	6.06 (55)	5.97 (55)
Area 3. Access to Sound Money	4.11 (100)	4.92 (93)	4.58 (95)	5.02 (93)	7.59 (67)	7.57 (78)	7.40 (84)	7.53 (84)
Area 4. Freedom to Trade Internationally	3.40 (82)	2.88 (88)	3.71 (94)	5.95 (85)	5.50 (109)	5.74 (99)	5.87 (98)	5.63 (99)
Area 5. Regulation of Credit, Labor, and Business	3.96 (89)	2.92 (103)	4.10 (98)	4.25 (110)	4.74 (107)	6.01 (88)	5.99 (93)	6.20 (86)

Unadjusted

	1980	1985	1990	1995	2000	2005	2008	2009
Summary Rating (Rank) ➤	4.82 (75)	4.13 (94)	4.24 (101)	5.53 (78)	5.95 (87)	6.05 (106)	5.92 (117)	6.04 (112)
	Rating Data	Rating Data	Rating Data	Rating Data	Rating Data	Rating Data	Rating Data	Rating Data
1. Size of Government	**5.83**	**3.79**	**3.58**	**7.01**	**5.77**	**4.60**	**4.10**	**4.73**
A. Government consumption	7.50 (14.50)	6.44 (18.10)	6.75 (17.06)	7.03 (16.08)	8.31 (11.76)	6.30 (18.60)	4.81 (23.65)	4.68 (24.08)
B. Transfers and subsidies	10.00 (0.00)	8.72 (5.20)						
C. Government enterprises and investment	0.00 (53.80)	0.00 (53.50)	2.00 (40.03)	8.00 (17.20)	4.00 (34.60)	2.00 (40.00)	2.00 (40.00)	4.00 (30.01)
D. Top marginal tax rate		0.00	2.00	6.00	5.00	5.50	5.50	5.50
(i) Top marginal income tax rate		0.00 (95)	3.00 (50)	8.00 (30)	7.00 (31)	8.00 (30)	8.00 (30)	8.00 (30)
(ii) Top marginal income and payroll tax rates			1.00 (57)	4.00 (45)	3.00 (46)	3.00 (46)	3.00 (48)	3.00 (48)
2. Legal Structure and Security of Property Rights	**6.13**	**5.85**	**5.21**	**5.41**	**6.15**	**6.10**	**5.97**	**5.89**
A. Judicial independence						4.90	4.51	4.18
B. Impartial courts				5.84	5.84	4.50	4.48	4.33
C. Protection of property rights						4.90	4.54	4.42
D. Military interference in rule of law and politics				7.81	6.67	6.70	6.67	6.67
E. Integrity of the legal system				4.11	8.33	8.30	8.33	8.33
F. Legal enforcement of contracts						6.10	6.11	6.11
G. Regulatory restrictions on sale of real property						7.10	7.17	7.17
3. Access to Sound Money	**4.11**	**4.92**	**4.58**	**5.02**	**7.59**	**7.60**	**7.40**	**7.53**
A. Money growth	5.94 (20.30)	7.92 (10.40)	4.00 (30.00)	4.48 (27.60)	8.72 (6.40)	7.30 (13.40)	7.18 (14.12)	7.99 (10.04)
B. Standard deviation of inflation	6.54 (8.66)	8.43 (3.93)	8.70 (3.26)	6.38 (9.06)	7.83 (5.43)	9.70 (0.80)	9.48 (1.29)	9.54 (1.16)
C. Inflation: most recent year	3.96 (30.20)	3.34 (33.28)	5.64 (21.82)	4.23 (28.86)	8.82 (5.92)	8.30 (8.63)	7.94 (10.28)	7.57 (12.14)
D. Freedom to own foreign currency bank accounts	0.00	0.00	0.00	5.00	5.00	5.00	5.00	5.00
4. Freedom to Trade Internationally	**3.67**	**2.89**	**3.73**	**5.95**	**5.50**	**5.90**	**6.00**	**5.75**
A. Taxes on international trade	4.87	4.70	4.53	5.26	4.96	4.90	4.92	4.92
(i) Revenues from trade taxes (% of trade sector)	4.87 (7.70)	5.80 (6.30)	5.00 (7.50)	4.60 (8.10)	2.07 (11.90)	2.10 (11.90)	2.07 (11.90)	2.07 (11.90)
(ii) Mean tariff rate		3.60 (32.00)	4.06 (29.70)	6.10 (19.50)	6.18 (19.10)	7.40 (12.90)	7.48 (12.60)	7.48 (12.60)
(iii) Standard deviation of tariff rates				5.08 (12.30)	6.64 (8.40)	5.30 (11.70)	5.21 (11.97)	5.21 (11.97)
B. Regulatory trade barriers						5.60	5.98	5.78
(i) Non-tariff trade barriers						4.90	5.75	5.35
(ii) Compliance cost of importing and exporting						6.30	6.22	6.22
C. Size of trade sector relative to expected	5.23	1.46	5.85	6.52	3.56	5.10	6.18	5.37
D. Black-market exchange rates	0.00	0.00	0.00	9.80	10.00	10.00	10.00	10.00
E. International capital market controls	0.00	0.00	0.00	0.00	0.77	3.70	2.89	2.67
(i) Foreign ownership/investment restrictions						7.40	5.79	5.34
(ii) Capital controls	0.00	0.00	0.00	0.00	0.77	0.00	0.00	0.00
5. Regulation of Credit, Labor, and Business	**4.35**	**3.21**	**4.10**	**4.25**	**4.74**	**6.10**	**6.14**	**6.32**
A. Credit market regulations	1.64	0.30	3.74	2.90	4.50	7.70	7.96	7.93
(i) Ownership of banks	0.00	0.00	0.00	0.00	0.00	8.00	8.00	8.00
(ii) Foreign bank competition						7.00	7.00	7.00
(iii) Private sector credit	0.93	0.89	7.21	4.69	4.51	6.70	6.86	6.74
(iv) Interest rate controls/negative real interest rates	4.00	0.00	4.00	4.00	9.00	9.00	10.00	10.00
B. Labor market regulations						5.80	5.20	5.80
(i) Hiring regulations and minimum wage						0.00	0.00	1.10
(ii) Hiring and firing regulations						5.10	4.14	4.51
(iii) Centralized collective bargaining						7.40	5.06	5.13
(iv) Hours regulations						8.70	8.70	10.00
(v) Mandated cost of worker dismissal						8.30	8.33	9.07
(vi) Conscription	10.00	5.00	5.00	5.00	5.00	5.00	5.00	5.00
C. Business regulations						5.00	5.27	5.21
(i) Price controls			0.00	4.00	4.00	6.00	6.00	6.00
(ii) Administrative requirements						4.20	3.80	3.90
(iii) Bureaucracy costs						3.00	5.81	5.55
(iv) Starting a business						8.10	8.68	8.75
(v) Extra payments/bribes/favoritism						4.60	3.92	3.64
(vi) Licensing restrictions						0.90	0.57	0.58
(vii) Cost of tax compliance						8.10	8.07	8.07

Thailand

Chain-Linked	1980		1985		1990		1995		2000		2005		2008		2009	
	Rating	(Rank)	Rating	(Rank)	Rating	(Rank)	Rating	(Rank)	Rating	(Rank)	Rating	(Rank)	Rating	(Rank)	Rating	(Rank)
Summary Rating (Rank) ➤	**6.19**	(25)	**6.21**	(30)	**6.97**	(26)	**7.19**	(25)	**6.52**	(60)	**6.92**	(55)	**7.04**	(49)	**6.96**	(48)
Area 1. Size of Government	6.01	(25)	5.58	(36)	7.36	(13)	7.76	(16)	6.84	(40)	7.12	(39)	7.42	(30)	7.08	(32)
Area 2. Legal Structure and Security of Property Rights	7.00	(28)	6.27	(35)	6.90	(33)	5.41	(64)	5.99	(52)	6.21	(53)	5.94	(59)	5.74	(62)
Area 3. Access to Sound Money	6.32	(49)	7.02	(35)	7.97	(32)	9.46	(24)	6.61	(96)	6.76	(93)	6.98	(87)	7.08	(87)
Area 4. Freedom to Trade Internationally	6.31	(35)	6.18	(39)	6.74	(32)	7.14	(36)	7.63	(38)	7.32	(35)	7.57	(29)	7.66	(18)
Area 5. Regulation of Credit, Labor, and Business	5.45	(46)	6.07	(34)	5.95	(41)	6.16	(42)	5.54	(86)	7.18	(35)	7.27	(27)	7.24	(28)

Unadjusted

	1980		1985		1990		1995		2000		2005		2008		2009	
Summary Rating (Rank) ➤	**6.09**	(26)	**6.10**	(32)	**6.82**	(19)	**7.10**	(26)	**6.52**	(60)	**6.84**	(70)	**6.95**	(60)	**6.87**	(65)
	Rating	Data	Rating	Data	Rating	Data	Rating	Data	Rating	Data	Rating	Data	Rating	Data	Rating	Data
1. Size of Government	**6.01**		**5.58**		**7.36**		**7.76**		**6.84**		**7.10**		**7.42**		**7.08**	
A. Government consumption	7.11	(15.81)	6.51	(17.86)	7.57	(14.26)	7.19	(15.57)	6.77	(17.00)	6.70	(17.20)	6.35	(18.42)	6.04	(19.47)
B. Transfers and subsidies	9.95	(0.70)	9.81	(1.20)	9.86	(1.00)	9.84	(1.10)	9.60	(1.96)	8.80	(5.00)	9.33	(2.97)	9.29	(3.09)
C. Government enterprises and investment	4.00	(31.90)	4.00	(32.00)	8.00	(15.20)	7.00	(21.60)	4.00	(37.20)	7.00	(24.70)	7.00	(24.06)	6.00	(26.80)
D. Top marginal tax rate	3.00		2.00		4.00		7.00		7.00		6.00		7.00		7.00	
(i) Top marginal income tax rate	3.00	(60)	2.00	(65)	4.00	(55)	7.00	(37)	7.00	(37)	6.00	(37)	7.00	(37)	7.00	(37)
(ii) Top marginal income and payroll tax rates					4.00	(55)	7.00	(37)	7.00	(37)	6.00	(37)	7.00	(37)	7.00	(37)
2. Legal Structure and Security of Property Rights	**6.52**		**5.85**		**6.43**		**5.41**		**5.99**		**6.20**		**5.94**		**5.74**	
A. Judicial independence							5.77		5.85		5.70		5.33		5.53	
B. Impartial courts							3.75		4.68		5.90		5.07		5.12	
C. Protection of property rights							3.60		4.42		7.10		5.46		4.85	
D. Military interference in rule of law and politics							6.96		6.67		6.70		5.83		5.83	
E. Integrity of the legal system							6.96		8.33		4.20		4.17		4.17	
F. Legal enforcement of contracts											6.10		6.11		6.11	
G. Regulatory restrictions on sale of real property											7.90		9.60		8.55	
3. Access to Sound Money	**6.32**		**7.02**		**7.97**		**9.46**		**6.61**		**6.80**		**6.98**		**7.08**	
A. Money growth	8.96	(5.20)	9.49	(−2.55)	8.69	(6.56)	9.42	(2.90)	8.71	(6.47)	8.50	(7.30)	9.33	(3.33)	8.97	(5.16)
B. Standard deviation of inflation	8.85	(2.87)	9.02	(2.45)	9.34	(1.66)	9.62	(0.96)	8.06	(4.86)	9.40	(1.49)	9.68	(0.79)	9.53	(1.17)
C. Inflation: most recent year	7.46	(12.70)	9.56	(2.18)	8.85	(5.77)	8.80	(6.01)	9.69	(1.57)	9.10	(4.54)	8.91	(5.47)	9.83	(−0.85)
D. Freedom to own foreign currency bank accounts	0.00		0.00		5.00		10.00		0.00		0.00		0.00		0.00	
4. Freedom to Trade Internationally	**6.31**		**6.18**		**6.55**		**6.87**		**7.63**		**7.30**		**7.57**		**7.66**	
A. Taxes on international trade	4.47		4.71		3.21		4.57		6.65		6.80		7.29		7.43	
(i) Revenues from trade taxes (% of trade sector)	5.40	(6.90)	5.67	(6.50)	6.40	(5.40)	7.67	(3.50)	9.06	(1.41)	9.30	(1.10)	9.53	(0.71)	9.55	(0.67)
(ii) Mean tariff rate	3.54	(32.30)	3.76	(31.20)	1.84	(40.80)	2.80	(36.00)	6.60	(17.00)	7.90	(10.60)	7.90	(10.50)	8.02	(9.90)
(iii) Standard deviation of tariff rates					1.40	(21.50)	3.24	(16.90)	4.28	(14.30)	3.30	(16.60)	4.46	(13.86)	4.73	(13.17)
B. Regulatory trade barriers							5.13		7.20		5.90		6.92		7.08	
(i) Non-tariff trade barriers							5.13		5.73		5.00		5.66		5.97	
(ii) Compliance cost of importing and exporting									8.66		6.80		8.18		8.18	
C. Size of trade sector relative to expected	7.88		6.58		9.37		10.00		10.00		10.00		10.00		10.00	
D. Black-market exchange rates	9.00		9.40		10.00		10.00		10.00		10.00		10.00		10.00	
E. International capital market controls	2.00		2.00		2.00		4.65		4.28		3.90		3.63		3.76	
(i) Foreign ownership / investment restrictions							7.30		7.02		6.30		5.72		5.99	
(ii) Capital controls	2.00		2.00		2.00		2.00		1.54		1.50		1.54		1.54	
5. Regulation of Credit, Labor, and Business	**5.29**		**5.88**		**5.80**		**6.01**		**5.54**		**6.80**		**6.85**		**6.81**	
A. Credit market regulations	6.67		8.65		8.26		7.28		7.04		9.00		9.00		8.74	
(i) Ownership of banks	8.00		8.00		8.00		8.00		5.00		8.00		8.00		8.00	
(ii) Foreign bank competition							5.55		3.75		8.00		8.00		8.00	
(iii) Private sector credit	8.02		7.96		8.78		9.23		9.17		10.00		10.00		8.97	
(iv) Interest rate controls / negative real interest rates	4.00		10.00		8.00		10.00		10.00		10.00		10.00		10.00	
B. Labor market regulations							4.98		5.39		4.30		5.40		5.61		5.70	
(i) Hiring regulations and minimum wage							5.77		3.94		6.70		6.70		6.67	
(ii) Hiring and firing regulations					7.01		7.01		4.60		4.70		5.69		5.81	
(iii) Centralized collective bargaining	7.93		7.93		7.93		7.93		6.45		6.10		6.28		6.34	
(iv) Hours regulations							6.27		6.51		10.00		10.00		10.00	
(v) Mandated cost of worker dismissal											5.00		4.99		5.36	
(vi) Conscription	0.00		0.00		0.00		0.00		0.00		0.00		0.00		0.00	
C. Business regulations							5.35		5.29		5.90		5.95		6.00	
(i) Price controls					4.00		5.00		3.00		4.00		4.00		4.00	
(ii) Administrative requirements									6.88		4.90		4.10		4.34	
(iii) Bureaucracy costs							6.77		3.98		2.20		4.23		4.51	
(iv) Starting a business							6.53		7.28		8.90		8.91		8.92	
(v) Extra payments / bribes / favoritism							3.11		5.31		5.90		4.98		4.85	
(vi) Licensing restrictions											8.40		8.35		8.36	
(vii) Cost of tax compliance											7.00		7.04		7.04	

Togo

Chain-Linked	1980		1985		1990		1995		2000		2005		2008		2009	
	Rating	(Rank)	Rating	(Rank)	Rating	(Rank)	Rating	(Rank)	Rating	(Rank)	Rating	(Rank)	Rating	(Rank)	Rating	(Rank)
Summary Rating (Rank) ➤	4.22	(90)	5.16	(64)	5.65	(51)	5.38	(83)	5.84	(92)	5.87	(101)	5.65	(105)	5.63	(108)
Area 1. Size of Government	1.60	(107)	3.80	(89)	6.43	(30)	6.86	(30)	8.44	(7)	8.70	(5)	8.50	(7)	8.13	(9)
Area 2. Legal Structure and Security of Property Rights	3.33	(65)	4.22	(74)	4.48	(70)	4.75	(94)	3.73	(108)	2.48	(120)	2.61	(122)	2.57	(123)
Area 3. Access to Sound Money	5.53	(80)	6.75	(49)	6.95	(49)	5.03	(92)	6.48	(98)	6.88	(90)	6.42	(100)	6.63	(105)
Area 4. Freedom to Trade Internationally									6.12	(89)	6.27	(84)	6.13	(87)	5.98	(86)
Area 5. Regulation of Credit, Labor, and Business	4.40	(78)	4.47	(81)	4.46	(87)	4.60	(98)	4.42	(112)	4.87	(118)	4.47	(120)	4.75	(119)

Unadjusted

	1980		1985		1990		1995		2000		2005		2008		2009	
Summary Rating (Rank) ➤	4.34	(88)	5.52	(54)	5.53	(59)	5.31	(86)	5.84	(92)	5.97	(108)	5.77	(121)	5.74	(123)
	Rating	Data	Rating	Data	Rating	Data	Rating	Data	Rating	Data	Rating	Data	Rating	Data	Rating	Data
1. Size of Government	**1.60**		**5.69**		**6.43**		**6.86**		**8.44**		**9.70**		**9.44**		**9.03**	
A. Government consumption	3.20	(29.11)	7.60	(14.18)	6.87	(16.65)	7.72	(13.76)	8.88	(9.82)	9.00	(9.50)	8.91	(9.70)	7.69	(13.85)
B. Transfers and subsidies			9.48	(2.40)							10.00	(0.30)	9.40	(2.69)	9.39	(2.74)
C. Government enterprises and investment	0.00	(71.70)	0.00	(73.90)	6.00	(28.80)	6.00	(25.80)	8.00	(16.80)	10.00	(12.50)	10.00	(12.50)	10.00	(12.50)
D. Top marginal tax rate																
(i) Top marginal income tax rate																
(ii) Top marginal income and payroll tax rates																
2. Legal Structure and Security of Property Rights	**3.33**		**4.22**		**4.48**		**4.75**		**3.73**		**2.50**		**2.61**		**2.57**	
A. Judicial independence																
B. Impartial courts							4.15		4.11		3.70		4.20		4.00	
C. Protection of property rights																
D. Military interference in rule of law and politics							3.90		1.67		0.10		0.00		0.00	
E. Integrity of the legal system							6.96		5.00		5.00		5.00		5.00	
F. Legal enforcement of contracts											3.10		3.15		3.15	
G. Regulatory restrictions on sale of real property											0.40		0.69		0.73	
3. Access to Sound Money	**5.53**		**6.75**		**6.95**		**5.03**		**6.48**		**6.90**		**6.42**		**6.63**	
A. Money growth	8.66	(6.68)	9.66	(−1.72)	9.03	(−4.84)	8.06	(9.71)	8.66	(6.69)	9.90	(−0.30)	8.60	(6.99)	8.10	(9.50)
B. Standard deviation of inflation	5.56	(11.11)	8.04	(4.90)	9.37	(1.58)	4.50	(13.74)	7.65	(5.88)	8.90	(2.66)	8.82	(2.96)	8.82	(2.95)
C. Inflation: most recent year	7.91	(10.47)	9.32	(3.40)	9.40	(2.98)	7.57	(12.17)	9.62	(1.89)	8.60	(6.80)	8.26	(8.68)	9.61	(1.95)
D. Freedom to own foreign currency bank accounts	0.00		0.00		0.00		0.00		0.00		0.00		0.00		0.00	
4. Freedom to Trade Internationally	**5.51**		**5.94**		**5.30**				**6.12**		**6.20**		**6.01**		**5.86**	
A. Taxes on international trade	1.73		4.27		3.87				7.60		7.40		7.52		7.52	
(i) Revenues from trade taxes (% of trade sector)	1.73	(12.40)	4.27	(8.60)	3.87	(9.20)					7.80	(3.30)	7.66	(3.50)	7.66	(3.50)
(ii) Mean tariff rate									7.60	(12.00)	7.10	(14.60)	7.62	(11.90)	7.62	(11.90)
(iii) Standard deviation of tariff rates											7.30	(6.80)	7.29	(6.78)	7.29	(6.78)
B. Regulatory trade barriers											6.30		6.34		6.40	
(i) Non-tariff trade barriers																
(ii) Compliance cost of importing and exporting											6.30		6.34		6.40	
C. Size of trade sector relative to expected	8.03		7.46		5.24		4.29		4.82		6.30		5.41		4.62	
D. Black-market exchange rates	9.60		9.80		9.20		9.80		10.00		10.00		10.00		10.00	
E. International capital market controls	0.00		0.00		0.00		0.00		0.00		0.80		0.77		0.77	
(i) Foreign ownership/investment restrictions																
(ii) Capital controls	0.00		0.00		0.00		0.00		0.00		0.80		0.77		0.77	
5. Regulation of Credit, Labor, and Business	**5.70**		**4.97**		**4.46**		**4.60**		**4.42**		**4.70**		**4.36**		**4.60**	
A. Credit market regulations	6.42		6.61		6.59		6.38		5.78		4.80		4.80		4.80	
(i) Ownership of banks	2.00		2.00		2.00		2.00		2.00		5.00		5.00		5.00	
(ii) Foreign bank competition																
(iii) Private sector credit	9.26		9.82		9.77		9.15		9.33		3.40		3.40		3.40	
(iv) Interest rate controls/negative real interest rates	8.00		8.00		8.00		8.00		6.00		6.00		6.00		6.00	
B. Labor market regulations											4.60		3.59		4.19	
(i) Hiring regulations and minimum wage											5.60		1.70		1.67	
(ii) Hiring and firing regulations																
(iii) Centralized collective bargaining																
(iv) Hours regulations											6.00		6.00		8.00	
(v) Mandated cost of worker dismissal											6.70		6.66		7.09	
(vi) Conscription			0.00		0.00		0.00		0.00		0.00		0.00		0.00	
C. Business regulations											4.70		4.70		4.81	
(i) Price controls							0.00		2.00		2.00		4.00		4.00		4.00
(ii) Administrative requirements																
(iii) Bureaucracy costs																
(iv) Starting a business											3.90		3.76		4.13	
(v) Extra payments/bribes/favoritism																
(vi) Licensing restrictions											4.00		4.07		4.15	
(vii) Cost of tax compliance											7.00		6.97		6.97	

Trinidad and Tobago

	1980	1985	1990	1995	2000	2005	2008	2009
Chain-Linked	Rating (Rank)	Rating (Rank)	Rating (Rank)	Rating (Rank)	Rating (Rank)	Rating (Rank)	Rating (Rank)	Rating (Rank)
Summary Rating (Rank) ➤	**5.07** (65)	**4.92** (78)	**5.64** (52)	**6.93** (31)	**7.18** (33)	**6.75** (65)	**6.83** (61)	**6.68** (64)
Area 1. Size of Government	5.48 (39)	3.79 (90)	6.31 (37)	7.04 (23)	7.05 (33)	7.17 (35)	7.40 (31)	7.41 (24)
Area 2. Legal Structure and Security of Property Rights	5.14 (45)	4.54 (64)	5.87 (46)	5.12 (77)	5.93 (56)	4.56 (91)	4.57 (93)	4.57 (91)
Area 3. Access to Sound Money	4.50 (98)	6.16 (82)	5.94 (75)	8.61 (37)	9.03 (38)	8.58 (59)	8.48 (53)	8.06 (72)
Area 4. Freedom to Trade Internationally	3.90 (74)	3.43 (81)	3.70 (95)	7.02 (42)	6.69 (73)	6.98 (52)	6.95 (58)	6.71 (58)
Area 5. Regulation of Credit, Labor, and Business	6.34 (19)	6.72 (13)	6.42 (26)	6.88 (15)	7.20 (14)	6.58 (58)	6.83 (47)	6.73 (53)

Unadjusted

	1980	1985	1990	1995	2000	2005	2008	2009
Summary Rating (Rank) ➤	**5.20** (61)	**5.05** (76)	**5.67** (53)	**6.97** (33)	**7.18** (33)	**7.06** (51)	**7.14** (48)	**6.99** (54)
	Rating Data	Rating Data	Rating Data	Rating Data	Rating Data	Rating Data	Rating Data	Rating Data
1. Size of Government	**5.38**	**3.79**	**6.31**	**7.04**	**7.05**	**7.20**	**7.40**	**7.41**
A. Government consumption	5.64 (20.81)	3.09 (29.49)	6.81 (16.84)	6.73 (17.11)	6.74 (17.10)	6.00 (19.70)	6.02 (19.53)	7.03 (16.11)
B. Transfers and subsidies	8.50 (6.00)	6.08 (14.90)	7.41 (10.00)	8.45 (6.20)	8.45 (6.20)	7.70 (8.90)	8.60 (5.65)	8.60 (5.65)
C. Government enterprises and investment	2.00 (47.60)	2.00 (40.60)	4.00 (34.60)	8.00 (16.70)	6.00 (28.67)	7.00 (23.60)	7.00 (23.59)	7.00 (23.59)
D. Top marginal tax rate		4.00	7.00	5.00	7.00	8.00	8.00	7.00
(i) Top marginal income tax rate		4.00 (50)	7.00 (35)	5.00 (38)	7.00 (35)	8.00 (30)	9.00 (25)	9.00 (25)
(ii) Top marginal income and payroll tax rates			7.00 (35)	5.00 (38)	7.00 (35)	8.00 (30)	7.00 (33)	5.00 (39)
2. Legal Structure and Security of Property Rights	**5.42**	**4.78**	**6.19**	**5.40**	**5.93**	**5.20**	**5.19**	**5.19**
A. Judicial independence						5.30	5.43	6.11
B. Impartial courts				6.47	6.28	5.20	4.92	4.72
C. Protection of property rights					5.30	6.00	5.86	5.36
D. Military interference in rule of law and politics				7.15	8.33	8.30	8.33	8.33
E. Integrity of the legal system				4.11	6.67	3.80	4.17	4.17
F. Legal enforcement of contracts						3.00	2.96	2.96
G. Regulatory restrictions on sale of real property						4.60	4.64	4.64
3. Access to Sound Money	**4.50**	**6.16**	**5.94**	**8.61**	**9.03**	**8.60**	**8.48**	**8.06**
A. Money growth	7.62 (11.88)	9.98 (−0.09)	9.06 (4.70)	8.76 (6.18)	8.83 (5.86)	8.20 (8.80)	7.43 (12.84)	7.85 (10.77)
B. Standard deviation of inflation	5.89 (10.27)	6.66 (8.34)	7.81 (5.47)	6.41 (8.98)	8.02 (4.95)	7.50 (6.33)	8.90 (2.76)	5.81 (10.48)
C. Inflation: most recent year	4.49 (27.53)	7.98 (10.10)	6.90 (15.49)	9.25 (3.75)	9.29 (3.56)	8.60 (6.89)	7.59 (12.05)	8.61 (6.97)
D. Freedom to own foreign currency bank accounts	0.00	0.00	0.00	10.00	10.00	10.00	10.00	10.00
4. Freedom to Trade Internationally	**4.24**	**3.78**	**3.85**	**7.30**	**6.69**	**7.10**	**7.06**	**6.81**
A. Taxes on international trade	7.87	6.40	6.12	6.99	5.40	7.80	7.71	7.71
(i) Revenues from trade taxes (% of trade sector)	7.87 (3.20)	6.20 (5.70)	8.20 (2.70)	8.87 (1.70)	3.20 (10.20)	9.10 (1.40)	9.17 (1.25)	9.17 (1.25)
(ii) Mean tariff rate		6.60 (17.00)	6.28 (18.60)	7.18 (14.10)	6.32 (18.40)	8.40 (7.80)	8.50 (7.50)	8.50 (7.50)
(iii) Standard deviation of tariff rates			3.88 (15.30)	4.92 (12.70)	6.68 (8.30)	6.00 (10.10)	5.47 (11.33)	5.47 (11.33)
B. Regulatory trade barriers					6.20	6.50	7.00	7.15
(i) Non-tariff trade barriers					6.20	5.70	6.64	6.49
(ii) Compliance cost of importing and exporting						7.40	7.37	7.80
C. Size of trade sector relative to expected	4.91	2.03	2.90	3.96	4.34	3.90	4.10	3.06
D. Black-market exchange rates	0.20	2.20	2.00	9.40	10.00	10.00	10.00	10.00
E. International capital market controls	0.00	0.00	0.00	8.00	7.53	7.10	6.50	6.15
(i) Foreign ownership/investment restrictions					8.15	7.40	6.84	6.14
(ii) Capital controls	0.00	0.00	0.00	8.00	6.92	6.90	6.15	6.15
5. Regulation of Credit, Labor, and Business	**6.47**	**6.77**	**6.07**	**6.50**	**7.20**	**7.30**	**7.58**	**7.47**
A. Credit market regulations	6.90	8.04	7.24	7.99	7.55	8.30	9.00	8.75
(i) Ownership of banks	5.00	8.00	8.00	8.00	8.00	8.00	8.00	8.00
(ii) Foreign bank competition					4.02	8.00	8.00	8.00
(iii) Private sector credit	8.81	8.12	7.71	9.98	9.98	10.00	10.00	10.00
(iv) Interest rate controls/negative real interest rates		8.00	6.00	6.00	9.00	7.00	10.00	9.00
B. Labor market regulations					7.15	7.50	7.48	7.51
(i) Hiring regulations and minimum wage					5.34	10.00	10.00	10.00
(ii) Hiring and firing regulations					5.80	5.30	4.69	4.86
(iii) Centralized collective bargaining					7.47	6.10	6.39	5.84
(iv) Hours regulations						10.00	10.00	10.00
(v) Mandated cost of worker dismissal						3.80	3.79	4.38
(vi) Conscription	10.00	10.00	10.00	10.00	10.00	10.00	10.00	10.00
C. Business regulations					6.88	6.10	6.26	6.15
(i) Price controls			4.00	6.00	6.00	6.00	6.00	6.00
(ii) Administrative requirements					7.47	3.30	3.95	4.11
(iii) Bureaucracy costs					7.70	4.70	4.95	4.97
(iv) Starting a business					6.63	8.60	8.62	8.61
(v) Extra payments/bribes/favoritism					6.60	4.80	4.92	5.05
(vi) Licensing restrictions						6.60	6.65	6.65
(vii) Cost of tax compliance						8.70	8.72	7.65

Tunisia

	1980	1985	1990	1995	2000	2005	2008	2009
Chain-Linked	Rating (Rank)	Rating (Rank)	Rating (Rank)	Rating (Rank)	Rating (Rank)	Rating (Rank)	Rating (Rank)	Rating (Rank)
Summary Rating (Rank) ➤	**5.09** (63)	**4.80** (82)	**5.48** (59)	**5.75** (73)	**6.03** (85)	**6.05** (90)	**5.98** (94)	**5.96** (101)
Area 1. Size of Government	4.87 (59)	4.48 (73)	5.81 (53)	4.56 (95)	5.28 (86)	5.17 (96)	5.08 (104)	5.25 (92)
Area 2. Legal Structure and Security of Property Rights	4.92 (47)	3.52 (82)	3.50 (83)	5.68 (54)	6.42 (44)	6.23 (52)	6.07 (53)	6.20 (49)
Area 3. Access to Sound Money	6.18 (56)	6.50 (65)	6.98 (47)	7.02 (56)	7.05 (77)	7.30 (83)	6.77 (93)	6.81 (96)
Area 4. Freedom to Trade Internationally	5.23 (50)	4.93 (61)	5.97 (49)	6.16 (80)	6.05 (92)	5.75 (98)	6.18 (84)	5.57 (102)
Area 5. Regulation of Credit, Labor, and Business	4.33 (83)	4.57 (77)	5.13 (65)	5.34 (69)	5.35 (96)	5.73 (100)	5.70 (102)	5.88 (100)

Unadjusted

	1980	1985	1990	1995	2000	2005	2008	2009
Summary Rating (Rank) ➤	**5.02** (71)	**4.73** (84)	**5.52** (60)	**5.80** (69)	**6.03** (85)	**6.49** (82)	**6.42** (92)	**6.40** (94)
	Rating Data	Rating Data	Rating Data	Rating Data	Rating Data	Rating Data	Rating Data	Rating Data
1. Size of Government	**4.19**	**3.86**	**5.81**	**4.56**	**5.28**	**5.20**	**5.14**	**5.31**
A. Government consumption	6.17 (19.03)	5.16 (22.46)	5.75 (20.45)	5.56 (21.11)	5.74 (20.50)	6.00 (19.60)	6.23 (18.83)	6.68 (17.28)
B. Transfers and subsidies	8.61 (5.60)	8.28 (6.80)	7.68 (9.00)	8.14 (7.34)	8.10 (7.47)	7.40 (10.00)	6.82 (12.19)	7.05 (11.33)
C. Government enterprises and investment	0.00 (53.10)	0.00 (52.80)	4.00 (35.90)	0.00 (50.70)	2.00 (47.40)	2.00 (44.40)	2.00 (44.40)	2.00 (44.40)
D. Top marginal tax rate	2.00	2.00				5.50	5.50	5.50
(i) Top marginal income tax rate	2.00 (62)	2.00 (62)				7.00 (35)	7.00 (35)	7.00 (35)
(ii) Top marginal income and payroll tax rates						4.00 (51)	4.00 (51)	4.00 (51)
2. Legal Structure and Security of Property Rights	**4.92**	**3.52**	**3.50**	**5.68**	**6.43**	**6.80**	**6.64**	**6.78**
A. Judicial independence						6.80	6.18	6.31
B. Impartial courts				6.71	6.99	6.60	6.19	6.69
C. Protection of property rights						7.40	6.98	7.31
D. Military interference in rule of law and politics				8.07	6.67	6.70	6.67	6.67
E. Integrity of the legal system				4.11	8.33	8.30	8.33	8.33
F. Legal enforcement of contracts						4.90	4.88	4.88
G. Regulatory restrictions on sale of real property						7.10	7.26	7.26
3. Access to Sound Money	**6.18**	**6.50**	**6.98**	**7.02**	**7.05**	**7.30**	**6.77**	**6.81**
A. Money growth	8.64 (6.80)	8.48 (7.61)	9.63 (1.86)	9.48 (2.60)	9.04 (4.82)	9.80 (1.10)	8.69 (6.54)	8.63 (6.86)
B. Standard deviation of inflation	8.63 (3.43)	8.25 (4.37)	9.20 (2.00)	9.62 (0.94)	9.75 (0.62)	9.80 (0.41)	9.36 (1.61)	9.37 (1.58)
C. Inflation: most recent year	7.44 (12.80)	9.28 (3.60)	9.10 (4.48)	8.96 (5.19)	9.41 (2.93)	9.60 (2.02)	9.01 (4.93)	9.23 (3.83)
D. Freedom to own foreign currency bank accounts	0.00	0.00	0.00	0.00	0.00	0.00	0.00	0.00
4. Freedom to Trade Internationally	**5.12**	**4.83**	**5.97**	**6.16**	**6.05**	**6.10**	**6.57**	**5.92**
A. Taxes on international trade	4.36	3.17	4.71	4.61	5.53	5.30	6.02	5.98
(i) Revenues from trade taxes (% of trade sector)	4.00 (9.00)	1.13 (13.30)	3.67 (9.50)	4.00 (9.00)	7.75 (3.37)	8.70 (2.00)	8.97 (1.54)	8.85 (1.72)
(ii) Mean tariff rate	4.72 (26.40)	5.20 (24.00)	4.50 (27.50)	4.50 (27.50)	3.88 (30.60)	7.30 (13.40)	5.70 (21.50)	5.70 (21.50)
(iii) Standard deviation of tariff rates			5.96 (10.10)	5.32 (11.70)	4.96 (12.60)	0.00 (26.00)	3.38 (16.56)	3.38 (16.56)
B. Regulatory trade barriers						6.60	6.89	7.10
(i) Non-tariff trade barriers						6.30	6.18	6.19
(ii) Compliance cost of importing and exporting						6.80	7.60	8.01
C. Size of trade sector relative to expected	6.63	5.16	6.54	6.21	5.74	5.70	7.02	5.97
D. Black-market exchange rates	6.40	7.60	8.40	9.80	10.00	8.80	9.49	7.16
E. International capital market controls	0.00	0.00	2.00	2.00	0.77	4.10	3.43	3.37
(i) Foreign ownership / investment restrictions						7.40	6.08	5.98
(ii) Capital controls	0.00	0.00	2.00	2.00	0.77	0.80	0.77	0.77
5. Regulation of Credit, Labor, and Business	**4.70**	**4.96**	**5.36**	**5.57**	**5.35**	**7.00**	**6.98**	**7.18**
A. Credit market regulations	4.89	5.58	7.21	7.27	6.93	7.90	8.17	8.06
(i) Ownership of banks	2.00	2.00	5.00	5.00	5.00	5.00	5.00	5.00
(ii) Foreign bank competition						8.00	8.00	8.00
(iii) Private sector credit	8.68	8.75	8.63	8.80	8.86	8.40	9.68	9.25
(iv) Interest rate controls / negative real interest rates	4.00	6.00	8.00	8.00		10.00	10.00	10.00
B. Labor market regulations						6.50	6.17	6.64
(i) Hiring regulations and minimum wage						7.20	7.20	7.23
(ii) Hiring and firing regulations						5.80	4.91	5.33
(iii) Centralized collective bargaining						6.00	4.80	5.48
(iv) Hours regulations						8.70	8.70	10.00
(v) Mandated cost of worker dismissal						8.40	8.42	8.79
(vi) Conscription	3.00	3.00	3.00	3.00	3.00	3.00	3.00	3.00
C. Business regulations						6.60	6.60	6.84
(i) Price controls			4.00	6.00	6.00	6.00	6.00	6.00
(ii) Administrative requirements						5.30	4.72	5.28
(iii) Bureaucracy costs						4.30	3.76	3.53
(iv) Starting a business						9.50	9.59	9.60
(v) Extra payments / bribes / favoritism						6.80	6.92	7.34
(vi) Licensing restrictions						7.50	7.74	7.78
(vii) Cost of tax compliance						7.00	7.44	8.39

Turkey

Chain-Linked	1980 Rating (Rank)	1985 Rating (Rank)	1990 Rating (Rank)	1995 Rating (Rank)	2000 Rating (Rank)	2005 Rating (Rank)	2008 Rating (Rank)	2009 Rating (Rank)
Summary Rating (Rank) ➤	3.95 (94)	5.08 (71)	5.14 (74)	5.72 (75)	5.75 (96)	6.36 (83)	6.91 (53)	6.84 (55)
Area 1. Size of Government	4.40 (73)	4.93 (59)	5.82 (52)	6.93 (26)	7.08 (31)	7.84 (18)	7.44 (29)	6.90 (40)
Area 2. Legal Structure and Security of Property Rights	5.82 (38)	6.11 (37)	4.68 (67)	4.85 (84)	5.39 (70)	6.50 (45)	5.61 (68)	5.59 (67)
Area 3. Access to Sound Money	0.78 (112)	2.68 (105)	3.87 (104)	3.21 (106)	3.57 (116)	4.84 (120)	8.57 (52)	8.91 (49)
Area 4. Freedom to Trade Internationally	3.85 (76)	5.78 (48)	5.66 (57)	7.41 (33)	7.15 (54)	6.63 (63)	6.41 (77)	6.40 (72)
Area 5. Regulation of Credit, Labor, and Business	5.01 (63)	5.92 (37)	5.60 (52)	6.26 (36)	5.58 (83)	6.00 (89)	6.54 (61)	6.41 (71)

Unadjusted

	1980 Rating Data	1985 Rating Data	1990 Rating Data	1995 Rating Data	2000 Rating Data	2005 Rating Data	2008 Rating Data	2009 Rating Data
Summary Rating (Rank) ➤	3.77 (99)	4.85 (81)	4.86 (88)	5.65 (76)	5.75 (96)	6.28 (95)	6.82 (75)	6.74 (75)
1. Size of Government	**4.40**	**4.93**	**5.82**	**6.93**	**7.08**	**7.80**	**7.44**	**6.90**
A. Government consumption	7.09 (15.89)	8.40 (11.44)	7.71 (13.78)	7.85 (13.30)	6.93 (16.43)	7.00 (16.30)	7.20 (15.53)	6.75 (17.06)
B. Transfers and subsidies	8.50 (6.00)	7.30 (10.40)	9.07 (3.90)	7.86 (8.36)	9.37 (2.81)	9.40 (2.80)	7.58 (9.38)	6.86 (12.04)
C. Government enterprises and investment	2.00 (40.00)	2.00 (45.50)	4.00 (31.70)	8.00 (16.50)	7.00 (22.80)	8.00 (15.70)	8.00 (19.38)	7.00 (21.65)
D. Top marginal tax rate	0.00	2.00	2.50	4.00	5.00	7.00	7.00	7.00
(i) Top marginal income tax rate	0.00 (75)	2.00 (63)	4.00 (50)	4.00 (55)	6.00 (45)	7.00 (40)	7.00 (35)	7.00 (35)
(ii) Top marginal income and payroll tax rates			1.00 (57)	4.00 (55)	4.00 (46)	7.00 (40)	7.00 (35)	7.00 (35)
2. Legal Structure and Security of Property Rights	**5.57**	**5.85**	**4.48**	**4.85**	**5.39**	**6.50**	**5.61**	**5.59**
A. Judicial independence				5.47	5.34	5.30	4.51	4.01
B. Impartial courts				6.62	6.51	4.70	4.01	4.17
C. Protection of property rights				4.25	3.43	6.30	4.83	5.08
D. Military interference in rule of law and politics				3.80	5.00	6.70	3.33	3.33
E. Integrity of the legal system				4.11	6.67	7.50	7.50	7.50
F. Legal enforcement of contracts						6.20	6.16	6.16
G. Regulatory restrictions on sale of real property						8.90	8.90	8.90
3. Access to Sound Money	**0.78**	**2.68**	**3.87**	**3.21**	**3.57**	**4.80**	**8.57**	**8.91**
A. Money growth	3.14 (34.30)	5.02 (24.88)	2.36 (38.20)	0.00 (50.41)	0.00 (81.91)	0.00 (59.30)	7.46 (12.68)	8.18 (9.10)
B. Standard deviation of inflation	0.00 (27.75)	5.71 (10.72)	3.11 (17.23)	2.84 (17.89)	4.27 (14.33)	1.40 (21.49)	8.92 (2.69)	8.73 (3.18)
C. Inflation: most recent year	0.00 (85.04)	0.00 (52.18)	0.00 (58.21)	0.00 (86.99)	0.00 (54.92)	8.00 (10.14)	7.91 (10.44)	8.75 (6.25)
D. Freedom to own foreign currency bank accounts	0.00	0.00	10.00	10.00	10.00	10.00	10.00	10.00
4. Freedom to Trade Internationally	**3.71**	**5.57**	**5.00**	**7.13**	**7.15**	**6.60**	**6.41**	**6.40**
A. Taxes on international trade	3.50	6.34	4.53	8.31	7.42	6.90	6.29	6.29
(i) Revenues from trade taxes (% of trade sector)	5.80 (6.30)	8.00 (3.00)	8.13 (2.80)	9.00 (1.50)	9.55 (0.67)	9.70 (0.40)	9.61 (0.58)	9.63 (0.56)
(ii) Mean tariff rate	1.20 (44.00)	4.68 (26.60)	5.46 (22.70)	8.20 (9.00)	8.58 (7.10)	9.50 (2.40)	8.06 (9.70)	8.06 (9.70)
(iii) Standard deviation of tariff rates			0.00 (35.70)	7.72 (5.70)	4.12 (14.70)	1.40 (21.60)	1.19 (22.02)	1.19 (22.02)
B. Regulatory trade barriers				7.60	6.98	6.60	7.13	7.07
(i) Non-tariff trade barriers				7.60	5.63	6.30	6.21	6.08
(ii) Compliance cost of importing and exporting					8.33	6.90	8.05	8.05
C. Size of trade sector relative to expected	0.00	3.89	2.67	4.64	5.56	5.60	4.52	3.99
D. Black-market exchange rates	6.80	9.40	9.60	9.60	10.00	10.00	10.00	10.00
E. International capital market controls	0.00	0.00	0.00	5.49	5.79	4.00	4.11	4.66
(i) Foreign ownership / investment restrictions				8.98	9.27	6.60	6.68	6.25
(ii) Capital controls	0.00	0.00	0.00	2.00	2.31	1.50	1.54	3.08
5. Regulation of Credit, Labor, and Business	**4.41**	**5.21**	**5.13**	**6.15**	**5.58**	**5.60**	**6.05**	**5.90**
A. Credit market regulations	3.99	6.65	5.41	7.59	6.41	6.50	7.47	6.67
(i) Ownership of banks	8.00	8.00	8.00	8.00	8.00	5.00	5.00	5.00
(ii) Foreign bank competition				7.82	5.10	6.00	6.00	6.00
(iii) Private sector credit	3.98	3.96	6.22	7.35	4.29	5.00	8.90	5.69
(iv) Interest rate controls / negative real interest rates	0.00	8.00	2.00	8.00		10.00	10.00	10.00
B. Labor market regulations			5.16	5.35	4.49	3.80	4.38	4.78
(i) Hiring regulations and minimum wage				6.35	3.38	4.40	5.60	5.57
(ii) Hiring and firing regulations			7.23	7.23	5.32	4.00	5.65	5.03
(iii) Centralized collective bargaining	7.24	7.24	7.24	7.24	6.57	6.40	6.85	7.11
(iv) Hours regulations				4.93	6.18	6.00	6.00	8.00
(v) Mandated cost of worker dismissal						1.20	1.19	1.97
(vi) Conscription	0.00	0.00	1.00	1.00	1.00	1.00	1.00	1.00
C. Business regulations				5.51	5.86	6.40	6.28	6.24
(i) Price controls			8.00	5.00	6.00	5.00	6.00	6.00
(ii) Administrative requirements					7.40	3.30	3.21	3.47
(iii) Bureaucracy costs				6.24	5.15	6.20	5.12	4.98
(iv) Starting a business				7.55	5.22	9.50	9.63	9.59
(v) Extra payments / bribes / favoritism				3.23	5.52	6.30	5.03	4.68
(vi) Licensing restrictions						7.10	7.46	7.43
(vii) Cost of tax compliance						7.20	7.50	7.50

Uganda

Chain-Linked	1980		1985		1990		1995		2000		2005		2008		2009	
	Rating	(Rank)	Rating	(Rank)	Rating	(Rank)	Rating	(Rank)	Rating	(Rank)	Rating	(Rank)	Rating	(Rank)	Rating	(Rank)
Summary Rating (Rank) ➤	3.42	(100)	3.01	(108)	3.00	(112)	5.17	(95)	6.57	(55)	6.85	(58)	7.12	(44)	7.10	(39)
Area 1. Size of Government			4.05	(84)	4.90	(75)	7.47	(18)	6.73	(45)	7.02	(44)	7.32	(32)	7.13	(30)
Area 2. Legal Structure and Security of Property Rights	2.76	(73)	2.93	(95)	2.44	(104)	4.35	(102)	4.60	(83)	5.11	(81)	4.95	(84)	5.14	(77)
Area 3. Access to Sound Money	1.04	(111)	0.10	(112)	0.28	(117)	4.62	(98)	9.30	(31)	8.70	(54)	8.79	(47)	8.40	(64)
Area 4. Freedom to Trade Internationally	4.54	(64)	3.73	(76)	2.95	(101)	4.95	(103)	6.88	(64)	6.40	(75)	7.27	(38)	7.56	(22)
Area 5. Regulation of Credit, Labor, and Business	4.25	(87)	4.23	(87)	4.46	(87)	4.47	(103)	5.36	(95)	6.74	(51)	7.00	(40)	7.05	(38)

Unadjusted

	1980		1985		1990		1995		2000		2005		2008		2009	
Summary Rating (Rank) ➤	3.21	(104)	3.02	(108)	2.93	(112)	5.19	(95)	6.57	(55)	6.76	(73)	7.02	(58)	7.01	(52)
	Rating	Data	Rating	Data	Rating	Data	Rating	Data	Rating	Data	Rating	Data	Rating	Data	Rating	Data
1. Size of Government			3.73		4.52		7.47		6.73		7.00		7.32		7.13	
A. Government consumption			7.20	(15.51)	9.57	(7.48)	8.68	(10.49)	7.50	(14.51)	7.20	(15.60)	7.97	(12.89)	7.85	(13.32)
B. Transfers and subsidies							9.20	(3.42)	8.94	(4.40)	7.90	(8.10)	8.30	(6.75)	8.67	(5.38)
C. Government enterprises and investment	2.00	(42.80)	4.00	(39.00)	2.00	(49.10)	6.00	(27.80)	4.00	(31.50)	7.00	(22.40)	7.00	(23.44)	6.00	(25.84)
D. Top marginal tax rate			0.00		2.00		6.00		6.50		6.00		6.00		6.00	
(i) Top marginal income tax rate			0.00	(70)	3.00	(50)	8.00	(30)	8.00	(30)	8.00	(30)	8.00	(30)	8.00	(30)
(ii) Top marginal income and payroll tax rates					1.00	(59)	4.00	(41)	5.00	(40)	4.00	(41)	4.00	(41)	4.00	(41)
2. Legal Structure and Security of Property Rights	2.76		2.93		2.44		4.35		4.60		4.80		4.68		4.85	
A. Judicial independence											4.60		3.69		3.99	
B. Impartial courts							5.54		4.41		4.10		4.37		4.58	
C. Protection of property rights											4.30		4.22		4.69	
D. Military interference in rule of law and politics							3.70		3.33		3.30		3.33		3.33	
E. Integrity of the legal system							4.11		6.67		6.70		5.83		5.83	
F. Legal enforcement of contracts											3.70		3.89		4.04	
G. Regulatory restrictions on sale of real property											7.00		7.39		7.49	
3. Access to Sound Money	1.04		0.00		0.28		4.62		9.30		8.70		8.79		8.40	
A. Money growth	3.12	(34.40)	0.00	(76.20)	0.00	(410.00)	5.96	(20.21)	8.73	(6.34)	8.60	(7.20)	7.77	(11.14)	7.97	(10.14)
B. Standard deviation of inflation	0.00	(33.80)	0.00	(40.83)	0.00	(52.40)	4.36	(14.10)	9.05	(2.39)	7.90	(5.36)	9.71	(0.73)	8.30	(4.25)
C. Inflation: most recent year			0.00	(120.35)	1.12	(44.38)	8.15	(9.23)	9.43	(2.83)	8.40	(8.15)	7.67	(11.63)	7.31	(13.45)
D. Freedom to own foreign currency bank accounts	0.00		0.00		0.00		0.00		10.00		10.00		10.00		10.00	
4. Freedom to Trade Internationally	4.33		3.73		2.95		5.05		6.88		5.90		6.72		6.99	
A. Taxes on international trade	7.93		3.13		3.39		5.38		5.43		5.70		7.01		7.04	
(i) Revenues from trade taxes (% of trade sector)	7.93	(3.10)	2.27	(11.60)	2.80	(10.80)	3.20	(10.20)	2.51	(11.23)	4.30	(8.50)	8.23	(2.66)	8.32	(2.52)
(ii) Mean tariff rate			4.00	(30.00)	3.98	(30.10)	6.58	(17.10)	8.34	(8.30)	7.50	(12.40)	7.48	(12.60)	7.48	(12.60)
(iii) Standard deviation of tariff rates							6.36	(9.10)			5.30	(11.70)	5.31	(11.72)	5.31	(11.72)
B. Regulatory trade barriers											3.30		5.19		5.43	
(i) Non-tariff trade barriers											4.10		5.44		5.92	
(ii) Compliance cost of importing and exporting											2.50		4.94		4.94	
C. Size of trade sector relative to expected	5.49		2.26		1.07		2.26		2.31		2.40		3.94		4.86	
D. Black-market exchange rates	0.00		5.00		2.00		9.40		10.00		10.00		10.00		10.00	
E. International capital market controls	0.00		0.00		0.00		0.00		8.46		8.20		7.49		7.63	
(i) Foreign ownership / investment restrictions											8.00		7.28		6.80	
(ii) Capital controls	0.00		0.00		0.00		0.00		8.46		8.50		7.69		8.46	
5. Regulation of Credit, Labor, and Business	4.72		4.70		4.46		4.47		5.36		7.30		7.61		7.66	
A. Credit market regulations	2.61		2.58		3.23		4.29		6.55		8.90		8.70		8.87	
(i) Ownership of banks	2.00		2.00		2.00		2.00		2.00		10.00		10.00		10.00	
(ii) Foreign bank competition											7.00		7.00		7.00	
(iii) Private sector credit	5.84		5.74		7.70		6.86		8.66		9.60		8.79		9.48	
(iv) Interest rate controls / negative real interest rates	0.00		0.00		0.00		4.00		9.00		9.00		9.00		9.00	
B. Labor market regulations											7.60		7.92		8.07	
(i) Hiring regulations and minimum wage											10.00		10.00		10.00	
(ii) Hiring and firing regulations											6.90		7.08		7.01	
(iii) Centralized collective bargaining											8.70		8.65		8.42	
(iv) Hours regulations											8.00		10.00		10.00	
(v) Mandated cost of worker dismissal											8.80		8.79		10.00	
(vi) Conscription	10.00		10.00		10.00		3.00		3.00		3.00		3.00		3.00	
C. Business regulations											5.60		6.22		6.04	
(i) Price controls							0.00		4.00		6.00		6.00		6.00		6.00	
(ii) Administrative requirements											3.80		4.50		4.86	
(iii) Bureaucracy costs											2.40		6.06		6.14	
(iv) Starting a business											8.10		8.31		8.21	
(v) Extra payments / bribes / favoritism											4.20		2.97		3.08	
(vi) Licensing restrictions											7.10		7.53		5.80	
(vii) Cost of tax compliance											7.30		8.20		8.20	

Ukraine

	1980	1985	1990	1995	2000	2005	2008	2009
Chain-Linked			Rating (Rank)	Rating (Rank)	Rating (Rank)	Rating (Rank)	Rating (Rank)	Rating (Rank)
Summary Rating (Rank) ➤				3.72 (121)	4.70 (118)	5.60 (108)	5.60 (107)	5.69 (105)
Area 1. Size of Government					4.59 (101)	4.96 (101)	5.87 (80)	5.72 (75)
Area 2. Legal Structure and Security of Property Rights				4.78 (89)	4.81 (79)	5.28 (77)	5.00 (82)	4.74 (87)
Area 3. Access to Sound Money			3.90 (103)	0.12 (121)	2.24 (122)	4.88 (119)	4.61 (121)	5.32 (121)
Area 4. Freedom to Trade Internationally				6.68 (61)	7.05 (61)	6.60 (66)	6.51 (73)	6.68 (59)
Area 5. Regulation of Credit, Labor, and Business			2.80 (113)	3.34 (119)	4.79 (106)	6.28 (67)	6.00 (92)	6.00 (97)

Unadjusted

	1980		1985		1990		1995		2000		2005		2008		2009	
Summary Rating (Rank) ➤							3.44 (122)		4.70 (118)		5.61 (124)		5.60 (125)		5.70 (125)	
	Rating	Data	Rating	Data	Rating	Data	Rating	Data	Rating	Data	Rating	Data	Rating	Data	Rating	Data
1. Size of Government									4.59		5.00		5.87		5.72	
A. Government consumption	4.65	(24.20)	4.41	(25.00)	5.16	(22.44)	3.58	(27.84)	3.59	(27.80)	4.40	(25.10)	5.19	(22.37)	5.10	(22.66)
B. Transfers and subsidies									6.26	(14.24)	4.00	(22.60)	3.80	(23.24)	3.26	(25.22)
C. Government enterprises and investment									4.00		4.00		7.00		7.00	
D. Top marginal tax rate									4.50		7.50		7.50		7.50	
(i) Top marginal income tax rate									5.00	(40)	10.00	(13)	10.00	(15)	10.00	(15)
(ii) Top marginal income and payroll tax rates									4.00	(44)	5.00	(38)	5.00	(40)	5.00	(40)
2. Legal Structure and Security of Property Rights							4.32		4.81		5.30		5.00		4.74	
A. Judicial independence							6.10		3.17		2.60		2.09		1.66	
B. Impartial courts							4.28		3.51		3.10		2.08		2.11	
C. Protection of property rights							1.22		2.38		3.90		3.09		2.66	
D. Military interference in rule of law and politics							5.67		8.33		8.30		8.33		8.33	
E. Integrity of the legal system									6.67		6.70		6.67		6.67	
F. Legal enforcement of contracts											5.30		5.34		5.34	
G. Regulatory restrictions on sale of real property											7.10		7.39		6.44	
3. Access to Sound Money					3.37		0.00		2.24		4.90		4.61		5.32	
A. Money growth									3.17	(34.15)	5.30	(23.70)	6.06	(19.70)	7.20	(13.98)
B. Standard deviation of inflation							0.00	(1158.31)	1.45	(21.38)	6.90	(7.64)	7.42	(6.44)	7.26	(6.86)
C. Inflation: most recent year					6.73	(16.34)	0.00	(415.53)	4.36	(28.20)	7.30	(13.52)	4.95	(25.23)	6.82	(15.89)
D. Freedom to own foreign currency bank accounts					0.00		0.00		0.00		0.00		0.00		0.00	
4. Freedom to Trade Internationally							6.20		7.05		6.60		6.51		6.68	
A. Taxes on international trade									7.62		6.70		8.16		8.79	
(i) Revenues from trade taxes (% of trade sector)									9.36	(0.96)	8.90	(1.70)	8.98	(1.53)	9.45	(0.83)
(ii) Mean tariff rate									7.90	(10.50)	8.60	(6.80)	8.90	(5.50)	9.08	(4.60)
(iii) Standard deviation of tariff rates									5.60	(11.00)	2.70	(18.20)	6.59	(8.53)	7.83	(5.43)
B. Regulatory trade barriers							2.52		5.51		4.80		5.13		4.86	
(i) Non-tariff trade barriers							2.52		4.03		4.60		4.94		4.40	
(ii) Compliance cost of importing and exporting									6.99		5.10		5.32		5.32	
C. Size of trade sector relative to expected					5.82		9.45		10.00		8.70		6.90		7.25	
D. Black-market exchange rates	0.00		0.00		0.00		9.40		7.78		10.00		10.00		10.00	
E. International capital market controls	0.00		0.00		0.00		3.43		4.34		2.70		2.35		2.49	
(i) Foreign ownership / investment restrictions									4.86		7.13		4.60		3.94		4.21	
(ii) Capital controls	0.00		0.00		0.00		2.00		1.54		0.80		0.77		0.77	
5. Regulation of Credit, Labor, and Business					3.45		3.25		4.79		6.30		6.02		6.03	
A. Credit market regulations					0.00		1.77		5.11		8.90		8.07		8.10	
(i) Ownership of banks					0.00		0.00		0.00		8.00		8.00		8.00	
(ii) Foreign bank competition							3.17		3.93		8.00		8.00		8.00	
(iii) Private sector credit							1.72		9.76		9.50		9.27		6.41	
(iv) Interest rate controls / negative real interest rates							0.00		7.00		10.00		7.00		10.00	
B. Labor market regulations							5.35		4.51		6.20		6.30		6.24	
(i) Hiring regulations and minimum wage							6.62		1.87		5.60		6.70		5.57	
(ii) Hiring and firing regulations					5.83		5.83		6.25		6.30		6.21		6.11	
(iii) Centralized collective bargaining							7.93		8.07		7.30		7.10		7.15	
(iv) Hours regulations							5.35		5.34		8.00		8.00		8.00	
(v) Mandated cost of worker dismissal											8.80		8.79		9.60	
(vi) Conscription							1.00		1.00		1.00		1.00		1.00	
C. Business regulations							2.64		4.75		4.00		3.70		3.76	
(i) Price controls					0.00		4.00		6.00		4.00		1.00		1.00	
(ii) Administrative requirements									6.27		2.60		2.81		2.65	
(iii) Bureaucracy costs							2.20		4.80		3.80		5.87		6.25	
(iv) Starting a business							3.73		2.87		8.20		8.57		9.06	
(v) Extra payments / bribes / favoritism							0.62		3.79		5.60		3.49		2.88	
(vi) Licensing restrictions											3.50		2.38		1.86	
(vii) Cost of tax compliance											0.00		1.75		2.64	

United Arab Emirates

	1980	1985	1990	1995	2000	2005	2008	2009
Chain-Linked	Rating (Rank)	Rating (Rank)	Rating (Rank)	Rating (Rank)	Rating (Rank)	Rating (Rank)	Rating (Rank)	Rating (Rank)
Summary Rating (Rank) ➤	**5.92** (35)	**6.79** (18)	**7.18** (21)	**6.77** (35)	**7.02** (40)	**7.22** (37)	**7.38** (27)	**7.26** (30)
Area 1. Size of Government	5.97 (27)	5.75 (33)	7.43 (11)	5.94 (65)	6.11 (65)	6.98 (46)	7.12 (36)	7.13 (30)
Area 2. Legal Structure and Security of Property Rights	2.06 (86)	5.85 (40)	5.79 (47)	5.83 (51)	6.56 (39)	6.66 (38)	6.90 (29)	6.65 (31)
Area 3. Access to Sound Money	6.64 (35)	7.64 (31)	7.91 (33)	7.76 (44)	7.75 (65)	7.60 (77)	7.88 (68)	8.44 (62)
Area 4. Freedom to Trade Internationally					8.22 (19)	8.74 (3)	8.68 (3)	7.96 (6)
Area 5. Regulation of Credit, Labor, and Business	5.31 (50)	6.26 (27)	6.37 (29)	6.34 (32)	6.46 (43)	6.15 (77)	6.33 (74)	6.17 (87)

	1980	1985	1990	1995	2000	2005	2008	2009
Unadjusted								
Summary Rating (Rank) ➤	**5.92** (33)	**6.78** (16)	**7.40** (8)	**6.89** (36)	**7.02** (40)	**7.49** (24)	**7.66** (13)	**7.54** (14)
	Rating Data	Rating Data	Rating Data	Rating Data	Rating Data	Rating Data	Rating Data	Rating Data
1. Size of Government	**5.19**	**5.00**	**7.43**	**5.94**	**6.11**	**7.00**	**7.12**	**7.13**
A. Government consumption	0.37 (38.73)	0.00 (41.76)	2.91 (30.10)	3.88 (26.80)	4.71 (23.97)	6.20 (18.90)	6.78 (16.94)	6.80 (16.89)
B. Transfers and subsidies			9.81 (1.20)	9.86 (1.00)	9.71 (1.55)	9.70 (1.60)	9.71 (1.55)	9.71 (1.55)
C. Government enterprises and investment			7.00 (21.40)	0.00 (55.70)	0.00 (56.90)	2.00 (49.10)	2.00 (48.70)	2.00 (48.70)
D. Top marginal tax rate	10.00	10.00	10.00	10.00	10.00	10.00	10.00	10.00
(i) Top marginal income tax rate	10.00 (0)	10.00 (0)	10.00	10.00 (0)	10.00 (0)	10.00 (0)	10.00 (0)	10.00 (0)
(ii) Top marginal income and payroll tax rates						10.00 (16)	10.00 (16)	10.00 (16)
2. Legal Structure and Security of Property Rights	**2.06**	**5.85**	**5.79**	**5.83**	**6.56**	**6.90**	**7.19**	**6.93**
A. Judicial independence						6.30	6.76	6.49
B. Impartial courts				6.92	7.55	6.30	7.00	6.21
C. Protection of property rights						6.80	7.45	6.71
D. Military interference in rule of law and politics				8.50	8.33	8.30	8.33	8.33
E. Integrity of the legal system				4.11	6.67	6.70	6.67	6.67
F. Legal enforcement of contracts						4.80	4.83	4.83
G. Regulatory restrictions on sale of real property						9.30	9.30	9.30
3. Access to Sound Money	**7.93**	**9.12**	**9.44**	**9.45**	**7.75**	**7.60**	**7.88**	**8.44**
A. Money growth	5.46 (22.70)	9.30 (−3.51)	9.27 (3.66)	8.90 (5.51)	8.87 (5.66)	6.60 (16.80)	7.14 (14.28)	7.71 (11.44)
B. Standard deviation of inflation	8.08 (4.79)	8.09 (4.78)	9.32 (1.69)		6.49 (8.78)	6.60 (8.45)	8.32 (4.21)	8.32 (12.17)
C. Inflation: most recent year	8.18 (9.10)	9.11 (4.46)	9.18 (4.10)		5.63 (21.83)	7.10 (14.29)	6.04 (19.80)	7.74 (−11.28)
D. Freedom to own foreign currency bank accounts	10.00	10.00	10.00	10.00	10.00	10.00	10.00	10.00
4. Freedom to Trade Internationally	**9.16**	**7.72**	**7.94**		**8.22**	**8.50**	**8.47**	**7.76**
A. Taxes on international trade	10.00	9.60	10.00		9.60	8.90	8.45	8.67
(i) Revenues from trade taxes (% of trade sector)	10.00 (0.00)	10.00 (0.00)	10.00 (0.00)		10.00 (0.00)	10.00 (0.00)	10.00 (0.00)	10.00 (0.00)
(ii) Mean tariff rate		9.20 (4.00)			9.20 (4.00)	9.00 (4.80)	9.00 (5.00)	9.02 (4.90)
(iii) Standard deviation of tariff rates						7.60 (6.10)	6.36 (9.10)	7.00 (7.50)
B. Regulatory trade barriers						8.10	8.62	8.63
(i) Non-tariff trade barriers						7.60	8.30	8.12
(ii) Compliance cost of importing and exporting						8.60	8.93	9.14
C. Size of trade sector relative to expected	7.70	5.86	6.57	7.43	7.22	9.20	8.51	5.00
D. Black-market exchange rates	10.00	10.00	10.00	10.00	10.00	10.00	10.00	10.00
E. International capital market controls	10.00	5.00	5.00	5.00	6.15	6.40	6.75	6.49
(i) Foreign ownership/investment restrictions						6.70	7.67	7.15
(ii) Capital controls	10.00	5.00	5.00	5.00	6.15	6.20	5.83	5.83
5. Regulation of Credit, Labor, and Business	**5.28**	**6.22**	**6.37**	**6.34**	**6.46**	**7.40**	**7.63**	**7.46**
A. Credit market regulations	6.85	6.17	6.49	6.36	6.86	7.80	7.90	7.81
(i) Ownership of banks	5.00	5.00	5.00	5.00	5.00	5.00	5.00	5.00
(ii) Foreign bank competition						8.00	8.00	8.00
(iii) Private sector credit	8.71	7.35	7.98	7.73	8.71	8.20	8.62	8.24
(iv) Interest rate controls/negative real interest rates						10.00	10.00	10.00
B. Labor market regulations						7.50	7.53	7.19
(i) Hiring regulations and minimum wage						10.00	10.00	10.00
(ii) Hiring and firing regulations						6.20	6.43	6.17
(iii) Centralized collective bargaining						8.50	8.53	8.34
(iv) Hours regulations						8.00	8.00	6.00
(v) Mandated cost of worker dismissal						2.20	2.21	2.65
(vi) Conscription	3.00	10.00	10.00	10.00	10.00	10.00	10.00	10.00
C. Business regulations						7.00	7.45	7.37
(i) Price controls			8.00	8.00	8.00	6.00	6.00	6.00
(ii) Administrative requirements						5.60	6.06	5.51
(iii) Bureaucracy costs						2.20	2.67	2.81
(iv) Starting a business						8.00	9.45	9.45
(v) Extra payments/bribes/favoritism						8.10	8.27	8.10
(vi) Licensing restrictions						9.20	9.82	9.81
(vii) Cost of tax compliance						9.90	9.87	9.87

United Kingdom

	1980	1985	1990	1995	2000	2005	2008	2009
Chain-Linked	Rating (Rank)	Rating (Rank)	Rating (Rank)	Rating (Rank)	Rating (Rank)	Rating (Rank)	Rating (Rank)	Rating (Rank)
Summary Rating (Rank) ➤	**6.73** (17)	**7.66** (7)	**8.14** (5)	**8.04** (6)	**8.25** (6)	**8.04** (8)	**7.78** (9)	**7.68** (8)
Area 1. Size of Government	3.94 (84)	4.61 (69)	5.65 (58)	5.42 (81)	6.13 (61)	6.29 (75)	6.02 (78)	5.68 (77)
Area 2. Legal Structure and Security of Property Rights	8.29 (19)	7.83 (21)	9.10 (17)	8.84 (14)	9.29 (6)	8.52 (12)	8.11 (15)	8.20 (12)
Area 3. Access to Sound Money	5.96 (68)	9.35 (10)	9.48 (12)	9.60 (15)	9.31 (30)	9.45 (29)	9.41 (24)	9.58 (12)
Area 4. Freedom to Trade Internationally	8.28 (6)	8.33 (6)	8.14 (10)	8.25 (10)	8.42 (12)	7.76 (19)	7.62 (26)	7.68 (15)
Area 5. Regulation of Credit, Labor, and Business	7.41 (5)	8.19 (2)	8.38 (2)	8.06 (4)	8.08 (3)	8.17 (10)	7.76 (18)	7.28 (27)

Unadjusted								
Summary Rating (Rank) ➤	**6.28** (21)	**7.15** (8)	**7.57** (6)	**8.03** (6)	**8.25** (6)	**8.06** (8)	**7.81** (10)	**7.71** (8)
	Rating Data	Rating Data	Rating Data	Rating Data	Rating Data	Rating Data	Rating Data	Rating Data
1. Size of Government	**3.94**	**4.61**	**5.65**	**5.42**	**6.13**	**6.30**	**6.02**	**5.68**
A. Government consumption	3.93 (26.62)	4.16 (25.85)	4.52 (24.63)	4.36 (25.18)	5.23 (22.22)	4.30 (25.30)	4.30 (25.37)	3.97 (26.49)
B. Transfers and subsidies	5.83 (15.80)	5.26 (17.90)	6.08 (14.90)	5.31 (17.70)	6.31 (14.05)	6.30 (14.00)	6.28 (14.15)	5.74 (16.14)
C. Government enterprises and investment	6.00 (29.10)	7.00 (23.50)	8.00 (15.30)	8.00 (16.40)	8.00 (16.40)	10.00 (4.20)	10.00 (13.69)	8.00 (18.26)
D. Top marginal tax rate	0.00	2.00	4.00	4.00	5.00	4.50	3.50	5.00
(i) Top marginal income tax rate	0.00 (83)	2.00 (60)	5.00 (40)	5.00 (40)	6.00 (40)	5.00 (41)	4.00 (41)	6.00 (40)
(ii) Top marginal income and payroll tax rates			3.00 (48)	3.00 (48)	4.00 (48)	4.00 (48)	3.00 (48)	4.00 (48)
2. Legal Structure and Security of Property Rights	**7.05**	**6.65**	**7.73**	**8.84**	**9.29**	**8.50**	**8.11**	**8.20**
A. Judicial independence				9.50	9.02	8.70	8.37	8.81
B. Impartial courts				8.88	9.02	8.40	7.01	6.98
C. Protection of property rights				7.08	8.44	9.10	7.65	7.92
D. Military interference in rule of law and politics				8.76	10.00	10.00	10.00	10.00
E. Integrity of the legal system				10.00	10.00	9.20	9.17	9.17
F. Legal enforcement of contracts						6.00	6.04	6.04
G. Regulatory restrictions on sale of real property						8.30	8.50	8.50
3. Access to Sound Money	**5.96**	**9.35**	**9.48**	**9.60**	**9.31**	**9.40**	**9.41**	**9.58**
A. Money growth	8.57 (7.17)	9.57 (2.17)	9.75 (1.27)	9.59 (2.06)	8.14 (9.31)	8.50 (7.30)	8.56 (7.18)	8.68 (6.61)
B. Standard deviation of inflation	9.04 (2.40)	9.01 (2.48)	9.45 (1.38)	9.30 (1.74)	9.69 (0.77)	9.80 (0.44)	9.86 (0.35)	9.75 (0.61)
C. Inflation: most recent year	6.23 (18.84)	8.82 (5.91)	8.72 (6.42)	9.51 (2.44)	9.41 (2.93)	9.40 (2.83)	9.20 (3.99)	9.89 (−0.55)
D. Freedom to own foreign currency bank accounts	0.00	10.00	10.00	10.00	10.00	10.00	10.00	10.00
4. Freedom to Trade Internationally	**8.47**	**8.53**	**8.21**	**8.19**	**8.42**	**7.80**	**7.62**	**7.68**
A. Taxes on international trade	8.89	9.05	8.41	8.63	9.18	8.40	8.03	8.22
(i) Revenues from trade taxes (% of trade sector)	9.53 (0.70)	9.60 (0.60)	9.60 (0.60)	9.60 (0.60)	9.78 (0.33)	9.60 (0.60)	9.61 (0.59)	9.44 (0.84)
(ii) Mean tariff rate	8.24 (8.80)	8.50 (7.50)	8.52 (7.40)	8.66 (6.70)	9.52 (2.40)	9.50 (2.70)	8.88 (5.60)	8.94 (5.30)
(iii) Standard deviation of tariff rates			7.12 (7.20)	7.64 (5.90)	8.24 (4.40)	6.10 (9.70)	5.61 (10.98)	6.29 (9.28)
B. Regulatory trade barriers				8.03	9.32	8.10	8.03	8.27
(i) Non-tariff trade barriers				8.03	8.97	7.20	7.15	7.34
(ii) Compliance cost of importing and exporting					9.67	8.90	8.91	9.20
C. Size of trade sector relative to expected	5.34	5.44	4.48	4.81	4.51	3.80	3.99	3.65
D. Black-market exchange rates	10.00	10.00	10.00	10.00	10.00	10.00	10.00	10.00
E. International capital market controls	10.00	10.00	10.00	9.45	9.10	8.50	8.03	8.24
(i) Foreign ownership/investment restrictions				8.89	9.75	8.60	7.72	8.15
(ii) Capital controls	10.00	10.00	10.00	10.00	8.46	8.50	8.33	8.33
5. Regulation of Credit, Labor, and Business	**6.00**	**6.62**	**6.79**	**8.08**	**8.08**	**8.30**	**7.89**	**7.40**
A. Credit market regulations	7.33	9.71	9.93	8.63	9.19	9.20	8.96	7.27
(i) Ownership of banks	10.00	10.00	10.00	10.00	10.00	10.00	10.00	10.00
(ii) Foreign bank competition				9.28	7.42	9.00	9.00	9.00
(iii) Private sector credit	8.00	9.12	9.79	6.36	10.00	8.00	6.85	1.07
(iv) Interest rate controls/negative real interest rates	4.00	10.00	10.00	10.00	10.00	10.00	10.00	9.00
B. Labor market regulations	6.67	6.79	7.24	7.22	6.92	8.50	7.98	8.19
(i) Hiring regulations and minimum wage				6.67	4.61	8.90	8.90	8.90
(ii) Hiring and firing regulations			7.39	7.39	4.90	5.80	5.22	5.36
(iii) Centralized collective bargaining	5.18	5.18	6.21	6.21	8.60	8.10	7.83	7.87
(iv) Hours regulations	4.84	5.19	5.37	5.85	6.51	10.00	8.00	8.00
(v) Mandated cost of worker dismissal						8.00	7.96	9.03
(vi) Conscription	10.00	10.00	10.00	10.00	10.00	10.00	10.00	10.00
C. Business regulations				8.39	8.13	7.10	6.71	6.73
(i) Price controls			9.00	9.00	8.00	4.00	6.00	6.00
(ii) Administrative requirements					7.93	3.80	3.33	3.43
(iii) Bureaucracy costs				7.78	8.03	5.90	2.21	1.98
(iv) Starting a business				8.07	7.73	9.60	9.58	9.58
(v) Extra payments/bribes/favoritism				8.70	8.97	9.00	7.87	8.08
(vi) Licensing restrictions						8.40	9.25	9.24
(vii) Cost of tax compliance						8.80	8.77	8.77

United States

Chain-Linked	1980 Rating (Rank)	1985 Rating (Rank)	1990 Rating (Rank)	1995 Rating (Rank)	2000 Rating (Rank)	2005 Rating (Rank)	2008 Rating (Rank)	2009 Rating (Rank)
Summary Rating (Rank) ➤	**8.03** (3)	**8.18** (3)	**8.43** (3)	**8.32** (4)	**8.45** (3)	**8.07** (4)	**7.89** (7)	**7.58** (10)
Area 1. Size of Government	5.17 (49)	6.05 (27)	6.71 (24)	6.88 (29)	7.03 (34)	7.13 (38)	6.88 (45)	6.49 (54)
Area 2. Legal Structure and Security of Property Rights	9.81 (1)	9.81 (4)	9.81 (12)	8.76 (15)	9.23 (9)	7.63 (21)	7.50 (22)	7.30 (26)
Area 3. Access to Sound Money	9.22 (5)	9.36 (9)	9.68 (6)	9.76 (3)	9.78 (2)	9.76 (1)	9.69 (2)	9.60 (11)
Area 4. Freedom to Trade Internationally	8.09 (8)	7.78 (11)	7.91 (13)	8.01 (18)	8.01 (25)	7.52 (26)	7.57 (29)	7.02 (44)
Area 5. Regulation of Credit, Labor, and Business	8.10 (2)	8.08 (3)	8.17 (4)	8.21 (3)	8.19 (2)	8.29 (8)	7.78 (17)	7.49 (20)

Unadjusted

	1980 Rating Data	1985 Rating Data	1990 Rating Data	1995 Rating Data	2000 Rating Data	2005 Rating Data	2008 Rating Data	2009 Rating Data
Summary Rating (Rank) ➤	**7.53** (5)	**7.66** (4)	**7.87** (3)	**8.30** (4)	**8.45** (3)	**8.09** (6)	**7.91** (7)	**7.60** (10)
1. Size of Government	**5.17**	**6.05**	**6.71**	**6.88**	**7.03**	**7.10**	**6.88**	**6.49**
A. Government consumption	5.53 (21.21)	5.45 (21.46)	5.66 (20.76)	6.18 (18.97)	6.59 (17.60)	6.30 (18.40)	6.10 (19.27)	6.02 (19.55)
B. Transfers and subsidies	7.17 (10.90)	6.73 (12.50)	6.68 (12.70)	6.32 (14.00)	6.54 (13.19)	6.70 (12.70)	6.44 (13.56)	5.94 (15.40)
C. Government enterprises and investment	8.00 (17.71)	8.00 (18.07)	8.00 (18.28)	8.00 (16.70)	8.00 (17.68)	8.00 (15.20)	8.00 (18.85)	7.00 (22.68)
D. Top marginal tax rate	0.00	4.00	6.50	7.00	7.00	7.50	7.00	7.00
(i) Top marginal income tax rate	0.00 (70-75)	4.00 (50-59)	7.00 (33-42)	7.00 (40-46)	7.00 (40-46)	8.00 (35-42)	7.00 (35-41)	7.00 (35-41)
(ii) Top marginal income and payroll tax rates			6.00 (36-45)	7.00 (42-49)	7.00 (42-49)	7.00 (37-44)	7.00 (37-43)	7.00 (37-43)
2. Legal Structure and Security of Property Rights	**8.35**	**8.35**	**8.35**	**8.76**	**9.23**	**7.60**	**7.50**	**7.30**
A. Judicial independence				8.30	8.02	6.60	7.24	6.62
B. Impartial courts				8.52	9.02	6.80	5.78	5.70
C. Protection of property rights				7.76	9.10	8.10	7.54	6.83
D. Military interference in rule of law and politics				9.23	10.00	6.70	6.67	6.67
E. Integrity of the legal system				10.00	10.00	8.30	8.33	8.33
F. Legal enforcement of contracts						7.30	7.33	7.33
G. Regulatory restrictions on sale of real property						9.60	9.61	9.61
3. Access to Sound Money	**9.22**	**9.36**	**9.68**	**9.76**	**9.78**	**9.80**	**9.69**	**9.60**
A. Money growth	9.25 (3.75)	9.11 (4.46)	9.86 (−0.72)	9.70 (1.51)	9.94 (−0.28)	9.90 (−0.40)	9.67 (1.64)	8.86 (5.72)
B. Standard deviation of inflation	9.54 (1.15)	9.04 (2.41)	9.71 (0.72)	9.74 (0.64)	9.84 (0.40)	9.80 (0.52)	9.84 (0.40)	9.63 (0.91)
C. Inflation: most recent year	8.10 (9.51)	9.30 (3.52)	9.13 (4.34)	9.60 (2.00)	9.32 (3.38)	9.30 (3.39)	9.23 (3.84)	9.93 (−0.36)
D. Freedom to own foreign currency bank accounts	10.00	10.00	10.00	10.00	10.00	10.00	10.00	10.00
4. Freedom to Trade Internationally	**8.07**	**7.76**	**7.77**	**7.87**	**8.01**	**7.50**	**7.57**	**7.02**
A. Taxes on international trade	8.90	8.77	8.23	8.41	8.12	8.40	8.41	8.46
(i) Revenues from trade taxes (% of trade sector)	9.27 (1.10)	8.87 (1.70)	9.00 (1.50)	9.20 (1.20)	9.44 (0.84)	9.50 (0.80)	9.56 (0.66)	9.57 (0.65)
(ii) Mean tariff rate	8.54 (7.30)	8.68 (6.60)	8.76 (6.20)	8.82 (5.90)	9.20 (4.00)	9.40 (3.20)	9.30 (3.50)	9.30 (3.50)
(iii) Standard deviation of tariff rates			6.92 (7.70)	7.20 (7.00)	5.72 (10.70)	6.30 (9.30)	6.37 (9.07)	6.50 (8.75)
B. Regulatory trade barriers				7.82	8.81	8.00	7.93	7.69
(i) Non-tariff trade barriers				7.82	8.12	6.70	6.52	6.03
(ii) Compliance cost of importing and exporting					9.50	9.30	9.35	9.35
C. Size of trade sector relative to expected	5.29	3.88	4.45	4.73	4.91	4.50	5.09	3.90
D. Black-market exchange rates	10.00	10.00	10.00	10.00	10.00	10.00	10.00	10.00
E. International capital market controls	8.00	8.00	8.00	8.39	8.21	6.70	6.44	5.08
(i) Foreign ownership/investment restrictions				8.78	9.49	7.30	6.73	6.32
(ii) Capital controls	8.00	8.00	8.00	8.00	6.92	6.20	6.15	3.85
5. Regulation of Credit, Labor, and Business	**6.82**	**6.80**	**6.83**	**8.23**	**8.19**	**8.40**	**7.89**	**7.60**
A. Credit market regulations	9.52	9.47	9.64	9.04	9.14	8.80	7.74	7.00
(i) Ownership of banks	10.00	10.00	10.00	10.00	10.00	10.00	10.00	10.00
(ii) Foreign bank competition				8.33	7.60	8.00	8.00	8.00
(iii) Private sector credit	8.55	8.40	8.93	8.79	9.43	7.30	2.95	0.00
(iv) Interest rate controls/negative real interest rates	10.00	10.00	10.00	10.00	10.00	10.00	10.00	10.00
B. Labor market regulations	7.74	7.74	7.68	7.46	7.17	9.10	9.20	9.10
(i) Hiring regulations and minimum wage				5.90	3.82	10.00	10.00	10.00
(ii) Hiring and firing regulations			7.15	7.15	6.65	7.00	7.27	7.05
(iii) Centralized collective bargaining	7.59	7.59	7.59	7.59	8.35	7.80	7.92	7.55
(iv) Hours regulations	5.63	5.63	5.98	6.67	7.01	10.00	10.00	10.00
(v) Mandated cost of worker dismissal						10.00	10.00	10.00
(vi) Conscription	10.00	10.00	10.00	10.00	10.00	10.00	10.00	10.00
C. Business regulations				8.21	8.26	7.20	6.73	6.69
(i) Price controls			9.00	9.00	8.00	7.00	6.00	6.00
(ii) Administrative requirements				7.92	4.30	3.99	4.13
(iii) Bureaucracy costs				7.48	8.15	5.90	2.30	2.58
(iv) Starting a business				8.43	8.40	9.80	9.80	9.79
(v) Extra payments/bribes/favoritism				7.91	8.82	7.20	7.10	6.47
(vi) Licensing restrictions						10.00	9.98	9.98
(vii) Cost of tax compliance						6.40	7.90	7.90

Uruguay

	1980	1985	1990	1995	2000	2005	2008	2009
Chain-Linked	Rating (Rank)	Rating (Rank)	Rating (Rank)	Rating (Rank)	Rating (Rank)	Rating (Rank)	Rating (Rank)	Rating (Rank)
Summary Rating (Rank) ➤	**5.95** (33)	**5.86** (39)	**6.17** (40)	**6.11** (60)	**6.68** (46)	**6.74** (66)	**6.67** (71)	**6.64** (68)
Area 1. Size of Government	7.82 (8)	7.01 (7)	7.67 (9)	7.48 (17)	6.53 (51)	7.50 (25)	7.07 (37)	6.50 (53)
Area 2. Legal Structure and Security of Property Rights	5.42 (40)	5.19 (57)	6.06 (43)	5.80 (52)	5.74 (62)	5.14 (80)	4.91 (85)	4.97 (83)
Area 3. Access to Sound Money	4.18 (99)	3.71 (101)	3.76 (105)	3.92 (101)	8.39 (48)	8.18 (64)	8.45 (54)	8.83 (53)
Area 4. Freedom to Trade Internationally	6.56 (32)	7.23 (18)	6.97 (31)	7.07 (40)	6.74 (72)	6.78 (59)	6.95 (58)	6.76 (53)
Area 5. Regulation of Credit, Labor, and Business	5.78 (36)	6.10 (33)	6.36 (30)	6.27 (35)	5.97 (62)	6.14 (79)	6.02 (90)	6.16 (88)

	1980	1985	1990	1995	2000	2005	2008	2009
Unadjusted								
Summary Rating (Rank) ➤	**6.11** (25)	**5.97** (35)	**6.24** (36)	**6.18** (58)	**6.68** (46)	**7.00** (56)	**6.93** (61)	**6.90** (62)
	Rating Data	Rating Data	Rating Data	Rating Data	Rating Data	Rating Data	Rating Data	Rating Data
1. Size of Government	**7.82**	**7.01**	**7.67**	**7.48**	**6.53**	**7.50**	**7.07**	**6.50**
A. Government consumption	7.61 (14.11)	6.64 (17.41)	6.83 (16.77)	7.49 (14.52)	7.40 (14.84)	7.90 (13.20)	7.53 (14.39)	7.10 (15.88)
B. Transfers and subsidies	7.66 (9.10)	7.41 (10.00)	6.87 (12.00)	5.42 (17.30)	5.20 (18.10)	6.60 (13.00)	6.73 (12.50)	6.39 (13.76)
C. Government enterprises and investment	6.00 (29.00)	4.00 (36.20)	7.00 (23.00)	7.00 (22.90)	6.00 (25.20)	8.00 (17.70)	7.00 (22.16)	6.00 (28.94)
D. Top marginal tax rate	10.00	10.00	10.00	10.00	7.50	7.50	7.00	6.50
(i) Top marginal income tax rate	10.00 (0)	10.00 (0)	10.00 (0)	10.00 (0)	10.00 (0)	10.00 (0)	9.00 (25)	9.00 (25)
(ii) Top marginal income and payroll tax rates					5.00 (36)	5.00 (36)	5.00 (45)	4.00 (45)
2. Legal Structure and Security of Property Rights	**5.61**	**5.38**	**6.28**	**6.00**	**5.74**	**5.80**	**5.59**	**5.66**
A. Judicial independence						6.60	6.99	7.11
B. Impartial courts				6.04	6.67	5.50	4.64	5.17
C. Protection of property rights					5.53	6.30	6.37	6.24
D. Military interference in rule of law and politics				7.24	8.33	8.20	6.67	6.67
E. Integrity of the legal system				6.96	5.00	4.20	4.17	4.17
F. Legal enforcement of contracts						3.90	3.88	3.88
G. Regulatory restrictions on sale of real property						6.40	6.42	6.42
3. Access to Sound Money	**4.18**	**3.71**	**3.76**	**3.92**	**8.39**	**8.20**	**8.45**	**8.83**
A. Money growth	1.45 (42.73)	2.98 (35.11)	0.00 (54.79)	2.99 (35.05)	8.49 (7.57)	6.90 (15.50)	6.72 (16.42)	8.09 (9.54)
B. Standard deviation of inflation	5.28 (11.81)	1.85 (20.37)	5.03 (12.43)	1.08 (22.30)	6.04 (9.89)	6.80 (8.11)	8.65 (3.38)	8.67 (3.33)
C. Inflation: most recent year	0.00 (54.76)	0.00 (74.02)	0.00 (100.39)	1.59 (42.03)	9.05 (4.76)	9.10 (4.70)	8.43 (7.86)	8.58 (7.10)
D. Freedom to own foreign currency bank accounts	10.00	10.00	10.00	10.00	10.00	10.00	10.00	10.00
4. Freedom to Trade Internationally	**6.93**	**7.41**	**7.31**	**7.41**	**6.74**	**7.00**	**7.14**	**6.94**
A. Taxes on international trade	4.07	4.97	5.94	7.83	7.72	7.70	7.83	7.80
(i) Revenues from trade taxes (% of trade sector)	4.07 (8.90)	6.13 (5.80)	6.27 (5.60)	8.20 (2.70)	8.71 (1.93)	8.40 (2.40)	8.84 (1.74)	8.73 (1.90)
(ii) Mean tariff rate		3.80 (31.00)	3.90 (30.50)	8.14 (9.30)	7.78 (11.10)	8.00 (9.90)	7.90 (10.50)	7.90 (10.50)
(iii) Standard deviation of tariff rates			7.64 (5.90)	7.16 (7.10)	6.68 (8.30)	6.70 (8.20)	6.76 (8.09)	6.77 (8.09)
B. Regulatory trade barriers					6.25	6.20	6.53	6.67
(i) Non-tariff trade barriers					6.25	5.70	5.87	6.14
(ii) Compliance cost of importing and exporting					6.70	7.20	7.20	7.20
C. Size of trade sector relative to expected	2.39	3.91	2.46	1.06	1.00	3.20	2.98	1.85
D. Black-market exchange rates	10.00	10.00	10.00	10.00	10.00	10.00	10.00	10.00
E. International capital market controls	10.00	10.00	10.00	10.00	8.74	7.60	8.34	8.38
(i) Foreign ownership/investment restrictions					9.02	6.70	8.21	8.29
(ii) Capital controls	10.00	10.00	10.00	10.00	8.46	8.50	8.46	8.46
5. Regulation of Credit, Labor, and Business	**6.00**	**6.36**	**6.20**	**6.11**	**5.97**	**6.50**	**6.43**	**6.54**
A. Credit market regulations	5.50	6.97	7.67	6.72	5.94	7.00	7.13	7.03
(i) Ownership of banks	5.00	5.00	5.00	5.00	5.00	2.00	2.00	2.00
(ii) Foreign bank competition					6.30	8.00	8.00	8.00
(iii) Private sector credit		7.91	10.00	9.15	7.25	9.10	9.52	9.13
(iv) Interest rate controls/negative real interest rates	6.00	8.00	8.00	6.00	5.00	9.00	9.00	9.00
B. Labor market regulations					5.89	6.40	6.18	6.59
(i) Hiring regulations and minimum wage					2.56	6.70	6.70	6.67
(ii) Hiring and firing regulations					4.12	3.30	2.95	3.37
(iii) Centralized collective bargaining					6.90	3.50	2.33	2.37
(iv) Hours regulations						8.00	8.00	10.00
(v) Mandated cost of worker dismissal						7.10	7.13	7.11
(vi) Conscription	10.00	10.00	10.00	10.00	10.00	10.00	10.00	10.00
C. Business regulations					6.07	6.10	5.98	6.01
(i) Price controls			4.00	6.00	6.00	6.00	6.00	6.00
(ii) Administrative requirements					6.75	3.50	3.41	3.46
(iii) Bureaucracy costs					6.48	5.00	4.63	4.53
(iv) Starting a business					5.00	7.60	7.50	7.48
(v) Extra payments/bribes/favoritism					6.11	7.50	7.11	7.40
(vi) Licensing restrictions						6.80	6.94	6.95
(vii) Cost of tax compliance						6.60	6.23	6.23

Venezuela

	1980	1985	1990	1995	2000	2005	2008	2009
Chain-Linked	Rating (Rank)	Rating (Rank)	Rating (Rank)	Rating (Rank)	Rating (Rank)	Rating (Rank)	Rating (Rank)	Rating (Rank)
Summary Rating (Rank) ➤	**6.29** (22)	**5.95** (38)	**5.45** (62)	**4.34** (116)	**5.61** (101)	4.74 (118)	4.30 (121)	4.23 (121)
Area 1. Size of Government	6.29 (21)	6.86 (10)	5.95 (46)	6.13 (60)	5.95 (73)	4.91 (104)	4.84 (107)	4.88 (101)
Area 2. Legal Structure and Security of Property Rights	6.11 (37)	5.16 (58)	5.60 (52)	3.84 (110)	3.75 (106)	3.11 (116)	2.91 (119)	2.64 (122)
Area 3. Access to Sound Money	7.40 (27)	8.34 (22)	4.74 (94)	1.93 (113)	5.56 (110)	5.10 (116)	5.30 (119)	5.35 (120)
Area 4. Freedom to Trade Internationally	7.25 (19)	4.82 (65)	6.50 (38)	5.30 (99)	7.13 (56)	5.48 (105)	3.52 (120)	2.98 (121)
Area 5. Regulation of Credit, Labor, and Business	4.59 (71)	4.91 (64)	4.57 (85)	4.48 (101)	5.68 (79)	5.08 (115)	4.91 (117)	5.30 (113)

Unadjusted								
Summary Rating (Rank) ➤	**6.61** (16)	**6.23** (26)	**5.63** (56)	**4.30** (116)	**5.61** (101)	4.72 (135)	4.28 (138)	4.28 (139)
	Rating Data	Rating Data	Rating Data	Rating Data	Rating Data	Rating Data	Rating Data	Rating Data
1. Size of Government	**6.29**	**6.86**	**5.95**	**6.13**	**5.95**	**4.90**	**4.84**	**4.88**
A. Government consumption	6.56 (17.68)	7.52 (14.44)	8.25 (11.95)	9.02 (9.32)	6.06 (19.39)	6.40 (18.40)	6.60 (17.57)	6.73 (17.13)
B. Transfers and subsidies	9.59 (2.00)	8.91 (4.50)	8.56 (5.80)	8.50 (6.01)	7.74 (8.79)	5.80 (16.00)	5.77 (16.01)	5.77 (16.01)
C. Government enterprises and investment	2.00 (45.60)	4.00 (35.80)	0.00 (65.20)	0.00 (58.30)	2.00 (42.36)	2.00 (42.40)	0.00	0.00 (56.38)
D. Top marginal tax rate	7.00	7.00	7.00	7.00	8.00	5.50	7.00	7.00
(i) Top marginal income tax rate	7.00 (45)	7.00 (45)	7.00 (45)	7.00 (34)	8.00 (35)	7.00 (34)	8.00 (34)	8.00 (34)
(ii) Top marginal income and payroll tax rates			7.00 (45)	7.00 (34)	8.00 (35)	4.00 (49)	6.00 (43)	6.00 (41)
2. Legal Structure and Security of Property Rights	**6.22**	**5.25**	**5.70**	**3.84**	**3.75**	**3.10**	**2.91**	**2.64**
A. Judicial independence				2.85	1.67	0.30	0.74	1.15
B. Impartial courts				2.90	3.67	0.90	1.30	1.22
C. Protection of property rights				3.72	3.40	2.30	1.80	1.26
D. Military interference in rule of law and politics				5.65	3.33	0.80	0.83	0.83
E. Integrity of the legal system				4.11	6.67	5.00	3.33	1.67
F. Legal enforcement of contracts						4.00	3.97	3.97
G. Regulatory restrictions on sale of real property						8.40	8.39	8.39
3. Access to Sound Money	**7.40**	**8.34**	**4.74**	**1.93**	**5.56**	**5.10**	**5.30**	**5.35**
A. Money growth	7.79 (11.04)	7.49 (12.53)	7.28 (13.58)	3.94 (30.28)	5.48 (22.60)	3.10 (34.40)	6.06 (19.72)	6.06 (19.72)
B. Standard deviation of inflation	7.02 (7.44)	7.94 (5.15)	0.00 (30.17)	3.77 (15.57)	0.00 (39.24)	5.50 (11.29)	6.42 (8.95)	6.06 (9.84)
C. Inflation: most recent year	4.80 (26.02)	7.92 (10.41)	1.66 (41.71)	0.00 (51.93)	6.76 (16.21)	6.80 (15.95)	3.71 (31.44)	4.28 (28.59)
D. Freedom to own foreign currency bank accounts	10.00	10.00	10.00	0.00	10.00	5.00	5.00	5.00
4. Freedom to Trade Internationally	**8.08**	**5.33**	**6.79**	**5.18**	**7.13**	**5.50**	**3.52**	**2.98**
A. Taxes on international trade	8.00	3.68	4.22	7.78	7.61	7.60	7.51	7.80
(i) Revenues from trade taxes (% of trade sector)	8.00 (3.00)	3.93 (9.10)	8.53 (2.20)	7.93 (3.10)	7.89 (3.16)	8.40 (2.30)	8.45 (2.33)	8.45 (2.33)
(ii) Mean tariff rate		3.42 (32.90)	3.88 (30.60)	7.32 (13.40)	7.30 (13.50)	7.40 (12.80)	7.34 (13.30)	7.50 (12.50)
(iii) Standard deviation of tariff rates			0.24 (24.40)	8.08 (4.80)	7.64 (5.90)	7.00 (7.40)	6.76 (8.11)	7.45 (6.38)
B. Regulatory trade barriers				4.57	5.68	4.00	2.65	2.67
(i) Non-tariff trade barriers				4.57	4.87	4.80	3.67	3.71
(ii) Compliance cost of importing and exporting					6.49	3.30	1.62	1.62
C. Size of trade sector relative to expected	6.27	4.75	6.56	5.06	4.23	5.40	4.26	2.51
D. Black-market exchange rates	10.00	5.00	10.00	1.60	10.00	5.10	0.00	0.00
E. International capital market controls	8.00	5.00	5.00	6.87	8.15	5.20	3.17	1.92
(i) Foreign ownership / investment restrictions				8.74	9.37	5.00	2.49	3.08
(ii) Capital controls	8.00	5.00	5.00	5.00	6.92	5.40	3.85	0.77
5. Regulation of Credit, Labor, and Business	**5.04**	**5.39**	**4.96**	**4.42**	**5.68**	**5.00**	**4.82**	**5.56**
A. Credit market regulations	6.09	6.92	6.00	5.98	7.57	9.00	8.25	9.00
(i) Ownership of banks	5.00	8.00	8.00	8.00	8.00	8.00	8.00	8.00
(ii) Foreign bank competition				7.60	6.15	8.00	8.00	8.00
(iii) Private sector credit	9.26	8.77	10.00	8.92	9.64	10.00	10.00	10.00
(iv) Interest rate controls / negative real interest rates	4.00	4.00	0.00	0.00	8.00	10.00	7.00	10.00
B. Labor market regulations			3.87	4.30	4.03	3.10	3.14	4.52
(i) Hiring regulations and minimum wage				4.85	4.07	3.30	3.30	2.23
(ii) Hiring and firing regulations			4.36	4.36	4.55	1.70	1.90	2.05
(iii) Centralized collective bargaining	7.24	7.24	7.24	7.24	5.83	4.30	4.49	4.81
(iv) Hours regulations				5.03	5.68	6.00	6.00	8.00
(v) Mandated cost of worker dismissal								10.00
(vi) Conscription	0.00	1.00	0.00	0.00	0.00	0.00	0.00	0.00
C. Business regulations				2.99	5.45	2.90	3.07	3.16
(i) Price controls				0.00	5.00	0.00	0.00	0.00
(ii) Administrative requirements					6.42	1.40	1.40	1.88
(iii) Bureaucracy costs				5.31	6.15	3.70	6.02	5.94
(iv) Starting a business				4.57	4.68	6.40	6.41	6.35
(v) Extra payments / bribes / favoritism				2.07	5.02	4.40	2.78	3.06
(vi) Licensing restrictions						4.30	4.58	4.59
(vii) Cost of tax compliance						0.30	0.32	0.32

Vietnam

	1980	1985	1990	1995	2000	2005	2008	2009
Chain-Linked						Rating (Rank)	Rating (Rank)	Rating (Rank)
Summary Rating (Rank) ➤								
Area 1. Size of Government								
Area 2. Legal Structure and Security of Property Rights								
Area 3. Access to Sound Money								
Area 4. Freedom to Trade Internationally								
Area 5. Regulation of Credit, Labor, and Business								

	1980	1985	1990	1995	2000	2005	2008	2009
Unadjusted								
Summary Rating (Rank) ➤						**6.38** (89)	**6.15** (104)	**6.48** (88)
					Rating Data	Rating Data	Rating Data	Rating Data
1. Size of Government						**6.60**	**6.27**	**6.73**
A. Government consumption					9.38 (8.09)	9.20 (8.80)	9.30 (8.38)	9.20 (8.73)
B. Transfers and subsidies								
C. Government enterprises and investment							4.00	4.00
D. Top marginal tax rate						4.00	5.50	7.00
(i) Top marginal income tax rate						5.00 (40)	6.00 (40)	7.00 (35)
(ii) Top marginal income and payroll tax rates						3.00 (52)	5.00 (42)	7.00 (35)
2. Legal Structure and Security of Property Rights						**5.80**	**6.01**	**5.92**
A. Judicial independence						4.10	4.64	4.78
B. Impartial courts						4.60	4.95	4.65
C. Protection of property rights						5.70	5.71	5.14
D. Military interference in rule of law and politics						5.00	5.00	5.00
E. Integrity of the legal system						6.70	6.67	6.67
F. Legal enforcement of contracts						6.40	6.51	6.51
G. Regulatory restrictions on sale of real property						8.30	8.56	8.73
3. Access to Sound Money						**6.30**	**5.25**	**5.94**
A. Money growth					6.96 (15.21)	7.90 (10.30)	8.10 (9.52)	7.75 (11.23)
B. Standard deviation of inflation						8.90 (2.76)	7.54 (6.15)	7.42 (6.44)
C. Inflation: most recent year						8.30 (8.27)	5.38 (23.12)	8.59 (7.05)
D. Freedom to own foreign currency bank accounts						0.00	0.00	0.00
4. Freedom to Trade Internationally						**6.80**	**6.87**	**7.08**
A. Taxes on international trade						5.80	5.56	6.90
(i) Revenues from trade taxes (% of trade sector)					8.18 (2.73)	8.20 (2.80)	8.16 (2.76)	8.16 (2.76)
(ii) Mean tariff rate						7.40 (13.20)	6.64 (16.80)	7.82 (10.90)
(iii) Standard deviation of tariff rates						1.90 (20.30)	1.87 (20.33)	4.72 (13.19)
B. Regulatory trade barriers						5.50	6.08	5.99
(i) Non-tariff trade barriers						4.30	5.15	4.97
(ii) Compliance cost of importing and exporting						6.70	7.01	7.01
C. Size of trade sector relative to expected						10.00	10.00	10.00
D. Black-market exchange rates						10.00	10.00	10.00
E. International capital market controls						2.80	2.71	2.50
(i) Foreign ownership/investment restrictions						5.50	5.43	5.00
(ii) Capital controls						0.00	0.00	0.00
5. Regulation of Credit, Labor, and Business						**6.40**	**6.34**	**6.70**
A. Credit market regulations						9.50	8.99	9.61
(i) Ownership of banks								
(ii) Foreign bank competition								
(iii) Private sector credit						9.10	8.99	9.23
(iv) Interest rate controls/negative real interest rates					10.00	10.00	9.00	10.00
B. Labor market regulations						5.40	5.35	5.71
(i) Hiring regulations and minimum wage						10.00	8.90	8.90
(ii) Hiring and firing regulations						5.40	5.94	5.78
(iii) Centralized collective bargaining						6.20	6.65	7.62
(iv) Hours regulations						8.70	8.70	10.00
(v) Mandated cost of worker dismissal						1.90	1.93	1.97
(vi) Conscription						0.00	0.00	0.00
C. Business regulations						4.20	4.68	4.78
(i) Price controls								
(ii) Administrative requirements						2.30	2.85	2.70
(iii) Bureaucracy costs						4.00	6.01	6.19
(iv) Starting a business						8.10	8.26	8.46
(v) Extra payments/bribes/favoritism						4.00	3.63	3.79
(vi) Licensing restrictions						7.00	7.31	7.52
(vii) Cost of tax compliance						0.00	0.00	0.00

Zambia

	1980	1985	1990	1995	2000	2005	2008	2009
Chain-Linked	Rating (Rank)	Rating (Rank)	Rating (Rank)	Rating (Rank)	Rating (Rank)	Rating (Rank)	Rating (Rank)	Rating (Rank)
Summary Rating (Rank) ➤	**5.08** (64)	**3.97** (98)	**3.52** (108)	**4.87** (99)	**6.63** (50)	**6.99** (52)	**7.30** (33)	**7.35** (25)
Area 1. Size of Government	2.56 (101)	3.15 (98)	3.97 (95)	6.43 (44)	6.63 (49)	7.32 (29)	7.96 (16)	8.12 (10)
Area 2. Legal Structure and Security of Property Rights	6.66 (31)	4.37 (68)	4.05 (77)	5.91 (46)	5.85 (60)	5.57 (68)	5.88 (63)	5.88 (58)
Area 3. Access to Sound Money	6.26 (52)	3.33 (103)	0.59 (116)	0.65 (120)	7.15 (75)	8.11 (66)	8.37 (57)	8.55 (60)
Area 4. Freedom to Trade Internationally	5.41 (49)	5.10 (58)	4.78 (77)	6.68 (61)	7.72 (34)	7.62 (24)	7.68 (21)	7.68 (15)
Area 5. Regulation of Credit, Labor, and Business	4.77 (68)	3.97 (92)	4.20 (97)	4.69 (97)	5.78 (71)	6.25 (69)	6.48 (64)	6.41 (71)

Unadjusted	1980	1985	1990	1995	2000	2005	2008	2009
Summary Rating (Rank) ➤	**5.18** (64)	**3.99** (98)	**3.45** (109)	**4.87** (100)	**6.63** (50)	**6.90** (62)	**7.21** (42)	**7.26** (38)
	Rating Data	Rating Data	Rating Data	Rating Data	Rating Data	Rating Data	Rating Data	Rating Data
1. Size of Government	**2.56**	**3.15**	**3.97**	**6.43**	**6.63**	**7.30**	**7.96**	**8.12**
A. Government consumption	2.47 (31.60)	3.60 (27.78)	4.96 (23.14)	7.28 (15.24)	8.53 (11.00)	8.20 (12.00)	7.94 (12.99)	6.59 (17.60)
B. Transfers and subsidies	7.77 (8.70)	8.99 (4.20)	8.91 (4.50)	9.43 (2.60)	10.00 (0.00)	9.00 (4.10)	9.91 (0.83)	9.91 (0.83)
C. Government enterprises and investment	0.00 (77.10)	0.00 (90.70)	2.00 (46.20)	2.00 (41.30)	0.00 (62.60)	4.00 (31.00)	6.00 (25.60)	8.00 (19.62)
D. Top marginal tax rate	0.00	0.00	0.00	7.00	8.00	8.00	8.00	8.00
(i) Top marginal income tax rate	0.00 (70)	0.00 (80)	0.00 (75)	7.00 (35)	8.00 (30)	8.00 (30)	8.00 (30)	8.00 (30)
(ii) Top marginal income and payroll tax rates								
2. Legal Structure and Security of Property Rights	**6.09**	**3.99**	**3.70**	**5.91**	**5.85**	**5.60**	**5.88**	**5.88**
A. Judicial independence				6.67	6.18	2.90	4.57	4.65
B. Impartial courts				4.85	4.86	5.00	4.18	4.63
C. Protection of property rights				4.77	3.23	6.00	5.78	5.24
D. Military interference in rule of law and politics				6.31	8.33	8.30	8.33	8.33
E. Integrity of the legal system				6.96	6.67	6.70	6.67	6.67
F. Legal enforcement of contracts						4.60	4.56	4.56
G. Regulatory restrictions on sale of real property						5.50	7.09	7.07
3. Access to Sound Money	**6.26**	**3.33**	**0.59**	**0.65**	**7.15**	**8.10**	**8.37**	**8.55**
A. Money growth	9.21 (3.95)	6.58 (17.10)	1.92 (40.40)	0.00 (58.52)	5.45 (22.73)	7.00 (15.10)	7.94 (10.30)	8.29 (8.57)
B. Standard deviation of inflation	8.18 (4.55)	4.96 (12.60)	0.43 (23.92)	0.00 (49.23)	8.35 (4.11)	9.10 (2.17)	8.02 (4.95)	8.58 (3.55)
C. Inflation: most recent year	7.65 (11.76)	1.77 (41.14)	0.00 (106.39)	2.62 (36.92)	4.79 (26.03)	6.30 (18.32)	7.51 (12.45)	7.32 (13.40)
D. Freedom to own foreign currency bank accounts	0.00	0.00	0.00	0.00	10.00	10.00	10.00	10.00
4. Freedom to Trade Internationally	**5.72**	**5.12**	**4.80**	**6.68**	**7.72**	**7.10**	**7.14**	**7.14**
A. Taxes on international trade	8.40	4.39	5.84	6.04	6.22	7.00	7.22	7.24
(i) Revenues from trade taxes (% of trade sector)	8.40 (2.40)	5.73 (6.40)	6.80 (4.80)	7.47 (3.80)	5.11 (7.33)	7.80 (3.30)	8.46 (2.31)	8.46 (2.31)
(ii) Mean tariff rate		3.04 (34.80)	4.88 (25.60)	4.88 (25.60)	7.06 (14.70)	7.10 (14.60)	7.24 (13.80)	7.28 (13.60)
(iii) Standard deviation of tariff rates				5.76 (10.60)	6.48 (8.80)	6.00 (10.00)	5.97 (10.07)	5.97 (10.06)
B. Regulatory trade barriers						3.40	4.06	4.68
(i) Non-tariff trade barriers						5.10	6.40	6.38
(ii) Compliance cost of importing and exporting						1.70	1.72	2.98
C. Size of trade sector relative to expected	10.00	8.58	7.94	7.80	5.02	6.30	6.07	5.75
D. Black-market exchange rates	0.00	2.40	0.00	9.40	10.00	10.00	10.00	10.00
E. International capital market controls	2.00	2.00	2.00	2.00	9.23	8.70	8.37	8.04
(i) Foreign ownership / investment restrictions						8.20	7.57	6.86
(ii) Capital controls	2.00	2.00	2.00	2.00	9.23	9.20	9.17	9.23
5. Regulation of Credit, Labor, and Business	**5.26**	**4.37**	**4.20**	**4.69**	**5.78**	**6.40**	**6.71**	**6.63**
A. Credit market regulations	4.04	1.70	2.39	3.34	6.95	6.80	7.88	7.88
(i) Ownership of banks	2.00	2.00	2.00	5.00	5.00	5.00	5.00	5.00
(ii) Foreign bank competition								
(iii) Private sector credit	6.13	3.10	5.18	5.03	7.86	7.40	9.64	9.64
(iv) Interest rate controls / negative real interest rates	4.00	0.00	0.00	0.00	8.00	8.00	9.00	9.00
B. Labor market regulations						6.90	6.30	6.47
(i) Hiring regulations and minimum wage						10.00	8.90	8.90
(ii) Hiring and firing regulations						8.20	5.66	5.71
(iii) Centralized collective bargaining						8.70	6.52	6.22
(iv) Hours regulations						4.70	6.70	8.00
(v) Mandated cost of worker dismissal						0.00	0.00	0.00
(vi) Conscription	10.00	10.00	10.00	10.00	10.00	10.00	10.00	10.00
C. Business regulations						5.60	5.96	5.53
(i) Price controls			0.00	2.00	2.00	4.00	4.00	4.00
(ii) Administrative requirements						5.30	4.58	4.65
(iii) Bureaucracy costs						5.50	5.78	5.52
(iv) Starting a business						8.60	9.12	9.13
(v) Extra payments / bribes / favoritism						2.90	4.59	4.54
(vi) Licensing restrictions						4.30	5.12	2.33
(vii) Cost of tax compliance						8.50	8.52	8.52

Zimbabwe

	1980	1985	1990	1995	2000	2005	2008	2009
Chain-Linked	Rating (Rank)	Rating (Rank)	Rating (Rank)	Rating (Rank)	Rating (Rank)	Rating (Rank)	Rating (Rank)	Rating (Rank)
Summary Rating (Rank) ➤	**4.93** (70)	**4.85** (81)	**5.05** (83)	**5.81** (70)	**4.59** (119)	**3.37** (123)	**4.03** (122)	**4.06** (122)
Area 1. Size of Government	6.90 (13)	5.48 (40)	5.57 (59)	7.00 (25)	5.85 (74)	5.12 (98)	4.56 (111)	4.06 (114)
Area 2. Legal Structure and Security of Property Rights	3.21 (67)	3.29 (88)	4.30 (75)	5.53 (59)	5.02 (76)	3.51 (110)	3.72 (108)	3.51 (113)
Area 3. Access to Sound Money	6.35 (48)	6.31 (73)	5.67 (83)	4.92 (95)	2.89 (119)	0.10 (123)	2.39 (123)	2.48 (123)
Area 4. Freedom to Trade Internationally	4.47 (65)	4.23 (72)	5.08 (68)	6.28 (76)	3.65 (121)	3.82 (120)	4.72 (115)	5.50 (103)
Area 5. Regulation of Credit, Labor, and Business	3.81 (92)	4.88 (66)	4.60 (83)	5.29 (70)	5.55 (85)	4.30 (121)	4.72 (119)	4.72 (120)

Unadjusted

	1980	1985	1990	1995	2000	2005	2008	2009
Summary Rating (Rank) ➤	**5.09** (69)	**5.00** (78)	**5.15** (74)	**5.82** (68)	**4.59** (119)	**3.38** (141)	**4.05** (139)	**4.08** (141)
	Rating Data	Rating Data	Rating Data	Rating Data	Rating Data	Rating Data	Rating Data	Rating Data
1. Size of Government	**6.90**	**5.48**	**5.57**	**7.00**	**5.85**	**5.10**	**4.56**	**4.06**
A. Government consumption	5.56 (21.10)	4.52 (24.65)	4.84 (23.56)	5.42 (21.57)	3.65 (27.60)	3.70 (27.40)	0.00 (43.28)	0.00 (43.28)
B. Transfers and subsidies	7.03 (11.40)	7.41 (10.00)	8.45 (6.20)	8.57 (5.73)	7.75 (8.77)	7.70 (8.80)	7.75 (8.77)	7.75 (8.77)
C. Government enterprises and investment	10.00 (12.70)	10.00 (14.50)	8.00 (18.60)	10.00 (11.80)	10.00 (6.20)	6.00 (29.90)	6.00 (29.90)	4.00 (31.78)
D. Top marginal tax rate	5.00	0.00	1.00	4.00	2.00	3.00	4.50	4.50
(i) Top marginal income tax rate	5.00 (45)	0.00 (63)	1.00 (60)	4.00 (45)	2.00 (53)	3.00 (46)	5.00 (36)	5.00 (36)
(ii) Top marginal income and payroll tax rates			1.00 (60)	4.00 (45)	2.00 (53)	3.00 (46)	4.00 (42)	4.00 (42)
2. Legal Structure and Security of Property Rights	**2.97**	**3.05**	**3.99**	**5.53**	**5.02**	**3.50**	**3.72**	**3.51**
A. Judicial independence				6.67	6.18	1.10	1.74	2.10
B. Impartial courts				7.25	7.35	2.10	2.73	3.16
C. Protection of property rights				4.77	3.23	1.40	1.70	1.95
D. Military interference in rule of law and politics				4.87	5.00	5.00	3.33	3.33
E. Integrity of the legal system				4.11	3.33	5.00	5.00	5.00
F. Legal enforcement of contracts						5.40	5.43	2.37
G. Regulatory restrictions on sale of real property						4.40	6.09	6.62
3. Access to Sound Money	**6.35**	**6.31**	**5.67**	**4.92**	**2.89**	**0.00**	**2.39**	**2.48**
A. Money growth	7.96 (10.19)	8.86 (5.70)	7.24 (13.79)	4.53 (27.34)	3.92 (30.39)	0.00 (224.10)	0.00 (457.94)	0.00 (457.94)
B. Standard deviation of inflation	8.75 (3.13)	7.68 (5.80)	8.38 (4.05)	7.28 (6.81)	2.64 (18.39)	0.00 (140.78)	0.00 (10732.62)	0.00 (10773.88)
C. Inflation: most recent year	8.69 (6.57)	8.70 (6.49)	7.05 (14.75)	7.86 (10.70)	0.00 (55.86)	0.00 (302.12)	9.55 (2.27)	4.93 (25.33)
D. Freedom to own foreign currency bank accounts	0.00	0.00	0.00	0.00	5.00	0.00	5.00	5.00
4. Freedom to Trade Internationally	**4.94**	**4.68**	**5.57**	**6.36**	**3.65**	**3.80**	**4.72**	**5.50**
A. Taxes on international trade	8.43	6.46	5.71	6.78	4.56	3.90	3.33	3.33
(i) Revenues from trade taxes (% of trade sector)	8.87 (1.70)	4.67 (8.00)	3.87 (9.20)	5.40 (6.90)	5.11 (7.33)	5.10 (7.30)	5.11 (7.33)	5.11 (7.33)
(ii) Mean tariff rate	8.00 (10.00)	8.26 (8.70)	7.98 (10.10)	8.16 (9.20)	5.72 (21.40)	6.70 (16.70)	4.88 (25.60)	4.88 (25.60)
(iii) Standard deviation of tariff rates			5.28 (11.80)		2.84 (17.90)	0.00 (71.70)	0.00 (54.83)	0.00 (54.83)
B. Regulatory trade barriers				3.68	5.86	3.10	2.95	3.45
(i) Non-tariff trade barriers				3.68	5.22	4.70	4.74	5.73
(ii) Compliance cost of importing and exporting					6.49	1.60	1.16	1.16
C. Size of trade sector relative to expected	6.05	5.08	4.95	8.01	5.33	10.00	5.67	8.29
D. Black-market exchange rates	0.00	1.60	7.00	9.80	0.00	0.00	10.00	10.00
E. International capital market controls	2.00	2.00	2.00	3.53	2.50	2.00	1.66	2.43
(i) Foreign ownership/investment restrictions				5.06	5.00	4.00	3.32	4.85
(ii) Capital controls	2.00	2.00	2.00	2.00	0.00	0.00	0.00	0.00
5. Regulation of Credit, Labor, and Business	**4.28**	**5.49**	**4.94**	**5.30**	**5.55**	**4.50**	**4.85**	**4.86**
A. Credit market regulations	4.45	4.65	6.16	5.89	6.58	5.30	5.84	5.60
(i) Ownership of banks	2.00	2.00	2.00	5.00	8.00	8.00	8.00	8.00
(ii) Foreign bank competition				4.75	6.77	9.00	9.00	9.00
(iii) Private sector credit	5.36	3.95	8.49	7.27	7.12	4.30	6.37	5.38
(iv) Interest rate controls/negative real interest rates	6.00	8.00	8.00	8.00	8.00	0.00	0.00	0.00
B. Labor market regulations			3.63	6.02	4.88	5.10	5.31	5.17
(i) Hiring regulations and minimum wage				5.85	3.52	8.90	10.00	6.67
(ii) Hiring and firing regulations			3.42	3.42	1.57	2.60	2.79	3.28
(iii) Centralized collective bargaining			4.49	4.49	2.45	2.80	3.06	3.05
(iv) Hours regulations				6.35	6.85	6.00	6.00	8.00
(v) Mandated cost of worker dismissal						0.00	0.00	0.00
(vi) Conscription	1.00	10.00	3.00	10.00	10.00	10.00	10.00	10.00
C. Business regulations				3.98	5.18	3.00	3.40	3.81
(i) Price controls			2.00	4.00	4.00	0.00	0.00	0.00
(ii) Administrative requirements					5.10	2.00	2.63	3.50
(iii) Bureaucracy costs				4.30	7.05	3.40	6.21	5.87
(iv) Starting a business				3.68	5.68	3.60	3.59	5.20
(v) Extra payments/bribes/favoritism				3.92	4.09	4.60	4.42	4.82
(vi) Licensing restrictions						0.00	0.00	0.00
(vii) Cost of tax compliance						7.60	6.97	7.29

Chapter 3
What Matters for Development—Freedom or Entitlement?

by Jean-Pierre Chauffour

> *How can we keep the government we create from becoming a Frankenstein that will destroy the very freedom we establish it to protect? Freedom is a rare and delicate plant*
>
> Milton Friedman, *Capitalism and Freedom*, p.2

Introduction

In reviewing the distinctive characteristics of the 13 economies that have been able to grow at more than 7% for periods of more than 25 years since 1950, the Commission on Growth and Development (2008) found that sustainable high economic growth requires, among other things, leadership and governance; engagement with the global economy; high rates of investment and savings; mobile resources, especially labor; and inclusiveness to share the benefits of globalization, provide access to the underserved, and deal with issues of gender inclusion. However, observing that successful economies display a number of commonalities and desirable features is of little help in understanding why and how those countries have been able to nurture and sustain these specific features over time. Why are certain countries better governed than others, save and invest more, have more flexible markets, or achieve greater inclusiveness? Are there some admittedly more fundamental common characteristics that could explain why, on average, certain countries create better institutions, promote better policies, and achieve better outcomes?

Although a general theory of economic growth continues to elude the economists (Easterly, 2001),[1] the idea

that differences in societies' institutional arrangements are the fundamental cause of differences in economic performance has gained enormous momentum in recent decades. Since the days of North and Thomas (1973), it has become clear that, while factor accumulation, innovation, and technological progress are the proximate factors that explain the mechanics of economic growth, they are *not* the causes of growth, they *are* growth. To locate the more fundamental determinants of growth, one needs to push the question back one step and ask why factor accumulation and innovation advance at different rates in different countries or groups of countries; why do countries differ in the level of schooling available, quality of infrastructure, health of the population, and other proximate factors of economic growth? The growing consensus is that the answer has to do with differences in institutions (e.g., the rule of law, the

Jean-Pierre Chauffour is Lead Economist, Middle East and North Africa Region, World Bank. The paper draws on his book, *The Power of Freedom: Uniting Human Rights and Development* (Cato Institute, 2009) and his paper "On the Relevance of Freedom and Entitlement in Development: New Empirical Evidence (1975–2007)" (World Bank, 2011). The chapter benefited from comments from participants in the Freedom Index Seminar hosted by the Cato Institute and co-sponsored by the Fraser Institute and the Friedrich Naumann

Foundation on May 25–27, 2011. The views expressed in this chapter are solely my own and should not be attributed to the World Bank, its Executive Directors, or the countries they represent. I can be contacted at: jchauffour@worldbank.org.

1 Broadly speaking, three theories of economic growth are usually discussed in the literature: the neoclassical growth theory, which emphasizes the accumulation of factors (labor and capital) and technological progress (exogenous or endogenous) as the primary determinants of growth (e.g., Solow, 1956; Mawkin, Romer and Weil, 1992); the geographic growth theory, which emphasizes climatic conditions, access to major markets, and other locational factors as key to explaining long-term economic development (e.g., Diamond, 1997; Sachs, 2001); and the institutional growth theory, which stresses the importance of a society's institutional framework, in particular the existence of a market-friendly environment for entrepreneurial activities, in the long-term performance of economies (e.g., North, 1990; Acemoglu and al., 2004).

property regime, and the participatory process) and differences in geography and other exogenous factors.[2]

Analyzing the genesis and development of institutions, some scholars have tried to push the issue back even further to ask why institutions differ across countries in the first place. Could it be that certain norms, values, and organizational principles in societies are conducive to better institutions? For instance, Acemoglu, Johnson, and Robinson (2004) suggest that political institutions and the distribution of resources are the fundamental determinants of institutions and therefore of growth. Chauffour (2009) hypothesizes that the extent to which political institutions and human interactions in society are formed around the concept of *freedom* constitutes one key determinant of growth, perhaps the ultimate cause for economic agents to actually create and accumulate.

Looking at the economic performance—good and bad—of more than 100 countries over the last 30 years, this chapter proposes to (1) re-examine the long-term relationship between freedom and economic growth; and (2) disentangle the respective role of economic freedom, civil, and political liberties, and the pursuit of economic, social and cultural rights on economic growth. In line with the analytical framework of the rights-based approach to development, the chapter conjectures that development is rooted in the protection of some fundamental rights. It further conjectures, however, that all so-called "rights" are not necessarily equal and that the individual rights at the root of sound institutions and sustainable economic growth may not necessarily coincide with the rights embedded in the instruments of international human-rights law. In particular, the rights that foster the pursuit of freedom (i.e., economic freedom, and civil and political liberties) and entitlement "rights" (i.e., right to food, housing, education, health, and so on) may lead to different institutions and development outcomes over the long run.

Concepts

The starting proposition is that, at the simplest level, economic development can be seen as the product of exogenous and endogenous factors. Exogenous factors are those factors that are *not* under the control of individuals,

such as geography, natural-resource endowment, ethno-linguistic homogeneity, and various other types of good and bad luck. Endogenous factors would correspond to factors that are influenced by individuals, alone or in associations. Those endogenous factors can in turn be divided between factors that are mainly the expression of free individual choices leading to market solutions, and factors that are the results of more coerced individual decisions leading to political solutions.

Freedom conditions would include all forms of economic freedom, civil rights, and political liberties. These are essentially "negative" rights in nature and are covered by the Universal Declaration of Human Rights and the UN International Covenant on Civil and Political Rights. In contrast, coercive conditions would include the regulations, taxations, and other forms of government interventions to provide for public goods and various entitlement rights. Beyond a certain threshold of government intervention, these entitlement rights are essentially "positive" rights in the spirit of the economic, social, and cultural rights as provided by the UN International Covenant on Economic, Social, and Cultural Rights (Box 3.1).

Of course, the problem of when exactly government intervention starts interfering with individual choices and the market is open to reasoned debate. In the final analysis in a democratic context, it is often believed that the scope of the state is a matter for the democratic process to decide. However, although societies may reveal different preferences regarding the trade-off between state intervention and economic freedom, majority rule may not necessarily lead to the optimal state, either from a normative or utilitarian perspective—especially when it violates the freedom of minorities (e.g., discrimination, expropriation, confiscatory taxation). Friedman notoriously pointed out that *market* solutions (that is, voluntary cooperation among responsible individuals) permit "unanimity without conformity" (that is, a system of effective proportional representation), whereas *political* solutions (even those with proportional representation) typically tend to produce the opposite: "conformity without unanimity" (1962: 33). From this position, he concluded that the wider the range of activities covered by the market, the fewer the issues on which explicitly political decisions were needed and, hence, required agreement. In turn, the fewer the issues on which agreement was necessary, the greater the likelihood of reaching agreement while maintaining a free society. Depending on the balance between market solutions and political solutions, individual opportunities to learn, own, work, save, invest, trade, protect, and so forth may vary greatly across countries and over time.

---

2   Acemoglu, Johnson, and Robinson, 2005; Alesina, Easterly, Devleeschauwer, Kurlat, and Wacziarg, 2003; Gallup, Sachs, and Mellinger, 1998; Frankel and Romer, 1999; Glaeser, La Porta, López-de-Silanes, and Shleifer, 2004; Knack and Keefer, 1997; Rodrik, Subramanian, and Trebbi, 2004.

In this understanding of the world, economic development could therefore be reduced to three fundamental sets of circumstances: (1) a set of exogenous conditions; (2) the degree of individual freedom and extent to which market solutions are used; and (3) the degree of state intervention and extent to which political solutions, including the intervention needed to protect individual freedom itself, are used. Certain countries may be able to sustain better institutions and outcomes over time because of a better mixed of these circumstances.

Development as economic freedom

Economic freedom is in itself part and parcel of the basic liberties that people have reason to value. As Sen puts it, "the freedom to exchange words, or goods, or gifts does not need defensive justification in terms of their favorable but distant effects; they are part of the way human beings in society live and interact with each other (unless stopped by regulation or fiat)" (1999: 61). Economic freedom in all its dimensions, therefore, has an intrinsic value irrespective of its impact on economic growth and development and this value is not limited to egotism and selfishness. Indeed,

freedom has been defined as "a state in which each can use his knowledge for his purposes" (Hayek, 1973: 55–56).

The main dimensions of economic freedom generally include the freedom to hold and legally acquire property; the freedom to engage in voluntary transactions, inside or outside a nation's borders; the freedom from government control of the terms on which individuals transact; the freedom from government expropriation of property (for example, by confiscatory taxation or unanticipated inflation); and the freedom to move freely within a country and across international boundaries. There are several theoretical reasons why institutions and policies guaranteeing economic freedom conceivably have the capacity to provide growth-enhancing incentives: they promote a high return on productive efforts through low taxation, an independent legal system, and the protection of private property; they enable talent to be allocated where it generates the highest value; they foster a dynamic, experimentally organized economy in which a large amount of business trial and error and competition among different players can take place because regulations and government enterprises are few;

Box 3.1: Negative and positive rights

The distinction between positive and negative rights is controversial and at the core of differing interpretations about human rights. Negative rights conceive of human rights in terms of liberties and "freedoms from." They derive primarily from seventeenth- and eighteenth-century reformist theories (i.e., those associated with the English, American, and French revolutions). Imbued with the political philosophy of liberal individualism and the related economic and social doctrine of *laissez-faire*, they are fundamentally civil and political in nature and opposed to government intervention in the quest for human dignity. In contrast, positive rights see human rights more in terms of claims, entitlements, and "rights to." They originated primarily in the nineteenth-century socialist tradition and were taken up by the revolutionary struggles and welfare movements of the early twentieth century. As a counterpoint to "negative" civil and political rights, they tend to favor state intervention for the purposes of providing economic, social, and cultural rights and ensuring the equitable distribution of the values or capabilities involved.

Acknowledging the intellectual challenge posed by the promotion of both negative and positive rights in international human-rights law, a number of scholars have tried to reconcile views by emphasizing the continuum between both sets of rights. First, positive rights have been defended on the grounds that the protection of negative rights also entails positive actions by the state that could be as costly as the realization of a number of positive rights (Alston, 2004). Second, positive rights have been promoted on the basis that all human rights involve a mix of negative and positive duties and entitlements. However, this line of argument tends to brush aside the fact that the fundamental distinction between positive and negative rights is about the essence of those rights and not, as has often been claimed, about the economic costs of implementing them. Hayek (1960) has elaborated on the good reasons for guaranteeing basic human rights, even if they are costly. Indeed, promoting and protecting negative rights that underpin economic freedom and civil and political liberties requires a government that is streamlined, yet strong and effective.

they facilitate predictable and rational decision making by means of a low and stable inflation rate; and they promote the flow of goods, capital, labor, and services to where preference satisfaction and returns are the highest (Berggren, 2003). Figure 3.1 illustrates the relationship between economic freedom (as measured by the Fraser Institute; Gwartney and Lawson, 2009) and per-capita GDP in more than 100 countries in 2007. Countries that enjoy high levels of economic freedom are those that are associated with higher levels of economic development.

Economic freedom and free markets give spontaneous satisfaction to people's demands and constitute the main engine for technological progress and economic growth. In turn, sustained and vigorous economic growth creates the conditions for achieving various human development goals, including economic, social, and cultural ones. Friedman argues that economic growth gives benefits far beyond the material: it brings "greater opportunity, tolerance of diversity, social mobility, commitment to fairness, and dedication to democracy" (2005: 4). And, conversely, when there is economic stagnation or decline, the citizen's "moral character" tends to decline accordingly, there being less tolerance, less openness, and less generosity to poor and disadvantaged people. Economic freedom is the recognition that being forced not to behave according to one's preferences is utility reducing and costly.

Development as civil and political liberties

Economic freedom is only one dimension of individual freedom. Other dimensions—such as those related to civil rights and political liberties—are equally fundamental. All three dimensions of freedom essentially aim at freeing human beings from various types of state and non-state violence and "unfreedoms." Sen (1999) takes the view that securing economic rights will not achieve the expected economic benefits in case of civil and political rights violations. When the state does not refrain from physically harming its citizens (through means ranging from arbitrary imprisonment to politically motivated killings), the resulting climate of fear and anxiety is unlikely to be conducive to investment and growth. Rodrik (2000) conjectures that democratic countries would favor higher-quality growth—that is, a more predictable long-term growth rate, greater short-term stability, better resilience to adverse shocks, and a more equitable distribution of wealth. Civil and political liberties would also usually be associated with greater gender equality, higher levels of female education, lower reproduction and lower infant mortality—all factors contributing to economic growth. Figure 3.2 shows the relationship between civil and political rights (as measured

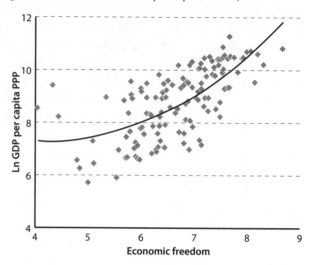

Figure 3.1: Economic freedom vs. per-capita income, 2007

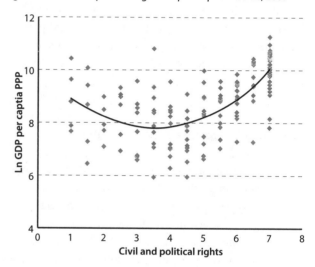

Figure 3.2: Civil and political rights vs. per-capita income, 2007

by Freedom House) and per-capita GDP in more than 100 countries in 2007. At a first glance, the relationship seems to be non-linear, where countries with low and high levels of civil and political rights register slightly higher levels of GDP per capita as compared to countries with intermediate levels of civil and political rights.

A number of theoretical arguments have been advanced to make the case that civil and political freedom and economic freedom are mutually reinforcing. (For an empirical examination of this issue, see Lawson and Clark, 2010.) Civil and political freedom is expected to facilitate the functioning of the market economy by developing a more predictable and stable institutional framework for engaging in productive transactions, including better protection of property rights. This has a positive influence on economic growth through higher savings and investment rates and through lower rents associated with corruption, government controls, and the lack of respect for the rule of law. Also, political rights and civil liberties are usually conducive to faster economic growth because of the need for political legitimacy on the part of the government undertaking economic reforms with possible short-term costs, the need for an independent judicial system to carry out a successful economic liberalization, and the fact that respect for property rights is most often achieved in societies where civil liberties and political rights are guaranteed.

Development as entitlement rights

To ensure the protection of the various forms of economic, civil, and political freedoms discussed above requires an efficient state—that is, a state able effectively to fulfill the core functions of government responsibility (such as the protection of persons, contracts, and properties; the maintenance of the rule of law and justice; and the provision of public goods). However, political circumstances (being democratic or undemocratic) often lead the state to take on a more ambitious range of activities to foster growth directly, promote development, and achieve a number of social objectives (such as reducing inequality or promoting social justice). Typically, those activities would involve political solutions—as opposed to market solutions—that entail an enlargement of the scope of the state and the creation of entitlements (for instance, to social security, health, education, food, housing, work, an adequate standard of living, and so forth). To deliver those entitlements, the state interferes with the market—for instance, to produce manufacturing goods directly (through state-owned enterprises), to supply services (such as education, health, energy, transport, telecommunications, and culture), to control prices (through wages, interest rates, rents, and commodities) or quantities (via credits, quotas, licensing, and other barriers to entry), and to redistribute income (through taxes, subsidies, and transfers).

The relationship between the size of government and economic growth has been extensively studied and tested in the literature, using many different econometric techniques, empirical settings, and samples of countries. But results presented in the literature have been mixed and inconclusive (Bayraktar and Moreno-Dodson, 2010). In a recent paper trying to explain why both the Scandinavian and the Anglo-Saxon welfare states seem able to deliver high growth rates for very different levels of government size, Bergh and Henrekson (2011) suggest that, first, countries with higher social trust levels are able to develop larger government sectors without harming the economy, and,

second, countries with large governments may compensate for high taxes and spending by implementing market-friendly policies in other areas. In his seminal paper, Barro (1991) concludes that government expenditure is positively linked to economic growth when the share of government expenditure (and, consequently, the tax rate) is low; but it then turns negative because of increasing inefficiencies as the share of expenditure increases, indicating a nonlinear relationship between government expenditure and growth. Such findings could be explained by the key initial role of the state in providing some fundamental public goods to protect liberty itself—economic freedom and civil and political rights. However, when the scope of the state expands to cover many economic and social areas, its impact on economic growth could turn negative. Figure 3.3 illustrates the relationship between entitlement rights (as measured by the Fraser Institute, see definition below) and per-capita GDP in more than 100 countries in 2007. There is no apparent clear relationship between the level of entitlement rights and the level of development.

Figure 3.3: Entitlement rights vs. per-capita income, 2007

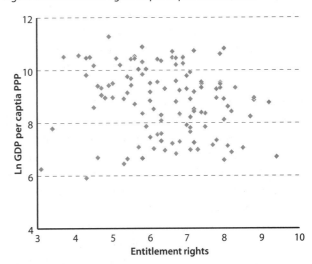

Data and model

Sources of data

The concepts of economic freedom, civil and political rights, and entitlements rights are notoriously difficult to quantify and attempts to grasp such complex subjects in one summary index can only be deceptive. Each concept is wide in scope (both breadth and depth) and impossible to summarize in one all-encompassing indicator. The best that can be done is to approach each concept through a combination of measurable indicators and proxies. The data used in this chapter includes the index of *Economic*

Freedom of the World of the Fraser Institute and the indices of *Civil Rights and Political Liberties* published by the Freedom House. These are among the few available databases that cover those concepts for a large sample of countries and a relatively long period of time in a comprehensive and consistent way.

Index of economic freedom

The index of economic freedom (EFW) used in this chapter is the simple average of four of the five areas of the index published in the Fraser Institute's *Economic Freedom of the World* (EFW), namely (2) Legal Structure and Security of Property Rights, (3) Access to Sound Money, (4) Freedom to Trade Internationally, and (5) Regulation of Credit, Labor, and Business.[3] In turn, each area consists of a number of components and sub-components. Area 2 measures the degree of judicial independence, impartial courts, protection of property rights, military inference in rule of law and the political process, integrity of the legal system, legal enforcement of contracts, and regulatory restrictions on the sale of real property. Area 3 measures money growth, standard deviation of inflation, rate of inflation, and freedom to own foreign currency bank accounts. Area 4 measures taxes on international trade, regulatory trade barriers, the size of the trade sector relative to expected, the black-market exchange rate, and the extent of international capital market controls. Area 5 measures credit market regulations, labor market regulations, and business regulations. The EFW index is constructed if the data is available on at least three out of the four areas of economic freedom; otherwise we marked the data as missing.

Index of entitlement rights

The index of entitlement rights (ER) is computed from Area 1: Size of Government of the index of *Economic Freedom of the World*. It is a rough proxy to measure the inclination of government to expand the scope of their activities in providing goods, services and entitlements. Area 1 includes general government consumption spending as a percentage of total consumption, transfers and subsidies as a percentage of GDP, government enterprises and investment, and top marginal tax rate. Because this measure is both broad and limited, it necessarily hides a lot of heterogeneity, especially regarding the quality of public expenditures and other forms of government intervention.

In particular, among small governments, the index cannot distinguish between failed states and more effective states. Among larger governments, the index cannot differentiate efficient welfare states from ineffective and wasteful rent-seeking states. Yet, the index aims at capturing the overall characteristic that governments with large public spending, transfers, and subsidies, numerous government enterprises, and high marginal tax rates are generally prone to provide various forms of entitlement.[4] The value of the index has been reversed so that the higher levels represent larger governments and, by extension, more extensive provisions of entitlement rights.

Index of civil and political rights

The index of civil and political rights (CPR) is computed as the simple average of Freedom House's Civil Rights (CR) and Political Liberties (PL) indices (Freedom House, 2011). Civil rights indicates whether citizens are able to participate freely in the political process: do they have the right to vote for distinct alternatives in legitimate elections, compete for public office, join political parties and organizations, as well as elect representatives that have a distinct impact on public policies and are accountable to the public? Political liberties allow for freedom of expression and belief, association and organization rights, rule of law and personal autonomy. The scale of the CPR index has been reversed from that of the Freedom House indices, so that the higher the rating, the higher the level of freedom. Because the indexes of civil rights and political liberties are highly correlated,[5] we create a joint index of civil and political rights (CPR).

Control variables

A number of control variables are used to depict exogenous factors: geography (Tropics), whether a country is landlocked (Pop100km), or remote (Remoteness). To control for geography, we use the data from Gallup, Sachs, and Mellinger (1998) on the extent of land located in the geographical tropics. To control for a country's being landlocked, we also use the data from Gallup, Sachs and Mellinger (1998) on the proportion of the country's

---

3   The publication and data tables are available from <http://www.freetheworld.com/>. See Exhibit 1.1 in this volume for full list of areas, components, and sub-components of the EFW Index.

4   For example, entitlement to healthcare, education, pension; to free or highly subsidized food, water, energy, and other goods and services; to public housing, controlled rents, or publicly guaranteed mortgages; to public employment, minimum wages; to protection from foreign and domestic competition through bans, quotas, and other limits to entry.

5   The Spearman rank correlation between the two indices over the period from 1970 to 2007 amounts to 0.93.

populations living within 100 km of the coastline or ocean-navigable river. To control for remoteness, we include a measure of the average distance to the world markets in line with the work of Redding and Venables (2004). We calculate as distance-weighted average GDP of all other countries in our sample. The measure of distance originates from the CEPII data base and represents the geographical distance between the capital cities.

Dummy variable

Finally, given the possible noise introduced by initial conditions in terms of natural resource endowments, we include a dummy variable for countries with subsoil assets (World Bank, 2006). We refer to this dummy variable as Resources. It should be noted, however, that the effects of natural endowments on long-term economic growth is unclear. Sachs and Warner (1997) find support for the hypothesis that countries rich in natural resources tend to grow more slowly. The authors include the ratio of natural resource (fuels and non-fuel primary products) exports to GDP in the base year and find it to be negatively correlated with economic growth. Similarly, Barro (1997), who includes a dummy variable for oil-rich countries in the growth regression finds it to be negative and statistically significant. However, several more recent studies found that the presence of natural resources does not necessarily present an impediment to higher growth; it depends on other policies pursued by the countries (e.g., Lederman and Maloney, 2007). The data on GDP per capita and the amount of net overseas development assistance per capita (ODI) originate from the World Bank World Development Indicators data base.[6]

Model

The methodology applied in this study follows closely that applied by Dawson (1998) who starts from the Mankiw, Romer, and Weil's (1992) human-capital-augmented version of the Solow's (1956) model:

$$Y_t = K_t^\alpha H_t^\beta (A_t L_t)^{1-\alpha-\beta}$$
$$\alpha, \beta > 0, \alpha + \beta < 1$$

where Y is aggregate output, K is physical capital, H is human capital, L is labor, and A is the level of (labor-augmenting) technology.

The model then relaxes the hypothesis of exogenous rates of growth of physical capital, human capital, and technology and assumes that these variables grow as

a function of the more fundamental determinants of accumulation that constitute economic freedom (EF), civil and political rights (CPR), entitlement rights (ER), and exogenous conditions. Given than the quantity and quality of physical capital and human capital human are notoriously difficult to measure and almost impossible to collect across countries on a timely and consistency basis, we bypass the estimation of the direct effects of EF, CPR, and ER on the accumulation of physical and human capital and estimate instead the following reduced form:

$$\Delta Y_i/Y = \alpha_0 + \alpha_1 Y_{i0} + \alpha_2 EF_{i0} + \alpha_3 \Delta EF_i/EF + \alpha_4 CPR_{i0} + \alpha_5 \Delta CPR_i/CPR + \alpha_6 ER_{i0} + \alpha_7 \Delta ER_i/ER + \alpha_8 X_i + \in_i$$

where $\Delta Y_i/Y$ is the average growth of per-capita GDP of country i; Y_0 is the initial level of GDP; EF_{i0}, CPR_{i0}, and ER_{i0} are the initial levels of the economic freedom index, civil and political rights index, and entitlement rights index, respectively. $\Delta EF_i/EF$, $\Delta CPR_i/CPR$, and $\Delta ER_i/ER$ are percentage point changes in the respective indexes over the period under investigation, while X_i is a vector of control variables determined by geography and natural resources (i.e., Tropics, Remoteness, Pop100K, and Resources). As indicated earlier, Tropics represents the extent of land located in the geographical tropics, Remoteness measures the average distance to world markets, Pop100K indicates the proportion of population living within 100 km of the coastline or ocean-navigable river, and Resources is a dummy variable for countries with subsoil assets.

Results

The results presented in this section are a best endeavor to test the theoretical discussion with available data. As already indicated, the multifaceted concepts of economic freedom, civil, and political rights, or entitlement rights are difficult to measure and the data used in the empirical analysis are necessarily imperfect proxies of the underlying concepts. And, the gaps between the conceptual framework and the measured concepts only complicate further the empirical verification of the ideas motivating the chapter. This caveat notwithstanding, the empirical analysis suggests that, for a given set of exogenous circumstances, respect for and promotion of economic freedom and civil and political rights are on average strongly associated with a country's per-capita income growth over the long run. In contrast, in most estimates, the extent to which the state expands its scope to provide entitlement rights does not add significant explanatory power in estimating countries' growth performance over the long run.

---

6 Database available from <http://data.worldbank.org/data-catalog/world-development-indicators>.

In the estimates where it does, the results would suggest that entitlement rights have a negative effect on economic growth. These findings are consistent in both the cross-section and panel estimates.

Cross-section estimates

Table 3.1 presents cross-section estimates of the model specification for about 100 countries (depending on data availability) over 30 years. The dependent variable is the average growth of the GDP per capita in constant US$ from 1975 to 2005. The various specifications allow for various combinations of variables to check the robustness of the estimated relationship. The first regression is similar to the specification employed by Gwartney, Holcome and Lawson (2006). Economic growth is mainly explained by the initial level of economic freedom and its growth over decades. This specification isolates the persistence of the impact of previous changes in economic freedom on economic growth. Using the same approach, we introduce the initial level and changes over time of the civil and political rights, and entitlement rights. In addition to the initial level of the GDP per capita we add the control variables as discussed in the previous section: Pop100km, Tropics, Resources, and Remoteness.

The results indicate that the level of economic freedom contributes to economic growth. We find that the level of economic freedom is consistently statistically significant across all specifications and has a positive impact on economic growth. For example, in the most comprehensive specification in the column 7 of table 3.1 our results indicate that a one-unit change in the initial level of economic freedom (on a scale of 1 to 10) is associated with an increase of almost one percentage point in the average economic growth rate during the period. As an example, Argentina with an economic freedom rating of 2.84 in 1975 could have expected an average growth rate one-percentage point higher than its actual growth rate over the period had its initial level of freedom been that of Turkey (3.84). A similar comparison can be made between Turkey and Israel (4.8) or Israel and Cyprus (5.9) or Cyprus and Singapore (7.0) and finally Singapore and Luxembourg (8.15).

The results indicate that the change in economic freedom over time also contributes to economic growth. Improvements in economic freedom have a persistent impact on economic growth as growth in economic freedom in previous decades affects economic growth to a larger extent than the more recent changes in economic freedom. Specifically, a unit increase in the economic freedom rating during the earlier decade results in more than a 1.3 percentage-point increase in the average growth rate over the whole period, while a unit increase in the economic freedom rating during the later decade results in a 0.9 percentage-point increase in the average economic growth rate over the entire period.

We also find the evidence of a positive impact of civil and political rights on economic growth. The initial level of civil and political rights is consistently statistically significant and positive across all regressions. A one-unit change in initial civil and political rights conditions on a scale of 1 to 8 (i.e., the difference between, say, Mongolia and Chile in 1975) increases average economic growth by more than 0.3 percentage point during the period (column 7 of table 3.1). A similar conclusion is reached if one compares the initial conditions of Chile (with a CPR of 2) and Egypt (CPR of 3), and then Egypt and Portugal (CPR of 4), Portugal and Monaco (CPR of 5), Monaco and Greece (CPR of 6), and finally Greece and the United States (CPR of 7). However, the results indicate that changes in civil and political rights conditions over time are not always associated with increased per-capita GDP. The coefficients of changes in civil and political rights are in some specifications statistically significant and positive, but the relationship is not robust to different specifications.

Finally, we do not find any robust relationship between entitlement rights and economic growth. The initial level of the entitlement right is negative and statistically significant in regression where only this variable has been included (column 3) and not statistically significant in other specifications. The change in entitlement rights seems to influence the average economic growth positively, but this relationship is not robust to the inclusion of economic freedom. In line with earlier literature, this may indicate that the role of the state on economic growth is ambiguous. When the state limits itself to the core functions of governmental responsibility, including the protection of various forms of freedom and the provision of key public goods, it is likely to have a strong positive influence on growth. However, when the state grows beyond the size needed to fulfill these core functions, it may dampen economic growth.

This nonlinear effect between government intervention and economic growth is not easy to test as there is no guarantee (and for that matter little evidence) that governments necessarily prioritize the core functions of government responsibility over other forms of government intervention. In other words, a country with a low ratio of government spending to GDP may not necessarily maintain the rule of law and justice or provide the core public

Table 3.1: Economic growth and economic freedom, civil and political rights, and economic and entitlement rights—cross-section estimates

	Coefficient	Coefficient	Coefficient	Coefficient	Coefficient	Coefficient	Coefficient
Column	1	2	3	4	5	6	7
EF	1.099***			0.946***	1.071***		0.969***
dEF 1985–1994	1.335***			1.250***	1.045***		1.375***
dEF 1995–2004	0.994***			0.827***	1.047***		0.928***
CPR		0.562***		0.428***		0.446***	0.332**
dCPR 1985–1994	0.426**		0.328*		0.335	0.230	
dCPR 1995–2004	0.267*		0.210		0.264*	0.127	
ER			−0.255*		−0.111	−0.192	−0.524
dER 1985–1994		0.013		0.108	0.029	0.121	
dER 1995–2004		0.016		0.308**	0.026	0.283*	
initial GDP per capita	−0.740***	−0.585***	−0.290**	−0.868***	−0.766***	−0.496***	−0.879***
Tropics	−1.694***	−2.179***	−2.413***	−1.660***	−1.803***	−2.343***	−1.748***
Resources	0.526	0.625	−0.099	1.041**	1.069**	0.616	1.360**
Pop100km	1.286***	1.660***	2.082***	0.813*	1.279***	1.599***	0.922*
Remoteness	−0.148**	−0.190**	−0.201**	−0.125*	−0.127*	−0.170**	−0.110
Constant	−5.202***	−1.281*	1.934**	−5.733***	−7.370***	0.181	−5.121***
No. of countries	98	109	105	97	98	103	97
Adjusted R-sq:	0.562	0.429	0.405	0.588	0.599	0.429	0.608

*** significant at 1%, ** significant at 5%, * significant at 10%.

Dependent variable: average annual growth of GDP per capita in constant US$ from 1975 to 2005.

goods that are necessary to protect fundamental freedoms and hence development. Conversely, a country with a large welfare state, while distorting incentives and dampening economic growth, may deliver those core functions of government responsibility perfectly. The methodology and data used in this chapter do not allow investigating this issue further. This would require additional research.

Consistent with economic theory and all previous studies, the results indicate that the initial level of GDP per capita is statistically significant and has the expected negative sign in all specifications. Poorer countries tend to grow faster. Also, all control variables except for Resources are statistically significant in all specifications and have the expected signs. We find that countries located in the tropical climate and far away from the world's biggest markets tend to grow more slowly than otherwise similar countries in different locations. We also find that higher proportion of coastal population is associated with faster growth. The impact of resources on growth turns out to be statistically significant and positive in three out of 7 regressions. This would suggest that, controlling for all other variables, countries that possess subsoil assets tend to grow faster. This is not necessarily inconsistent with the findings of some previous studies that found a negative impact of resource abundance on economic growth. It has been argued that abundant natural resources might lead to greater corruption and inefficient bureaucracies or that the governments in resource-rich economies are more likely to follow some form of state-led development policies or tend to waste the rents through profligate or inappropriate consumption. However, our various indicators of freedom might be controlling for these factors already, hence our results indicate that given two economies with the same level of economic freedom and other attributes, the economy that is in addition abundant in natural resources will tend to grow faster.

Table 3.2: Economic growth and economic freedom, civil and political rights, and economic and entitlement rights—panel estimates

	Coefficient	Coefficient	Coefficient	Coefficient	Coefficient	Coefficient	Coefficient	Coefficient
Column	1	2	3	4	5	6	7	8
initial EF	1.415***			1.152***		1.358***	1.116***	2.671***
dEF(−1)	1.032**			1.039**		1.069**	1.072**	−0.193
initial CPR		1.087***		0.737***	0.979***		0.691***	0.941**
dCPR(−1)		0.519*		0.700**	0.548*		0.699**	0.548*
initial ER			−0.711***		−0.546***	−0.428**	−0.353*	−1.469***
dER(−1)			0.008		−0.071	0.312	0.188	0.213
initial GDP per capita	−1.072***	−1.436***	−0.659***	−1.181***	−1.014***	−1.048***	−1.149***	−8.474***
Tropics	−2.752***	−3.647***	−3.407***	−2.418***	−3.325***	−3.109***	−2.733***	
Resources	1.471*	3.925***	0.196	2.623***	2.195***	1.613**	2.659***	
Remoteness	−0.241***	−0.445***	−0.336***	−0.243***	−0.328***	−0.245***	−0.246***	
Constant	−4.021**	−0.863	6.591***	−6.283***	1.585	−1.922	−4.406**	
No. of obs.	511	624	573	508	564	511	508	508
No. of countries	121	136	121	121	121	121	121	121
R-sq within	0.087	0.146	0.162	0.118	0.170	0.102	0.131	0.237
R-sq between	0.435	0.308	0.280	0.425	0.340	0.426	0.418	0.075
R-sq overall	0.138	0.146	0.102	0.173	0.159	0.147	0.178	0.004

*** significant at 1%, ** significant at 5%, * significant at 10%.

Dependent variable: average annual growth of GDP per capita in constant USD over 5 year intervals from 1975 to 2005.

Panel estimates

Table 3.2 presents estimates of the relationship between economic freedom and economic growth in a panel of data from 1975 to 2005. The average economic growth is measured over five-year intervals (as the index of *Economic Freedom of the World* is only available every five years from 1975 to 2000). Data on economic freedom is available for 121 countries. As in the cross-section estimates, the dependent variable is explained by the initial levels of the various exogenous variables (EF, CPR, and ER), the changes of those variables in the previous periods (to avoid the problem of endogeneity), and a similar set of control variables.[7]

The panel-data estimates are consistent with the cross-section estimates. We find a robust positive relationship between the initial level of economic freedom and its growth in the previous period. In addition, we find a similar relationship between economic growth and civil and political rights. Both the initial level and changes in the civil and political rights in the previous period contribute positively to the economic growth. This relationship is robust to the inclusion of the indicator of economic freedom. In contrast to the cross-section estimates, we find this time a robust negative relationship between the initial level of entitlement rights and economic growth in all specifications, while we still do not find any statistically significant impact of the change in entitlement rights on economic growth.

All the control variables are statistically significant in most specifications and have the same signs as in the

---

7   We drop the Pop100km variable as it was consistently not statistically significant in the panel regression estimates.

cross section estimates presented in table 3.1. Column 8 of table 3.2 presents the results based on the fixed-effects estimation. The only difference in this specification is that the growth of economic freedom in the previous period does not seem to affect economic growth in the current period. The overall fit of the fixed-effects regression is poor and it does not seem to be the appropriate way to model the economic growth since the heterogeneity of the data set is driven by cross-country variation and not by time-series variation.

Conclusions

Freedom and entitlement are largely different paradigms for thinking about the fundamentals of economic development. Depending on the balance between free choices and more coerced decisions, individual opportunities to learn, own, work, save, invest, trade, protect, and so forth could vary greatly across countries and over time. The empirical findings in this chapter suggest that fundamental freedoms are paramount to explain long-term economic growth.

For a given set of exogenous conditions, countries that favor free choice—economic freedom and civil and political liberties—over entitlement rights are likely to achieve higher sustainable economic growth and to achieve many of the distinctive proximate characteristics of success identified by the Commission on Growth and Development (2008). In contrast, pursuing entitlement rights through greater state coercion is likely to be deceptive or self-defeating in the long run.

These findings provide potentially important policy lessons for all countries. For developed countries, they suggest that prioritizing economic freedom over social entitlements could be an effective way to reform the welfare state and make it more sustainable and equitable in the long run. For middle-income countries (such as countries in the midst of the Arab Spring and in Asia and Latin America), they indicate that the quest for civil and political rights and for economic freedom could create the conditions for new social contracts. For low-income countries, they provide an opportunity to reflect on the achievements under the Millennium Development Goals (MDG) and the potential role that economic freedom and other fundamental freedoms could play in a post-2015 MDG development agenda.

References

Acemoglu, Daron, and Simon Johnson (2005). Unbundling Institutions. *Journal of Political Economy* 113, 5 (October): 949–95.

Acemoglu, Daron, Simon Johnson, and James A. Robinson (2004). *Institutions as the Fundamental Cause of Long-Run Growth*. NBER Working Paper No. 10481. National Bureau of Economic Research.

Barro, Robert J. (1991). Economic Growth in a Cross-Section of Countries. *Quarterly Journal of Economics* 106, 2 (May): 407–43.

Bayraktar, Nihal, and Blanca Moreno-Dodson (2010). *How Can Public Spending Help You Grow? An Empirical Analysis for Developing Countries*. World Bank Policy Research Paper 5367. World Bank.

Berggren, Niclas (2003). The Benefits of Economic Freedom: A Survey. *The Independent Review* 8, 2: 193–211.

Bergh, Andreas, and Magnus Henrekson (2011). *Government Size and Growth: A Survey and Interpretation of the Evidence*. Working Paper No. 858. Research Institute of Industrial Economics (IFN).

Chauffour, Jean-Pierre (2009). *The Power of Freedom: Uniting Human Rights and Development*. Cato Institute.

Chauffour, Jean-Pierre (2011). *On the Relevance of Freedom and Entitlement in Development: New Empirical Evidence (1975–2007)*. Policy Research Working Paper 5660. World Bank.

Commission on Growth and Development (2008). *The Growth Report: Strategies for Sustained Growth and Inclusive Development*. World Bank. <http://www.growthcommission.org/index.php>.

Easterly, William (2001). *The Elusive Quest for Growth: Economists' Adventures and Misadventures in the Tropics*. MIT Press.

Frankel, Jeffrey, and David Romer (1999). Does Trade Cause Growth? *American Economic Review* 89, 3: 379–99.

Freedom House (2011). *Freedom in the World 2011 Survey Release*. <http://www.freedomhouse.org/images/File/fiw/Tables%2C%20Graphs%2C%20etc%2C%20FIW%202011_Revised%201_11_11.pdf>.

Friedman, Benjamin M. (2005). *The Moral Consequences of Economic Growth*. Knopf.

Friedman, Milton (1962). *Capitalism and Freedom*. University of Chicago Press.

Gallup, John Luke, Jeffrey D. Sachs, and Andrew D. Mellinger (1998). *Geography and Economic Development*. NBER Working Paper Series No. w6849. National Bureau of Economic Research.

Gwartney, James, and Robert A. Lawson (2009). *Economic Freedom of the World: 2009 Annual Report*. Fraser Institute. <http://www.freetheworld.com/2009/reports/world/EFW2009_BOOK.pdf>.

Hayek, Friedrich A. (1960). *The Constitution of Liberty*. University of Chicago Press.

Hayek, Friedrich A. (1973). *Law, Legislation and Liberty, Vol. 1: Rules and Order*. University of Chicago Press.

Lawson, Robert A., and J.R. Clark (2010). Examining the Hayek-Friedman Hypothesis on Economic and Political Freedom. *Journal of Economic Behavior & Organization* 74, 3: 230–39.

Lederman D., and W.F. Maloney (Eds.) (2007). *Natural Resources: Neither Curse nor Destiny*. World Bank and Stanford University Press.

Mankiw, N. Gregory, David Romer, and David N. Weil (1992). A Contribution to the Empirics of Economic Growth. *Quarterly Journal of Economics* 107, 2 (May): 407–37.

North, Douglass C. (1990). *Institutions, Institutional Change and Economic Performance*. Cambridge University Press.

North, Douglass C., and R.P. Thomas (1973). *The Rise of the Western World: A New Economic History*. Cambridge University Press.

Redding, S., and A.J. Venables (2004). Economic Geography and International Inequality. *Journal of International Economics* 62, 1: 53–82.

Rodrik, D. (2000). *Institutions for High-Quality Growth: What They Are and How to Acquire Them*. NBER Working Paper No. 7540. National Bureau of Economic Research.

Romer, P. M. (1989). *What Determines the Rate of Growth and Technical Change?* World Bank Research Working Paper No. 279. World Bank.

Sachs, Jeffrey D., and Andrew M. Warner (1997). Fundamental Sources of Long Run Growth. *American Economic Review* 87, 2 (May): 184–88.

Sala-i-Martin, X. (1997). I Just Ran Two Million Regressions. *American Economic Review* 87, 2: 178–83.

Sen, Amartya (1999). *Development as Freedom*. Oxford University Press.

Solow, Robert M. (1956). A Contribution to the Theory of Economic Growth. *Quarterly Journal of Economics* 70, 1 (February): 65–94.

World Bank (2006). *Where is the Wealth of Nations? Measuring Capital for the 21st Century*. World Bank.

Chapter 4
Does Economic Freedom Promote Women's Well-being?

By Michael D. Stroup

Introduction

Over the last few decades, more and more countries have been adopting the political and economic institutions that promote greater economic freedom. For example, many Eastern European countries have been moving towards market economies after the dissolution of the Soviet Union. There has been the remarkable rise of the Asian Tiger economies of the Pacific Rim countries. Today, even China is dabbling with localized, free-market areas. To varying degrees these governments are:

1 decreasing the size and scope of government allocations of resources,

2 establishing and protecting private property rights,

3 insulating their sovereign money from political influences,

4 opening up their economies to international markets, and

5 decreasing the scope of regulatory control over private commerce.

Economic Freedom of the World

These notable events have created a grand social experiment for economists to examine in this new millennium. The Fraser Institute compiles and publishes an annual index of economic freedom in each country (Gwartney, Hall, and Lawson, 2010) that aids the cross-country analysis of this global phenomenon. The index published in *Economic Freedom of the World*, (EFW index), is made up of various metrics reflecting the extent to which each country has implemented the five categories of institutions noted above that promote economic freedom.

Many empirical studies using the EFW index reveal that a country's economic freedom is highly correlated with its level of economic prosperity, capital investment, and rate of economic growth (Dawson, 1998; Gwartney, Holcombe, and Lawson, 1999; Gwartney, Lawson, and Holcombe, 2006; Hall, Sobel, and Crowley, 2010). Other studies have even shown that the EFW index, or its constituent components, is positively correlated with many non-monetary measures of social welfare such as maintaining peaceful relations between nations (Gartzky, 2007; Hall and Lawson, 2009) and various measures of individual well-being (Norton, 1998, 2003; Stroup, 2007).

However, one can ask whether this increase in prosperity and well-being has also generated a more equitable allocation of these benefits within society. Scully (2002) has found that economic freedom is correlated with more equal distributions of income across countries, but does economic freedom promote the well-being of typically under-served groups in a society? For example, would women find that living in a market-based economy tends to support their pursuit of a better quality of life? Stroup (2008) used selected measures of women's well-being from the World Bank Indicators database to find evidence that some aspects of women's well-being were positively correlated to the country's level of economic freedom.

Evidence from the UN Development Program's Gender Inequality Index

The empirical analysis in this chapter examines whether a beneficial link between economic freedom and women's welfare remains evident when using the Gender Inequality Index (GI index). This index comprises various measures of women's well-being and is compiled by the United Nations Development Program (United Nations, 2010). Simple correlations between these measures of women's well-being and the values of the EFW index are examined and regression analysis is employed to determine if a relationship between economic freedom and women's well-being remains after controlling for per-capita income, and religious and regional ethnic differences across countries. The results indicate that women living in those developing countries embracing the institutions of economic freedom might be encouraged, since empirical evidence implies that those institutions that promote economic freedom have relatively better metrics of women's well-being, as defined by the United Nations Development Program.

How economic freedom promotes women's well-being

Before examining the data, one might ask: Why would a society characterized by greater economic freedom be relatively more beneficial for a woman's pursuit of well-being? After all, market-based economies have been roundly criticized as a heartless arrangement of political and economic institutions that ignore the innate value of individuals as human beings (Stiglitz, 1996; Stiglitz et. al., 2006; Posner, 2009). This criticism has been especially pointed regarding those groups considered disenfranchised in society (Stiglitz, 2002), such as women (Gibson-Graham, 1996).

Yet, a competing theory that economic freedom benefits women may be explained as a simple case of supply of, and demand for, valuable human capital. Consider the demand side. Individuals in a market-based society engage in voluntary commerce within a highly competitive economy. In an economic environment characterized by private property rights and the rule of law, individual prosperity can only be achieved by providing a product or service of sufficient value that the buyer voluntarily pays more than the seller's cost of providing it. Neither the profits from making good economic decisions nor the losses of making bad economic decisions are shared by any third parties to the exchange. This means the incentives for seeking out and exploiting mutual gains from trade are maximized, making everyone in a society more keenly aware how significant lost economic opportunities (or "opportunity cost" in economic parlance) can be when pursuing one's own prosperity.

One particularly prominent opportunity cost is the loss of the value of female human capital in the key economic processes of innovation, production, and distribution within a nation's economy. The recognition of, and demand for, female human capital is expected to be higher in any society where a greater level of economic

accountability is imposed on those who ignore such opportunity costs by practicing intolerant and prejudicial behavior. Market-based societies economically punish those who practice such behavior, as they are forced to bear all of the forgone benefits arising from their choice. The more enlightened and tolerant individuals enjoy the full benefits of their impartiality. This makes it much more difficult for individuals in a market-based society to sustain a persistent undervaluation of female human capital.

Next, consider the supply side. As stated earlier, the level of economic freedom has been found to be highly correlated with prosperity and economic growth. Parents of more prosperous families find it easier to release the labor of their children to pursue education or technical training, rather than keeping them home to support the family with their unskilled labor. In a society where the value of female human capital is highly demanded, both male and female children of these families would be expected to attain higher levels of education and training. A greater supply of female human capital helps the individual woman as well as the society in which she lives. It creates a more productive labor force with greater economic potential for the whole economy, while enhancing a woman's ability to identify and exploit a larger set of economic opportunities for avoiding any resilient pockets of intolerance and bigotry left in society.

Therefore, an increase in both the supply of, and demand for, female human capital can increase a woman's ability to achieve greater individual prosperity while enhancing the well-being of all women. This would naturally place greater pressure on men to recognize women's equal standing in the various non-economic facets of society as well. If women's well-being is found to be correlated with the level of economic freedom in a country, then this would be evidence that the cold-hearted institutions of markets could truly unite the noble goals of an enlightened and tolerant society with the self-centered goals of individual prosperity—thus demonstrating Adam Smith's insight of how people voluntarily interact in the market as if "led by an invisible hand to promote an end which was no part of his [or her] intention" (1776, par. IV.2.9).

Measuring women's well-being

When there are conflicting theoretical models of whether or not greater economic freedom promotes the well-being of women, the question of which theory fits best requires an empirical investigation. Do countries with greater economic freedom generally exhibit superior measures of women's well-being, such that a female living in a market-based society is more likely to achieve a higher quality of life? The following cross-country analysis compares the value of the EFW index with the level of various non-monetary measures of women's well-being, as developed by the United Nations Development Program. In their annual Human Development Report (UNDP, 2010), the UNDP examines and quantifies the relative progress that countries are making in advancing human development around the world. They also examine the respective impacts of various political, economic, and cultural changes on women's well-being in each country.[1]

A key founder of UNDP project was the late Mahub ul Haq. Like other prominent social scientists, such as Nobel Laureate Amartya Sen, ul Haq felt that traditional measures of economic prosperity (like GDP per capita) reflected only a narrow aspect of an individual's true level of well-being. Indeed, he writes, "the basic purpose of development is to enlarge people's choices (and) create an enabling environment for people to enjoy long, healthy and creative lives" (UNDP, 2010: <http://hdr.undp.org/en/humandev/>).

While the annual UNDP reports consistently question the efficacy of markets in promoting non-monetary aspects of individual well-being, their reports do compile a useful database of socio-economic measures reflecting the level of individual well-being in each country. Indeed, the UNDP encourages social scientists to use this data for research into various global human development issues. These measures range from educational attainment and literacy rates to health-care access and mortality rates to various indicators of economic and political opportunity like labor-force participation rates and minority representation in government.

In this light, the UNDP has developed a Gender Inequality (GI) Index[2] designed to reveal each country's relative performance in promoting the well-being of women. The value of the GI index ranges from 0 to 1, with higher values indicating a greater level of gender inequality in a society. The GI index comprises five measures reflecting the level of female achievement in three basic categories of women's well-being:[3]

1 Reproductive Health (maternal mortality ratio and adolescent fertility rate),

2 Empowerment (female parliamentary representation and educational attainment), and

3 Labor Market (female labor force participation rate).

Whether these five measures adequately reflect a woman's well-being is not questioned in this analysis. These and similar measures are widely used to reflect women's well-being in the economic development literature on gender inequality. The GI index and its various components are simply examined to determine if greater economic freedom are properly correlated with those measures that the UNDP deems as vital to women's well-being.

The Fraser Institute's EFW index comprises various economic and political measures that reflect the presence of institutional structures in a country that promote economic freedom. These measures are grouped into the five categories listed in the introduction, above, and are aggregated into a single index. The scale of the EFW index runs from 0 (least economic freedom) to 10 (most economic freedom).

Examining the data

Figure 4.1 reveals a histogram which illustrates the relationship between the GI index from the 2010 report and the EFW index. Assuming that the institutions of economic freedom in a society take time to influence these measures of women's well-being, the EFW index values used in these histograms are the average between the 1995 and 2008 EFW index (the latest year available).[4] The countries are arranged in order of economic freedom index value, with the quartile of the least free countries on the left and the quartile of the freest countries on the right. A higher GI index value indicates greater inequality for women, such that the histogram reveals how the average value of the GI index continuously declines as the average value of economic freedom rises across the quartiles. This relationship lends support to the theory that greater economic freedom promotes the women's well-being.

However, a more careful examination would also look at how well each component of the GI index is correlated with the level of EFW index in a country. A similarly constructed histogram in Figure 4.2 reveals how the percent of female seats in national parliament and the percent of female adults with a secondary education both consistently

---

1   Unless otherwise indicated, all measures used in this analysis come from the UNDP report, which gleans country data from the databases of organizations like UNICEF, the World Health Organization, and similar international databases.

2   This is not to be confused with an older UNDP index, called the Gender Development Index, which the GI index now replaces.

3   The UNDP data can be freely downloaded in Excel format at <http://hdr.undp.org/en/statistics/data/>.

4   This sample includes data from all countries in the GI index for which data exists in the EFW index.

Figure 4.1: Gender Inequality Index compared to EFW Index (larger is more unequal)

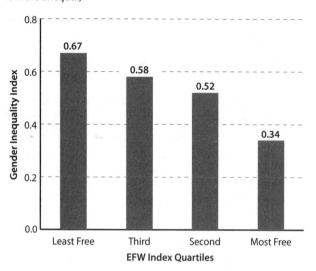

Figure 4.2: Percentage of female adults with secondary education (■) and female seats in parliament (▩) compared to EFW Index

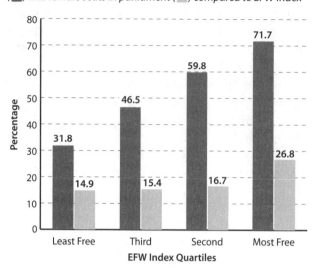

increase with the value of the EFW index.[5] Figure 4.3 shows how maternal mortality (per 100,000 births) and adolescent fertility per 1,000 females age 15–19[6] both consistently decline with the value of the EFW index. However, Figure 4.4 illustrates that the rate at which women participate in the labor force does not appear to have any meaningful correlation with the value of the EFW. This last result is discussed in more detail, below.

Controlling for other influences

The preceding empirical examination shows that higher levels of the EFW index are correlated with lower, more beneficial, ratings on four of the five measures that make up the GI index, as well as with a lower, more beneficial, level on the GI index itself. This intriguing evidence implies that countries with more economic freedom generally tend to promote the well-being of women, at least as measured by the GI index. Yet one must be careful to control for other influences that could produce similar statistical results.

Cultural differences across ethnic regions of the world and arising from religious traditions embedded in a country's historical roots affect women's well-being. As Blau et al. state: "Social forces such as religion, ideology, and culture also influence women's status, especially through

their effect on the labor market activity" (2006: 377). For example, women living in theocratic Muslim nations likely face more restrictive female labor laws and educational opportunities than women living in non-Muslim nations. Women living in former European colonies dominated by Catholic beliefs might have relatively less influence over how many children they will bear or what stage in their life they might want to have children (World Bank, 2000).

It would be helpful to try to control for such influences when statistically uncovering the relationship between economic freedom and various measures of women's well-being. Regression analysis is a useful statistical procedure that is often employed in social science research to hold constant such extraneous influences. In this light, a separate linear regression was run using each of the five UNDP measures, and the Gender Inequality Index itself, as dependent variables. Each equation uses the same specification. The explanatory variables used in each regression include:

- the EFW index, expressed as the average of the 1995 and 2008 index values;

- the percent of the population that is Muslim;

- the percent of the population that is Catholic or Orthodox;

- a dummy variable for each of the geographical regions of the world, as defined by the United Nations and the World Bank: North America, Latin America, Western Europe, Middle East, sub-Saharan Africa, East Asia, and South Asia.

---

5 For the purposes of inclusiveness, the following histograms use the UNDP measures for all available countries, which may reflect data from some countries not included in the GI index.

6 See UNDP, 2010: Technical notes <http://hdr.undp.org/en/media/HDR_2010_EN_TechNotes_reprint.pdf> for a description of the HDR indices, indicators, and calculations.

Figure 4.3: Maternal mortality rate and adolescent fertility rate compared to EFW Index

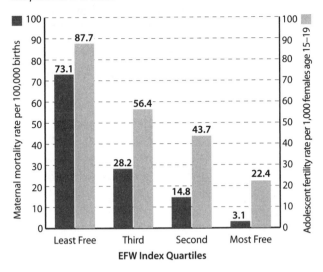

Figure 4.4: Female labor-force participation rate (%) compared to EFW Index

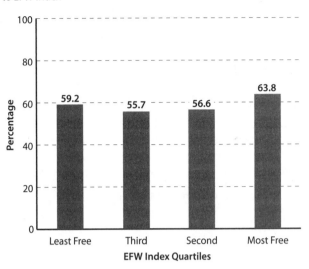

Additionally, women in more prosperous countries may be able to pursue a greater scope of opportunities for individual advancement than women in less prosperous countries. As mentioned earlier, the EFW index is highly correlated with the level of prosperity in a country. If economic prosperity promotes women's well-being, this would imply that the level of economic freedom in a country might have both a direct and an indirect influence on women's well-being. Therefore, a second specification was run for each of these six dependent variables that includes the Gross Domestic Product (GDP) per person, expressed as the average of 1995 and 2005 levels of GDP per person, measured in thousands of year-2000 US dollars.

Interpreting the results

Table 4.1 reveals the statistical results from two linear regression specifications (with and without income) for each of the six dependent variables. In each case, the same number of countries was used in both regressions for direct comparability of the results. All countries were included in each sample for which data was available.

First, consider the regression results for the GI index. The coefficient estimate for the EFW index was statistically significant in explaining the observed variation in the GI Index at the traditional 5% level, both with and without the income variable present in the specification. The average value of the GI Index in this sample of 111 countries was 0.53. The coefficient estimate for the EFW variable in the specification without the income variable is –0.06. The negative sign indicates that

higher EFW index values are associated with lower GI index values, supporting the theory that economic freedom appears to have a beneficial influence on women's well-being.

The coefficient estimate for EFW indicates that a one-point increase in the EFW index would result in a decline in the GI index of –0.06. To put the magnitude of this beneficial impact into context, consider the histogram displayed in figure 4.1. The difference in the average EFW index value for the middle two quartiles was 0.59. If a one unit increase in the EFW index can be expected to decrease the GI index by –0.06, this 0.59 increase in the EFW index is expected to produce a 0.035 decrease the GI index (–0.06 times 0.59). The difference in the GI index value between these same quartiles was 0.06 (the difference between 0.58 and 0.52). This implies that the expected benefit from the observed increase in the EFW index values between these middle two quartiles may explain about 58% the actual difference in the GI index between the these same quartiles (because 0.035 is 58% of 0.06). In other words, after controlling for potential ethnic differences across regions and for religious differences across countries, over half the difference between the GI index values between these two quartiles could be explained by the differential in the average levels of economic freedom between the two groups of countries.

However, some of the estimated impact of the EFW index on the GI index may not be directly attributable to the level of economic freedom in a society. This possibility arises because the income variable was not included in the specification referred to above. If economic freedom promotes prosperity, which in turn promotes women's

Table 4.1: The impact of economic freedom on women's well-being

	Equation 1a Gender Inequality Index	Equation 1b Gender Inequality Index	Equation 2a Female representation in parliament (% of seats)	Equation 2b Female representation in parliament (% of seats)
Number of Countries	111	111	117	117
Mean Dependent Variable	0.53	0.53	18.42	18.42
EFW Index	−0.06**	−0.03**	3.96**	2.34*
GDP per capita		−0.01**		0.30**
Percent Muslim	0.14**	0.11**	−6.72*	−5.49
Percent Catholic or Orthodox	0.02	−0.01	−3.59	−2.10
R-squared	0.80	0.84	0.27	0.30
No. of significant regions**	3	1	0	0

	Equation 3a Adult women with secondary education (%)	Equation 3b Adult women with secondary education (%)	Equation 4a Maternal mortality (per 100,000 births)	Equation 4b Maternal mortality (per 100,000 births)
Number of Countries	113	113	118	118
Mean Dependent Variable	52.26	52.26	299.71	299.71
EFW Index	5.44**	4.88*	−112.80**	−131.41**
GDP per capita		0.09		3.37
Percent Muslim	−27.98**	−27.57**	273.59**	288.03**
Percent Catholic or Orthodox	−10.60	−10.18	49.78	66.41
R-squared	0.61	0.61	0.73	0.73
No. of significant regions**	4	4	1	1

	Equation 5a Adolescent fertility (per 1,000 females age 15-19)	Equation 5b Adolescent fertility (per 1,000 females age 15-19)	Equation 6a Female labor force participation (%)	Equation 6b Female labor force participation (%)
Number of Countries	119	119	119	119
Mean Dependent Variable	53.25	53.25	58.61	58.61
EFW Index	−7.91**	−6.64*	−0.05	−1.83
GDP per capita		−0.22		0.33**
Percent Muslim	22.40**	21.43**	−22.50**	−21.05**
Percent Catholic or Orthodox	6.10	4.99	−9.68**	−8.02**
R-squared	0.73	0.73	0.54	0.56
No. of significant regions**	2	1	2	1

Note: * denotes significance at the 10% level, and ** denotes significance at the 5% level.

well-being, then some or all of the observed impact of EFW index could be only *indirectly* attributable to the influence of economic freedom via its impact on economic prosperity. In this light, table 4.1 also reveals the results from adding the income variable to the GI index regression. The coefficient estimate on per-capita income was found to be negative and significant, as expected. While the presence of income in the equation did not diminish the statistical significance of the EFW index, the magnitude of the coefficient estimate diminished from –0.06 to –0.02. This implies that the level of economic freedom still retains some direct impact on women's well-being, even after controlling for differences in prosperity across countries. Using this estimate of the *direct* impact of EFW index, it appears that economic freedom still explains almost 20% of the observed difference in the GI index between the middle two quartiles in figure 4.1.

Next, consider the five different measures of women's well-being that make up the GI index. Among those regressions excluding the income variable, the EFW index was found to be beneficial to women's well-being and statistically significant at the 5% level in four of the five measures. Only Female Labor Force Participation was not significantly influenced by the level of the EFW index (which is discussed further, below). When income was included in these specifications, it was found to be significant for only two variables (Female Representation in Parliament and Labor Force Participation). The EFW index was found to remain beneficial and significant at the 5% level for only one of the five dependent variables (Maternal Mortality). Interestingly, the magnitude of the coefficient increased after including the income variable. The EFW coefficient estimates for the remaining three dependent variables were found to be significant at only the 10% level. In each case, the EFW index retained a beneficial impact but the magnitude of their respective impacts was diminished.

It is worth briefly summarizing the impact of the various control variables. Palaez (2009) examined the EFW index for Islamic nations and found that, as a group, these countries have exhibited a decline in the level of economic freedom over the last decade or so. Even after controlling for the level of economic freedom, the coefficient estimate for the Percent Muslim Population variable was found to be statistically significant at the 5% level for 14 of the 18 regressions. In each of these cases, the coefficient estimate had a detrimental impact on the GI index and on each of the five component measures of women's well-being. The coefficient estimates for the Percent Catholic

Population variable were found to be statistically significant for only two of the 18 regressions (in both equations, for Labor Force Participation) and exhibited a detrimental impact in both cases. Finally, one or more regional dummy variables were found to be significant in 10 of the 12 regression equations.

Reconsidering female labor force participation

Why would the measure of labor force participation appear to be the only uncorrelated component of the GI index when compared to the average level of economic freedom in a country? There are many possible explanations. First, there may be one or more omitted explanatory variables in the specification. As Blau et. al. explain: "Factors that influence the supply of female labor include the relative value of market earnings as compared to time spent in household production, which is itself strongly influenced by fertility rates (and) the availability of goods and services for purchase" (2006: 377). The fertility influence could be reflected by including the UNDP fertility rate as an explanatory variable. The market earnings influence could be reflected by the level of human capital, or educational attainment, evident among women. Therefore, the UNDP secondary education variable could be included as an explanatory variable.

Second, cross-country studies in the development economics literature note that different stages of a country's level of economic development can influence women's willingness to join the labor force outside the home. Blau et. al. state: "Part of the explanation for differences in labor force activity by gender is that countries, and more generally regions, are in various stages of economic development, ranging from agricultural to industrial to post-industrial" (2006: 373). For example, Mammen and Paxson (2000) find that female labor force participation is generally higher in less-developed agricultural economies and generally declines among those countries that have transformed into more industrial economies.

Therefore, the share of a country's GDP arising from the agricultural and manufacturing sectors could also be included in the specification to reflect this impact. The agricultural and manufacturing sector's percentage value-added to GDP are each calculated as the average between 1995 and 2005 values. Both variables are available from the World Bank Development Indicators database (World Bank, 2010: table 1), and are included as a ratio of agriculture to manufacturing sectors to reflect any potential non-linear influence on female labor force participation.

Table 4.2: The impact of economic freedom on female labor force participation rates

	Equation 7a Female labor force participation (%)	Equation 7b Female labor force participation (%)	Equation 8a Ratio of female-to-male labor force participation rates (%)	Equation 8b Ratio of female-to-male labor force participation rates (%)
Number of Countries	94	94	94	94
Mean Dependent Variable	57.8	57.8	71.94	71.94
Percentage change EFW	0.05	0.13*	0.12**	0.18**
GDP per capita		0.39**		0.30*
Adolescent fertility	−0.11**	−0.10**	−0.12**	−0.11**
Female secondary education	−0.10	−0.13**	−0.06	−0.09
Ratio agriculture/manufacturing	1.52	1.37	1.60	1.49
Percent Muslim	−20.01**	−19.56**	−26.06**	−25.71**
Percent Catholic or Orthodox	−7.63*	−6.13	−8.31*	−7.13*
R-squared	0.60	0.63	0.69	0.71
No. of significant regions**	2	1	2	1

* denotes significance at the 10% level, and ** denotes significance at the 5% level.

Third, while initially examining the influence of the EFW index on the five components of the GI index, the EFW index was included in one of two forms: the average level and the percentage change in levels between 1995 and 2008. While the average level appeared to be reasonably robust in statistical significance across the five components, the percentage change variable was rarely significant—except in explaining the female labor force participation rate. In this case, the percentage change in EFW index was weakly significant at the 10% level. In this light, the change in EFW index is used in place of the average level, which has proven to be statistically insignificant.

Table 4.2 reveals the results of using a specification derived from the above discussion to explain the level of the UNDP's measure of the female labor force participation rate. The mean value of female labor force participation in this sample was about 58%. Additionally, the ratio of female-to-male labor force participation rates is also used as an explanatory variable (the male variable is available from the same UNDP report). The mean value of this ratio indicates that the average female labor force participation rate is only 72% that of men.

When controlling for income, the percentage change in the EFW index is significant at the 10% level for the female labor force participation rate equation, and significant at the 5% for the ratio of female-to-male participation rates equation. An increase in the percentage change of the EFW index of one percentage point increases the female labor force participation rate by 0.13, and increases the ratio of female-to-male participation rates by 0.18. Given that the average change in the EFW index in the sample was 14%, this implies that the average increase in the level of economic freedom across countries from 1995 to 2008 has improved female labor force participation by 1.8% (14 times 0.13) and improved the ratio of female-to-male participation rates by 2.5% (14 times 0.18).

Conclusion

Would a woman living in a relatively more market-based society find that the institutional characteristics of economic freedom tend to support or hinder her pursuit of a better life? Using the United Nations Development Project data on women's well-being, this empirical examination yields some encouraging evidence. Women living in countries exhibiting more economic freedom appear to enjoy higher levels of well-being.

This conclusion is supported by examining the correlation between the value of the EFW index and the various socioeconomic measures of the Gender Inequality Index (GI index) used by the United Nations Development Project (UNDP, 2010). This index is designed to reflect the degree of progress that each country has made in promoting the well-being of women. It is made up of five components collated into three categories: Reproductive Health (maternal mortality and adolescent fertility), Empowerment (female parliamentary representation and educational attainment), and Labor Market (female labor force participation rate).

First, examining simple histograms of the GI index and its components with the average level of EFW index between 1995 and 2008 revealed beneficial correlations existed for all but the female labor force participation rate. Second, simple regression analysis results indicated that, even when controlling for cross-country differences in income, religious influences, and geographical regions, the level of economic freedom appears to exert a beneficial influence over the GI index, as well as over four of its five components (again excepting female labor force participation rates). Third, when the percentage increase in the EFW index over the same period is used in place of the level of EFW index, and other pertinent control variables were included based on models used in the economic development literature, increases in the EFW index were found to improve the labor force participation rate of women, as well as improve the ratio of female-to-male labor force participation rates.

For example, when considering the direct influences (after controlling for cross-country differences in per-capita incomes) exhibited by economic freedom in a country, a one-point increase in the average EFW index was found to be associated with:

- a decline in the UNDP Gender Inequality (GI) index of 0.03 when the sample average is 0.53;

- a decline in the maternal death rate by 131 women per 100,000 births when the sample average is 300;

- a reduction of over six births per 1,000 births to females age 15–19 when the sample average is 53;

- an increase of almost five percentage points in the percentage of women with a secondary education when the sample average is 52%;

- an increase of two percentage points in the number of women holding seats in parliament in the legislative branch of a national government when the sample average is 18%.

Clearly, the regression specifications used in this empirical analysis to explain observed variation in the GI index components can be improved upon, by using unique specifications pertaining to each particular measure of women's well-being. The above empirical analyses simply illustrates that a more thorough investigation is warranted into the apparently beneficial relationship between economic freedom and women's well-being.

Appendix: List of the countries and the regression equations in which they were included

All countries were included for which data were available for all variables employed in each regression analysis.

	Equations						
Albania	1	2	3	3	4	5	
Algeria	1	2	3	3	4	5	6
Argentina	1	2	3	3	4	5	6
Australia	1	2	3	3	4	5	6
Austria	1	2	3	3	4	5	6
Bahamas		2		3	4	5	
Bahrain	1	2	3	3	4	5	
Bangladesh	1	2	3	3	4	5	6
Belgium	1	2	3	3	4	5	6
Belize	1	2	3	3	4	5	6
Benin	1	2	3	3	4	5	6
Bolivia	1	2	3	3	4	5	6
Botswana	1	2	3	3	4	5	6
Brazil	1	2	3	3	4	5	6
Bulgaria	1	2	3	3	4	5	
Burundi	1	2	3	3	4	5	6
Cameroon	1	2	3	3	4	5	6
Canada	1	2	3	3	4	5	
Central African Rep.	1	2	3	3	4	5	6
Chad		2		3	4	5	
Chile	1	2	3	3	4	5	6
China	1	2	3	3	4	5	6
Colombia	1	2	3	3	4	5	6
Congo, Dem. Republic	1	2	3	3	4	5	
Congo, Republic	1	2	3	3	4	5	6
Costa Rica	1	2	3	3	4	5	6
Côte d'Ivoire	1	2	3	3	4	5	6
Croatia	1	2	3	3	4	5	6
Cyprus	1	2	3	3	4	5	6

	Equations						
Czech Republic	1	2	3	3	4	5	6
Denmark	1	2	3	3	4	5	6
Dominican Republic	1	2	3	3	4	5	6
Ecuador	1	2	3	3	4	5	
Egypt	1	2	3	3	4	5	6
El Salvador	1	2	3	3	4	5	6
Estonia	1	2	3	3	4	5	6
Fiji			3	3	4	5	6
Finland	1	2	3	3	4	5	6
France	1	2	3	3	4	5	
Germany	1	2	3	3	4	5	6
Ghana	1	2	3	3	4	5	6
Greece	1	2	3	3	4	5	
Guatemala	1	2	3	3	4	5	6
Guinea-Bissau		2		3	4	5	
Guyana	1	2	3	3	4	5	6
Haiti	1	2	3	3	4	5	
Honduras	1	2	3	3	4	5	6
Hong Kong			3		4	5	6
Hungary	1	2	3	3	4	5	6
Iceland	1	2	3	3	4	5	
India	1	2	3	3	4	5	6
Indonesia	1	2	3	3	4	5	6
Iran	1	2	3	3	4	5	6
Ireland	1	2	3	3	4	5	6
Israel	1	2	3	3	4	5	
Italy	1	2	3	3	4	5	6
Jamaica	1	2	3	3	4	5	6
Japan	1	2	3	3	4	5	

Appendix, continued: List of the countries and the regression equations in which they were included

All countries were included for which data were available for all variables employed in each regression analysis.

	Equations									Equations						
Jordan	1	2	3	3	4	5	6	Romania	1	2	3	3	4	5	6
Kenya	1	2	3	3	4	5	6	Russia	1	2	3	3	4	5	
Korea, South	1	2	3	3	4	5	6	Rwanda	1	2	3	3	4	5	6
Kuwait	1	2	3	3	4	5		Senegal	1	2	3	3	4	5	6
Latvia	1	2	3	3	4	5	6	Sierra Leone	1	2	3	3	4	5	
Lithuania	1	2	3	3	4	5	6	Singapore	1	2	3	3	4	5	6
Luxem.	1	2	3	3	4	5	6	Slovak Republic	1	2	3	3	4	5	6
Madagascar		2		3	4	5		Slovenia	1	2	3	3	4	5	6
Malawi	1	2	3	3	4	5	6	South Africa	1	2	3	3	4	5	6
Malaysia	1	2	3	3	4	5	6	Spain	1	2	3	3	4	5	6
Mali	1	2	3	3	4	5	6	Sri Lanka	1	2	3	3	4	5	6
Malta	1	2	3	3	4	5		Sweden	1	2	3	3	4	5	6
Mauritius	1	2	3	3	4	5	6	Switzerland	1	2	3	3	4	5	
Mexico	1	2	3	3	4	5	6	Syria	1	2	3	3	4	5	6
Morocco	1	2	3	3	4	5	6	Tanzania		2		3	4	5	
Namibia	1	2	3	3	4	5	6	Thailand	1	2	3	3	4	5	6
Nepal	1	2	3	3	4	5	6	Togo	1	2	3	3	4	5	6
Netherlands	1	2	3	3	4	5	6	Trinidad & Tobago	1	2	3	3	4	5	6
New Zealand	1	2	3	3	4	5		Tunisia	1	2	3	3	4	5	6
Nicaragua	1	2	3	3	4	5	6	Turkey	1	2	3	3	4	5	6
Norway	1	2	3	3	4	5	6	Uganda	1	2	3	3	4	5	6
Pakistan	1	2	3	3	4	5	6	Ukraine	1	2	3	3	4	5	6
Panama	1	2	3	3	4	5	6	United Arab Emirates	1	2	3	3	4	5	6
Papua New Guinea	1	2	3	3	4	5	6	United Kingdom	1	2	3	3	4	5	6
Paraguay	1	2	3	3	4	5	6	United States	1	2	3	3	4	5	6
Peru	1	2	3	3	4	5	6	Uruguay	1	2	3	3	4	5	6
Philippines	1	2	3	3	4	5	6	Venezuela	1	2	3	3	4	5	6
Poland	1	2	3	3	4	5	6	Zambia	1	2	3	3	4	5	6
Portugal	1	2	3	3	4	5	6	Zimbabwe	1	2	3	3	4	5	6

References

Blau, Francine, Marianne Ferber, and Anne Winkler (2006). *The Economics of Women, Men and Work*. Fifth Edition. Pearson-Prentice Hall.

Dawson, John (1998). Institutions, Investment and Growth: New Cross-Country and Panel Data Evidence. *Economic Inquiry* 36, 4: 603–19.

Esposito, Alfredo, and Peter Zaleski (1999). Economic Freedom and the Quality of Life. *Constitutional Political Economy* 10: 185–97.

Gartzke, Erik (2007). The Capitalist Peace. *American Journal of Political Science* 51, 1: 166–91.

Gibson-Graham, J.K. (1996). *The End of Capitalism (As We Knew It): A Feminist Critique of Political Economy*. Blackwell.

Gwartney, James, Joshua Hall, and Robert Lawson (2010). *Economic Freedom of the World: 2010 Report*. Fraser Institute.

Gwartney, James, Randall Holcombe, and Robert Lawson (1999). Economic Freedom and the Environment for Growth. *Journal of Institutional and Theoretical Economics* 155, 4: 1–21.

Gwartney, James, Robert Lawson, and Randall Holcombe (2006). Institutions and the Impact of Investment on Growth. *Kyklos* 59, 2: 255–76.

Hall, Joshua, Russell Sobel, and George Crowley (2010). Institutions, Capital and Growth. *Southern Economic Journal* 77, 2: 385–405.

Norton, Seth (1998). Poverty, Property Rights and Human Well-being: A Cross-national Study. *Cato Journal* 18, 2: 233–45.

Norton, Seth (2003). Economic Institutions and Human Well-Being: A Cross-National Analysis. *Eastern Economic Journal* 29, 1: 23–40.

Palaez, Rolando (2009). Economic Freedom: A Comparative Study. *Journal of Economics and Finance* 33, 3: 246–58.

Posner, Richard (2009). *A Failure of Capitalism: The Crisis of '08 and the Descent into Depression*. Harvard University Press.

Sculy, G.W. (2002). Economic Freedom, Government Policy and the Trade-Off between Equity and Economic Growth. *Public Choice* 113, 1-2: 7–96.

Stiglitz, Joseph (1996). *Whither Socialism?* MIT Press.

Stiglitz, Joseph (2002). Employment, Social Justice and Societal Wellbeing. *International Labor Review* 141: 9–29.

Stiglitz, Joseph, Jose Antonio Ocampo, Shari Spiegel, Ricardo French-Davis, and Deepak Nayyar (2006). *Stability with Growth: Macroeconomics, Liberalization and Development*. Oxford University Press.

Stroup, Michael D. (2007). Economic Freedom, Democracy and the Quality of Life: An Empirical Analysis. *World Development* 35, 1: 52–66.

Stroup, Michael D. (2008). Separating the Influence of Capitalism and Democracy on Women's Well-Being. *Journal of Economic Behavior and Organization* 67, 3-4: 560–72.

United Nations Development Program [UNDP] (2010). *Human Development Report: 2010*. Oxford University Press. Also available on-line at <http://hdr.undp.org/en>.

World Bank (2000). Removing Social Barriers and Building Social Institutions. In *World Development Report, 2000/2001: Attacking Poverty* (World Bank, 2000): 177–31.

World Bank (2010). *World Development Indicators*. CD-ROM. World Bank.

Appendix
Explanatory Notes and Data Sources

Area 1: Size of Government: Expenditures, Taxes, and Enterprises

A General government consumption spending

This component is measured as general government consumption spending as a percentage of total consumption. The rating for this component is equal to: $(V_{max} - V_i) / (V_{max} - V_{min})$ multiplied by 10. The V_i is the country's actual government consumption as a proportion of total consumption, while the V_{max} and V_{min} were set at 40 and 6 respectively. The 1990 data were used to derive the maximum and minimum values for this component. Countries with a larger proportion of government expenditures received lower ratings. In contrast, as the ratio approaches the maximum value, the ratio moves toward zero. • **Sources** World Bank, *World Development Indicators* (various issues); International Monetary Fund, *International Financial Statistics* (various issues); United Nations National Accounts.

B Transfers and subsidies as a percentage of GDP

This component is measured as general government transfers and subsidies as a share of GDP. The rating for this component is equal to: $(V_{max} - V_i) / (V_{max} - V_{min})$ multiplied by 10. The V_i is the country's ratio of transfers and subsidies to GDP, while the V_{max} and V_{min} values are set at 37.2 and 0.5 respectively. The 1990 data were used to derive the maximum and minimum values for this component. The formula will generate lower ratings for countries with larger transfer sectors. When the size of a country's transfer sector approaches that of the country with the largest transfer sector during the 1990 benchmark year, the rating of the country will approach zero. • **Sources** International Monetary Fund, *Government Finance Statistics Yearbook* (various years); World Bank, *World Development Indicators* (various issues); International Monetary Fund, *International Financial Statistics* (various issues); United Nations National Accounts.

C Government enterprises and investment

Data on the number, composition, and share of output supplied by State-Operated Enterprises (SOEs) and government investment as a share of total investment were used to construct the zero-to-10 ratings. Countries with more government enterprises and government investment received lower ratings. When there were few SOEs and government investment was generally less than 15% of total investment, countries were given a rating of 10. When there were few SOEs other than those involved in industries where economies of scale reduce the effectiveness of competition (e.g., power generation) and government investment was between 15% and 20% of the total, countries received a rating of 8. When there were, again, few SOEs other than those involved in energy and other such industries and government investment was between 20% and 25% of the total, countries were rated at 7. When SOEs were present in the energy, transportation, and communication sectors of the economy and government investment was between 25% and 30% of the total, countries were assigned a rating of 6. When a substantial number of SOEs operated in many sectors, including manufacturing, and government investment was generally between 30% and 40% of the total, countries received a rating of 4. When numerous SOEs operated in many sectors, including retail sales, and government investment was between 40% and 50% of the total, countries were rated at 2. A rating of zero was assigned when the economy was dominated by SOEs and government investment exceeded 50% of total investment. In some cases, this rating was estimated from the *Global Competitiveness Report* questions: "State-owned enterprises in your country: (1 = Play a dominant role in the economy ; 7 = Have little or no role in the economy)", and "State-owned enterprises in your country: (1 = Are heavily favoured over private sector competitors ; 7 = Compete on an equal basis with the private sector)." • **Sources** International Monetary Fund, *Government Finance Statistics Yearbook* (various issues); World Bank, *World Development Indicators* (various issues); International Monetary Fund, *International Finance Statistics* (various issues); World Economic Forum, *Global Competitiveness Report* (various issues); United Nations National Accounts; European Bank for Reconstruction and Development, Transition Indicators.

D Top marginal tax rate

i Top marginal income tax rate

Countries with higher marginal tax rates that take effect at lower income thresholds received lower ratings based on the matrix below. The income threshold data were converted from local currency to 1982/1984 US dollars (using beginning-of-year exchange rates and the US Consumer Price Index). These figures include sub-national rates if applicable.

ii Top marginal income and payroll tax rates

Countries with higher marginal income and payroll (wage) tax rates that take effect at lower income thresholds received lower ratings based on the matrix below. The income threshold data were converted from local currency to 1982/1984 US dollars (using beginning-of-year exchange rates and the US Consumer Price Index). These figures include sub-national rates if applicable.

Top Marginal Tax Rate	Income Threshold at Which the Top Marginal Rate Applies (1982–1984 US$)			
	< $25,000	$25,000 – $50,000	$50,000 – $150,000	> $150,000
< 20%	10	10	10	10
21% – 25%	9	9	10	10
26% – 30%	8	8	9	9
31% – 35%	7	7	8	9
36% – 40%	5	6	7	8
41% – 45%	4	5	6	7
46% – 50%	3	4	5	5
51% – 55%	2	3	4	4
56% – 60%	1	2	3	3
61% – 65%	0	1	2	2
66% – 70%	0	0	1	1
> 70%	0	0	0	0

Sources PricewaterhouseCoopers, *Worldwide Tax Summaries Online*, <http://www.pwc.com/extweb/pwcpublications.nsf/doc id/9B2B76032544964C8525717E00606CBD>; PricewaterhouseCoopers, *Individual Taxes: A Worldwide Summary* (various issues).

Area 2: Legal Structure and Security of Property Rights

Note The ratings for Area 2 from 1970 to 1995 are the same as the Area V ratings from *Economic Freedom of the World: 2001 Annual Report*. Please see that report for methodological details.

A Judicial independence

This component is from the *Global Competitiveness Report* question: "Is the judiciary in your country independent from political influences of members of government, citizens, or firms? No—heavily influenced (= 1) or Yes—entirely independent (= 7)." The question's wording has varied slightly over the years. All variables from the *Global Competitiveness Report* were converted from the original 1-to-7 scale to a 0-to-10 scale using this formula: $EFW_i = ((GCR_i - 1) \div 6) \times 10$. • **Source** World Economic Forum, *Global Competitiveness Report* (various issues), <http://www.weforum.org/en/initiatives/gcp/index.htm>.

B Impartial courts

This component is from the *Global Competitiveness Report* question: "The legal framework in your country for private businesses to settle disputes and challenge the legality of government actions and/or regulations is inefficient and subject to manipulation (= 1) or is efficient and follows a clear, neutral process (= 7)." The question's wording has varied slightly over the years. • **Note** The "Rule of Law" ratings from the World Bank's Governance Indicators Project have been used to fill in countries omitted in the primary data source since 1995. • **Sources** World Economic Forum, *Global Competitiveness Report* (various issues), <http://www.weforum.org/en/initiatives/gcp/index.htm>; World Bank, *Governance Indicators* (various years), <http://www.worldbank.org/wbi/governance/govdata/>.

Area V ratings from *Economic Freedom of the World: 2001 Annual Report*

V a • Countries with more secure property rights received higher ratings. The data for 1999 are from the IMD, *World Competitiveness Report, 2000*. No reliable data were available for 1995. The data from 1980 to 1990 are from PRS Group, *International Country Risk Guide* (various issues). The 1970 and 1975 data are from Business Environment Risk Intelligence (BERI). The ICRG did not provide ratings for Barbados, Benin, Burundi, Central African Republic, Chad, Estonia, Latvia, Lithuania, Mauritius, Slovenia and Ukraine. We rated these countries based on the ratings for similar countries (in parentheses): for Barbados (Bahamas), Mauritius (Botwsana), Estonia, Latvia, and Lithuania (Poland and Russia), Slovenia (Czech Republic and Slovakia), Ukraine (Bulgaria and Russia), Benin, Burundi, Central African Republic, and Chad (Cameroon, Republic of Congo, Gabon, Mali, and Niger). • While the original rating scale for the ICRG data was zero to 10, BERI data were on a one-to-four scale. We used regression analysis from the two sources during the initial overlapping year 1982 to merge the two data sets and place the 1970 and 1975 ratings on a scale comparable to that used for the other years. Likewise, regression analysis between the 1999 IMD data and the 1990 ICRG data was used to splice in the new data set. • Because of inconsistencies in the ICRG ratings over time, all ratings were adjusted using the maximum and minimum procedure used in other components in order to make the component consistent over time. The following formula was used to place the figures on a 0-to-10 scale: $(V_i - V_{min})/(V_{max} - V_{min})$ multiplied by 10. V_i is the country's actual value for the component. V_{max} and V_{min} were set at 10 and 2 standard deviations below the average, respectively. • **Sources** IMD, *World Competitiveness Report, 2000*; PRS Group, *International Country Risk Guide* (various issues), and Business Environment Risk Intelligence.

V b • Countries with legal institutions that were more supportive of rule of law received higher ratings. The data from 1980 to 1999 on the rule of law are from PRS Group, *International Country Risk Guide* (various issues). In certain years, the ICRG did not provide ratings for Barbados, Benin, Burundi, Central African Republic, Chad, Estonia, Latvia, Lithuania, Mauritius, Slovenia and Ukraine. In those cases, we rated these countries based on the ratings for similar countries (in parentheses): Barbados (Bahamas), Mauritius (Botwsana), Estonia, Latvia, and Lithuania (Poland and Russia), Slovenia (Czech Republic and Slovakia), Ukraine (Bulgaria and Russia), Benin, Burundi, Central African Republic, and Chad (Cameroon, Republic of Congo, Gabon, Mali, and Niger). • Because of inconsistencies in the ICRG ratings over time, all ratings were adjusted each year using the maximum and minimum procedure used in other components in order to make the component more consistent over time. The following formula was used to place the figures on a 0-to-10 scale: $(V_i - V_{min})/(V_{max} - V_{min})$ multiplied by 10. V_i is the country's actual value for the component. V_{max} and V_{min} were set at 10 and 2 standard deviations below the average, respectively. • **Source** PRS Group, *International Country Risk Guide* (various issues).

C   Protection of property rights

This component is from the *Global Competitiveness Report* question: "Property rights, including over financial assets, are poorly defined and not protected by law (= 1) or are clearly defined and well protected by law (= 7)."   •   **Note** This replaces previous *Global Competitiveness Report* question on protection of intellectual property.   •   **Source** World Economic Forum, *Global Competitiveness Report* (various issues), <http://www.weforum.org/en/initiatives/gcp/index.htm>.

D   Military interference in rule of law and the political process

This component is based on the *International Country Risk Guide*, Political Risk Component G., Military in Politics: "A measure of the military's involvement in politics. Since the military is not elected, involvement, even at a peripheral level, diminishes democratic accountability. Military involvement might stem from an external or internal threat, be symptomatic of underlying difficulties, or be a full-scale military takeover. Over the long term, a system of military government will almost certainly diminish effective governmental functioning, become corrupt, and create an uneasy environment for foreign businesses."   •   **Note** The "Political Stability and Absence of Violence" ratings from the World Bank's Governance Indicators Project have been used to fill in countries omitted in the primary data source since 1995.   •   **Sources** PRS Group, *International Country Risk Guide* (various issues), <http://www.prsgroup.com/ICRG.aspx>; World Bank, *Governance Indicators* (various years), <http://www.worldbank.org/wbi/governance/govdata/>.

E   Integrity of the legal system

This component is based on the *International Country Risk Guide,* Political Risk Component I., for Law and Order: "Two measures comprising one risk component. Each sub-component equals half of the total. The 'law' sub-component assesses the strength and impartiality of the legal system, and the 'order' sub-component assesses popular observance of the law."   •   **Source** PRS Group, *International Country Risk Guide* (various issues), <http://www.prsgroup.com/ICRG.aspx>.

F   Legal enforcement of contracts

This component is based on the World Bank's *Doing Business* estimates for the time and money required to collect a clear-cut debt. The debt is assumed to equal 200% of the country's per-capita income where the plaintiff has complied with the contract and judicial judgment is rendered in his favor. Zero-to-10 ratings were constructed for (1) the time cost (measured in number of calendar days required from the moment the lawsuit is filed until payment) and (2) the monetary cost of the case (measured as a percentage of the debt). These two ratings were then averaged to arrive at the final rating for this sub-component. The formula used to calculate the zero-to-10 ratings was: $(V_{max} - V_i) / (V_{max} - V_{min})$ multiplied by 10. V_i represents the time or money cost value. The values for V_{max} and V_{min} were set at 725 days and 82.3% (1.5 standard deviations above average) and 62 days (1.5 standard deviations below average) and 0%, respectively. Countries with values outside the range marked off by V_{max} and V_{min} received ratings of either zero or ten, accordingly.   •   **Source** World Bank, *Doing Business* (various issues), <http://www.doingbusiness.org/>.

G   Regulatory restrictions on the sale of real property

This sub-component is based on the World Bank's *Doing Business* data on the time measured in days and monetary costs required to transfer ownership of property that includes land and a warehouse. Zero-to-10 ratings were constructed for (1) the time cost (measured in number of calendar days required to transfer ownership) and (2) the monetary cost of transferring ownership (measured as a percentage of the property value). These two ratings were then averaged to arrive at the final rating for this sub-component. The formula used to calculate the zero-to-10 ratings was: $(V_{max} - V_i) / (V_{max} - V_{min})$ multiplied by 10. V_i represents the time or money cost value. The values for V_{max} and V_{min} were set at 265 days and 15% (1.5 standard deviations above average) and 0 days and 0%, respectively. Countries with values outside the range marked off by V_{max} and V_{min} received ratings of either zero or ten, accordingly.   •   **Source** World Bank, *Doing Business* (various issues), <http://www.doingbusiness.org/>.

Area 3: Access to Sound Money

A Money growth

The component measures the average annual growth of the money supply in the last five years minus average annual growth of real GDP in the last ten years. The M1 money supply figures were used to measure the growth rate of the money supply. The rating is equal to: $(V_{max} - V_i) / (V_{max} - V_{min})$ multiplied by 10. V_i represents the average annual growth rate of the money supply during the last five years adjusted for the growth of real GDP during the previous ten years. The values for V_{min} and V_{max} were set at zero and 50%, respectively. Therefore, if the adjusted growth rate of the money supply during the last five years was zero, indicating that money growth was equal to the long-term growth of real output, the formula generates a rating of 10. Ratings decline as the adjusted growth in the money supply increases toward 50%. When the adjusted annual money growth is equal to (or greater than) 50% a rating of zero results.   •   **Sources** World Bank, *World Development Indicators* (various issues); International Monetary Fund, *International Financial Statistics* (various issues); United Nations National Accounts.

B Standard deviation of inflation

The component measures the standard deviation of the inflation rate over the last five years. Generally, the GDP deflator was used as the measure of inflation for this component. When these data were unavailable, the Consumer Price Index was used. The following formula was used to determine the zero-to-10 scale rating for each country: $(V_{max} - V_i) / (V_{max} - V_{min})$ multiplied by 10. V_i represents the country's standard deviation of the annual rate of inflation during the last five years. The values for V_{min} and V_{max} were set at zero and 25%, respectively. This procedure will allocate the highest ratings to the countries with least variation in the annual rate of inflation. A perfect 10 results when there is no variation in the rate of inflation over the five-year period. Ratings will decline toward zero as the standard deviation of the inflation rate approaches 25% annually.   •   **Sources** World Bank, *World Development Indicators* (various issues); International Monetary Fund, *International Financial Statistics* (various issues).

C Inflation: Most recent year

Generally, the CPI was used as the measure of inflation for this component. When these data were unavailable, the GDP deflator inflation rate was used. The zero-to-10 country ratings were derived by the following formula: $(V_{max} - V_i) / (V_{max} - V_{min})$ multiplied by 10. V_i represents the rate of inflation during the most recent year. The values for V_{min} and V_{max} were set at zero and 50%, respectively—the lower the rate of inflation, the higher the rating. Countries that achieve perfect price stability earn a rating of 10. As the inflation rate moves toward a 50% annual rate, the rating for this component moves toward zero. A zero rating is assigned to all countries with an inflation rate of 50% or more.   •   **Sources** World Bank, *World Development Indicators* (various issues); International Monetary Fund, *International Financial Statistics* (various issues).

D Freedom to own foreign currency bank accounts

When foreign currency bank accounts were permissible without restrictions both domestically and abroad, the rating was 10; when these accounts were restricted, the rating was zero. If foreign currency bank accounts were permissible domestically but not abroad (or vice versa), the rating was 5.   •   **Source** International Monetary Fund, *Annual Report on Exchange Arrangements and Exchange Restrictions* (various issues).

Area 4: Freedom to Trade Internationally

A Taxes on international trade

i International trade tax revenues (% of trade sector)

This sub-component measures the amount paid in taxes on international trade as a share of exports and imports. The formula used to calculate the ratings for this sub-component was: $(V_{max} - V_i) / (V_{max} - V_{min})$ multiplied by 10. V_i represents the revenue derived from taxes on international trade as a share of the trade sector. The values for V_{min} and V_{max} were set at zero and 15%, respectively. This formula leads to lower ratings as the average tax rate on international trade increases. Countries with no specific taxes on international trade earn a perfect 10. As the revenues from these taxes rise toward 15% of international trade, ratings decline toward zero. • **Note** Except for two or three extreme observations, the revenues from taxes on international trade as a share of the trade sector are within the zero-to-15% range.) • **Sources** International Monetary Fund, *Government Finance Statistics Yearbook* (various issues); International Monetary Fund, *International Financial Statistics* (various issues).

ii Mean tariff rate

This sub-component is based on the unweighted mean of tariff rates. The formula used to calculate the zero-to-10 rating for each country was: $(V_{max} - V_i) / (V_{max} - V_{min})$ multiplied by 10. V_i represents the country's mean tariff rate. The values for V_{min} and V_{max} were set at 0% and 50%, respectively. This formula will allocate a rating of 10 to countries that do not impose tariffs. As the mean tariff rate increases, countries are assigned lower ratings. The rating will decline toward zero as the mean tariff rate approaches 50%. • **Note** Except for two or three extreme observations, all countries have mean tariff rates within this range from 0% to 50%.) • **Sources** World Trade Organization, *World Tariff Profiles* (various issues).

iii Standard deviation of tariff rates

Compared to a uniform tariff, wide variation in tariff rates exerts a more restrictive impact on trade and, therefore, on economic freedom. Thus, countries with greater variation in their tariff rates should be given lower ratings. The formula used to calculate the zero-to-10 ratings for this component was: $(V_{max} - V_i) / (V_{max} - V_{min})$ multiplied by 10. V_i represents the standard deviation of the country's tariff rates. The values for V_{min} and V_{max} were set at 0% and 25%, respectively. This formula will allocate a rating of 10 to countries that impose a uniform tariff. As the standard deviation of tariff rates increases toward 25%, ratings decline toward zero. • **Note** Except for a few very extreme observations, the standard deviations of the tariff rates for the countries in our study fall within this 0%-to-25% range.) • **Source** World Trade Organization, *World Tariff Profiles* (various issues).

B Regulatory Trade Barriers

i Non-tariff trade barriers

This sub-component is based on the *Global Competitiveness Report* survey question: "In your country, tariff and non-tariff barriers significantly reduce the ability of imported goods to compete in the domestic market." The question's wording has varied slightly over the years. • **Source** World Economic Forum, *Global Competitiveness Report* (various issues), <http://www.weforum.org/en/initiatives/gcp/index.htm>.

ii Compliance cost of importing and exporting

This sub-component is based on the World Bank's *Doing Business* data on the time (i.e., non-money) cost of procedures required to export or import a full, 20-foot container of dry goods that contains no hazardous or military items. Countries where it takes longer to export or import are given lower ratings. Zero-to-10 ratings were constructed for (1) the time cost to export a good (measured in number of calendar days required) and (2) the time cost to import a good (measured in number of calendar days required). These two ratings were then averaged to arrive at the final rating for this sub-component. The formula used to calculate the zero-to-10 ratings was: $(V_{max} - V_i) / (V_{max} - V_{min})$ multiplied by 10. V_i represents the time cost value. The values for V_{max}

and V_{min} were set at 62 (export) and 80 (import) days (1.5 standard deviations above average) and 2 (export) days (1.5 standard deviations below average) and 0 (import) days. Countries with values outside of the V_{max} and V_{min} range received ratings of either zero or ten, accordingly.   •   **Source** World Bank, *Doing Business* (various issues), http://www.doingbusiness.org/.

C   Size of the trade sector relative to expected

Regression analysis was used to derive an expected size of the trade sector based on the population and geographic size of the country and its location relative to the concentration of world GDP. The actual size of the trade sector was then compared with the expected size for the country. If the actual size of the trade sector is greater than expected, this figure will be positive. If it is less than expected, the number will be negative. The percent change of the negative numbers was adjusted to make it symmetrical with the percent change of the positive numbers. The following formula was used to place the figures on a zero-to-10 scale: $(V_i - V_{min}) / (V_{max} - V_{min})$ multiplied by 10. V_i is the country's actual value for the component. V_{max} and V_{min} were set at 100% and minus 50%, respectively. (**Note** Minus 50% is symmetrical with positive 100%.) This procedure allocates higher ratings to countries with large trade sectors compared to what would be expected, given their population, geographic size, and location. On the other hand, countries with small trade sectors relative to the expected size receive lower ratings. Additional details are available in the short paper: Joshua C. Hall, Robert Lawson, and Chuck Skipton, Estimating the Size of the Trade Sector in the Economic Freedom of the World Index, *Economics Bulletin* 31, 1 (2011): 466–72; <http://www.accessecon.com/Pubs/EB/2011/Volume31/EB-11-V31-I1-P45.pdf>   •   **Sources** World Bank, *World Development Indicators* (various issues); International Monetary Fund, *International Financial Statistics* (various issues); United Nations National Accounts.

D   Black-market exchange rates

This component is based on the percentage difference between the official and the parallel (black) market exchange rate. The formula used to calculate the zero-to-10 ratings for this component was the following: $(V_{max} - V_i) / (V_{max} - V_{min})$ multiplied by 10. V_i is the country's black-market exchange rate premium. The values for V_{min} and V_{max} were set at 0% and 50%, respectively. This formula will allocate a rating of 10 to countries without a black-market exchange rate; that is, those with a domestic currency that is fully convertible without restrictions. When exchange-rate controls are present and a black market exists, the ratings will decline toward zero as the black market premium increases toward 50%. A zero rating is given when the black market premium is equal to, or greater than, 50%.   •   **Sources** *MRI Bankers' Guide to Foreign Currency* (various issues).

E   International capital market controls

i   Foreign ownership/investment restrictions

This sub-component is based on the following two *Global Competitiveness Report* questions: "How prevalent is foreign ownership of companies in your country? 1 = Very rare , 7 = Highly prevalent"; and "How restrictive are regulations in your country relating to international capital flows? 1 = Highly restrictive, 7 = Not restrictive at all".   •   **Source** World Economic Forum, *Global Competitiveness Report* (various issues), <http://www.weforum.org/en/initiatives/gcp/index.htm>.

ii   Capital controls

The International Monetary Fund reports on up to 13 types of international capital controls. The zero-to-10 rating is the percentage of capital controls not levied as a share of the total number of capital controls listed, multiplied by 10.   •   **Source** International Monetary Fund, *Annual Report on Exchange Arrangements and Exchange Restrictions* (various issues).

Area 5: Regulation of Credit, Labor, and Business

A   Credit market regulations

i   Ownership of banks

Data on the percentage of bank deposits held in privately owned banks were used to construct rating intervals. Countries with larger shares of privately held deposits received higher ratings. When privately held deposits totaled between 95% and 100%, countries were given a rating of 10. When private deposits constituted between 75% and 95% of the total, a rating of 8 was assigned. When private deposits were between 40% and 75% of the total, the rating was 5. When private deposits totaled between 10% and 40%, countries received a rating of 2. A zero rating was assigned when private deposits were 10% or less of the total.   •   **Sources** James R. Barth, Gerard Caprio, Jr. and Ross Levine, *Bank Regulation and Supervision* (various years); James R. Barth, Gerard Caprio, and Ross Levine, *Rethinking Bank Regulation: Till Angels Govern* (2006).

ii   Foreign bank competition

If a country approved all or most foreign bank applications and if foreign banks had a large share of the banking sector assets, then the country received a higher rating according to table below.

Foreign Bank License Denial Rate (Denials/Applications)

		0%	0%–49%	50%–100%
Foreign bank assets as a share of total banking sector assets	80%–100%	10	8	5
	40%–79%	9	7	4
	0%–39%	8	6	3

Sources James R. Barth, Gerard Caprio, Jr. and Ross Levine, *Bank Regulation and Supervision* (various years); James R. Barth, Gerard Caprio, and Ross Levine, *Rethinking Bank Regulation: Till Angels Govern* (2006).

iii   Private sector credit

This sub-component measures the extent to which government borrowing crowds out private borrowing. If data are available, this sub-component is calculated as the government fiscal deficit as a share of gross saving. Since the deficit is expressed as a negative value, higher numerical values result in higher ratings. The formula used to derive the country ratings for this sub-component was $(-V_{max} - V_i) / (V_{max} + V_{min})$ multiplied by 10. V_i is the ratio of deficit to gross investment, and the values for V_{max} and V_{min} are set at 0 and −100.0% respectively. The formula allocates higher ratings as the deficit gets smaller (i.e., closer to zero) relative to gross saving. If the deficit data are not available, this sub-component is instead based on the share of private credit to total credit extended in the banking sector. Higher values are indicative of greater economic freedom. Thus, the formula used to derive the country ratings for this sub-component was $(V_i - V_{min}) / (V_{max} - V_{min})$ multiplied by 10. V_i is the share of the country's total domestic credit allocated to the private sector and the values for V_{max} and V_{min} are set at 99.9% and 10.0%, respectively. The 1990 data were used to derive the maximum and minimum values for this component. The formula allocates higher ratings as the share of credit extended to the private sector increases.   •   **Note** In previous editions, this component was based only on the ratio of private credit to total credit in the banking sector. The database has been updated back to 1990 using this new methodology.   •   **Sources** World Bank, *World Development Indicators* (various issues); International Monetary Fund, *International Financial Statistics* (various issues).

iv   Interest rate controls / negative real interest rates

Data on credit-market controls and regulations were used to construct rating intervals. Countries with interest rates determined by the market, stable monetary policy, and positive real deposit and lending rates received higher ratings. When interest rates were determined primarily by market forces and the real rates were positive, countries were given a rating of 10. When interest rates were primarily market-determined but the real rates were sometimes slightly negative (less than 5%) or the differential between the deposit and lending rates was large (8% or more), countries received a rating of 8. When the real deposit or lending rate was persistently negative by a single-digit amount or the differential between them was regulated by the government, countries were rated at 6. When the deposit and lending rates were fixed by the government and the real rates were often negative by single-digit amounts, countries were assigned a rating of 4. When the real deposit or lending rate was persistently negative by a double-digit amount, countries received a rating of 2. A zero rating was assigned when the deposit and lending rates were fixed by the government and real rates were persistently negative by double-digit amounts or hyperinflation had virtually eliminated the credit market.   •   **Source** World Bank, *World Development Indicators* (various issues); International Monetary Fund, *International Financial Statistics* (various issues).

B Labor market regulations

i Hiring regulations and minimum wage

This sub-component is based on the World Bank's *Doing Business* Difficulty of Hiring Index, which is described as follows: "The difficulty of hiring index measures (i) whether fixed-term contracts are prohibited for permanent tasks; (ii) the maximum cumulative duration of fixed-term contracts; and (iii) the ratio of the minimum wage for a trainee or first-time employee to the average value added per worker. An economy is assigned a score of 1 if fixed-term contracts are prohibited for permanent tasks and a score of 0 if they can be used for any task. A score of 1 is assigned if the maximum cumulative duration of fixed-term contracts is less than 3 years; 0.5 if it is 3 years or more but less than 5 years; and 0 if fixed-term contracts can last 5 years or more. Finally, a score of 1 is assigned if the ratio of the minimum wage to the average value added per worker is 0.75 or more; 0.67 for a ratio of 0.50 or more but less than 0.75; 0.33 for a ratio of 0.25 or more but less than 0.50; and 0 for a ratio of less than 0.25." Countries with higher difficulty of hiring are given lower ratings.   •   **Source** World Bank, *Doing Business* (various issues), <http://www.doingbusiness.org/>.

ii Hiring and firing regulations

This sub-component is based on the *Global Competitiveness Report* question: "The hiring and firing of workers is impeded by regulations (= 1) or flexibly determined by employers (= 7)." The question's wording has varied slightly over the years.   •   **Source** World Economic Forum, *Global Competitiveness Report* (various issues), <http://www.weforum.org/en/initiatives/gcp/index.htm>.

iii Centralized collective bargaining

This sub-component is based on the *Global Competitiveness Report* question: "Wages in your country are set by a centralized bargaining process (= 1) or up to each individual company (= 7)." The question's wording has varied slightly over the years.   •   **Source** World Economic Forum, *Global Competitiveness Report* (various issues), <http://www.weforum.org/en/initiatives/gcp/index.htm>.

iv Hours regulations

This sub-component is based on the World Bank's *Doing Business* Rigidity of Hours Index, which is described as follows: "The rigidity of hours index has 5 components: (i) whether there are restrictions on night work; (ii) whether there are restrictions on weekly holiday work; (iii) whether the work week can consist of 5.5 days; (iv) whether the work week can extend to 50 hours or more (including overtime) for 2 months a year to respond to a seasonal increase in production; and (v) whether paid annual vacation is 21 working days or fewer. For questions (i) and (ii), when restrictions other than premiums apply, a score of 1 is given. If the only restriction is a premium for night work and weekly holiday work, a score of 0, 0.33, 0.66 or 1 is given according to the quartile in which the economy's premium falls. If there are no restrictions, the economy receives a score of 0. For questions (iii), (iv) and (v), when the answer is no, a score of 1 is assigned; otherwise a score of 0 is assigned."   •   **Note** This component was previously called "Mandated cost of hiring a worker" and was based on the World Bank's *Doing Business* data on the cost of all social security and payroll taxes and the cost of other mandated benefits including those for retirement, sickness, health care, maternity leave, family allowance, and paid vacations and holidays associated with hiring an employee. Because of pressure from the International Labour Organization, this measure was dropped from the *Doing Business* project. In order to maintain as much consistency over time as possible, we have revised the dataset back to 2002 with these data replacing the previous values.   •   **Source** World Bank, *Doing Business* (various issues), <http://www.doingbusiness.org/>.

v   Mandated cost of worker dismissal

This sub-component is based on the World Bank's *Doing Business* data on the cost of the advance notice requirements, severance payments, and penalties due when dismissing a redundant worker. The formula used to calculate the zero-to-10 ratings was: $(V_{max} - V_i) / (V_{max} - V_{min})$ multiplied by 10. V_i represents the dismissal cost (measured in weeks of wages). The values for V_{max} and V_{min} were set at 108 weeks (1.5 standard deviations above average) and 0 weeks, respectively. Countries with values outside the range marked off by V_{max} and V_{min} received ratings of either zero or ten, accordingly.   •   **Source** World Bank, *Doing Business* (various issues), <http://www.doingbusiness.org/>.

vi   Conscription

Data on the use and duration of military conscription were used to construct rating intervals. Countries with longer conscription periods received lower ratings. A rating of 10 was assigned to countries without military conscription. When length of conscription was six months or less, countries were given a rating of 5. When length of conscription was more than six months but not more than 12 months, countries were rated at 3. When length of conscription was more than 12 months but not more than 18 months, countries were assigned a rating of 1. When conscription periods exceeded 18 months, countries were rated zero. If conscription was present, but apparently not strictly enforced or the length of service could not be determined, the country was given a rating of 3. In cases where it is clear conscription is never used, even though it may be possible, a rating of 10 is given. If a country's mandated national service includes clear non-military options, the country was given a rating of 5.   •   **Source** International Institute for Strategic Studies, *The Military Balance* (various issues); War Resisters International, *World Survey of Conscription and Conscientious Objection to Military Service*, <http://www.wri-irg.org/programmes/world_survey/>.

C   Business regulations

i   Price controls

The more widespread the use of price controls, the lower the rating. The survey data of the International Institute for Management Development's (IMD) *World Competitiveness Yearbook* (various editions) were used to rate the countries (mostly developed economies) covered by this report. For other countries, other sources were used to categorize countries. Countries were given a rating of 10 if no price controls or marketing boards were present. When price controls were limited to industries where economies of scale may reduce the effectiveness of competition (e.g., power generation), a country was given a rating of 8. When price controls were applied in only a few other industries, such as agriculture, a country was given a rating of 6. When price controls were levied on energy, agriculture, and many other staple products that are widely purchased by households, a rating of 4 was given. When price controls applied to a significant number of products in both agriculture and manufacturing, the rating was 2. A rating of zero was given when there was widespread use of price controls throughout various sectors of the economy.   •   **Sources** International Institute for Management Development (IMD), *World Competitiveness Yearbook* (various issues), European Bank for Reconstruction and Development, *Transition Indicators*.

ii   Administrative requirements

This sub-component is based on the *Global Competitiveness Report* question: "Complying with administrative requirements (permits, regulations, reporting) issued by the government in your country is (1 = burdensome, 7 = not burdensome)."   •   **Source** World Economic Forum, *Global Competitiveness Report* (various issues), <http://www.weforum.org/en/initiatives/gcp/index.htm>.

iii Bureaucracy costs

This sub-component is based on the *Global Competitiveness Report* question: "Standards on product/service quality, energy and other regulations (outside environmental regulations) in your country are: (1 = Lax or non-existent, 7 = among the world's most stringent)". • **Source** World Economic Forum, *Global Competitiveness Report* (various issues), <http://www.weforum.org/en/initiatives/gcp/index.htm>.

iv Starting a business

This sub-component is based on the World Bank's *Doing Business* data on the amount of time and money it takes to start a new limited-liability business. Countries where it takes longer or is more costly to start a new business are given lower ratings. Zero-to-10 ratings were constructed for three different variables: (1) time (measured in days) necessary to comply with regulations when starting a limited liability company; (2) money costs of the fees paid to regulatory authorities (measured as a share of per-capita income); and (3) minimum capital requirements, that is, funds that must be deposited into a company bank account (measured as a share of per-capita income). These three ratings were then averaged to arrive at the final rating for this sub-component. The formula used to calculate the zero-to-10 ratings was: $(V_{max} - V_i) / (V_{max} - V_{min})$ multiplied by 10. V_i represents the variable value. The values for V_{max} and V_{min} were set at 104 days, 317%, and 1017% (1.5 standard deviations above average) and 0 days, 0%, and 0%, respectively. Countries with values outside the range marked off by V_{max} and V_{min} received ratings of either zero or 10, accordingly. • **Source** World Bank, *Doing Business* (various issues), <http://www.doingbusiness.org/>.

v Extra payments / bribes / favouritism

This sub-component is based on the *Global Competitiveness Report* questions. [1] "In your industry, how commonly would you estimate that firms make undocumented extra payments or bribes connected with the following: A–Import and export permits; B–Connection to public utilities (e.g., telephone or electricity); C—Annual tax payments; D—Awarding of public contracts (investment projects); E—Getting favourable judicial decisions. Common (= 1) Never occur (= 7)"? [2] "Do illegal payments aimed at influencing government policies, laws or regulations have an impact on companies in your country: 1 = Yes, significant negative impact, 7 = No, no impact at all"? [3] "To what extent do government officials in your country show favouritism to well-connected firms and individuals when deciding upon policies and contracts: 1 = Always show favouritism, 7 = Never show favouritism"? • **Source** World Economic Forum, *Global Competitiveness Report* (various issues), <http://www.weforum.org/en/initiatives/gcp/index.htm>.

vi Licensing restrictions

This sub-component is based on the World Bank's *Doing Business* data on the time in days and monetary costs required to obtain a license to construct a standard warehouse. Zero-to-10 ratings were constructed for (1) the time cost (measured in number of calendar days required to obtain a license) and (2) the monetary cost of obtaining the license (measured as a share of per-capita income). These two ratings were then averaged to arrive at the final rating for this sub-component. The formula used to calculate the zero-to-10 ratings was: $(V_{max} - V_i) / (V_{max} - V_{min})$ multiplied by 10. V_i represents the time or money cost value. The values for V_{max} and V_{min} were set at 363 days and 2763% (1.5 standard deviations above average) and 56 days (1.5 standard deviations below average) and 0%, respectively. Countries with values outside the range marked off by V_{max} and V_{min} received ratings of either zero or ten, accordingly. • **Source** World Bank, *Doing Business* (various issues), <http://www.doingbusiness.org/>.

vii Cost of tax compliance

This sub-component is based on the World Bank's *Doing Business* data on the time required per year for a business to prepare, file, and pay taxes on corporate income, value added or sales taxes, and taxes on labor. The formula used to calculate the zero-to-10 ratings was: $(V_{max} - V_i) / (V_{max} - V_{min})$ multiplied by 10. V_i represents the time cost (measured in hours) of tax compliance. The values for V_{max} and V_{min} were set at 892 hours (1.5 standard deviations above average) and 0 hours, respectively. Countries with values outside the range marked off by V_{max} and V_{min} received ratings of either zero or ten, accordingly. • **Source** World Bank, *Doing Business* (various issues), <http://www.doingbusiness.org/>.

About the Authors

James D. Gwartney

James Gwartney holds the Gus A. Stavros Eminent Scholar Chair at Florida State University, where he directs the Stavros Center for the Advancement of Free Enterprise and Economic Education. He is the coauthor of *Economics: Private and Public Choice* (Cengage/South-Western Press, 2011), a widely used principles of economics text that is now in its 13th edition. He is also coauthor of an economics primer, *Common Sense Economics: What Everyone Should Know about Wealth and Prosperity* (St. Martin's Press, 2010). His publications have appeared in both professional journals and popular media such as the *Wall Street Journal* and the *New York Times*. He served as Chief Economist of the Joint Economic Committee of the US Congress during 1999/2000. In 2004, he was the recipient of the Adam Smith Award of the Association of Private Enterprise Education for his contribution to the advancement of free-market ideals. He is a past President of the Southern Economic Association and the Association of Private Enterprise Education. His Ph.D. in economics is from the University of Washington.

Robert A. Lawson

Robert Lawson is the Jerome M. Fullinwider Chair in Economic Freedom in the O'Neil Center for Global Markets and Freedom in the Cox School of Business at Southern Methodist University. Prior to taking a position at SMU, he taught at Auburn University, Capital University, and Shawnee State University. Lawson has numerous professional publications in journals such as *Public Choice, Journal of Economic Behavior and Organization, Cato Journal, Kyklos, Journal of Labor Research, Journal of Institutional and Theoretical Economics*, and *European Journal of Political Economy*. Lawson has served as president of the Association of Private Enterprise Education and is a member of the Mont Pelerin Society. He earned his B.S. in economics from the Honors Tutorial College at Ohio University and his M.S. and Ph.D. in economics from Florida State University.

Joshua C. Hall

Joshua C. Hall is an assistant professor in the Department of Economics and Management at Beloit College in Beloit, Wisconsin. He earned his B.A. and M.A. in economics from Ohio University and his Ph.D. from West Virginia University. Formerly an economist for the Joint Economic Committee of the US Congress, he has published numerous policy studies and professional publications. Professor Hall's research has appeared in journals such as the *Atlantic Economic Journal, Cato Journal, Journal of Economic Behavior and Organization, Journal of Economic Education, Journal of Labor Research, Southern Economic Journal*, and *Public Finance Review*.

About the Contributors

Jean-Pierre Chauffour

Jean-Pierre Chauffour is lead economist in the World Bank's Middle East and North Africa Region, where he works on regionalism, competitiveness, and economic integration issues. Prior to joining the World Bank in 2007, he spent 15 years at the IMF, where he held various positions, including mission chief in the African Department and representative to the WTO and United Nations in Geneva. Mr. Chauffour has extensive economic policy experience and has worked in many areas of the developing world, most extensively in the Middle East, Africa, and Eastern Europe. He holds a master in economics and a master in money, banking, and finance from the Panthéon-Sorbonne University in Paris. He is the author of *The Power of Freedom: Uniting Human Rights and Development* (Cato Institute, 2009) and has recently co-edited two books: *Preferential Trade Agreement Policies for Development: A Handbook* (World Bank, 2011) and *Trade Finance during the Great Trade Collapse* (World Bank, 2011).

Michael Stroup

Michael Stroup is currently a professor of economics at Stephen F. Austin State University (SFASU), where he has also served as Associate Dean of the Rusche College of Business and the Director of the MBA program. He earned his Ph.D. in economics from Florida State University, his M.A. in economics from the University of Washington, and his B.S. in Economics from Montana State University. Professor Stroup has written many articles in scholarly journals, such as *Public Choice, Journal of Economic Behavior and Organization, Kyklos, World Development, Journal of Applied Economics, Journal of Economics and Finance, Applied Financial Economics,* and *Economics Letters.* His latest research focuses on using international panel data to quantify the beneficial impact that economic and political freedoms have on various non-monetary measures of individual well-being in society, particularly in the areas of health, education, women's well-being and the environment. While at SFASU, Professor Stroup taught both undergraduate and graduate economics courses, co-authored two instructor's manuals for Michael Parkin's highly successful principles of economics textbook, and earned teaching excellence and research excellence awards.

Acknowledgments

As always, we are grateful for the intellectual and financial assistance of the Fraser Institute and Brent Skinner, the Institute's president & CEO. Without the assistance and guidance of both Michael Walker, former Executive Director of the Fraser Institute, and the late Milton Friedman, this project would never have gotten off the ground.

The members of the Economic Freedom Network again provided valuable support for this report. Our thanks also go to Kathy Makinen and Joe Connors at Florida State University, both of whom provided us with research assistance. We are grateful for the hard work of many at the Fraser Institute who help with the project, including especially Fred McMahon and Jean-François Minardi. Also, thanks to Ian Vasquez at the Cato Institute for his continued support. Steve Knack (World Bank) and Irene Mia (World Economic Forum) were instrumental in helping secure data from their respective organizations.

Thanks also go to the Charles G. Koch Charitable Foundation and Searle Freedom Trust for their support.

James Gwartney, Robert Lawson & Joshua Hall

About the Members of the Economic Freedom Network

Co-publishers of *Economic Freedom of the World*

Afghanistan • Afghanistan Economic and Legal Studies Organization (AELSO)

AELSO is a non-governmental think-tank that aims to introduce and promote a free-market economy, the rule of law, and good governance to the people of Afghanistan.

e-mail: <ramizpoor@hotmail.com>

Albania • Albanian Center for Economic Research (ACER)

The Albanian Center for Economic Research is a public-policy institute that focuses on research and advocacy. In addition to providing policy-makers and academics with applied economic research, it works to build public understanding of economic development issues.

e-mail: <zpreci@icc-al.org> • website: <http://www.acer.org.al>

Argentina • Fundación Libertad

Fundación Libertad is a private, non-profit institution working towards two main goals: the research and distribution of public-policy issues (specifically in socio-economic and business areas) and the promotion of the concept of a free-market society. Founded in Rosario, Argentina, in 1988 by a group of businessmen, professionals, and intellectuals, the Foundation has developed its activities with the support of more than 200 private companies. Its projects include courses, lectures, seminars, research, studies, and publications as well as a strong permanent presence in the media, through columns, and television and radio programs produced by the Foundation. These projects have focused on economic policies, education, regulations, and public spending. Outstanding guest speakers have delivered lectures and conferences for the Fundación Libertad; these include Peruvian writer Mario Vargas Llosa, Nobel-prize-winning economists such as Gary Becker, Douglass North, Robert Lucas, and James Buchanan, historian Paul Johnson, Nobel Peace Prize Laureate Lech Walesa, and other intellectuals like Jean François Revel. Fundación Libertad has also led the creation of REFUNDAR, a network of Argentine foundations made up of ten organizations, located in the country's major cities. This network has helped us spread our ideas all over the country and is affiliated with similar international organizations.

e-mail: <fundacion@libertad.org.ar> • website: <http://www.libertad.org.ar>

Armenia • Centre of Political, Legal and Economic Researches and Forecasting (PLERF)

PLERF is a non-governmental organization created in 2002. Its mission is to assist the development of an effective socio-economic policy; to establish a free-market-based economy; and to contribute to the development of democracy in the Republic of Armenia. PLERF organizes seminars and conferences related to its goals and carries out research, independent estimations of social and economic reforms, government policy in certain spheres, and assessment of the transition process, and surveys among experts and policy makers.

e-mail: <khachatryanvahagn@yahoo.com>

About the Economic Freedom Network

If you have questions about the Economic Freedom Network, please contact Jean-François Minardi via e-mail to <freetheworld@fraserinstitute.org> or via telephone +1.514.281.9550 ext. 306.

Australia • **Institute of Public Affairs**

Established in 1943, the IPA is Australia's oldest and largest private-sector think-tank. Its aim is to foster prosperity and full employment, the rule of law, democratic freedoms, security from crime and invasion, and high standards in education and family life for the Australian people. To identify and promote the best means of securing these values, the IPA undertakes research, organizes seminars, and publishes widely.

e-mail: ipa@ipa.org.au • website: <http://ipa.org.au>

Austria • **TIGRA®**

TIGRA® is the premier Austrian think-tank on governance research. Headquartered in Salzburg, it was founded to study and advance effective and efficient economic policies. TIGRA® organizes workshops and publishes papers and reports. Their mission is "From analysis to action." TIGRA® is a network of experts who provide effective market solutions to policy-makers. Special emphasis is put on knowledge management, monitoring the scope and quality of regulations ("cutting red tape"), and setting benchmarks.

e-mail: bendl@erwin.tc.

Azerbaijan • **Center for Economic and Political Research**

The Center for Economic and Political Research, Azerbaijan, is a non-profit, non-governmental, research institute founded in 1994. Its mission is to facilitate the country's democratization and economic liberalization and to increase the role of civil society. The main objectives of the Center's activities are analyzing the economic situation and progress of market reforms, political processes, foreign political relations, and regional economic and political tendencies. The Center also conducts sociological surveys and holds conferences, round-tables, and seminars on different aspects of economic and political reforms in the country.

e-mail: cesd.az@gmail.com • website: <http://www.cesd.az/>

Bahamas • **The Nassau Institute**

The Nassau Institute is an independent, non-political, non-profit institute that promotes economic growth, employment, and entrepreneurial activity. It believes that this can best be achieved with a free-market economy and a decent society—one that embraces the rule of law, the right of private property, the free exchange of property and services, and the individual virtues of self-control, commitment, and good will.

e-mail: joan@nassauinstitute.org • website: <http://www.nassauinstitute.org>

Bangladesh • **Making Our Economy Right (MOER)**

MOER, founded in 1991, is the country's lone free-market institute and continues the struggle to promote free-market capitalism against all odds. The concept of individual freedom and free markets determining the supply of goods, services, and capital is little understood in Bangladesh. For the past 50 years or so, Fabian socialism and the doctrines of Karl Marx were the basis of our country's economy. MOER contributes free-market, libertarian articles in English and Bangla newspapers. We also moderate a weekly radio talk show that focuses on liberalization of the economy. MOER also publishes books both in Bangla and in English for free distribution to libraries and others with the support of the International Policy Network of London. MOER's fourth book, published this year, *Clamoring for Free Market Freedom in Bangladesh*, has a foreword by Nobel laureate Milton Friedman. The book is a compilation of articles by Nizam Ahmad.

Belarus • **Scientific Research Mises Center**

Scientific Research Mises Center was founded in 2001. Its mission is to advance ideas and ideals of a free-market democratic society based on individual choice and personal responsibility and to create an open community of people who share those ideas. The Center promotes the original ideas of limited government, individual liberty, and private property through publications and discussion forums and conferences. The goal of the Center is to demonstrate the power of private institutions, both for-profit and non-profit, to create a good society and to foster the understanding that free choice of a fully informed individual is the foundation for a just, prosperous, and open society.

e-mail: liberti@belsonet.net • website: <http://liberty-belarus.info>

Belgium • Centre for the New Europe

The Centre for the New Europe (CNE) is a European research institute based in Brussels that promotes a market economy, personal liberty, and creativity and responsibility in an ordered society. CNE is founded on the belief that European integration can work only in a society led by a spirit of democratic capitalism. The Centre develops policy alternatives, encourages economic growth and deregulation, seeks new market-based solutions for social and environmental concerns, and promotes individual freedom, choice and responsibility.

e-mail: **info@cne.org** • website: <http://www.cne.org>

Bolivia • Política Publicas para la Libertad (POPULI)

POPULI's mission is to generate and promote public policies, in accordance with the country's social and economic realities, within the field of private enterprise, under the principle of state subsidiarity, preserving property rights, human rights, and strengthening the concept of liberty. Its vision is to generate and promote a benchmark of public policies while maintaining institutional independence and a strong commitment to the values of a free society.

e-mail: **populi@populi-bo.org** • website: <http://www.populi.org.bo/>

Brazil • Instituto Liberal do Rio de Janeiro

Instituto Liberal was founded to persuade Brazilians of the advantages of a liberal order. It is a non-profit institution supported by donations and the sponsorship of private individuals and corporations. Its by-laws provide for a Board of Trustees and forbid any political or sectarian affiliations. The institute publishes books, organizes seminars, and elaborates policy papers on subjects related to public policy.

e-mail: **ilrj@gbl.com.br** • website: <http://www.institutoliberal.org.br>

Bulgaria • Institute for Market Economics

Established in 1993, the Institute for Market Economics (IME) is the first independent economic think-tank in Bulgaria. It is a private, registered, non-profit corporation that receives international support and is widely respected for its expertise. IME designs and promotes solutions to the problems that Bulgaria is facing in its transition to a market economy, provides independent assessment and analysis of the government's economic policies, and supports an exchange of views on market economics and relevant policy issues.

e-mail: **mail@ime.bg** • website: <http://www.ime.bg>

Burkina Faso • Le Centre des Affaires Humaines (CEDAH)

Le Centre des Affaires Humaines (CEDAH) is a free-market educational and research public-policy think-tank founded in December 2007 in Burkina Faso. CEDAH is an independent, non-profit organization with no affiliations to any political party. It is financed entirely by contributions from individuals, organizations, and foundations. In order to protect its research independence, it does not accept grants from the government of Burkina Faso or political parties. The mission of CEDAH is to propose original and innovative solutions for the crafting of efficient public policies, using successful reforms applied elsewhere as models. CEDAH studies how markets function with the aim of identifying the mechanisms and institutions that foster the prosperity and long-term welfare of all the individuals that make up our society.

e-mail: **info@cedahburkina.com**

Cambodia • The Cambodia Institute of Development Study

The Cambodia Institute of Development Study (CIDS) is a non-profit, independent, local research institute founded in December 2004. The Institute's mission is to provide high-quality research on the local and provincial levels in the specialized areas of economics, natural resources and environment, agriculture and rural development, and public finance and governance, within the context of world integration. Its objectives are to generate and disseminate research on the national and provincial economies, and to enhance the capacity and promote the professional development of local resources by providing training and practical research opportunities.

e-mail: **info@cids-cambodia.org** • website: <http://www.cids-cambodia.org/>

Canada • **The Fraser Institute**

Our vision is a free and prosperous world where individuals benefit from greater choice, competitive markets, and personal responsibility. Our mission is to measure, study, and communicate the impact of competitive markets and government interventions on the welfare of individuals. Founded in 1974, we are an independent Canadian research and educational organization with locations throughout North America and international partners in over 80 countries. Our work is financed by tax-deductible contributions from thousands of individuals, organizations, and foundations. In order to protect its independence, the Institute does not accept grants from government or contracts for research.

e-mail: info@fraserinstitute.org • websites: <http://www.fraserinstitute.org>, <http://www.freetheworld.com>

Chile • **Instituto Libertad y Desarrollo**

Instituto Libertad y Desarrollo is a private think-tank wholly independent of any religious, political, financial, or governmental groups. It is committed to the free market and to political and economic freedom. It publishes studies and analyses of public-policy issues.

e-mail: lyd@lyd.org • website: <http://www.lyd.com>

China • **Center for China & Globalization**

The Center for China & Globalization (CCG) is a non-profit and independent think-tank. It has a pool of first-class scholars, business leaders, and experts in government, addressing issues on the challenges and opportunities of positioning China in the process of globalization. CCG conducts timely strategic analysis and feasibility studies of policy-making options for China's economic development and social progress. The top-level experts, Chinese and foreign alike, help assess the regional and global implications of China's rise in the context of international political and economic reconfiguration. CCG aims to become the leading international think-tank for China's society and business community and seeks to remain independent, objective, and constructive in all its research activities.

e-mail: ccg@ccg.org.cn • website: <http://www.CCG.org.cn/en/>

Colombia • **Instituto de Ciencia Política**

Since 1987, the Instituto de Ciencia Política (ICP) has established itself as a center of democratic thought and an association of free men and women united by a common affection for an intellectual identity with the principles, values, and feelings that constitute democracy as a political, economic, social, and cultural system, and united also by their desire to act constantly and efficiently towards overcoming the lack of stability and mistakes of our political sector, in order to achieve economic, political, social, and environmental development.

ICP, as an influential think tank in the nation, has been able, through its studies, recommendations, and debates, to mediate decisively in the new directions and measures taken on different occasions by public authorities, as well as in the formation of new national political thought, favorable to the market economy, economic openness, necessary privatizations, and the modernization of the State. The institution is not, nor aspires to be, a new political party or movement, and it is independent of parties, religions, and governments. Its mission is to consecrate the free-market economy, competition, and individual initiative, as well as the reduction of State intervention and control to the minimum indispensable, as fundamental principles.

e-mail: info@icpcolombia.org • website: <http://www.icpcolombia.org/index.php>

Costa Rica • **Instituto para la Libertad y el Análisis de Políticas**

The Instituto para la Libertad y el Análisis de Políticas (INLAP—Institute for Liberty and Public Policy Analysis) is a non-profit, non-partisan organization created to defend and promote individual liberty through analysis of public policy and educational activities. Its specific objectives are to increase awareness of the moral foundations of liberty and to promote liberty as an individual right necessary to achieve the highest levels of economic and human development; and to foster changes in social organization and public policies by influencing the thinking of policy makers, community leaders, and citizens. INLAP produces timely analyses of proposed laws, decrees, and regulations, and its recommendations provide guidance for elected officials who seek to achieve greater individual liberty and creativity and a more productive economy. It also conducts detailed studies of well-meant public policies that may ultimately have unintended adverse effects. The Institute's studies and recommendations are published in books, journals, and newspapers, appear as position papers and bulletins, and are also available via our website.

e-mail: **inlapp@racsa.co.cr**

Côte d'Ivoire • Audace Institut Afrique

Audace Institut Afrique (AIA) is a think-tank that aims to promote classical liberalism, the theory and politics of the market economy, and the philosophy of the Austrian school in Africa. The Insitute wishes to initiate reflections on the economic and political freedoms in Africa through the organization of symposia, seminars, conferences, workshops, training at the university, and a research program.

e-mail: **institut@audace-afrique.org** • website: <http://www.audace-afrique.com/index.php>

Croatia • The Institute of Economics

The Institute of Economics, Zagreb, established in 1939, is a major scientific and research institution for the study of economic processes and the application of contemporary theories in economics. The Institute's objective is the economic and social advance of Croatia. Research encompasses both macroeconomics and microeconomics, policy issues (including specialized areas such as business economics), current economic trends, methods of economic analysis, development of human resources, spatial and regional economics, international economics and technological development, and investment project planning. Researchers from inside and outside the Institute work together on research projects. The Institute employs 40 full-time researchers, the majority of whom have completed specialized training courses in foreign countries. Results of the Institute's research activities are published in books, reports, and studies as well as in scientific journals. The Institute maintains close contact with international organizations, professional associations, institutes, and universities.

email: **eizagreb@eizg.hr** • website: <http://www.eizg.hr/>

Czech Republic • Liberální Institut

Liberální Institut is an independent, non-profit organization for the development and application of classical liberal ideas: individual rights, private property, rule of law, self-regulating markets, and delineated government functions. It is financed by its various activities and by donations from individuals and private corporations.

e-mail: **eva.horova@libinst.cz** • website: <http://www.libinst.cz>

Denmark • Center for Politiske Studier (CEPOS)

The Center for Politiske Studier (Center for Political Studies) was founded in 2004 as an independent, non-profit think-tank based in Copenhagen. It seeks to promote a free and prosperous society by conducting research that will foster the policies, institutions, and culture that will best support a market economy, rule of law, and a civil society consisting of free and responsible individuals. It does so by producing academic studies and policy analyses aimed partly at general political debates and partly at the political process in areas such as welfare, taxation, regulation, education, entrepreneurship, health care, the environment, and the organization of the public sector.

e-mail: **info@cepos.dk** • website: <http://www.cepos.dk>

Dominican Republic • Fundación Economía y Desarrollo, Inc.

The Fundación Economía y Desarrollo, Inc. (FEyD) is a private, non-profit organization dedicated to fostering competitive markets, private enterprise, and strategies that promote economic development. To meet its objectives, FEyD has several regular publications in the most important newspapers in the country. It also produces a one-hour television program called "Triálogo," which is broadcast three times a week and explains studies of the performance of the Dominican economy and its sectors.

Ecuador • Instituto Ecuatoriano de Economía Política

The Instituto Ecuatoriano de Economía Política (IEEP) is a private, independent, non-profit institution that defends and promotes the classical liberal ideals of individual liberty, free markets, limited government, property rights, and the rule of law. The IEEP achieves its mission through publications, seminars, and workshops that debate socio-economic and political issues. The IEEP's funding comes from voluntary donations, membership subscriptions, and income from sales of its publications.

e-mail: **info@ieep.org.ec** • website: <http://www.ieep.org.ec>

France • Institut Economique Molinari

The Molinari Economic Institute (MEI) is a research and education think-tank. It aims to initiate and stimulate an economic approach to the analysis of public policy. It was named after Gustave de Molinari, a Franco-Belgian economist and journalist; he himself has worked all his life to promote this approach. The MEI has set a mission to propose alternative and innovative solutions favorable to the prosperity of all individuals in society. The MEI is a non-profit organization funded by voluntary contributions of its members: individuals, corporations, or other foundations. Affirming its intellectual independence, it accepts no government funding or support from political parties.

website: <http://www.institutmolinari.org>

Georgia • Society for Disseminating Economic Knowledge: New Economic School

The Society was founded in 2001. The goal of the Society is to disseminate and promote free-market ideas and to create a resource center promoting free-market economics for students, young scientists, teachers, and other interested parties. Through publications, conferences, seminars, lectures, panel workshops, summer and winter schools, scientific Olympiads, and competitions, the Society seeks to disseminate classical liberal ideas.

email: **office@nesgeorgia.org** • website: <http://www.nesgeorgia.org>

Germany • Liberales Institut

The Liberales Institut (Liberty Institute), based in Potsdam, is the think-tank of the Friedrich-Naumann-Foundation. It spreads free-market ideas through the publication of classical liberal literature, the analysis of current political trends, and the promotion of research. The Institute organizes conferences and workshops to stimulate an intellectual exchange among liberals around the world.

e-mail: **libinst@freiheit.org** • website: <http://www.freiheit.org>

Ghana • The Institute of Economic Affairs

The Institute of Economic Affairs (IEA), Ghana, was founded in October 1989 as an independent, non-governmental institution dedicated to the establishment and strengthening of a market economy and a democratic, free, and open society. It considers improvements in the legal, social, and political institutions as necessary conditions for sustained economic growth and human development. The IEA supports research and promotes and publishes studies on important economic, socio-political, and legal issues in order to enhance understanding of public policy.

e-mail: **iea@ieaghana.org** • website: <http://www.ieagh.org/>

Guatemala • Centro de Investigaciones Económicas Nacionales

The Centro de Investigaciones Económicas Nacionales (CIEN—the Center for Research on the National Economy) was established in Guatemala in 1982. It is a private, non-partisan, not-for-profit, public-policy institute, funded by the sale of its books and periodical publications, income from conferences and seminars, and the support it receives from its members and the public. The Center's program is devoted to the technical study of economic and social problems that impede the stable development of the nation. Its members, staff, research associates, and supporters share the principles of a social order of free and responsible individuals interacting through a market economy functioning within the rule of law.

e-mail: **cien@cien.org.gt** • website: <http://www.cien.org.gt>

Guinea • InafEcon—Institute of African Economics

The Institute of African Economics aims to promote and stimulate economic research and training in Guinea and other African countries through organizing conferences, congresses, seminars, and courses, publishing technical and scientific studies, granting scholarships and prizes, and advising sound economic policy. By doing so, the Institute would like to help reverse the tendencies of afro-pessimism and the marginalization of African continent in worldwide cultural, scientific, and commercial exchanges through the ownership by the African public (academics, political leaders, civil servants, corporate managers, and civil society) of the development challenges in a world integrated globally between the North, the South, the East, and the West.

e-mail: inafecon@inafecon.org • website: <http://www.inafecon.org/index.php?lang=en>

Haiti • Institut de Recherche pour la Liberté Économique et la Prospérité (IRLEP)

L'Institut de Recherche pour la Liberté Économique et la Prospérité (IRLEP), Haiti, was founded in 2004. It is a non-partisan, non-profit, research and educational organization devoted to improving the quality of life in Haiti through economic growth and development. Through publications and conferences, IRLEP promotes the principles and concepts of individual rights, limited government, competition, free trade, and physical and intellectual property rights. IRLEP does not accept funding and subsidies from public institutions and political parties.

e-mail: irlephaiti@yahoo.com

Honduras • Centro de Investigaciones Economicas y Sociales (CIES)

website: <www.cies.cohep.com>

Hong Kong • Hong Kong Centre for Economic Research

The Hong Kong Centre for Economic Research is an educational, charitable trust established in 1987 to promote the free market in Hong Kong by fostering public understanding of economic affairs and developing alternative policies for government. The Centre publishes authoritative research studies and is widely recognized as the leading free-market think-tank in Asia. It has been influential in persuading public opinion and the government in Hong Kong to liberalize telecommunications, open up air-cargo handling franchises, privatize public housing, adopt a fully funded provident scheme instead of a pay-as-you-go pension scheme, remove the legally sanctioned fixing of deposit interest rates by banks, and adopt market mechanisms for protecting the environment.

e-mail: hkcer@econ.hku.hk • website: <http://www.hku.hk/hkcer/>

Hungary • Szazadveg Foundation

The Szazadveg Foundation is a non-profit organization performing political and economic research, and advisory and training activities. This think-tank is independent of the government or any political parties and has been operating as a foundation since its establishment in 1990. Szazadveg publishes the results of its research to the public at large and also provides professional services to economic institutions, political and civil organizations, political parties, and the government.

e-mail: varkonyi@szazadveg.hu • website: <http://www.szazadveg.hu>

Iceland • Centre for Social and Economic Research (RSE)

The Centre for Social and Economic Research (RSE) is an independent, non partisan, non-profit organization in Reykjavik, Iceland, founded in 2004. Its mission is to promote an understanding of private property and free-market ideas for a progressive, democratic society. RSE achieves its mission through programs of publication and conferences. Its work is assisted by a council of academic advisors of the highest standard from various academic fields. RSE is funded entirely by voluntary contributions from its supporters.

website: <http://www.rse.is>

India • Centre for Civil Society

The Centre for Civil Society (CCS) is an independent, non-profit, research and educational organization inaugurated on August 15, 1997 and devoted to improving the quality of life for all citizens of India. The CCS maintains that, having earlier attained their political independence from an alien state, the Indian people must now seek economic, social, and cultural independence from the Indian state. This can work from two directions simultaneously: a "mortar" program of building or rebuilding the institutions of civil society and a "hammer" program of readjusting the size and scope of the political society. The CCS conducts monthly dialogues on topical issues to introduce classical liberal philosophy and market-based solutions into public debate. It has published *Agenda for Change*, a volume in 17 chapters that outlines policy reforms for the Indian government, Israel Kirzner's *How Markets Work*, and *Self-Regulation in the Civil Society*, edited by Ashok Desai. It organizes Liberty and Society seminars for college students and journalists.

e-mail: ccs@ccs.in • website: <http://www.ccsindia.org>

Indonesia • The Institute for Development of Economics and Finance

Indonesian Development of Economics and Finance (INDEF) is an NGO founded in Jakarta in 1996. It is a source of information in economics for policy makers, press, students and business.

e-mail: Indef@indo.net.id • website: <http://home.indo.net.id/~indef/>

Ireland • Open Republic Institute

The Open Republic Institute (ORI) is Ireland's only platform for public-policy discussion that is specifically interested in individual rights within the context of open-society and open-market ideas. The ORI works within a non-political framework to provide public-policy analysis and new policy ideas to government, public representatives, civil servants, academics, students, and citizens.

website: <http://www.openrepublic.org>

Israel • Jerusalem Institute for Market Studies

The Jerusalem Institute for Market Studies (JIMS) was founded in 2003 in Jerusalem, Israel, as an independent non-profit, economic policy think-tank. The mission of JIMS is to promote market solutions and limited government in Israel and the region. In order to spread free-market ideas, JIMS conducts original research and publishes public-policy papers and editorials. JIMS also runs a wide range of educational programs that target elementary school students, high school students, college students, and young professionals.

e-mail: corinne.sauer@jims-israel.org • website: <http://www.jims-israel.org>

Italy • Centro Einaudi

The Centro di Ricerca e Documentazione "Luigi Einaudi" was founded in 1963 in Turin, Italy, as a free association of businessmen and young intellectuals to foster individual freedom and autonomy, economic competition, and the free market. The Centro is an independent, non-profit institute financed by contributions from individuals and corporations, by the sale of its publications, and by specific research commissions. The Centro carries on research activities, trains young scholars and researchers, organizes seminars, conferences and lectures, and publishes monographs, books, and periodicals, including: the quarterly journal, *Biblioteca della libertà*; *Rapporto sull'economia globale e l'Italia* (*Report on the global economy and Italy*); *Rapporto sul risparmio e sui risparmiatori in Italia* (*Report on savings and savers in Italy*); and *Rapporto sulla distribuzione in Italia* (*Report on the retail trade in Italy*—published also in English).

e-mail: segreteria@centroeinaudi.it • website: <http://www.centroeinaudi.it>

Jordan • Young Entrepreneurs Association

The Young Entrepreneurs Association (YEA) is a non-profit organization that aims to help small and medium-sized Jordanian companies become investor- and market-ready, and develop their ideas to facilitate the growth of their business. The YEA aims to foster fellowship and the exchange of ideas among entrepreneurs; educate and train entrepreneurs; and be the voice for the entrepreneurial community as a whole. For entrepreneurial activities to succeed in Jordan, the YEA must act as an advocate for legislative change, thereby helping shape, through rules and regulation, a favorable business environment for startups and expanding businesses.

e-mail: director@yea.com.jo • website: <http://www.yea.com.jo>

Kazakhstan • **Central Asian Free Market Institute**

The Central Asian Free Market Institute is an independent think-tank. Its mission is to increase the individual freedom and responsibility of people in Central Asia. That includes strengthening the institutions of the market economy, property, and the rule of law.

Email: **office@freemarket.kg** • website: **<http://www.freemarket.kg/>**

Kenya • **African Research Center for Public Policy and Market Process**

The African Research Center for Public Policy and Market Process, Kenya, is the first research center founded in Africa by the African Educational Foundation for Public Policy and Market Process, an independent educational organization registered in the United States. The primary mission of the Center and the Foundation is to promote ideas about free markets and voluntary associations in Africa. The Center conducts research on all aspects of free markets, voluntary association, and individual liberty, and publishes the results to as wide an audience as possible. The Center also organizes seminars and conferences to examine liberty and enterprise in Africa.

e-mail: **kimenyi@kippra.or.ke**

Korea • **Center for Free Enterprise**

The Center for Free Enterprise (CFE) is a foundation committed to promoting free enterprise, limited government, freedom and individual responsibility, the rule of law, and restraint of violence. Funded by the members of the Federation of Korean Industries (FKI), the CFE was founded as a non-profit, independent foundation on April 1, 1997, at a time of economic crisis in Korean society. The CFE has concentrated on championing a free economy through books and reports on public policies, statistics, and analyses. In workshops and policy forums, the CFE has put forward alternatives to policies proposed as solutions for issues facing Korean society.

e-mail: **csn@cfe.org** • website: **<http://www.cfe.org>**

Kosovo • **Group for Legal and Political Studies**

The Group for Legal and Political Studies is a non-profit organization, based in Kosovo. The Group's main aim is to provide a qualitative and highly competitive research environment with the intention to offer a new perspective for the reform, democratization, and development of the governing system of Kosovo.

E-mail: **office@legalpoliticalstudies.org** • website: **<http://www.legalpoliticalstudies.org>**

Kyrgyz Republic • **Economic Policy Institute—Bishkek Consensus**

The Economic Policy Institute—Bishkek Consensus (EPI), Kyrgyzstan, was created in December of 2003 as a non-profit, non-partisan, independent institute with developed partnerships and cooperative relationships with government, business, the international community, civil society, and the news media. EPI's mission is to promote economic, social, and governance reforms in Kyrgyzstan, involving institutions of civil society to elaborate and execute the reforms, developing local potential and using the best international experience. Its strategic position is to be an independent and highly objective source of information and research on public-policy issues, as well as an unbiased forum for collaboration of diverse interest groups in the reform of public policy.

e-mail: **office@epi.kg** • website: **<http://www.epi.kg>**

Lithuania • **Lithuanian Free Market Institute**

The Lithuanian Free Market Institute (LFMI) is an independent, non-profit organization established in 1990 to advance the ideas of individual freedom and responsibility, free markets, and limited government. Since its inception, LFMI has been at the forefront of economic thought and reform in Lithuania. Not only has LFMI helped frame policy debates by conducting research and creating reform packages on key issues, it has also conducted extensive educational campaigns and played a key "behind-the-scenes" role in helping to craft and refine legislative proposals. LFMI promoted the idea of a currency board and provided decisive input to the Law on Litas Credibility; it led the creation of the legal and institutional framework for the securities market and contributed significantly to the country's privatization legislation; and it initiated and participated in the policy-making process on private, fully funded, pension insurance. LFMI's recommendations were adopted in legislation on commercial banks, the Bank of Lithuania, credit unions, insurance, and foreign investment. LFMI significantly influenced the improvement of company, bankruptcy and competition law.

e-mail: **lfmi@freema.org** · website: <http://www.freema.org>

Luxembourg · D'Letzeburger Land

E-mail: **info@mmp.lu** · website: <http://www.land.lu/index.php/home.html>

Malaysia · Institute for Democracy and Economic Affairs (IDEAS)

IDEAS is Malaysia's first think-tank dedicated to promoting market-based solutions to public policy challenges. We are an independent not-for-profit organization. As a cross-partisan think-tank, we work across the political spectrum. Our purpose is to advance market-based principles, and we are not bound by party politics, race, or religion. Our office is in Bukit Tunku, Kuala Lumpur, just minutes away from Parliament. We achieve our aims by working with an extensive network of experts who share our ideals.

e-mail: **admin@ideas.org.my** · website: <http://ideas.org.my/>

Mexico · Centro de Investigación para el Desarrollo A.C.

Centro de Investigación para el Desarrollo A.C. (CIDAC) is an independent, not-for-profit research institution devoted to the study of Mexico's economy and political system. Its philosophy is that Mexico's economy can be made viable only through a greater, more efficient, and more competitive private sector. CIDAC was founded in 1980 as an executive training facility for the financial sector at large (public and private, banking and business). It received an endowment from Banamex, then Mexico's largest private bank. In 1983, immediately after the expropriation of the private banks, CIDAC changed its mandate from teaching to research. Over the last five years, CIDAC has held over 40 conferences for businessmen and its professionals continuously address academic, policy, and business forums. CIDAC has also published 19 books on various economic, political, and policy issues, 45 monographs, and over 500 op-ed pieces in Mexican, American, and European papers and magazines.

E-mail: **info@cidac.org** · website: <http://www.cidac.org>

Mongolia · Open Society Forum

The Open Society Forum is an independent, non-governmental, organization founded in 2004. The Forum's goals are to provide quality policy research and analysis and broad public access to information resources pertaining to governance, economic, and social policies. It focuses on economic freedom, land reform, rule of law, freedom of media, campaign financing, nomadic pastoralism, privatization, the shadow economy, and education policy. The Forum conducts research and holds conferences to encourage public participation in policy formulation.

e-mail: **osf@forum.mn** · website: <http://www.forum.mn>

Montenegro · The Center for Entrepreneurship and Economic Development (CEED)

The Center for Entrepreneurship and Economic Development is the first non-governmental, non-partisan free-market center established in Montenegro. Its mission is to educate entrepreneurs about private ownership, democratic society, free markets, and the rule of law through a number of programs, initiatives, publications, and events. The Center was established to meet the demand for business knowledge by pioneering entrepreneurs, who needed training to operate in a new environment after the break-up of the former Yugoslavia.

e-mail: **ceed@t-com.me** · website: <http://www.visit-ceed.org.me/>

Nepal · The Prosperity Foundation

Samriddhi, the Prosperity Foundation, envisions a free and prosperous Nepal where individuals can live a dignified life in a vibrant and democratic society with equal access to opportunities and respect for the rule of law. Its mission is to promote ideas of freedom—civil, political and economic—through public-policy recommendations (based on independent research), educational programs, and public participation for a free and prosperous Nepal.

e-mail: **info@samriddhi.org** · website: <http://www.samriddhi.org>

New Zealand • **The New Zealand Business Roundtable**

The New Zealand Business Roundtable is made up of the chief executives of about 60 of New Zealand's largest businesses. Its aim is to contribute to the development of sound public policies that reflect New Zealand's overall interests. It has been a prominent supporter of the country's economic liberalization.

e-mail: **nzbr@nzbr.org.nz** • website: <http://www.nzbr.org.nz>

Nigeria • **Initiative of Public Policy Analysis**

The Initiative of Public Policy Analysis (IPPA) is a private, non-profit organization involved in research, education, and publication on matters affecting the freedom of individuals. Its objective is to provide market-oriented analysis of current and emerging policy issues, with a view to influencing the public debate and the political decision-making process.

e-mail: **info@ippanigeria.org** • website: <http://www.ippanigeria.org>

Norway • **Center for Business and Society Incorporated (Civita)**

Civita, the first market-oriented think-tank in Norway, was established in 2004. It strives for increased consensus on important principles of the market economy and their implications for welfare, freedom, and democracy. Civita is also dedicated to promoting personal responsibility and civil society to achieve larger, more important roles in society's development. To communicate its ideas to the public, it conducts research, publishes reports, and holds seminars and conferences.

e-mail: **civita@civita.no** • website: <http://www.civita.no>

Oman • **International Research Foundation (IRF)**

The International Research Foundation (IRF), Sultanate of Oman, was established in 2005 as a non-governmental, independent, non-profit think-tank based in Oman to conduct research on domestic and international economic issues with an emphasis on the Arab World. The IRF has set its research and public-affairs agenda on a collegial basis, relying on the input of its research staff, its editorial board, and its senior fellows. It maintains a working arrangement with governmental and non-governmental organizations in the region and other parts of the world. IRF is the regional member of the Fraser Institute's Economic Freedom Network.

The vision of IRF is to create wealth and jobs through the promotion of economic freedom. Its mission is to measure, research, and communicate to a global audience the impact of competitive markets on the welfare of individuals. The Board of Trustees of the IRF consists of high-profile private-sector members from different organizations. IRF has initiated the establishment of a network of academic researchers to facilitate research projects, which will help in its endeavor to research economic issues affecting the daily life of individuals.

e-mail: **azzan@ociped.com** • website: <www.irfoman.org>

Pakistan • **Alternate Solutions Institute**

Alternate Solutions Institute, founded in 2003, is the first free-market think-tank in Pakistan. Its mission is (1) to seek solutions to challenges pertaining to the economy, law, education, and health in accordance with the principles of classical liberalism; and (2) to promote the implementation of these solutions. The Institute aims to promote the concept of a limited, responsible government in Pakistan under the rule of law protecting life, liberty, and property of all of its citizens without any discrimination. The Institute conducts research and holds seminars, workshops, and conferences to educate interested students, teachers, and journalists about the principles of classical liberalism.

e-mail: **info@asinstitute.org** • website: <http://asinstitute.org>

Palestine • **Pal-Think for Strategic Studies**

Pal-Think for Strategic Studies is an independent, non-profit, institute in Gaza, Palestine. It was established in March 2007. Pal-Think's mission is to promote peace, freedom, and prosperity through debates on public issues, producing policy recommendations for the decision-makers in Palestine and the Middle East. The main objective of Pal-Think is to conduct research on thematic issues that serve as a basis for policy debates on matters that are important to the Palestinians, the region, and the international community.

To achieve its vision of being a leading think-tank in Palestine and the Middle East, Pal-Think also organizes conferences, workshops, round-table discussions, and other events on specific issues in Palestine and the region to deepen the understanding by the various constituencies and to provide appropriate policy solutions.

e-mail: info@palthink.org • website: <http://www.palthink.org>

Panama • Fundación Libertad

The Fundación Libertad, Panama, is a non-profit foundation engaged in the promotion and development of liberty, individual choice, and voluntary cooperation and in the reduction of the size of government. Fundación Libertad was founded in 2001 by members of professional and business organizations to promote free enterprise and democracy and to address issues affecting the freedom of the common citizen including the increasing discretionary power of the state and the proliferation of legislation fostering discrimination and establishing privileges, all of which are contrary to the spirit of democratic capitalism. Fundación Libertad has drawn initial support from sister organizations such as Centro de Divulgación del Conocimiento Económico (CEDICE) in Caracas, Venezuela, and the Centro de Investigación y Estudios Nacionales (CIEN) in Guatemala.

Email: info@fundacionlibertad.org.pa • website: <http://www.fundacionlibertad.org.pa>

Peru • Centro de Investigación y Estudios Legales (CITEL)

CITEL was organized in 1989. Its principal field is the economic analysis of law. To that end, it conducts research on different legal institutions, publishes books, and organizes seminars and colloquia.

E-mail: info@citel.org • website: <http://www.citel.org/>

Philippines • The Center for Research and Communication

The Center for Research and Communication (CRC) has, since 1967, conducted research and published works on domestic and international economic and political issues that affect the Asia-Pacific region. It provides forums for discussion and debate among academicians, businessmen, civil officials, and representatives of other sectors that shape public opinion and chart the course of policies. CRC is the main research arm of the University of Asia and the Pacific in Metro Manila.

e-mail: crcfound@yahoo.com

Poland • Centrum im. Adama Smitha

The Centrum im. Adama Smitha (the Adam Smith Research Centre—ASRC) is a private, non-partisan, non-profit, public-policy institute. It was founded in 1989 and was the first such institute in Poland and in Eastern Europe. The ASRC promotes a free and fair market economy, participatory democracy, and a virtuous society. Its activities in research and development, education, and publishing cover almost all important issues within the areas of economy and social life. The ASRC acts as a guardian of economic freedom in Poland. More than 50 experts are associated with the ASRC.

e-mail: 1989@smith.pl • website: <http://www.smith.org.pl/pl/>

Portugal • Causa Liberal

Causa Liberal is an independent, non-partisan, non-profit organization of Portuguese individuals who share the principles of the classical liberal tradition and wish to further its application in modern-day Portugal. Its mission is to defend the principles of the free society and its building blocks: individual rights, the rule of law, free markets, and private property. Its primary goals are to establish and consolidate a network of individuals with an interest in the study, discussion, and promotion of the classical liberal tradition, and to advance free-market ideas and policies in Portugal.

e-mail: causaliberal@yahoo.com • website: <http://www.causaliberal.net>

Romania • **Romania Think Tank**

Romania Think Tank is an independent research institute founded in 2003. The Think Tank is funded entirely by its founding members. Its objective is to promote the development of free markets, low taxation, reduction of bureaucracy, free trade, and the stimulation of foreign investment. To this end, the Romania Think Tank publishes numerous articles in the Romanian and international media, and studies and analyzes issues relevant to the development of a free-market economy in Romania.

e-mail: **office@rtt.ro** • website: <http://www.thinktankromania.ro/>

Russia • **Institute of Economic Analysis**

The Institute of Economic Analysis is a macroeconomic research institute that analyzes the current economic situation and policies and provides expert analysis of acts, programs, and current economic policy. It will offer advice to Russian government bodies, enterprises, and organizations and prepares and publishes scientific, research, and methodological economic literature. It also conducts seminars, conferences, and symposia on economic topics. The Institute is an independent, non-governmental, non-political, non-profit research center that works closely with leading Russian and international research centers. Its research focuses on macroeconomic, budget, and social policies.

e-mail: **iea@iea.ru** • website: <http://www.iea.ru>

Serbia • **Free Market Center (FMC)**

Free Market Center (FMC) is a non-profit, non-governmental organization founded in 2001. It is the only free-market think-tank in Serbia. The Center promotes the understanding and acceptance of ideas like individual liberty, the free-market economy, limited government, and peaceful cooperation. To that end, the FMC strives to achieve greater involvement in redirecting the attention not only of leading thinkers but also of members of the public, entrepreneurs, policy-makers, and students to the role of free markets and the proper role of government. Through publications, discussion forums, and conferences, the Center seeks to disseminate classical liberal ideas.

e-mail: **fmc@yubc.net** • website: <http://www.fmc.org.rs/>

Slovak Republic • **The F.A. Hayek Foundation**

The F.A. Hayek Foundation is an independent and non-partisan, non-profit organization that provides a forum for the exchange of opinions among scholars, businessmen, and policy-makers on the causes of, and solutions to, economic, social, and political problems. It proposes practical reforms of the economy, education, social security, and legislation as the Slovak Republic is transformed into an open society. Education of high-school and university students is a large part of its activities. The F.A. Hayek Foundation promotes classical liberalism, which was virtually absent until 1989: market economy, reduced role for government, rule of law and individual choice, responsibilities and rights to life, liberty, and property.

e-mail: **hayek@hayek.sk** • website: <http://www.hayek.sk>

South Africa • **The Free Market Foundation of Southern Africa**

The Free Market Foundation is an independent policy research and education organization founded in 1975 to promote the principles of limited government, economic freedom, and individual liberty in Southern Africa. Funding is received from members (corporate, organizational and individual), sponsorships, and the sale of publications.

e-mail: **fmf@mweb.co.za** • website: <http://www.freemarketfoundation.com/>

Spain • **Fundació Catalunya Oberta**

Fundació Catalunya Oberta (Open Catalonia Foundation) was founded in 2001 with the objective of promoting, analyzing, and extending the values of the open society, freedom, democracy, and the market economy. It also defends the rights of Catalonia as a nation, especially in the cultural and economic fields. It is a private foundation, espousing liberal ideology, with no political connections, whose aim is to influence public opinion in a civil society. The Foundation organizes a range of activities every year and publishes a number of reports. Moreover, the Foundation awards a 10,000-euro yearly prize to prestigious journalists from all over the world, in which their endeavours in favor of democracy and freedom is rewarded.

e-mail: fund@fco.cat • website: <http://www.catalunyaoberta.cat/>

Sudan • Nile Institute of Economic Studies

e-mail: nileinstitute@gmail.com • website: <http://web.me.com/durra1/Site/NileInstituteofEconomicStudies.html>

Sri Lanka • The Pathfinder Foundation

The Pathfinder Foundation has replaced the Center for Policy Research. Through informed and well-researched information, it seeks to challenge old ideas and the conventional wisdom, stimulate debate, change public attitudes, and seek new and innovative solutions to the economic and social problems of Sri Lanka.

e-mail: info@pathfinderfoundation.org • website: <http://www.pathfinderfoundation.org/>

Sweden • Timbro

Timbro is a Swedish think-tank that encourages public opinion to favor free enterprise, a free economy, and a free society. Timbro publishes books, papers, reports, and the magazine, *Smedjan*. It also arranges seminars and establishes networks among people. Founded in 1978, Timbro is owned by the Swedish Free Enterprise Foundation, which has as its principals a large number of Swedish companies and organizations.

e-mail: info@timbro.se • website: <http://www.timbro.se>

Switzerland • Liberales Institut

The Liberales Institut is a forum where the basic values and concepts of a free society can be discussed and questioned. The Institute's aim is the establishment of free markets as the best way towards the goals of openness, diversity, and autonomy. The Liberales Institut is not associated with any political party. Through publications, discussion forums, and seminars, it seeks to develop and disseminate classical liberal ideas.

e-mail: libinst@libinst.ch • website: <http://www.libinst.ch/>

Tajikistan • Tajikistan Free Market Centre

The long-term objectives of the Tajikistan Free Market Centre are: advancement and protection of values of individualism and personal freedom; dissemination and advocacy of ideas about the priority of private property and the free market; advancement of the principle of a limited state (non-interference of the state in the personal and economic life of the individual); training and support of activists and the organizations that are supporters of ideas of individual and economic freedom.

e-mail: freemarket.tj@gmail.com • website: <http://www.freemarket.tj/>

Trinidad and Tobago • Arthur Lok Jack Graduate School of Business, University of the West Indies

The Arthur Lok Jack Graduate School of Business was created in 1989 as a channel partner for developing managerial talent for the business community in Trinidad and Tobago. Its mission is to empower people and organizations in developing nations to optimize their performance capabilities and international competitiveness through development and deployment of consulting; education, research, and training resources. One of the Institute's core services are business and academic research in areas of real concern to business managers, enabling them to improve their ability to manage successfully in the face of increasingly complex markets.

e-mail: r.balgobin@gsb.tt • website: <http://www.lokjackgsb.org/>

Turkey • Association for Liberal Thinking

The Association for Liberal Thinking is a non-profit, non-governmental organization seeking to introduce the liberal democratic tradition into Turkey. The Association promotes the understanding and acceptance of ideas like liberty, justice, peace, human rights, equality, and tolerance. It also encourages academic writing on liberal themes to help the Turkish people assess contemporary domestic and international changes and attempts to find effective solutions to Turkey's problems within liberal thought. The Association for Liberal Thinking is not involved in day-to-day politics and has no direct links to any political party or movement. Instead, as an independent intellectual group, it aims to set broader political agendas so as to contribute to the liberalization of economics and politics in Turkey.

e-mail: info@liberal-dt.org.tr · website: <http://www.liberal.org.tr/>

Ukraine · The Ukrainian Center for Independent Political Research

The Ukrainian Center for Independent Political Research (UCIPR) was established in early 1991 as a non-profit, non-partisan, and non-governmental research institution that would increase awareness of democracy among the Ukrainian people and analyze domestic and international politics and security. The UCIPR is politically independent; it does not accept any funding from either the state or any political party. The UCIPR publishes books and research papers on Ukraine's domestic and foreign policy, the economy in transition, security, relations with neighboring states, the Crimean dilemma, interethnic relations, and the freedom of the news media. The Center has hosted a number of national and international conferences and workshops.

e-mail: ucipr@ucipr.kiev.ua · website: <http://www.ucipr.kiev.ua/>

United Kingdom · Institute of Economic Affairs (IEA)

The mission of the Institute of Economic Affairs (IEA) is to improve public understanding of the foundations of a free and harmonious society by expounding and analyzing the role of markets in solving economic and social problems, and bringing the results of that work to the attention of those who influence thinking. The IEA achieves its mission by a high-quality publishing program; conferences, seminars, and lectures on a range of subjects; outreach to school and college students; brokering media introductions and appearances; and other related activities. Incorporated in 1955 by the late Sir Antony Fisher, the IEA is an educational charity, limited by guarantee. It is independent of any political party or group, and is financed by sales of publications, conference fees, and voluntary donations.

e-mail: iea@iea.org.uk · website: <http://www.iea.org.uk/>

United States of America · Cato Institute

Founded in 1977, the Cato Institute is a research foundation dedicated to broadening debate about public policy to include more options consistent with the traditional American principles of limited government, individual liberty, free markets, and peace. To that end, the Institute strives to achieve greater involvement by the intelligent, concerned, lay public in questions of policy and the proper role of government through an extensive program of publications and seminars.

e-mail: ivasquez@cato.org · website: <http://www.cato.org/>

Venezuela · The Center for the Dissemination of Economic Knowledge (CEDICE)

The Center for the Dissemination of Economic Knowledge is a non-partisan, non-profit, private association dedicated to the research and promotion of philosophical, economic, political, and social thinking that focuses on individual initiative and a better understanding of the free-market system and free and responsible societies. To this end, CEDICE operates a library and bookstore, publishes the series, *Venezuela Today*, and other studies, provides economic training for journalists, and conducts special events and community programs.

e-mail: cedice@cedice.org.ve · website: <http://www.cedice.org.ve/>

Vietnam · Research Center for Entrepreneurship Development

The Research Center for Entrepreneurship Development, founded in 2004, is a non-government research and educational organization devoted to the entrepreneurial development of the private sector in Vietnam. Its mission is to study the development of policies that create the most favorable institutional and policy environment for entrepreneurial development of the private sector in Vietnam. Through publications, discussion forums, and conferences, the Center seeks to disseminate and encourage appropriate polices and entrepreneurial development.

e-mail: rced@rced.com.vn · website: <http://www.rced.com.vn>

Zambia • The Zambia Institute for Public Policy Analysis (ZIPPA)

The mission of the Zambia Institute for Public Policy Analysis is to promote wider appreciation of the key role of free markets and competition in economic development. Zambia, though peaceful and stable, is currently mired in a combination of protracted poverty, the HIV/AIDS pandemic, political animosities following a disputed election, and skepticism about economic liberalization. In this depressing environment, ZIPPA wants to play a constructive role by promoting realistic economic policies and by suggesting solutions that have been successfully applied in other countries to similar economic problems.

e-mail: zippamail@gmail.com